D1256454

WOODROW WILSON
A Bibliography of
His Times and Presidency

TWENTIETH-CENTURY PRESIDENTIAL BIBLIOGRAPHY SERIES
Richard Dean Burns and Peter H. Buckingham, *Series Editors*

Volumes Published
WOODROW WILSON
Peter H. Buckingham, *Compiler*

HARRY S. TRUMAN
Richard Dean Burns, *Compiler*

Volumes in Preparation
THEODORE ROOSEVELT / WILLIAM HOWARD TAFT
John C. Dobson, *Compiler*

WARREN G. HARDING / CALVIN COOLIDGE
Richard Dean Burns, *Compiler*

HERBERT HOOVER
Richard Dean Burns, *Compiler*

DWIGHT DAVID EISENHOWER
R. Alton Lee, *Compiler*

WOODROW WILSON
A Bibliography of
His Times and Presidency

Compiled by
Peter H. Buckingham

SR *Scholarly Resources Inc.*
Wilmington, Delaware

The paper used in this publication meets the minimum requirements of the American National Standard for permanence of paper for printed library materials, Z39.48, 1984.

©1990 by Scholarly Resources Inc.
All rights reserved
First published 1990
Printed and bound in the United States of America

Scholarly Resources Inc.
104 Greenhill Avenue
Wilmington, DE 19805-1897

Library of Congress Cataloging-in-Publication Data

Buckingham, Peter H., 1948–
  Woodrow Wilson : a bibliography of his times and presidency / compiled by Peter H. Buckingham.
       p. cm.
    ISBN 0-8420-2291-0
    1. United States—Politics and government—1913–1921— Bibliography. 2. Wilson, Woodrow, 1856–1924—Bibliography. I. Title.
Z1244.B83   1989
[E766]   89-10966
016.97391'3—dc20   CIP

LIBRARY
ALMA COLLEGE
ALMA, MICHIGAN

Contents

Chapter 7   Domestic Affairs: Politics, Progressives, the Press, and Administrative and Legal   153

Chapter 8   Domestic Affairs: Radicalism and the Red Scare   199

Contents

Preface

Bibliographers accumulate more than piles of index cards and computer printer hard copies, because projects such as this one are team efforts requiring the services of dedicated professionals and the forbearance of colleagues and loved ones. I would like to thank Richard Dean Burns, series editor, and Scholarly Resources for asking me to participate in the presidential series. I also would like to thank Scholarly Resources' Tricia Andryszewski for her editorial assistance. Librarians at the University of Texas at Austin and the Austin Public Library deserve acknowledgment for their hours of time and trouble. I owe a special debt of gratitude to the staff of the Scarborough-Phillips Library at St. Edward's University, especially Eileen Shockett, Carla Felsted, and Ming Pei-Eades, for sharing their resources with me. My colleagues John Houghton and Dean Joe O'Neal at New College, St. Edward's, provided invaluable practical and moral support. Thanks to Lu Harper of the Emanuel Northrup Library at Linfield College for her eleventh-hour assistance.

When this bibliography was first proposed three years ago, my wife, Ann, created a special computer program that helped me to organize a mountain of material. Without her perseverance, love, and encouragement this project would not have been possible.

Introduction

Most scholars believe that the period they are examining is among the most important in history. Regardless of whether Woodrow Wilson was or was not, as Arthur S. Link claims, "the prophet and pivot of the twentieth century," there can be little doubt that the years of the Wilson presidency witnessed events that had important consequences. In domestic affairs, it was a time of continued Progressive reform activity. In foreign affairs, crises with Mexico and concern over the political and economic stability of Central America and the Caribbean created controversy. The outbreak of World War I in Europe forced Wilson to devote even more attention to foreign policy as he attempted to safeguard the national interest while preparing the American people for possible military intervention. American entry into the war necessitated the total mobilization of national resources and led to the wholesale persecution of dissidents by the government, patriotic groups, and vigilantes. An atmosphere of mass hysteria, the Bolshevik Revolution, and labor unrest spawned a Red Scare in the postwar period. The president's determination to implement an international settlement based on the principle of "peace without victory" pointed toward a way to prevent future wars through collective security. Tragically, for both Wilson and the country, partisanship and the reluctance of many to accept the new responsibilities of greatly enhanced U.S. economic and military power brought about an American rejection of the peace settlement.

During the hotly contested presidential campaign of 1912, Wilson was called many things, among them "a long-haired bookworm of a professor." Hair length aside, he was just that, an academic with only two years of political experience as governor of New Jersey. Wilson's father wanted him to be a minister, but he studied law as the best means of entering politics. Quickly bored with legal work, he earned his doctorate at Johns Hopkins University and embarked on a brilliant career in higher education. An inspiring teacher, Wilson wrote general histories as well as books and essays on political science, and he did pioneering work in the study of public administration. He put his theories on administration to the test as president of Princeton University and helped to turn that institution into a great university before resigning because of differences with the regents. A "bookworm of a professor"—yes, but also quite probably the best intellectually prepared of our presidents. He never published another book after 1902, but he remained a man of letters, writing his own speeches, messages, personal correspondence and state papers on a portable typewriter and refusing to employ ghostwriters to manufacture quotations on his behalf.

Wilson was a man of great religious faith. On receiving the Democratic nomination for president in 1912, he declared characteristically: "I am a Presbyterian and believe in predestination and election. It was Providence that did the work." Once elected, he told his campaign chairman: "Before we proceed I wish it clearly understood that I owe you nothing." Taken aback, his manager reminded the president-elect of his service during the campaign, to which Wilson replied: "God ordained that I should be the next President of the United States. Neither you nor any other mortal could have prevented that!" Wilson cannot be understood without an appreciation of the Calvinism that fueled his righteousness. Even in his last days, when his health had been broken and his program for peace lay in ruins, he told friends that "I have seen fools resist Providence before, and I have seen their destruction. . . . That we shall prevail is as sure as God reigns."

While Woodrow Wilson suffered throughout his life from the burden of thinking that he was always right, he also had a sharp and sometimes self-deprecating sense of humor. He once recited a favorite risqué limerick to Charles Evans Hughes:

> There was a young man of Siberia
> Whose life grew drearier and drearier,
> So he burst from his cell
> With a hell of a yell
> And eloped with the Mother Superior.

As he watched Wilson's political ambitions grow, Hughes came to see the rhyme, in a figurative sense, as autobiographical. Wilson was a complex man emotionally, and he described his nature as a struggle between his Irish blood—generous, impulsive, and passionate—and his Scotch blood—canny, tenacious, and cold. He liked to compare himself to a dormant volcano, placid on the outside but boiling deep within.

No president, with the possible exception of Richard M. Nixon, has had his physical and mental health more closely studied than has Wilson, despite the fact that most of his medical records have been destroyed. Alexander and Juliette George began the controversy more than thirty years ago with the publication of *Woodrow Wilson and Colonel House: A Personality Study*. Their psychoanalytic biography postulated that the two great influences on Wilson were his own inner turbulence and the ideas of his friend Colonel Edward M. House, whose calculated playing to the president's vanity made him a power in his own right. In 1967 an extraordinary book surfaced that had been written in the 1930s by Sigmund Freud and William C. Bullitt. This study painted an extremely critical portrait of Wilson as a narcissist with a messiah complex. The problem was that Freud had never met Wilson, and the erratic Bullitt had initiated the project as a way of paying Wilson back for disappointing him during the Paris Peace Conference. Edwin A. Weinstein, a medical doctor and historian, examined Wilson in a more systematic fashion in *Woodrow Wilson: A Medical and Psychological Biography*. This work chronicles Wilson's life, devoting special attention to his major illnesses.

Wilson drove himself relentlessly during his academic career and suffered the first of a series of strokes in 1896. He had exhibited the symptoms of hypertension for years but denied the importance of his stroke out of a belief that illness was grounded in immorality. Wilson never was the same again. He became even more energetic and less relaxed, criticizing his colleagues without remorse while giving up such pleasures as billiards and bicycling. His only exercise was golf, which he called "an ineffectual attempt to put an elusive ball into an obscure hole with implements ill-adapted to the purpose." He grew impulsive and arbitrary after another stroke in 1904. Two years later he awoke blind in one eye, giving every indication that he was suffering from a severe disease of the arteries. Advised by his doctor to stop working, he pressed on instead with his ambitious reforms at Princeton. When the regents turned down his plan to democratize college life, he became depressed and had an affair with a married woman. Threatened with the loss of his wife's love and feeling immoral, Wilson embarked on a mission to purify politics. He was elected governor of New Jersey in 1910 and president of the United States two years later in what he described as "a sort of political miracle." The death of his wife touched off a prolonged period of depression, but again he bounced back, remarrying and steering the country through a difficult period of diplomatic neutrality.

Silently, the ravages of emotional tension, high blood pressure, and cerebral and retinal artery disease continued. In April 1919, during a critical phase of the Paris Peace Conference, Wilson contracted influenza with manifestations of cerebral and cardiac involvement. The story of what happened next is well known: The president returned home with a far-from-perfect peace treaty that provided for a League of Nations with collective security arrangements designed to prevent future wars. He faced a hostile Republican-controlled Senate concerned over the proposed "great departure" from American isolationism, angry over the president's high-handed ways, and eager for partisan gain.

Not appreciated until recently is that by this time the president was suffering from cerebral arteriosclerosis (hardening of the arteries of the brain), which helps to explain the fatal lapses in judgment and memory so noticeable to his doctor and other close associates. Willing to accept only mild Senate reservations about what he considered to be his treaty, Wilson took his case to the American people, embarking on an exhausting whirlwind tour of the western states. Not surprisingly, Wilson fell ill during the tour and was rushed back to Washington. Within one week he suffered a massive stroke that led to the complete paralysis of the left side of his body and the loss of vision in the left half-fields in both eyes. Bedridden, with his wife acting as an intermediary between himself and the outside world, this shell of a man continued to deny that anything was wrong, even as he boiled complex questions down to simple black-and-white answers. His demand that loyal Senate Democrats vote against the treaty with the Republican reservations ensured tragic defeat.

Measuring Wilson's greatness as a president is a difficult task. What began as a parlor game in the late 1940s has evolved into a more systematic measurement of the opinions of American historians, who are asked periodically to rank the chief executives. Arthur M. Schlesinger's original poll of fifty-four authorities taken in 1948 ranked Wilson fourth in the category "great" behind Lincoln, Washington, and Franklin D. Roosevelt. In 1962 he asked seventy-five historians for their opinions, and once again Wilson finished fourth. A more extensive survey taken ten years later revealed that Wilson had slipped to sixth place, with liberals giving him much higher marks than conservatives. He remained at number six, in the "near great category," in the most recent polling (1981–82) sandwiched between Teddy Roosevelt and Andrew Jackson. The authors of that study observed, though, that there was a generation gap when it came to Wilson. Older historians gave him a higher ranking than younger historians, which means that his reputation may slip further in the coming years.

How does one explain the decline in Wilson's reputation? Younger scholars may have less faith in the liberal state that Wilson did so much to erect. Also, the polls consistently gave Wilson the highest marks for his domestic leadership of the New Freedom reform program and his role as organizer of victory in World War I. There has been a great deal of scholarship in recent years on Wilson's sanctioning of wartime terrorism against German Americans and other dissident groups as well as his acquiescence in the Red Scare of 1919–20. Then there was the president's significant role in the disastrous defeat of the Treaty of Versailles. In the years after World War II, many people, historians included, believed that Wilson had been vindicated by the creation of the United Nations. Perhaps Wilson's reputation has declined in proportion to the American loss of faith in international organization. In the aftermath of Vietnam, the future of collective security seems shaky once again.

The Wilson years marked the close of the Progressive era, a time when the American upper-middle class responded to what Richard M. Abrams has called "the burden of progress." In spite of a sound economy and remarkable material progress, there was a sense that all was not right with American liberal institutions. Woodrow Wilson summed up the feeling best when he explained: "Our life contains every great thing, and it contains it in rich abundance. But the evil has come with the good. . . . We have squandered a great part of what we might have used. . . . We have not hitherto stopped thoughtfully enough to count the human cost. . . . There has been something crude and heartless and unfeeling in our haste to succeed and be great. . . . We have come now to the sober second thought." The problem was progress itself. The Progressive movement, well under way when Wilson came to the White House, was an effort to act on this sober second thought, to conserve the best of the American past and present while eliminating the injustices brought by the Industrial Revolution. Progressives such as Theodore Roosevelt argued that the marketplace had to yield to an expanded government that, with its agencies of experts, would bring order to the economy. But another group of Progressives, led by Woodrow Wilson, disagreed with that approach. Wilson believed that greatly expanded government would lead to the ruin of American individualism and that federal power should only be used to impose truly open market conditions, thereby restoring competition. The government could then step back and watch, as he put it, "a free and fair field" once again.

Wilson put his ideas to the test with his New Freedom program, reforming the market system by foiling "the special interests." There was meaningful tariff reform in the Federal Reserve Act of 1913, which gave the government some power to moderate the business cycle. Congress created the Federal Trade Commission to end unfair business practices and passed the Clayton Act to prohibit practices that reduced competition. It was a dazzling legislative accomplishment, but Wilson had begun to change his mind about the role of government. He came to see that interest-group politics were not necessarily a bad thing, especially at election time. Desperate to convert his 40 percent share of the 1912 popular vote to the majority he would need against the reunited Republican party and understanding the need to use government to mobilize the country in the event of war, he courted farmers, labor unions, and social workers by pushing for special interest legislation, which he had denounced just a few years earlier. The strategy worked, but it marked Wilson's bow to the trend toward corporate ascendency and group politics, and it tied the Progressive movement in a Gordian knot.

"You may feel assured," Wilson had said in 1912, "of my entire comprehension of the ambitions of the negro race and my willingness and desire to deal with that race fairly and justly." Northern black Republicans, disappointed that Progressives such as Theodore Roosevelt and William Howard Taft had done little for them, flocked to Wilson as a man with a keen sense of morality and justice. Although he was a brilliant man in many ways, Wilson was also a southerner and a racist who believed that segregation of the races was necessary to preserve racial purity. Ignoring his campaign promise, he presided over the further segregation of government facilities in Washington. He did receive a delegation of black leaders, but he ordered them out of his office because he did not like their tone. The president applauded the most popular movie made during his tenure, D. W. Griffith's *The Birth of a Nation*, which depicted the dramatic confrontation between the supposedly heroic Ku Klux Klan and maniacal blacks during Reconstruction. The film, he said, was like "writing history in lightning."

Much has been done in recent years to bring the activities of women into focus: women in trade unions, women's contribution to World War I, and the final successful drive to write women's suffrage into the Constitution. Like so many Progressive males in a generation preoccupied with the rites of manliness, Wilson was reluctant to accept suffragettes into the Progressive coalition, because he was a firm believer that a woman's place was in the home. By the time he became president, women could vote in eleven states, but progress had been painfully slow. In 1915 the National American Woman Suffrage Association elected educator/organizer Carrie Chapman Catt as its president. Armed with a $2-million war chest, Catt created a "Winning Plan" of coordinated state campaigns and mass lobbying to win a federal suffrage amendment by the end of 1920. Through Catt's efforts the suffrage movement placed tremendous pressure on Wilson to reverse his conservative view of women.

During the Civil War, leaders of the first women's rights crusade had agreed to suspend their activities to work for the war effort, believing that once the slaves had been emancipated and enfranchised that suffrage would follow for women as well. Vowing not to repeat that mistake during World War I, the suffragettes redoubled their efforts. Alice Paul's Woman's Party applied militant tactics to Wilson, picketing the White House with signs reading "Kaiser Wilson" and accusing the president of hypocrisy for fighting a war "to make the world safe for democracy" while denying the vote to half the population at home. The riots and jailings that became a part of the picketing aroused sympathy and embarrassed the president. Arrested women were force-fed to prevent hunger strikes. Alice Paul was tossed into a psychiatric ward. The hunger strikes and other actions of the Woman's Party were criticized by moderates as counterproductive, but, on 9 January 1918, President Wilson asked Democrats to vote for a suffrage amendment "as an act of right and justice to the women of the country and of the world." It quickly passed the House but stalled in the Senate, so the president personally lobbied the amendment through. He had been pragmatic enough to change his mind and contributed much to the passage of the Nineteenth Amendment.

Wilson once remarked that it would be "the irony of fate" if his administration was remembered chiefly for its foreign policy. An avalanche of books, articles, and dissertations on Wilsonian diplomacy bears witness to the growing importance of events beyond American borders. Wilson, like most Americans, had thought but little about foreign affairs. He came to the presidency quite critical of the blustering and militaristic big-stick mentality of Theodore Roosevelt and of the crass dollar diplomacy of the Taft administration. He was soon forced to turn his attention to Mexico, where a revolution presented the prospect of great change and a concomitant threat to American investments. The violent overthrow of the revolution's first president, Francisco Madero, shocked Wilson, who responded by withholding diplomatic recognition from the government of Victoriano Huerta as part of a campaign to force a change in regimes. He sent U.S. marines to the Mexican port of Veracruz on a trivial pretext, an act that both contributed to Huerta's departure and alienated much of Latin America. The succeeding government of Venustiano Carranza not only failed to reunite the country but also denounced Wilson for his interference in Mexican affairs. The objections grew louder when Wilson ordered General John J. Pershing into Mexico to capture Pancho Villa after a murderous raid across the border into Columbus, New Mexico. Wilson's chauvinism kept him from calling off the futile chase for more than nine months. An overweening pride also led him to send the marines into Haiti in 1915 and into the Dominican Republic and Nicaragua in 1916.

Exaltation mixed with calculation in Wilson's thoughts during the prolonged period of American neutrality, while Europe bloodied itself in "The Great War." He asked the impossible from his country: to remain impartial in thought as well as in deed toward a conflict about which most people held passionate convictions. For a long time, historians tried to prove that events changed policy, that German atrocities, murderous U-boats, and British propaganda led America into the war. Recent scholarship indicates that he was unneutral from the outset, feeling that a triumphant German victory would bring the disaster of universal militarism. All along he sympathized with the Entente powers, especially with France and Britain. Since public opinion was not ready for war, Wilson waited. Privately he said: "I am not justified in forcing my opinion upon the people of the United States and bringing them into a war which they do not understand." In public he took a consistent stance for neutrality. "There is such a thing as a man being too proud to fight" he told a crowd in 1915 following the sinking of the *Lusitania*. Germany's desperate gamble of early 1917 changed the president's public position. Hoping to starve out the Entente, the German High Command decided to wage all-out U-boat warfare in the Atlantic. The small regular American army would make little difference, since it might take years to train, organize, and dispatch a real fighting force. Once the sinkings began, Wilson realized that the pride of the American people would demand war.

Wilson's dream of a just and lasting peace has long been debated. For years he has been under attack by the influential realist school of historians, which contends that he was far too idealistic in his approach. As George Frost Kennan, the dean of this school, remarked: "This was the sort of peace you got when you allowed war hysteria and impractical idealism to lie down together in your mind, like the lion and the lamb; when you indulged yourself in the colossal conceit of thinking that you could suddenly make international life over into what you believed to be your own image." Thus, in trying to create peace without victory, Wilson wrecked the balance of power in Europe and set the stage for another war. Nonsense, says the great Wilson scholar and defender Arthur S. Link. Wilson had a realistic vision of the future, but he was unable to carry it out completely because of his limited power. However, the peace treaty did incorporate his liberal ideals. Belgium was restored, Alsace-Lorraine was returned to France, and a viable

Polish state came into being along with other countries based on the right of self-determination. Most importantly, the work of the peace conference could be improved upon in the future by the League of Nations. It is absurd, Link argues, to blame World War II on Wilson, because the later conflict was primarily due to the results of the Great Depression.

It is interesting to note that in recent years, in his search for allies against the realist critique, Link has lavished praise on the New Left and on other revisionists for their appreciation of Wilson's shrewd understanding of the needs of the American system. They see Wilson's diplomacy as part of a larger movement made by a thoughtful elite to expand American overseas exports and investments to compensate for the ending of the American frontier. Perhaps the key to understanding the president's "irony of fate" lies in the realization that the Wilsonian peace manifests the inevitable clash between idealism and realism at a crucial turning point in history. In the end, Wilson's great successes and failings were those of an imperfect product of an evolving civilization seeking a more rational and peaceful world order.

Peter H. Buckingham

Chronology—Woodrow Wilson

1856   —Woodrow Wilson was born 28 December at Staunton, Augusta County, Virginia. Christened Thomas Woodrow Wilson, he was the third child of the Reverend Joseph Ruggles Wilson and Janet Woodrow Wilson.

1858   —Family moved to Augusta, Georgia. Wilson did not learn his letters until age nine and did not learn to read before age eleven or twelve because of developmental dyslexia.

1867–70   —Attended Mr. Derry's Classical School, in Augusta.

1870–73   —Moved to Columbia, South Carolina, where Mrs. Joseph R. Russell tutored Woodrow privately in Latin and Greek.

1873–74   —Entered Davidson College, a small Presbyterian school near Charlotte, North Carolina, and dropped out after suffering from severe depression and abandoning plans to become a minister.

1875–79   —Attended Princeton University, earning an undergraduate degree. As a class leader he was active in student literary and debating activities, sang in the Glee Club, and managed and organized football and baseball teams.

1877   —Published his first article, "Prince Bismarck," in *Nassau Literary Magazine*.

1878   —Wrote prize-winning essay, "William, Earl of Chatham," published in *Nassau Literary Magazine*.

1879   —Wrote "Cabinet Government in the United States," published in *International Review*.

1879–80   —Entered University of Virginia's law school, excelling in debate but struggling with the work load. Dropped out due to poor health.

1880   —Oration on John Bright published in *University of Virginia Magazine*. Text of debate arguing against Roman Catholicism as a menace to American institutions published in *University of Virginia Magazine*. Article "Mr. Gladstone—A Character Sketch," written under pen name Atticus, published in *University of Virginia Magazine*.

1881   —Recuperated at home in Wilmington, North Carolina, from illness that was partly dyspepsia and partly psychosomatic. Proposed marriage to first cousin Harriet Woodrow and was rejected. Studied law, published articles on the New South in the New York *Evening Post*, and wrote several letters to newspaper editors.

1882–83   —Admitted to state bar of Georgia, and entered into practice with Edward I. Renick in Atlanta. Appeared before a presidential tariff commission to argue against protectionism. Neglected law practice to study history and political science. Began courtship of Ellen Louise Axson of Savannah, Georgia.

1883–85   —Entered Johns Hopkins University to study for Ph.D. under Herbert Baxter Adams and Richard T. Ely.

1885   —Published first book, *Congressional Government.*

    —24 June: Married Ellen Louise Axson.

1885–88   —Appointed associate professor of history and political science at Bryn Mawr College. Sole history professor at women's college.

1886   —16 April: First daughter, Margaret, born.

    —Ph.D. granted from Johns Hopkins University, using *Congressional Government* as his thesis.

1887   —28 August: Second daughter, Jessie Woodrow, born.

1888   —April: Death of mother, Janet Woodrow Wilson.

1888–90   —Appointed to chair of history and political economy at Wesleyan University. Lectured at Johns Hopkins University and throughout New England.

1889   —Published *The State: Elements of Historical and Practical Politics*, considered his greatest scholarly achievement.

    —16 October: Third daughter, Eleanor Randolph, born.

1890–1902   —Occupied chair of jurisprudence and politics at Princeton University.

1893   —Published "Mr. Cleveland's Cabinet" in *Review of Reviews. An Old Master and Other Political Essays* and a historical study of sectionalism and the Civil War, *Division and Reunion*, were also published.

1896   —*Mere Literature and Other Essays* and *George Washington* were published.

    —May: Suffered stroke (misdiagnosed as neuritis) that caused weakness of right arm and hand (right upper extremity). Had difficulty writing for almost one year.

1897	—"Mr. Cleveland's Cabinet" and "The Making of the Nation" were both published in *Atlantic Monthly*.
1901	—Published essay, "When a Man Comes of Himself," in book form.
1902	—*A History of the American People* published in five volumes.
1902–10	—Served as president of Princeton University, where he brought about many educational reforms.
1903	—21 January: Death of father, Joseph R. Wilson.
	—Published article, "States' Rights," in *Cambridge Modern History*.
1904	—Statement on tutorial system published in *Princeton Alumni Weekly*.
	—June: Suffered stroke that caused weakness of right upper extremity.
1905	—Statement on Princeton preceptorial system published in the *Independent*.
1906	—28 May: Suffered stroke that caused loss of vision in left eye and weakness in right upper extremity.
	—Recuperated in England. Proposed controversial "quad" plan requiring students to live in colleges rather than dorms.
1907	—November: Suffered from periodic weakness and numbness in fingers of right hand.
	—Published article "Politics from 1857 to 1907" in *Atlantic Monthly*.
1908	—Article "The States and the Federal Government" appeared in *North American Review*, and book *Constitutional Government in the United States* published.
	—July: Suffered two attacks of what was diagnosed as neuritis.
1909	—Article "The Tariff Make-Believe" published in *North American Review*, and "What Is College For?" published in *Scribner's*.
1910	—Article "Living Principles of Democracy" published in *Harper's Weekly*, and "Hide and Seek Politics" published in *North American Review*.
	—15 September: Nominated as Democratic party candidate for governor of New Jersey.
	—23 October: Resigned from Princeton.
	—November: Elected governor.
	—December: Suffered recurrent weakness of right hand.
1911	—17 January: Inaugurated governor of New Jersey. Called for regulation of corporations, employers' liability legislation, ballot reform, a primary election system, a public utilities commission, tax reform, and a corrupt-practices act.

1912 —26 February: Delivered first annual message to New Jersey legislature.

—2 April: Vetoed sixteen bills.

—2 July: Nominated as Democratic party candidate for president on forty-sixth ballot.

—4 November: Received 6,286,214 popular votes and 435 electoral votes to become twenty-seventh president.

1913 —1 March: Resigned as governor of New Jersey.

—4 March: Inaugurated president.

—11 March: Refused to recognize Victoriano Huerta government of Mexico.

—8 April: Appeared before Congress to make dramatic request for tariff revisions.

—April: Suffered attack of what was diagnosed as neuritis.

—23 June: Appeared before Congress to urge currency reform.

—27 August: Appeared before Congress to discuss Mexico policy.

—3 October: Signed tariff bill.

—27 October: Addressed the Southern Commercial Congress at Mobile, Alabama, on Latin America, pledging that the United States "will never again seek one additional foot of territory by conquest."

—2 December: Appeared before Congress to make first annual address.

—23 December: Signed Federal Reserve Act.

1914 —20 January: Addressed Congress on issue of trusts and monopolies.

—7 April: Signed Colombian-American treaty providing recompense for the Canal Zone, a pact that the Senate rejected.

—20 April: Addressed Congress on crisis with Mexico.

—22 April: Ordered seizure of the Customs House at Veracruz by the U.S. Navy.

—May: Vascular pathology in renal arteries observed.

—4 August: World War I began in Europe.

—6 August: Death of wife, Ellen Axson Wilson.

—19 August: Issued proclamation of neutrality.

—8 December: Delivered second annual address to Congress, urging development of the merchant marine, conservation legislation, greater self-government for the Philippines, and national defense measures.

1915–19   —Suffered periodic severe headaches, most probably associated with hypertension.

1915   —28 January: Returned immigration bill to House on ground that it would violate human rights by denying asylum to refugees.

—10 February: Sent note to Germany about freedom of the seas.

—13 May, 9 June, 21 July: Notes sent to Germany protesting the sinking of the *Lusitania*.

—May to September: Suffered periodic weakness of right hand.

—7 October: Announced engagement to Edith Bolling Galt.

—19 October: Recognized Venustiano Carranza government of Mexico.

—21 October: Denounced the British blockade of neutral ports in Europe.

—7 December: Delivered third annual address to Congress, discussing neutrality, Mexico, Pan-Americanism, preparedness, antiradicalism, farm credits, and transportation.

—18 December: Married Edith Bolling Galt.

1916   —27 January to 3 February: Made several speeches on war and national defense.

—22 February: Gave memorandum to Lord Grey proposing a conference to end the war.

—15 March: Ordered troops under the command of General John J. Pershing into Mexico to pursue Pancho Villa.

—19 April: Delivered address to Congress on crisis with Germany over U-boat warfare.

—4 May: Germany offered assurances on the rights of neutrals.

—16 June: Renominated for president by the National Democratic Convention at St. Louis.

—17 July: Signed the Federal Farm Loan Act.

—29 August: Delivered address to Congress making recommendations designed to thwart a threatened railroad strike.

—3 September: Signed the Adamson railway wage law.

—7 September: Signed bill creating U.S. Shipping Board.

—7 November: Narrowly reelected president with 9 million popular votes and 277 electoral votes.

1916   —5 December: Delivered fourth annual address to Congress, discussing railroad legislation, promotion of foreign trade, Puerto Rico, and revision of the corrupt-practices acts.

     —18 December: Sent message to belligerents "proposing that soundings be taken" on peace.

1917   —22 January: Reported to Senate on peace efforts.

     —29 January: Vetoed immigration restriction bill, because it included provisions for literacy testing.

     —3 February: Delivered address to Congress on Germany's renewed U-boat warfare.

     —26 February: Asked Congress for authority to arm merchant ships.

     —4 March: Denounced "a little group of willful men" in the Senate for blocking the armed-ship bill.

     —5 March: Inaugurated president for second term.

     —2 April: Delivered address to Congress asking for declaration of war against Germany.

     —6 April: Signed proclamation declaring war on Germany.

     —18 May: Signed selective draft act.

     —19 May: Announced food control program.

     —4 December: Delivered fifth annual address to Congress, asking for declaration of war against Austria-Hungary.

     —7 December: War declared on Austria-Hungary.

     —26 December: Issued declaration placing railroads under government control.

1918   —4 January: Delivered address to Congress justifying government takeover of railroads.

     —8 January: Delivered address to Congress on Fourteen Points for peace.

     —11 February: Delivered address to Congress on prospects for peace.

     —16 May: Signed the sedition amendment to the Espionage Act, sanctioning the most severe restrictions on freedom of speech and the press in American history.

     —27 May: Delivered address to Congress on war finance and noted that "politics is adjourned."

     —22 July: Announced that telegraph and telephone systems were to be placed under government control.

—26 July: Issued statement on civil liberties in wartime.

—30 September: Addressed Senate, urging passage of women's suffrage amendment.

—October: Exchanged diplomatic notes with Germany and Austria-Hungary on the restoration of peace.

—25 October: Issued statement asking American people to vote for Democrats to strengthen his position of leadership.

—11 November: Delivered address to Congress announcing Armistice.

—2 December: Delivered sixth annual message to Congress, announcing that he would go to Paris to discuss the peace settlement.

—4 December: Departed for Europe to attend Paris Peace Conference.

—14–30 December: Visited France and Great Britain.

1919   —3–6 January: Visited Italy, where he made several speeches.

—18 January: Delivered address at opening of Paris Peace Conference.

—14 February: Presented report to conference on the plan for the League of Nations.

—15 February: Departed France for the United States.

—24 February: Addressed meeting in Boston, discussing hopes for peace.

—4 March: Addressed meeting in New York City, along with former President William Howard Taft, on the need for the League.

—5 March: Departed for Europe to return to peace conference.

—3–7 April: Suffered from severe influenza, which impaired functioning of brain and heart.

—23 April: Issued statement on controversy with Italy over the Adriatic region.

—28 April: Presented the revised League of Nations Covenant to peace conference.

—28 June: Signed Treaty of Versailles and departed Europe.

—8 July: Returned to the United States.

—10 July: Delivered address to Senate asking for ratification of Treaty of Versailles.

—29 July: Sent Tripartite Treaty of Guarantee to Senate.

—8 August: Addressed Congress on subject of the economy.

1919   —19 August: Discussed Versailles treaty with the Senate Foreign Relations Committee at the White House.

—4–25 September: Traveled 8,000 miles on tour of Western cities, explaining the treaty and the League and rallying support for ratification. Suffered severe headaches, double vision, and heart problems.

—25 September: Suffered temporary paralysis of left side.

—26 September: Abandoned trip on advice of physician.

—3 October: Suffered massive stroke with permanent paralysis of left side, restricted vision, and mental disability.

—25 October: Issued statement threatening to intervene in strike by United Mine Workers.

—27 October: Vetoed Volstead Act.

—17 November: Told Senate Democratic Minority Leader Gilbert M. Hitchcock that he could not accept the Henry Cabot Lodge reservations to Article Ten of the League Covenant.

—19 November: Senate voted to reject the Treaty of Versailles, with or without the Lodge reservations.

—2 December: Sent seventh annual message to Congress, discussing railroads, the balance of trade, foreign markets, tariff revision, farm problems, the economy, and labor.

—9 December: Issued statement urging striking coal miners to accept settlement.

—24 December: Issued proclamation returning railroads to private control.

1920   —8 January: Wrote letter explaining to Democrats that he did not object to interpretive reservations to the Versailles treaty provided that they did not alter the League Covenant.

—13 February: Accepted forced resignation of Secretary of State Robert Lansing.

—19 March: Senate voted to return Treaty of Versailles to Wilson unratified.

—24 May: Sent message to Congress requesting approval for an American mandate over Armenia.

—27 May: Vetoed House resolution declaring peace with former Central Powers.

—1 June: Senate rejected Armenian mandate proposal.

—30 July: Demanded that striking miners return to work.

—2 November: Warren G. Harding wins presidency in landslide viewed as a repudiation of Wilson.

—7 December: Sent eighth annual message to Congress.

—10 December: Awarded Nobel Peace Prize.

1921   —3 January: Vetoed bill extending term of War Finance Corporation.

—3 March: Vetoed House emergency tariff bill.

—4 March: Expiration of presidential term. Moved to home at 2340 S Street.

—10 October: Urged Senate Democrats not to ratify the Treaty of Berlin, the separate peace with Germany.

—11 November: Rode in funeral procession of Unknown Soldier.

1922   —15 January and 11 November: Spoke to crowd in front of home on subject of peace.

1923–24   —Suffered further deterioration of eyesight.

1923   —8 August: Accompanied body of President Harding from White House to Capitol.

—August: Published article "The Road away from Revolution" in *Atlantic Monthly*.

—10 November: Addressed radio audience on Armistice Day.

—11 November: Told crowd gathered at his home that the principles he stood for would triumph.

1924   —31 January: Collapsed into final illness.

—3 February: Death of Woodrow Wilson.

—6 February: Interred in Bethlehem Chapel, Washington Cathedral.

1961   —28 December: Death of Edith Bolling Wilson. Interred in Washington Cathedral.

Introduction to the Bibliography

The years of the Wilson presidency (1913–1921) marked a turning point in American life. While the United States had been a great industrial power for some time, there was still a sense of innocence and simplicity about government and about life in general when Woodrow Wilson took office. By the time he tottered into retirement, the Progressive movement had run its course, the country had played a vital role in winning World War I, and Americans were caught up in a postwar malaise seething with bitterness and anger. The Wilson era left mixed legacies of accomplishments and failures and of idealism and disillusionment that still reverberate today.

The purpose of this bibliography is to put between the covers of a single volume a survey of the most important written materials chronicling and analyzing the events of the Wilson period. While much has been written about Wilson's presidency and times, it is apparent that there is ample room for more original research and new interpretations.

Basic Design

This bibliography is arranged by subject matter, with each chapter covering such associated topics as domestic, foreign, and military matters. Researchers should begin by consulting the extensive table of contents. Chapter topics are further divided into more specialized sections and subsections. These subdivisions have been extensively cross-referenced with associated topics in other chapters. The author index lists the writers in alphabetical order, and the subject index refers to material that may appear in several different topical areas.

This bibliography does not pretend to be definitive; it is, rather, a comprehensive survey of the basic literature on the Wilson years. Scholarly and popular books, articles, and doctoral dissertations make up most of the entries. Major published and microfilmed documents are also listed, although researchers would do well to consult local and university libraries for special collections of documents and other primary sources. Most unpublished versions of dissertations that were subsequently published are not included, although some have been retained if the original work was substantially altered or printed in a much-truncated form.

The annotations are more descriptive than judgmental, and they concentrate on the Wilson period rather than on the work as a whole. Thus, an entry on Progressive chief executives would focus on material relevant to the Wilson presidency, and one on the history of music would highlight chapters concerning the period from 1913 to 1921. Annotations also include information on such amenities as photographs, illustrations, notes, bibliographies, appendixes, and indexes to give researchers a better idea of the work's scholarly value.

Supplementary Research Tools

By the time this book reaches the hands of its intended audience, many new materials will have been published. Researchers should be aware that it will be necessary for them to become their own bibliographers. Fortunately, there are several sources to assist with this, although none is completely satisfactory.

One excellent source is *America: History and Life*, an annotated bibliography of English-language periodical literature on American and Canadian history (Part A), which is published several times a year along with indexes to book reviews and dissertations and cross references to subject matter (Parts B, C, and D). Usually one or two years lapse before an article can be listed. Because the series relies on volunteer labor (scholars are given free subscriptions to the material they annotate), not every issue of every periodical is covered, although the coverage is impressive. For foreign-language journals, consult *Historical Abstracts*, for which the same caveats apply. Three times a year the American Historical Association puts out *Recently Published Articles* for all areas of history, including American. Entries are not annotated, and there is no index.

Reviews in American History is an excellent quarterly publication containing thoughtful review essays prepared by leading scholars on important new history books. Coverage is highly selective and based on what the majority of the readership might find most interesting. Many scholarly journals publish brief reviews of recent works, but again it can take years for the notice to see the light of day. Reviews are of uneven quality, because some academics are more interested in grinding their own axes than in presenting fair-minded descriptions and commentary.

Finally, a few words are in order about computer-assisted bibliographic searches. Many scholars now own or have access to personal computers with modem hardware designed to communicate with data banks. Private and government-sponsored databases allow bibliographic searches to be made from home or office with speed and convenience. DIALOG Information Retrieval Service, for example, offers access to hundreds of databases, among them *Book Review Index, Books in Print, America: History and Life, Historical Abstracts, LISA,* and *Social Scisearch*. Search options include author/title (with or without abstracts) and complete texts of articles and documents. However, there are a few serious drawbacks. Database searches are expensive, requiring membership fees, training sessions, and charges for using the system computed by the minute. While many libraries subscribe to retrieval services, researchers should understand that librarians must parcel out their computer time and money to many patrons. Even with training, it takes experience to become an effective user, and even then operators must realize that no database, no matter how large, can be comprehensive. Richard Dean Burns, series editor of this presidential bibliography series, offers prudent advice in his guide to compilers: "Computer searches may help but are not a substitute for the more traditional techniques."

Woodrow Wilson

Materials dealing with Woodrow Wilson's life, early years, academic career, family, health, gubernatorial term, and postpresidential years comprise this chapter. Strictly separating Wilson's life from his presidency is an impossible and rather arbitrary task; therefore, readers should also consult Chapter 2 for materials that concentrate on his actions and policies as president.

A number of excellent overviews of Wilson's life have been written. See David D. Anderson, *Woodrow Wilson* (#0001); John Morton Blum, *Woodrow Wilson and the Politics of Morality* (#0006); John A. Garraty, *Woodrow Wilson: A Great Life in Brief* (#0017); Arthur S. Link, *Woodrow Wilson: A Brief Biography* (#0029); and Arthur Walworth, *Woodrow Wilson* (#0036). Link is the preeminent Wilson scholar, having devoted over thirty years to his subject. His masterful five-volume political biography, *Wilson* (#0026), covers Wilson's career and his times in great detail up to 1916. The first volume, *Wilson: The Road to the White House* (#0027), examines the period from 1902 to 1912.

While most older biographies have been omitted from this study, readers will find some useful. William B. Hale, author of *Woodrow Wilson: The Story of His Life* (#0022), was Wilson's campaign manager, and he interviewed Wilson about his early life. Ray S. Baker, *Woodrow Wilson: Life and Letters* (#0003), wrote an eight-volume authorized biography that ends with the Armistice. Josephus Daniels, *The Life of Woodrow Wilson, 1856–1924* (#0011), contributes an uncritical insider's account as does Joseph P. Tumulty, *Woodrow Wilson as I Know Him* (#0035). Two distinguished journalists wrote early biographies: David Lawrence, *The True Story of Woodrow Wilson* (#0023), and William

Allen White, *Woodrow Wilson, The Man, His Times, and His Task* (#0038).

Wilson's early life has not escaped the attention of historians. See John M. Mulder, *Woodrow Wilson: The Years of Preparation* (#0047), and George C. Osborn, *Woodrow Wilson: The Early Years* (#0049). Both accounts deal with Wilson's academic career as does Henry W. Bragdon, *Woodrow Wilson: The Academic Years* (#0056). Many of Wilson's classmates and colleagues wrote about his university years, among them Hardin Craig, *Woodrow Wilson at Princeton* (#0059); Winthrop Daniels, *Recollections of Woodrow Wilson* (#0061); and Bliss Perry, *And Gladly Teach* (#0071).

Several works concentrate on Wilson's family life. Frances W. Saunders, *Ellen Axson Wilson: First Lady between Two Worlds* (#0091), has written an excellent biography of Wilson's first wife. Edith Bolling Wilson has received more attention, in large part because of her role as an intermediary between her husband and the outside world during Wilson's illness of 1919–20. See Alden Hatch, *Edith Bolling Wilson, First Lady Extraordinary* (#0083), and Ishbel Ross, *Power with Grace: The Life Story of Mrs. Woodrow Wilson* (#0090). Letters between Wilson and his second wife are excerpted in Edwin Tribble, ed., *A President in Love: The Courtship Letters of Woodrow Wilson and Edith Bolling Galt* (#0094). The second Mrs. Wilson tells her own story in *My Memoir* (#0096). Wilson's daughter Eleanor Wilson McAdoo writes about her childhood in *The Woodrow Wilsons* (#0086) and presents a volume of revealing family letters, *The Priceless Gift* (#0087). Mary A. Hulbert, *The Story of Mrs. Peck* (#0084), discreetly discusses her controversial friendship with Wilson.

President Wilson and his granddaughter, Ellen Wilson McAdoo. *Library of Congress.*

Wilson's health, both physical and mental, has been examined by a number of writers. Edwin A. Weinstein, *Woodrow Wilson: A Medical and Psychological Biography* (#0116), details Wilson's health problems and their effects on his work. Alexander and Juliette George, *Woodrow Wilson and Colonel House: A Personality Study* (#0019), examine Wilson's personal makeup and his relationship with Edward House. The Georges attack Weinstein's book in a number of articles, (#0103–0105), while Arthur Link defends it. Most controversial of all is Sigmund Freud and William C. Bullitt, *Thomas Woodrow Wilson, Twenty-eighth President of the United States: A Psychological Study* (#0102), a disappointing book full of Bullitt's vitriol.

Researchers serious about examining the life and times of Woodrow Wilson will want to consult the primary sources. The Library of Congress has microfilmed its collection of *Woodrow Wilson Papers* (#0138), providing a 3-volume index (#0123) to the series, which runs to 540 reels. Several major university libraries have purchased the series, and it is available through interlibrary loan. Arthur S. Link et al., eds., *The Papers of Woodrow Wilson* (#0133), provide many documents not previously available to scholars. Now approaching completion, this series is unsurpassed in the care with which it has been assembled and annotated. Researchers also should consult Wilson's *Constitutional Government in the United States* (#0125) and *Congressional Government: A Study in American Politics* (#0124) because of their seminal importance. Wilson's other major writings, *Division and Reunion* (#0126), *George Washington* (#0127), *The State: Elements of Historical and Practical Politics* (#0136), *When a Man Comes to Himself* (#0137), and *A History of the American People* (#0128), are readily available in various editions published over the years. John Wells Davidson, ed., *A Crossroads of Freedom: The 1912 Campaign Speeches of Woodrow Wilson* (#0120), is an important source for what Wilson said during the election.

Wilson's brief tenure as governor of New Jersey is chronicled in David W. Hirst, *Woodrow Wilson, A Reform Governor* (#0142). See also a contemporary article by Burton J. Hendrick, "Woodrow Wilson: Political Leader" (#0141).

The final tragic years following Wilson's retirement are examined in Mary U. Archer, "Woodrow Wilson: The Post Presidential Years" (#0148), and Gene Smith, *When the Cheering Stopped: The Last Years of Woodrow Wilson* (#0153). Peter H. Buckingham, *International Normalcy: The Open Door Peace with the Former Central Powers, 1921–1929*

(#0149), contains material on Wilson's efforts to block ratification of the separate peace with Germany in 1921.

Autobiographical and Biographical Materials

GENERAL

Materials relating strictly to Wilson's presidency may be found in Chapter 2.

0001 Anderson, David D. *Woodrow Wilson.* Boston: Twayne, 1978.

The most complex of presidents, Wilson fused realism and idealism, often with mixed results. While his failures, both public and private, outweighed his successes, he was a great man. Notes, bibliography, index.

0002 Annin, Robert E. *Woodrow Wilson: A Character Study.* New York: Dodd, Mead, 1925.

Although Wilson was a public figure who had unique talents and the highest of aims, faulty perspectives, both personal and political, prevented him from being truly effective. The author finds "disturbing constants" throughout Wilson's career concerning his "mental equipment."

0003 Baker, Ray S. *Woodrow Wilson: Life and Letters.* 8 vols. Garden City, NY: Doubleday, Doran, 1927–1939.

This authorized biography, based on the Wilson papers and the author's conversations with the president, ends with the Armistice of 1918. An ardent Wilsonian, Baker's hero worship and his erratic documentation detract from a work that still should be considered an important source. Photographs, notes, index.

0004 Bellot, Hugh H. *Woodrow Wilson.* London: Athlone, 1955.

In this extended essay, Wilson is seen as an earnest man of great natural ability who was bored by detail. An astute politician, Wilson could sway multitudes with his words.

0005 Black, Harold G. *The True Woodrow Wilson.* New York: Fleming Revell, 1946.

Wilson is seen as a man of strong likes and dislikes whose real nature was revealed only in his private life. He deserves to be ranked in the company of Washington, Jefferson, and Lincoln. Index.

0006 Blum, John Morton. *Woodrow Wilson and the Politics of Morality*. Boston: Little, Brown, 1956.

While Wilson's domestic program was a magnificent accomplishment, it was hardly original, since the foundations of it had been laid by others, and it had certain nostalgic qualities. His faith in liberal constitutionalism has not been completely justified, but his greatest triumph was that he taught us that America had to play a leading part in world affairs. Bibliography, index.

0007 Bradford, Gamaliel. *The Quick and the Dead*. Boston: Houghton Mifflin, 1931.

One chapter contains a brief biography of Wilson.

0008 Cranston, Ruth. *The Story of Woodrow Wilson*. New York: Simon and Schuster, 1945.

A lifelong Wilsonian and friend of the family, the author's admiration for the president only increased as a result of her research. Wilson's life was devoted to service, democracy, responsibility, and noblesse oblige. Appendix, index.

0009 Curti, Merle. "Woodrow Wilson's Concept of Human Nature." *Midwest Journal of Political Science* 1 (1957): 1–19.

A liberal Calvinist, Wilson believed that people were capable of living up to their absolute moral standards. His inflexible standards, combined with his misunderstanding of cultural relativism and his forsaking of realism, led to his downfall. Notes.

0010 Dabney, Virginius. "The Human Side of Woodrow. Wilson." *Virginia Quarterly Review* 32 (1956): 508–24.

Wilson's character was contradictory in many ways. Few realized that he had a great sense of humor. His illness affected his judgment, shortened his temper, and led to a series of breaks with friends. Notes.

0011 Daniels, Josephus. *The Life of Woodrow Wilson, 1856–1924*. Philadelphia: Winston, 1924.

Wilson's faithful secretary of the navy writes favorably of his chief as the epic figure of their era, whose failure to get the Treaty of Versailles through the Senate does not detract from his stature. Index.

0012 Diamond, William. *The Economic Thought of Woodrow Wilson*. Baltimore: Johns Hopkins University Press, 1943.

Economics played an important role in Wilson's thought. By the time he became president, Wilson had a sophisticated understanding of foreign economic policy. Notes, bibliography, index.

0013 Easum, Chester V. "Woodrow Wilson in Commemoration of the 100th Anniversary of His Birth on 28 December 1956" (in German). *Jahrbüch für Amerikastudien* [West Germany] 2 (1957): 8–18.

Although Wilson was an idealist with a strong Calvinist background, he was more of a realist than is generally recognized. He led the United States into the fight against militarism and autocracy, neither to combat monarchy nor at the behest of commercial interests. Notes, bibliography.

0014 Eaton, William D.; Read, Harry C.; and McKenna, Edmond. *Woodrow Wilson: His Life and Work*. N.p.: J. Thomas, 1924.

Three leading journalists combined forces to produce this uncritical biography of Wilson, whose domestic program was designed to perfect democracy and whose foreign policy was dedicated to world peace. Photographs.

0015 Ferrell, Robert H. "Woodrow Wilson: Man and Statesman." *Review of Politics* 18 (1956): 131–45.

Wilson's greatness has held up after forty years. His tragedy was that, with victory in sight, his personal weaknesses surfaced so that the Treaty of Versailles fell short of ratification. Notes.

0016 Fosdick, Raymond B. "Personal Recollections of Woodrow Wilson." In Earl Latham, ed. *The Philosophy and Policies of Woodrow Wilson*. Chicago: University of Chicago Press, 1958, pp. 28–45.

Upon meeting the future president at Princeton in 1903, the author found that Wilson was a deeply religious man. Passionate sincerity and precision of mind made him a great orator.

0017 Garraty, John A. *Woodrow Wilson: A Great Life in Brief*. New York: Knopf, 1956.

Wilson was a great man, a brilliant politician, and a high-minded statesman. He lived too much within himself and never seems to have found inner peace.

0018 ——. "Woodrow Wilson: A Study in Personality." *South Atlantic Quarterly* 56 (1957): 176–85.

Wilson's personality was such that he felt less at ease with individuals than he did with groups. He was an extremely demanding boss and friend, and he could not work at all with subordinates who disagreed with him. He was completely comfortable only when he was with his family. Notes.

0019 George, Alexander L., and George, Juliette L. *Woodrow Wilson and Colonel House: A Personality Study*. New York: John Day, 1956.

The two great influences on Wilson were his own "inner turbulence" and the ideas of his friend Colonel House, whose calculated playing to the president's vanity made him a power in his own right. Notes, index.

0020 Gershov, Z. M. *Woodrow Wilson* [in Russian]. Moscow: Mysl', 1983.

Wilson is viewed as a tool of American capitalism who implemented reforms to co-opt the class struggle and cloaked American imperialism in idealistic phrases. Notes.

0021 Gilbert, Clinton. *The Mirrors of Washington*. New York: Putnam's, 1921.

One chapter in this series of stinging portraits by a Washington journalist is on Wilson, who is viewed as strange and self-absorbed. Illustrations.

0022 Hale, William Bayard. *Woodrow Wilson: The Story of His Life*. Garden City, NY: Doubleday, 1912.

This campaign biography is useful, because Wilson discussed his childhood with the author. Photographs.

0023 Lawrence, David. *The True Story of Woodrow Wilson*. New York: Doran, 1924.

Wilson lived and died "unexplained and unrevealed." He was a Christian idealist who disliked the popular press and granted fewer personal interviews than any other modern president.

0024 Link, Arthur S. "The Higher Realism of Woodrow Wilson." In Arthur S. Link. *The Higher Realism of Woodrow Wilson and Other Essays*. Nashville: Vanderbilt University Press, 1971, pp. 127–39.

Wilson was a supreme realist in his three public careers as educator, governor, and president of the United States. He lived in Christian faith and demonstrated the power of his brand of higher realism.

0025 ——. "A Portrait of Wilson." *Virginia Quarterly Review* 32 (1956): 833–51.

Wilson cannot be understood without an appreciation of his religious convictions. His strong need for affection, his egotism, and his reliance on intuition were other key aspects of his character. Notes.

0026 ——. *Wilson*. 5 vols. Princeton: Princeton University Press, 1947.

This five-volume political biography carries Wilson's life up to the spring of 1916. Meticulously researched, it must still be considered the best secondary source on Wilson. Individual volumes are cited elsewhere. Photographs, notes, bibliography, index.

0027 ——. *Wilson: The Road to the White House*. Princeton: Princeton University Press, 1947.

Volume I of Link's Wilson biography (#0026) disposes of Wilson's formative years in one chapter to concentrate on the Princeton years, the governorship of New Jersey, and the presidential campaign of 1912. By 1912, the once-conservative Wilson had emerged as the heir of the Populist-William Jennings Bryan tradition. Notes, bibliography, index.

0028 ——. "Woodrow Wilson: The American as Southerner." In Arthur S. Link. *The Higher Realism of Woodrow Wilson and Other Essays*. Nashville: Vanderbilt University Press, 1971, pp. 21–37.

Southerners were quick to claim Wilson as one of their own, beginning in 1885. In turn, Wilson brought the South back into the mainstream of American politics, benefiting the South and the whole country. Notes.

0029 ——. *Woodrow Wilson: A Brief Biography*. Cleveland: World, 1963.

The author's scholarship on Wilson's life is abridged for the general reader. Bibliography, index.

0030 ——. "Woodrow Wilson and His Presbyterian Inheritance." In Arthur S. Link. *The Higher Realism of Woodrow Wilson and Other Essays*. Nashville: Vanderbilt University Press, 1971, pp. 3–20.

Wilson's Presbyterian heritage played an important part in his life and thought. Wilson would bring the Scottish and Scotch-Irish legacy to politics, society, and culture. Notes.

0031 ——. "Woodrow Wilson: Presbyterian in Government." In George L. Hunt, ed.

Calvinism and the Political Order. Philadelphia: Westminster, 1965, pp. 157–74.

Wilson's Calvinistic Presbyterianism is examined to illustrate how vital his faith was to his world outlook.

0032 ———. *Woodrow Wilson: A Profile*. New York: Hill and Wang, 1968.

To introduce readers to Wilson the man, as opposed to Wilson the Ray Stannard Baker myth (see #0003), excerpts from previously published works are presented along with an essay by Link on the idealism and realism of Wilson. Bibliography.

0033 McKinley, Silas B. *Woodrow Wilson: A Biography*. New York: Praeger, 1957.

Wilson was a great man whose faults caused him to make tragic mistakes. Partisanship and stubbornness aroused violent opposition to him. His failures in Mexico, preparedness, and the Treaty of Versailles were offset by his domestic reforms, his wartime leadership, and his vision of peace. Photographs, bibliography, index.

0034 Schulte, Nordholt J. W. "The Religion of Woodrow Wilson" (in Dutch). *Tijdschrift voor Geschiedenis* [Netherlands] 98 (1985): 43–55.

Wilson's Presbyterian roots played a vital role in his outlook. He viewed America as a Christian nation destined to lead the world. His religion-based optimism was not realistic. Notes.

0035 Tumulty, Joseph P. *Woodrow Wilson as I Know Him*. Garden City, NY: Doubleday, Page, 1921.

Wilson's private secretary writes about his boss as a man who was too sincere to be a backslapping politician and who governed with both a great heart and a great mind. Appendix, index.

0036 Walworth, Arthur. *Woodrow Wilson*. 2 vols. Boston: Houghton Mifflin, 1965.

Revised after it won the Pulitzer Prize in 1958, this well-written account reveres Wilson as a prophet who was ahead of his time as an educator, a social reformer, and an advocate of world peace. Notes, bibliography, index.

0037 Wells, Wells [pseud.]. *Wilson the Unknown: An Explanation of an Enigma of History*. New York: Scribner's, 1931.

A master of inductive reasoning, Wilson became "the dogmatic dictator of Democracy." Notes, appendixes, index.

0038 White, William Allen. *Woodrow Wilson, The Man, His Times, and His Task*. Boston: Houghton Mifflin, 1924.

Neither a god nor a fiend, Wilson was a middle-aged academic driven by Calvinism. He was a sincere man with pure motives, but he had a "reptilian personality." Appendix.

0039 Wilson, Woodrow. *A Day of Dedication: The Essential Writings & Speeches of Woodrow Wilson*. Edited by Albert Fried. New York: Macmillan, 1965.

An extended biographical essay precedes judicious selections from Wilson's writings and speeches between 1877 and 1923 to explain his political philosophy. Bibliography.

0040 ———. *The Political Thought of Woodrow Wilson*. Edited by E. David Cronon. New York: Bobbs–Merrill, 1965.

A chronology of Wilson's life is presented along with documents illuminating his political ideas, arranged topically. Bibliography, index.

0041 ———. *Wilson*. Edited by John Braeman. Englewood Cliffs, NJ: Prentice-Hall, 1972.

An introductory essay, a chronology, and excerpts from essential speeches and writings provide an overview of Wilson's life and work. Judgments by Wilson's contemporaries and historians round out this volume from the Great Lives Observed series. Bibliography, index.

0042 ———. *The Wilson Years*. Edited by Frances Farmer. New York: Oceana, 1956.

Excerpts from letters, speeches, and documents are cut and pasted together with brief comments from the editor. Bibliography.

0043 ———. *Woodrow Wilson's Own Story*. Edited by Donald Day. Boston: Little, Brown, 1952.

Bits and pieces of Wilson's articles, addresses, public statements, and letters are strung together in chronological order with a narrative to form an autobiography of sorts. Index.

WILSON'S EARLY YEARS

0044 Bober, Robert A. "Young Woodrow Wilson: The Search for Immortality." Ph.D. dissertation, Case Western Reserve University, 1981.

Wilson's frustrated father passed on a great desire for achievement to his son, a boy who failed to meet impossibly high standards. Eschewing the ministry, Wilson turned to academia in his search for heroic immortality. DAI 41:3232-A.

0045 Gatewood, Willard B., Jr. "Woodrow Wilson: The Formative Years, 1856–1880." *Georgia Review* 21 (1967): 3–13.

A study of Wilson's early years is essential to the understanding of such a complex figure.

0046 Harris, Irving D. "The Psychologies of Presidents." *History of Childhood Quarterly* 3 (1976): 337–50.

Like other people, presidents are shaped by the positions they hold in their families as children. Wilson is among those studied, and he fits the pattern of first sons, who are more likely to lead the country into war. Notes.

0047 Mulder, John M. *Woodrow Wilson: The Years of Preparation*. Princeton: Princeton University Press, 1978.

Wilson was strongly influenced by his father, a Presbyterian minister, who taught his son that the greatest purpose in life was to serve mankind. Woodrow Wilson chose to carry out that mission as a writer and educator and later in government service. He violated his own understanding of politics as the art of compromise when he saw basic moral issues at stake. Photographs, notes, bibliography, index.

0048 Osborn, George C. "The Influence of Joseph Ruggles Wilson on His Son Woodrow Wilson." *North Carolina Historical Review* 32 (1955): 519–43.

Wilson's father was his most intimate companion and most generous critic. Above all, Joseph Wilson gave his son a yearning for knowledge.

0049 ———. *Woodrow Wilson: The Early Years*. Baton Rouge: Louisiana State University Press, 1968.

Wilson's life from birth to 1902 is covered. The late-blooming and prudish young Wilson was caught between his domineering father and a mother equally determined to possess him. His idealism is traced through his writings as a student and a teacher. Notes, bibliography, index.

0050 ———. "Woodrow Wilson: The Evolution of a Name." *North Carolina Historical Review* 34 (1961): 507–16.

As a boy he was "Tommy," but he probably decided to use "Woodrow" as a first name in remembrance of his first love, Harriet Woodrow, in 1881.

0051 ———. "Woodrow Wilson as a Young Lawyer, 1882–1883." *Georgia Historical Quarterly* 4 (1957): 126–42.

Wilson quickly abandoned his career as a lawyer in Atlanta, because that city had too many attorneys, and because he found himself more interested in history and political science. Notes.

0052 Patterson, Archibald W. *Personal Recollections of Woodrow Wilson and Some Reflections upon His Life and Character*. Richmond, VA: Whittet and Shepperson, 1929.

The author met "T. W." Wilson in 1879 at the University of Virginia, where he was much admired although usually quite reserved.

0053 Weisenburger, Francis P. "The Middle Western Antecedents of Woodrow Wilson." *Mississippi Valley Historical Review* 23 (1936): 375–90.

Both sides of Wilson's family came from Ohio. His ancestors were very active in Ohio politics and in the ministry.

0054 Wilson, Theodore R. "The Birth of Greatness: A Psychological and Sociological Study of the Influences upon Woodrow Wilson during his Formative Years." Ph.D. dissertation, University of Pennsylvania, 1960.

The influences on Wilson during the first twenty-six years of his life are examined. Analyses of Wilson as a schizoid personality and explanations of him in terms of repressed feelings toward his father are criticized. The stress and frustration he felt during his early years may have led to severe health problems later in life. DAI 21:733.

WILSON'S ACADEMIC CAREER

0055 Axson, Stockton. "Woodrow Wilson as a Man of Letters—Three Public Lectures Delivered at the Rice Institute." *Rice Institute Pamphlet* 22 (1935): 195–270.

Wilson's brother-in-law discusses the effects of heredity and environment on Wilson as well as Wilson as a political philosopher and a literary historian.

0056 Bragdon, Henry W. *Woodrow Wilson: The Academic Years*. Cambridge, MA: Harvard University Press, 1967.

Wilson's days as a student, professor, and president of Princeton are analyzed. His study of American politics, his leadership on campus, and his powers of persuasion all helped to prepare him for the presidency. Photographs, notes, bibliography.

0057 Chitwood, John C. "Selected Studies in the History of American Public Administration Thought from Wilson to Waldo: A Sociology of Knowledge Perspective." 2 vols. Ph.D. dissertation, Ohio State University, 1980.

Wilson's theories on American public administration are included in this survey of public administration literature. DAI 41:3254-A.

0058 Cooper, John M., Jr. "Woodrow Wilson: The Academic Man." *Virginia Quarterly Review* 58 (1982): 38–53.

Wilson was one of the most successful academics of his time. His presidency at Princeton served as a bridge between the scholarly life and politics. Parallels between his two careers can be taken too far, since he did many things differently in politics from the way he did them in academia.

0059 Craig, Hardin. *Woodrow Wilson at Princeton*. Norman: University of Oklahoma Press, 1960.

Wilson's reforms at Princeton were designed to make the university serve mankind better. His ideas were ahead of his time. Illustrations, notes, index.

0060 Daniel, Marjorie L. "Woodrow Wilson—Historian." *Mississippi Valley Historical Review* 21 (1934): 361–74.

Although Wilson's special field was political science, he wrote *A History of the American People* (#0128), the first general history of the United States since the Civil War. Although the work has many defects, Wilson should be judged a good historian.

0061 Daniels, Winthrop. *Recollections of Woodrow Wilson*. New Haven, CT: Yale University Press, 1944.

Wilson's longtime friend and academic ally recalls some of the character traits that made Wilson a forceful presence before his political career began.

0062 Gottlieb, Kevin C. "The Political Philosophy of Woodrow Wilson as President of Princeton, 1902 to 1910." Ph.D. dissertation, Syracuse University, 1970.

Wilson's political philosophy during his presidency at Princeton reveals much about his concepts of leadership, statesmanship, public opinion, individualism, and law. DAI 31:2990-A.

0063 Grzybowski, Kazimierz. "Woodrow Wilson on Law, State and Society." *George Washington Law Review* 30 (1962): 808–52.

Wilson's notes for law classes he taught at Princeton University are examined for what they reveal about the future president's attitudes toward the law.

0064 Hruska, Thomas J., Jr. "Woodrow Wilson: The Organic State and His Political Theory." Ph.D. dissertation, Claremont Graduate School, 1978.

By focusing on Wilson's theories concerning "the organic state," the author finds an underlying consistency in his thought even after his conversion from conservatism to Progressivism. DAI 39:3802-A.

0065 Kirwan, Kent A. "The Crisis of Identity in the Study of Public Administration: Woodrow Wilson." *Polity* 9 (1977): 321–43.

Recent students of public administration have rejected Wilson's theories as erroneous but have failed to present viable alternative models. A reexamination of Wilson's ideas has yielded a new appreciation of his work in this field.

0066 Kurz, Alexander T., Jr. "The Epistemology of Public Administration: An Epistemic View." Ph.D. dissertation, University of Southern California, 1986.

Ninety-five years of selected public administration literature is analyzed, including Wilson's 1887 paper, "The Study of Administration" (#0133). DAI 47:2310-A.

0067 Lewis, McMillan. *Woodrow Wilson of Princeton*. Narbeth, PA: Livingston, 1952.

Wilson's twenty years at Princeton foreshadowed his successes and failures as president of the United States. He welcomed the opportunity to be the Democratic nominee for governor of New Jersey so that he could exit academia honorably.

0068 Link, Arthur S. "Woodrow Wilson and the Study of Administration." *Proceedings of the American Philosophical Society* 112 (1968): 431–33.

Wilson's journal article on public administration published in 1887 (#0133) broke new ground in the field and established his expertise. He went on to implement public administration studies at Johns Hopkins University and to publish a textbook. Notes.

0069 Mulder, John M. "Wilson the Preacher: The 1905 Baccalaureate Sermon." *Journal of Presbyterian History* 51 (1973): 267–84.

Wilson's baccalaureate address at Princeton in 1905 reveals his strongly held faith and how he applied it.

0070 Myers, William S., ed. *Woodrow Wilson: Some Princeton Memories*. Princeton: Princeton University Press, 1946.

Faculty members who served with Wilson, and then under him during his Princeton presidency, discuss his contributions to intellectual life.

0071 Perry, Bliss. *And Gladly Teach*. Boston: Houghton Mifflin, 1935.

Wilson's colleague at Princeton in the 1890s remembers his friend as an admirer of Grover Cleveland and a man of sincere Christian faith and noble character. His tragic fault was excessive self-confidence. Index.

0072 Rabin, Jack, and Bowman, James S., eds. *Politics and Administration: Woodrow Wilson and American Public Administration*. New York: Marcel Dekker, 1984.

Seventeen essays explore Wilson's role as the father of the study and practice of modern American public administration. Notes, bibliography, index.

0073 Reid, Edith G. *Woodrow Wilson: The Caricature, the Myth, and the Man*. New York: Oxford University Press, 1934.

Writing at the behest of Wilson's daughters, the author presents a remarkable portrait of the man's private side when he was a student and, later, a professor. Index.

0074 Sears, Louis M. "Woodrow Wilson." In William T. Hutchinson, ed. *The Marcus W. Jernegan Essays in American Historiography*. Chicago: University of Chicago Press, 1937, pp. 102–21.

Wilson deserves inclusion as an important historian because of his subsequent political career. As a historian greatness was within his grasp, but he never fully seized it.

0075 Silverthorne, C. Allan. "Crisis and Renewal in American Public Administration: The Role of Organization Development." Ph.D. dissertation, University of California, Los Angeles, 1986.

Surveying self-critical literature in public administration, the author includes Woodrow Wilson's contribution to the origins of the field. DAI 47:2311-A.

0076 Stillman, Richard J., III. "Woodrow Wilson and the Study of Administration: A New Look at an Old Essay." *American Political Science Review* 67 (1973): 582–88.

Wilson's essay "The Study of Administration" (1887) (#0133) introduced the country to the concept of public administration. His theories were affected profoundly by Social Darwinism and the crying need for reform, but his study raised more questions than it answered.

0077 Taggart, Robert J. "Woodrow Wilson and Curriculum Reform." *New Jersey History* 93 (1975): 99–114.

As president of Princeton, Wilson hoped to implement reforms that would generalize the curriculum, replace snobbish eating clubs, and change the role of the graduate school. These ideas met with a storm of criticism. Notes.

0078 Thorsen, Niels A. "The Political and Economic Thought of Woodrow Wilson, 1875–1902." Ph.D. dissertation, Princeton University, 1981.

Wilson's course of study at Johns Hopkins University (1883–1885) was the most important influence on his intellectual development. As a political scientist, he tried to recast old ideas of American liberal democracy in the light of the Industrial Revolution, outlining the new science of public administration in the process. DAI 41:4816-A.

0079 Turner, Henry A. "Woodrow Wilson as Administrator." *Public Administration Review* 16 (1956): 249–57.

Wilson tested his theories of administration as president of Princeton, reorganizing the university, changing instructional methods, and raising the standards of scholarship. His pattern at Princeton and the White House was one of success followed by failure. As chief executive he forged the Democratic party into an instrument of service for the state, and thus he deserves recognition as a great president.

0080 Veysey, Laurence R. "The Academic Mind of Woodrow Wilson." *Mississippi Valley Historical Review* 49 (1963): 613–34.

Wilson's educational reforms at Princeton are discussed. The author contends that Wilson believed that higher education was best pursued in an ivory tower away from the corrupting influences of the world. Notes.

WILSON FAMILY

0081 Cutler, Charles L., Jr. " 'My Dear Mrs. Peck.' " *American History Illustrated* 6 (1971): 4–9ff.

While serving as president of Princeton, Wilson struck up a friendship with Mary Hulbert Peck. They wrote more than 200 letters to each other until his remarriage, when the correspondence ended at the insistence of the second Mrs. Wilson.

0082 Elliott, Margaret R. A. *My Aunt Louisa and Woodrow Wilson*. Chapel Hill: University of North Carolina Press, 1944.

The younger sister of Wilson's first wife discusses his private side, that of a man who laughed, joked, and played with his daughters.

0083 Hatch, Alden. *Edith Bolling Wilson, First Lady Extraordinary*. New York: Dodd, Mead, 1961.

Based largely on published sources, this book finds little fault with Edith Wilson, seeing her as bright, witty, and charming as well as generally misunderstood.

0084 Hulbert, Mary A. *The Story of Mrs. Peck: An Autobiography*. New York: Minton, Balch, 1933.

Estranged from her second husband, Mary Allen Hulbert Peck developed a deep platonic friendship with Woodrow Wilson.

0085 James, Edith. "Edith Bolling Wilson: A Documentary View." In Mabel E. Deutrich and Virginia C. Purdy, eds. *Clio Was a Woman: Studies in the History of American Women.* Washington, DC: Howard University Press, 1980, pp. 234–40.

The letters of Edith Bolling Wilson are used as an example of the sources that can be used to study a president's wife. She is seen here as a woman fighting to balance her private needs and her public obligations.

0086 McAdoo, Eleanor Wilson. *The Woodrow Wilsons*. New York: Macmillan, 1937.

Wilson's daughter writes lovingly of her father, covering the period from the time of her childhood until the death of her mother in August 1914. Photographs.

0087 ———, ed. *The Priceless Gift*. New York: McGraw-Hill, 1962.

Wilson's daughter presents letters that reveal her father's private side. Wilson freely expressed his intimate feelings and emotions to those he loved. Photographs, index.

0088 Maddox, Robert J. "Mrs. Wilson and the Presidency." *American History Illustrated* 7 (1973): 36–44.

During Wilson's protracted period of illness in 1919 to 1920, Mrs. Wilson became a surrogate president.

0089 Phifer, Gregg. "Edith Bolling Wilson: Gatekeeper Extraordinary." *Speech Monographs* 38 (1971): 277–89.

For a time during Wilson's incapacitation in 1919–20, Mrs. Wilson acted as a regent, reading every message intended for the president. Notes.

0090 Ross, Ishbel. *Power with Grace: The Life Story of Mrs. Woodrow Wilson*. New York: G. P. Putnam's Sons, 1975.

A woman of strong prejudices, Edith Wilson was ambitious for her husband, but not for herself. During his illness of 1919–20 her protective instincts came to the fore, as she became a self-appointed courier between her husband and the world. Bibliography, index.

0091 Saunders, Frances W. *Ellen Axson Wilson: First Lady between Two Worlds*. Chapel Hill: University of North Carolina Press, 1985.

In this biography of Wilson's first wife, the author portrays Ellen Axson Wilson as a latent feminist who helped her husband in his career while pursuing her own avocation as a painter. Mrs. Wilson had an "extraordinary understanding of political issues and of human nature." Photographs, notes, bibliography, index.

0092 ———. "Love and Guilt: Woodrow Wilson and Mary Hulbert." *American Heritage* 30 (1979): 69–77.

Wilson's relationship with Mary Hulbert (from 1907 to 1915) is examined in light of his first wife's death and his decision to remarry.

0093 Shachtman, Tom. *Edith and Woodrow: A Presidential Romance*. New York: Putnam, 1981.

Throughout their loving relationship, Wilson relied on the advice of Edith Galt. While Wilson's advisers believed that the nation would have been better off without Mrs. Wilson during the president's illness, the author believes that she made a positive contribution.

0094 Tribble, Edwin, ed. *A President in Love: The Courtship Letters of Woodrow Wilson and Edith Bolling Galt*. Boston: Houghton, Mifflin, 1981.

Bits and pieces from some 250 letters Wilson and Galt wrote to one another are edited into a narrative. The result, the author states, reveals Wilson's "romantic exuberance, sometimes overdone."

0095 Weaver, Judith L. "Edith Bolling Wilson as First Lady: A Study in the Power of

Personality, 1919–1920." *Presidential Studies Quarterly* 15 (1985): 51–76.

Following Wilson's massive stroke of October 1919, his wife acted as the president's doorkeeper, barring entrance to those she did not trust or like. This group included the president's three key advisers, Joseph Tumulty, Edward House, and Robert Lansing. Above all, she wanted to be on the closest terms with her husband. Notes.

0096 Wilson, Edith Bolling. *My Memoir.* Indianapolis: Bobbs-Merrill, 1939.

Wilson's second wife discusses her early life, her courtship with Wilson, and her days as First Lady. During Wilson's illness of 1919–20, she undertook a "stewardship" on doctor's orders, screening material that her husband was to see without making decisions herself. Photographs, index.

PICTORIAL BIOGRAPHIES

0097 Ions, Edmund. *Woodrow Wilson: The Politics of Peace and War.* New York: American Heritage, 1972.

The life and times of Wilson are presented through photographs, cartoons, and paintings accompanied by a narrative. Index.

0098 Johnson, Gerald W. *Woodrow Wilson.* New York: Harper, 1944.

The life of Wilson is depicted through photographs in this work published during the Wilsonian revival of World War II. Photographs.

WILSON'S HEALTH

See also Chapter 5, *Health Issues.*

0099 Brodie, Bernard. "A Psychoanalytic Interpretation of Woodrow Wilson." *World Politics* 9 (1957): 413–22.

Alexander and Juliette George's book (#0019) on Wilson and Edward House is "completely satisfactory" as a psychoanalytic biography, although House's character is not nearly so well illuminated as is that of Wilson.

0100 Cocks, Geoffrey, and Crosby, Travis, eds. *Readings in the Method of Psychology, Psychoanalysis, and History.* New Haven, CT: Yale University Press, 1987.

This anthology presents several essays on Wilson and psychohistory, including one by

Robert C. Tucker and others by the Georges and by Edwin Weinstein, James Anderson, and Arthur Link cited below. Notes, bibliography, index.

0101 Feerick, John D. *From Failing Hands: The Story of Presidents' Succession.* New York: Fordham University Press, 1965.

Chapter 13 contains a brief discussion of the circumstances surrounding the "Wilson Inability" of 1919–20. Notes, appendixes, bibliography, index.

0102 Freud, Sigmund, and Bullitt, William C. *Thomas Woodrow Wilson, Twenty-eighth President of the United States: A Psychological Study.* Boston: Houghton Mifflin, 1967.

Written in 1932, revised in 1939, and published after the death of Wilson's widow, this study is extremely critical of Wilson as a narcissist. It should be used with caution, because Bullitt was a bitterly disappointed Wilsonian, and because Freud never met his subject personally. Index.

0103 George, Alexander L., and George, Juliette L. "Dr. Weinstein's Interpretation of Woodrow Wilson: Some Preliminary Observations." *Psychohistory Review* 8 (1979): 71–72.

Since little of Wilson's medical record has survived, Edwin Weinstein's conclusions (#0117 and #0118) about the president's health are not grounded in fact. Weinstein and Arthur Link will not reveal the evidence they found for their assertion that Wilson suffered "a probable virus encephalopathy" at the Paris Peace Conference.

0104 George, Juliette L., and George, Alexander L. " 'Woodrow Wilson and Colonel House': A Reply to Weinstein, Anderson, and Link." *Political Science Quarterly* 96 (1981): 641–65.

Edwin Weinstein's interpretations (#0117 and #0118) of Wilson's medical problems are open to question, since the authors have produced their own expert, a professor of medicine, who disagrees. Link has compromised the objectivity of the Wilson papers by including such controversial material.

0105 George, Juliette L.; Marmor, Michael F.; and George, Alexander L. "Issues in Wilson Scholarship: References to Early 'Strokes' in the Papers of Woodrow Wilson." *Journal of American History* 70 (1984): 845–53.

Taking issue with the findings of Arthur Link and Edwin Weinstein (#0118) concerning the strokes that Wilson suffered in 1896, 1906, and 1907, the authors contend that this is a questionable theory which should not be presented as fact. Notes.

0106 Gilbert, Robert E. "Death and the American President" (in Italian). *Politico* [Italy] 42 (1977): 719–41.

A study of the personal statistics of presidents, vice presidents, and defeated candidates reveals that they lived shorter lives than did other white males, while members of Congress and the Supreme Court lived longer than the general white male population. Notes.

0107 Grayson, Cary T. *Woodrow Wilson: An Intimate Memoir.* New York: Holt, Rinehart and Winston, 1960.

Wilson's physician wrote this memoir in 1924, although it was not published for forty-six years. The author writes that he saw Wilson "more constantly and more intimately than any other man during those eleven years" from 1913 to 1924.

0108 Handy, Craighill, and Handy, Elizabeth. *Woodrow Wilson's Heritage and Environment.* Philadelphia: Dorrance, 1969.

The influences of heritage and environment on Wilson's character are examined through the use of "genethnics." Notes, bibliography.

0109 Hoffs, Joshua A. "Comments on Psychoanalytic Biography, with Special Reference to Freud's Interest in Woodrow Wilson." *Psychoanalytic Review* 56 (1969): 402–14.

Freud actually wrote little aside from the introduction to the study of Wilson that he published with William C. Bullitt (#0102), although the book is consistent in most respects with his previous work in psychoanalytic biography. As a whole, psychoanalytic biography is controversial, but it can be valuable if done properly.

0110 Lewis, Thomas T. "Alternative Psychological Interpretations of Woodrow Wilson." *Mid-America* 65 (1983): 71–85.

Over the years many diverse psychological interpretations of Wilson have been proposed, the most important of which are discussed. Notes.

0111 Link, Arthur S. "The Case for Woodrow Wilson." In Arthur S. Link. *The Higher Realism of Woodrow Wilson and Other Essays.* Nashville: Vanderbilt University Press, 1971, pp. 140–54.

While some of the data in the Freud-Bullitt study (#0102) of Wilson is accurate, the authors distort and abuse evidence in their haste to prove Wilson neurotic. The study says more about its authors than it does about its subject.

0112 Park, Bert E. *The Impact of Illness on World Leaders.* Philadelphia: University of Pennsylvania Press, 1986.

The effects of Wilson's health on his leadership are examined in this work, which also analyzes Franklin D. Roosevelt, Winston Churchill, Adolf Hitler, and Paul von Hindenburg. Photographs, notes, bibliography, index.

0113 Riccards, Michael P. "The Presidency: In Sickness and in Health." *Presidential Studies Quarterly* 7 (1977): 215–31.

The effects of disease, including Wilson's, on presidential decision making are examined. Stress and ailments brought with them to the White House account for the shortened lifespans of post-Civil War presidents. Notes.

0114 Ross, Dorothy. "Woodrow Wilson and the Case for Psychohistory." *Journal of American History* 69 (1982): 659–68.

Using Edwin Weinstein's work (#0116) as a springboard, a case is made for psychohistory. While psychobiography has been criticized for not meeting the standards of historical scholarship, it can contribute to our understanding by expanding the base of evidence, illuminating patterns of cause and action, and sharpening the questions that should be asked.

0115 Tuchman, Barbara W. "Can History Use Freud? The Case of Woodrow Wilson." *Atlantic Monthly* 219 (February 1967): 39–44.

Freud and Bullitt (see #0102) had high hopes for the "new diplomacy" and blamed Wilson for its failure. Their notion that Wilson had no original thoughts is absurd as is their assumption that the president had enough power to make a just peace.

0116 Weinstein, Edwin A. *Woodrow Wilson: A Medical and Psychological Biography.* Princeton: Princeton University Press, 1981.

The author chronicles Wilson's life, giving special attention to his major illnesses including strokes, headaches, hypertension, influenza, and cardiac problems. The cerebral dysfunctions that came about as a result of a series of strokes, the author concludes, led ultimately to the defeat of the Treaty of Versailles. Photographs, notes, bibliography, index.

0117 ———. "Woodrow Wilson's Neurological Illness." *Journal of American History* 57 (1970): 324–51.

Wilson developed cerebral vascular disease in 1896, a condition which eventually caused his major stroke of 1919. The seriousness of this illness was kept a secret by Wilson's doctor. Notes.

0118 Weinstein, Edwin A.; Anderson, James W.; and Link, Arthur S. "Woodrow Wilson's Political Personality: A Reappraisal." *Political Science Quarterly* 93 (1979): 585–98.

Fire is concentrated on the Georges' *Woodrow Wilson and Colonel House* (#0019), which distorts Wilson's relationship with his father to make a point about his political personality. Notes.

WILSON'S SPEECHES AND PAPERS

0119 Bailey, Kenneth M. "Woodrow Wilson: The Educator Speaking." Ph.D. dissertation, University of Iowa, 1970.

Wilson's educational ideas and his rhetoric are examined. As an administrator his emphasis shifted from the written word to verbal communication, and he demonstrated a keen understanding of the theory of persuasion. He preferred to appeal to reason, using precise and appropriate language. DAI 31:1406-A.

0120 Davidson, John Wells, ed. *A Crossroads of Freedom: The 1912 Campaign Speeches of Woodrow Wilson.* New Haven, CT: Yale University Press, 1956.

The compiler presents Wilson's most important campaign speeches in chronological order with a brief commentary. Illustrations, notes, index.

0121 La Fontaine, Charles V. "God and Nation in Selected U.S. Presidential Inaugural Addresses, 1789–1945, Part I." *Journal of Church and State* 18 (1976): 39–60.

Presidential inaugural addresses are religious statements constituting periodic national statements of faith. Wilson's addresses are among those examined. Notes.

0122 ———. "God and Nation in Selected U.S. Presidential Inaugural Addresses, 1789–1945, Part II." *Journal of Church and State* 18 (1976): 503–21.

The views of select presidents (including Wilson) on God in their inaugural addresses are analyzed. Wilson's addresses were like those of Lincoln in that he emphasized restoration of grace. Notes.

0123 Library of Congress. *Index to the Woodrow Wilson Papers.* 3 vols. Washington, DC: Government Printing Office, 1973.

Strictly an index of names, this work is useful chiefly to check whether a document has been included in the Library of Congress's microfilm edition of the Wilson papers (#0138).

0124 Wilson, Woodrow. *Congressional Government: A Study in American Politics.* Boston: Houghton Mifflin, 1885.

Wilson's first book, which he used as his doctoral dissertation, examines the functioning of American government as well as its defects. The text is reproduced in Volume IV of *The Papers of Woodrow Wilson* (#0133) along with reviews of the work. Other volumes contain information on the composition of chapters and comments from friends and colleagues.

0125 ———. *Constitutional Government in the United States.* New York: Columbia University Press, 1908.

Based on lectures that Wilson gave at Columbia in 1907 and 1908, the book reveals an interest in the expanded role of the presidency, based not only on the work of dynamic chief executives such as Grover Cleveland and Theodore Roosevelt but also on Wilson's own leadership of Princeton University. Because of its importance, this work is reprinted in full in the eighteenth volume of *The Papers of Woodrow Wilson* (#0133).

0126 ———. *Division and Reunion, 1829–1889.* New York: Longmans, Green, 1893.

Wilson discusses the importance of sectionalism in American history and how the tragic War between the States united America into a powerful new whole.

0127 ———. *George Washington.* New York: Harper, 1896.

Originally written as a series of essays that Wilson dashed off because he needed money, this work offers little to recommend itself except for what it reveals about the attempt to marry history and literature.

0128 ———. *A History of the American People.* 5 vols. New York: Harper, 1902.

This popular history contains numerous factual errors but nonetheless made Wilson famous among the literate sectors of the public.

0129 ———. *International Ideals: Speeches and Addresses Made during the President's European Trip*. New York: Harper, 1919.

This is a collection of speeches made before cheering throngs in Europe, as Wilson prepared to make peace and convince the world to accept the "new diplomacy."

0130 ———. *Mere Literature and Other Essays*. Boston: Houghton Mifflin, 1896.

Wilson's essays on history and literature are reprinted in this volume.

0131 ———. *The New Freedom: A Call for the Generous Energies of a People*. Garden City, NY: Doubleday, Page, 1918.

Wilson's campaign manager, William Bayard Hale, put together this volume based on stenographic reporting of speeches from the 1912 campaign.

0132 ———. *An Old Master and Other Political Essays*. New York: Scribner's, 1893.

Reprinted here are essays on Adam Smith, the study of politics, political sovereignty, democracy in America, and constitutional government.

0133 ———. *The Papers of Woodrow Wilson*. Edited by Arthur S. Link et al. Princeton: Princeton University Press, 1967–.

A model of scholarly editing, this multivolume work contains many of Wilson's published writings, letters sent and received, as well as diaries and other primary accounts of his activities. Index.

0134 ———. *The Politics of Woodrow Wilson: Selections from His Speeches and Writings*. Edited by August Heckscher. New York: Harper, 1956.

Wilson's political philosophy is illuminated by his early writings and his speeches as president of Princeton, governor of New Jersey, and president of the United States.

0135 ———. *The Public Papers of Woodrow Wilson*. 6 vols. Edited by Ray Stannard Baker and William E. Dodd, Jr. New York: Harper, 1925–1927.

Superseded by the microfilmed Wilson papers from the Library of Congress (#0138) and by the published papers edited by Arthur Link and his staff (#0133), these volumes contain Wilson's speeches, messages, and public papers.

0136 ———. *The State: Elements of Historical and Practical Politics*. Boston: Heath, 1889.

This survey of the advances in Western political institutions is considered by some to be Wilson's greatest scholarly achievement.

0137 ———. *When a Man Comes to Himself*. New York: Harper, 1901.

Wilson discusses his desire for political leadership in this slender volume first published as an essay in *Century* magazine earlier in 1901.

0138 ———. *Woodrow Wilson Papers*. Washington, DC: Library of Congress, 1973.

The Wilson papers in the Library of Congress have been copied onto 540 reels of microfilm, available for purchase or loan. Microfilm.

Wilson's Gubernatorial Career

0139 Buenker, John D. "Urban, New-Stock Liberalism and Progressive Reform in New Jersey." *New Jersey History* 87 (1969): 79–104.

Wilson's gubernatorial term is discussed as part of a larger trend of Progressive reform in New Jersey, which was often supported by city bosses.

0140 Ellis, Mary Louise. "Tilting on the Piazza: Emmet O'Neal's Encounter with Woodrow Wilson, September 1911." *Alabama Review* 39 (1986): 83–95.

The governor of Alabama, Emmet O'Neal, blasted the Progressive political reforms of initiative, recall, and referendum at the governors' conference of 1911. Hosting the conference, New Jersey's Governor Woodrow Wilson maneuvered to paper over the controversy, because he supported the Progressive measures. Notes.

0141 Hendrick, Burton J. "Woodrow Wilson: Political Leader." *McClure's Magazine* 38 (December 1911): 217–31.

Although hardly an objective analysis, this is probably the best contemporary essay on Wilson's gubernatorial period. Wilson is seen as an active and energetic governor.

0142 Hirst, David W. *Woodrow Wilson, A Reform Governor*. Princeton: Van Nostrand, 1965.

Edited primary sources are used to detail Woodrow Wilson's rise to the governorship of New Jersey. After hearing Wilson's inaugural address as president of Princeton, journalist George Harvey set out to make him governor and then president. Wilson learned the game of politics quickly and ably. Notes, bibliography, index.

0143 Link, Arthur S. "Woodrow Wilson in New Jersey." In Arthur S. Link. *The Higher Realism of Woodrow Wilson and Other Essays*. Nashville: Vanderbilt University Press, 1971, pp. 45–59.

Wilson stamped his character on Princeton during his eight-year presidency of the university. As governor of New Jersey, he brought hope and vision to politics while transforming the governmental structure of the state. Notes.

0144 Luthin, Reinhard H. *American Demagogues: Twentieth Century*. Boston: Beacon, 1954.

The author presents portraits of modern demagogues from James M. Curley to Joe McCarthy, including Frank Hague, boss of Jersey City and political enemy of Governor Woodrow Wilson.

0145 Mahoney, Joseph F. "Backsliding Convert: Woodrow Wilson and the 'Seven Sisters.' " *American Quarterly* 18 (1966): 71–80.

If Wilson was converted by Louis Brandeis from a moralistic to an institutional approach to curbing monopolies, it was not reflected in the "Seven Sisters" antitrust campaign in New Jersey. Rather, the Seven Sisters represented an attempt to marry Wilson's idea of corporate moral responsibility with the Brandeisian theory of regulated competition.

0146 Noble, Ransom E., Jr. *New Jersey Progressivism before Wilson*. Princeton: Princeton University Press, 1946.

Wilson was not the first Progressive in New Jersey politics. Many Republicans with new ideas paved the way for his Progressive administration. Notes, index.

0147 Reynolds, John F. "Testing Democracy: Electoral Participation and Progressive Reform in New Jersey, 1888–1919." Ph.D. dissertation, Rutgers University, 1980.

Progressive reforms under Governor Wilson were designed to make voting a more intelligent and disinterested process, but they led instead to a decline in voter participation. DAI 41:1736-A.

Postpresidential Years

0148 Archer, Mary U. "Woodrow Wilson: The Post Presidential Years." Ph.D. dissertation, St. Louis University, 1963.

This work concentrates on Wilson as an ex-president rather than on his personal life or medical problems. While he regretted the failure of the Senate to approve the Treaty of Versailles, he never wavered in his conviction that he had been right. He spent his last years playing the part of a prophet-politician. DAI 25:35.

0149 Buckingham, Peter H. *International Normalcy: The Open Door Peace with the Former Central Powers, 1921–1929*. Wilmington, DE: Scholarly Resources, 1983.

While Wilson shunned involvement in politics during his retirement, he tried to rally opposition to the Treaty of Berlin ending the German-American state of war, because he regarded this treaty as a stain on American honor. Notes, bibliography, index.

0150 Clark, James C. *Faded Glory: Presidents Out of Power*. New York: Praeger, 1985.

Wilson's postpresidential years were difficult for him personally, but he lived long enough to see his popularity rise again. Bibliography, index.

0151 Colby, Bainbridge. *The Close of Woodrow Wilson's Administration and the Final Years*. New York: Kennerly, 1930.

Wilson's last secretary of state, who offered the president a partnership in his law firm, discusses the postpresidential years.

0152 Naveh, Eyal J. "The Martyr Image in American Political Culture (Lincoln, Sermons, Obituaries)." Ph.D. dissertation, University of California, 1986.

Between the Civil War and the 1920s only Lincoln became a national martyr. While some people regarded Wilson as a martyr, he was not a second Lincoln. DAI 47:2712-A.

0153   Smith, Gene. *When the Cheering Stopped: The Last Years of Woodrow Wilson.* New York: William Morrow, 1964.

Wilson's last years of illness, defeat, bitterness, and withdrawal are detailed in this popular work. Photographs, notes, bibliography, index.

Overview of the Wilson Presidency

There is little doubt that Woodrow Wilson stands among the most important presidents in American history, although many might disagree with Richard Nixon's verdict that "Wilson was our greatest President of this century." Superbly prepared to be chief executive and imbued with the determination to carry out his Progressive reform program, Wilson exerted masterful leadership of Congress in pressing for the New Freedom designed to harmonize conflicting classes and interests. In foreign affairs, he was equally determined to lead, using the government both in the search for new markets abroad and to intervene where revolution or political disorder threatened American interests. During the period of American neutrality, and once the United States had plunged into the war, Wilson exercised his presidential powers with increasing vigor, contributing to the rise of the "imperial presidency." Although materials on important domestic and foreign policy issues are presented in subsequent chapters, readers interested in a broader view of the Wilson presidency should consult John M. Cooper, Jr., *The Warrior and the Priest: Woodrow Wilson and Theodore Roosevelt* (#0163); Herbert Hoover, *The Ordeal of Woodrow Wilson* (#0177); and the essays in Earl Latham, ed., *The Philosophy and Policies of Woodrow Wilson* (#0184). Many of the collected articles of Arthur S. Link, *The Higher Realism of Woodrow Wilson* (#0185), deal with his presidency. Volumes II to V of Link's *Wilson* (#0026) examine the politics and diplomacy of the period in rich detail—*Wilson: The New Freedom* (#0188) covers the first two years of the first term, *Wilson: The Struggle for Neutrality, 1914–1915*

(#0189) looks at the period immediately following the outbreak of war in Europe, *Wilson: Confusions and Crises, 1915–1916* (#0187) discusses the crucial months of late 1915 to early 1916, and *Wilson: Campaigns for Progressivism and Peace, 1916–1917* (#0186) examines the 1916 election and the growing crisis with Germany.

Works focusing on Wilson's role as a leader include John M. Blum, *The Progressive Presidents* (#0213); George C. Edwards III and Stephen J. Wayne, *Presidential Leadership: Politics and Policy Making* (#0216); and Clinton L. Rossiter, *The American Presidency* (#0235). Americans have a fondness for lists, and some historians have assembled presidential rankings based on polls of colleagues. For a summary of these efforts, see Gary M. Maranell, "The Evaluation of Presidents: An Extension of the Schlesinger Polls" (#0247). The most ambitious undertaking is Robert K. Murray and Tim H. Blessing, "The Presidential Performance Study: A Progress Report" (#0249). The polls rank Wilson in the "near great" category, although older historians give him higher marks than do younger ones.

Wilson understood the importance of public opinion and the press for effective leadership. See Elmer E. Cornwell, Jr., "The Press Conferences of Woodrow Wilson" (#0259) and *Presidential Leadership of Public Opinion* (#0257), as well as a doctoral dissertation by Patricia A. Grim, "From Strict Neutrality to the Fourteen Points: Woodrow Wilson's Communication Strategies in World War I" (#0219). Wilson's masterful handling of Congress is examined by Arthur S. Link,

Woodrow Wilson delivers his first inaugural address, 4 March 1913. *Herbert Hoover Presidential Library.*

"Woodrow Wilson and the Democratic Party" (#0267), and by Arthur MacMahon, "Woodrow Wilson as a Legislative Leader and Administrator" (#0268).

Wilson Presidency

Autobiographical and biographical materials on Wilson may be found in Chapter 1. Other references to Wilson's role as president may be found in Chapter 9, *Wilson and Foreign Affairs*, and Chapter 10, *Wilsonian Diplomacy*.

GENERAL ACCOUNTS

0154 Alsop, Em B. *The Greatness of Woodrow Wilson*. New York: Rinehart, 1956.

In commemoration of the centennial of Wilson's birth, the editor compiled a series of laudatory essays from scholars such as Arthur Link and world leaders including Madame Chiang Kai-shek and Dag Hammarskjöld. Bibliography.

0155 Bell, H. C. F. *Woodrow Wilson and the People*. Garden City, NY: Doubleday, Doran, 1945.

The author begins this uncritical biography with Wilson's presidency of Princeton. One of the strongest factors in his public life, the author concludes, was a "sustained effort to establish and maintain contact with the people." Bibliographic essay, index.

0156 Block, Harold B. *The True Woodrow Wilson: Crusader for Democracy*. New York: Fleming H. Revell, 1946.

Only Washington, Jefferson, and Lincoln exceeded Wilson in presidential greatness, the author argues. He agrees with David Lloyd George that Wilson's was "a glorious failure." Index.

0157 Blum, John M. "Woodrow Wilson: A Study in Intellect." *Confluence* 5 (1957): 367–75.

Wilson's intellect was rooted firmly in the nineteenth century, not the twentieth. He believed that the naturally superior Anglo-Saxon race had a duty to make over the world. The president failed to understand how the world was changing and expected too much from people. Notes.

0158 Bolling, John R. *Chronology of Woodrow Wilson*. New York: Frederick A. Stokes, 1927.

The author presents a detailed chronology of Wilson's life together with his most important presidential speeches. Photographs, appendix.

0159 Buehrig, Edward H. "Idealism and Statecraft." *Confluence* 5 (1956): 252–63.

Analyzing the tension between idealism and statecraft, the author focuses on Wilson, who tried to make justice and security compatible. Notes.

0160 Bundy, McGeorge. "Woodrow Wilson and a World He Never Made." *Confluence* 5 (1957): 281–90.

Like Franklin Roosevelt and Dwight Eisenhower, Woodrow Wilson was driven by a special sense of mandate. As a result, he did not pay enough attention to garnering bipartisan support for his foreign policy decisions. Notes.

0161 Canfield, Leon H. *The Presidency of Woodrow Wilson: Prelude to a World in Crisis*. Rutherford, NJ: Fairleigh Dickinson University Press, 1966.

Writing as a historian, but also as a Wilsonian, the author sees Wilson as "the victim of his enemies." Photographs, notes, bibliography, index.

0162 Carleton, William G. "The Ungenerous Approach to Woodrow Wilson." *Virginia Quarterly Review* 44 (1968): 161–81.

Wilson has been overly criticized by writers in recent years who have failed to appreciate his Progressive achievements, his realism, his work toward the creation of the League of Nations, and his effective political style.

0163 Cooper, John M., Jr. *The Warrior and the Priest: Woodrow Wilson and Theodore Roosevelt*. Cambridge, MA: Harvard University Press, 1983.

Roosevelt and Wilson reinvigorated the presidency. Wilson practiced politics more conventionally than Roosevelt and achieved many reforms during his first term. It is too simple to label Roosevelt a realist and Wilson an idealist. Between them, they redefined American politics. Notes, index.

0164 Cronon, E. David. "Woodrow Wilson." In Morton Borden, ed. *America's Eleven Greatest Presidents*. Chicago: Rand McNally, 1971, pp. 202–25.

Like Lincoln, Wilson was great in his leadership and tragic because he could not convince Americans to adopt his noble dream. While Wilson shares responsibility for the U.S. failure to adopt the League of Nations Covenant, his achievements outweigh this failing. Bibliography.

0165 Daniels, Jonathan. "The Long Shadow of Woodrow Wilson." *Virginia Quarterly Review* 32 (1956): 481–93.

While the popular image of Wilson is that of a professor-statesman, he was also a shrewd politician. He was the first president to carry American idealism to the world.

0166 DeJouvenel, Bertrand. "Woodrow Wilson." *Confluence* 5 (1957): 320–31.

Far too concerned with "doing good," Wilson did not think problems through clearly or pay enough attention to facts. His idea of national self-determination helped to spawn fascism. Notes.

0167 De Madariaga, Salvador. "Wilson and the Dream of Reason." *Virginia Quarterly Review* 32 (1956): 594–98.

Wilson was a great visionary who was less to blame for the failure of permanent peace than were the times in which he lived.

0168 DeSantis, Vincent P. *The Shaping of Modern America: 1877–1916*. Boston: Allyn and Bacon, 1973.

In a chapter on Wilson, the author argues that the abandonment of the New Freedom and the acceptance of Roosevelt's New Nationalism hold the key to understanding his presidency. Bibliography, index.

0169 Dodd, William E. *Woodrow Wilson and His Work*. Garden City, NY: Doubleday, 1921.

Wilson is ranked as the "third great American dreamer," behind Jefferson and Lincoln. Notes.

0170 Elletson, D. H. *Roosevelt and Wilson: A Comparative Study*. London: Murray, 1965.

In comparing and contrasting the presidencies of the two Progressive presidents, the author judges Wilson an enigma who exhibited such diverse characteristics as coldness, egotism, pride, hatefulness, and tenderness. Bibliography, index.

0171 Ferrell, Robert H. "Woodrow Wilson: Man and Statesman." *Review of Politics* 18 (1956): 131–45.

A great statesman, Wilson enacted Progressive reforms and provided wartime leadership, but his character defects caught up with him when he tried to force Congress to accept the peace treaty strictly on his own terms.

0172 Goldman, Eric. *Rendezvous with Destiny: A History of Modern American Reform*. New York: Knopf, 1953.

Wilson plays a key role in this classic history of liberal reformers. Wilson stole Roosevelt's thunder and became the idol of most Progressives only to become their devil during the fight over the Treaty of Versailles. Notes, bibliographic essay, index.

0173 Hansen, Alvin H. "Woodrow Wilson as an Economic Reformer." *Virginia Quarterly Review* 32 (1956): 566–78.

Wilson was both a Jeffersonian liberal and a conservative reformer. His programs led to bigger government and less political power for big business. Industrialization and urbanization, he believed, had brought about problems that only the state could solve. Notes.

0174 Harley, J. Eugene, ed. *Woodrow Wilson Still Lives—His World Ideas Triumphant*. Los Angeles: Center for International Understanding, 1944.

Written as Americans began to think about the formation of the United Nations, the editor assembled tributes to Wilson by his daughter, Herbert Hoover, Cordell Hull, Ray Stannard Baker, and others. Bibliography.

0175 Hawley, Ellis W. *The Great War and the Search for a Modern Order, A History of the American People and Their Institutions, 1917–1933*. New York: St. Martin's Press, 1979.

The author begins his survey with a general analysis of the Wilson years. Like those who followed them, Wilson and his reconstruction managers failed in their search for "ordering mechanisms" able to orchestrate continuing economic prosperity, a just social order, and world peace. Bibliographic essay, index.

0176 Herring, Pendleton. "Woodrow Wilson: A President's Reading." *Historic Preservation* 27 (1975): 38–42.

Wilson's reading habits were surveyed as part of a project to gather a collection of his favorite books. Photographs.

0177 Hoover, Herbert C. *The Ordeal of Woodrow Wilson*. New York: McGraw-Hill, 1958.

Hoover views Wilson's life as a Greek tragedy. A born crusader, Wilson had trouble choosing the lesser of evils and was impatient with honest criticism. Photographs, index.

0178 Johnson, Gerald W. "Wilson the Man." *Virginia Quarterly Review* 32 (1956): 494–508.

Wilson should be understood in terms of his background as a Scotch Presbyterian. He believed that action in the international arena should conform to universal law. Notes.

0179 Johnson, Theodore R. "The Memorialization of Woodrow Wilson." Ph.D. dissertation, George Washington University, 1979.

Wilson's image in the many memorials written about him between 1921 and 1971 is examined. His image is that of a moral man motivated by a special sense of American mission in the world. DAI 40:2201-A.

0180 Katz, Milton. "Woodrow Wilson and the Twentieth Century." *Confluence* 5 (1956): 229–38.

Wilson was the first president to understand the new mood of the twentieth century and its implications for making America a great power. Notes.

0181 Kerney, James. *The Political Education of Woodrow Wilson*. New York: Century, 1926.

This friendly account by a New Jersey publisher chronicles Wilson's transformation "from a conservative Democrat to a very militant two-fisted Radical, and, with the coming of war, into an equally two-fisted Autocrat." Photographs, index.

0182 Kirk, Russell. "Wilson: Abstraction, Principle, and the Antagonist World." *Confluence* 5 (1956): 204–15.

Wilson was more a conservative reformer than a Progressive. His failures came from not being conservative enough. Notes.

0183 Knight, Lucian L. *Woodrow Wilson: The Dreamer and the Dream*. Atlanta: Johnson-Dallis, 1924.

This brief early biography of Wilson portrays the president as "a lamb of sacrifice upon the altar of reconciliation." Index.

0184 Latham, Earl, ed. *The Philosophy and Policies of Woodrow Wilson*. Chicago: University of Chicago Press, 1958.

Sixteen essays on Wilson's presidency are presented under such headings as the president and his education, the New Freedom, foreign policy, and Wilson in perspective. Essays that appear only in this collection are cited separately in the appropriate categories. Notes, index.

0185 Link, Arthur S. *The Higher Realism of Woodrow Wilson and Other Essays*. Edited by Dewey W. Grantham. Nashville: Vanderbilt University Press, 1971.

Twenty of the twenty-four essays by Link in this volume pertain to either Wilson or the Wilson era. Notes, index.

0186 ———. *Wilson: Campaigns for Progressivism and Peace, 1916–1917*. Princeton: Princeton University Press, 1965.

Volume V of *Wilson* (see #0026) covers the presidential campaign of 1916 when Wilson forged a Progressive coalition that carried him to victory, efforts to mediate an end to the Great War, and the crisis with Germany that led to the declaration of war. Photographs, notes, appendix, index.

0187 ———. *Wilson: Confusions and Crises, 1915–1916*. Princeton: Princeton University Press, 1964.

Volume IV of *Wilson* (see #0026) covers the period from the fall of 1915 to the spring of 1916, during which time the president tried to steer a middle course in the preparedness controversy, keep control of the Democratic party, and deal with crises with Germany over neutral rights and with Mexico over the punitive expedition against Pancho Villa. Photographs, notes, bibliography, index.

0188 ———. *Wilson: The New Freedom*. Princeton: Princeton University Press, 1956.

Volume II (see #0026) of what the author calls an "admixture of history with biography" covers the first two years of the Wilson presidency. The president's relations with Congress and with the Democratic party are analyzed along with the crisis with Mexico and various components of the New Freedom including tariff reform, the Federal Reserve Act of 1913, and antitrust legislation. Photographs, notes, bibliography, index.

0189 ———. *Wilson: The Struggle for Neutrality, 1914–1915*. Princeton: Princeton University Press, 1960.

Volume III of Link's five-volume study of Wilson (see #0026) covers the fifteen months beginning with the outbreak of World War I in Europe, when the president and his advisers laid the foundation for neutrality as Britain and Germany both encroached on American rights. Problems in Mexico, the Caribbean, and the Far East are also examined. Photographs, notes, bibliography, index.

0190 ———. *Woodrow Wilson and the Progressive Era, 1910–1917*. New York: Harper & Row, 1954.

The election of 1912 and the politics and diplomacy of the Wilson presidency up to American entry into the war are analyzed. Wilson strengthened the presidency, formulating a complete legislative program and working closely with his party in Congress to see it through. Notes, bibliography, index.

0191 Martin, Laurence W. "Necessity and Principle: Woodrow Wilson's Views." *Review of Politics* 22 (1960): 96–114.

The natural tension that exists between the needs for international cooperation and for national security must be reconciled by statesmen. Wilson's emphasis on morality in foreign policy necessitated a fundamental reexamination of American interests. Notes.

0192 Mervin, David. "Woodrow Wilson and Presidential Myths." *Presidential Studies Quarterly* 11 (1981): 559–64.

A study of Wilson's activities over a period of six months during his first term reveals a mixture of work and relaxation—not the schedule of a workaholic. Notes.

0193 Mothner, Ira. *Woodrow Wilson: Champion of Peace*. New York: Franklin Watts, 1969.

This brief examination of Wilson's presidency finds the chief executive to have been an idealist who refused to compromise his vision of world peace.

0194 Pisney, Raymond F., ed. *Woodrow Wilson in Retrospect*. Verona, VA: McClure, 1978.

Addresses on the Wilson presidency given under the auspices of the Woodrow Wilson Birthplace Foundation between 1940 and 1959 are reprinted.

0195 Pomeroy, Earl S. "Woodrow Wilson: The End of His First Century." *Oregon Historical Quarterly* 57 (1956): 315–32.

Wilson found satisfaction in impersonal relations with crowds, substituting this for personal friendships. It was his misfortune that there was no John Wilkes Booth at Versailles' Hall of Mirrors, because he became the loneliest and most tragic of all presidents.

0196 Seymour, Charles. "Woodrow Wilson: A Political Balance Sheet." *Proceedings of the American Philosophical Society* 101 (1957): 135–41.

Wilson had many more accomplishments than failures. His great record as a domestic reformer and as a war leader outshines his failure to push through the Treaty of Versailles. Notes.

0197 Skau, George H. "Woodrow Wilson's Impact on the American Presidency." In Philip C. Dolce and George H. Skau, eds. *Power and the Presidency*. New York: Charles Scribner's Sons, 1976, pp. 75–87.

Wilson's leadership in domestic affairs was unprecedented in its success. He was also successful in foreign affairs until 1918. He demonstrated the need for positive leadership from the White House. Photographs, bibliography, index.

0198 Sklar, Martin J. "Woodrow Wilson and the Political Economy of United States Liberalism." *Studies on the Left* 1 (1960): 17–47.

Puritanism and Smithian-Manchestrian economics were the forces behind Wilson's determination to strengthen government. This conceptual framework was both realistic and moralistic. Notes.

0199 Slosson, Preston W. *The Great Crusade and After, 1914–1928*. New York: Macmillan, 1930.

Students will find this early scholarly social history of America during the Wilson years to be still useful. Illustrations, photographs, notes, bibliographic essay.

0200 Thompson, Charles W. *Presidents I've Known and Two Near Presidents*. Indianapolis: Bobbs-Merrill, 1929.

This gossipy memoir contains six chapters on Wilson, a man who suffered from his failure to heed advice and from a tendency to take criticism personally.

0201 Valentine, Alan. *1913: America between Two Worlds*. New York: Macmillan, 1962.

This book is a popular survey of America in 1913, the year "the familiar world" vanished and the Acquisitive Age began.

0202 Vexler, Robert I., ed. *Woodrow Wilson, 1856–1924*. Dobbs Ferry, NY: Oceana, 1969.

A chronology of Wilson's life is presented along with a documentary record of his presidency from the first inaugural address to the seventh annual message, of 1919. Bibliography, index.

0203 Vinogradov, K. B., and Sergeev, V. V. "Woodrow Wilson in War and Peace" (in Russian). *Novaia i Noveishaia Istoriia* [USSR] (1975): 122–34.

Wilson is examined from a Soviet Marxist perspective and found to be a leader whose tenure ended in political disaster.

0204 Wise, Jennings C. *Woodrow Wilson, Disciple of Revolution*. New York: Paisley, 1938.

Wilson is viewed as a man of overweening ambition who was selfish, disloyal, and somehow responsible for the success of the Bolshevik Revolution. Appendix.

THE WHITE HOUSE

0205 Durbin, Louise. *Inaugural Cavalcade*. New York: Dodd, Mead, 1971.

Presidential inaugurations are put into historical perspective. Wilson's first was a festive affair, while his second was somber and tense with the greatest concern for the safety of the president since 1864. Photographs, bibliography, index.

0206 Klapthor, Margaret B. *Official White House China: 1789 to the Present*. Washington, DC: Smithsonian Institution Press, 1975.

Presidential china settings are examined chronologically, including the services used during the Wilson administration. Photographs, index.

0207 Seale, William. *The President's House*. 2 vols. Washington, DC: White House Historical Association, 1987.

Two chapters discuss Ellen Wilson's remodeling of the White House, her death, the widower's household, Wilson's remarriage, the war, and the president's illness. Notes, bibliography.

0208 Smith, Marie. *Entertaining in the White House*. Washington, DC: Acropolis, 1967.

This social history of the White House includes a chapter on Wilson. Three weddings were held in the executive mansion, although not the president's. Also presented are menus and the second Mrs. Wilson's favorite recipes. Illustrations, index.

0209 Starling, Edmund W., and Sugrue, Thomas. *Starling of the White House*. New York: Simon and Schuster, 1946.

The head of the White House Secret Service detail that guarded presidents from Wilson to FDR discusses Wilson's courtship of Edith Bolling Galt, the presidential election campaign of 1916, the war, the peace conference, and Wilson's illness. Photographs.

0210 Truman, Margaret. *White House Pets*. New York: David McKay, 1969.

President Truman's daughter takes a light-hearted look at presidential pets. Photographs.

Presidential Leadership

See Chapter 4, *Business, Government Policies*; *Economics, Government Policies*; and *Wilson and Labor*, and Chapter 7, for specific aspects of Wilson's executive leadership.

0211 Balch, Stephen H. "Do Strong Presidents Really Want Strong Legislative Parties?" *Presidential Studies Quarterly* 7 (1977): 231–38.

Wilson did not want a strong legislative party, because he was a strong president. Consequently he worked to undermine congressional leadership in his own party. Notes.

0212 Bishirjian, Richard J. "Croly, Wilson, and the American Civil Religion." *Modern Age* 23 (1979): 33–38.

The beliefs of Woodrow Wilson and Herbert Croly about millenarianism are compared and contrasted.

0213 Blum, John M. *The Progressive Presidents*. New York: Norton, 1980.

A chapter on Wilson emphasizes that, despite his failings, the president embodied the best hopes of liberalism. Like Theodore Roosevelt's, his policies revealed both the risks and the advantages of his particular use of the presidency and exposed the contradictions and advantages of his purpose. Bibliography, index.

0214 Corwin, Edward S. *The President: Office and Powers, 1787–1957*. 4th ed. New York: New York University Press, 1957.

In this legal history of the presidency, Wilson's ideas on presidential prerogatives in foreign affairs, war powers, and congressional relations are discussed. Notes, index.

0215 Dimock, Marshall E. "Wilson the Domestic Reformer." *Virginia Quarterly Review* 32 (1956): 546–66.

Wilson surpassed all presidents before him in his attention to economics. He made an important contribution to the American traditions of aiding private business and avoiding outright government ownership. Notes.

0216 Edwards, George C., III, and Wayne, Stephen J. *Presidential Leadership: Politics and Policy Making*. New York: St. Martin's, 1985.

Wilson succeeded in enacting his legislative agenda because of his presidential leadership and his public oratory. Like Franklin Roosevelt, he used the presidency as a podium, but he did not manipulate the press the way FDR did. Notes, appendix, index.

0217 Frisch, Michael L. "Urban Theorists, Urban Reform, and American Political Culture in the Progressive Period." *Political Science Quarterly* 97 (1982): 295–315.

Wilson's belief that government should play a strong role in reforming society is examined as one of the more important contributions of Progressive political thought. Notes.

0218 Goldsmith, William M. *The Growth of Presidential Power: A Documented History*. 3 vols. New York: Chelsea, 1974.

Volume III discusses the Progressive impact on the presidency and Wilson's legislative leadership in domestic affairs. Wilson's role as world leader is also covered. Notes, bibliography, index.

0219 Grim, Patricia A. "From Strict Neutrality to the Fourteen Points: Woodrow Wilson's Communication Strategies in World War I." Ph.D. dissertation, University of Pittsburgh, 1983.

As president, Wilson was very adept in the use of quotations, slogans, phrases, and metaphors to influence public opinion on the war. His ministerial style and missionary themes convinced the public that the United States should become a world mediator. DAI 45:343-A.

0220 Heckscher, August. "Wilson-Style Leadership." *Confluence* 5 (1957): 332–40.

Wilson was careful to tailor his message to the particular audience to be addressed. The president hoped to use his style of leadership to move people to do great things. His style never changed, even after his crushing defeat over the Versailles treaty. Notes.

0221 ———. "Woodrow Wilson: An Appraisal and Recapitulation." In Earl Latham, ed. *The Philosophy and Policies of Woodrow Wilson*. Chicago: University of Chicago Press, 1958, pp. 244–59.

Wilson was a deliberate and artful stylist, a man with the strongest of moral commitments, and a great liberal.

0222 Henry, Laurin L. *Presidential Transitions*. Washington, DC: Brookings Institution, 1960.

The William Howard Taft-Wilson transition reflected nineteenth-century innocence and simplicity, while the Wilson-Warren Harding transition mirrored the bitterness and anger of the postwar malaise. Notes, index.

0223 Herring, Pendleton. *Presidential Leadership: The Political Relations of Congress and the Chief Executive*. New York: Farrand and Rinehart, 1940.

Like Theodore Roosevelt before him, Wilson clashed bitterly with Congress during the last years of his second term. Presidential leadership is a necessity, but the chief executive cannot be successful without the strong support of Congress. Notes, appendixes, index.

0224 Howard, Vincent W. "Woodrow Wilson, the Press, and Presidential Leadership: Another Look at the Passage of the Underwood Tariff, 1913." *Centennial Review* 24 (1980): 167–84.

While Wilson could have relied on patronage power, a Democratic majority in Congress, and support from Progressive Republicans to obtain passage of the Underwood tariff, he took the opportunity to deliver his message in person to Congress and signed the bill into law during an ornate ceremony, thereby asserting strong presidential leadership. Notes.

0225 Jackson, Carlton. *Presidential Vetoes, 1792–1945*. Athens: University of Georgia Press, 1967.

Chapter 12 discusses Presidents Taft and Wilson. President Wilson vetoed the Burnett-Dillingham immigration bill, because it would have required a literacy test. He also exercised his veto power several times during and after the war.

0226 Koenig, Louis W. *The Chief Executive*. 3d ed. New York: Harcourt Brace Jovanovich, 1975.

The country would be better off with a stronger president, a better Congress, and a reorganized party system, the author argues, referring to Wilson in passing. Notes, bibliography, index.

0227 Kundanis, George. "Ardent Advocates of Action: The Idea of Strong Presidential Leadership in the United States, 1885–1965." Ph.D. dissertation, University of Wisconsin, Madison, 1982.

Chapter 2 contains a discussion of Wilson as an advocate of action. He believed that the president should be an independent man of high morals and integrity. DAI 43:2777-A.

0228 Link, Arthur S. "Woodrow Wilson and American Traditions." In Russell H. Lucas, ed. *Outstanding American Statesmen*. Cambridge, MA: Schenkman, 1970, pp. 17–33.

Wilson made his greatest contribution to the presidency as a teacher to the likes of Herbert Hoover, Bernard Baruch, FDR, Cordell Hull, Allen and John Foster Dulles, and Dwight Eisenhower.

0229 Longaker, Richard P. "Woodrow Wilson and the Presidency." In Earl Latham, ed. *The Philosophy and Policies of Woodrow Wilson*. Chicago: University of Chicago Press, 1958, pp. 67–81.

Franklin Roosevelt, Harry Truman, and Dwight Eisenhower all learned from Wilson's presidency. They learned from his adroit leadership and initiative in the 1913 legislative campaign, but they also learned that caution was necessary as a result of the president's disastrous clash with Congress of 1919.

0230 Loss, Richard. "Alexander Hamilton and the Modern Presidency: Continuity or Discontinuity?" *Presidential Studies Quarterly* 12 (1982): 6–26.

While some have suggested that Hamilton's writings foreshadowed the modern theory of presidential power, the author finds that

Theodore Roosevelt and Woodrow Wilson boiled the complex theories of Hamilton down to a quest for power, ignoring his interests in natural law, religion, moderation, and virtue. Notes.

0231 McKown, Paul. "Certain Domestic Policies of Woodrow Wilson." Ph.D. dissertation, University of Pennsylvania, 1932.

Wilson's style of presidential leadership on such domestic issues as women's rights, prohibition, the role of labor, conservation, and the tariff is examined. As he grew confident in his ability to use government to solve the problems of modern society, Wilson evolved from a decentralist to a centralist.

0232 Marion, David E. "Alexander Hamilton and Woodrow Wilson on the Spirit and Form of a Responsible Republican Government." *Review of Politics* 42 (1980): 309–28.

While Wilson and Hamilton have been compared in their preference for strong executive leadership, their broader visions differed. Wilson's was based on democratic and egalitarian principles.

0233 Noble, Charles. "Wilson's Choice: The Political Origins of the Modern American State." *Comparative Politics* 17 (1985): 313–36.

Presidential leadership is especially important during times of active reform such as the Progressive era. Wilson faced many problems in dealing with various reform movements during his presidency. Notes.

0234 Rosenman, Samuel, and Rosenman, Dorothy. *Presidential Style: Some Giants and a Pygmy in the White House*. New York: Harper & Row, 1976.

Wilson was among the "giant" presidents, because he insisted on frank, open discussion and decision on public affairs while exerting leadership and taking responsibility. His successor, Warren G. Harding, by contrast, was a pygmy. Notes, index.

0235 Rossiter, Clinton L. *The American Presidency*. 2d ed. New York: Harcourt, Brace and World, 1960.

Wilson was the best prepared of presidents, both morally and intellectually. His leadership during his first term brought government to a new height, but, while he was a great wartime leader, in the end he lost control of Congress, the country, and himself. Appendixes, bibliography, index.

0236 Seltzer, Alan L. "Woodrow Wilson as 'Corporate Liberal': Toward a Reconsideration of Left Revisionist Historiography." *Western Political Quarterly* 30 (1977): 183–212.

New Left revisionists are wrong, it is asserted, in dismissing Wilson as a "corporate liberal." The president's antitrust policy was heartfelt and energetic.

0237 Skau, George H. "Woodrow Wilson and the American Presidency: Theory and Practice." Ph.D. dissertation, St. John's University, 1969.

Young Wilson preferred the British form of cabinet government to the American constitutional system, but he revised his opinions on the presidency early in the Progressive era. During his first term in the White House, he exhibited great leadership ability in domestic reforms, but his temperament prevented him from carrying out the peace process successfully. DAI 30:1121-A.

0238 Tugwell, Rexford G., and Cronin, Thomas E., eds. *The Presidency Reappraised*. New York: Praeger, 1974.

A collection of essays on the evolution of the presidency are presented, several of which discuss Woodrow Wilson. Bibliography, index.

0239 Turner, Henry A. "Woodrow Wilson: Exponent of Executive Leadership." *Western Political Quarterly* 4 (1951): 97–115.

More constructive legislation was passed under Wilson's leadership than under any other president until FDR, because Wilson led and controlled Congress. His view of the presidency was that of an Americanized prime minister. Once he lost sway over Congress in 1918, he lost his effectiveness.

0240 Warren, Sidney. *The President as World Leader*. Philadelphia: Lippincott, 1964.

Wilson elevated the presidency to an international institution, seeking to win the admiration of the world. He did not succeed in jolting the American people out of their isolationism. Notes, bibliography, index.

0241 Younger, Edward. "Woodrow Wilson: The Making of a Leader." *Virginia Magazine of History and Biography* 64 (1956): 387–401.

Wilson was neither an opportunist nor an idealist, but rather a man applying ideas and plans formulated long before his public career. To him leadership meant persuasion and action. He insisted that a leader should not compromise, because the people would join a righteous cause.

WILSON'S PRESIDENTIAL RANKING

0242 Amlund, Curtis A. "President-Ranking: A Criticism." *Midwest Journal of Political Science* 8 (1964): 309–14.

Attempts to rank the presidents have not been very satisfactory, because presidential greatness is difficult to measure.

0243 Bailey, Thomas A. *Presidential Greatness: The Image and the Man from George Washington to the Present*. New York: Appleton-Century, 1966.

Like Jefferson, Wilson was more a great man than a great president. He led America "into the fog and bog of disillusionment and frustration." He was great for his first six years in office but only near-great if his last years are considered as well. Bibliography, appendix, index.

0244 ————. *The Pugnacious Presidents*. New York: Free Press, 1980.

Most presidents have had to deal with either war or the threat of conflict, including Wilson, who intervened in Mexico, the Caribbean, and Europe. Notes, bibliography, index.

0245 Carleton, William G. "A New Look at Woodrow Wilson." *Virginia Quarterly Review* 38 (1962): 545–66.

Wilson has not yet achieved a high place in world history, because he is judged by a higher standard than others. Far from being an uncompromising and naive idealist, Wilson was a shrewd diplomat-politician. He deserves a great place in history. Notes.

0246 Kynerd, Tom. "An Analysis of Presidential Greatness and 'Presidential Rating.'" *Southern Quarterly* 9 (1971): 309–29.

The methodology, criteria, objectivity, shortcomings, and usefulness of the president rating done by Arthur Schlesinger, Thomas Bailey, Clinton Rossiter, and others are examined. There is no systematic, objective, or scientific basis for rating presidents. Notes.

0247 Maranell, Gary M. "The Evaluation of Presidents: An Extension of the Schlesinger Polls." *Journal of American History* 57 (1970): 104–13.

Arthur Schlesinger's presidential polls are reprinted along with a 1968 survey of 571 historians. The historians based their judgments less on idealism, flexibility, practicality, and control over events than on accomplishments. Tables.

0248   Maranell, Gary M., and Doddler, Richard A. "Political Orientation and the Evaluation of Presidential Prestige: A Study of American Historians." *Social Science Quarterly* 51 (1970): 415–21.

To update the Schlesinger polls, 571 members of the Organization of American Historians were surveyed by questionnaire and follow-up. Wilson finished sixth in prestige, although liberal and conservative historians reacted to him very differently. Notes, tables.

0249   Murray, Robert K., and Blessing, Tim H. "The Presidential Performance Study: A Progress Report." *Journal of American History* 70 (1983): 535–55.

A 1981–82 poll of 846 historians ranked Wilson as "near great," between Theodore Roosevelt and Andrew Jackson. Older historians gave Wilson higher marks than did younger ones, but there was very little difference between the "top 75" historians and other respondents. Notes, tables.

0250   Rossiter, Clinton L. "The Presidents and the Presidency." *American Heritage* 7 (1956): 28–33ff.

While Rossiter does not separate the presidents into categories, it is clear from his remarks that he regards Wilson as great.

0251   Schlesinger, Arthur M., Sr. "Rating the Presidents: A Rating by 75 Historians." *New York Times Magazine*, 29 July 1962.

Updating his 1948 poll, the author finds that seventy-five historians rated Wilson fourth (behind Lincoln, Washington, and FDR), just as others had done before them.

0252   ———. "The U.S. Presidents." *Life* (1 November 1948): 65.

A 1948 poll of fifty-four authorities on American history ranked Wilson fourth in greatness, behind Lincoln, Washington, and FDR.

0253   Simonton, Dean K. *Why Presidents Succeed: A Political Psychology of Leadership.* New Haven, CT: Yale University Press, 1987.

Presidential success is examined from the viewpoint of a political psychologist considering such factors as motivation, cognitive style, intelligence, childhood experience, performance in elections and on the job,

popularity, and greatness. Notes, bibliography, index.

0254   Wells, Ronald. "American Presidents as Political and Moral Leaders: A Report on Four Surveys." *Fides et Historia* 11 (1978): 39–53.

Results of polls taken in 1977 of professors of American studies in the United States and Britain were similar not only to each other but also to the Schlesinger surveys. Notes, table.

Wilson and the Press

See also Chapter 7, *Public Opinion and the Press.*

0255   Bloomfield, Douglas M. "Joe Tumulty and the Press." *Journalism Quarterly* 42 (1965): 413–21.

Wilson's secretary, Joseph Tumulty, was the first real presidential press secretary, meeting with newspaper reporters daily and keeping the lines of communication open during the war. Notes.

0256   Boaz, John K. "The Presidential Press Conference." Ph.D. dissertation, Wayne State University, 1969.

Press conferences of twentieth-century presidents are analyzed, including those of Wilson. DAI 32:6580-A.

0257   Cornwell, Elmer E., Jr. *Presidential Leadership of Public Opinion.* Bloomington: Indiana University Press, 1965.

Wilson exhibited a great talent for enlisting public support for his programs. With regard to the League, his failure was tactical, not strategic. His innovations included the formal press conference and the propagandistic Creel committee. Notes, index.

0258   ———. "The Presidential Press Conference: A Study of Institutionalization." *Midwest Journal of Political Science* 4 (1960): 370–89.

Wilson's contribution to the institutionalization of the presidential news conference is mentioned in passing. Notes.

0259   ———. "The Press Conferences of Woodrow Wilson." *Journalism Quarterly* 39 (1962): 292–300.

The first president to hold regular press conferences, Wilson used these meetings to mold public opinion and assert leadership over Congress. Transcripts of fifty-seven press conferences exist today. Notes.

0260 Juergens, George. *News from the White House: The Presidential-Press Relationship in the Progressive Era.* Chicago: University of Chicago Press, 1981.

Wilson disliked popular journalism and fought with the press over coverage of his family. Newsmen did not care for the president either, and Wilson put an end to his regular press conferences in 1915. He enjoyed good press, because Joseph Tumulty handled reporters with skill. Photographs, notes, bibliography, index.

President as Commander in Chief

0261 Spector, Ronald. " 'You're Not Going to Send Soldiers over There Are You!': The American Search for an Alternative to the Western Front, 1916–1917." *Military Affairs* 36 (1972): 1–4.

American officials seriously considered not sending troops to the western front, and President Wilson studied plans that would have launched an offensive in Eastern Europe. Notes.

0262 Trask, David F. "Remarks for the Bicentennial Lecture Series: Woodrow Wilson and the Coordination of Force and Diplomacy." *SHAFR Newsletter* 12 (1981): 12–19.

To be successful in modern warfare, the commander in chief must coordinate force and diplomacy. Wilson succeeded in doing so during the war, but he failed when making the peace.

0263 ———. "Woodrow Wilson and International Statecraft: A Modern Assessment." *Naval War College Review* 36 (1983): 57–68.

Wilson agonized over American entry into World War I, because he thought that modern warfare was obsolete. He shrewdly watched over American interests, finally entering the conflict to gain influence over the peace process. He put too much faith in public opinion and in his ideal of collective security. Notes.

0264 ———. "Woodrow Wilson and the Reconciliation of Force and Diplomacy: 1917–1918." *Naval War College Review* 27 (1975): 23–31.

Many writers have underestimated Wilson's ability to coordinate military force and diplomacy. In many ways no president was a better wartime commander in chief.

Wilson and Congress

See Chapter 11, *Politics,* for Wilson's wartime relations with Congress.

0265 Dimock, Marshall E. "Woodrow Wilson as Legislative Leader." *Journal of Politics* 19 (1957): 3–19.

Analyzing Wilson's effectiveness as a legislative leader, the author shows how the president used the force of his personality, his education, and his values in the art of persuasion. Notes.

0266 Hendrix, J. A. "Presidential Addresses to Congress: Woodrow Wilson and the Jeffersonian Tradition." *Southern Speech Journal* 31 (1966): 285–94.

Wilson's address before the opening session of Congress in April 1913 helped to establish his strong authority and ended a 113-year hiatus in the practice of presidents speaking before the legislative branch. Notes.

0267 Link, Arthur S. "Woodrow Wilson and the Democratic Party." *Review of Politics* 18 (1956): 146–56.

Although he began his presidency as leader of the Progressive forces within the Democratic party, Wilson also worked with conservatives and with party bosses to line up support for his foreign policy and administrative reforms. Notes.

0268 MacMahon, Arthur W. "Woodrow Wilson as a Legislative Leader and Administrator." *American Political Science Review* 50 (1956): 641–76.

A great admirer of the parliamentary form of government, Wilson used the presidency to influence Congress. Notes.

0269 ———. "Woodrow Wilson: Political Leader and Administrator." In Earl Latham, ed. *The Philosophy and Policies of Woodrow Wilson*. Chicago: University of Chicago Press, 1958, pp. 100–22.

Wilson exerted presidential leadership by influencing Congress selectively, collaborating whenever possible, using the Democratic party rather than a Progressive coalition, working through caucuses, and appealing to public opinion.

President Wilson poses with his cabinet, 1917. Front row, l. to r.: Secretary of Commerce William C. Redfield, Secretary of State Robert Lansing, Secretary of Agriculture David F. Houston, the president, Secretary of the Treasury William G. McAdoo, Postmaster General Albert S. Burleson. Back row, l. to r.: Secretary of the Navy Josephus Daniels, Secretary of Labor William B. Wilson, Secretary of War Newton D. Baker, Attorney General Thomas W. Gregory, Secretary of the Interior Franklin K. Lane. *Library of Congress.*

Administration Personalities: Political, Military, and Diplomatic

Persons who played important roles during the Wilson era in national politics, military affairs, and diplomacy are grouped together in this chapter. Important individuals not listed here may be found in other chapters. For industrialists, see Chapter 4, *Business Leaders;* for union leaders, see Chapter 4, *Labor, Personalities.* For civil rights leaders, see Chapter 6, *Minority Groups, Leaders and Organizations;* for women leaders, see Chapter 6, *Women, Feminism, Radical Women,* and *The Suffrage Movement;* for radical leaders, see Chapter 8, *Radical Ideologies, Anarchism, Syndicalism, Socialism,* and *Communism.* Additional entries on Progressive politicians may be found in Chapter 7, *The Progressive Movement* and *New Freedom.* Chapter 7 also contains information on persons involved in *State and Local Politics.* See Chapter 7, *Supreme Court Justices,* for works on persons in the judicial branch, including Wilson's adviser Louis D. Brandeis. Chapter 11 contains entries on personalities prominent during World War I under *Mobilization, Propaganda, Civil Liberties, Politics,* and *The Military Dimension.* For persons involved with the Paris Peace Conference, see Chapter 12, *Preparations* and *General Accounts.*

Readers will note that materials on past and future presidents active in politics and administration during the Wilson years, including Herbert Hoover, Franklin D. Roosevelt, Theodore Roosevelt, and William Howard Taft, are highly selective, having been chosen because they contain significant material on the period from 1912 to 1921. See also the bibliographies listed in Chapter 13.

Executive Branch

GENERAL

0270   Fenno, Richard F., Jr. *The President's Cabinet: An Analysis in the Period from Wilson to Eisenhower.* Cambridge, MA: Harvard University Press, 1959.
Wilson treated his cabinet members as departmental administrators. He delegated authority in domestic affairs and initiated matters relating to foreign policy. While he sometimes asked for the opinions of his cabinet, he often ignored its advice or used it merely as a sounding board. Notes, index.

0271   Vexler, Robert I. *The Vice Presidents and Cabinet Members.* 2 vols. Dobbs Ferry, NY: Oceana, 1975.
Thumbnail biographies of all the vice presidents and cabinet officials are presented, including those of members of the Wilson administration. Bibliographies, index.

NEWTON D. BAKER

See also Chapter 11, *Mobilization.*

0272 Baker, Newton D. *Why We Went to War.* New York: Harper, 1936.

Still a champion of Wilsonian internationalism in the isolationist 1930s, Baker defends intervention on practical as well as on idealistic grounds.

0273 Beaver, Daniel R. *Newton D. Baker and the American War Effort, 1917–1919.* Lincoln: University of Nebraska Press, 1966.

The secretary of war's role in mobilizing the American war machine is examined, including his condoning of the repression of those who opposed the war. Notes, bibliography, index.

0274 Cramer, Clarence H. *Newton D. Baker: A Biography.* Cleveland: World, 1961.

In the first full-length biography of Wilson's secretary of war, the author portrays Baker as a humanitarian and an idealist who remained unwavering in his Wilsonianism. Photographs, notes, bibliography, index.

0275 Palmer, Frederick. *Newton D. Baker.* 2 vols. New York: Dodd, Mead, 1931.

Secretary of War Baker's effective work in helping to put a large army in the field during World War I is examined. Photographs, notes, index.

BERNARD BARUCH

See also Chapter 11, *Mobilization.*

0276 Baruch, Bernard M. *Baruch.* 2 vols. New York: Holt, Rinehart and Winston, 1957–1960.

Volume II covers Baruch's involvement in politics and government service. He regards his friend Woodrow Wilson as one of the greatest men in history. While he was close to Wilson, Baruch could not convince the stricken president to compromise with the Republicans on the Treaty of Versailles. Photographs, index.

0277 Coit, Margaret L. *Mr. Baruch.* Boston: Houghton Mifflin, 1957.

The author details Baruch's work as "Dr. Facts," chairman of the powerful War Industries Board. As a member of the reparation commission at the Paris Peace Conference, Baruch fought against reparations designed to cripple Germany and emerged as Wilson's most intimate adviser

following the banishment of Colonel Edward House. Photographs, notes, bibliography, index.

0278 Cuff, Robert D. "Bernard Baruch: Symbol and Myth in Industrial Mobilization." *Business History Review* 43 (1969): 115–33.

Baruch gained an unwarranted reputation as the war's industrial czar, a reputation based more on the work of press agents than on the reality that big corporations retained considerable powers. Notes.

0279 Grant, James. *Bernard M. Baruch: The Adventures of a Wall Street Legend.* New York: Simon and Schuster, 1983.

This biography concentrates on the financial career of Baruch, who brought a "trader's flexibility to national politics." Photographs, notes, index.

0280 Schwarz, Jordan A. *The Speculator: Bernard M. Baruch in Washington, 1917–1965.* Chapel Hill: University of North Carolina Press, 1981.

The author finds that Baruch had "an instinct for power, publicity, and prestige" and dreamed of being a power broker for the Democratic presidential nomination. Baruch failed in his principal public purpose of educating people about the need to plan for economic stabilization. Notes, bibliography, index.

0281 White, William L. *Bernard Baruch: Portrait of a Citizen.* New York: Harcourt, Brace, 1950.

White devotes one chapter to Baruch's service in Washington during World War I and his relationship with Woodrow Wilson. Bibliography.

ALBERT S. BURLESON

See also Chapter 8, *The Red Scare, General Studies* and Chapter 11, *Civil Liberties, Government.*

0282 Anderson, Adrian N. "Albert Sidney Burleson: A Southern Politician in the Progressive Era." Ph.D. dissertation, Texas Technological College, 1967.

Congressman Burleson served effectively as postmaster general during Wilson's administration. He also acted as Wilson's political adviser and liaison with Congress. DAI 28:4071-A.

0283 ———. "President Wilson's Politician: Albert Sidney Burleson of Texas." *Southwestern Historical Quarterly* 77 (1974): 339–54.

A political appointee, Postmaster General Burleson loyally supported Wilson in order to keep his job. Power politics interested him more than Progressive reforms. Notes.

GEORGE CREEL

See also Chapter 11, *Propaganda*.

0284 Creel, George. *Rebel at Large: Reflections of Fifty Crowded Years.* New York: Putnam's, 1947.

Wilson's propaganda chief insists that he engaged in no press manipulation, just provided information, and that censorship was completely voluntary. In the end, Wilson was neither bamboozled by the Allies at Paris nor naive politically; rather, he was sold out by the Henry Cabot Lodge clique.

JOSEPHUS DANIELS

0285 Daniels, Jonathan. *The End of Innocence.* Philadelphia: J. B. Lippincott, 1954.

Daniels writes about the two men he most admired: Franklin D. Roosevelt and his father, Josephus Daniels. Index.

0286 Daniels, Josephus. *The Cabinet Diaries of Josephus Daniels, 1913–1921.* Edited by E. David Cronon. Lincoln: University of Nebraska Press, 1963.

Although diaries for the years 1914 and 1916 are missing, this source is valuable for understanding the workings of the cabinet and Washington during the Wilson years. Notes, index.

0287 ———. *The Wilson Era.* 2 vols. Chapel Hill: University of North Carolina Press, 1946.

In this massive memoir, Wilson's secretary of the navy finds the president to have been "the most distinguished figure of an age." Unlike most other contemporaries and historians, Daniels found Wilson to be easy to understand, because he always meant what he said. Photographs, index.

0288 Jenkins, Innis L. "Josephus Daniels and the Navy Department, 1913–1916: A Study in Military Administration." Ph.D. dissertation, University of Maryland, 1960.

Wilson appointed Josephus Daniels navy secretary in 1913. Formerly a journalist as well as a politician, Daniels was able to use his skills of persuasion and communication to convince both Congress and the public to finance a modernized, expanded navy. His reorganization of navy administration was generally quite successful. DAI 22:1963.

0289 Morrison, Joseph L. *Josephus Daniels: The Small-d Democrat.* Chapel Hill: University of North Carolina Press, 1966.

In this biography of the provincial North Carolina editor who became Wilson's secretary of the navy and, later, his chief defender, the author concludes that Daniels "lived a life free of anti-climax." Photographs, notes, index.

0290 Thelander, Theodore A. "Josephus Daniels and the Publicity Campaign for Naval and Industrial Preparedness before World War I." *North Carolina Historical Review* 43 (1966): 316–32.

Daniels created a Naval Consulting Board to publicize naval expansion and preparedness, an effort which was aided by the budding advertising industry. Notes.

0291 Urofsky, Melvin I. "Josephus Daniels and the Armor Trust." *North Carolina Historical Review* 45 (1968): 237–63.

Distrustful of large corporations, Navy Secretary Daniels favored creation of a government naval armor factory to force down prices. While the plant never became operational, prices did fall. Notes.

CARTER GLASS

0292 Glass, Carter. "The Opposition to the Federal Reserve Bank Bill." *Proceedings of the Academy of Political Science* 30 (1971): 37–43.

In this reprint of a 1913 article Glass refutes opposition to the bill, which he helped to author.

0293 Smith, Rixey, and Beasley, Norman. *Carter Glass: A Biography.* New York: Longmans, Green, 1939.

Congressman Glass played an important role in the origination of the Federal Reserve system. He later served as Wilson's secretary of the treasury from 1918 to 1920, until his election to the Senate.

HERBERT C. HOOVER

See also Chapter 11, *Mobilization.*

0294 Anderson, Howard Clifford. "Herbert Hoover: A Study of Historical Revisionism." Ph.D. dissertation, Illinois State University, 1984.

Hoover served on various relief committees during the Wilson administration. The primary focus of this dissertation, however, is on changing interpretations of Hoover, particularly of Hoover during his presidency. DAI 46:243-A.

0295 Best, Gary D. "Food Relief as Price Support: Hoover and American Pork, January-March 1919." *Agricultural History* 45 (1971): 79–84.

After the war, Hoover faced the problem of continuing government price supports for pork in the face of cheap meat flooding into Europe from Argentina and other sources. Under the guise of keeping order in Europe, Congress granted relief appropriations to underwrite the continued export of American food. Notes.

0296 ———. "Herbert Hoover's Technical Mission to Yugoslavia, 1919–1920." *Annals of Iowa* 42 (1974): 443–59.

Following the shutdown of the American Relief Administration, Herbert Hoover attempted to keep technical experts on the job in Eastern Europe to coordinate transportation. The problems involved in the Yugoslav sector are detailed up to when the mission concluded its work in the fall of 1920. Notes.

0297 ———. *The Politics of American Individualism: Herbert Hoover in Transition, 1918–1921.* Westport, CT: Greenwood, 1975.

Hoover had gained respect as a great administrator by 1919, and he was mentioned prominently as a presidential candidate. He supported Warren G. Harding after assurances that the GOP nominee favored the League of Nations. Notes, bibliography, index.

0298 Burner, David. *Herbert Hoover: A Public Life.* New York: Knopf, 1978.

Several chapters are devoted to Hoover's work in the Food Administration saving Europe from starvation, his plan to use food to fight Bolshevism, and the 1920 presidential campaign. Notes, bibliography, index.

0299 Chávez, Leo E. "Herbert Hoover and Food Relief: An Application of American Ideology." Ph.D. dissertation, University of Michigan, 1976.

Hoover used food relief to fight Bolshevism and to promote the Open Door as an alternative to military force. He hoped Europe would embrace the American model for the good of mankind. DAI 37:3847-A.

0300 Gelfand, Lawrence E., ed. *Herbert Hoover: The Great War and Its Aftermath, 1914–1923.* Iowa City: University of Iowa, 1979.

This collection of essays includes work on Hoover concerning war organization and the Food Administration, his thoughts on the Treaty of Versailles and the Bolshevik Revolution, and his postwar public image. Notes, index.

0301 Guth, James L. "Herbert Hoover, the U.S. Food Administration, and the Dairy Industry, 1917–1918." *Business History Review* 55 (1981): 170–87.

Hoover tried to mediate the milk question during the war through investigative commissions and talks between milk producers and dealers, which at least showed consumers that the government cared about high wartime milk prices. Notes.

0302 Hall, Tom G., Jr. "Cheap Bread from Dear Wheat: Herbert Hoover, the Wilson Administration, and the Management of Wheat Prices, 1916–1920." Ph.D. dissertation, University of California, Davis, 1970.

As head of the Food Administration, Herbert Hoover skillfully manipulated the wheat market to balance the interests of consumers, farmers, and the war effort. DAI 31:4674-A.

0303 Hoff-Wilson, Joan. *Herbert Hoover: Forgotten Progressive.* Boston: Little, Brown, 1975.

Hoover's activities during the Progressive era, including his wartime service to Wilson, are examined briefly. Bibliography, index.

0304 Hoover, Herbert C. *An American Epic: Famine in Forty-Five Nations: The Battle on the Front Line, 1914–1923.* 3 vols. Chicago: Regnery, 1961.

Hoover examines World War I and its tragic aftermath in terms of food and starvation and how he organized relief efforts. Appendix, index.

0305 ———. *Memoirs*. 3 vols. New York: Macmillan, 1951–52.

In Volume I, Hoover discusses his work with Belgian relief, the creation of the Food Administration, and the American Peace Commission. President Wilson, Hoover writes, ended up at odds with Allied leaders because he "was too great a man to employ European methods." Photographs, index.

0306 Nelsen, Clair E. "The Image of Herbert Hoover as Reflected in the American Press." Ph.D. dissertation, Stanford University, 1956.

The author stresses that this is an analysis of Hoover's public image, not a biography. Chapter 1 recounts his career through 1920. Overall, newspapers treated Hoover quite favorably. DAI 16:1892.

0307 Winters, Donald L. "The Hoover-Wallace Controversy during World War I." *Annals of Iowa* 39 (1969): 586–97.

Hoover and Henry C. Wallace parted ways over government efforts to increase hog production during the war.

EDWARD M. HOUSE

See also Chapter 1, *Autobiographical and Biographical Materials,* Chapter 10, *Wilsonian Diplomacy,* and Chapter 12, *Preparations* and *Paris Peace Conference, General Accounts.*

0308 Koenig, Louis W. *The Invisible Presidency*. New York: Rinehart, 1960.

This work contains short biographies of powerful presidential assistants including Colonel House, the "Sphinx in a Soft Hat." House suffered from a sense of "overwhelming self-importance."

0309 Medved, Michael. *The Shadow Presidents: The Secret History of the Chief Executives and Their Top Aides.* New York: Times, 1979.

Chapter 5 covers the "singular friendship" between Wilson and House. Thanks to the colonel's tireless cultivation of writers and academics, he received favorable reviews as a selfless public servant, when he was really devious, insincere, and contemptuous of democracy. Photographs, bibliography.

0310 Reinertson, John. "Colonel House, Woodrow Wilson and European Socialism, 1917–1919." Ph.D. dissertation, University of Wisconsin, 1971.

Wilson and Colonel House were ready to make tacit alliances with socialist parties in Europe in order to build democracy. Bolsheviks on the left and nationalists on the right were too strong for the House-Wilson scheme, one that was less idealistic than radical, to succeed. DAI 31:6528-A.

0311 Richardson, Rupert N. *Colonel Edward M. House: The Texas Years, 1858–1912.* Abilene: Hardin-Simmons University Press, 1964.

Long before he met Woodrow Wilson, Colonel House wielded great political influence in Texas, exhibiting a gift for inspiring greatness in others. Notes, bibliography, index.

0312 Rifkind, Robert S. "The Colonel's Dream of Power." *American Heritage* 10 (1959): 62–64ff.

Colonel House published a novel under an assumed name about a dashing young man who becomes a heroic American dictator. Notes.

0313 Seymour, Charles. "End of a Friendship." *American Heritage* 14 (1963): 4–9ff.

In 1938 the dying Colonel House revealed his side of the story of the breakup of the Wilson-House friendship in 1919, with the proviso that it not be discussed for twenty-five years, a promise kept by the author of this article.

0314 ———. *The Intimate Papers of Colonel House Arranged as a Narrative.* 4 vols. Boston: Houghton Mifflin, 1926–1928.

Sixty years after its publication this is still a very useful work on Wilson's close friend and adviser. The author characterizes their relationship as an "extraordinary partnership." Photographs, index.

DAVID F. HOUSTON

0315 Houston, David F. *Eight Years with Wilson's Cabinet.* 2 vols. Garden City, NY: Doubleday, Page, 1926.

Wilson's secretary of agriculture recalls his tenure in detail. Houston concludes that Wilson "was nervous only about the possibility of being wrong." His one-track mind and his long background as a cloistered academic, the author observes, were traits which hampered the president's thinking. Photographs, appendix, index.

FRANKLIN K. LANE

0316 Lane, Franklin K. *The Letters of Franklin K. Lane, Personal and Political.* Edited by Anne W. Lane and Louise H. Wall. Boston: Houghton Mifflin, 1922.

This collection of letters includes a generous selection from Lane's years as secretary of the interior during Wilson's tenure.

0317 Olson, Keith W. *Biography of a Progressive: Franklin K. Lane, 1864–1921.* Westport, CT: Greenwood, 1979.

Franklin Lane, secretary of the interior from 1913 to 1920, was known for his integrity, his belief in conservation, and his Progressivism, which was conservative in that he believed that the capitalist system needed only modification to function for the benefit of all. Notes, bibliography, index.

0318 ———. "Woodrow Wilson, Franklin K. Lane, and the Wilson Cabinet Meetings." *Historian* 32 (1970): 270–75.

Lane's charge that Wilson did not make good use of his cabinet is refuted. Notes.

WILLIAM G. McADOO

0319 Broesmale, John J. *William Gibbs McAdoo: A Passion for Change, 1863–1917.* Port Washington, NY: Kennikat, 1973.

Wilson's emphasis on the search for foreign markets and on flexibility in trade policy allowed his secretary of the treasury to be an innovator. Photographs, notes, bibliography, index.

0320 McAdoo, William G. *Crowded Years: The Reminiscences of William G. McAdoo.* Boston: Houghton Mifflin, 1921.

Wilson's ambitious son-in-law, who served as secretary of the treasury, includes chapters on implementing the Federal Reserve system, neutrality, and financing the war. Although he admired Wilson greatly, McAdoo concludes that he never really knew him well. Illustrations, photographs, index.

0321 Shook, Dale N. "William G. McAdoo and the Development of National Economic Policy, 1913–1918." Ph.D. dissertation, University of Cincinnati, 1975.

McAdoo made the Treasury Department an important agency of national economic development. During the war he helped to forge the business-government partnership that was instrumental in winning the war for the Allies. DAI 36:6268-A.

THOMAS R. MARSHALL

0322 Brown, John E. "Woodrow Wilson's Vice President: Thomas R. Marshall and the Wilson Administration, 1913–1921." Ph.D. dissertation, Ball State University, 1970.

A loyal supporter of President Wilson throughout his eight-year tenure as vice president, Marshall earned the president's appreciation for his political skills and patriotism. Overshadowed by an activist and domineering president, Marshall still exhibited his very real talents at an important time in American history. DAI 31:4664-A.

0323 Marshall, Thomas R. *Recollections of Thomas R. Marshall: A Hoosier Salad.* Indianapolis: Bobbs-Merrill, 1925.

Anecdotes and homespun philosophy dominate this volume. Marshall believed that, after the war, Wilson erred in assuming that the American people would support him. Photographs, index.

A. MITCHELL PALMER

See also Chapter 8, *The Red Scare.*

0324 Coben, Stanley A. *A. Mitchell Palmer: Politician.* New York: Columbia University Press, 1963.

Before the war, Palmer was a "champion of the underprivileged," but he became a "liberal demagogue" and chief inquisitor of the Red Scare after caving in to public criticism. Palmer became "one of the most dangerous men in our history," because he abandoned his principles to follow the mob. Photographs, notes, bibliography, index.

FRANKLIN D. ROOSEVELT

0325 Coady, Joseph W. "Franklin D. Roosevelt's Early Washington Years (1913–1920)." Ph.D. dissertation, St. John's University, 1968.

Roosevelt's eight years as assistant secretary of the navy under Wilson and his experience as the vice presidential standard-bearer for the Democrats in 1920 shaped his outlook in many ways. He gained administrative experience, watched Wilson firsthand, learned about foreign affairs, minorities, and the working class, and developed a pragmatic political style that would later serve him well. DAI 30:1103-A.

0326 Freidel, Frank. *Franklin D. Roosevelt.* Vol. 1, *The Apprenticeship.* Boston: Little, Brown, 1952.

Volume I of this massive biography contains material on Roosevelt's tenure as assistant secretary of the navy. Notes, bibliography, index.

0327 Nash, Gerald D. "Franklin D. Roosevelt and Labor: The World War I Origins of Early New Deal Policy." *Labor History* 1 (1960): 39–52.

Roosevelt drew heavily on his experience as assistant secretary of the navy under Wilson for his New Deal labor policies. During World War I, Roosevelt drew up policies for the Shipbuilding Labor Adjustment Board and the National War Labor Board. Notes.

0328 Van Everen, Brooks. "Franklin D. Roosevelt and the German Problem: 1914–1945." Ph.D. dissertation, University of Colorado, 1970.

Roosevelt's thinking about Germany during his presidency was shaped by his experiences during the Wilson administration, when he served as assistant secretary of the navy. DAI 31:4696-A.

0329 Young, Lowell T. "Franklin D. Roosevelt and Imperialism." Ph.D. dissertation, University of Virginia, 1970.

As assistant secretary of the navy under Wilson, FDR exhibited imperialist attitudes toward Mexican and Caribbean affairs. DAI 31:4698-A.

JOSEPH TUMULTY

0330 Blum, John Morton. *Joe Tumulty and the Wilson Era*. Boston: Houghton Mifflin, 1951.

The author regards Tumulty and his boss, Woodrow Wilson, as naive for believing that the League could solve the world's problems, when their political experience should have showed them that people are wicked and unreasonable. Photographs, notes, bibliography, index.

OTHERS

0331 Daniel, Robert L. "The Friendship of Woodrow Wilson and Cleveland H. Dodge." *Mid-America* 43 (1961): 182–96.

Although Wilson did not care for businessmen usually, he and Dodge, a New York millionaire, became lifelong friends. Dodge's philanthropy and Wilson's idealism gave the two men common ground. Notes.

0332 Wilhelm, Clarke L. "William B. Wilson: The First Secretary of Labor." Ph.D. dissertation, Johns Hopkins University, 1967.

William Wilson was a strong and effective labor advocate serving a sympathetic administration. Under his influence, government became involved in mediation. He was in charge of mobilizing labor for the war effort, and he promoted collective bargaining, a minimum wage, and an eight-hour day. However, his efforts to unify labor for the Democrats in 1916 were unsuccessful. DAI 28:4587-A.

Diplomats

WILLIAM JENNINGS BRYAN

See also Chapter 9, *Foreign Affairs: Bilateral Relations*.

0333 Anderson, David D. *William Jennings Bryan*. Boston: Twayne, 1981.

Bryan was an important force in modern liberalism, struggling to maintain democratic values in urban and industrial America. Notes, bibliography, index.

0334 Bryan, William Jennings, and Bryan, Mary Baird. *Memoirs*. Chicago: John C. Winston, 1925.

Bryan's wife finished a very rough first draft to complete this memoir, which includes a chapter comparing and contrasting him to Wilson and several chapters on his tenure as secretary of state. Photographs, appendix, index.

0335 Challener, Richard. "William Jennings Bryan." In Norman A. Graebner, ed. *An Uncertain Tradition: American Secretaries of State in the Twentieth Century*. New York: McGraw-Hill, 1961, pp. 79–100.

Bryan's outlook was that of rural, midwestern America. His provincial ideas had little to do with the real world by the time he became secretary of state. He approached all issues on the basis of good versus evil.

0336 Cherny, Robert W. *A Righteous Cause: The Life of William Jennings Bryan*. Boston: Little, Brown, 1985.

Above all, the author asserts, Bryan was a crusader. While he was certainly not an intellectual, most recent presidents have not been, either. Photographs, bibliography, index.

0337 Clements, Kendrick A. "William Jennings Bryan and Democratic Foreign Policy, 1896–1915." Ph.D. dissertation, University of California, Berkeley, 1970.

The devoutly religious Bryan believed in the American mission to become a model of democracy for all the world to follow. He had to compromise his principles when he became secretary of state, and he did a fair job as a result. DAI 31:6510-A.

0338 Coletta, Paolo E. "Bryan, Anti-Imperialism and Missionary Diplomacy." *Nebraska History* 44 (1963): 167–87.

Bryan's anti-imperialism of the late 1890s and early 1900s changed during his tenure as secretary of state, when he accepted the practice of Dollar Diplomacy.

0339 ———. "Bryan Briefs Lansing." *Pacific Historical Review* 27 (1958): 383–96.

Following his resignation as secretary of state in 1915, William Jennings Bryan wrote a briefing for his successor, Robert Lansing, which is published here in full.

0340 ———. " 'The Most Thankless Task': Bryan and the California Alien Land Legislation." *Pacific Historical Review* 36 (1967): 163–87.

Wilson's many distractions caused Bryan to lose out in his bid to intervene on behalf of Japanese in California, victims of discriminatory legislation. Notes.

0341 ———. "The Patronage Battle between Bryan and Hitchcock." *Nebraska History* 49 (1968): 121–37.

Longtime political rivals Bryan and Gilbert C. Hitchcock fought over Nebraska patronage during Wilson's first term, a battle which Bryan eventually lost following his resignation as secretary of state.

0342 ———. "Secretary of State William Jennings Bryan and 'Deserving Democrats.' " *Mid-America* 48 (1966): 75–98.

Bryan freely delivered jobs to incompetent but "deserving" party loyalists as secretary of state, a policy which brought him much grief. Notes.

0343 ———. *William Jennings Bryan.* 3 vols. Lincoln: University of Nebraska Press, 1969.

Volume II covers the Great Commoner's part in the 1912 election and the New Freedom as well as his tenure as secretary of state. Volume III details Bryan's activities in the anti-preparedness campaign, prohibitionism, women's suffrage, the Treaty of Versailles, and postwar issues. Photographs, bibliography, index.

0344 ———. "William Jennings Bryan and Currency and Banking Reform." *Nebraska History* 45 (1964): 31–57.

Bryan's thoughts on money and banking are outlined from bimetalism to the Federal Reserve system, the latter of which might not have become reality without his support.

0345 Daniels, Roger. "William Jennings Bryan and the Japanese." *Southern California Quarterly* 48 (1966): 227–40.

While Bryan was sincere in his attempt to negotiate a fair settlement of problems with Japan over immigration and land ownership in California, his efforts came to little good. Notes.

0346 Ginger, Ray. *William Jennings Bryan: Selections.* Indianapolis: Bobbs-Merrill, 1967.

Ginger uses selections from the Bryan papers and other sources to show that the young Bryan, the very model of a liberal politician, and the old Bryan, Ku Klux Klan apologist and Scopes trial prosecutor, were the same man. Bibliography, index.

0347 Glad, Paul W. "Bryan and the Urban Progressives." *Mid-America* 39 (1957): 169–79.

As a leader of the rural wing of the Progressive movement, Bryan worked to produce a program after the urban wing demonstrated the necessity of change. Notes.

0348 Kaplan, Edward S. "The Latin American Policy of William Jennings Bryan, 1913–1915." Ph.D. dissertation, New York University, 1970.

As secretary of state, Bryan practiced imperialism and Dollar Diplomacy, policies he had criticized under Republican administrations, especially in regard to Central America and the Caribbean. DAI 31:4088-A.

0349 Koenig, Louis W. *A Political Biography of William Jennings Bryan.* New York: Putnam's, 1971.

This sympathetic biography contains a chapter on Bryan as secretary of state and one on his activities as a private citizen during World War I. Notes, bibliography, index.

0350 Levine, Lawrence W. *Defender of the Faith: William Jennings Bryan, the Last Decade, 1915–25.* New York: Oxford University Press, 1965.

Following his resignation as secretary of state, Bryan continued to work for Progressive causes even as he turned to fundamentalism. Photographs, notes, bibliography, index.

0351 Smith, Willard H. "William Jennings Bryan and Racism." *Journal of Negro History* 54 (1969): 127–49.

While Bryan tolerated some racial minorities, he supported the strict segregation of blacks, failing to see the paradox of fighting for increased popular rule while denying equal rights. Notes.

0352 ———. "William Jennings Bryan and the Social Gospel." *Journal of American History* 53 (1966): 41–60.

Bryan's reputation as a Christian fundamentalist is misleading, since he advocated the Progressive social gospel.

WILLIAM C. BULLITT

See also Chapter 11, *The Bolshevik Revolution, American Reactions* and Chapter 12, *Russian Question.*

0353 Farnsworth, Beatrice. *William C. Bullitt and the Soviet Union.* Bloomington, Indiana University Press, 1967.

Bullitt's mission to Russia in March 1919 and his repudiation by Wilson at Paris are discussed. Notes, bibliography, index.

BAINBRIDGE COLBY

See also Chapter 1, *Postpresidential Years.*

0354 Israel, Fred L. "Bainbridge Colby and the Progressive Party, 1914–1916." *New York History* 40 (1959): 33–46.

A political idealist, Colby refused to follow Theodore Roosevelt back into the Republican party. Notes.

0355 Novick, Joel R. "Bainbridge Colby, Profile in Progressivism." Ph.D. dissertation, New York University, 1970.

Colby remained loyal to his Progressive principles throughout the Wilson period, bringing many Progressive Republicans with him

into the president's camp in 1916. DAI 31:4686-A.

0356 Smith, Daniel M. *Aftermath of War: Bainbridge Colby and Wilsonian Diplomacy, 1920–21.* Philadelphia: American Philosophical Society, 1970.

Wilson had great moral and intellectual respect for his last secretary of state. He was a responsible administrator and the president's principal adviser on foreign affairs, coming to achieve a relationship with Wilson akin to Colonel Edward House's. Notes, bibliography, index.

0357 ———. "Bainbridge Colby and the Good Neighbor Policy, 1920–1921." *Mississippi Valley Historical Review* 50 (1963): 55–78.

Colby did pioneering work for the Good Neighbor policy during his brief tenure as secretary of state, touring lands to the south and eschewing intervention. Notes.

JAMES W. GERARD

See also Chapter 9, *Germany.*

0358 Gerard, James W. *My First Eighty-Three Years in America.* Garden City, NY: Doubleday, 1951.

Wilson's ambassador to Germany finds the president and William Randolph Hearst to have been "the most difficult for me to fathom."

0359 ———. *My Four Years in Germany.* New York: Doran, 1917.

The American ambassador to Germany during the period of U.S. neutrality looks back on four frustrating years of diplomatic service.

0360 Troisi, James L. "Ambassador Gerard and American-German Relations, 1913–1917." Ph.D. dissertation, Syracuse University, 1978.

As ambassador to Germany from 1913 to 1917, Gerard was outspoken and insensitive, but he labored under difficult circumstances, as he did not have the support of Wilson, Edward House, or Robert Lansing. Commercial and humanitarian efforts were his strong areas. He was neither a great failure nor a great success. DAI 39:3784-A.

JOSEPH C. GREW

0361 Grew, Joseph C. *Turbulent Era: A Diplomatic Record of Forty Years, 1904–1945.* Edited by Walter Johnson. 2 vols. Boston: Houghton Mifflin, 1952.

Grew's diaries contain extensive observations on wartime Germany (1914–1917), the Department of State during American participation in the war, and the Paris Peace Conference, where this career diplomat served as secretary-general of the American commission and American secretary on the international secretariat. After the war, Grew served as minister to Denmark, which position he developed into an early listening post on Soviet Russia. Photographs, notes, index.

0362 Heinrichs, Waldo H., Jr. *American Ambassador: Joseph C. Grew and the Development of the United States Diplomatic Tradition.* Boston: Little, Brown, 1966.

The author devotes three chapters to Grew's early diplomatic career during the Wilson years. Photographs, notes, index.

ROBERT LANSING

See also Chapter 10, *Wilsonian Diplomacy* and Chapter 12, *Paris Peace Conference, General Accounts.*

0363 Baker, George W. "Robert Lansing and the Purchase of the Danish West Indies." *Social Studies* 57 (1966): 64–71.

Lansing played a large part in the acquisition of the Danish West Indies to improve national security against the Central Powers.

0364 Barany, George. "Wilsonian Central Europe: Lansing's Contribution." *Historian* 28 (1966): 224–51.

A believer in the traditional idea of balance of power, Lansing had some influence in steering the president toward a realistic settlement of Central Europe's postwar political problems. Notes.

0365 Brands, Henry W., Jr. "Unpremeditated Lansing: His 'Scraps.' " *Diplomatic History* 9 (1985): 25–33.

Lansing's books of private notes reveal an emotional side to a man widely regarded as emotionless. Privately, he expressed contempt for many of his contemporaries. Notes.

0366 Hartig, Thomas H. "Robert Lansing: An Interpretive Biography." Ph.D. dissertation, Ohio State University, 1974.

A conservative, bourbon Democrat who developed a realistic attitude toward foreign affairs prior to joining the Wilson administration, Lansing was a Germanophobe from 1914 onward. He became secretary of state through luck, but Wilson increasingly operated outside of departmental channels during his tenure. DAI 35:5301.

0367 Lazo, Dimitri D. "A Question of Loyalty: Robert Lansing and the Treaty of Versailles." *Diplomatic History* 9 (1985): 35–53.

While many have argued that Lansing's forced resignation came because he overstepped his bounds during Wilson's incapacitation, the secretary himself traced it to his differences with the president over the Treaty of Versailles. Notes.

0368 Smith, Daniel M. "Robert Lansing." In Norman A. Graebner, ed. *An Uncertain Tradition: American Secretaries of State in the Twentieth Century.* New York: McGraw-Hill, 1961, pp. 101–27.

Lansing was a successful secretary of state. He helped to make the Panama Canal secure, approached Mexico realistically, defended national security by urging war against Germany, and adjusted American interests in the Far East to fit the new reality of Japan.

0369 ———. "Robert M. Lansing and the Wilson Interregnum, 1919–1920." *Historian* 21 (1959): 135–61.

The relationship between Wilson and Lansing began to strain at the Paris Peace Conference and deteriorated further during Wilson's lengthy illness. Wilson forced his resignation after Lansing acted independently as secretary of state. Notes.

0370 Smith, Ephraim K., Jr. "Robert Lansing and the Paris Peace Conference." Ph.D. dissertation, Johns Hopkins University, 1972.

Lansing still managed to exert influence over the peace settlement, although Wilson often disregarded his advice. An opponent of the League of Nations, the secretary of state at least offered the American delegation alternatives to the president's plans. DAI 36:6870-A.

0371 U.S. Department of State. *Papers Relating to the Foreign Relations of the United States: The Lansing Papers, 1914–1920.* 2 vols. Washington, DC: Government Printing Office, 1939–40.

The most important documents from the Lansing papers at the Department of State are reprinted. Index.

0372 Živojinović, Dragan. "Robert Lansing's Comments on the Pontifical Peace Note of August 1, 1917." *Journal of American History* 56 (1969): 556–71.

Lansing advised Wilson to reject Pope Benedict XV's peace proposals, since they were grounded in fear of leftist encroachments on Catholicism and might save the Central Powers from military defeat. Notes.

HENRY MORGENTHAU, JR.

See also Chapter 9, *Middle East.*

0373 Lebow, Richard N. "The Morgenthau Peace Mission of 1917." *Jewish Social Studies* 32 (1970): 267–85.

Morgenthau's plans to negotiate Turkey out of the war were sabotaged by the British and the Zionists in spite of support from Wilson and Lansing. Notes.

0374 Lifschutz, B. "The Pogroms in Poland of 1918–1919, the Morgenthau Commission and the American State Department." *Zion* [Israel] 23 (1958): 66–97.

When American Jewish organizations urged the government to protest the new Polish government's pogroms against Jews, the State Department refused at first. The Morgenthau commission's subsequent report presented a careful assessment of the anti-Jewish violence. Notes.

0375 Morgenthau, Henry, Jr. *All in a Lifetime.* Garden City, NY: Doubleday, Page, 1922.

Wilson's ambassador to Turkey idealizes America's role in the Near East and discusses his work at the Paris Peace Conference.

0376 ———. *Ambassador Morgenthau's Story.* Garden City, NY: Doubleday, Page, 1919.

Writing when America was considering an Armenian mandate, the ambassador discusses the plight of the Christian minority and what he and private groups did to help them.

WALTER HINES PAGE

See also Chapter 9, *Great Britain and Its Dominions* and Chapter 10, *Wilsonian Diplomacy* and *Wartime Relations, Entente.*

0377 Cooper, John M., Jr. *Walter Hines Page: The Southerner as American, 1855–1918.* Chapel Hill: University of North Carolina Press, 1977.

Page's southern background, writing career, service as ambassador to Britain, and quarrels with other members of the administration are examined. Photographs, notes, bibliography, index.

0378 Gregory, Ross. "The Superfluous Ambassador: Walter Hines Page's Return to Washington, 1916." *Historian* 28 (1966): 389–404.

Page's recall to Washington from London in 1916 did little good for either his reputation or the pro-British cause. Notes.

0379 ———. *Walter Hines Page: Ambassador to the Court of St. James's.* Lexington: University of Kentucky Press, 1970.

The author concludes that, while he was talented and colorful, Page's impact "was not nearly so great as his admirers have contended." Furthermore, his zeal for the British cause led honorable men to take dishonorable positions. Photographs, notes, bibliography, index.

0380 Hendrick, Burton J. *The Life and Letters of Walter H. Page.* 3 vols. Garden City, NY: Doubleday, Page, 1922–1925.

This work is as much a collection of the ambassador's letters as a biography. The author finds that Page preached "Americanism of the loftiest kind." Photographs, index.

0381 Kihl, Mary R. "A Failure of Ambassadorial Diplomacy: The Case of Page and Spring-Rice, 1914–1917." Ph.D. dissertation, Pennsylvania State University, 1968.

Ambassador to Britain Walter Page and British Ambassador to America Sir Cecil Spring-Rice were increasingly bypassed in the tense years of American neutrality. Wilson's friend and adviser Colonel Edward House undermined Page both by personal mistrust and by traveling to Britain himself and establishing important contacts there. Although Ambassadors Page and Spring-Rice were capable men, they both had personal traits that aroused suspicion in their respective governments. DAI 29:4427-A.

0382 Weaver, Frederick H. "Walter H. Page and the Progressive Mood." Ph.D. dissertation, Duke University, 1968.

Page's long career as a journalist before he became ambassador to London is examined as an example of the Progressive spirit. DAI 30:3417-A.

PAUL S. REINSCH

See also Chapter 9, *China* and Chapter 10, *Wartime Relations, Asia.*

0383 Pugach, Noel H. *Paul S. Reinsch: Open Door Diplomat in Action.* Millwood, NY: KTO, 1979.

Wilson's minister to China, Paul S. Reinsch, believed that if America exported wealth, know-how, and technology to China, the economic prosperity of both countries would be ensured. While many of his assumptions were wrong, and he was largely unsuccessful, he was a dynamic and original proponent of some of the popular political philosophies of the time, including Progressivism and disarmament. Reinsch resigned when Wilson sided with Japan on the Shantung question at the peace talks.

0384 Reinsch, Paul S. *An American Diplomat in China.* Garden City, NY: Doubleday, 1922.

The American minister to China from 1913 until Wilson acquiesced in Japanese encroachments at the Paris Peace Conference in 1919 discusses commercial interests and his efforts to protect China.

0385 Scanlan, Patrick J. "No Longer a Treaty Port: Paul S. Reinsch and China, 1913–1919." Ph.D. dissertation, University of Wisconsin, 1973.

Reinsch's Progressivism blinded him to the Chinese desire for true territorial integrity and an end to special privileges for foreigners. This lack of understanding led him to oppose China's basic aspirations while exaggerating the importance of the United States to the Chinese. DAI 34:2533.

HENRY WHITE

See also Chapter 12, *Paris Peace Conference, General Accounts.*

0386 Nevins, Allan. *Henry White: Thirty Years of American Diplomacy.* New York: Harper and Brothers, 1930.

Nevins finds White to have been an able diplomat, as loyal when he served Theodore Roosevelt as when he went to Paris with Wilson. White understood America's expanding world role better than most. Photographs, notes, appendix, index.

BRAND WHITLOCK

0387 Crunden, Robert M. *A Hero in Spite of Himself: Brand Whitlock in Art, Politics, and War.* New York: Knopf, 1969.

Author, Progressive, mayor of Toledo, and diplomat, Whitlock was Wilson's minister to Belgium. He revered the president until the bitter fight over the Treaty of Versailles. The author concludes that Whitlock "symbolized the saving virtues of a humanitarian civilization." Notes, bibliographic essay, index.

0388 Davidson, John W. "Brand Whitlock and the Diplomacy of Belgian Relief." *Prologue* 2 (1970): 145–60.

Whitlock's role as a conciliator among the Belgium relief groups—and the Germans—led to the perception that he was weak. Notes.

0389 Southern, David W. "The Ordeal of Brand Whitlock, Minister to Belgium, 1914–1922." *Northwest Ohio Quarterly* 41 (1969): 113–26.

Whitlock's writings reveal a Progressive's agony over the horrors of war as well as details of how the Committee for the Relief of Belgium worked and did not work. Notes.

0390 Tager, Jack. *The Intellectual as Urban Reformer: Brand Whitlock and the Progressive Movement.* Cleveland: Case Western Reserve University Press, 1968.

Whitlock was a sincere Jeffersonian who was unconcerned with the declining status of his class. His disillusion with Progressivism and with Wilson's new diplomacy soured him on reform and America. Notes, bibliography, index.

0391 Thorburn, Neil. "What Happened to Brand Whitlock's Progressivism?" *Northwest Ohio Quarterly* 40 (1968): 153–60.

The Progressive politician and muckraker moved to the political right as a result of his wartime experiences and the imperfect peace of Versailles. Notes.

0392 Whitlock, Brand. *The Letters and Journal of Brand Whitlock.* Edited by Allan Nevins. 2 vols. New York: Appleton-Century, 1936.

A wealth of material is included concerning Whitlock's service as ambassador to Belgium.

HENRY LANE WILSON

See also Chapter 9, *Mexico.*

0393 Blaisdell, Lowell L. "Henry Lane Wilson and the Overthrow of Madero." *Southwestern Social Science Quarterly* 43 (1962): 126–35.

The ambassador embarrassed President Wilson by conspiring with Victoriano Huerta to overthrow Mexico's President Francisco Madero.

0394 Masingill, Eugene F. "The Diplomatic Career of Henry Lane Wilson in Latin America." Ph.D. dissertation, Louisiana State University, 1957.

Wilson's ambassador to Mexico, H. L. Wilson, was caught in the crossfire when the president chose not to recognize Huerta, whom Ambassador Wilson had encouraged, as president of Mexico in 1913. Wilson was dismissed later that year, even though his record as a diplomat had been good. DAI 17:1741.

0395 Wilson, Henry Lane. *Diplomatic Episodes in Mexico, Belgium and Chile.* Garden City, NY: Doubleday, Page, 1927.

Written "to correct misleading accounts of important events," this account offers a spirited defense of H. L. Wilson's activities during the Mexican Revolution. He concludes that Woodrow Wilson "was badly or not fully informed" of events leading to the overthrow of Francisco Madero. Appendix, index.

OTHERS

0396 Coolidge, Harold J., and Lord, Robert H. *Archibald Cary Coolidge: Life and Letters.* Boston: Houghton Mifflin, 1932.

A Harvard history professor, Coolidge undertook diplomatic missions for the Wilson administration to Archangel and Vienna during World War I. The book contains excerpts from a diary kept while Coolidge was at the Paris Peace Conference. Photographs, appendix, index.

0397 Crane, Katharine. *Mr. Carr of State: Forty-Seven Years in the Department of State.* New York: St. Martin's, 1960.

Wilbur J. Carr was director of the consular service in the Department of State under Wilson. The author includes material on Carr's dealings with Secretaries William Jennings Bryan, Robert Lansing, and Bainbridge Colby as well as administration battles with Congress over appropriations. Photographs, notes, index.

0398 Darnell, Michael R. "Henry P. Fletcher and American Diplomacy, 1902–1929." Ph.D. dissertation, University of Colorado, 1972.

A career diplomat, Fletcher served as American ambassador to Chile and then Mexico during Wilson's tenure. Fletcher was consistent in his defense of the Monroe Doctrine and the rights of Americans doing business in foreign countries. DAI 33:1633-A.

0399 Dulles, Eleanor Lansing. *Chances of a Lifetime.* Englewood Cliffs, NJ: Prentice-Hall, 1980.

The sister of John Foster and Allen Dulles includes a chapter on her trip to Paris during the peace conference. Index.

0400 Fosdick, Raymond B. *Chronicle of a Generation: An Autobiography.* New York: Harper's, 1958.

The first undersecretary-general of the League of Nations details his organizational efforts during the Paris Peace Conference and describes his "long and occasionally intimate" association with Woodrow Wilson. Index.

0401 Fox, Frank W. *J. Reuben Clark: The Public Years.* Provo: Brigham Young University Press, 1980.

This is a thorough biography of the Republican diplomat who was a member of the Mormon First Presidency for almost thirty years. Taft's Mexican policy, fashioned largely by Clark, was wise in comparison to Wilson's, the author finds. During the war Clark worked in the office of the attorney general, where he resisted what he considered to be significant abuses of executive authority. Notes, bibliographic essay, index.

0402 Gaines, Anne-Rosewell J. "Political Reward and Recognition: Woodrow Wilson Appoints Thomas Nelson Page Ambassador to Italy." *Virginia Magazine of History and Biography* 89 (1981): 328–40.

Wilson had known the wealthy writer Thomas Nelson Page since their days together at the University of Virginia. The president appointed him ambassador to Italy in spite of his ties to Presidents Taft and Roosevelt, and Page carried out his duties loyally. Notes.

0403 Harbaugh, William H. *Lawyer's Lawyer: The Life of John W. Davis.* New York: Oxford University Press, 1973.

Wilson tapped this lawyer-congressman for a post in the Justice Department and then named him ambassador to Great Britain in 1918. He was always the Wall Street lawyer, growing more conservative with the years. Photographs, notes, index.

0404 Kohlenberg, Gilbert C. "David Rowland Francis: American Businessman in Russia." *Mid-America* 40 (1958): 195–217.

Much more a businessman than a diplomat, the last American ambassador to czarist Russia worked to renew a commercial and maritime treaty and used his embassy to aid American capitalist ventures. Notes.

0405 Lamont, Thomas W. *Across World Frontiers*. Cambridge, MA: Harvard University Press, 1951.

A partner in J. P. Morgan and Company, Lamont undertook several diplomatic assignments for the Wilson administration. He discusses the Paris Peace Conference, where he represented the U.S. Treasury Department. Although an admirer of President Wilson, Lamont concludes that he made several "lamentable blunders." Index.

0406 Megargee, Richard. "The Diplomacy of John Bassett Moore: Realism in American Foreign Policy." Ph.D. dissertation, Northwestern University, 1963.

Moore was counselor of the Department of State, a member of the Permanent Court of Arbitration, and a professor of international law during the Wilson years. A realist in foreign policy, Moore was unsuccessful in his attempts to implement practical internationalism while serving in the Wilson administration. DAI 24:3715.

0407 Mitchell, Kell F., Jr. "Frank L. Polk and the Paris Peace Conference, 1919." Ph.D. dissertation, University of Georgia, 1966.

Polk was under secretary of state from 1915 to 1920 and head of the American delegation during the second half of the Paris Peace Conference. Generally supportive of Wilson, Polk rarely asserted his own views. Although he participated in many negotiations and strategy sessions, he had little real effect on the final settlements. DAI 27:3404-A.

0408 Nicolson, Harold. *Dwight Morrow*. New York: Harcourt, Brace, 1935.

Morrow was "a model for the completely civilized man." A corporate lawyer and partner in the J. P. Morgan Company, he helped the Allies to obtain American financing and coordinated common economic efforts and European reconstruction. Photographs, index.

0409 Petrov, Vladimir. *A Study in Diplomacy: The Story of Arthur Bliss Lane*. Chicago: Regnery, 1971.

The opening chapter describes Lane's apprenticeship in diplomacy as a young foreign service officer serving in Rome and Warsaw during the Wilson administration. Index.

0410 Posey, John P. "David Hunter Miller at the Paris Peace Conference, November, 1918-May, 1919." Ph.D. dissertation, University of Georgia, 1961.

David Miller, an adviser on international law, was actively involved in all aspects of the peace settlement and helped to compose an early draft of the Covenant of the League of Nations. Miller's *My Diary at the Peace Conference of Paris*, a primary source for this paper, provides a unique, intelligent viewpoint and some facts unavailable elsewhere. DAI 23:2110.

0411 Pruessen, Ronald W. "John Foster Dulles and Reparations at the Paris Peace Conference, 1919: Early Patterns of Life." *Perspectives in American History* 8 (1974): 381–410.

Dulles played a significant role at the peace conference, urging the Allies to compromise on German reparations. His experience there left him an economic internationalist. Notes.

0412 Prisco, Salvatore, III. *John Barrett, Progressive Era Diplomat: A Study of a Commercial Expansionist, 1887–1920*. University: University of Alabama Press, 1973.

Director-general of the Pan-American Union from 1907 to 1920, Barrett's career is examined as an example of Progressivism in the diplomatic corps. Notes, bibliography, index.

0413 Stephenson, George M. *John Lind of Minnesota*. Minneapolis: University of Minnesota Press, 1935.

Lind's role as Wilson's representative during the 1913 crisis with Mexico is covered in this biography.

0414 Stiller, Jesse Herbert. "George S. Messersmith: A Diplomatic Biography." Ph.D. dissertation, City University of New York, 1984.

Messersmith joined the U.S. foreign service in 1914. His most notable achievements came after the Wilson era. DAI 45:280-A.

0415 Swerczek, Ronald E. "The Diplomatic Career of Hugh Gibson, 1908–1938." Ph.D. dissertation, University of Iowa, 1972.

A career diplomat, Gibson's service during World War I in Brussels, London, Washington, and Paris allowed him to advance up the professional ladder rapidly. DAI 33:3563-A.

0416 Watts, James F. "The Public Life of Breckinridge Long, 1916–1944." Ph.D. dissertation, University of Missouri, 1964.

Breckinridge Long served under Wilson as assistant secretary of state from 1917 to 1920. DAI 25:5897.

0417 Wilson, Hugh. *The Education of a Diplomat.* New York: Longmans, Green, 1938.

This career diplomat details his learning experiences in prewar Berlin and Vienna.

Military Officers

TASKER BLISS

See also Chapter 12, *Paris Peace Conference, General Accounts.*

0418 Palmer, Frederick. *Bliss, Peacemaker: The Life and Letters of General Tasker Howard Bliss.* New York: Dodd, Mead, 1934.

A plenipotentiary on the American Commission to Negotiate Peace at Paris, General Bliss represented the military viewpoint and was often critical of the peacemakers.

0419 Trask, David F. *General Tasker Howard Bliss and the 'Sessions of the World,' 1919.* Philadelphia: American Philosophical Society, 1966.

The general's role as a diplomat and adviser to the president at the Paris Peace Conference is examined.

ROBERT L. BULLARD

0420 Bullard, Robert L. *Personalities and Reminiscences of the War.* Garden City, NY: Doubleday, Page, 1925.

Major General Bullard discusses his role in the American Expeditionary Force during World War I. Index.

0421 Millett, Allan R. *The General: Robert L. Bullard and Officership in the United States Army, 1881–1925.* Westport, CT: Greenwood, 1975.

Bullard saw action at the Mexican border and in France. At the end of the war he was a lieutenant general and an army commander. Photographs, notes, bibliography, index.

GEORGE C. MARSHALL

0422 Marshall, George C. *Memoirs of My Services in the World War, 1917–1918.* Edited by James L. Collins, Jr. Boston: Houghton Mifflin, 1976.

This manuscript, discovered in an attic after Marshall's death, details his duties as a staff officer during the war. Photographs, notes, index.

0423 Pogue, Forrest C. *George C. Marshall.* Vol. 1, *Education of a General, 1880–1939.* New York: Viking, 1963.

Volume I of the definitive Marshall biography includes chapters on World War I and the Armistice. Photographs, notes, bibliography, index.

JOHN J. PERSHING

See also Chapter 9, *Mexico.*

0424 Goedeken, Edward A. "The Dawes-Pershing Relationship during World War I." *Nebraska History* 65 (1984): 108–29.

Charles Dawes's friendship with John J. Pershing propelled him through the ranks to the positions of general purchasing agent and head of the General Purchasing Board. Notes.

0425 Pershing, John J. *My Experiences in the World War.* 2 vols. New York: Stokes, 1931.

While critical of the Wilson administration for its lack of military preparedness, Pershing was grateful to the president for giving him the freedom to make military policy. Photographs, appendix, index.

0426 Smythe, Donald. "The Early Years of John J. Pershing, 1860–1882." *Missouri Historical Review* 58 (1963): 1–20.

Pershing's early life in Missouri reveals the energy, dedication, and methodical nature that marked his career as one of America's greatest soldiers.

0427 ———. *Guerilla Warrior: The Early Life of John J. Pershing*. New York: Scribner's, 1973.

Pershing's life up to 1917 is discussed, including his command of the force sent into Mexico to punish Pancho Villa. Notes, bibliography, index.

0428 ———. "John J. Pershing: A Study in Paradox." *Military Review* 49 (1969): 66–72.

Pershing exhibited a martial nature but disliked the army early in his career. His officers either loved or hated him, and he was a racist. Cold on the outside, Pershing wept over the death and illness of his troops.

0429 ———. "Pershing and Counterinsurgency." *Military Review* 46 (1966): 85–92.

Pershing's handling of the Moros in the Philippine campaign is used to demonstrate that Americans can run successful counterinsurgency operations.

0430 ———. *Pershing: General of the Armies*. Bloomington: Indiana University Press, 1986.

Pershing's almost autonomous command of the American Expeditionary Force is examined. He was a man of great personal strength who overestimated American military power and had little understanding of politics or diplomacy. Notes, bibliography, index.

0431 ———. "Pershing's Great Personal Tragedy." *Missouri Historical Review* 60 (1966): 320–35.

Pershing's family perished in a house fire at the Presidio in San Francisco in August 1915, while the general was serving in El Paso, Texas. He was never the same after this tragedy.

0432 Vandiver, Frank E. *Black Jack: The Life and Times of John J. Pershing*. 2 vols. College Station: Texas A & M University, 1977.

Much more an old-fashioned portrait than a life-and-times study, this massive biography paints a largely favorable picture of the American Expeditionary Force commander. Photos, maps, notes, bibliography, index.

EDDIE RICKENBACKER

0433 Adamson, Hans C. *Eddie Rickenbacker*. New York: Macmillan, 1946.

This popular biography emphasizes "Rickenbacker the Crusader."

0434 Rickenbacker, Edward V. *Rickenbacker*. Englewood Cliffs, NJ: Prentice-Hall, 1967.

Rickenbacker chronicles "preaching money, munitions and men" before American entrance into the war as well as his service with the Ninety-Fourth Aero Pursuit Squadron and the famous Hat-in-the-Ring Squadron. Photographs, index.

WILLIAM S. SIMS

0435 Morison, Elting E. *Admiral Sims and the Modern American Navy*. Boston: Houghton Mifflin, 1941.

Admiral William S. Sims was the wartime commander of U.S. naval forces in European waters and the instigator of several reforms designed to improve naval fire power. Notes, bibliography, index.

0436 Parsons, Edward B. "Admiral Sims' Mission in Europe in 1917–1919 and Some Aspects of United States Naval and Foreign Wartime Policy." Ph.D. dissertation, State University of New York, Buffalo, 1971.

Commander of naval forces in Europe during the period of American participation in the war, Sims was frustrated by President Wilson's determination to keep as much American strength in reserve as possible in order to wield greater political clout at the forthcoming peace conference. DAI 32:3224-A.

LEONARD WOOD

See also Chapter 7, *Elections, 1920.*

0437 Clifford, J. Garry. "Leonard Wood, Samuel Gompers, and the Plattsburg Training Camps." *New York History* 52 (1971): 169–89.

Gompers resented Wood's Plattsburg training camps as elitist, because they were aimed at preparing the upper class for war. Wood opened the program to the working class, and Gompers approved the idea of selective service so long as labor could participate in local draft boards. Notes.

0438 Hagedorn, Hermann. *Leonard Wood: A Biography*. 2 vols. New York: Hager, 1931.

Volume II details Wood's part in the preparedness campaign, GOP maneuvering against Wilson, and Wood's wartime service. Wood wanted power, the author concludes, but he did not understand politics and had no talent for it.

0439 Lane, Jack C. *Armed Progressive: General Leonard Wood.* San Rafael, CA: Presidio, 1978.

The Progressive movement influenced Wood, who developed a modern professional army while attempting to convert Americans to the idea that citizenship entailed a military obligation. The author concludes that Wood was "a man mostly full of himself." Photographs, notes, bibliography, index.

0440 ———. "Leonard Wood and the Shaping of American Defense Policy, 1900–1920." Ph.D. dissertation, University of Georgia, 1963.

Leonard Wood was chief of staff of the army from 1910 until 1914, but he criticized many of Wilson's policies and was not even given a command in World War I. Wood believed wholeheartedly in building American military power, and he campaigned for preparedness and universal military training. He opposed all of Wilson's strategies for peace. DAI 25:1175.

OTHERS

0441 Coffman, Edward M. *The Hilt of the Sword: The Career of Peyton C. March.* Madison: University of Wisconsin Press, 1966.

Chief of staff during World War I, March epitomized a new breed of military manager. Photographs, notes, bibliography, index.

0442 Ohl, John K. " 'Old Iron Pants': The Wartime Career of General Hugh S. Johnson, 1917–1918." Ph.D. dissertation, University of Cincinnati, 1971.

Johnson's wartime involvement with selective service and the War Industries Board prepared him for a major role in FDR's New Deal. DAI 32:3222-A.

0443 Weyant, Jane G. "The Life and Career of General William V. Judson, 1865–1923." Ph.D. dissertation, Georgia State University, 1981.

Military attaché and chief of the American military mission to Russia during a critical period of the Russian Revolution, Judson advocated the establishment of regular channels of communications with the Bolsheviks, a stance which led to his recall. DAI 44:1898-A.

Congressional and Political Leaders

See also Chapter 2, *Wilson and Congress*; Chapter 7, *National Politics*; Chapter 9, *Congress and Foreign Policy*; Chapter 11, *Politics*; and Chapter 12, *Ratification Controversy.*

0444 Livingston, Ellis N. "Senate Investigating Committees, 1900–1938." Ph.D. dissertation, University of Minnesota, 1953.

Senate investigations between 1900 and 1938 were not objective enough to produce useful information and were frequently misused as political weapons. The investigations of Brandeis's appointment to the Supreme Court and of the Treaty of Versailles are included. DAI 13:1174.

ALBERT BEVERIDGE

0445 Bowers, Claude G. *Beveridge and the Progressive Era.* New York: Literary Guild, 1932.

Imperialist, Republican, Progressive, and historian, Beveridge opposed the League of Nations not for partisan reasons but because it would place limits on American nationalism. Unlike Theodore Roosevelt and Henry Cabot Lodge, who held Wilson in contempt, Beveridge's "intellectual poise" led him to the conclusion that the president was "a master politician." Photographs, notes, index.

0446 Braeman, John. *Albert J. Beveridge: American Nationalist.* Chicago: University of Chicago Press, 1971.

Wilson skillfully undercut the Republicans politically with his Progressive reforms. Beveridge, a diehard imperialist, fought against Wilson's foreign policy. Notes, bibliography, index.

0447 ———. "Albert J. Beveridge and the First National Child Labor Bill." *Indiana Magazine of History* 60 (1964): 1–36.

Beveridge fought long and hard for a national child labor bill and helped to lay the groundwork for a constitutional defense of subsequent social and economic legislation.

0448 Levine, Daniel. "The Social Philosophy of Albert J. Beveridge." *Indiana Magazine of History* 58 (1962): 101–16.

Beveridge advocated a strong, centralist brand of Progressivism. Racism and a yearning for order explain his national chauvinism and imperialism.

0449 Thompson, J. A. "An Imperialist and the First World War: The Case of Albert J. Beveridge." *Journal of American Studies* [Great Britain] 5 (1971): 133–50.

Beveridge evolved from an imperialist at the turn of the century to an isolationist by the time of the Treaty of Versailles. Notes.

WILLIAM E. BORAH

See also Chapter 12, *Ratification Controversy*.

0450 Burke, Robert E. "Hiram Johnson's Impressions of William E. Borah." *Idaho Yesterdays* 17 (1973): 2–11.

Johnson expressed both admiration for Borah and frustration with him in these excerpts from his colorful diaries and letters to his family.

0451 Church, Frank. "Borah the Statesman." *Idaho Yesterdays* 9 (1965): 2–9.

Borah's long career in the Senate is analyzed. His faith in the wisdom of American principles, the Constitution, and the founding fathers still deserves our consideration.

0452 Johnson, Claudius O. *Borah of Idaho*. Seattle: University of Washington, 1967.

Published originally in 1936, this edition contains a new introduction. Borah was a Progressive, but he was conservative about the Constitution and about governmental power, which explains his opposition to Wilson's new diplomacy. Illustrations, notes, index.

0453 McKenna, Marian C. *Borah*. Ann Arbor: University of Michigan Press, 1961.

Like Woodrow Wilson, William Borah was a man of high principles who disagreed with the president over methods. Bibliography, index.

0454 Maddox, Robert James. *William E. Borah and American Foreign Policy*. Baton Rouge: Louisiana State University Press, 1969.

The first four chapters deal with the Wilsonian period. Borah was much more interested in fighting against perceived deviations from traditional American ideals than

in formulating programs of his own. Bibliographic essay, index.

0455 Vinson, John Chalmers. *William E. Borah and the Outlawry of War*. Athens, GA: University of Georgia Press, 1957.

In this study of Borah's crusades from 1917 to 1931, the author explains that the Idaho senator battled against the League and other internationalist peace schemes because he felt they would "ultimately destroy the Republic." Notes, bibliography, index.

CHAMP CLARK

0456 Morrison, Geoffrey F. "A Political Biography of Champ Clark." Ph.D. dissertation, St. Louis University, 1972.

Speaker of the House from 1911 to 1919, Clark almost received the nomination for the presidency in 1912, but differences with Bryan led the Great Commoner to throw his support to Wilson. DAI 33:1655-A.

WILL HAYS

See also Chapter 7, *Elections, 1920* and Chapter 11, *Politics*.

0457 Hays, Will H. *Memoirs*. Garden City, NY: Doubleday, 1955.

The national chairman of the Republican party (1918–1920) details Wilson's "playing politics in wartime," as well as the treaty fight and the 1920 election. The Treaty of Versailles went unratified due to "the clash, not of ideas or ideals, but of temperaments." Index.

CHARLES EVANS HUGHES

See also Chapter 7, *Elections, 1916*.

0458 Danelski, David J., and Tulchin, Joseph S., eds. *The Autobiographical Notes of Charles Evans Hughes*. Cambridge, MA: Harvard University Press, 1973.

As the title implies, the work is fragmentary, but the editors have tried to round the autobiography out with material from the Hughes papers and from government documents. Photographs, notes, appendix, index.

0459   Glad, Betty. *Charles Evans Hughes and the Illusions of Innocence.* Urbana: University of Illinois Press, 1966.

The author sets out to prove the thesis that Hughes's nineteenth-century mind was ill-suited for the task of making America a responsible world power, although he did demonstrate considerable political realism. Notes, bibliography, index.

0460   Perkins, Dexter. *Charles Evans Hughes and American Democratic Statesmanship.* Boston: Little, Brown, 1955.

A conservative at heart, Hughes was converted to the Progressive cause by Theodore Roosevelt. He returned to politics after serving on the Supreme Court because he found Wilson's foreign policy to be weak and ineffective. His 1916 election campaign showed him at his worst. Bibliography, index.

0461   Pusey, Merlo J. *Charles Evans Hughes.* 2 vols. New York: Macmillan, 1951.

Volume I contains material on Hughes's role as a Republican party leader and on the 1916 presidential election. Notes, appendix, index.

HIRAM JOHNSON

See also Chapter 12, *Ratification Controversy.*

0462   Boyle, Peter G. "The Study of an Isolationist: Hiram Johnson." Ph.D. dissertation, University of California, Los Angeles, 1970.

Although Senator Johnson voted to declare war in 1917, he opposed the president's idealistic war aims and repressive domestic policies. Johnson also criticized the American intervention in the Russian civil war and the Treaty of Versailles. DAI 31:5311-A.

0463   Burke, Robert E., ed. *The Diary Letters of Hiram Johnson, 1917–1945.* 7 vols. New York: Garland, 1983.

These seven volumes contain letters written by Hiram Johnson, Republican senator from California, Progressive, and an irreconcilable foe of the Wilsonian peace. Volume I contains a wealth of material on the war and the treaty controversy as well as a biographical sketch. Index.

0464   DeWitt, Howard A. "Hiram W. Johnson and Economic Opposition to Wilsonian Diplomacy: A Note." *Pacific Historian* 19 (1975): 15–23.

Fear that a cabal of capitalists would reap the rewards of heightened American internationalism caused Johnson to oppose Wilson's peace diplomacy. Notes.

0465   ———. "Hiram W. Johnson and World War I: A Progressive in Transition." *Southern California Quarterly* 56 (1974): 295–305.

Johnson feared that Wilson was becoming too powerful at the expense of Congress during the war and the treaty-making process. His evolution into a Progressive isolationist illustrates how the war changed many reformers. Notes.

0466   Fitzpatrick, John J., III. "Senator Hiram W. Johnson: A Life History, 1866–1945." Ph.D. dissertation, University of California, Berkeley, 1975.

Johnson's outlook on the world and his struggle against senatorial and presidential foes were rooted in his ambiguous feelings toward his father. This love-hate relationship led to mental depressions, a quarrelsome personality, and limited effectiveness as a national political figure. DAI 36:3923-A.

0467   Le Pore, Herbert P. "Prelude to Prejudice: Hiram Johnson, Woodrow Wilson, and the California Alien Land Law Controversy of 1913." *Southern California Quarterly* 61 (1979): 99–110.

In 1913, California, under Governor Hiram Johnson, passed a law prohibiting aliens from owning land, ostensibly to prevent Japanese domination of agriculture. Although President Taft had discouraged a similar law in 1911, Wilson chose not to challenge this racist legislation, possibly in order to win California's support in the 1916 election.

0468   Lincoln, A. " 'My Dear Friend and Champion': Letters between Theodore Roosevelt and Hiram Johnson in 1918." *California Historical Society Quarterly* 48 (1969): 19–36.

Running mates in the 1912 election, the two men continued to regard one another with high esteem and were united in 1918 by a loathing for Wilson.

0469   Lowet, Richard C. "Hiram Johnson: The Making of an Irreconcilable." *Pacific Historical Review* 41 (1972): 505–26.

Johnson hated the war and the League, because he feared that they would corrupt democracy and the Progressive movement as well as interfere with national self-determination. Notes.

0470 ———. "Hiram Johnson and the Progressive Denouement, 1910–1920." Ph.D. dissertation, University of California, Berkeley, 1969.

Consistent in his Progressivism, Johnson failed to redirect the spirit of the Bull Moose party back into the Republican mainstream after 1912. While he opposed Wilson's peace plan because he thought that it would wreck the Progressive movement, his own brand of isolationism contributed to the Progressive denouement. DAI 30:4377.

0471 Olin, Spencer C., Jr. *California's Prodigal Son: Hiram Johnson and the Progressives, 1911–1917*. Berkeley: University of California Press, 1968.

California's Hiram Johnson was a powerful, effective and popular governor. A Progressive, he opposed special interest groups and any attempt to exploit California's resources for strictly private gain. He built a powerful political machine without using it for corrupt ends. Notes, bibliography, index.

ROBERT M. LA FOLLETTE

See also Chapter 7, *State and Local Politics*.

0472 Kennedy, Padraic C. "La Follette's Foreign Policy." *Wisconsin Magazine of History* 46 (1963): 287–93.

La Follette veered away from his endorsement of American imperialism, when it became evident to him that most of the world was not benefiting from it.

0473 Kent, Alan E. "Portrait in Isolationism: The La Follettes and Foreign Policy." Ph.D. dissertation, University of Wisconsin, 1957.

Robert La Follette, Sr., opposed American involvement in World War I, because he felt that it would end the domestic reform movement and propel the nation toward a bigger, more imperialistic government. War also seemed to him a poor way to resolve international problems. DAI 17:885.

0474 La Follette, Belle C., and La Follette, Fola. *Robert M. La Follette*. 2 vols. New York: Macmillan, 1953.

La Follette's wife and daughter wrote this massive biography from his papers. Photographs, bibliography, index.

0475 Manning, Eugene A. "Old Bob La Follette: Champion of the People." Ph.D. dissertation, University of Wisconsin, 1966.

During the Wilson era, La Follette believed that conspiracies lay behind important events. For example, he suggested that American entry into World War I was masterminded by the munitions industry and by financiers. DAI 27:1761-A.

0476 Thelen, David P. *Robert M. La Follette and the Insurgent Spirit*. Boston: Little, Brown, 1976.

La Follette is portrayed as a clever yet sincere politician who opposed World War I for moral reasons. Notes, index.

HENRY CABOT LODGE

See also Chapter 12, *Ratification Controversy*.

0477 Garraty, John A. *Henry Cabot Lodge: A Biography*. New York: Knopf, 1953.

Lodge was a genuine conservative and a strong partisan who led the opposition to Wilson's foreign policy, not just during the treaty fight but throughout the president's tenure. Photographs, notes, bibliography, index.

0478 Mervin, David. "Henry Cabot Lodge and the League of Nations." *Journal of American Studies* [Great Britain] 4 (1971): 201–16.

Politics dictated Lodge's opposition to the League of Nations, a concept he supported in theory. An advocate of congressional power, he hoped to cut the presidency down to size by defeating the Treaty of Versailles. Notes.

0479 Schriftgiesser, Karl. *The Gentleman from Massachusetts: Henry Cabot Lodge*. Boston: Little, Brown, 1944.

Lodge is portrayed as a partisan bent on sabotaging Wilson's work. Bibliography, index.

0480 Widenor, William C. *Henry Cabot Lodge and the Search for an American Foreign Policy*. Berkeley: University of California Press, 1980.

Although Lodge wanted the United States to become a responsible world power, he was a man flawed deeply by cynicism. His bitter treaty fight with Wilson caused him to lose "his vaunted grasp of American political realities." Notes, bibliography, index.

GEORGE W. NORRIS

0481 Lief, Alfred. *Democracy's Norris: The Biography of a Lonely Crusader*. New York: Stackpole, 1939.

Norris was "a free Republican" who grew disillusioned with Wilson quickly over the tariff issue. The Nebraskan resented Wilson's arrogance and his "grand illusion of international statesmanship." Photographs, notes, index.

0482 Lowitt, Richard. *George W. Norris*. Vol. 2, *The Persistence of a Progressive, 1913–1933*. Urbana: University of Illinois Press, 1971.

This Nebraska senator persisted in the Progressive cause long after Wilson and others had abandoned it. During Wilson's second term, Norris blamed the president for economic extravagance, enhanced corporate power, the 1918 sedition act, and the Red Scare. His hatred of Wilson turned "into a bitterness that passed the bounds of mere political opposition." Photographs, notes, bibliography, index.

0483 ———. "A Neglected Aspect of the Progressive Movement: George W. Norris and Public Control of Hydro-Electric Power, 1913–1919." *Historian* 27 (1965): 350–65.

In the course of a campaign to diminish the House speaker's powers, Norris adopted managerial views that he applied to the issue of hydroelectric power. Notes.

0484 Neuberger, Richard L., and Kahn, Stephen B. *Integrity: The Life of George W. Norris*. New York: Vanguard, 1937.

This uncritical biography details Norris's bitter feud with Wilson. Illustrations, bibliography, index.

0485 Norris, George W. *Fighting Liberal: The Autobiography of George W. Norris*. New York: Macmillan, 1945.

Norris found that his misgivings over the New Freedom were more than offset by his sympathies for the president's objectives. Wilson blundered badly in not taking the people and the Congress into his confidence during the peacemaking process after the war. Norris voted for the Senate reservations to the Treaty of Versailles because he "did not like the map making." Photographs, index.

0486 Zucker, Norman L. *George W. Norris: Gentle Knight of American Democracy*. Urbana: University of Illinois Press, 1966.

In this political biography of a man who began his career as a Republican with "tinges of Populism," the author argues that Norris combined the best qualities of William Jennings Bryan and Robert La Follette. Norris was "a moral idealist in politics." Notes, bibliography, index.

0487 ———. "The Political Philosophy of George W. Norris." Ph.D. dissertation, Rutgers University, 1961.

Nebraskan George Norris was a congressman from 1903 to 1918, and a senator from 1913 to 1942. A Progressive Republican who supported the 1912 Bull Moose movement, Norris's political philosophy could be called an uninspired version of the "new individualism." Norris believed government should ensure social justice while restraining the worst aspects of big business. Norris opposed both entry into World War I and the League of Nations. DAI 22:312.

THEODORE ROOSEVELT

See also Chapter 7, *Elections, 1920*.

0488 Blakey, George T. "Calling a Boss a Boss: Did Roosevelt Libel Barnes in 1915?" *New York History* 60 (1979): 195–216.

William Barnes, Jr., sued Theodore Roosevelt for $50,000 in 1915, claiming that Roosevelt wrongly labeled him a corrupt political boss. New York State Supreme Court records reveal that Roosevelt used the trial to expound against bossism and political machines and to try to regain some of his popularity.

0489 Dyer, Thomas G. "Aaron's Rod: Theodore Roosevelt, Tom Watson, and Anti-Catholicism." *Research Studies* 44 (1976): 60–68.

In 1915, Roosevelt chastised Watson severely for the Georgian's anti-Catholic remarks.

0490 Olson, William C. "Theodore Roosevelt's Conception of an International League." *World Affairs Quarterly* 29 (1959): 329–53.

While Roosevelt had advocated the idea of a league of nations as far back as 1905, he denounced Wilson's vision as a throwback to the Holy Alliance and helped Senator Henry Cabot Lodge to defeat the Treaty of Versailles. Notes.

0491 Roosevelt, Theodore. *The Foes of Our Own Household*. New York: Doran, 1917.

The former president rails against antiwar opponents, especially the "immorality and absurdity" of the socialists. He urges all Americans, women included, to go all out for the war effort.

0492 ———. *The Letters of Theodore Roosevelt*. Edited by Elting E. Morison, et al. 8 vols. Cambridge, MA: Harvard University Press, 1951–1954.

The final two volumes contain letters from the 1912 campaign and reveal Roosevelt's growing frustration with Wilson's domestic and foreign policies. Index.

0493 Schmidt, Patricia Blix. "New Letters on Progressive Politics: Teddy Roosevelt to Governor McGovern." *Milwaukee History* 7 (1984): 30–45.

Roosevelt kept in touch with Wisconsin politics and Progressive issues through his correspondence with Governor Francis E. McGovern during Wilson's first term.

0494 Sellen, Robert W. "Opposition Leaders in Wartime: The Case of Theodore Roosevelt and World War I." *Midwest Quarterly* 9 (1968): 225–42.

Roosevelt became outspokenly critical of Wilson's war policies and, just before his death in 1919, of the League of Nations. Many of Roosevelt's bombastic pronouncements are quoted.

ELIHU ROOT

See also Chapter 12, *World Court* and *Ratification Controversy*.

0495 Dubin, Martin D. "Elihu Root and the Advocacy of a League of Nations, 1914–1917." *Western Political Quarterly* 19 (1966): 439–55.

The conservative Republican elder statesman played an important part in the prewar debate over a possible international league to keep the peace, with Root airing his concern that such idealistic schemes would infringe on American national sovereignty. Notes.

0496 Jessup, Philip C. *Elihu Root*. 2 vols. New York: Dodd, Mead, 1983.

Holder of many high offices, Root played the role of GOP elder statesman during the Wilson presidency. Although he opposed the "Wilson League," Root endorsed the Versailles treaty with reservations. Photographs, bibliography, appendix, index.

0497 Leopold, Richard W. *Elihu Root and the Conservative Tradition*. Boston: Little, Brown, 1954.

The author concludes that Root understood better than Wilson that the League was

not acceptable to the American people because it broke too sharply with the past. Bibliographic essay, index.

0498 Muth, Edwin A. "Elihu Root: His Role and Concepts Pertaining to United States Policies of Intervention." Ph.D. dissertation, Georgetown University, 1966.

Elihu Root's long public career included serving as a senator from New York from 1909 to 1915. He generally favored intervention in foreign affairs, although he criticized Wilson's actions in Mexico. After America's entry into the war, Wilson sent him to Russia to attempt to directly influence events there. He fought American participation in the League of Nations as presented by Wilson. DAI 27:3818-A.

WILLIAM HOWARD TAFT

See also Chapter 7, *Elections, 1912* and Chapter 12, *Ratification Controversy*.

0499 Pringle, Henry F. *The Life and Times of William Howard Taft*. 2 vols. New York: Farrar and Rinehart, 1939.

Taft's biographer devotes much attention to the 1912 presidential election and to Wilson's years in the White House. While Taft considered himself a friend of the League of Nations idea, his dislike of Wilson hardened into hatred during the treaty fight. Photographs, bibliography, index.

OSCAR W. UNDERWOOD

See also Chapter 7, *New Freedom*.

0500 Johnson, Evans C. "Oscar Underwood and the Hobson Campaign." *Alabama Review* 16 (1963): 125–40.

Underwood's campaign for the Senate in 1913 against prohibitionist Richmond Hobson is examined, a bitter and expensive contest which Underwood won with ease.

0501 ———. *Oscar W. Underwood: A Political Biography*. Baton Rouge: Louisiana State University Press, 1980.

A senator from Alabama, Underwood supported much of the New Freedom for pragmatic political reasons. His willingness to accept the Versailles treaty with reservations and even to drop the League angered President Wilson and revealed Underwood to be "a broker of interests." Notes, bibliography, index.

0502 Toradash, Martin. "Underwood and the Tariff." *Alabama Review* 20 (1967): 115–30.

The high point of Underwood's thirty-year congressional career came in 1913, when he played a key role in moderate tariff reform legislation. Notes.

OTHERS

0503 Allen, Howard W. "Miles Poindexter and the Progressive Movement." *Pacific Northwest Quarterly* 53 (1962): 114–22.

Poindexter was a sincere Progressive who endorsed the repression of the Left during the war and the Red Scare.

0504 ———. *Poindexter of Washington: A Study in Progressive Politics.* Carbondale: Southern Illinois University Press, 1981.

World War I transformed this Washington senator from a Progressive into an antilabor, antiradical reactionary. Notes, index.

0505 Arnett, Alex M. *Claude Kitchin and the Wilson War Policies.* Boston: Little, Brown, 1937.

Written to counter "malignant propaganda" against this North Carolina congressman and House majority leader, this study contrasts Wilsonian idealism with realistic "Kitchinism." The many diatribes against Kitchin as a result of his opposition to Wilson's war policies cut his career and his life short. Illustrations, notes, bibliography, index.

0506 Bailey, Richard R. "Morris Sheppard of Texas: Southern Progressive and Prohibitionist." Ph.D. dissertation, Texas Christian University, 1980.

A southern Progressive with a special interest in tariff revision, Sheppard helped to push through the Underwood-Simmons tariff. A loyal supporter of Wilson, the Texas Democrat authored the prohibition amendment to the Constitution. DAI 41:3693-A.

0507 Bellush, Bernard. *He Walked Alone: A Biography of John Gilbert Winant.* The Hague: Mouton, 1968.

The author writes admiringly of Winant, a Republican from New Hampshire who served as an air officer during World War I and went on to become governor of his home state and Franklin

Roosevelt's ambassador to Britain during World War II. Notes, bibliography, index.

0508 Billington, Monroe. "T. P. Gore and Agricultural Legislation." *Agricultural History* 31 (1957): 29–39.

Senator Thomas P. Gore called for government help for rural areas before World War I, but opposed it during the New Deal. Notes.

0509 ———. *Thomas P. Gore: The Blind Senator from Oklahoma.* Lawrence: University of Kansas Press, 1967.

Although he supported Wilson's New Freedom program and his Mexico policy, this Oklahoma senator lined up with Progressive pacifists in opposing military preparedness. Gore broke with the president over the war, favoring the Treaty of Versailles only with reservations. Notes, bibliography, index.

0510 Bowden, Robert D. *Boies Penrose: Symbol of an Era.* New York: Greenberg, 1937.

Penrose succeeded in becoming a powerful politician "without benefit of ethics or acquisition." The author concludes that this last and greatest of the bosses left behind no legislative accomplishments of lasting consequence. Photographs, index.

0511 Brown, Kenny L. "A Progressive from Oklahoma: Senator Robert Latham Owen, Jr." *Chronicles of Oklahoma* 62 (1984): 232–65.

A Progressive Democrat and an ally of Wilson, Owen supported the New Freedom and the League of Nations, although he would have accepted the reservations that the president found so distasteful. Notes.

0512 Brownlow, Louis. *A Passion for Politics: The Autobiography of Louis Brownlow.* 2 vols. Chicago: University of Chicago Press, 1955.

A journalist appointed by Woodrow Wilson as a commissioner of the District of Columbia, Brownlow relates his disagreement with the president over strategy for dealing with suffragettes picketing the White House. Photographs, index.

0513 Cashin, Edward L. "Thomas E. Watson and the Catholic Laymen's Association of Georgia." Ph.D. dissertation, Fordham University, 1962.

Former Populist Thomas Watson attempted in the last years of his life to attract a following based on anti-Catholicism. Many of his ideas were adopted by the Georgia Ku Klux

Klan. The Catholic Laymen's Association had methodically discredited him by the time of his death, in 1922. DAI 23:4331.

0514 Cleaver, Charles G. "Frank B. Kellogg: Attitudes and Assumptions Influencing His Foreign Policy Decisions." Ph.D. dissertation, University of Minnesota, 1956.

Careful analysis of Kellogg's writings and speeches reveals his underlying beliefs and assumptions: for example, a distaste for change combined with faith in progress. His attitudes toward the League of Nations, armament, and nonrecognition of Communist Russia are examined. DAI 20:1336.

0515 Coker, William Sidney. "Pat Harrison: The Formative Years." *Journal of Mississippi History* 25 (1963): 251–78.

A member of the House of Representatives and then the Senate during Wilson's presidency, Harrison supported the president's foreign policy and much of his Progressive agenda, where it did not clash with states' rights.

0516 Connally, Tom. *My Name Is Tom Connally: As Told to Alfred Steinberg*. New York: Crowell, 1954.

A Democratic member of the House Foreign Affairs Committee during World War I, Connally admired Wilson and loathed Henry Cabot Lodge. Photographs, index.

0517 Cook, Charles O. "Arkansas's Charles Hillman Brough, 1876–1935: An Interpretation." Ph.D. dissertation, University of Houston, 1980.

Charles Brough, a history Ph.D. at twenty-one, eloquently espoused a coherent but unrealistically optimistic vision of a new, prosperous South. As governor of Arkansas from 1917 to 1921, his effectiveness was restricted by a preference for rhetoric over accomplishment. DAI 42:344-A.

0518 De Chambrun, Clara Longworth. *The Making of Nicholas Longworth: Annals of an American Family*. New York: Ray Long and Richard Smith, 1933.

House Republican leader Nicholas Longworth's sister strings together long quotations from family letters including Longworth's opinions on preparedness, the war, the Volstead Act, and his opposition to the Wilsonian peace. Photographs.

0519 Duke, Escal F. "The Political Career of Morris Sheppard, 1875–1941." Ph.D. dissertation, University of Texas, 1958.

Texas senator Morris Sheppard was a steadfast supporter of almost all of Wilson's policies. He particularly championed humanitarian Progressive legislation such as women's suffrage, child welfare, and prohibition. DAI 19:1353.

0520 Elliott, Lawrence. *Little Flower: The Life and Times of Fiorello La Guardia*. New York: William Morrow, 1983.

The biography of New York's beloved Fiorello La Guardia contains material on his time as a newcomer in Congress during the Wilson administration. "Congress had never seen his like before," the author observes, "and some congressmen did not like what they saw." Bibliography, index.

0521 Fausold, Martin L. *James W. Wadsworth, Jr.: The Gentleman from New York*. Syracuse: Syracuse University Press, 1975.

An aristocratic congressman and later a senator from New York, Wadsworth fought a Republican rearguard action against the New Freedom and became a strong reservationist on the Versailles treaty. Photographs, notes, appendixes, bibliography, index.

0522 Ferrell, Henry C. "Claude A. Swanson of Virginia." Ph.D. dissertation, University of Virginia, 1964.

Virginia senator Claude Swanson supported Wilson. He fought sincerely for the Progressive legislation his constituents wanted, and he excelled, when necessary, at arranging compromises. DAI 25:3533.

0523 Flynt, Wayne. *Duncan Upshaw Fletcher: Dixie's Reluctant Progressive*. Tallahassee: Florida State University Press, 1971.

Fletcher was a social conservative and pragmatic liberal senator from Florida who became a pro-Wilson administration regular, leading the fight for the Federal Farm Loan Act of 1916. He had a long political career, the author believes, because his actions "mirrored the average Floridian's opinion." Notes, bibliography, index.

0524 Fortenberry, Joseph E. "James Kimble Vardaman and American Foreign Policy, 1913–1919." *Journal of Mississippi History* 35 (1973): 127–40.

This Mississippi senator was a persistent critic of military preparedness and of the campaign to intervene in the European war, knowing full well that this would cost him his political career. Notes.

0525 Forth, William S. "Wesley L. Jones: A Political Biography." Ph.D. dissertation, University of Washington, 1962.

Wesley Jones was a Progressive Republican senator best known for his loyalty to his party and his constituents. He supported most of Wilson's Progressive legislation, but he opposed the administration's racism and intervention in Mexico. Primarily interested in domestic affairs, he was lukewarm about the war and uninvolved in the peace. DAI 24:265.

0526 Gieske, Millard L. "The Politics of Knute Nelson, 1912–1920." Ph.D. dissertation, University of Minnesota, 1965.

Senior Republican Senator Knute Nelson placed a high value on friendship. Although his primary loyalty was to his farming constituency, the rich and powerful were also among his friends. He increasingly, though inconsistently, opposed the far left. DAI 26:5525.

0527 Gilderhus, Mark T. "Senator Albert B. Fall and 'The Plot against Mexico.'" *New Mexico Historical Review* 48 (1973): 299–311.

While Fall and a group of U.S. oil companies denied charges that they conspired to bring about American intervention against the Mexican government in 1919, evidence of the plot exists.

0528 Grantham, Dewey W., Jr. *Hoke Smith and the Politics of the New South.* Baton Rouge: Louisiana University Press, 1958.

A Georgia Democrat who served in the Senate from 1911 to 1921, Smith embodied much of what the New South stood for. Notes, bibliography, index.

0529 Grollman, Catherine A. "Cordell Hull and His Concept of a World Organization." Ph.D. dissertation, University of North Carolina, Chapel Hill, 1965.

Congressman Hull believed that lower tariffs could boost worldwide prosperity, ensuring peace. He campaigned for an international free trade organization and disparaged the League of Nations for its noneconomic slant. DAI 26:3901.

0530 Harris, Ted C. "Jeannette Rankin: Suffragist, First Woman Elected to Congress, and Pacifist." Ph.D. dissertation, University of Georgia, 1972.

First elected to the House in 1916 from Montana, Rankin fought against the war and for legislation benefiting women, children, workers, and consumers. DAI 33:5089-A.

0531 Haughton, Virginia F. "John Worth Kern and Wilson's New Freedom: A Study of a Senate Majority Leader." Ph.D. dissertation, University of Kentucky, 1973.

Senate majority leader from 1913 to 1917, Kern played a key part in passage of Wilson's New Freedom agenda. No philosopher, he excelled in the behind-the-scenes mechanics of the legislature. DAI 35:1593-A.

0532 ———. "John W. Kern: Senate Majority Leader and Labor Legislation, 1913–1917." *Mid-America* 57 (1975): 184–94.

Co-author of the Kern-McGillicuddy workman's compensation act of 1916, Kern was a strong backer of laws protecting working people. Notes.

0533 Holmes, William F. *The White Chief: James Kimble Vardaman.* Baton Rouge: Louisiana State University Press, 1970.

Vardaman, a Democratic senator from Mississippi, moved left to Progressivism during Wilson's first term, generally supporting the presidential program of reforms. The senator's refusal to bow to wartime hysteria cost him his Senate seat in 1918. Index, bibliographic essay, notes.

0534 Holt, Wythe W. "The Senator from Virginia and the Democratic Floor Leadership: Thomas S. Martin and Conservatism in the Progressive Era." *Virginia Magazine of History and Biography* 83 (1975): 3–21.

A conservative supporter of Wilson, Martin sacrificed his position as Democratic floor leader to preserve the seniority system in 1913. Four years later, Wilson acquiesced in his re-election to the post. Notes.

0535 Hutchinson, William T. *Lowden of Illinois: The Life of Frank O. Lowden.* 2 vols. Chicago: University of Chicago Press, 1957.

In this biography of the wartime governor of Illinois, the author shows "Win the War Lowden" to be an excellent example of old guard Republicans who "out-Wilsoned Wilson in their belligerence toward the Central Powers." Notes, index.

0536 Huthmacher, J. Joseph. *Senator Robert F. Wagner and the Rise of Urban Liberalism.* New York: Atheneum, 1968.

The first portion of this biography covers New York during the Progressive period, when Wagner worked in the "polyglot politics of Tammany Hall," an experience that shaped his cultural liberalism. Photographs, notes, bibliography, index.

0537 Ingle, Homer L. "Pilgrimage to Reform: A Life of Claude Kitchin." Ph.D. dissertation, University of Wisconsin, 1967.

Democratic North Carolina Congressman Claude Kitchin became the majority leader in 1915. He was an advocate of free trade, but he opposed Wilson over preparedness and entry into the war. He wrote an excess profits tax into the revenue code, but he suffered a stroke in 1920 and was unable to prevent the bill's repeal. DAI 28:1032-A.

0538 Johnson, Carolyn W. *Winthrop Murray Crane: A Study in Republican Leadership, 1892–1920*. Northampton, MA: Smith College, 1967.

Crane was a Taft supporter and a power in the Republican party. He pleaded with the GOP to support American entry into the League of Nations. Notes, bibliography.

0539 Johnson, William G. "The Senatorial Career of Henry Algernon Du Pont." *Delaware History* 13 (1969): 234–51.

Du Pont pushed through the volunteer act of 1914 and helped to bolster the army as part of the preparedness campaign. The old guard Republican did not, by and large, use his position to further the interests of the Du Pont Corporation. Notes.

0540 Karlin, Jules A. *Joseph M. Dixon of Montana*. 2 vols. Missoula: University of Montana Press, 1974.

This biography of a Montana newspaper publisher and Republican politician contains a useful portrait of Montana during the Great War. Photographs, notes, bibliography, index.

0541 Keating, Edward. *The Gentleman from Colorado: A Memoir*. Denver: Sage, 1964.

A Democratic congressman from Colorado, Keating was a "Wilson man" who voted against the war and conscription but still had the support of the president. Index.

0542 La Borde, Adras. *National Southerner: Ransdell of Louisiana*. New York: Benziger, 1951.

A senator from Louisiana during the Wilson years, James Ransdell battled the president over the tariff on foreign sugar while supporting the administration on the war issue. Deploring Wilson's peace policies, Ransdell urged the president to take Theodore Roosevelt

with him to the Paris Peace Conference. Photographs.

0543 Larson, Bruce L. *Lindbergh of Minnesota: A Political Biography*. New York: Harcourt Brace Jovanovich, 1973.

A Progressive Republican, Charles A. Lindbergh, Sr., was a man of deep convictions who was always independent. The author finds that "in the sense of wanting bold and deep change, he was radical." Photographs, notes, bibliography, index.

0544 Levine, Ervin L. *Theodore Francis Green: The Rhode Island Years, 1906–1936*. Providence: Brown University Press, 1963.

This biography of the New Deal-era governor of Rhode Island contains material on Rhode Island politics during the Wilson years. Notes, bibliography, index.

0545 Longworth, Alice Roosevelt. *Crowded Hours: Reminiscences*. New York: Charles Scribner's, 1933.

The daughter of Theodore Roosevelt and wife of longtime Republican House leader Nicholas Longworth details the political struggles of the Wilson years. Her viewpoint reflects the hatred her family felt for Wilson. Photographs, index.

0546 Manners, William. *Patience and Fortitude: Fiorello La Guardia*. New York: Harcourt Brace Jovanovich, 1976.

First elected to Congress in 1917, La Guardia commanded forces on the Italian front during the war. Photographs, bibliography, index.

0547 Margulies, Herbert F. *Senator Lenroot of Wisconsin: A Political Biography 1900–1929*. Columbia: University of Missouri Press, 1977.

The junior partner of Robert La Follette in Wisconsin politics, Irvine Lenroot broke with his friend over the war issue. His style and philosophy kept him out of the spotlight. The author regards Lenroot as a moderate in an era of revolutionaries and reactionaries. Notes, bibliography, index.

0548 Masterson, Thomas D. "David J. Lewis of Maryland: Formative and Progressive Years, 1869–1917." Ph.D. dissertation, Georgetown University, 1976.

This powerful Maryland congressman became the "Father of the Parcel Post" and fought for a number of other Progressive acts during Wilson's presidency. DAI 38:5641-A.

0549 Meriwether, Lee. *Jim Reed: "Senatorial Immortal."* Webster Grove, MO: Mark Twain Society, 1948.

This completely uncritical biography highlights the irreconcilable Missourian's fight against the Treaty of Versailles. Photographs, illustrations, index.

0550 Milner, Cooper. "The Public Life of Cordell Hull: 1907–1924." Ph.D. dissertation, Vanderbilt University, 1960.

Democrat Cordell Hull served in Congress almost continuously from 1907 to 1933. His career was devoted principally to tax and tariff legislation. During World War I, he was an adviser to the IRS and the Treasury Department. DAI 22:239.

0551 Mullen, Arthur F. *Western Democrat.* New York: Wilfred Funk, 1940.

This autobiography of a leading William Jennings Bryan Democrat from Nebraska argues that, if Champ Clark had been elected president instead of Wilson, the United States would have stayed out of the war. Photographs.

0552 Neal, Nevin E. "A Biography of Joseph T. Robinson." Ph.D. dissertation, University of Oklahoma, 1958.

Robinson began his years as senator from Arkansas in 1913. An admirable, if not first-rank, conservative southern statesman, he supported most of Wilson's policies, particularly regulation of big business and care of natural resources. DAI 19:1731.

0553 Nethers, John L. *Simeon D. Fess: Educator & Politician.* Brooklyn: Pageant-Poseidon, 1973.

Fess was a successful educator who developed a Chautauqua program to keep Antioch College afloat. He became a congressman during the Wilson years to boost his own income, supporting prohibition and women's suffrage. Photographs, notes, bibliography, index.

0554 Osborn, George C. *John Sharp Williams.* Baton Rouge: Louisiana State University Press, 1943.

A friend and ardent supporter of Woodrow Wilson, this senator from Mississippi became embittered by the defeat of the Versailles treaty. Index, bibliographic essay, notes.

0555 Ramage, Thomas W. "Augustus Owsley Stanley: Early Twentieth Century Kentucky Democrat." Ph.D. dissertation, University of Kentucky, 1968.

Governor of Kentucky and then senator from that state during the Wilson years, Stanley was a moderate Progressive who fought against what he considered to be excessive government interference with individual liberties. DAI 30:1484-A.

0556 Sayre, Ralph M. "Albert Baird Cummins and the Progressive Movement in Iowa." Ph.D. dissertation, Columbia University, 1958.

Republican Senator Albert Cummins detested Wilson and opposed him on most major war issues. He was particularly interested in resolving the problems of railroad transportation. DAI 19:313.

0557 Sheldon, Richard N. "Richmond Pearson Hobson as a Progressive Reformer." *Alabama Review* 25 (1972): 243–61.

This Alabama congressman unsuccessfully tried to parlay his strong support of Progressive legislation into a Senate seat in 1914. Moderate views on race and women's suffrage lost him the congressional primary two years later. Notes.

0558 Simkins, Francis B. *Pitchfork Ben Tillman, South Carolinian.* Baton Rouge: Louisiana State University Press, 1974.

Tillman dominated South Carolina politics for many years from his seat in the Senate. When he ran into political trouble in 1918, President Wilson intervened on his behalf, but Tillman died before the fall elections. Notes, bibliography, index.

0559 Smith, Thomas H. "The Senatorial Career of Atlee Pomerene of Ohio." Ph.D. dissertation, Kent State University, 1966.

Pomerene served as Democratic senator from Ohio between 1911 and 1923. Known as a foe of special interests and of the alliance between big business and government, he also opposed labor, prohibition, and national women's suffrage. He supported Wilson on most war issues and fought for the League of Nations. DAI 28:607-A.

0560 Symonds, Merrill S. "George Higgins Moses of New Hampshire—The Man and the Era." Ph.D. dissertation, Clark University, 1955.

New Hampshire journalist George Moses was elected to the Senate in 1918, where he immediately joined the fight against the League of Nations. DAI 15:1842.

0561 Thompson, Alice A. "The Life and Career of William L. Igoe, the Reluctant Boss, 1879–1953." Ph.D. dissertation, St. Louis University, 1980.

William Igoe served as a congressman during Wilson's presidency, opposing participation in World War I. DAI 41:3236-A.

0562 Timmons, Bascom N. *Garner of Texas: A Personal History*. New York: Harper and Brothers, 1948.

This friendly biography includes a chapter on the Wilson years, when John Nance Garner was House whip. Although Congressman Garner had a stormy relationship with Wilson, he admired him greatly. Illustrations.

0563 Towne, Ruth W. *Senator William J. Stone and the Politics of Compromise*. Port Washington, NY: Kennikat, 1979.

Democratic chairman of the Senate Foreign Relations Committee, Stone was a spokesman for Wilson in foreign policy, until he opposed the arming of merchant ships against German U-boats. The author speculates that if Stone had lived the Versailles treaty might have passed under his leadership. Notes, bibliography, essay, index.

0564 Towns, Stuart. "Joseph T. Robinson and Arkansas Politics, 1912–1913." *Arkansas Historical Quarterly* 24 (1965): 291–307.

In 1913, Robinson served in turn as a congressman, governor, and senator from Arkansas as a result of special circumstances.

0565 Trow, Clifford W. "Senator Albert B. Fall and Mexican Affairs: 1912–1921." Ph.D. dissertation, University of Colorado, 1966.

Fall, a Republican senator from New Mexico, urged the administration to use military force to establish a protectorate in Mexico. He opposed Wilson's noninterventionism at every turn and attempted to win support from the public as well as from Congress and businessmen. Fall had economic interests in Mexico and eventually found himself aligned with the oil companies holding Mexican investments. DAI 28:1382-A.

0566 Waller, Robert A. *Rainey of Illinois: A Political Biography*. Urbana: University of Illinois Press, 1977.

A rural Progressive, Henry T. Rainey used his seat on the House Ways and Means Committee to help pass Wilson's New Freedom legislation. Notes, bibliography, index.

0567 Ward, Robert D. "Stanley Hubert Dent and American Military Policy, 1916–1920." *Alabama Historical Quarterly* 33 (1971): 177–89.

Like many southerners, the Alabama Democratic congressman fought preparedness and conscription, although he reluctantly supported Wilson during American participation in the war. Opposition to militarism after the war may have cost him his seat in the 1920 election.

0568 Watson, James E. *As I Knew Them*. Indianapolis: Bobbs-Merrill, 1936.

In this memoir of the longtime Republican senator from Indiana, Watson blames Woodrow Wilson for the many shortcomings in the Treaty of Versailles. He concludes that Wilson was "just another idealistic college professor who had beautiful dreams." Photographs, index.

0569 Wayman, Dorothy G. *David I. Walsh: Citizen-Patriot*. Milwaukee: Bruce, 1952.

The powerful Massachusetts Democrat, who served as governor during World War I until his election to the Senate, broke with Wilson over the Treaty of Versailles. Index.

0570 Woodward, C. Vann. *Tom Watson, Agrarian Rebel*. New York: Macmillan, 1938.

Watson's journey from radical Populist to antiwar agitator and reactionary is examined.

4

Domestic Affairs:
Agriculture, Business, the
Economy, and Labor

Americans were preoccupied with domestic affairs during Wilson's first term. Farmers enjoyed a golden age of prosperity but also faced many problems connected with modernization. Concerned with the decline in the quality of rural life, Progressives sought, with mixed results, to bring back the supposed virtues of preindustrial America. Not all farmers shared in the general prosperity; many who felt exploited by shippers and by the market system turned to the Socialist party and the Nonpartisan League. Business issues attracted the interest of Progressive reformers eager to undercut the appeal of the Socialist party among the working class by mitigating the grosser abuses of the American system. Business leaders often worked with the Progressives, finding that they had common interests in fine-tuning capitalism and helping business to expand on a multinational level. They also implemented scientific management schemes and used industrial psychology to make their enterprises more efficient and profitable.

The nineteenth-century belief in minimum government was further eroded during the Wilson years, as political leaders saw the need for federal manipulation of the economy. American entry into World War I created new challenges for economic organization. The postwar period brought the long period of prosperity to a halt, as business and government groped for ways to readjust. Organized labor continued to challenge the ascendancy of big business while seeking its place in the national political establishment. Some unions scorned this approach, preferring to confront capitalists

with direct action. After World War I a wave of strikes swept over the country, with workers trying to hold on to their many gains and corporations working to roll back the union movement. Wilson's presidency ended with little hope for the harmony of interests that the Progressives had hoped would follow their crusade.

For the impact of technology on the American farmer, see Reynold M. Wik, "Benjamin Holt and the Intervention of the Track-Type Tractor" (#0588) and "Henry Ford's Tractors and American Agriculture" (#0589), and a doctoral dissertation by Robert C. Williams, "Fordson, Farmall, and Poppin' Johnny: The Development and Impact of the American Farm Tractor" (#0590). The Progressive country life movement is examined by David B. Danbom, *The Resisted Revolution: Urban America and the Industrialization of Agriculture, 1900–1930* (#0593), and by William L. Bowers, *The Country Life Movement in America, 1900–1920* (#0591). The agricultural protest movement has attracted the attention of a number of scholars, among them Gavin Burbank, *When Farmers Voted Red: The Gospel of Socialism in the Oklahoma Countryside, 1910–1924* (#0595). For the impact of the Nonpartisan League, see Robert L. Morlan, *Political Prairie Fire: The Nonpartisan League, 1915–1922* (#0599), and dissertations by Scott A. Ellsworth, "Origins of the Nonpartisan League (North Dakota)" (#0596), and Kathleen D. Moum, "Harvest of Discontent: The Social Origins of the Nonpartisan League, 1880–1922" (#0600).

The impact of scientific management on business is examined in Daniel Nelson, *Managers and Workers: Origins of the New Factory System in the United States, 1880–1920* (#0617). Albro Martin examines the negative impact of Progressive reforms on the railroad industry in *Enterprise Denied: Origins of the Decline of American Railroads, 1897–1917* (#0615). Many biographies and monographs on industrial leaders have been published. Henry Ford, the most prominent industrialist of the Wilson years, is examined by Anne Jardim, *The First Henry Ford: A Study in Personality and Business Leadership* (#0628); David L. Lewis, *The Public Image of Henry Ford: An American Folk Hero and His Company* (#0631); Allan Nevins and Frank E. Hill, *Ford* (#0636); and Reynold M. Wik, *Henry Ford and Grass-Roots America* (#0642). For two very different interpretations of foreign expansion, see a doctoral dissertation by Paul P. Abrahams, "The Foreign Expansion of American Finances and Its Relationship to the Foreign Economic Policies of the United States, 1907–1921" (#0643), and William H. Becker, *The Dynamics of Business-Government Relations: Industry and Exports* (#0651). How extensive was business support for Progressive reforms? Robert H. Wiebe, *Businessmen and Reform: A Study of the Progressive Movement* (#0665), argues that businessmen were prominent in shaping reforms that affected them. Two studies by Gabriel Kolko, *Railroads and Regulation, 1877–1916* (#0659) and *The Triumph of Conservatism: A Reinterpretation of American History, 1900–1916* (#0660), view Progressivism as a form of political capitalism that helped conservative big business to fasten a permanent hold on the economy. This thesis is rebutted by Robert W. Harbeson, "Railroads and Regulation, 1877–1916: Conspiracy or Public Interest?" (#0657). James Weinstein, *The Corporate Ideal in the Liberal State, 1900–1918* (#0663), postulates that many businessmen understood that government regulation of business could mean prosperity and stability.

The economy is examined in the classic study by Harold U. Faulkner, *The Decline of Laissez-Faire, 1897–1917* (#0686), and a doctoral dissertation by John E. Hollitz, "The Challenge of Abundance: Reactions to the Development of a Consumer Economy, 1890–1920" (#0687). See also Martin J. Sklar, *The Corporate Reconstruction of American Capitalism, 1890–1916* (#0693). Burton I. Kaufman explores economic expansionism in *Efficiency and Expansion: Foreign Trade Organization in the Wilson Administration, 1913–1921* (#0701). Wilson's acceptance of business concentration during his second term is the subject of a monograph by Melvin I. Urofsky, *Big Steel and the Wilson Administration: A Study of Business-Government Relations* (#0707).

American labor during the Wilson years has been examined by a number of historians, many of whom (not surprisingly) write from a leftist, revisionist, or feminist perspective. The prolific Philip S. Foner contributes two detailed volumes from his *History of the Labor Movement in the United States* (#0716 and #0717). For Wilson's labor policies, see the doctoral dissertation by Manfred F. Boemeke, "The Wilson Administration, Organized Labor, and the Colorado Coal Strike, 1913–1914" (#0728), and John S. Smith, "Organized Labor and Government in the Wilson Era, 1913–1921" (#0732). The impact of Ford's innovative policies on his workers is examined in Stephen Meyer III, *The Five Dollar Day: Labor Management and Social Control in the Ford Motor Company, 1908–1921* (#0736), while Bruno Ramirez, *When Workers Fight: The Politics of Industrial Relations in the Progressive Era, 1898–1916* (#0739), analyzes the effects of collective bargaining. Labor activities in politics and foreign policy are scrutinized by Marc Karson, *American Labor Unions and Politics, 1900–1918* (#0749), and by Ronald Radosh, *American Labor and United States Foreign Policy* (#0751).

On the Progressives' concern about child labor, see Walter I. Trattner, *Crusade for the Children: A History of the National Child Labor Committee and Child Labor Reform* (#0757). Many books have been published on women and labor in recent years. Among the best are Sarah Eisenstein, *Give Us Bread but Give Us Roses: Working Women's Consciousness in the United States, 1890 to the First World War* (#0766); Philip S. Foner, *Women and the American Labor Movement* (#0767); Maureen W. Greenwald, *Women, War and Work: The Impact of World War I on Women Workers in the United States* (#2990); and Leslie W. Tentler, *Wage-Earning Women: Industrial Work and Family Life in the United States, 1900–1930* (#0788).

John H. M. Laslett, *Labor and the Left: A Study of Socialist and Radical Influences in the American Labor Movement, 1881–1924* (#0800), examines the question of why socialism was not more appealing to workers. One reason, surely, was the influence of Samuel Gompers, longtime president of the American Federation of Labor. He tells his story in *Seventy Years of Life and Labor: An Autobiography* (#0804). See also Harold Livesay, *Samuel Gompers and Organized Labor in America* (#0808), and Philip Taft, *The A.F.L. in the Time of Gompers* (#0812). The Industrial Workers of the World took à very different approach to labor organization: syndicalism.

Because of its ideological nature and close association with the Socialist party, material on the IWW has been placed in Chapter 8, *Radical Ideologies, Syndicalism.*

Agriculture

GENERAL

0571 Rasmussen, Wayne D., ed. *Agriculture in the United States: A Documentary History.* 4 vols. New York: Random House, 1975.

Volume III covers topics in the Wilson years including farm tenancy, farm loans, World War I, and changes in farming and farm life. Index.

0572 Roet, Jeffrey B. "Agricultural Settlement on the Dry Farming Frontier, 1900–1920." Ph.D. dissertation, Northwestern University, 1982.

Farmers tended to settle near railroad lines and to initially plant the crops they were familiar with, even when they were inappropriate to their new soil and climate. Where there was insufficient rain for either wheat- or corn-based agriculture, a farming-grazing system eventually developed. DAI 43:2100-A.

0573 Schapsmeier, Edward L., and Schapsmeier, Frederick H. *Encyclopedia of American Agricultural History.* Westport, CT: Greenwood, 1975.

Entries germane to the Wilson years include those on Wilson's agricultural policies, farm leaders, legislation, and political movements. Index.

0574 Scott, Roy V. "American Railroads and Agricultural Extension, 1900–1914: A Study in Railway Developmental Techniques." *Business History Review* 39 (1965): 74–98.

Railroads helped farmers indirectly through the establishment of model farms and by advocating county agents, running educational trains, and contributing to youth organizations and fairs.

0575 Smith, Marvanna S. *Chronological Landmarks in American Agriculture.* Washington, DC: Government Printing Office, 1979.

This chronology includes important agricultural events that happened during the Wilson administration.

0576 Tweton, D. Jerome. "The Golden Age of Agriculture: 1897–1917." *North Dakota History* 37 (1970): 41–55.

The right economic climate and weather conditions helped farmers to prosper in the period between the Spanish-American War and World War I, as production remained steady and urban demand for food rose. Notes.

0577 Waugh, Frederick V., and Ogren, Kenneth E. "An Interpretation of Changes in Agricultural Marketing Costs." *American Economic Review* 51 (1961): 213–27.

Food pricing and marketing costs since 1913 are examined including the effects of World War I and the postwar economic slump.

GOVERNMENT POLICIES

0578 Baker, Gladys L. *The County Agent.* Chicago: University of Chicago Press, 1939.

Included is a discussion of the Smith-Lever act, which formalized cooperative agricultural extension work. Bibliography, index.

0579 Hochheiser, Sheldon. "The Evolution of U.S. Food Color Standards, 1913–1919." *Agricultural History* 55 (1981): 385–91.

The Department of Agriculture launched a program to test synthetic food colors following enactment of the Food and Drug Act, because most dyes used in food products were unsafe. Notes.

0580 Link, Arthur S. "The Federal Reserve Policy and the Agricultural Depression of 1920–1921." In Dewey W. Grantham, ed. *The Higher Realism of Woodrow Wilson and Other Essays.* Nashville: Vanderbilt University Press, 1971, pp. 330–48.

Farm prices dropped sharply without warning late in 1920, leading agrarian spokesmen to lash out at the Federal Reserve Board. The price decline occurred because of a drop in exports, overexpansion in production, less government purchasing, and deflation. Notes.

0581 McDean, Harry C. "Professionalism, Policy, and Farm Economists in the Early Bureau of Agricultural Economics." *Agricultural History* 57 (1983): 64–82.

Economists replaced agronomists in the Department of Agriculture under the leadership of Henry C. Taylor after World War I, thus bringing about modern forecasting techniques. Notes.

0582 Reid, Bill G. "Agrarian Opposition to Franklin K. Lane's Proposal for Soldier Settlement, 1918–1921." *Agricultural History* 41 (1967): 167–79.

Secretary of the Interior Franklin K. Lane endorsed a bill introduced by Wyoming Congressman Frank W. Mondell to give land previously passed over as unworkable to World War I veterans. A powerful coalition that included farmers, the Department of Agriculture, and farm editors helped to defeat the proposal. Notes.

0583 ———. "Colonies for Disabled Veterans in Minnesota." *Minnesota History* 39 (1965): 241–51.

After World War I, disabled veterans were resettled in farm colonies, an experiment which resulted in much suffering, because the handicapped were expected to work on clear-cut, eroded land.

0584 ———. "Franklin K. Lane's Idea for Veterans' Colonization, 1918–1921." *Pacific Historical Review* 33 (1964): 447–61.

Lane's plan to give war veterans their own farms included provisions for government scrutiny to ensure that the land was being farmed.

0585 ———. "Proposals for Soldier Settlement during World War I." *Mid-America* 46 (1964): 172–86.

Secretary of the Interior Franklin K. Lane drew up a scheme for returning war veterans to settle on farms, but objections from commercial agricultural interests killed it.

INDUSTRIALIZATION

0586 Cavert, William L. "The Technological Revolution in Agriculture, 1910–1955." *Agricultural History* 30 (1956): 18–27.

In 1910 animals provided most nonhuman farm power; by 1955 mechanical power predominated. Other changes chronicled include greater emphasis on farm management, specialization, greater interest in location, and larger farm units. Notes.

0587 Johnson, Diane. *Edwin Brown Ford: Scientist, Administrator, Gentleman.* Madison: University of Wisconsin Press, 1974.

A researcher at the University of Wisconsin, Ford began to supply cultures of nitrogen-fixing bacteria to growers of legumes in 1914, resulting in increased yields. Notes, index.

0588 Wik, Reynold M. "Benjamin Holt and the Invention of the Track-Type Tractor." *Technology and Culture* 20 (1979): 90–107.

Holt developed crawler-tractors in response to the new large-scale farms of California. Notes.

0589 ———. "Henry Ford's Tractors and American Agriculture." *Agricultural History* 38 (1964): 79–86.

The many flaws in the Fordson tractor made these farming devices less popular and less profitable than the Model T, but they convinced many farmers of the need for mechanized vehicles.

0590 Williams, Robert C. "Fordson, Farmall, and Poppin' Johnny: The Development and Impact of the American Farm Tractor." Ph.D. dissertation, Texas Tech University, 1981.

First handcrafted in the late nineteenth century, by 1918 tractors were in mass production. The transformation of agriculture wrought by tractors threw millions of laborers out of work and favored large, one-crop tracts over small, diverse farms. DAI 42:4557-A.

COUNTRY LIFE MOVEMENT

See also Chapter 7, *The Progressive Movement.*

0591 Bowers, William L. *The Country Life Movement in America, 1900–1920.* Port Washington, NY: Kennikat, 1974.

The Progressive country life movement was an attempt to bring back the supposed virtues of country life to modern America. The campaign to make rural life more attractive was undercut by forces working to make agriculture more modern. Appendix, notes, bibliography, index.

0592 ———. "Country-Life Reform, 1900–1920: A Neglected Aspect of Progressive Era History." *Agricultural History* 45 (1971): 211–21.

Leaders of the country life movement failed to understand how agriculture was changing as a result of industrial technology. Too much emphasis on education and not enough on imaginative solutions to rural problems also limited the movement's effectiveness. Notes.

0593 Danbom, David B. *The Resisted Revolution: Urban America and the Industrialization of Agriculture, 1900–1930.* Ames: Iowa State University Press, 1979.

Seeking to raise the rural standard of living, the country life movement reformed education and agriculture. Notes, bibliography, index.

0594 Swanson, Merwin R. "The American Country Life Movement, 1900–1940." Ph.D. dissertation, University of Minnesota, 1972.

To halt the decline in the quality of rural life, a movement developed to enhance community vitality. The country life movement peaked just after World War I, and, while reformers were on the right track in looking beyond the economic aspects of farm policy, they never came up with really effective programs. DAI 33:3562-A.

AGRICULTURAL DISCONTENT

See also Chapter 8, *Socialism*.

0595 Burbank, Gavin. *When Farmers Voted Red: The Gospel of Socialism in the Oklahoma Countryside, 1910–1924*. Westport, CT: Greenwood, 1976.

Farmers made the Socialist party a major political power in Oklahoma during the Progressive era. The farmers' pietistic Christianity and their discontent with the system made evolutionary socialism seem appealing. Notes, bibliography, index.

0596 Ellsworth, Scott A. "Origins of the Nonpartisan League (North Dakota)." Ph.D. dissertation, Duke University, 1982.

Originating in North Dakota in 1915, the Nonpartisan League represented the interests of a majority of farmers and laborers in the Midwest and the West. Exploiting an almost universal grievance of farmers, the need for improved grain marketing, the league enlisted leaders from both the agrarian wing of the Socialist party and the equity movement. This dissertation focuses on the organizational roots of the Nonpartisan League. DAI 43:3683-A.

0597 Guth, James L. "The National Board of Farm Organizations: Experiment in Political Cooperation." *Agricultural History* 48 (1974): 418–40.

An umbrella group of several farmers' organizations, the board failed to sway Congress due to internal bickering and a distinct lack of sympathy on the part of the executive branch. Notes.

0598 Iaz'kov, E. F. "The Development of Agricultural Cooperatives and Their Role in the Farmers' Movement in the USA after World War I (1918–1923)" (in Russian). *Vestnik Moskovskogo Universiteta* [USSR] (1969): 35–52.

Agricultural cooperatives developed during the Progressive era. With prices dropping after the war the Farm Bureau Federation worked to centralize existing co-ops, but the co-op movement collapsed during the 1920s. Notes.

0599 Morlan, Robert L. *Political Prairie Fire: The Nonpartisan League, 1915–1922*. Minneapolis: University of Minnesota Press, 1955.

The Nonpartisan League began as a farmer-labor revolt against banks and big business and became an important political force in midwestern politics. Notes, bibliography, index.

0600 Moum, Kathleen D. "Harvest of Discontent: The Social Origins of the Nonpartisan League, 1880–1922." Ph.D. dissertation, University of California, 1986.

Strong community relationships and common economic problems engendered the phenomenal early success of the Nonpartisan League. However, the league's opponents were eventually able to use the same deep sense of community against the organization. DAI 47:3169-A.

0601 Saloutos, Theodore. "The Rise of the Nonpartisan League in North Dakota, 1915–1917." *Agricultural History* 20 (1946): 43–61.

The origins of the Nonpartisan League in North Dakota are examined along with the battle against patriotic groups during World War I. Notes.

0602 Saloutos, Theodore, and Hicks, John D. *Agricultural Discontent in the Middle West, 1900–1939*. Madison: University of Wisconsin Press, 1951.

The origins and consequences of broad-based farmer discontent are analyzed, including movements active during the Wilson years. Notes, index.

LOCAL AND REGIONAL STUDIES

0603 Anderson, James D. "The Southern Improvement Company: Northern Reformers' Investment in Negro Cotton Tenancy, 1900–1920." *Agricultural History* 52 (1978): 111–31.

Northerners with humanitarian intentions tried to help blacks become landowning farmers, but the scheme proved unworkable. Notes.

0604 Ashmen, Roy. "Price Determination in the Butter Market: The Elgin Board of Trade, 1872–1917." *Agricultural History* 36 (1962): 156–62.

Dairymen founded the board as a way of marketing butter and cheese more profitably. While the Elgin board's price of butter became the national benchmark for a time, the board was closed in 1917 after Chicago dealers took control. Notes.

0605 Lovin, Hugh T. "The Farmer Revolt in Idaho, 1914–1922." *Idaho Yesterdays* 20 (1976): 2–15.

Angry over the lack of support for irrigation projects, Idaho farmers banded together in the Progressive party.

0606 Saloutos, Theodore. *Farmer Movements in the South, 1865–1933*. Berkeley: University of California Press, 1960.

Chapters on the New Freedom, southern agriculture, cotton, and the war are included in this survey of farm protest movements. Notes, bibliography, index.

0607 Stroup, Rodger E. "John L. McLaurin: A Political Biography." Ph.D. dissertation, University of South Carolina, 1980.

John McLaurin, who had been active in state politics since 1885, helped to establish the North Carolina cotton warehouse system between 1912 and 1917. DAI 42:349-A.

Business

GENERAL

See also Chapter 11, *Mobilization*.

0608 Abrahams, Paul P. "American Bankers and the Economic Tactics of Peace: 1919." *Journal of American History* 56 (1969): 572–83.

While the Wilson administration insisted on halting public loans to the Allies, repayment of war debts, and a return to normal trade conditions after the Armistice, many bankers saw the need for an international consortium to rebuild war-torn areas. Their concern led to the Edge act of 1919, but this export banking scheme collapsed when the government refused to cooperate. Notes.

0609 Corn, Joseph. "Selling Technology: Advertising Films and the American Corporation, 1900–1920." *Film and History* 11 (1981): 49–58.

During the Progressive era and the wartime period, large corporations made short films that advertised their wares outright or educated the public in ways that promoted products indirectly.

0610 Edwards, James D. "Public Accounting in the United States from 1913–1928." *Business History Review* 32 (1958): 74–101.

The federal income tax and the federal revenue act of 1917 led to the growth of public accounting and the professionalization of the field. Notes.

0611 Grant, H. Roger. *Insurance Reform: Consumer Action in the Progressive Era*. Ames: Iowa State University Press, 1979.

Progressives were active in several states in the consumer crusade to reform the insurance industries. Corporate leaders cooperated with these movements, seeking to channel the reform impulse toward the federal level because they found national laws less objectionable than a maze of state and local regulations. Notes, bibliography, index.

0612 Hounsell, David A. "From the American System to Mass Production: The Development of Manufacturing Technology in the United States, 1850–1920." Ph.D. dissertation, University of Delaware, 1978.

The final chapter discusses Henry Ford and the rise of the first full-blown system of mass production—the assembly line of the Progressive era. DAI 39:7484-A.

0613 Liebenau, Jonathan M. "Scientific Ambitions: The Pharmaceutical Industry, 1900–1920." *Pharmacy in History* 27 (1985): 3–11.

Technicians and scientists came to work for the growing pharmaceutical industry during the Progressive era, resulting in new products, new methods of testing, and the standardization of druggists' formulas. Notes.

0614 Lynch, Edmund C. "Walter Dill Scott: Pioneer Industrial Psychologist." *Business History Review* 42 (1968): 149–70.

During the Progressive era Scott helped business to adopt psychology. During the war he devised a complex rating system to help the military pick officers.

0615 Martin, Albro. *Enterprise Denied: Origins of the Decline of American Railroads, 1897–1917.* New York: Columbia University Press, 1971.

Unwarranted interference in the vital railroad business by Progressives stunted growth and led to a decline in the vitality of management. The government was forced to take over the railroads during World War I, because reforms and regulations had weakened them. Tables, appendix, notes, bibliography, index.

0616 Navin, Thomas R. "The 500 Largest American Industrials in 1917." *Business History Review* 44 (1970): 360–86.

United States Steel tops this listing of the biggest companies ranked by assets, followed by Standard Oil of New Jersey, Bethlehem Steel, and Armour. Notes.

0617 Nelson, Daniel. *Managers and Workers: Origins of the New Factory System in the United States, 1880–1920.* Madison: University of Wisconsin Press, 1975.

Factory owners embraced scientific management because it promised higher profit and lower costs while satisfying worker demands for better working conditions. Notes, index.

0618 Pugach, Noel H. "American Shipping Promoters and the Shipping Crisis of 1914–1916: The Pacific & Eastern Steamship Company." *American Neptune* 35 (1975): 166–82.

The Pacific and Eastern Steamship line, created in response to the wartime shortage of cargo vessels, was a failure, because speculators squandered their resources quarreling with one another. Notes.

0619 Samson, Peter E. "The Emergence of a Consumer Interest in America, 1870–1930." Ph.D. dissertation, University of Chicago, 1980.

Industrialization brought the development of consumer interest organizations and publications. Intellectuals criticized business's practice of simultaneously exploiting and catering to customers. DAI 41:3235-A.

0620 Tenopir, Carol. "Characteristics of Corporations that Founded Libraries, 1910–1921." *Special Libraries* 76 (1985): 43–52.

Special libraries created by corporations came about as a result of either economic expansion or new management, since new companies seldom engaged in such undertakings.

0621 Wiebe, Robert H. "Business Disunity and the Progressive Movement, 1901–1914."

Mississippi Valley Historical Review 44 (1958): 664–85.

The Progressive movement was able to advance its cause because the business community was not unified. Notes.

BUSINESS LEADERS

0622 Curry, Mary E. "Creating an American Institution: The Merchandising Genius of J. C. Penney." Ph.D. dissertation, American University, 1980.

J. C. Penney's sound and innovative business practices underlay his phenomenal success. His principles included low prices, cash-only sales, cooperative buying, centralized departments, good communication throughout all levels of the organization, management training, and respect for the ideas of managers. DAI 41:2733-A.

0623 Davidson, Gordon W. "Henry Ford: The Formation and Course of a Public Figure." Ph.D. dissertation, Columbia University, 1966.

Although Henry Ford lacked both education and insight, his views were widely reported in the press, and he was considered for public office. His fame and success gave him a blind faith in his own intuition which eventually harmed his business. DAI 27:435-A.

0624 Henry, Lyell D., Jr. "Alfred W. Lawson, the Forgotten 'Columbus of the Air.'" *Journal of American Culture* 7 (1984): 93–99.

A noted baseball organizer and magazine publisher, Lawson also founded the first national passenger airline.

0625 Hessen, Robert A. "A Biography of Charles M. Schwab, Steel Industrialist." Ph.D. dissertation, Columbia University, 1969.

The dynamic president of United States Steel was forced to resign, but he then worked to make Bethlehem Steel into a major corporate rival through the use of innovative technology and aggressive sales techniques overseas. During the war, Wilson appointed him to direct the national shipbuilding program. DAI 32:6341-A.

0626 Hyser, Raymond M. "A Study in Cooperative Management: The Business Career of James W. Ellsworth (1849–1925)." Ph.D. dissertation, Florida State University, 1983.

Ellsworth made himself wealthy in the 1880s by selling coal to the railroads, and he later operated his own coal mines. He came to believe in a paternalistic style of cooperation between management and labor and so provided his workers with decent housing and services. In 1907 he moved to his hometown of Hudson, Ohio, intending to transform it into a model town. He eventually won the cooperation of residents, reopening the Western Reserve Academy in 1916 as part of his plan. DAI 44: 844-A.

0627 Jacobson, D. S. "The Political Economy of Industrial Location: The Ford Motor Company at Cork, 1912–26." *Irish Economic and Social History* 4 (1977): 36–55.

In 1917, Henry Ford built a factory in Cork, Ireland, to manufacture tractors. In doing so the American industrialist drove a hard bargain with Great Britain and the Irish Free State. Notes.

0628 Jardim, Anne. *The First Henry Ford: A Study in Personality and Business Leadership.* Cambridge, MA: MIT Press, 1970.

Henry Ford anticipated John Maynard Keynes with his concept of mass production and his belief that lower prices and greater markets would allow wages to rise indefinitely. Notes, index.

0629 Klein, John William. "The Role and Impact of Rockefeller Philanthropy during the Progressive Era." Ph.D. dissertation, Fordham University, 1980.

Between 1900 and 1920, John D. Rockefeller and his associates instituted, with questionable long-range motives, a wide range of philanthropic ventures of unquestionable immediate benefit. The generous philanthropy did not seriously dilute Rockefeller's fortune, and it won him enormous respect and political power. The public also became more willing to accept giant and influential private fortunes. DAI 41:1187-A.

0630 Lacey, Robert. *Ford: The Men and the Machine.* Boston: Little, Brown, 1986.

This massive anecdotal history discusses the Ford family, portraying its founding father as an industrial genius who was also paranoid and something of a lunatic. Index.

0631 Lewis, David L. *The Public Image of Henry Ford: An American Folk Hero and His Company.* Detroit: Wayne State University Press, 1976.

The public worshipped Ford, because he succeeded through hard work and creativeness rather than by manipulating money or people, and because he retained the common touch. Notes, index.

0632 May, Martha. "The Historical Problem of the Family Wage: The Ford Motor Company and the Five Dollar Day." *Feminist Studies* 8 (1982): 399–424.

Ford's motives for implementing the five-dollar day for workers were complex. His reasons included stabilization of the work force, discouragement of unionization and strikes, and modernization. Notes.

0633 Mayer, Robert S. "The Influence of Frank A. Vanderlip and the National City Bank on American Commerce and Foreign Policy, 1910–1920." Ph.D. dissertation, Rutgers University, 1968.

Between 1910 and 1920, American industry was producing a surplus and needed to export more goods. Foreign branches of American banks were endorsed by the government to facilitate trade. Vanderlip of the National City Bank cooperated with the American government only when its goals coincided with the profitability of his bank. While urging military intervention to protect his own investments, Vanderlip at times worked with foreign governments against U.S. goals. DAI 29:2187-A.

0634 Meyer, Stephen. "Adapting the Immigrant to the Line: Americanizing in the Ford Factory, 1914–1921." *Journal of Social History* 14 (1980): 67–82.

The Ford Sociological Department and the Ford English School were paternalistic attempts to Americanize immigrant workers, programs the company dropped in 1920 to save money. Notes.

0635 Morgan, George T., Jr. "The Gospel of Wealth Goes South: John Henry Kirby and Labor's Struggle for Self-Determination, 1901–1916." *Southwestern Historical Quarterly* 75 (1971): 186–97.

Lumber magnate Kirby used the social gospel and charitable work as part of his campaign to break the union movement in eastern Texas. Notes.

0636 Nevins, Allan, and Hill, Frank E. *Ford.* 2 vols. New York: Scribner's, 1957.

Ford is portrayed as an industrialist autocrat who believed in the future of high wages and cheap goods as well as the immorality of mere money-making. Notes, appendix, index.

0637 Nye, David E. *Henry Ford: "Ignorant Idealist."* Port Washington, NY: Kennikat, 1979.

Ford was America's greatest hero, whose life incorporated the national experience. Only Wilson, William Jennings Bryan, Charles Evans

Hughes, and Theodore Roosevelt garnered more publicity between 1914 and 1920. Notes, bibliography, index.

0638 Scoufelis, Aristides. "The Public Views and Charitable Contributions of American Big Businessmen toward Learning, Culture, and Human Welfare, 1910–1932." Ed.D. dissertation, Columbia University, 1985.

The philanthropy of fifty-eight prominent businessmen as described in a variety of publications reveals something of their characters and motivations. Many of their bequests reveal a thoughtful humanitarian philosophy particularly directed toward education. DAI 46:778-A.

0639 Sevitch, Benjamin. "The Rhetoric of Paternalism: Elbert H. Gary's Argument for the Twelve-Hour Day." *Western Speech* 35 (1971): 15–23.

Gary's paternalism toward workers contributed to the postwar strike by steelworkers enraged by his insistence on perpetuating the twelve-hour day. Notes.

0640 Stern, Sheldon M. "The Evolution of a Reactionary: Louis Arthur Coolidge, 1900–1925." *Mid-America* 57 (1975): 89–105.

A prewar Progressive, Coolidge moved to the right politically as a result of World War I, the Russian Revolution, and the expansion of government. His Sentinels of the Republic fought against laws designed to protect children and female laborers and to enhance educational opportunities. Notes.

0641 Taniguchi, Nancy J. "Perceptions and Realities: Progressive Reform and Utah Coal." Ph.D. dissertation, University of Utah, 1985.

The Wilson administration's demand that businesses cooperate with one another during World War I reversed years of Progressive trust-busting. In the case of the Utah coal industry, the result was a new oligopoly. DAI 46:3140-A.

0642 Wik, Reynold M. *Henry Ford and Grass-Roots America.* Ann Arbor: University of Michigan Press, 1972.

Henry Ford's Model T automobile and Fordson tractor had a major impact on rural America. Ford became a hero to many farmers, who also believed his questionable political ideas. Photographs, notes, bibliography, index.

FOREIGN EXPANSION

See also *Economic Diplomacy*, below, and Chapter 9.

0643 Abrahams, Paul P. "The Foreign Expansion of American Finances and Its Relationship to the Foreign Economic Policies of the United States, 1907–1921." Ph.D. dissertation, University of Wisconsin, 1967.

Expansion of American banking to foreign countries accelerated economic internationalism and affected Wilson's diplomatic views. DAI 28:4980-A.

0644 Cartensen, Fred V., and Werking, Richard Hume. "International Harvester in Russia: The Washington-St. Petersburg Connection." *Business History Review* 57 (1983): 347–66.

Washington did not help International Harvester to market its products in Russia because of pressure from competing businesses, although the American government could have done little in any case. Notes.

0645 DeNovo, John A. "The Movement for an Aggressive American Oil Policy Abroad, 1918–1920." *American Historical Review* 61 (1956): 854–76.

Americans were complacent about oil supplies in 1918, but that attitude changed to anxiety by 1920. Oil interests convinced the government and the public that securing foreign sources of oil was a matter of national security. Notes.

0646 Harrison, Benjamin T. "Chandler Anderson and American Foreign Relations (1896–1928)." Ph.D. dissertation, University of California, Los Angeles, 1969.

A leading authority on international arbitration with excellent State Department connections, Anderson specialized in representing Americans doing business in Latin America who sought special concessions from the American government. During the Wilson years, he represented Wall Street's interests in Mexico. DAI 30:3399-A.

0647 Hutchins, John G. B. "The American Shipping Industry since 1914." *Business History Review* 28 (1954): 105–27.

Public subsidies helped the U.S. merchant marine move from fourth to first place in the world in the period under study. Railroads and trucking led to a decline in intercoastal and coastwise shipping. Notes.

0648 Mazuzan, George T. " 'Our New Gold Goes Adventuring': The American International Corporation in China." *Pacific Historical Review* 43 (1974): 212–32.

The American International Corporation worked to gain a foothold in the China market in 1916 to 1917, but it failed to make much progress as a result of its business methods and protests from the Entente powers. Notes.

GOVERNMENT POLICIES

See also Chapter 7, *The Progressive Movement, New Freedom*, and *State and Local Politics*.

0649 Auddell, Robert M., and Cain, Louis P. "Public Policy, the Consent Decree, and the Meatpacking Industry." Part I, "Public Policy toward 'The Greatest Trust in the World.' " *Business History Review* 55 (1981): 217–42.

Charges by the Federal Trade Commission in 1919 that five major meat packers engaged in unfair competition against other firms were not completely well-founded. A settlement negotiated with the Justice Department and subsequent legislation changed little. Notes.

0650 Schultze, Quentin J. "Legislating Morality: The Progressive Response to American Outdoor Advertising, 1900–1917." *Journal of Popular Culture* 17 (1984): 37–44.

Progressive reformers fought attempts by advertisers to use billboards to sell goods to immigrants. Notes.

GOVERNMENT-BUSINESS RELATIONS

See also *Economics, Government Policies*, below, and Chapter 7, *The Progressive Movement, New Freedom*, and *State and Local Politics*.

0651 Becker, William H. *The Dynamics of Business-Government Relations: Industry and Exports, 1893–1921*. Chicago: University of Chicago Press, 1982.

New Left revisionists have not studied the economic basis of business decisions closely enough in their rush to judge U.S. foreign economic policy. Small firms supported government intervention in the development of foreign markets, while big firms opposed such aid, since they had more to lose. Tables, appendixes, notes, bibliography, index.

0652 Cuff, Robert D. "Woodrow Wilson's Missionary to American Business, 1914–1915." *Business History* 43 (1969): 545–51.

Impressed with newspaper reporter Charles Ferguson's writings on the need for business to become more humane, Wilson gave

him a job in the Commerce Department as a missionary to business.

0653 Doezema, William R. "Railroad Management and the Interplay of Federal and State Regulation, 1885–1916." *Business History Review* 50 (1976): 153–78.

Railroad leaders did not support federal regulation as a ploy to co-opt more strict laws at the state level until late in the Progressive era. Notes.

0654 Ershkowitz, Herbert. *The Attitude of Business toward American Foreign Policy, 1900–1916*. University Park: Pennsylvania State University Press, 1967.

This brief account describes business opinions about and business influence on foreign policy during the Progressive era. Notes, bibliography.

0655 Graebner, William. "The Coal-Mine Operator and Safety: A Study of Business Reform in the Progressive Period." *Labor History* 14 (1973): 483–505.

Mine owners and operators quickly took control of the movement for mine safety, looking to the federal government to provide safety standards only so long as the mine owners had a major say in any oversight agencies. Notes.

0656 ———. *Coal-Mining Safety in the Progressive Period: The Political Economy of Reform*. Lexington: University Press of Kentucky, 1976.

Coal mine owners and operators lobbied for uniform state safety regulations to bring order to their business and to co-opt more radical reforms. Notes, bibliography, index.

0657 Harbeson, Robert W. "Railroads and Regulation, 1877–1916: Conspiracy or Public Interest?" *Journal of Economic History* 27 (1967): 230–42.

The author attacks the work of Gabriel Kolko for his thesis that the railroad industry supported federal regulation solely because it was in their interest. Notes.

0658 Kerr, K. Austin. *American Railroad Politics, 1914–1920: Rates, Wages, and Efficiency*. Pittsburgh: University of Pittsburgh Press, 1968.

Shippers, rather than the railroads, gained the most from control by the Interstate Commerce Commission. The business-government relationship was complicated by numerous interest groups seeking to protect their constituents. Notes, bibliography, index.

0659 Kolko, Gabriel. *Railroads and Regulation, 1877–1916.* Princeton: Princeton University Press, 1965.

Railroads supported federal regulation of their industry to make it more orderly and to fight off more substantive reforms at the state level. Progressivism was a form of political capitalism, whereby business used the expanded power of government for its own ends. Notes, bibliography, index.

0660 ———. *The Triumph of Conservatism: A Reinterpretation of American History, 1900–1916.* Chicago: Quadrangle, 1963.

Conservative big business triumphed by supporting Progressives such as Wilson. Federal regulation of the economy preserved existing power and economic relations; therefore, it was conservative in effect as well as in purpose. Notes, index.

0661 McCulley, Richard T. "The Origins of the Federal Reserve Act of 1913: Banks and Politics during the Progressive Era, 1897–1913." Ph.D. dissertation, University of Texas, 1980.

Economic interests, ideology, and politics all played important roles in Wall Street's drive to fulfill Alexander Hamilton's vision of a centralized banking system based on a partnership between government and financiers. DAI 42:1284-A.

0662 Sobel, Robert. *The Age of Giant Corporations: A Microeconomic History of American Business, 1914–1970.* Westport, CT: Greenwood, 1972.

The rise of the giant corporation is examined. A key event was the intertwining of business and political power during World War I, which led to further government-business cooperation in the postwar period. Tables, notes, bibliography, index.

0663 Weinstein, James. *The Corporate Ideal in the Liberal State, 1900–1918.* Boston: Beacon, 1968.

By the end of the Progressive period, the foundations for the liberal state had been formulated and developed by "the more sophisticated leaders of America's largest corporations and financial institutions." These businessmen recognized that a government active in economic matters could assure stability and prosperity and that the ideal for the future was a responsible social order. Notes, index.

0664 ———. "Organized Business and the City Commission and Manager Movements." *Journal of Southern History* 28 (1962): 166–82.

Conservative business interests supported commission and manager city government to fight radicalism and labor. Notes.

0665 Wiebe, Robert H. *Businessmen and Reform: A Study of the Progressive Movement.* Cambridge, MA: Harvard University Press, 1962.

Businessmen were very active in the Progressive movement, often contributing important ideas. On issues affecting business they played dominant roles in shaping reform measures. Notes, bibliography, index.

ORGANIZATIONS

0666 Bennett, Dianne, and Graebner, William. "Safety First: Slogan and Symbol of the Industrial Safety Movement." *Journal of the Illinois State Historical Society* 68 (1975): 243–56.

Illinois Steel's Robert J. Young coined the slogan "Safety First" as part of a campaign for safety on the job, which Progressives hoped would result in conservation of manpower and greater efficiency.

0667 Gable, Richard W. "Birth of an Employers' Association." *Business History Review* 33 (1959): 535–45.

Originally created to promote business views about tariffs, the National Association of Manufacturers quickly evolved into an antilabor force. Notes.

0668 Gitelman, H. M. "Management's Crisis of Confidence and the Origin of the National Industrial Conference Board, 1914–1916." *Business History Review* 58 (1984): 153–77.

The conference board was created to promote the interests of business against those of labor unions and reformist politicians through carefully orchestrated publicity campaigns. Notes.

0669 Lorence, James J. "The American Asiatic Association, 1898–1925: Organized Business and the Myth of the China Market." Ph.D. dissertation, University of Wisconsin, 1970.

The American Asiatic Association was created by businessmen to publicize the potential of the Asian market and the Open Door policy. Once this educational goal had been achieved, the organization began to decline but revived briefly between 1913 and 1916 under the presidency of Willard Straight. DAI 31:2313-A.

0670 Silver, James W. "The Hardwood Producer Comes of Age." *Journal of Southern History* 23 (1957): 427–53.

The American lumber industry matured quickly during the Progressive era. The Hardwood Manufacturers Institute brought about cooperation between government and business. Notes.

0671 Steigerwalt, A. K. "The NAM and the Congressional Investigations of 1913: A Case Study in the Suppression of Evidence." *Business History Review* 34 (1960): 335–44.

Published reports by congressional committees investigating the lobbying practices of the National Association of Manufacturers were tainted, because their star witness was later proven to be a liar. Notes.

0672 Werking, Richard Hume. "Bureaucrats, Businessmen, and Foreign Trade: The Origins of the United States Chamber of Commerce." *Business History Review* 52 (1978): 321–41.

The government played a greater role than business did in creating the national chamber, which was meant to coordinate the efforts of merchants, industrialists, and government officials. Notes.

LOCAL AND REGIONAL STUDIES

See also Chapter 7, *State and Local Politics.*

0673 Atwood, Roy A. "Interlocking Newspaper and Telephone Company Directorates in Southeastern Iowa, 1900–1917." *Annals of Iowa* 47 (1984): 255–69.

Newspapers took over the telephone business in Iowa to drum up more business by using the telephone to collect news and promote advertising. Notes.

0674 Beilke, William E. "Colorado's First Oil Shale Rush, 1910–1930." Ph.D. dissertation, University of Colorado, Boulder, 1984.

Although the government retained control of most Colorado oil shale lands, private corporations also scrambled for ownership, not always legally. All of the oil shale ventures eventually failed, as cheaper oil sources were discovered. DAI 45:2231-A.

0675 Blackford, Mansel G. "Banking and Bank Legislation in California, 1890–1915." *Business History Review* 47 (1973): 482–507.

Bankers formed interest groups to lobby for legislation and to bring order to their profession. Notes.

0676 ———. "Businessmen and the Regulation of Railroads and Public Utilities in California during the Progressive Era." *Business History Review* 44 (1970): 307–19.

Government regulation of railroads and public utilities was favored by businessmen seeking order and an end to unfair practices. Consumers also benefited from these Progressive reforms. Notes.

0677 ———. *The Politics of Business in California, 1890–1920.* Columbus: Ohio State University Press, 1977.

Diverse business interests in California ranging from agriculture to banking all favored economic integration to promote stabilization and orderliness. Notes, bibliography, index.

0678 Brownlee, W. Elliot, Jr. "Income Taxation and Capital Formation in Wisconsin, 1911–1929." *Explorations in Economic History* 8 (1970): 77–102.

Wisconsin Progressivism did the state's economy more harm than good, because it stunted growth. Notes.

0679 ———. *Progressivism and Economic Growth: The Wisconsin Income Tax 1911–1929.* Port Washington, NY: Kennikat, 1974.

Rural Progressives used the income tax to force industry to pay for expanding government services, a ploy which slowed economic growth. Notes, appendix, index.

0680 Cochran, Thomas C., and Ginger, Ray. "The American-Hawaiian Steamship Company, 1899–1919." *Business History Review* 28 (1954): 343–65.

This steamship company provides an example of how innovative businessmen made transportation profitable during the Progressive era. Notes.

0681 Heidebrecht, Paul H. "Faith and Economic Practice: Protestant Businessmen in Chicago, 1900–1920." Ph.D. dissertation, University of Illinois, 1986.

Socially prominent capitalists in the early twentieth century imposed their business-oriented world views on American Protestantism, permanently changing it. The effort made by a group of Chicago businessmen to apply Christian ethics to social problems was insidiously pro-wealth. DAI 47:2482-A.

0682 McConachie, Alexander S. "The 'Big Cinch': A Business Elite in the Life of a City, Saint Louis, 1895–1915." Ph.D. dissertation, Washington University, 1976.

The downtown community, dominated by the St. Louis business elite, was not a closed group: many of humble origins and many born outside the region rose to prominence. During the Progressive era, middle- and working-class associations differed with the Big Cinch establishment over ways to improve urban life and politics. DAI 37:2383-A.

0683 Roberts, Joe D. "An Economic and Geographic History of Cushing, Oklahoma, from Its Origins through the Oil Boom Years, 1912–1917." Ph.D. dissertation, University of Minnesota, 1976.

Cushing was an oil boomtown that spent windfall revenues wisely on public works. Following its short-lived boom, the town became a refining and pipeline center. Consistent throughout its history was its absolute faith in laissez-faire capitalism. DAI 37:3859-A.

0684 Tripp, Mary E. "Longleaf Pine Lumber Manufacturing in the Altamaha River Basin, 1865–1918." Ph.D. dissertation, Florida State University, 1983.

By 1918, a large part of the southern forests had already been exploited. The importance of rivers and ports declined, as the railroads became more accessible. DAI 44: 2226-A.

0685 Whitley, Donna J. "Fuller E. Callaway and Textile Mill Development in LaGrange, 1895–1920." Ph.D. dissertation, Emory University, 1984.

Fuller E. Callaway, already a successful merchant, built not only a textile mill, but also a worker's community to go with it. He tried to keep the workers happy, but relations with the old town were often rocky. DAI 45:1847-A.

Economics

GENERAL

See also Chapter 7, *The Progressive Movement* and *New Freedom*, and Chapter 11, *Mobilization* and *Readjustment*.

0686 Faulkner, Harold U. *The Decline of Laissez-Faire, 1897–1917.* New York: Holt, Rinehart and Winston, 1951.

The rise of finance capitalism and economic imperialism were among the institutional changes affecting capitalism during this time of great prosperity. Progressive reforms designed to help the nation adjust to the Industrial Revolution are also discussed. Photographs, notes, appendix, bibliography, index.

0687 Hollitz, John E. "The Challenge of Abundance: Reactions to the Development of a Consumer Economy, 1890–1920." Ph.D. dissertation, University of Wisconsin, Madison, 1981.

Industrialization boosted the production of goods by so much that the nineteenth-century concept of supply and demand was turned on its head. Advertising, used to create demand, began to assume its modern form before 1920. Also by 1920, a rudimentary consumer philosophy had developed to reconcile traditional ethical, religious, and economic values with the new abundance of goods. DAI 42:3273-A.

0688 Pilgrim, John D. "The Upper Turning Point of 1920: A Reappraisal." *Explorations in Economic History* 11 (1974): 271–98.

The economy improved in 1920 after a sharp postwar downturn caused by government monetary policies and the inelasticity of supply.

0689 Pope, Daniel. "American Economists and the High Cost of Living: The Late Progressive Era." *Journal of the History of the Behavioral Sciences* 17 (1981): 75–87.

Rising living costs concerned American economists during Wilson's first term, to the point that they saw individualism and the family threatened.

0690 Roose, Kenneth D. "The Production Ceiling and the Turning-Point of 1920." *American Economic Review* 48 (1958): 348–56.

Production ceilings as factors in the turning of business cycles are discussed, using 1920 as an example.

0691 Saul, S. B. "The American Impact on British Industry, 1895–1914." *Business History Review* 3 (1960): 19–38.

American competition shook British manufacturers out of complacency during the Progressive era, as evidenced in the machine tool and electrical engineering industries. Notes.

0692 Shinkawa, Kensaburo. "The Emergence of American 'State Capitalism,' 1913–1940."

Ph.D. dissertation, University of Maryland, 1968.

During the Wilson era, privately organized business and economic groups set the stage for increasing government manipulation of the economy. DAI 29:3083-A.

0693 Sklar, Martin J. *The Corporate Reconstruction of American Capitalism, 1890–1916*. New York: Cambridge University Press, 1988.

The period from 1890 to 1916 marked the transition of industrial capitalism from its proprietary-competitive stage to the beginning of its corporate administered stage. The corporate reconstruction of American capitalism brought about fundamental changes reflected in laws, institutions, thinking, and habits. Notes, bibliography, index.

0694 Soule, George H. *Prosperity Decade: From War to Depression, 1917–1929*. New York: Holt, Rinehart and Winston, 1947.

The opening chapters of this economic survey examine wartime economic mobilization and the postwar boom, depression, and eventual recovery. Photographs, notes, bibliography, index.

ANTITRUST POLICIES

See also Chapter 7, *New Freedom.*

0695 Burns, Malcolm R. "The Competitive Effects of Trust Busting: A Portfolio Analysis." *Journal of Political Economy* 85 (1977): 717–39.

Stock prices and finance theory are used to show the effect of corporate dissolutions on investors.

0696 Gordon, David. "The Beef Trust: Antitrust policy and the Meat Packing Industry, 1902–1922." Ph.D. dissertation, Claremont Graduate School, 1983.

The "beef trust" survived continual legal assaults from the federal government between 1902 and 1922. The Supreme Court finally confirmed certain regulations in 1922. DAI 44:1549-A.

0697 Himmelberg, Robert F. "Business, Anti-Trust Policy, and the Industrial Board of the Department of Commerce, 1919." *Business History Review* 42 (1968): 1–23.

The industrial board created by the Department of Commerce in 1919 was an attempt by business groups to turn back the clock on

antitrust efforts while the president occupied himself with the Paris Peace Conference.

GOVERNMENT POLICIES

0698 Beckhardt, Benjamin H. *The Federal Reserve System*. New York: Columbia University Press, 1972.

The origins of the Federal Reserve system, its operation during World War I, and postwar attempts to curb inflation are among the topics covered in this history of the Federal Reserve. Tables, notes, index.

0699 Ingle, H. Larry. "The Dangers of Reaction: The Repeal of the Revenue Act of 1918." *North Carolina History Journal* 44 (1967): 72–88.

The excess-profits tax might have restructured the economic classes and financed the war, but its author, the ailing Progressive Claude Kitchin, could not stop the repeal campaign. Notes.

0700 Ise, John. *The United States Oil Policy*. New Haven, CT: Yale University Press, 1926.

Oil policy increasingly concerned the Wilson administration as a result of wartime mobilization and America's growing energy needs. Notes, index.

0701 Kaufman, Burton I. *Efficiency and Expansion: Foreign Trade Organization in the Wilson Administration, 1913–1921*. Westport, CT: Greenwood, 1974.

The Wilson administration understood the opportunity presented by World War I for expansion into new markets and helped American business make the most of the situation. Tables, notes, bibliography, index.

0702 ———. "The Organizational Dimension of United States Economic Foreign Policy, 1900–1920." *Business History Review* 46 (1972): 17–44.

As part of the effort to make businesses more competitive and efficient, organizations were developed to push for foreign trade. Despite Wilson's doubts about such projects, Congress passed the Webb-Pomerene act and the Edge act, which helped banking houses in their activities abroad. Notes.

0703 Lewis, James A. "Diplomacy and Gold: American Attitudes toward the Role of Government in World Recovery from Versailles to the First New Deal." Ph.D. dissertation, University of Chicago, 1984.

The gold standard was fundamental to post-World War I efforts to stabilize international finance. However, intense nationalism and sheer complexity undermined economic reconstruction. DAI 45:3435-A.

0704 Noble, Charles I. "The Class Origins of the Modern State, 1877–1916." Ph.D. dissertation, University of California, Berkeley, 1979.

The New Freedom is examined as an example of conservative reform. Wilson chose "to work within the parameters established by conservative capital rather than lead workers and small farmers against capital." DAI 41:386-A.

0705 Sharfman, I. L. *The Interstate Commerce Commission: A Study in Administrative Law and Procedure.* 5 vols. New York: Commonwealth Fund, 1931–1937.

The expanded authority of the ICC during the Wilson administration is examined along with the commission's major cases. Index.

0706 Taussig, Frank W. *The Tariff History of the United States.* New York: Putnam's, 1931.

Still an important source of information, this work includes material on the Underwood-Simmons tariff of 1913. Notes, appendix, index.

0707 Urofsky, Melvin I. *Big Steel and the Wilson Administration: A Study of Business-Government Relations.* Columbus: Ohio State University Press, 1969.

Wilson violated a major tenet of his New Freedom platform by accepting business concentration as politically expedient and necessary for wartime mobilization. Notes, bibliography, index.

ECONOMIC DIPLOMACY

See also Chapter 9.

0708 Kaufman, Burton I. "United States Trade and Latin America: The Wilson Years." *Journal of American History* 58 (1971): 342–63.

The Wilson administration sought the increase of exports to Latin America. The withdrawal of Germany and Britain from some markets after 1914 provided additional openings, and the government helped to set up conferences with Latin Americans. Notes.

0709 Scheiber, Harry N. "World War I as Entrepreneurial Opportunity: Willard Straight and the American International Corporation." *Political Science Quarterly* 84 (1969): 486–511.

Straight hoped to use the war to crack open the vast potential for trade with Asia through the American International Corporation. Notes.

Labor

GENERAL

0710 Bradley, Harold C. "Frank P. Walsh and Postwar America." Ph.D. dissertation, St. Louis University, 1966.

Frank Walsh resigned from the War Labor Board after the war and campaigned for government intervention to prevent unemployment and other labor problems. A strong advocate of self-determination, he became disillusioned with the League of Nations when nothing was done for small nations outside the Austro-Hungarian empire, particularly Ireland. Walsh is representative of Wilson-era idealists who felt betrayed and disappointed by postwar events. DAI 27: 2978-A.

0711 Brody, David. *Workers in Industrial America: Essays on the 20th Century Struggle.* New York: Oxford University Press, 1980.

Five essays on the changing nature of work and the work force include material on the Wilson era. Notes.

0712 Calvi, Giulia. "The Boss's Space and the Worker's Time: Some Working Hypotheses on Early 20th Century America" (in Italian). *Movimento Operaio e Socialista* [Italy] 3 (1980): 81–90.

The reactions of workers to the reorganization of the workplace in eastern factories are compared with the discontents of poor farmers and rural laborers in the West. Notes.

0713 Commons, John R., et al. *History of Labor in the United States.* 4 vols. New York: Macmillan, 1918–1935.

Several writers from the Wisconsin School of Labor History collaborated on this massive work. Volume III covers wages, hours, and working conditions in the years 1900–1930. Notes, bibliography, index.

0714 Dubofsky, Melvyn. *Industrialism and the American Worker, 1865–1920.* Arlington Heights, IL: Harlan Davidson, 1985.

The last quarter of this survey deals with labor during the Wilson years, a time when organized labor had an opportunity to build powerful organizations capable of challenging big business in the national political arena. Annotated bibliography, index.

0715 Fisher, Paul. "A Forgotten Gentry of the Fourth Estate." *Journalism Quarterly* 33 (1956): 167–74.

The "forgotten gentry" is the tramp printer, a skilled itinerant who provided extra labor when needed. Once unions succeeded in establishing a six-day work week, the tramp was no longer needed. Notes.

0716 Foner, Philip S. *History of the Labor Movement in the United States.* Vol. VI, *On the Eve of America's Entrance into World War I, 1915–1916.* New York: International, 1982.

Henry Ford's five-dollar day, strikes in copper mines, steel mills, oil refineries, and the New York transit system, unionism in the garment industry and among women, railroad workers, and racism are among the topics covered. Notes, index.

0717 ———. *History of the Labor Movement in the United States.* Vol. VII, *Labor and World War I, 1914–1918.* New York: International, 1987.

The author examines in detail the Socialist party during the war, labor's road to war, the roles played by women, blacks, and the Industrial Workers of the World (IWW), and the severe wartime repression. Notes, index.

0718 Fones-Wolf, Elizabeth. "The Politics of Vocationalism: Coalitions and Industrial Education in the Progressive Era." *Historian* 46 (1983): 39–55.

Fundamental disagreement between organized labor, manufacturers, and middle-class reformers over vocational education undercuts the argument that these groups were allied during the Progressive era. Notes.

0719 Gordon, Gerald R. "The AFL, the CIO and the Quest for a Peaceful World Order, 1914–1946." Ph.D. dissertation, University of Maine, 1967.

Before World War I, American and European labor shared an idealistic vision of international pacifism and fraternalism. During the war, American labor came to believe that the war was a necessary fight for worldwide democracy which would bring world peace. However, labor, along with the rest of the nation, became disillusioned during the 1920s. DAI 28:3109-A.

0720 Green, James R. *The World of the Worker: Labor in Twentieth Century America.* New York: Hill and Wang, 1980.

The rank-and-file worker's struggle for freedom in the workplace is examined. Bibliography, index.

0721 Krydner, Elizabeth A. G. "Humanizing the Industrial Workplace: The Role of the Early Personnel Manager: 1897–1920." Ph.D. dissertation, Bowling Green State University, 1982.

Personnel managers were influential players in both humanization of the workplace and labor/management disputes. Twenty-seven personnel managers are scrutinized and portrayed as complex human beings responding to complex problems in the American tradition of moral reform. Other histories are criticized for ignoring the role of personnel managers and for oversimplifying the motives of reformers. DAI 43:1265-A.

0722 Montgomery, David. "The 'New Unionism' and the Transformation of Workers' Consciousness in America, 1909–1922." *Journal of Social History* [Great Britain] 7 (1974): 509–35.

A new unionism with syndicalist leanings but independent from the IWW emerged by 1920 among miners, railroad and shipyard workers, and factory hands. In a reply, James R. Green presents an alternative interpretation of the tendencies toward syndicalism. Notes.

0723 ———. "Whose Standards? Workers and the Reorganization of Production in the United States, 1900–1920" (in French). *Mouvement Social* [France] (1978): 101–27.

The Progressive era witnessed a series of showdowns between labor and management over the reshaping of the workplace. Scientific management schemes and strikes both became commonplace as workers struggled to supplant traditional craft union lines and many companies sought to wreck unions.

0724 Palmer, Bryan. "Class, Conception and Conflict: The Thrust for Efficiency, Managerial Views of Labor and the Working Class Rebellion, 1903–1922." *Review of Political Economy* 7 (1975): 31–49.

Scientific management techniques squeezed the American worker and led to a number of strikes.

0725 Peterson, Joyce S. "A Social History of Automobile Workers before Unionization, 1900–1933." Ph.D. dissertation, University of Wisconsin, Madison, 1976.

Mass production brought many changes to the workplace including division of labor, rigid discipline, and the hiring of immigrants and rural native-born Americans. Union organizing in the auto industry was especially difficult, but workers tried to organize nonetheless. DAI 37:6706.

0726 Shapiro, Stanley. "The Passage of Power: Labor and the New Social Order." *Proceedings of the American Philosophical Society* 120 (1976): 464–74.

The Left gained a share of power in Britain after World War I but not in the United States, the key difference being American labor's lack of power. Notes.

WILSON AND LABOR

See also Chapter 11, *Mobilization*.

0727 Best, Gary D. "President Wilson's Second Industrial Conference, 1919–20." *Labor History* 16 (1975): 505–20.

The conference tackled the idea of industrial democracy (the use of shop committees as vehicles for employee representation), which industrialists would use to erect company unions. Notes.

0728 Boemeke, Manfred F. "The Wilson Administration, Organized Labor, and the Colorado Coal Strike, 1913–1914." Ph.D. dissertation, Princeton University, 1983.

Wilson's Progressive vision of harmony between labor and management led him to insist during the Colorado coal strike that there must be genuine democracy in the workplace. This marked the beginning of a new role for government, that of impartial mediator. DAI 44:3463-A.

0729 Hurwitz, Haggai. "Ideology and Industrial Conflict: President Wilson's First Industrial Conference of October 1919." *Labor History* 18 (1977): 509–24.

This conference had no chance of success, because even moderate unions made militant demands, and industrialists were not

about to give up any of their private property rights. Notes.

0730 Jensen, Billie B. "Woodrow Wilson's Intervention in the Coal Strike of 1914." *Labor History* 15 (1974): 63–77.

At the request of the governor of Colorado, Wilson dispatched federal troops to the scene of a bitter coal strike. Notes.

0731 Jones, Dallas L. "The Wilson Administration and Organized Labor, 1912–1919." Ph.D. dissertation, Cornell University, 1954.

Wilson came into the White House believing in the right of labor to organize and the need for legislation to protect workers from the grosser injustices of capitalism. With the exception of its actions during the 1919 steel strike, his administration did nothing to deprive workers of their rights. DAI 15:108.

0732 Smith, John S. "Organized Labor and Government in the Wilson Era, 1913–1921: Some Conclusions." *Labor History* 3 (1962): 265–86.

That Wilson included labor in his legislative agenda is shown by many laws passed during his first term and by his courting of Samuel Gompers. William B. Wilson's appointment as the first secretary of labor brought about closer cooperation between the American Federation of Labor and the government. Notes.

BUSINESS AND LABOR

See also *Business Leaders* and *Business, Organizations*, elsewhere in this chapter.

0733 Blacksilver, Jack. "George Gunton: Pioneer Spokesman for a Labor-Big Business Entente." *Business History Review* 31 (1957): 1–31.

Although Gunton was a strong union man, the interdependence of labor and capital led him to advocate a moderate brand of unionism. Notes.

0734 Gitelman, H. M. "Being of Two Minds: American Employers Confront the Labor Problem, 1915–1919." *Labor History* 25 (1984): 189–216.

Meeting semiannually, beginning in 1915, business representatives never reached a consensus on the problem of growing worker unrest. Notes.

0735 Green, Marguerite. *The National Civic Federation and the American Labor Movement, 1900–1925*. Washington, DC: Catholic University of America Press, 1956.

Progressives formed the NCF to bring labor and capital together so that they might work shoulder to shoulder instead of against one another. Notes, bibliography, index.

0736 Meyer, Stephen, III. *The Five Dollar Day: Labor, Management and Social Control in the Ford Motor Company, 1908–1921*. Albany: State University Press of New York, 1981.

Ford used the five-dollar day to control workers at the plant and at home by attaching strings to the higher wage. Increased worker militancy was the result of this benevolent despotism. Notes, bibliography, index.

0737 Morgan, George T., Jr. "No Compromise—No Recognition: John Henry Kirby, the Southern Lumber Operators' Association and Unionism in the Piney Woods, 1906–1916." *Labor History* 10 (1969): 193–204.

Rallying lumber operators to a stance of no compromise with the Brotherhood of Timberworkers in Texas and Louisiana, John Henry Kirby broke this union movement in 1916 after it became affiliated with the Industrial Workers of the World. Notes.

0738 Nelson, Daniel. " 'A Newly Appreciated Art': The Development of Personnel Work at Leeds and Northrup, 1915–1923." *Business History Review* 44 (1970): 520–35.

Personnel departments and company unions were introduced in many corporations between 1915 and 1923 to increase efficiency and undercut labor unions. Leeds and Northrup developed the most comprehensive programs in these areas. Notes.

0739 Ramirez, Bruno. *When Workers Fight: The Politics of Industrial Relations in the Progressive Era, 1898–1916*. Westport, CT: Greenwood, 1978.

Management found collective bargaining appealing because it contained labor, while labor favored it as a powerful new tool. Politicians, too, found it acceptable because it kept labor-management conflicts from erupting into violence. Notes, bibliography, index.

0740 Wakstein, Allen M. "The Origins of the Open Shop Movement, 1919–1920." *Journal of American History* 51 (1964): 460–75.

Wartime cooperation between employers and workers in the name of national security breathed new life into the open shop movement, which industrialists used to break the power of unions in the postwar period. Notes.

0741 Weinstein, James. "Big Business and the Origins of Workmen's Compensation." *Labor History* 8 (1967): 156–74.

Business leaders endorsed workmen's compensation as a relatively inexpensive way to undercut labor discontent. Notes.

GOVERNMENT LEGISLATION AND LABOR POLICIES

See also Chapter 7, *New Freedom*.

0742 Auerbach, Jerold S. "Progressives at Sea: The La Follette Act of 1915." *Labor History* 2 (1961): 344–60.

The Seamen's Act of 1915, sponsored by Senator Robert La Follette, is illustrative of the breadth of the Progressive movement. The motives of the various groups that supported the bill included higher wages for seamen and the exclusion of Orientals (labor), racism (southerners), national security (imperialists), and justice for sailors (humanitarians). Notes.

0743 Krivy, Leonard P. "American Organized Labor and the First World War, 1917–1918: A History of Labor Problems and the Development of a Government War Labor Program." Ph.D. dissertation, New York University, 1965.

Samuel Gompers organized the American Alliance for Labor and Democracy after American entry into World War I. Under pressure from the war, the government agreed to numerous labor demands. Various other agencies were formed in the first year of the war to address the problem of mobilizing sufficient labor, but only the War Labor Administration (headed by William B. Wilson) had the centralized power, skills, and knowledge to find solutions. DAI 29:544-A.

0744 Listikov, S. V. "Trade Unions and the Ideological and Political Struggle over the Plumb Plan" (in Russian). *Amerikanskii Ezhegodnik* [USSR] (1980): 92–117.

The 1919 Plumb plan for the nationalization of railroads was turned down by bankers, right wingers, and a group of trade unions. Notes.

0745 White, W. Thomas. "Railroad Labor Relations in the Great War and After, 1917–1921." *Journal of the West* 25 (1986): 36–43.

Railroad maintenance workers received better wages during the war, when the government took over operations. When the railroad companies took back control, their status dropped, leading them to support the Plumb plan and fight for what they had lost.

0746 Wood, Norman J. "Industrial Relations Policies of American Management, 1900–1933." *Business History Review* 34 (1960): 403–20.

This period witnessed a complete transformation in American industrial relations. Notes.

INVESTIGATIVE COMMISSIONS AND COMMITTEES

0747 Adams, Graham, Jr. *Age of Industrial Violence, 1910–15: The Activities and Findings of the United States Commission on Industrial Relations.* New York: Columbia University Press, 1966.

The commission's examination of several violent confrontations between labor and management is analyzed, as is the internal strife over the commission's final report. Notes, bibliography, index.

0748 Kerr, Thomas J. "New York Factory Investigating Commission and the Progressives." Ph.D. dissertation, Syracuse University, 1965.

The New York State Factory Investigating Commission was established after a factory fire killed 146 workers. The commission was highly effective in the areas of labor reform, administrative innovation, social research, and education. Various nationally prominent individuals, including Samuel Gompers, served on the commission. DAI 27:165-A.

LABOR AND POLITICS

See also Chapter 7, *Elections,* Chapter 8, *The Red Scare,* and Chapter 11, *Mobilization.*

0749 Karson, Marc. *American Labor Unions and Politics, 1900–1918.* Carbondale: Southern Illinois University Press, 1958.

The American Federation of Labor and the Industrial Workers of the World are among the Progressive era labor movements examined. The roles of churches and the Socialist party in the union movement are also studied. Notes, bibliography, index.

LABOR AND FOREIGN POLICY

0750 Levenstein, Harvey L. "The United States Labor Movement and Mexico, 1910–1951." Ph.D. dissertation, University of Wisconsin, 1966.

The American Federation of Labor established close relationships with Mexican labor groups during the Wilson era. Each group hoped to strengthen its own power to influence both domestic and foreign policy. DAI 27:731-A.

0751 Radosh, Ronald. *American Labor and United States Foreign Policy.* New York: Random House, 1969.

Organized labor began cooperating with the federal government in foreign policy matters during the Wilson years in return for general recognition, thus setting precedents that would be followed during the Cold War. Notes, index.

0752 Toth, Charles W. "The Pan American Federation of Labor: Its Political Nature." *Western Political Quarterly* 18 (1965): 615–20.

The Pan American Federation of Labor was a creature of Samuel Gompers. The organization never functioned very well, in part because of Gompers's close relationship with the American government and the dictatorial nature of most Latin American governments. Notes.

0753 ———. "Samuel Gompers, Communism, and the Pan American Federation of Labor." *The Americas* 23 (1967): 273–78.

Anticommunism was a prime motive behind Gompers's creation of the Pan American Federation of Labor to battle left-wing influences south of the border. Notes.

0754 ———. "Samuel Gompers, World Peace, and the Pan American Federation of Labor." *Caribbean Studies* 7 (1967): 59–64.

Gompers hoped to use the Pan American Federation of Labor to promote international cooperation and collective security. Notes.

CHILD LABOR

See also Chapter 7, *The Progressive Movement,* and *Legal.*

0755 Lea, Arden J. "Cotton Textiles and the Federal Child Labor Act of 1916." *Labor History* 16 (1975): 485–94.

Textile manufacturers supported the conservative Keating-Owen act as a means of using the federal government to help stabilize prices. Notes.

0756 Speakman, Joseph M. "Unwilling to School: Child Labor and Its Reform in Pennsylvania in the Progressive Era." Ph.D. dissertation, Temple University, 1976.

Second only to Alabama in the number of child laborers employed at the turn of the century, Pennsylvania passed several child labor laws during the Progressive era. Elitist reformers were motivated by a mixture of humanitarianism and urge toward social control. DAI 37:2385-A.

0757 Trattner, Walter I. *Crusade for the Children: A History of the National Child Labor Committee and Child Labor Reform.* Chicago: Quadrangle, 1970.

The National Child Labor Committee led the movement for child labor reform, effectively allying itself with other such organizations and with concerned Progressives. Notes, bibliography, index.

0758 Walker, Roger W. "The A.F.L. and Child-Labor Legislation: An Exercise in Frustration." *Labor History* 11 (1970): 323–40.

A mixture of humanitarian concerns and self-interest motivated the American Federation of Labor to support the Progressive crusade to mitigate the tragedy of child labor. Notes.

WOMEN WORKERS

See also Chapter 6, *Women* and *Immigration*, Chapter 7, *Legal*, Chapter 8, *Syndicalism* and *Socialism*, and Chapter 11, *Women*.

0759 Aldrich, Mark, and Albelda, Randy. "Determinants of Working Women's Wages during the Progressive Era." *Explorations in Economic History* 17 (1980): 323–41.

Progressives disagreed over the solution to the problem of women's low wages. The unskilled nature of the work they did, physical limitations, their usual inability to relocate, and nativism were among the special problems women faced. Notes.

0760 Asher, Nina L. "Dorothy Jacobs Bellanca: Feminist Trade Unionist, 1894–1946." Ph.D. dissertation, State University of New York, Binghamton, 1982.

Vice president of the Amalgamated Clothing Workers of America from its founding in 1914 until she died in 1946, Dorothy Jacobs

Bellanca combined feminism with unionism. DAI 43:1650-A.

0761 Calvi, Giulia. "Women in Industry: Work and Sociability in America, 1900–1915" (in Italian). *Quaderni Storici* [Italy] 17 (1982): 817–51.

Women's social experiences on the job freed them from the traditional authorities of parents and ethnicity, a factor that suffragettes and union organizers did not appreciate.

0762 Clement, Alice M. "Margaret Dreier Robins and the Dilemma of the Women's Trade Union League: Organization versus Legislation." Ph.D. dissertation, University of California, Davis, 1984.

Robins, wealthy president of the Women's Trade Union League from 1907 to 1922, transformed the league from an instrument for the organization of women's unions into one seeking to protect women through the enactment of laws. DAI 45:2627-A.

0763 Davis, Allen F. "The Women's Trade Union League: Origins and Organization." *Labor History* 5 (1964): 3–17.

The Women's Trade Union League, founded to help women establish trade unions, was a prime example of how reformers and labor moderates worked together during the prewar era.

0764 Dye, Nancy Schrom. *As Equals and as Sisters: Feminism, the Labor Movement and the Women's Trade Union League of New York.* Columbia: University of Missouri Press, 1980.

Wealthy women and working women worked together in the Women's Trade Union League, although it retreated to reformism from its original goal of union organizing. Notes, bibliography, index.

0765 ———. "Feminism or Unionism? The New York Women's Trade Union League and the Labor Movement." *Feminist Studies* 3 (1975): 111–25.

The Women's Trade Union League tried to integrate women into the union movement, organizing unskilled workers into craft unions on the AFL model. A different approach might have better served feminist interests. Notes.

0766 Eisenstein, Sarah. *Give Us Bread but Give Us Roses: Working Women's Consciousness in the United States, 1890 to the First World War.* London: Routledge and Kegan Paul, 1983.

Working women developed an ideology based on prevailing ideas of how women should behave and on their own practical experiences. Appendix, notes, bibliography, index.

0767 Foner, Philip S. *Women and the American Labor Movement*. 2 vols. New York: Free Press, 1979–80.

Both volumes contain a wealth of information on working women during the Wilson years. Notes, bibliography, index.

0768 Frederickson, Mary E. "A Place to Speak Our Minds: The Southern School for Women Workers." Ph.D. dissertation, University of North Carolina, Chapel Hill, 1981.

Social problems, organizations, and reforms of the Wilson years are discussed as they apply to the Southern School for Women Workers, which was founded in 1927. DAI 42:2818-A.

0769 Glenn, Susan A. "The Working Life of Immigrants: Women in the American Garment Industry, 1880–1920." Ph.D. dissertation, University of California, Berkeley, 1983.

Jewish immigrant garment workers were more assertive than were most female laborers, demanding better working conditions, higher wages, and more opportunity. The particular combination of old-world background and immigrant conditions tended to push young women who still lived at home, rather than married women, into the work force. DAI 45: 919-A.

0770 Gurowsky, David. "Factional Disputes within the ILGWU, 1919–1928." Ph.D. dissertation, State University of New York, Binghamton, 1978.

After World War I, radical and conservative wings of the International Ladies Garment Workers Union engaged in a ruinous factional dispute that saw membership drop by two thirds in a ten-year period. The left wing was not controlled by the Communist party but rather by Jewish and Italian socialists alienated by leaders more interested in power than in substantial change. DAI 38:5004-A.

0771 Jacoby, Robin Miller. "The Women's Trade Union League and American Feminism." *Feminist Studies* 3 (1975): 126–40.

The Women's Trade Union League hoped to improve working conditions for women by lobbying state legislatures and Congress for suffrage, a strategy which would give women the political clout necessary for their legislative agenda. Notes.

0772 Kennedy, Susan Estabrook. " 'The Want It Satisfies Demonstrates the Need of It': A Study of *Life and Labor* of the Women's Trade Union League." *International Journal of Women's Studies* [Canada] 3 (1980): 391–406.

Life and Labor's efforts at educating female workers in union organizing are analyzed.

0773 Kirkby, Diane E. "Alice Henry: The National Women's Trade Union League of America and Progressive Labor Reform." Ph.D. dissertation, University of California, Santa Barbara, 1982.

A leading figure in the national Women's Trade Union League, Alice Henry worked for suffrage, protective labor laws, the organization of unions, education, and the right of women to act independently from men. Her Australian background shaped many of her ideas. DAI 44:265-A.

0774 ———. " 'The Wage Earning Woman and the State': The National Women's Trade Union League and Protective Labor Legislation, 1903–1923." *Labor History* 28 (1987): 54–74.

State laws passed during the Progressive era governing hours, wages, and sanitary and safety conditions for the good of working women helped to exclude them from the labor force and restricted their job opportunities in many areas. Notes.

0775 Klaczynska, Barbara M. "Working Women in Philadelphia—1900–1930." Ph.D. dissertation, Temple University, 1975.

Ethnic and native-born working women in Philadelphia are studied to determine how family and community affected their behavior in the work force. DAI 36:6264-A.

0776 Landes, Elisabeth M. "The Effect of State Maximum-Hours Laws on the Employment of Women in 1920." *Journal of Political Economy* 88 (1980): 476–94.

Women workers, especially immigrants, lost jobs and work hours when state maximum-hours laws were enforced in 1920.

0777 Lieberman, Jacob A. "Their Sisters' Keepers: The Women's Hours and Wages Movement in the United States, 1890–1925." Ph.D. dissertation, Columbia University, 1971.

Women's groups and social reformers undertook a successful campaign to limit the hours of working women during the Progressive era and made headway with improving minimum wages and working conditions as well. DAI 32:5154-A.

0778 McCreesh, Carolyn D. "On the Picket Line: Militant Women Campaign to Organize Garment Workers, 1880–1917." Ph.D. dissertation, University of Maryland, 1975.

In the long struggle to organize women garment workers into unions, by 1917 working women had pushed middle-class labor organizers to the periphery of their garment industry unions. DAI 37:1174-A.

0779 Malino, Sarah S. "Faces across the Counter: A Social History of Female Department Store Employees, 1870–1920." Ph.D. dissertation, Columbia University, 1982.

Although beginning pay was low and hours were long, department store work was generally less physically harmful and often more secure than factory work. Department store work also raised the hope of advancement into management or buyer positions. DAI 43:1654-A.

0780 Milden, James W. "Women, Public Libraries, and Library Unions: The Formative Years." *Journal of Library History* 12 (1977): 150–58.

During the period 1917–1920, many local unions of library workers were formed, only to fade away during the Red Scare. Notes.

0781 Nadel, Stanley. "Reds versus Pinks: A Civil War in the International Ladies Garment Workers Union." *New York History* 66 (1985): 48–72.

Communists almost took over the ILGWU after World War I. Moderate socialists felt compelled to call on New York City officials for help and to work out a deal with management to keep the radicals from taking control. Notes.

0782 Scharnau, Ralph. "Elizabeth Morgan, Crusader for Labor Reform." *Labor History* 14 (1973): 340–51.

Motivated by revisionist socialism, Morgan organized women workers of Chicago into trade unions and an important political force. Notes.

0783 Schofield, Ann. "Rebel Girls and Union Maids: The Woman Question in the Journals of the AFL and IWW, 1905–1920." *Feminist Studies* 9 (1983): 335–58.

Publications of the moderate AFL and the radical IWW shared attitudes of paternalism and sexism, although the IWW's "rebel girl" was portrayed as more of an activist. Notes.

0784 Sharpless, John, and Rury, John. "The Political Economy of Women's Work, 1900–1920." *Social Science History* 4 (1980): 317–46.

Women had several disadvantages in attempting to create unions, among them the absence of social contacts outside of the factory, the fact that many worked only intermittently, and pressures on ethnic females to remain at home. Notes.

0785 Srole, Carole. " 'A Position that God Has Not Particularly Assigned to Men': The Feminization of Clerical Work, Boston, 1860–1915." Ph.D. dissertation, University of California, Los Angeles, 1984.

The shift to a corporate economy, the proliferation of typewriters, the availability of appropriately educated women, the lower wages expected by women, and the ease and safety of clerical compared to factory work all contributed to the feminization of clerical work. Changing family structures and social values underlay many women's decisions to become clerical workers. DAI 45:2631-A.

0786 Tannen, Michael B. "Women's Earnings, Skill, and Nativity in the Progressive Era." *Explorations in Economic History* 19 (1982): 128–55.

Women immigrants made more money in manufacturing for their level of skill than did native-born women. When retailing trades are factored in, the native women seem to have earned more, on average. Notes.

0787 Tax, Meredith. *The Rising of the Women: Feminist Solidarity and Class Conflict, 1880–1917*. New York: Monthly Review, 1980.

Women who were active in the socialist, feminist, and trade union movements between 1880 and World War I failed to develop lasting relationships across class lines. They could only succeed by working together. Notes, index.

0788 Tentler, Leslie W. *Wage-Earning Women: Industrial Work and Family Life in the United States, 1900–1930*. New York: Oxford University Press, 1979.

Women who worked did so, on the average, for six to eight years between when they left school and when they got married. Low wages, long hours, and hard work all reinforced the notion that domestic life was preferable, because women at least had some power within that separate sphere. Notes, bibliography, index.

IMMIGRANTS AND LABOR

See also Chapter 6, *Hispanic Americans and Asian Americans*, *Women*, and *Immigration*, and

Chapter 8, *Syndicalism, Socialism, Communism,* and *The Red Scare.*

0789 Asher, Robert. "Union Nativism and the Immigrant Response." *Labor History* 23 (1982): 325–48.

The nativism of organized labor applied to eastern and southern European immigrants restricted where the newcomers could be unionized. Leftist organizers of immigrant origins played a large part in bringing unions and immigrants together. Notes.

0790 Everling, Arthur C. "Tactics over Strategy in the United Mine Workers of America: Internal Politics and the Question of the Nationalization of the Mines, 1908–1923." Ph.D. dissertation, Pennsylvania State University, 1976.

The UMW was divided into two factions: conservatives who sought to convince mine owners that the union could discipline the work force and radicals who wanted political solutions to the problems of workers. Socialists failed to organize their forces well and did not gain strength until the mounting discontents of the post-World War I period. DAI 37:7269-A.

0791 Fenton, Edwin. "Italian Immigrants in the Stoneworkers' Union." *Labor History* 3 (1962): 188–207.

While many Italian immigrants did not join labor unions, they were not opposed to unionization. When they were treated as equals, as in the stoneworkers' union, they joined in large numbers. Notes.

0792 Lane, A. T. "American Trade Unions, Mass Immigration and the Literacy Test, 1900–1917." *Labor History* 25 (1984): 5–25.

Demands by the American Federation of Labor for literacy testing as a means of cutting back on immigration intensified during the period from 1906 to 1917 as a result of economic slowdowns. Notes.

0793 Mellinger, Philip J. "In the Beginnings of Modern Industrial Unionism in the Southwest: Labor Trouble among Unskilled Copper Workers, 1903–1917." Ph.D. dissertation, University of Chicago, 1978.

Unskilled copper workers, many of them immigrants from Mexico and Europe, fought for better wages, working conditions, and job opportunities. While the copper companies and the government broke the IWW and the Western Federation of Miners during World War I, workers did not lose all that they had fought for. DAI 39:6298-A.

0794 Pacyga, Dominic A. "Villages of Packinghouses and Steel Mills: The Polish Worker on Chicago's South Side, 1880 to 1921." Ph.D. dissertation, University of Illinois, Chicago Circle, 1981.

Thousands of Polish immigrants settled in south Chicago in the late nineteenth century. Primarily employed as unskilled labor in stockyards and steel mills, they maintained a powerful sense of tradition and community. By the Wilson era, they had begun to struggle for better living and working conditions. A steel strike in 1919 and a packinghouse strike in 1921 were both actively supported by Chicago's Polish community. DAI 42:4555-A.

0795 Reisler, Mark. *By the Sweat òf Their Brow: Mexican Immigrant Labor in the United States, 1900–1940.* Westport, CT: Greenwood, 1976.

Mexicans were attracted to the southwestern United States by employers seeking unskilled labor. Although immigration restriction legislation was passed in 1917, the needs of the war dictated that Mexicans be admitted temporarily. Notes, bibliography, index.

BLACK WORKERS

See also Chapter 6, *Blacks.*

0796 Finney, John D. "A Study of Negro Labor during and after World War I." Ph.D. dissertation, Georgetown University, 1967.

When America entered the war, a huge number of blacks migrated north to fill jobs in industry. However, neither white labor nor the government showed much concern for the black workers, and they failed to organize their own union. As a result, blacks were exploited and discriminated against. DAI 28:3107-A.

LABOR RADICALISM

See also Chapter 8, *Syndicalism, Socialism, Communism,* and *The Red Scare,* and Chapter 11, *Civil Liberties.*

0797 Dick, William M. *Labor and Socialism in America: The Gompers Era.* Port Washington, NY: Kennikat, 1972.

The division between organized labor and socialism was not an inevitable result of the American political climate. It came because of decisions made by labor leaders, notably by Samuel Gompers.

0798 Goldberg, Barry H. "Beyond Free Labor: Labor, Socialism and the Idea of Wage Slavery, 1890–1920." Ph.D. dissertation, Columbia University, 1979.

Wage slavery, a term used by trade unionists and socialists which implied that wage earners were no better off than slaves, is examined as an idea and for what it says about Progressive era radicals and labor theorists. DAI 40:1648-A.

0799 Grubbs, Frank L. "Council and Alliance Labor Propaganda, 1917–1919." *Labor History* 7 (1966): 156–72.

During World War I, the socialist-pacifist People's Council battled against a prowar propaganda arm of the AFL, but both organizations found themselves on the same losing side after the war when the government turned on labor. Notes.

0800 Laslett, John H. M. *Labor and the Left: A Study of Socialist and Radical Influences in the American Labor Movement, 1881–1924.* New York: Basic Books, 1970.

American exceptionalism is used to explain the failure of socialism in America, since workers made relatively high wages thanks to the efforts of pragmatic unions and lacked class consciousness. Notes, bibliography, index.

0801 Listikov, S. V. "The Socialist Movement's Ideological Influence on Trade Unions, 1916–1919" (in Russian). *Amerikanski Ezhegodnik* [USSR] (1981): 209–29.

Socialists exerted an antimilitarist influence on trade unions during World War I (in part because of the Bolshevik Revolution), but not much thereafter. Notes.

0802 Nash, Michael H. *Conflict and Accommodation: Coal Miners, Steel Workers, and Socialism, 1890–1920.* Westport, CT: Greenwood, 1982.

Steelworkers turned to the Socialist party during violent strikes, but returned to the Democratic and Republican parties when employers made significant concessions. Coal miners never found socialism appealing, since the United Mine Workers represented their demands effectively. Appendixes, notes, bibliography, index.

0803 O'Neill, William L. "Labor Radicalism and *The Masses*." *Labor History* 7 (1966): 197–208.

The complex relations between the leftist literary journal *The Masses* and labor radicals are examined.

PERSONALITIES

Samuel Gompers

0804 Gompers, Samuel. *Seventy Years of Life and Labor: An Autobiography.* Edited by Nick Salvatore. New Haven, CT: Yale University Press, 1984.

Gompers's massive autobiography, which includes material on the Wilson period, has been edited into readable form. Photographs, index.

0805 Greenbaum, Fred. "The Social Ideas of Samuel Gompers." *Labor History* 7 (1966): 35–61.

Gompers bequeathed pragmatism, a narrow conceptual framework of labor organization, voluntarism, and anti-intellectualism to the union movement. Notes.

0806 Levenstein, Harvey. "Samuel Gompers and the Mexican Labor Movement." *Wisconsin Magazine of History* 51 (1968): 155–63.

Gompers paid close attention to the union movement in Mexico—to keep it out of the hands of his rival, the IWW. Notes.

0807 Levine, Daniel. "Gompers and Racism: Strategy of Limited Objectives." *Mid-America* 43 (1961): 106–13.

Gompers opposed the campaign for racial equality, because he feared that it would interfere with bread-and-butter union issues such as higher wages and better working conditions. Notes.

0808 Livesay, Harold. *Samuel Gompers and Organized Labor in America.* Boston: Little, Brown, 1978.

Although Gompers did not trust Wilson, he supported him in 1912 and seemingly was rewarded with the Clayton Act. During the war this patriotic labor leader supported the president to the point of worship. Bibliography, index.

0809 Mandel, Bernard. *Samuel Gompers: A Biography.* Yellow Springs, OH: Antioch Press, 1963.

Gompers's place in the union movement is chronicled along with his relationship with Woodrow Wilson. Photographs, notes, index.

0810 ———. "Samuel Gompers and the Negro Workers, 1886–1914." *Journal of Negro History* 40 (1955): 34–60.

Gompers's views on blacks reflect his evolution from a labor agitator to a conservative bureaucrat. He began with relatively progressive views and retreated to acceptance of Jim Crow. Notes.

0811 Radosh, Ronald. "The Development of the Corporate Ideology of American Labor Leaders, 1914–1933." Ph.D. dissertation, University of Wisconsin, 1967.

Samuel Gompers wanted organized labor to be recognized as an economic and political partner to owners and management, promoting economic stability. He favored at-large congressional elections so that each economic, rather than geographic, sector would be represented. DAI 28:3121-A.

0812 Taft, Philip. *The A.F.L. in the Time of Gompers*. New York: Harper, 1957.

The founding of the AFL and the early years of the union are examined, including Gompers's rejection of socialism and industrial unionism. Notes, bibliography, index.

0813 Whittaker, William G. "Samuel Gompers, Labor, and the Mexican-American Crisis of 1916: The Carrizal Incident." *Labor History* 17 (1976): 551–67.

Gompers and the AFL acted as intermediaries between Mexico and the United States after American prisoners were taken at Carrizal in 1916. These efforts averted a war. Notes.

Others

See also Chapter 6, *Women*, and Chapter 8, *Syndicalism*, *Socialism*, and *Communism*.

0814 Ameringer, Oscar. *If You Don't Weaken: The Autobiography of Oscar Ameringer*. Norman: University of Oklahoma Press, 1983.

A German-born labor journalist and organizer for the Socialist party, Ameringer details life in prewar Oklahoma, wartime Milwaukee, and during the Red Scare. Index.

0815 Frost, Richard H. *The Mooney Case*. Stanford, CA: Stanford University Press, 1968.

Convicted of the dynamite bombing of a Preparedness Day parade, Tom Mooney spent over twenty years in jail but did not achieve full martyrdom in spite of his receiving an unfair trial in an atmosphere of near-hysteria. Photographs, notes, index.

0816 Howlett, Charles F. "Brockwood Labor College and Worker Commitment to Social Reform." *Mid-America* 61 (1979): 47–66.

In 1919, William Fincke founded a college to train labor leaders in reforms that went beyond the AFL's ideas. Notes.

0817 Mal'kov, V. L. "Tom Mooney: Prisoner of San Quentin" (in Russian). *Novaia i Noveishaia Istoriia* [USSR] (1975): 101-15.

Tom Mooney's career as a socialist and a labor organizer is examined along with his trial for setting off a deadly explosion in San Francisco in 1916. Notes.

UNIONS

Mill Workers

0818 Carlton, David L. "Mill and Town: The Cotton Mill Workers and the Middle Class in South Carolina, 1880–1920." Ph.D. dissertation, Yale University, 1977.

Two new groups emerged in South Carolina between 1880 and 1920: "town people," who were middle-class businessmen and professionals, and "mill people," white wage earners working in factories. Child labor laws and educational reforms were Progressive measures aimed at exposing the children of mill people to middle-class socialization. DAI 38:3676-A.

Miners

0819 Byrkit, James W. *Forging the Copper Collar: Arizona's Labor-Management War of 1901–1920*. Tucson: University of Arizona Press, 1982.

As Arizona evolved from a frontier area to an industrial center during the Progressive era, labor and management clashed repeatedly, a struggle climaxed by the Bisbee deportations of 1917. Notes, bibliography, index.

0820 Kluger, James R. *The Clifton-Morenci Strike: Labor Difficulty in Arizona 1915–1916*. Tucson: University of Arizona Press, 1970.

The strike of Mexican and Indian copper miners was not a violent one. The strikers repudiated the Western Federation of Miners in return for specific concessions. Photographs, notes, bibliography, index.

0821 Lunt, Richard D. *Law and Order vs. the Miners: West Virginia, 1907–1933*. Hamden, CT: Archon, 1979.

The struggle of West Virginia miners to unionize is examined. The mine owners had the power of the law on their side, especially after

World War I, when antiradicalism made effective organization even more difficult. Notes, bibliography, index.

0822 Singer, Alan J. " 'Which Side Are You On?': Ideological Conflict in the United Mine Workers of America, 1919–1928." Ph.D. dissertation, Rutgers University, 1982.

After World War I, Communists, Progressives, professional union organizers, and coal miners contributed to the formation of the United Mine Workers of America. DAI 43: 1268-A.

Steelworkers
See also Chapter 8, *The Red Scare.*

0823 Brody, David. *Labor in Crisis: The Steel Strike of 1919.* Philadelphia: Lippincott, 1965.

Labor leaders seeking to organize the steel industry faced a hostile and powerful coalition of interests bent on stopping them by any means. Notes, bibliography, index.

0824 ———. *Steelworkers in America: The Nonunion Era.* Cambridge, MA: Harvard University Press, 1960.

During the Progressive era scientific management took power away from skilled workers, and wages declined as a result. Control of the workplace was at stake in the subsequent battles between labor and management, including the great steel strike of 1919. Notes, bibliography, index.

Others
See also *Samuel Gompers*, above, Chapter 6, *Women*, and Chapter 8, *Syndicalism, Socialism, Communism*, and *The Red Scare.*

0825 Cooper, Patricia A. "From Hand Craft to Mass Production: Men, Women and Work Culture in American Cigar Factories, 1900–1919." Ph.D. dissertation, University of Maryland, 1981.

Some cigar manufacturers employed skilled, unionized craftsmen, while others used less-skilled, non-union women. Competitiveness between the two groups was set aside during World War I, when labor shortages gave labor the upper hand. Although some gains were made by the united workers, success was short-lived, because in 1919 new technology began to eclipse the craft of hand rolling cigars. DAI 43:241-A.

0826 ———. "The 'Traveling Fraternity': Union Cigar Makers and Geographic Mobility, 1900–1919." *Journal of Social History* 17 (1983): 127–38.

Cigar makers followed the market, going from one job to another with the help and understanding of their unions. Notes.

0827 Kimeldorf, Howard. "Working Class Culture, Occupational Recruitment, and Union Politics." *Social Forces* 64 (1985): 359–76.

Longshoremen's unions on the west coast were radical, while those on the east coast were conservative. This was due to the different political cultures in different ideological communities prior to World War I.

0828 Murphy, Marjorie. "From Artisan to Semi-Professional: White Collar Unions among Chicago Public School Teachers, 1870–1930." Ph.D. dissertation, University of California, Davis, 1981.

The Loeb rule of 1915 severed the long-standing bonds between teachers and trade unions. The National Education Association, primarily concerned with professionalizing teaching, became the only organized agency dealing with grievances. DAI 42:3721-A.

0829 Russell, Jack. "The Coming of the Line: The Ford Highland Park Plant, 1910–1914." *Radical America* 12 (1978): 28–45.

When the continuous assembly line came to Ford's huge Highland Park factory, it resulted in worker discontent and high turnovers, factors which led Henry Ford to implement the five-dollar day in 1914. Notes.

STRIKES

See also Chapter 8, *Syndicalism* and *The Red Scare*, and Chapter 11, *Civil Liberties.*

0830 Bucki, Cecelia F. "Dilution and Craft Tradition: Bridgeport, Connecticut Munitions Workers: 1915–1919." *Social Science History* 4 (1980): 105–24.

Skilled workers in Bridgeport responded with strikes to technological innovations that downgraded their status and wages. Notes.

0831 Eklund, Monica. "Massacre at Ludlow." *Southwest Economy and Society* 4 (1978): 21–30.

The Ludlow coal miners' strike of 1913–14 led to tragedy, when the National Guard and associated goons destroyed an encampment of strikers, killing many women and children.

0832 Ensley, Phillip C. "The Interchurch World Movement and the Steel Strike of 1919." *Labor History* 13 (1972): 217–30.

The Interchurch World Movement, having failed to mediate the steel strike, probed the causes of labor unrest. Business withdrew support from the movement following several critical reports. Notes.

0833 Ernst, Eldon G. "The Interchurch World Movement and the Great Steel Strike of 1919–1920." *Church History* 39 (1970): 212–23.

The Interchurch World Movement hoped to promote a solution to the angry labor-management confrontations of the postwar period through the social gospel. The pro-labor reports it published failed to ignite an active movement. Notes.

0834 Goldberg, David J. "Immigrants, Intellectuals and Industrial Unions: The 1919 Textile Strikes and the Experience of the Amalgamated Textile Workers of America in Passaic and Paterson, New Jersey, and Lawrence, Massachusetts." Ph.D. dissertation, Columbia University, 1984.

The Amalgamated Textile Workers of America sought to organize an ethnically and ideologically diverse group of workers into one powerful union. The group threw its greatest efforts into the strikes in Passaic and Paterson, New Jersey, and Lawrence, Massachusetts. DAI 45:3198-A.

0835 Graham, John. "Upton Sinclair and the Ludlow Massacre." *Colorado Quarterly* 21 (1972): 55–67.

Sinclair responded to the Ludlow massacre of striking miners in 1914 by picketing the offices of John D. Rockefeller in New York, where he was jailed. His book *King Coal* is based on his research of the coal strike.

0836 Montgomery, David. "Immigrants, Industrial Unions, and Social Reconstruction in the United States, 1916–1923." *Labour* [Canada] (1984): 101–13.

The years 1916 to 1922 witnessed the biggest wave of work stoppages in American history owing to the changing nature of collective capitalism and the willingness of workers to strike for their demands.

0837 Tobin, Eugene M. "Direct Action and Conscience: The 1913 Paterson Strike as an Example of the Relationship between Labor Radicals and Liberals." *Labor History* 20 (1979): 73–88.

Labor radicals and liberals formed an uneasy alliance in the wake of judicial high-handedness. Notes.

LOCAL AND REGIONAL STUDIES

See also Chapter 8, *The Red Scare* and *Local and Regional Studies.*

0838 Arnold, Dexter P. " 'A Row of Bricks': Worker Activism in the Merrimack Valley Textile Industry, 1912–1922." Ph.D. dissertation, University of Wisconsin, Madison, 1985.

Workers in Boston-area mill towns were involved in a number of strikes in the ten-year period under examination, the most famous of which occurred in Lawrence. Workers learned that to win considerable changes in the workplace they had to whip up mass protests and build solid unions. DAI 46:504-A.

0839 Cornford, Daniel A. "Lumber, Labor and Community in Humboldt County, California, 1850–1920." Ph.D. dissertation, University of California, Santa Barbara, 1983.

The AFL edged out the IWW in unionizing Humboldt county lumber workers. Employers used techniques such as scientific management and welfare capitalism to keep the union on the defensive. DAI 45:608-A.

0840 Dubofsky, Melvyn. "Organized Labor and the Immigrant in New York City, 1900–1918." *Labor History* 2 (1961): 182–201.

Gompers and the AFL fought against socialist unions in the needle trades, whose workers were primarily immigrants. Notes.

0841 ———. *When Workers Organize: New York City in the Progressive Era.* Amherst: University of Massachusetts Press, 1968.

Union activists concentrated on organization rather than on working for reform legislation. The war helped the union movement, but it did not bring workers either security or status. Notes, bibliography, index.

0842 Greenberg, Jaclyn. "Industry in the Garden: A Social History of the Canning Industry and Cannery Workers in the Santa Clara Valley, California, 1870–1920." Ph.D. dissertation, University of California, Los Angeles, 1985.

The motives and attitudes of women cannery workers changed as their community changed and as factory working conditions deteriorated while production increased. Katherine Edson of the Industrial Welfare Commission tried to solve some of the problems, but the workers conducted several strikes from 1917 to 1919. DAI 46:1060-A.

0843 Havira, Barbara S. "Factories and Workers in Three Michigan Towns: 1880–1920." Ph.D. dissertation, Michigan State University, 1986.

Small-town factories and labor relations differed in character from their big-city counterparts. Continual face-to-face contact between owners and labor combined with awareness of mutual dependence to reduce conflicts and unionization. DAI 47:3543-A.

0844 Lindner, Barbara J. "Working-Class Culture and Unionization in North La Crosse, Wisconsin." Ph.D. dissertation, Bowling Green State University, 1983.

An unsuccessful 1915 unionizing attempt was affected by the ethnicity, class, and skill levels of rubber mill workers. DAI 44: 2554-A.

0845 Long, Durward. "The Open-Closed Shop Battle in Tampa's Cigar Industry, 1919–1921." *Florida Historical Quarterly* 47 (1968): 101–21.

Inflation and consequent cost-of-living increases led Tampa cigar factory hands to ask for wage hikes. Efforts to break the cigar makers' unions were followed by strikes which failed to prevent open shops. Notes.

0846 Maroney, James C. "Organized Labor in Texas." Ph.D. dissertation, University of Houston, 1975.

Organized labor in Texas, primarily skilled craftsmen, rejected both the conservatism of the AFL and the radicalism of the IWW and the Western Federation of Miners. Aspiring to middle-class status, the union men embraced the Progressive movement and were thoroughgoing racists. DAI 36:4713-A.

0847 Saxton, Alexander. "San Francisco Labor and the Populist and Progressive Insurgencies." *Pacific Historical Review* 34 (1965): 421–38.

San Francisco's labor unions supported the Progressive movement, adding an ethnic, working-class element to the reform thrust. Notes.

0848 Schwieder, Dorothy A. "A Social and Economic Study of Iowa's Coal Mining Population, 1895–1925." Ph.D. dissertation, University of Iowa, 1981.

Immigrants were drawn to coal mining as ready employment, despite poor living and working conditions. Coal camps typically lacked much social or religious life, and jobs were not secure. The mine workers' strong union was the largest in Iowa. DAI 42:2266.

0849 Tripp, Joseph F. "Progressive Labor Laws in Washington State (1900–1925)." Ph.D. dissertation, University of Washington, 1973.

Washington state enacted many Progressive labor laws between 1900 and 1925, including child labor laws, workmen's compensation, and a minimum wage for women. Humanitarian concerns and the goal of ending class antagonisms were the primary motives for the pioneering labor statutes. DAI 34:5084-A.

0850 Weber, Debra A. "The Struggle for Stability and Control in the Cotton Fields of California: Class Relations in Agriculture, 1919–1942." Ph.D. dissertation, University of California, Los Angeles, 1986.

Beginning in 1919, specialized cotton farms allowed the creation of stable communities of cotton workers. Most were Mexican and used the Mexican Revolution as a model for their labor struggles. DAI 47:2293-A.

0851 White, William T. "A History of Railroad Workers in the Pacific Northwest, 1883–1934." Ph.D. dissertation, University of Washington, 1981.

During the Wilson era, skilled railway workers in the Northwest benefited from national labor successes, particularly the Adamson act of 1916. Shop craft workers joined the American Federation of Labor, while oppressive unskilled railroad jobs went largely to nonunionized immigrants. DAI 42:5224-A.

0852 Yellowitz, Irwin. *Labor and the Progressive Movement in New York State, 1897–1916.* Ithaca, NY: Cornell University Press, 1965.

Organized labor was an integral part of the Progressive movement in New York. The impulse for reform began to fade in 1914, long before America went to war. Notes, bibliography, index.

5

Domestic Affairs: Arts and Literature, Health, Society and Popular Culture, Science and Technology, and Environment

The years of the Wilson presidency were marked by often-bitter controversies in the arts, culture, and the sciences and by tragedy in the field of health care. It was also a time when educators and religious leaders continued to struggle with the problem of modernization and when the national pastime, baseball, faced a crisis that mirrored the commotion of Wilson's last years in office.

Frank Lloyd Wright was the dominant personality in the field of architecture. See Volume III of William Jordy's study *American Buildings and Their Architects* (#0856) for an overview of the period as well as more specialized works by H. Allen Brooks, *The Prairie School: Frank Lloyd Wright and His Midwest Contemporaries* (#0853), and Leonard K. Eaton, *Two Chicago Architects and Their Clients: Frank Lloyd Wright and Howard Van Doren Shaw* (#0854).

On the deep divisions in American culture, see Peter Conn, *The Divided Mind: Ideology and Imagination in America, 1898–1917* (#0871). Maxwell Geismar, *The Last of the Provincials: The American Novel, 1915–1925: H. L. Mencken, Sinclair Lewis, Willa Cather, Sherwood Anderson, F. Scott Fitzgerald* (#0881), analyzes how novelists reflected the social transformation of the period.

Films took on added importance during the Wilson years. See Lay May, *Screening Out

the Past: The Birth of Mass Culture and the Motion Picture Industry* (#0925). The work of the controversial and brilliant D. W. Griffith is examined in a number of articles, among them John Hope Franklin, *"Birth of a Nation: Propaganda as History"* (#0915). For the role of movies in wartime, see Michael T. Isenberg, *War on Film: The American Cinema and World War I, 1914–1941* (#0920).

The shift away from realism in art reflected the changing social values of the period. See Milton Brown, *American Painting from the Armory Show to the Depression* (#0947); Abraham A. Davidson, *Early American Modernist Painting, 1910–1935* (#0949); and Lloyd Goodrich, *Pioneers of Modern Art in America: The Decade of the Armory Show, 1910–1920* (#0950).

For an excellent overview of the conflict among intellectuals, see Henry May, *The End of American Innocence: A Study of the First Years of Our Own Time, 1912–1917* (#0983). Among the many works on cultural radicalism are Edward Abrahams, *The Lyrical Left: Randolph Bourne, Alfred Stieglitz, and the Origins of Cultural Radicalism in America* (#0959); Bruce Clayton, *Forgotten Prophet: The Life of Randolph Bourne* (#0963); Leslie Fishbein, *Rebels in Bohemia: The Radicals of "The Masses," 1911–1917* (#0969); and Robert E. Humphrey, *Children of Fantasy: The First Rebels *of Greenwich Village* (#0977). Pragmatism is examined by George Dykhuizen, *The Life and Mind of John Dewey* (#0968), and David Marcell, *Progress and Pragmatism: James, Dewey, Beard, and the American Idea of Progress* (#0981).

The influenza pandemic of 1918–19, which killed over twenty million people, was a catastrophic event overshadowed by the Great War. See Alfred W. Crosby, Jr., *Epidemic and Peace* (#1015). James G. Burrow, *Organized Medicine in the Progressive Era: The Move toward Monopoly* (#1011), and Ronald L. Numbers, *Almost Persuaded: American Physicians and Compulsory Health Insurance, 1912–1920* (#1028), both examine the medical profession. The impact of Freudianism is analyzed by John C. Burnham, *Psychoanalysis and American Medicine, 1894–1918: Medicine, Science, and Culture* (#1009), and Nathan G. Hale, Jr., *Freud and the Americans: The Beginnings of Psychoanalysis in the United States, 1876–1917* (#1019).

Progressive reformers expended considerable energy on behalf of children. See LeRoy Ashby, *Saving the Waifs: Reformers and Dependent Children* (#1062); Dominick Cavallo, *Muscles and Morals: Organized Playgrounds and Urban Reform, 1880–1920* (#1070); and Susan Tiffin, *In Whose Best Interest? Child Welfare Reform in the Progressive Era* (#1107).

Social change produced controversy in American churches during the Wilson years. For an overview, see William R. Hutchison, *The Modernist Impulse in American Protestantism* (#1136). The Catholic response to modernism is examined by Joseph M. McShane, *"Sufficiently Radical": Catholicism, Progressivism, and the Bishop's Program of 1919* (#1148). William G. McLoughlin, Jr., *Billy Sunday Was His Real Name* (#1146), contributes a biography of the popular fundamentalist.

Baseball was the most popular spectator sport in America during Wilson's time. Steven A. Riess, *Touching Base: Professional Baseball and American Culture in the Progressive Era* (#1183), explains the relationship between the game and Progressive cultural ideology. Eliot Asinof, *Eight Men Out* (#1170), chronicles the scandal of 1919 in which members of the Chicago White Sox were paid by gamblers to lose the World Series—and almost destroyed American faith in professional sport. The life of Jack Johnson, the great black boxing champion, is examined by Al-Tony Gilmore, *Bad Nigger! The National Impact of Jack Johnson* (#1173).

The spheres of science and politics often blurred together during the Progressive era. Samuel Haber, *Efficiency and Uplift: Scientific*

Management in the Progressive Era, 1890–1920 (#1200), examines how reformers used scientific management to effect social control. Engineers were caught between the impulse to use their expertise for the good of society and the needs of business. See Edwin T. Layton, Jr., *The Revolt of the Engineers: Social Responsibility and the American Engineering Profession* (#1207).

Concern over the environment was an important part of the Progressive reform thrust. Samuel P. Hays, *Conservation and the Gospel of Efficiency: The Progressive Conservation Movement, 1890–1920* (#1220), presents an insightful overview. For the origins of the National Park Service, see Horace M. Albright and Robert Cahn, *The Birth of the National Park Service: The Founding Years, 1913–33* (#1215).

Arts and Literature

ARCHITECTURE

0853 Brooks, H. Allen. *The Prairie School: Frank Lloyd Wright and His Midwest Contemporaries*. Toronto: University of Toronto Press, 1972.

The Prairie School of architecture peaked in the years before World War I, although it continued afterward. The school spurned ornamentation, preferring simple, precise lines and flat roofs. Brooks describes the movement's architects and buildings as well as its philosophy. Photographs, bibliography, index.

0854 Eaton, Leonard K. *Two Chicago Architects and Their Clients: Frank Lloyd Wright and Howard Van Doren Shaw*. Cambridge, MA: MIT Press, 1969.

Wright's revolutionary architectural style and Shaw's conservative one attracted slightly different groups of clients. Wright's clients were generally less conventional, less educated, less wealthy, and less socially active. Photographs, notes, appendix, bibliography, index.

0855 Engel, Martin. "Frank Lloyd Wright and Cubism: A Study in Ambiguity." *American Quarterly* 19 (1967): 24–38.

Wright is compared with the cubists because they both successfully synthesized the functional and the romantic. Photographs, floor plans, and a reproduction of *The Musician's Table* are included as evidence for the comparison.

0856 Jordy, William H. *American Buildings and Their Architects.* Vol. III, *Progressive and Academic Ideals at the Turn of the Twentieth Century.* Garden City, NY: Doubleday, 1972.

The author explores the works and thought of the most influential Progressive architects between 1880 and World War I.

0857 Kaufman, Edgar, Jr. "Crisis and Creativity: Frank Lloyd Wright, 1904–1914." *Journal of the Society of Architectural Historians* 25 (1966): 292–96.

A series of personal tragedies between 1908 and 1914, including marital strife, a house fire, and public criticism of his work, led Wright to pursue the Tokyo Imperial Hotel project with great zeal.

THEATER

0858 Auster, Albert. "Chamber of Diamonds and Delight: Actresses, Suffragists and Feminists in the American Theater, 1890–1920." Ph.D. dissertation, State University of New York, Stony Brook, 1981.

Sometimes inadvertently, women in theater furthered female awareness of both their plight and their possibilities for emancipation. Relationships between feminists and actresses are explored, focusing on Mary Shaw, Lillian Russell, and Ethel Barrymore. DAI 42:4552-A.

0859 Bigsby, C. W. E. *A Critical Introduction to Twentieth Century American Drama.* Vol. I, *1900–1940.* New York: Cambridge University Press, 1982.

Playwrights and directors began to dominate actors in twentieth-century American drama. Theater groups such as the Living Newspaper and the Provincetown Players and playwrights including Eugene O'Neill, Thornton Wilder, Lillian Hellman, and Clifford Odets are examined.

0860 Bloomfield, Maxwell. "Muckraking and the American Stage: The Emergence of Realism, 1905–1917." *South Atlantic Quarterly* 66 (1967): 165–78.

Journalistic muckraking led to theatrical realism, with reform as the underlying message. Notes.

0861 Gottlieb, Lois C. "The Double Standard Debate in Early 20th Century American Drama." *Michigan Academician* 7 (1975): 441–52.

Three plays from the Progressive era dealing with the double standard in male-female relations are analyzed.

0862 Harap, Louis. "Jews in American Drama." *American Jewish Archives* 36 (1984): 136–51.

Jews were most often portrayed as stereotypical clowns in American drama at the turn of the century, but by the end of the Progressive era they were being taken seriously. Notes.

0863 Henderson, Jerry. "Nashville in the Decline of Southern Legitimate Theatre during the Beginning of the Twentieth Century." *Southern Speech Journal* 29 (1963): 26–33.

By 1918 vaudeville and movies had all but killed legitimate theater as a cultural force in Nashville. Notes.

0864 Sarlos, Robert K. "Dionysos in 1915: A Pioneer Theatre Collective." *Theatre Research International* [Great Britain] 3 (1977): 33–53.

The Provincetown Players, founded by George Cook, rotated the jobs of playwrights, actors, and stagehands, the first company to practice this collectivism.

LITERATURE

0865 Aaron, Daniel. *Writers on the Left: Episodes in American Literary Communism.* New York: Harcourt, Brace and World, 1961.

After World War I, alienated and radical writers including Floyd Dell and Max Eastman were drawn to communism both as an ideal and as it was practiced in Russia. Notes, index.

0866 Alexander, A. John. "The First World War in American Thought." Ph.D. dissertation, American University, 1951.

Examining ideas about World War I held by important groups up to 1919, the author finds consistency in Catholic attitudes and changing perceptions among Protestants. The split between John Dewey and Randolph Bourne is examined, along with socialist attitudes. The ideas of historians are covered in detail as well. DAI 36:468-A.

0867 Alexander, Ruth A. "Midwest Main Street Literature: Symbol of Conformity." *Rocky Mountain Social Science Journal* 5 (1968): 1–12.

Midwest Main Street literature does not necessarily present an accurate portrayal of life as it was, because many writers were more concerned with the theme of conformity than with historical realism. Notes.

0868 Anderson, Hilton. "Edith Wharton and the Vulgar American." *Southern Quarterly* 7 (1968): 17–22.

Wharton includes many vulgar American characters in her Progressive-era novels. She especially loathed vulgar American tourists. Notes.

0869 Baker, John D. "John Dos Passos, Chronicler of the American Left." Ph.D. dissertation, Case Western Reserve University, 1971.

The early novels of John Dos Passos are an important source of social history. A sensitive observer, he wrote of the deeds, motives, and lives of American radicals of all stripes. DAI 32:3191-A.

0870 Blake, Casey N. "Beloved Community: The Cultural Criticism of Randolph Bourne, Van Wyck Brooks, Waldo Frank, and Lewis Mumford." Ph.D. dissertation, University of Rochester, 1987.

The four leading "young American" critics were influenced by pragmatism and by the English romantic tradition of cultural criticism. Preoccupied with self, they hoped to merge themselves into their surroundings through culture. DAI 48:206-A.

0871 Conn, Peter. *The Divided Mind: Ideology and Imagination in America, 1898–1917*. New York: Cambridge University Press, 1983.

American culture between 1898 and 1917 was characterized by a deeply divided, revolutionary-counterrevolutionary ideology. Conn discusses this schism in light of various writers and other innovators including Jack London, Kate Chopin, Edith Wharton, Booker T. Washington, Frank Lloyd Wright, and Alfred Stieglitz. Illustrations, notes, index.

0872 Connor, James R. "Pen and Sword: World War I Novels in America." Ph.D. dissertation, University of Wisconsin, 1961.

Between 1916 and 1922, novels on World War I were generally patriotic, both reflecting and propagating the theory that it was a just war against barbarism. After 1922, the war was perceived more as tragedy. Throughout, some novelists treated the war as mere adventure. DAI 21:3075.

0873 Cooperman, Stanley. *World War I and the American Novel*. Baltimore, MD: Johns Hopkins University Press, 1967.

The psychological and cultural impact of World War I reverberated in American novels for decades. Hemingway, e.e. cummings, Faulkner, Willa Cather, and Archibald MacLeish were all affected. Notes, bibliography, index.

0874 Crowe, M. Karen. "Southern Horizons: The Autobiography of Thomas Dixon: A Critical Edition." Ph.D. dissertation, New York University, 1982.

Dixon wrote *The Clansman* as part of a Reconstruction trilogy that became an enormously influential film of the Wilson era. The North Carolina lawyer, legislator, minister, and writer counted Wilson as an acquaintance. DAI 43:800-A.

0875 Dillon, Richard T. "Some Sources for Faulkner's Version of the First Air War." *American Literature* 44 (1973): 629–37.

William Faulkner's writings on aerial combat in World War I may well have been inspired by Elliot White Springs and James Warner Bellah.

0876 Dunkel, William P. "Between Two Worlds: Max Eastman, Floyd Dell, John Reed, Randolph Bourne, and the Revolt against the Genteel Tradition." Ph.D. dissertation, Lehigh University, 1976.

Progressive-era cultural rebels denounced the genteel tradition as bankrupt. Groping toward a new philosophy, they embraced socialism, science, pragmatism, Progressive education, high living, feminism, and modern art. While they helped to destroy the old traditions, they were not completely prepared to accept the sweeping changes brought about by the modern world. DAI 37:7269-A.

0877 Erisman, Fred. "L. Frank Baum and the Progressive Dilemma." *American Quarterly* 20 (1968): 616–23.

Baum's writings early in the Progressive period reflect his enthusiasm for the reform movement, but growing disenchantment led him to retreat into fantasy stories based on traditional values. Notes.

0878 Fenton, Charles A. "A Literary Fracture of World War I." *American Quarterly* 12 (1960): 119–32.

Looking at the members of the American Academy of Arts and Letters, the author finds that almost all of them were supporters of the Allies at the outset of World War I, and many were willing to criticize Wilson for his attempted neutrality. Notes.

0879 Fine, David M. "Attitudes toward Acculturation in the English Fiction of the Jewish Immigrant, 1900–1917." *American Jewish Historical Quarterly* 63 (1973): 45–56.

Many immigrant novelists wrote with the assumption that assimilation into WASP culture was part of the Americanization process. Sidney Nyburg and Abraham Cahan show how this process resulted in guilt and boredom.

0880 Fretz, Lewis A. "Upton Sinclair and World War I." *Political Science* 25 (1973): 2–12.

While he had long decried capitalist wars, Sinclair supported American entry into the European war as necessary to create a new world. His postwar novel *Jimmie Higgins* shows his disillusionment with that goal. Notes.

0881 Geismar, Maxwell. *The Last of the Provincials: The American Novel, 1915–1925: H. L. Mencken, Sinclair Lewis, Willa Cather, Sherwood Anderson, F. Scott Fitzgerald.* Boston: Houghton Mifflin, 1947.

Each novelist in the title both illuminates and is illuminated by the social transformation of the period—the ascendancy of the industrialized city over traditional rural life. Appendix, bibliography, index.

0882 Hamblen, Abigail A. "Edith Wharton in New England." *New England Quarterly* 38 (1965): 239–44.

Wharton's novels set in New England, *Ethan Frome* (1911) and *Summer* (1917), reflect her status as an outsider to the region, as they depict residents in a negative light.

0883 Hernandez, Pelayo H. "North America Seen by Ramón Pérez de Ayala and Julio Camba" (in Spanish). *Cuadernos Hispanoamericanos* [Spain] (1981): 71–80.

The Spanish writers Pérez and Camba's impressions of their extended visits to the United States during Wilson's tenure as president comment on American materialism, art, science, sexuality, humor, women, classes, and the importance of money.

0884 Hofstadter, Richard. *The Progressive Historians: Turner, Beard, Parrington.* New York: Knopf, 1968.

American historiography at the beginning of the Progressive era is examined, and the effects of the reform impulse on leading historians are analyzed. Notes, bibliography, index.

0885 Hoopes, James E. "Van Wyck Brooks: His Early Life and Work." Ph.D. dissertation, Johns Hopkins University, 1973.

Brooks theorized about creating an American cultural community through socialism in his quest for a viable center or middle ground in American life. DAI 36:7590-A.

0886 Horlacher, Friedrich W. "Economics and the Novel: Henry George and Robert Herrick." *New England Quarterly* 55 (1982): 416–31.

Charges that Robert Herrick's 1914 novel *Clark's Field* was based on the work of Henry George are not valid. This novel of social criticism leaves George far behind. Notes.

0887 Joost, Nicholas. *Years of Transition, "The Dial," 1912–1920.* New York: Barre Publishers, 1967.

The Dial was a conservative cultural publication which became more tolerant of radicalism until World War I. Thorstein Veblen's advocacy of a revolution to technocracy almost plunged the publication into financial ruin. Photographs, notes, index.

0888 Kelley, Karol L. "Self-Made Man? True Woman? Historical Approaches to the Creation of American Success Models." Ph.D. dissertation, Bowling Green State University, 1981.

Using a computer and viewing literature as "a body of rhetoric presenting certain sexually political ideals and values which centered around a main character," novels popular between 1850 and 1920 are analyzed. Unlike other studies of the masculine and feminine ideal, this approach finds little difference between traits of successful fictional men and women. DAI 42:346-A.

0889 Kwiat, Joseph J. "Theodore Dreiser's Creative Quest: Early 'Philosophical' Beliefs and Artistic Values." *Arizona Quarterly* 37 (1981): 265–74.

Dreiser was an important novelist whose writings reflected the trauma and confusion of a changing America during and after the Progressive era. Notes.

0890 Langlois, Karen S. "A Search for Significance: Mary Austin: The New York Years." Ph.D. dissertation, Claremont Graduate School, 1987.

Known primarily as a western writer, Mary Austin spent the years from 1910 to 1920 in New York. She worked as a playwright and became somewhat involved in politics, particularly the suffrage movement. However, she had numerous conflicts with publishers and disliked New York critics, and she ultimately decided to return to the West. DAI 47:4173-A.

0891 Lenz, William E. "*The Leatherwood God*: William Dean Howells' Confidence Man." *Old Northwest* 8 (1982): 119–30.

Howells's 1916 novel *The Leatherwood God* centers around an evangelical confidence man, a symbol of both the distrust and the optimism felt on the western frontier.

0892 Love, Glen A. "*Winesburg, Ohio* and the Rhetoric of Silence." *American Literature* 40 (1968): 38–57.

Sherwood Anderson's *Winesburg, Ohio*, written in 1919, uses silence to symbolize the loss of individualism in the industrial age. Notes.

0893 Lynn, Kenneth S. "Hemingway's Private War." *Commentary* 72 (1981): 24–33.

World War I had a major impact on the life of Ernest Hemingway, who wrote about it brilliantly in the 1920s.

0894 O'Brien, Sharon. "'The Thing Not Named': Willa Cather as a Lesbian Writer." *Signs* 9 (1984): 576–99.

There is more to lesbianism than sex preference. Cather's published writings masked her lesbianism at a time when such a thing was considered morally wrong. Notes.

0895 Oehlschaeger, Fritz H. "Civilization as Emasculation: The Threatening Role of Women in the Frontier Fiction of Harold Bell Wright and Zane Grey." *Midwest Quarterly* 22 (1981): 346–60.

The western novels of Wright and Grey equate women with civilization, two emasculating forces threatening their masculine heroes. Both authors compared the ideal woman with a man's tame horse.

0896 O'Neill, William L., ed. *Echoes of Revolt: "The Masses," 1911–1917*. Chicago: Quadrangle, 1966.

The art, articles, and poems of the radical magazine *The Masses* selected for this volume include the works of Max Eastman, Floyd Dell, Sherwood Anderson, John Reed, Art Young, and many others. Illustrations.

0897 Plante, Patricia R. "Edith Wharton and the Invading Goths." *Midcontinent American Studies Journal* 5 (1962): 18–23.

Wharton's World War I era novels are examined for the effects they had on American and French culture.

0898 Potter, Hugh. "Paul Rosenfeld: Criticism and Prophecy." *American Quarterly* 22 (1970): 82–94.

An art and literary critic, Paul Rosenfeld was a major contributor to the literary magazine *The Seven Arts*, published briefly in 1916–17. The arts, he believed, enhanced national life as well as expressed it. Notes.

0899 San Juan, Epifanio, Jr. "Vision and Reality: A Reconsideration of Sherwood Anderson's *Winesburg, Ohio*." *American Literature* 35 (1963): 137–55.

Anderson's 1919 novel *Winesburg, Ohio* influenced literature through its author's craftsmanship. Notes.

0900 Schmidt, Peter. "Wilderness Novels in the Progressive Era." *Journal of Popular Culture* 3 (1969): 72–90.

Nature played a prominent part in the novels of many Progressive writers, including Jack London, although the wilderness portrayed was peaceful and passive. Notes.

0901 Seavey, Ormond. "D. H. Lawrence and 'The First Dummy American.'" *Georgia Review* 39 (1985): 113–28.

Lawrence wrote about the America he so disliked, focusing on Benjamin Franklin as a symbol of an optimism and belief in hard work that he did not share.

0902 Sedgwick, Ellery, III. "The American Genteel Tradition in the Early Twentieth Century." *American Studies* 25 (1984): 49–67.

The *Atlantic Monthly* typified the genteel tradition in the years 1909–1919. Mostly written by women, the magazine's tone was liberal and Progressive, nostalgic about the past, hostile to much of the present, and not optimistic about the future of culture. Notes.

0903 Singer, David. "David Levinsky's Fall: A Note on the Liebman Thesis." *American Quarterly* 19 (1967): 696–706.

East European Jewish immigrants were already being secularized along ethnic lines at the expense of their religious faith by the time they reached America, a point made in Abraham

Cahan's 1917 novel *The Rise of David Levinsky*. Notes.

0904　Springer, Haskell S. "*The Leatherwood God*: From Narrative to Novel." *Ohio History* 74 (1965): 191–202.

　　William Dean Howells's last novel, *The Leatherwood God*, which came out in 1918, was based on another work by the same name published fifty years earlier.

0905　Storey, James B. "The Popular Novel and Culture in the Progressive Era." Ph.D. dissertation, University of Oklahoma, 1971.

　　Philosophers and popular culture wrestled with similar issues during the Progressive era, including the role of big business in America, the failings of religion, the new status of women, and basic social injustices. Novels reveal a deep disenchantment with the materialism and business values of the age. Still, optimism over the probability of future solutions reigned in the end. DAI 32:6355-A.

0906　Walsh, Jeffrey. *American War Literature 1914 to Vietnam*. New York: St. Martin's Press, 1982.

　　The experience of World War I created its own tradition of war fiction and poetry in the greater context of twentieth-century American war literature. Notes, index.

0907　Warner, Richard H. "A Contemporary Sketch of Jack London." *American Literature* 38 (1966): 376–80.

　　A brief description of Jack London written by Marshall Bond in 1916 is reproduced. It notes London's fondness for socialism, the Klondike, and his hometown of Oakland, California.

0908　Warren, Robert Penn. "Homage to Theodore Dreiser on the Centenary of His Birth." *Southern Review* 7 (1971): 345–410.

　　Dreiser's greatness is examined along with the environment that influenced him. His writings are compared and contrasted with those of other writers of the Progressive period.

0909　Wertheim, Arthur F. " 'The Fiddles Are Tuning': The Little Renaissance in New York City, 1908–1917." Ph.D. dissertation, New York University, 1970.

　　New York's artistic and literary renaissance is examined, including the socialist and anarchist writers, the apolitical iconoclasts, the cultural nationalists, and the modernists. World War I sent the movement into a rapid downward spiral but paved the way for a new movement in the 1920s. DAI 32:5167-A.

0910　West, Michael D. "Sherwood Anderson's Triumph: 'The Egg.' " *American Quarterly* 20 (1968): 675–93.

　　"The Egg," a Sherwood Anderson short story written in 1918, is seen as his most brilliant creation. Anderson used biblical phrasing and Freudianism to examine the failings of the American dream. Notes.

FILMS

See also Chapter 6, *Blacks*, and Chapter 11, *Propaganda*.

0911　Cripps, Thomas. "The Birth of a Race Company: An Early Stride toward a Black Cinema." *Journal of Negro History* 59 (1974): 28–37.

　　Blacks responded to the racism of *Birth of a Nation* by making films of their own, projects which failed but indicated a willingness to try. Notes.

0912　————. "The Reaction of the Negro to the Motion Picture *Birth of a Nation*." *Historian* 25 (1963): 344–62.

　　The film *Birth of a Nation* was yet another reminder to blacks of the racism of the Progressive era. Notes.

0913　Ewen, Elizabeth. "City Lights: Immigrant Women and the Rise of the Movies." *Signs*, suppl. 5 (1980): 45–65.

　　Early movie themes dwelling on poverty and the struggle of life attracted immigrant women to the theater and contributed to a generation gap between women immigrants and their more Americanized daughters. Notes.

0914　Fisher, Robert. "Film Censorship and Progressive Reform: The National Board of Censorship of Motion Pictures, 1909–1922." *Journal of Popular Film* 4 (1975): 143–56.

　　The board took a libertarian stance on the censorship of films, campaigning for education as a means of controlling smut.

0915　Franklin, John Hope. "*Birth of a Nation*: Propaganda as History." *Massachusetts Review* 20 (1979): 417–34.

　　The 1915 film *Birth of a Nation* was designed as white Democratic party propaganda.

As propaganda it succeeded, but the film was not accurate historically. Notes.

0916 Gallagher, Brian. "Racist Ideology and Black Abnormality in *The Birth of a Nation*." *Phylon* 43 (1982): 68–76.

In *Birth of a Nation*, blacks are portrayed as slaves to excess. Race hatred and innovative film techniques made this movie popular with whites as well as controversial.

0917 Gehring, Wes D. "Chaplin and the Progressive Era: The Neglected Politics of a Clown." *Indiana Social Studies Quarterly* 34 (1981): 10–18.

Charlie Chaplin made twelve films in 1916 and 1917 with such Progressive themes as bossism, poverty, antiunionism, and prohibitionism.

0918 Hansen, Miriam, and Christadler, Martin. "David Wark Griffith's *Intolerance* (1916): Concerning the Relationship of Motion Pictures and History in the Progressive Era" (in German). *Amerikastudien* [West Germany] 21 (1976): 7–37.

Intolerance is examined as a reflection of what America had become by 1916: preoccupied with love, power, and violence. Notes.

0919 Higashi, Sumiko. "The Silent Screen Heroine: A Study of the Popular Image of Woman, 1914–1929." Ph.D. dissertation, University of California, Los Angeles, 1974.

Analysis of 150 silent films reveals popular images of women rooted in the Victorian stereotypes of the virgin and the vamp. DAI 35:4383-A.

0920 Isenberg, Michael T. *War on Film: The American Cinema and World War I, 1914–1941*. Rutherford, NJ: Fairleigh Dickinson University Press, 1981.

Documentaries and fictional treatments of World War I presented a positive and simplistic view of the war, laced with traditional values. After the war, films exhibited a studied ambiguity. Notes, bibliography, index.

0921 Karina, Stephen J. "With Flaming Sword: The Reactionary Rhetoric of Thomas Dixon." Ph.D. dissertation, University of Georgia, 1978.

A former Christian socialist, Dixon wrote novels about Reconstruction justifying segregation, works that D. W. Griffith used in his movie *Birth of a Nation*. DAI 39:7484-A.

0922 Kirby, Jack T. "D. W. Griffith's Racial Portraiture." *Phylon* 39 (1978): 118–27.

Griffith used racial and ethnic stereotypes in many of his 400 films. Jews, Italians, Hispanics, Orientals, and Native Americans all were depicted according to the conventions of the day. The image of blacks in such famous movies as *Birth of a Nation* was negative and racist, although not as viciously so as in other films. Notes.

0923 Knock, Thomas J. "'History with Lightning': The Forgotten Film *Wilson*." *American Quarterly* 28 (1976): 523–43.

Darryl F. Zanuck produced *Wilson* in 1944 on the assumption that the U.S. failure to join the League of Nations contributed to World War II and that an international organization was essential to prevent another world war. The film was expensive, and it was a commercial flop. Republicans saw it as pro-Roosevelt propaganda.

0924 McCarthy, Kathleen D. "Nickel Vice and Virtue: Movie Censorship in Chicago, 1907–1915." *Journal of Popular Film* 5 (1976): 37–55.

Chicago Progressives used film censorship to regulate morality because of their sincere concern for young people.

0925 May, Lary. *Screening Out the Past: The Birth of Mass Culture and the Motion Picture Industry*. New York: Oxford University Press, 1980.

Victorian sexual mores, class inhibitions, and the work ethic were screened out of American culture by commercial motion pictures during the Wilson years. Photographs, appendixes, notes, index.

0926 Moore, John H. "South Carolina's Reaction to the Photoplay *The Birth of a Nation*." *Proceedings of the South Carolina Historical Association* (1963): 30–40.

Although South Carolinians did not care much for Thomas Dixon's novel and subsequent play *The Clansman*, they approved of the film derived from it. Still, the movie did not lead to a resurgence of the Ku Klux Klan in South Carolina, as it did in many other areas.

0927 Mould, David H., and Berg, Charles M. "Fact and Fantasy in the Films of World War One." *Film and History* 14 (1984): 50–60.

Since actual combat footage was rare and the battles undramatic, wartime films were full of staged fighting and oversimplifications.

0928 Palmer, R. Barton. "William S. Hart's *Hell's Hinges*: An Ideological Approach to the Early Western." *Canadian Review of American Studies* [Canada] 16 (1985): 255–70.

William S. Hart's 1916 film *Hell's Hinges* broke new ground by employing the ideology of good against evil and reflected other Progressive social and political thinking as well. Notes.

0929 Silverman, Joan L. "*The Birth of a Nation*: Prohibition Propaganda." *Southern Quarterly* 19 (1981): 23–30.

D. W. Griffith, who had made several films advocating prohibition, made the point in *Birth of a Nation* that blacks would abuse alcohol if they could get it, so booze should be banned. Notes.

0930 Sloan, Kay. "Sexual Warfare in the Silent Cinema: Comedies and Melodramas of Woman Suffragism." *American Quarterly* 33 (1981): 412–36.

The image of suffragettes in early films was overwhelmingly negative. Women's groups countered with their own films, beginning in 1912 and 1913, that portrayed suffragettes as moral, beautiful, romantic, and dedicated to family life. Notes.

0931 Soderbergh, Peter A. " 'Aux Armes': The Rise of the Hollywood War Film, 1916–1930." *South Atlantic Quarterly* 65 (1966): 509–22.

The movie industry did not make war films during World War I out of the belief that the public would be interested in such a tragic subject.

0932 Stryker-Rodda, Harriet. "Scott and Van Altena, Masters of the Song Slide." *Journal of Long Island History* 5 (1965): 17–27.

To keep the attention of early movie audiences while films were being repaired and reels were being changed, men like John D. Scott and Edward Van Altena developed song slides complete with scenic pictures and photographs of pretty girls.

0933 Tucker, Jean E. "Voices from the Silents." *Quarterly Journal of the Library of Congress* 37 (1980): 387–412.

D. W. Griffith's 1916 film *Intolerance* is recalled by several people who were involved with the production. While this lengthy and intricate movie failed at the box office, it was an artistic success. Notes.

MUSIC

0934 Blesh, Rudi. "Scott Joplin." *American Heritage* 26 (1975): 26–32ff.

The talented black pianist published many ragtime tunes during the Progressive era, although he spent his last years in poverty trying to market his *Treemonisha*, a folk opera.

0935 Boller, Paul F., Jr. "The Sound of Silents." *American Heritage* 36 (1985): 98–107.

Birth of a Nation was the first silent film to have its own musical score, in 1915. After that, many more were written, although few endured.

0936 Brown, Janet. "The 'Coon-Singer' and the 'Coon Song': A Case Study of the Performer-Character Relationship." *Journal of American Culture* 7 (1984): 1–8.

The racism and sexism of the Progressive era kept Sophie Tucker and Bert Williams from performing as anything but fools and coons.

0937 Davis, Ronald L. *A History of Music in American Life.* Vol. II, *The Gilded Years, 1865–1920.* Huntington, NY: Krieger, 1980.

Davis examines music in its social context, including the pretentiousness of early American opera devotees, the rising popularity of the symphony, and the growth of popular styles such as musical theater, blues, and jazz. The careers of composers Edward Alexander MacDowell and Charles Ives are charted. Bibliography, index.

0938 Hennessey, Thomas J. "From Jazz to Swing: Black Jazz Musicians and Their Music, 1917–1935." Ph.D. dissertation, Northwestern University, 1973.

During the period under study jazz was transformed from local black folk music to a more structured musical form with national popularity. Many local styles existed before 1917, but the next few years saw records and radio fuse black and white musical forms together. DAI 34:5870-A.

0939 Rossiter, Frank R. "Charles Ives and American Culture: The Process of Development, 1874–1921." Ph.D. dissertation, Princeton University, 1970.

Before 1921, Ives had little influence on music or on the larger culture; rather, his social class and its culture influenced him profoundly. He was not an insurance man to support his music, but because his own values demanded it. DAI 31:6529-A.

0940 Salzman, Eric. "Charles Ives, American." *Commentary* 46 (1968): 37–43.

A brief biography of the controversial composer Charles Ives explains his major innovations in the years just before World War I.

0941 Tirro, Frank. *Jazz: A History.* New York: Norton, 1977.

Tirro's approach combines musicology, cultural anthropology, and cultural history. Two chapters discuss jazz from 1900 through the 1920s. Photographs, appendixes, bibliography, index.

0942 Tischler, Barbara L. "Music Modernism and American Cultural Identity." Ph.D. dissertation, Columbia University, 1983.

American composers were generally evaluated either according to European standards or according to the moral and cultural effects of their music. Despite several organized attempts to establish an American music, it was only with the increasing acceptance of modern music that a truly American music began to take hold. DAI 44:2557-A.

0943 Turner, Frederick W. "Black Jazz Artists: The Dark Side of Horatio Alger." *Massachusetts Review* 10 (1969): 341–53.

The Horatio Alger myth of riches for talented artists from humble backgrounds did not apply to early black jazz artists, who made little money until whites discovered the pleasures of their music. Even then, they made much less money than did many whites with less talent.

0944 ———. *Remembering Song: Encounters with the New Orleans Jazz Tradition.* New York: Viking Press, 1982.

This cultural history traces the folk origins and evolution of jazz, emphasizing personalities such as Bunk Johnson and Jim Robinson.

0945 Williams, Martin T. *Jazz Masters of New Orleans.* New York: Macmillan, 1967.

Williams details the lives of the great jazz innovators and the New Orleans culture that nourished them.

PAINTING

0946 Agee, William C. *Synchromism and Color Principles in American Painting, 1910–1930.* New York: Knoedler, 1965.

The influence of synchromism on artists such as Thomas Hart Benton has been overlooked. The movement was more widespread than is commonly believed.

0947 Brown, Milton. *American Painting from the Armory Show to the Depression.* Princeton: Princeton University Press, 1955.

Between 1913 and 1929, changing American social values were reflected in a shift away from realism in art. European trends became more influential. Photographs, notes, bibliography, index.

0948 Canaday, John, et al. "Fiftieth Anniversary of the New York Armory Show." *Art in America* 51 (1963): 30–63.

Several writers contribute short pieces on the background and momentous consequences of the 1913 New York Armory show.

0949 Davidson, Abraham A. *Early American Modernist Painting, 1910–1935.* New York: Harper and Row, 1981.

A surprising and important feature of early American modernism was the suddenness of its arrival in 1910. Coverage includes the Stieglitz group; the Arensberg circle; color painters; early exhibitions, collectors, and galleries; precisionism; and the Independents. Photographs, notes, bibliography, index.

0950 Goodrich, Lloyd. *Pioneers of Modern Art in America: The Decade of the Armory Show, 1910–1920.* New York: Whitney Museum, 1946.

This catalogue covers an exhibition of thirty-four artists active between 1908 and 1932. Goodrich also comments on the Armory show of 1913, the New York art world of previous years, and various galleries, organizations, and art magazines of the period. Photographs, index.

0951 Hills, Patricia. "John Sloan's Images of Working-Class Women: A Case Study of the Roles and Interrelationships of Politics, Personality, and Patrons in the Development of Sloan's Art, 1905–1916." *Prospects* [Great Britain] 5 (1980): 157–96.

John Sloan became a socialist during the Progressive period. While he contributed to *The Masses*, his realist paintings were not political, because he continued to think of art as neutral. Notes.

0952 Homer, William I., and Organ, Violet. *Robert Henri and His Circle*. Ithaca, NY: Cornell University Press, 1969.

Robert Henri was an influential art teacher and a great artist. A Progressive in spirit, he had very mixed feelings about the rebellion touched off by the Armory show. Photographs, notes, bibliography, index.

0953 Hyland, Douglas K. S. "Agnes Ernst Meyer, Patron of American Modernism." *American Art Journal* 12 (1980): 64–81.

A sincere and tireless patron of the arts, Agnes Meyer organized showings of modern art and managed a gallery that helped to popularize modernism during the Progressive era. Notes.

0954 Knight, Christopher. "On Native Ground." *Art in America* 71 (1983): 166–73.

Three years after the Armory show of 1913, the Forum Exhibition of Modern American Painters was formed to make the public aware of American modernists.

0955 Levin, Gail. *Synchromism and American Color Abstraction: 1910–1925*. New York: Braziller, 1978.

This exhibition catalogue presents the paintings of Morgan Russell and Stanton MacDonald-Wright, founders of synchromism, along with paintings by other synchromist artists.

0956 Neil, J. Meredith. "The Impact of the Armory Show." *South Atlantic Quarterly* 79 (1980): 375–85.

The end of the nineteenth century in art came with the 1913 Armory show, which paved the way for twentieth-century modernism. Still, the modernist rebels were not accepted easily by the public. Notes.

0957 Saunier-Olier, Jacqueline. "In the Wake of the Armory Show: Immaculates and Objectivists." *Revue Française d'Études Américaines* [France] 4 (1979): 51–65.

The New York Armory show of 1913 brought cubism and abstract art to America from Europe, paving the way for radical movements in art and poetry.

0958 Zilczer, Judith. "Alfred Stieglitz and John Quinn: Allies in the American Avant-Garde." *American Art Journal* 17 (1985): 18–33.

Photographer Stieglitz and lawyer Quinn worked together to promote modern art, with the former offering to exhibit the works of promising artists and the latter buying their paintings. Notes.

PHILOSOPHY AND INTELLECTUALS

See also Chapter 7, *Public Opinion and the Press*, and Chapter 11, *Propaganda*.

0959 Abrahams, Edward. *The Lyrical Left: Randolph Bourne, Alfred Stieglitz, and the Origins of Cultural Radicalism in America*. Charlottesville: University Press of Virginia, 1986.

Bourne and Stieglitz were committed to the liberation of self, cultural pluralism, and a new kind of nationalism, all of which formed the basis of the "Lyrical Left." Notes, bibliography, index.

0960 Abrahamson, James L. "David Starr Jordan and American Antimilitarism." *Pacific Northwest Quarterly* 67 (1976): 76–87.

Using eugenic and euthenic theories rather than moral arguments, Jordan argued that war destroys the best of youth while fostering authoritarianism. In spite of misgivings, he supported Wilson's intervention in the European war on the ground that Germany could not be mollified by diplomatic means. Notes.

0961 Bourke, Paul F. "Philosophy and Social Criticism: John Dewey, 1910–1920." *History of Education Quarterly* 15 (1975): 3–16.

Dewey strove during this period to reformulate long-standing issues of logic and epistemology while researching the social history of philosophy.

0962 ———. "The Social Critics and the End of American Innocence, 1907–1921." *Journal of American Studies* [Great Britain] 3 (1969): 57–72.

The generation of 1912, including Herbert Croly, Walter Weyl, Walter Lippmann, Van Wyck Brooks, and Randolph Bourne, tried to apply academics to society outside of the university setting.

0963   Clayton, Bruce. *Forgotten Prophet: The Life of Randolph Bourne*. Baton Rouge: Louisiana University Press, 1984.

The life of this brilliant radical essayist is examined, including his opposition to World War I and his flamboyant, sad personal life. Photographs, notes, index.

0964   Cywar, Alan S. "An Inquiry into American Thought and the Determinate Influence of Political, Economic, and Social Factors in the Early Twentieth Century: Bourne, Dewey, DuBois, Nearing, Veblen, and Weyl." Ph.D. dissertation, University of Rochester, 1972.

This work explores the relationship that evolved during the Progressive era between social scientific thought and economic institutions that were political in nature. DAI 33:3529-A.

0965   ———. "John Dewey: Toward Domestic Reconstruction." *Journal of the History of Ideas* 30 (1969): 385–400.

By 1915, Dewey had shifted his emphasis from voluntary organizations to education as a vehicle for reform. After the war he saw the need for both strong government and industrial democracy.

0966   ———. "John Dewey in World War I: Patriotism and International Progressivism." *American Quarterly* 21 (1969): 578–94.

Like many other liberal or radical intellectuals, Dewey was profoundly moved by the horrors of World War I. Notes.

0967   Dorfman, Joseph; Gruchy, Allan G.; and Sweezy, Paul M. "Veblen Centenary Round Table." *American Economic Review* 48 (1958): 1–29.

Three brief articles pay tribute to Thorstein Veblen. Dorfman looks at Veblen the gifted writer, while Gruchy examines Veblen's economic thought, especially as contained in the 1923 work *Absentee Ownership and Business Enterprise in Recent Times*. Sweezy covers some of Veblen's other writings and his thoughts on class struggle.

0968   Dykhuizen, George. *The Life and Mind of John Dewey*. Carbondale: Southern Illinois Press, 1973.

Dewey was more a celebrity than an expounder of a systematic philosophy. Still, he wrote much about philosophy and made great contributions to education. Photographs, notes, index.

0969   Fishbein, Leslie. *Rebels in Bohemia: The Radicals of "The Masses," 1911–1917*. Chapel Hill: University of North Carolina Press, 1982.

Prewar radical intellectuals naively attempted to combine revolutionary Marxism with the Freudian preoccupation with self. The result was a belief system that left them unprepared to deal with the real world. Photographs, notes, bibliography, index.

0970   Frederickson, George M. "Thorstein Veblen: The Last Viking." *American Quarterly* 11 (1959): 403–15.

While Veblen pretended to be completely objective, he could not escape his Norwegian cultural heritage of anarchy. Notes.

0971   Fuchsman, Kenneth A. "Desire and Intelligence: Randolph Bourne and the Cycle of Progressivism." Ph.D. dissertation, Rutgers University, 1982.

Like other political liberals and radicals, Bourne was forced to lower his expectations of social progress. The stages of his career are used to illustrate the life cycle of the Progressive movement. DAI 43:900-A.

0972   Hoeveler, John D., Jr. "The New Humanism: An Aspect of Twentieth Century American Thought." Ph.D. dissertation, University of Illinois, Urbana-Champaign, 1971.

The origins of the new humanism during the Progressive era are discussed, including the work of such intellectuals as Irving Babbitt, Paul Elmer More, and Stuart Sherman. DAI 32:4228-A.

0973   Hoopes, James. "The Culture of Progressivism: Croly, Lippmann, Brooks, Bourne, and the Idea of American Artistic Decadence." *Clio* 7 (1977): 91–111.

Young intellectuals of this period regarded social reform as an art form and looked toward the day when freedom of expression would be absolute. Their interest in the art of society plunged them into politics and, ultimately, dissatisfaction. Notes.

0974   Howlett, Charles F. "Democracy's Ambassador to the Far East: John Dewey's Quest for World Peace." *Pacific Historian* 20 (1976): 388–406.

Seeing the importance of the Far East to future U.S. policies, Dewey visited the Orient after World War I, where he spoke for democracy as the best means of human cooperation. Notes.

0975 ———. "John Dewey and the Crusade to Outlaw War." *World Affairs* 138 (1976): 336–55.

Dewey's interest in pacifism and the outlawing of war began in the aftermath of World War I, a conflict that he had supported.

0976 ———. "Troubled Philosopher: John Dewey and American Pacifism, 1917–1945." Ph.D. dissertation, State University of New York, Albany, 1974.

Pragmatist Dewey supported World War I by arguing that it involved the intelligent use of force. Randolph Bourne's severe criticism of Dewey contributed to Dewey's reexamination of his position after the war, when he embraced pacifism. DAI 35:1579-A.

0977 Humphrey, Robert E. *Children of Fantasy: The First Rebels of Greenwich Village.* New York: Wiley, 1978.

Greenwich Village bohemians of the Wilson years rejected Victorian values and kept their cultural rebellion alive by eschewing social action and retreating to an isolated world of liberated sexuality. Photographs, notes, bibliography, index.

0978 Lasch, Christopher. *The New Radicalism in America, 1889–1963: The Intellectual as Social Type.* New York: Knopf, 1965.

Beginning around the turn of the century, radical intellectuals began to identify themselves with the underclass rather than with the overprivileged. Culture was believed to be inseparable from politics. The author describes the life and thought of various radical intellectuals, including the writers and editors of the *New Republic*. Notes, index.

0979 Lears, T. J. Jackson. *No Place of Grace: Antimodernism and the Transformation of American Culture, 1880–1920.* New York: Pantheon, 1981.

Antimodernists were mostly middle- and upper-class intellectuals who took a skeptical view of progress, as opposed to the optimism assumed by most social thinkers. The author re-examines the Progressive cultural transformation from a psychological and philosophical standpoint and in light of the antimodernists including Frank Norris, Edith Wharton, Henry Adams, and Henry James. Notes, index.

0980 McCormick, John S. "A Beleagured Minority: The Young Intellectuals and American Mass Society, 1910–1920." Ph.D. dissertation, University of Iowa, 1973.

Young intellectuals such as Randolph Bourne, Van Wyck Brooks, Waldo Frank, and Harold E. Stearns came to maturity with the rise of mass society and the relaxation of class distinctions. Self-absorbed and isolated, their ideas were sometimes perceptive but often shallow. DAI 34:5878-A.

0981 Marcell, David W. *Progress and Pragmatism: James, Dewey, Beard, and the American Idea of Progress.* Westport, CT: Greenwood, 1974.

William James, John Dewey, and Charles Beard met the intellectual challenge of their period by melding pragmatism with Progressivism. Notes, bibliography, index.

0982 Mathews, F. H. "The Americanization of Sigmund Freud: Adaptions of Psychoanalysis." *Journal of American Studies* 1 (1967): 39–62.

While many intellectuals rejected Freud's ideas as immoral during the Progressive era, some reworked his ideas to fit the American idiom. His popularity stemmed from the idea that psychoanalysis could be used to help society.

0983 May, Henry F. *The End of American Innocence: A Study of the First Years of Our Own Time, 1912–1917.* New York: Knopf, 1959.

Progressive-era optimism necessitated a backlash of disillusion, which would have occurred with or without World War I. Small groups of intellectuals and artists were the first to acknowledge the inevitable displacement of traditional values by the modern world. Conservative and radical ideology illuminate the two sides of prewar social rumblings. Notes, bibliography, index.

0984 ———. "The Rebellion of the Intellectuals." *American Quarterly* 8 (1956): 114–26.

The years 1912–1917 are portrayed as a period of intellectual restlessness that spilled over into politics and literature. Notes.

0985 Moreau, John A. "Bourne, a Biography." Ph.D. dissertation, University of Virginia, 1964.

Randolph Bourne was a leader of the radical intellectual movement of the Progressive era. He wrote literary criticism and political editorials for *New Republic* and other journals. Bourne died in the 1918 influenza epidemic at the age of 32. DAI 25:2949.

0986 Morris, Charles. *The Pragmatic Movement in American Philosophy*. New York: Braziller, 1970.

Morris analyzes the pragmatist writings of Charles Sanders Peirce, William James, John Dewey, and George H. Mead and the divergences and congruities of their ideas. Notes, appendix, bibliography, index.

0987 Namasaka, Boaz N. "William E. B. Du Bois and Thorstein B. Veblen: Intellectual Activists of Progressivism, a Comparative Study, 1900–1930." Ph.D. dissertation, Claremont Graduate School, 1971.

Du Bois and Veblen both advocated socialism to achieve an equitable society. Nothing less than a drastic shifting of the values of American culture, they believed, could bring about true equality of opportunity. DAI 32: 2579-A.

0988 Pickens, Donald K. *Eugenics and the Progressives*. Nashville: Vanderbilt University Press, 1968.

The Darwinian idea of natural selection and, implicitly, natural superiority, combined with naturalistic philosophy to inspire eugenic thought. Eugenicists believed that nature was a hierarchy, not a democracy, and therefore the reproductive and economic precedence of some men over others was desirable. The effect of environment on behavior was believed to be minimal. Notes, bibliography, index.

0989 Quandt, Jean B. *From Small Town to the Great Community: The Social Thought of Progressive Intellectuals*. New Brunswick, NJ: Rutgers University Press, 1970.

Jane Addams, William Allen White, and John Dewey were among the Progressive intellectuals who believed that cities should and could recreate the spirit and ethics of a small town. The author correlates these American thinkers with their European counterparts. Although their social ideals were worthy, no practical or sufficient means of transforming urban life were proposed.

0990 Robinson, Ira. "Cyrus Adler, Bernard Revel and the Prehistory of Organized Jewish Scholarship in the United States." *American Jewish History* 69 (1980): 497–505.

Bernard Revel founded the Society of Jewish Academicians in 1916 to synthesize modern science with Orthodox Jewish beliefs. A group headed by Cyrus Adler created the American Academy for Jewish Research in 1920 as an alternative to Revel's organization. Notes.

0991 Shanley, Kevin M. "Reinhold Niebuhr and Relations between Germany and America (1916–1956)." Ph.D. dissertation, State University of New York, Albany, 1984.

A second generation German American, Reinhold Niebuhr was a professor of Christianity who wrote frequently about relations between Germany and America. Although torn by loyalty to his ancestral country, Niebuhr decided to support American entry into World War I. DAI 45:921-A.

0992 Stromberg, Roland N. "Redemption by War: The Intellectuals and 1914." *Midwest Quarterly* 20 (1979): 211–27.

Most artists and intellectuals supported World War I from its outset in 1914, even though they were stereotyped as pacifists.

0993 Winterrle, John. "John Dewey and the First World War: A Study in Pragmatic Acquiescence." *North Dakota Quarterly* 35 (1967): 15–22.

Dewey supported the war, because he thought it would bring about a new world order. His writings display a consistent belief in pragmatism, not opportunism. Notes.

POETRY

0994 Blanshard, Brand. "Eliot at Oxford." *Southern Review* 21 (1985): 889–98.

A classmate remembers that the poet T. S. Eliot attended Oxford briefly from 1914 to 1915 and also what Eliot studied.

0995 Guillaume, Bernice F. "The Life and Work of Olivia Ward Bush (Banks), 1869–1944." Ph.D. dissertation, Tulane University, 1983.

Bush's response as a literary artist and as an Afro-American/Native American to her times is explored. DAI 44:2861-A.

0996 Hart, James A. "American Poetry of the First World War and the Book Trade." *Bibliographic Society of America Papers* 61 (1967): 209–24.

The period 1915 to 1918 witnessed a decline in the publication of fiction and a rising interest in poetry, as people embraced the heroic and the consoling. Before long, though, the public put poetry aside in favor of prose. Notes.

0997 Hartley, Lois. "Edgar Lee Masters, Political Essayist." *Journal of the Illinois State Historical Society* 57 (1964): 249–60.

Reading Masters's political essays can contribute to a greater understanding of his other writings. A Jeffersonian democrat, Masters held out hope that Woodrow Wilson would appoint him to a judgeship. Notes.

0998 Healey, Claire. "Amy Lowell Visits London." *New England Quarterly* 46 (1973): 439–53.

Poet Amy Lowell was inspired by her meetings with European imagists, such as Ezra Pound. Her plans to publish anthologies of imagist works ran into opposition from Pound. Notes.

0999 Healy, J. J. "*The Dial* and the Revolution in Poetry, 1912–1917: A Study in Controversy." *British Association for American Studies Bulletin* [Great Britain] (1965): 48–60.

Two rival magazines in Chicago waged a war of words over the new poetry, with *Poetry: A Magazine of Verse* supporting the movement and *The Dial* opposing it.

1000 Kennedy, Richard S. "E. E. Cummings at Harvard: Verse, Friends, Rebellion." *Harvard Library Bulletin* 25 (1977): 253–91.

Cummings's five years at Harvard (1911–1916) witnessed his transformation from a naive youth to a rebellious figure developing a unique poetic style. Notes.

1001 Myers, Neil. "Sentimentalism in the Early Poetry of William Carlos Williams." *American Literature* 37 (1966): 458–70.

After 1915, William Carlos Williams tempered his sentimental tendencies to the point that readers began to feel a rare intimacy with his poetic thoughts. Notes.

1002 Sears, John F. "Robert Frost and the Imagists: The Background of Frost's 'Sentence Sounds.' " *New England Quarterly* 54 (1981): 467–80.

Between 1913 and 1916, Robert Frost distanced himself from the imagist poets by developing his own theory of sentence sounds. Notes.

1003 Self, Robert T. "The Correspondence of Amy Lowell and Barrett Wendell, 1915–1919." *New England Quarterly* 47 (1974): 65–86.

The Lowell-Wendell letters reveal much about poetry and literature during the Wilson years, a time when the old guard and literary radicals were beginning to discuss their differences. Notes.

1004 Sokol, B. J. "What Went Wrong between Robert Frost and Ezra Pound." *New England Quarterly* 49 (1976): 521–41.

Pound introduced Frost to the London literary scene in 1913, but the two had a falling out over Pound's less-than-flattering review of Frost's first volume of poetry. Notes.

Health Issues

See also Chapter 1, *Wilson's Health,* Chapter 6, *Women,* and Chapter 7, *The Progressive Movement* and *Legal.*

1005 Anderson, Oscar E. *The Health of a Nation: Harvey W. Wiley and the Fight for Pure Food.* Chicago: University of Chicago Press, 1958.

Wiley battled for pure food laws, but hostile manufacturers and food processors, an indifferent public, and an ineffective government kept much of America's food impure. Notes, bibliography, index.

1006 Buckley, Kerry W. "Behaviorism and the Professionalization of American Psychology: A Study of John Broadus Watson, 1878–1958." Ph.D. dissertation, University of Massachusetts, 1982.

John Watson believed that behaviorism—the observation, prediction, and possible control of actual behavior as distinct from theoretical thought processes—could benefit the businessman as well as the scientist. He put theory into practice in 1920 when, forced to resign from Johns Hopkins University, he became an advertising psychologist. His career is also interesting viewed as a creative response to problems of industrialization. DAI 42:5219-A.

1007 Buhler-Wilkerson, Karen A. "False Dawn: The Rise and Decline of Public Health Nursing, 1900–1930." Ph.D. dissertation, University of Pennsylvania, 1984.

Public health nurses were typically paid by the wealthy to minister to the poor. As immigration tapered off, infectious diseases became less problematic, hospitals provided more health care, and public concern for the poor lessened, these nurses were believed to be no longer needed. DAI 45:1497-A.

1008 Burnham, John C. "The Progressive Era Revolution in American Attitudes toward Sex." *Journal of American History* 59 (1973): 885–903.

Progressive reformers and their allies in the social hygiene movement battled the Victorian double standard and the reluctance of Americans to discuss sexuality. They were thoroughgoing elitists who felt that they knew what was best for the masses. Notes.

1009 ———. *Psychoanalysis and American Medicine, 1894–1918: Medicine, Science and Culture.* New York: International Universities Press, 1967.

In the years before World War I, Freud's ideas spread to America from Europe, changing as psychotherapists strained his works through a Progressive filter. Bibliography, index.

1010 Burns, Chester R. "Richard Clarke Cabot (1868–1939) and the Reformation in American Medical Ethics." *Bulletin of the History of Medicine* 51 (1977): 353–68.

In 1916, Cabot found himself in hot water with the Massachusetts Medical Society for his criticisms of doctors' ethics. An advocate of patients' rights, he became a pioneer of modern medical ethics. Notes.

1011 Burrow, James G. *Organized Medicine in the Progressive Era: The Move toward Monopoly.* Baltimore, MD: Johns Hopkins University Press, 1977.

During the Progressive era, physicians began to form politically powerful organizations which commanded increasing public respect. The profession became more unified as it participated in and came to dominate health reforms.

1012 Camfield, Thomas M. "Psychologists at War: The History of American Psychology and the First World War." Ph.D. dissertation, University of Texas, Austin, 1969.

Psychologists exploited the war to further their study of the human mind. Their efforts furthered the military cause, won public plaudits, and enhanced the professional standing of psychologists. DAI 30:5370-A.

1013 Cassedy, James H. "Muckraking and Medicine: Samuel Hopkins Adams." *American Quarterly* 16 (1964): 85–99.

Adams had abandoned muckraking journalism to concentrate on health education by 1914. He became a respected critic of the way in which medicine was practiced in the United States.

1014 Cornebise, Alfred E. *Typhus and Doughboys: The American Polish Typhus Relief Expedition, 1919–1921.* Newark: University of Delaware Press, 1982.

The American Polish Typhus Relief Expedition was dispatched to help the Poles cope with a raging epidemic. Specialists from the armed services advised medical officials, educated citizens in cleanliness, and ran refugee camps. The Gilcrest mission served as a prototype for later humanitarian operations. Notes, bibliography, index.

1015 Crosby, Alfred W., Jr. *Epidemic and Peace, 1918.* Westport, CT: Greenwood, 1976.

Over twenty million persons perished in the influenza pandemic of 1918–19. The war diverted public attention from this catastrophe, and its impact was further reduced by the fact that only 2 to 3 percent of those who contracted the virus died. Charts, tables, notes, index.

1016 Curtis, Patrick A. "Eugenic Reformers, Cultural Perceptions of Dependent Populations, and the Care of the Feebleminded in Illinois, 1909–1920." Ph.D. dissertation, University of Illinois, Chicago Circle, 1983.

Between 1910 and 1920, influential eugenic reformers began to treat the feebleminded as individuals rather than as a defective group to be isolated from society and prevented from reproducing. The term "feebleminded" actually referred to anyone perceived as low, dirty, and dangerous. DAI 44:1548-A.

1017 English, Peter C. *Shock, Physiological Surgery, and George Washington Crile: Medical Innovation in the Progressive Era.* Westport, CT: Greenwood, 1980.

George Washington Crile experimented with ways to avoid postsurgical shock. Of necessity, many improvements were tested on actual patients, including a process called "physiological surgery." Crile, whose career lasted from 1888 until 1918, was also active as a Progressive reformer. Notes, bibliography, index.

1018 Gordon, Ann D. "Investigating the *Eastland* Accident." *Chicago History* 10 (1981): 74–85.

On 24 July 1915, the *Eastland* steamship overturned near Chicago, touching off a public outcry, but the Steamboat Inspection Service made only cursory inquiries into the tragedy.

1019 Hale, Nathan G., Jr. *Freud and the Americans: The Beginnings of Psychoanalysis in the United States, 1876–1917*. New York: Oxford University Press, 1971.

Freud challenged the new, civilized morality Americans had developed to discipline their sexuality. Psychoanalysis became a tool for dealing with problems created by the new morality. Notes, bibliography, index.

1020 Howell, Joel D. "Early Perceptions of the Electrocardiogram from Arrhythmia to Infarction." *Bulletin of the History of Medicine* 58 (1984): 83–98.

During the Progressive era James Herrick was quick to see the clinical applications of the electrocardiograph, using it to diagnose heart attacks. Notes.

1021 Klaus, Alisa C. "Babies All the Rage: The Movement to Prevent Infant Mortality in the United States and France, 1890–1920." Ph.D. dissertation, University of Pennsylvania, 1986.

A declining birthrate further decreased by the war deaths of a large percentage of young men forced the French government to take all possible action to improve the infant mortality rate. With no such pressures, the American government, politicians, and male physicians were relatively unconcerned about infant mortality, so it became a women's issue. DAI 47:3855-A.

1022 Leavitt, Judith Walzer. "Birthing and Anesthesia: The Debate over Twilight Sleep." *Signs* 6 (1980): 147–64.

Women tried to take back control over the birthing process with the promotion of scopolamine. The twilight sleep movement (1914–15) demanded that each woman be allowed to choose the kind of delivery she wanted.

1023 Lederer, Susan E. "Hideyo Noguchi's Luetin Experiment and the Antivivisectionists." *Isis* 76 (1985): 31–48.

To improve medicine's ability to diagnose syphilis, Hideyo Noguchi of the Rockefeller Institute outraged antivivisectionists by injecting orphans and hospital patients with luetin, an extract of the disease. Notes.

1024 ———. " 'The Right and Wrong of Making Experiments on Human Beings': Udo J. Wile and Syphilis." *Bulletin of the History of Medicine* 58 (1984): 380–97.

A 1916 report by Professor Wile that he had taken brain tissue from insane syphilitics for an experiment touched off controversy. Notes.

1025 Leys, Ruth. "Meyer, Watson, and the Dangers of Behaviorism." *Journal of the History of the Behavioral Sciences* 20 (1984): 128–49.

The stormy relationship between Professors John Watson and Adolf Meyer is examined, a collaboration that ended when Meyer forced Watson to leave Johns Hopkins over differences concerning behaviorism.

1026 Miller, Lawrence G. "Pain, Parturition, and the Profession: Twilight Sleep in America." In Susan Reverby and David Rosner, eds. *Health Care in America: Essays in Social History*. Philadelphia: Temple University Press, 1979, pp. 19–44.

The National Twilight Sleep Association advocated the use of anesthesia during labor during the Wilson years. While the movement met with failure, it led to the idea that childbirth was a medical condition as opposed to a natural event. Notes.

1027 Noyes, William R. "Influenza Epidemic, 1918–1919: A Misplaced Chapter in United States Social and Institutional History." Ph.D. dissertation, University of California, Los Angeles, 1968.

The war overshadowed the influenza epidemic, but the epidemic was a great crisis in public health nevertheless, jolting the medical profession and creating great human suffering. DAI 30:05050.

1028 Numbers, Ronald L. *Almost Persuaded: American Physicians and Compulsory Health Insurance, 1912–1920*. Baltimore, MD: Johns Hopkins University Press, 1978.

The American Association for Labor Legislation sponsored the first campaign for a compulsory health insurance bill. Gradual attrition of support from medical professionals doomed this early effort. Photographs, notes, bibliography, index.

1029 O'Donnell, John M. "The Origins of Behaviorism: American Psychology, 1870–1920." Ph.D. dissertation, University of Pennsylvania, 1979.

Academic psychology became a behavioral science during the Progressive era. An explosive mixture of philosophy, physiology, and social science, psychology became grounded in behaviorism, which shaped its intellectual development. DAI 40:3493-A.

1030 O'Toole, Coleen K. "The Search for Purity: A Retrospective Policy Analysis of the Decision to Chlorinate Cincinnati's Public Water

Supply, 1890–1920." Ph.D. dissertation, University of Cincinnati, 1986.

Any decision to alter a municipal water supply involves scientific, medical, and environmental uncertainties, now as well as in the past. A variety of social, political, and scientific factors affected the decision by Cincinnati and other cities to begin chlorination in the early twentieth century. DAI 47:2295-A.

1031 Persico, Joseph E. "The Great Swine Flu Epidemic of 1918." *American Heritage* 27 (1976): 28–31ff.

The great influenza pandemic may have started at Fort Riley, Kansas, whence doughboys picked it up and carried it to Europe.

1032 Pettit, Dorothy A. "A Cruel Wind: America Experiences Pandemic Influenza, 1918–1920." Ph.D. dissertation, University of New Hampshire, 1976.

More people died from influenza than died on the battlefields of World War I. The famous postwar apathy Americans felt may have been primarily the result of this pandemic, not disillusion with Wilson's policies. DAI 37: 7273-A.

1033 Pivar, David J. "Cleansing the Nation: The War on Prostitution, 1917–21." *Prologue* 12 (1980): 29–40.

Social hygienists and the government worked during World War I to implement the "American plan," a two-pronged campaign designed to control the spread of venereal disease and to stamp out prostitution. Notes.

1034 Rogers, Naomi. "Screen the Baby, Swat the Fly: Polio in the Northeastern United States, 1916." Ph.D. dissertation, University of Pennsylvania, 1986.

Despite consistent evidence that there was no link between poverty and polio, reformers focused their antipolio crusade on sanitation in the slums. DAI 47:4496-A.

1035 Rosen, George. "The Efficiency Criterion in Medical Care, 1900–1920." *Bulletin of the History of Medicine* 50 (1976): 28–44.

Medical charities paved the way in the application of scientific management to the practice of medicine. Notes.

1036 Ross, Irwin. "The Influenza Epidemic of 1918." *American History Illustrated* 3 (1968): 12–17.

The Spanish influenza pandemic of 1918 claimed over twenty-one million lives, including a million in North America. Coming just as World War I ended, this plague did not receive much media coverage.

1037 Rothman, David J. *Conscience and Convenience: The Asylum and Its Alternatives in Progressive America*. Boston: Little, Brown, 1980.

Progressive reformers put their faith in modern therapeutic treatments for mental deviants. Notes, index.

1038 Samuelson, Franz. "World War Intelligence Testing and the Development of Psychology." *Journal of the History of the Behavioral Sciences* 13 (1977): 274–82.

Government IQ testing during World War I used poor methodology, but at least the psychologists in the project wanted to use their skills in public service. Notes.

1039 Sanford, Wayne L. "The Influenza Epidemic of 1918 and Its Effects on the Military." *Indiana Medical Historical Quarterly* 9 (1983): 16–22.

The influenza epidemic had a large impact on how American doughboys were trained and transported. While there was no cure, medical personnel did experiment with preventive measures.

1040 Smith, Michael L. "Surveying El Dorado: The Social Role of California's Scientific Community, 1850–1915." Ph.D. dissertation, Yale University, 1983.

The typical nineteenth-century scientist was a naturalist-explorer who was accessible to the public. However, during the twentieth century, American science was transformed to fit a managerial model emphasizing standardized training, specialization, and laboratory research. California scientists, isolated from the East, maintained a regional scientific community that focused on outdoor research and profoundly affected American environmental science. DAI 47:2292-A.

1041 Teller, Michael E. "The American Tuberculosis Crusade, 1889–1917: The Rise of a Modern Health Campaign." Ph.D. dissertation, University of Chicago, 1985.

The tuberculosis crusade used education, sanitation measures, and the construction of facilities for diagnosis and treatment to reduce deaths. Lower economic groups were not substantially helped. Although it was not particularly effective, the tuberculosis crusade was an important model for later public health programs. DAI 46:2791-A.

1042 Von Mayarhauser, Richard T. "The Triumph of Utility: The Forgotten Clash of American Psychologies in World War I." Ph.D. dissertation, University of Chicago, 1986.

During the war, psychologists veered away from exploring the roots of behavior in order to establish practical applications for psychology. The Committee of Classification of Personnel in the army provided vocational testing and recommendations, while the Committee on Psychological Examining administered intelligence tests as an adjunct to medical diagnosis. DAI 47:1861-A.

1043 Walker, Forrest A. "Compulsory Health Insurance: 'The Next Great Step in Social Legislation.' " *Journal of American History* 56 (1969): 290–304.

A group of doctors and intellectuals fought hard for compulsory national health insurance. The proposal's association with precedents in Germany, Wilson's lack of interest, and opposition from the medical establishment, the American Federation of Labor, and insurance companies doomed it. Notes.

1044 Waserman, Manfred. "The Quest for a National Health Department in the Progressive Era." *Bulletin of the History of Medicine* 49 (1975): 353–80.

Regarding health as a resource to be preserved with government help, Progressives tried and failed to create a national health department.

1045 Young, James H. "Botulism and the Ripe Olive Scare of 1919–1920." *Bulletin of the History of Medicine* 50 (1976): 372–91.

Canned olives caused many cases of deadly botulism in 1919–20. To contain public fears, the National Canners Association worked with the government. The offending cans were removed from stores, and the association made recommendations for new, stricter food processing laws. Notes.

Society and Popular Culture

1046 Bailey, Beth L. "Conventions of Desire: Courtship in 20th Century America." Ph.D. dissertation, University of Chicago, 1986.

Chapter 1 details courtship between 1900 and 1920, when the practice of calling on a lady at home was replaced by dating. DAI 47:1856-A.

1047 Bush, Gregory W. "Lord of Attention: Gerald Stanley Lee and the Search for the Heroic Personality in the American Crowd." Ph.D. dissertation, St. Louis University, 1983.

Lee, a former Congregational minister, was well known between 1910 and World War I for his theories on crowd psychology. He championed advertising and believed that the public adulation of some men as heroes was actually a "democratic market mechanism." DAI 47:635-A.

1048 Couvares, Francis G. "Work, Leisure and Reform in Pittsburgh: The Transformation of an Urban Culture." Ph.D. dissertation, University of Michigan, 1980.

Forms of recreation changed parallel to society's movement toward urban industrialization. Nationwide networks of leisure entrepreneurs developed. DAI 41:2257-A.

1049 Dimeglio, John E. "A Vaudevillian's America." Ph.D. dissertation, University of Maine, 1971.

Vaudeville was the most popular form of entertainment during the Progressive era. Audiences represented the whole spectrum of American society and the American spirit itself. Vaudevillians were highly mobile and were only as successful as their talents allowed. DAI 32:4511-A.

1050 Erenberg, Lewis A. "Everybody's Doin' It: The Pre-World War I Dance Craze, the Castles and the Modern American Girl." *Feminist Studies* 3 (1975): 155–70.

Latin and black American dance forms were incorporated into the mainstream of popular dance in the prewar period, a reflection of larger cultural changes. Dancer Irene Castle gained notoriety as the new American woman, young and carefree while still remaining innocent. Notes.

1051 ———. *Steppin' Out: New York Nightlife and the Transformation of American Culture: 1890–1930.* Westport, CT: Greenwood, 1981.

The "dance craze" peaked in the cabarets of Manhattan during the Wilson years, bringing about a new social interaction between men and women as well as between different social classes. Photographs, notes, bibliography, indexes.

1052 Farrell, James J. *Inventing the American Way of Death, 1830–1920.* Philadelphia: Temple University Press, 1980.

By 1920, death was no longer a family affair, but rather the province of a variety of professionals including doctors, funeral directors, and cemetery owners. Tables, notes, index.

1053 Flautz, John T. "An American Demagogue in Barssom." *Journal of Popular Culture* 1 (1967): 263–75.

Edgar Rice Burroughs wrote a popular trilogy of books between 1912 and 1919 sustained by demagogic political fantasies.

1054 Gilkeson, John S., Jr. "A City of Joiners: Voluntary Associations and the Formation of the Middle Class in Providence, 1830–1920." Ph.D. dissertation, Brown University, 1981.

Using the records of middle-class associations as well as diaries and newspapers, Chapters 5 and 6 examine the struggles of middle-class reformers against the problems of industrialization between 1890 and 1920. This self-defined class maintained cohesion through clubs, national networks of clubs, and recreational centers. The roots of the consumer society are examined. DAI 42:4906-A.

1055 Hantover, Jeffrey P. "The Boy Scouts and the Validation of Masculinity." *Journal of Social Issues* 34 (1978): 184–95.

The Boy Scout organization was created during the Progressive era to preserve traditional tenets of masculinity, which were believed to be under fire from feminism and urbanization.

1056 Horowitz, Daniel. "Frugality or Comfort: Middle-Class Styles of Life in the Early Twentieth Century." *American Quarterly* 37 (1985): 239–59.

Home economist Ellen H. Richards urged her mostly middle-class readers to preserve traditional values, while Martha Bruère thought that the middle classes should indulge themselves with material things as long as they stayed within their means, the latter argument reflecting the feelings of the majority. Notes.

1057 Rotundo, Edward A. "Manhood in America: The Northern Middle Class, 1770–1920." Ph.D. dissertation, Brandeis University, 1982.

Derived from diaries and letters from the American Northeast, this study divides ideals of manhood into three periods. From 1850 through 1920, differences between the idealized man and the idealized woman lessened. DAI 43:1267-A.

1058 Rydell, Robert W. "All the World's a Fair: America's International Expositions, 1876–1916." Ph.D. dissertation, University of California, Los Angeles, 1980.

During Wilson's presidency, there was a fair in San Francisco in 1915 and one in San Diego in 1915–16. Anthropologist-approved exhibits of nonwhite village life and other promotions managed to convey to millions the idea that white lifestyles represented progress, and therefore superiority, over nonwhite lifestyles. This gave ideological support to both racism and imperialism. DAI 41:3696-A.

1059 Simmons, Christina C. " 'Marriage in the Modern Manner': Sexual Radicalism and Reform in America, 1914–1941." Ph.D. dissertation, Brown University, 1982.

Victorian ideals of sexual purity and strict separation of gender roles came to be called Victorian repression in the twentieth century. Advocates of birth control, sex education, and women's sexuality in and out of marriage appeared. Modern marriage, called "companionate," evolved. Instead of being members of a class separate from men, women came to be, in many regards, second-class men. DAI 43:3686-A.

1060 Weyeneth, Robert R. "Moral Spaces: Reforming the Landscape of Leisure in Urban America, 1850–1920." Ph.D. dissertation, University of California, Berkeley, 1984.

Progressives constructed utilitarian parks and community centers in an attempt to impose order and uniformity on urban leisure. Although the parks were well used, they had little effect on moral behavior. Various profit-making recreational opportunities became available to all income levels. DAI 46:1071-A.

1061 Zaretsky, Eli S. "Progressive Thought on the Impact of Industrialization on the Family and Its Relation to the Emergence of the Welfare State, 1890–1920." Ph.D. dissertation, University of Maryland, 1980.

The works of Jane Addams, Mary Richmond, Charlotte Perkins Gilman, William I. Thomas, and Florian Znaniecki on industrialization and the family are discussed to illustrate how Progressives inadvertently furthered selfish individualism through their advocacy of a welfare state. DAI 40:5564-A.

EDUCATION

1062 Ashby, LeRoy. *Saving the Waifs: Reformers and Dependent Children, 1890–1917.* Philadelphia: Temple University Press, 1984.

Progressive reformers were both moved by the plight of abused and neglected children and concerned with social control. Five different children's programs are examined. Notes, bibliography, index.

1063 ———. " 'Straight from Youthful Hearts': Lone Scout, and the Discovery of the Child, 1915–1924." *Journal of Popular Culture* 9 (1976): 775–93.

The Lone Scouts of America was created in 1915 and published a journal illustrative of the values of Progressive-era youth, such as community service, hard work, and perseverance. Racism and militarism were also apparent in this offshoot of the Boy Scouts. Notes.

1064 Auerbach, Jerold S. "Enmity and Amity: Law Teachers and Practitioners, 1900–1922." *Perspectives in American History* 5 (1971): 551–601.

Law professors were zealous in their reform spirit, while the legal profession as a whole wanted to change only slowly. The scholars wanted to use the law to bring about social justice, while many lawyers saw legal codes as a way to control the masses. Notes.

1065 Barnard, Harry V., and Best, John Hardin. "Public Education in the United States, 1918–1945." *Current History* 41 (1961): 22–27.

Federal programs of aid to education have been shaped in large part by times of crisis. During World War I, the Smith-Hughes Act started financial aid to vocational education, thus setting a precedent for future programs.

1066 Bartow, Beverly. "Isabel Bevier at the University of Illinois and the Home Economics Movement." *Journal of the Illinois State Historical Society* 72 (1979): 21–38.

Between 1900 and 1921, Bevier pioneered in the field of home economics, the science of domestic management. Notes.

1067 Beck, Earl R. "The German Discovery of American Education." *History of Education Quarterly* 5 (1965): 3–13.

German education experts did not like American high schools and universities but had some good things to say about adult education and elementary schools.

1068 Beltz, Lynda. "Never Too Old for New Ventures: Ida M. Tarbell's 'Second Profession.' " *Pennsylvania Magazine of History and Biography* 99 (1975): 476–89.

With muckraking out of fashion by 1915, journalist Ida Tarbell began a new career as a Chautauqua and lyceum speaker. Notes.

1069 Berrol, Selma C. "Education in New York City: 1900–1920." *Illinois Quarterly* 35 (1973): 20–30.

Public schools helped to assimilate immigrant children into the urban American scene at a time when the city was undergoing rapid growth.

1070 Cavallo, Dominick. *Muscles and Morals: Organized Playgrounds and Urban Reform, 1880–1920.* Philadelphia: University of Pennsylvania Press, 1981.

While play organizers did want to control urban youth, this was not necessarily a characteristic of the Progressive impulse. Rather, these and other reformers of the era hoped to create a balance between collectivism and individualism. Photographs, notes, bibliography, index.

1071 ———. "Social Reform and the Movement to Organize Children's Play during the Progressive Era." *History of Childhood Quarterly* 3 (1976): 509–22.

Progressive reformers used children's play to battle against individualism, to Americanize immigrant children, and to socialize youth in a modern setting.

1072 Cohen, Sol. "The Industrial Education Movement, 1906–1917." *American Quarterly* 20 (1968): 95–110.

Many Progressives supported the idea of industrial education in public schools to better prepare students for life. Junior high schools were created for vocational training, and many schools divided students onto academic and vocational tracks. Notes.

1073 Corley, Florence F. "Higher Education for Southern Women: Four Church-Related Women's Colleges in Georgia, Agnes Scott, Shorter, Spelman, and Wesleyan, 1900–1920." Ph.D. dissertation, Georgia State University, 1985.

Two women from each college illustrate the effect of education on their lives. White and black, and northern and southern colleges are contrasted. DAI 46:3842-A.

1074 Danbom, David B. "Rural Education Reform and the Country Life Movement, 1900–1920." *Agricultural History* 53 (1979): 462–74.

The country life movement hoped to use education to improve rural life. Country people were slow to adopt the liberal arts curriculum, in part because they did not trust the urban reformers. Notes.

1075 Diggins, John P. "John Dewey in Peace and War." *American Scholar* 50 (1981): 213–30.

Dewey's support for America's entrance into the war did not jibe with his pragmatic philosophy. If pragmatism was the solution to the crisis of historical knowledge, why did history seem to demonstrate the extreme limitations of the pragmatic approach?

1076 Fee, Elizabeth. "Competition for the First School of Hygiene and Public Health." *Bulletin of the History of Medicine* 57 (1983): 339–63.

Harvard, Yale, Columbia, and Johns Hopkins vied for funding from the Rockefeller Foundation for the first school of public health research and education, with Hopkins winning the honor thanks to the work of William Henry Welch. Notes.

1077 Fine, William F. "Progressive Evolutionism and American Sociology, 1890–1920." Ph.D. dissertation, University of Iowa, 1976.

Sociologists embraced progressive evolutionism during the Progressive era as a reaction against Social Darwinism. This movement to create a discipline grounded in science was driven by a desire to guide social change. While the activist philosophy dropped away, progressive evolutionism played an important role in the development of modern sociology. DAI 37:3127-A.

1078 Fuller, Wayne E. "Changing Concepts of the Country School as a Community Center in the Midwest." *Agricultural History* 58 (1984): 423–41.

To bring the old rural sense of community to burgeoning urban areas, Progressive reformers made city schools into community centers. Rural schools were reformed through consolidation, thus diminishing what was left of community in the countryside. Notes.

1079 Gordon, Lynn D. "Women with Missions: Varieties of College Life in the Progressive Era." Ph.D. dissertation, University of Chicago, 1980.

The interests of college women, who represented almost half of all undergraduates by 1920, are revealed by letters, articles, speeches, papers, and fiction. College women were most active in movements to better family life, from fair wages to child labor laws, and also, as might be expected, women's suffrage. DAI 41:3233-A.

1080 Hall, Margaret A. "A History of Women Faculty at the University of Washington, 1896–

1970." Ph.D. dissertation, University of Washington, 1984.

During the Wilson era, women faculty members at the University of Washington were almost entirely relegated to fields such as nursing and were typically given nontenured, low-paying positions. DAI 45:610-A.

1081 Herder, Dale M. "Haldeman-Julius, the Little Blue Books, and the Theory of Popular Culture." *Journal of Popular Culture* 4 (1971): 881–91.

To further the causes of happiness and civilization, Emanuel Haldeman-Julius published inexpensive reprints of classic books for the working class.

1082 Howlett, Charles. "The Pragmatist as Pacifist: John Dewey's Views on Peace Education." *Teachers College Record* 83 (1982): 435–51.

Dewey switched from support of World War I to pacifism, leading him to design an educational curriculum that deemphasized nationalism in favor of peace through international law. Notes.

1083 Jenkins, William D. "Housewifery and Motherhood: The Question of Role Change in the Progressive Era." In Mary Kelley, ed. *Woman's Being, Woman's Place: Female Identity and Vocation in American History*. Boston: G. K. Hall, 1979, pp. 142–53.

Home economics, which became a formal discipline taught in high schools and colleges during the Progressive era, added formal recognition to the science of housekeeping, but it also reinforced the notion that a woman's place was in the home. Notes.

1084 Kaplan, Thomas J. "From Theory to Practice in American Educational Reform, 1900–1925." Ph.D. dissertation, University of Wisconsin, Madison, 1979.

Disciples of John Dewey's educational theories were active in Wisconsin during the Progressive era. They had a mixed record in their educational reform efforts, because administrators were interested only in practical results, not grand theories. DAI 40:4716-A.

1085 Karnes, Thomas L. "Hiram Bingham and His Obsolete Shibboleth." *Diplomatic History* 3 (1979): 39–57.

Professor Hiram Bingham attacked the Monroe Doctrine as obsolete in 1913 and 1914, causing thoughtful Americans to take another look at the longtime policy. Bingham later backtracked, claiming American intervention was necessary on occasion. Notes.

1086 Kennedy, Thomas C. "Charles A. Beard in Midpassage." *Historian* 30 (1968): 179–98.

A strong supporter of American entry into the war in 1917, Charles A. Beard became an isolationist by the 1930s. Notes.

1087 Kraus, Michelle P. "Personnel Research: History and Policy Issues: Walter Van Dyke Bingham and the Bureau of Personnel Research." Ph.D. dissertation, Carnegie-Mellon University, 1982.

Industry in this period wanted effective but inexpensive expertise in testing and selecting employees. Walter Van Dyke Bingham sought to reconcile academically sound psychological testing with business's need for the quick and the cheap. Bingham's relationship with business compromised quality in favor of profit. DAI 44:636-A.

1088 Levstik, Frank R. "A History of the Education and Treatment of the Mentally Retarded in Ohio, 1787–1920." Ph.D. dissertation, Ohio State University, 1981.

The fledgling science of genetics perpetuated prejudices against the mentally retarded, and forced sterilization was common. The mentally retarded were believed to be inherently antisocial, and they were generally institutionalized to separate them from the larger society. Some vocational training was available. DAI 42:822-A.

1089 Link, William A. "Public Schooling and Social Change in Rural Virginia." Ph.D. dissertation, University of Virginia, 1981.

Reformers in the late nineteenth century considered compulsory, enlightened education crucial to relieving racial and economic problems in the South. The creation of a school bureaucracy, vocational education, and overall stabilization of the Virginia school system after its haphazard beginnings are discussed. DAI 42:3721-A.

1090 Lybarger, Michael. "Origins of Modern Social Studies." *History of Education Quarterly* 23 (1983): 455–68.

A Progressive-era committee chaired by Thomas J. Jones pioneered the development of the modern social studies curriculum. The new educational plans were based in part on ideas designed to keep blacks as a docile labor force, and the Committee on Social Studies hoped to use these plans to rationalize inequality. Notes.

1091 McArthur, Benjamin. "The Chicago Playground Movement: A Neglected Feature of Social Justice." *Social Service Review* 49 (1975): 376–95.

Social workers, businessmen, and civic leaders combined forces to organize the playground movement to preserve social order, preserve the home, and protect children while instilling them with patriotism.

1092 McCaffrey, Donna T. "The Origins and Early History of Providence College through 1947." Ph.D. dissertation, Providence College, 1983.

Providence College is a small liberal arts college supported by the Dominican Province of St. Joseph, the Diocese of Providence, and the Catholic community. The development of the college through its first five presidents is detailed, including the tenure of the first, Albert D. Casey, from 1919 through 1921. DAI 45:3728-A.

1093 Mead, David. "1914: The Chautauqua and American Innocence." *Journal of Popular Culture* 1 (1968): 339–56.

The Chautauqua of popular education and culture had its greatest year of growth in 1914. It was so influential that it delayed the end of American innocence by many years.

1094 Morgan, Alda C. M. "Academic Freedom in Higher Education: An Historical and Theological Examination of Its Place and Function in the Light of Five Cases." Ph.D. dissertation, Graduate Theological Union, 1984.

The author equates academic freedom with the search for truth, asserting that it "represents the deepest human values of the professor's work and sanctions his claims for cultural and social authority." Five specific cases are presented, two of which occurred during Wilson's presidency. DAI 45:1315-A.

1095 Nethers, John L. "Simeon D. Fess: Educator and Politician." Ph.D. dissertation, Ohio State University, 1964.

Simeon Fess was president of Antioch College from 1907 through 1917, and he also served as a Republican congressman for four terms, beginning in 1912. Fess opposed Wilson on numerous issues, including the League of Nations. DAI 25:6575.

1096 Payne, Kenneth W., and Murray, Stephen O. "Historical Inferences from Ethnohistorical Data: Boasian Views." *Journal of* *the History of the Behavioral Sciences* 19 (1983): 335–40.

In 1914–1916, the American Anthropological Association rejected the notion that folklore could be used to help reconstruct pre-Columbian history in North America in spite of the strong case the Boasians made for it.

1097 Reese, William J. "The Control of Urban School Boards during the Progressive Era: A Reconsideration." *Pacific Northwest Quarterly* 68 (1977): 164–73.

When citywide school boards took control of public education away from neighborhood elites, the socioeconomic profile of the controlling group remained constant. Notes.

1098 ———. "Progressive School Reform in Toledo: 1898–1921." *Northwest Ohio Quarterly* 47 (1975): 44–59.

The modern public school system of Toledo was born during the Progressive era, with reformers creating innovative programs for the handicapped and kindergartners while instilling the children with patriotism.

1099 Roitman, Joel M. "The Progressive Movement: Education and Americanization." Ph.D. dissertation, University of Cincinnati, 1981.

Immigrants from Southern and Eastern Europe spurred the Progressives to transform education from "the three Rs" to an instrument of cultural change designed to Americanize immigrants. DAI 42:2265-A.

1100 Schultze, Quentin J. " 'An Honorable Place': The Quest for Professional Advertising Education, 1900–1917." *Business History Review* 56 (1982): 16–32.

The campaign to include advertising in the business curriculum was complicated by the reluctance of independent academic institutions to make the desired changes and by the reluctance of businessmen to commit themselves to hiring graduates from such programs. Notes.

1101 Scult, Mel. "Mordecai Kaplan, the Teachers Institute, and the Foundations of Jewish Education in America." *American Jewish Archives* 38 (1986): 57–84.

The Jewish education movement was spurred between 1904 and 1916 by Mordecai Kaplan, who headed the Teachers Institute at the Jewish Theological Seminary of America. Samson Benderly and Solomon Schecter also played important parts in this educational crusade.

1102 Shapiro, Michael S. "Froebel in America: A Social and Intellectual History of the Kindergarten Movement, 1848–1918." Ph.D. dissertation, Brown University, 1980.

The traditional transmission of values and skills from parent to child, the romantic Froebelian ideas on early childhood education, and Protestantism all conflicted regarding the best treatment of young children. The Froebelian movement was internally consistent until 1918. It affected the philosophy of early education, including the thought of John Dewey. DAI 41:5224-A.

1103 Spring, Joel. "Education and Progressivism." *History of Education Quarterly* 10 (1970): 53–71.

In education, many Progressives advocated a cooperative approach rather than a concern with traditional individualism. Vocational curricula, junior high schools, and systematic educational planning all came out of this era. Notes.

1104 Stanfield, John H. "The 'Negro Problem' within and beyond the Institutional Nexus of Pre-World War I Sociology." *Phylon* 43 (1982): 187–201.

Blacks were not allowed into professional sociological societies in the Progressive era, and their ideas were ignored by white sociologists who perceived blacks as inferior beings.

1105 Sweeney, Raymond S. "Public Education in Maryland in the Progressive Era." *Maryland History Magazine* 62 (1967): 28–46.

Reformers made many changes in Maryland's public education system during the Progressive era, taking learning out of the hands of politicians and upgrading the status of educators.

1106 Taggart, Robert J. "Pierre S. Du Pont and the Great School Fight of 1919–1921." *Delaware History* 17 (1977): 155–78.

Du Pont fought for a centralized state school system, promising democracy but instead giving control to professional educators.

1107 Tiffin, Susan. *In Whose Best Interest? Child Welfare Reform in the Progressive Era.* Westport, CT: Greenwood, 1982.

Social workers and philanthropists were moved to help dependent and neglected children, because they regarded children as saviors of society who could provide the country with a stable future. While many children were helped, an underlying tension between the conflicting goals of social stability and social justice limited the movement's effectiveness. Notes, bibliography, index.

1108 Urban, Wayne. "Organized Teachers and Educational Reform during the Progressive Era, 1890–1920." *History of Education Quarterly* 16 (1976): 35–52.

Teacher organizations in urban areas fought against centralization and curricular changes advocated by Progressive reformers. Notes.

1109 ———. *Why Teachers Organized.* Detroit: Wayne State University Press, 1982.

Teachers in urban areas organized for better wages and to protect their seniority, becoming a politicized special interest group in the process. Notes, bibliography, index.

1110 Wish, Harvey. "Negro Education and the Progressive Movement." *Journal of Negro History* 49 (1964): 184–200.

Blacks had little chance to get an education during the Progressive era except in the area of industrial training. Black educators, especially W. E. B. DuBois and the NAACP, fought for improvement, as did a few concerned whites. Notes.

RELIGION

1111 Abell, Aaron I. *American Catholicism and Social Action: A Search for Social Justice, 1865–1950.* Notre Dame, IN: University of Notre Dame Press, 1963.

A chapter is included on Catholics interested in Progressive reforms during the Wilson era. Notes, bibliography, index.

1112 Ahlstrom, Sydney E. "Continental Influence on American Christian Thought since World War I." *Church History* 27 (1958): 256–72.

In this examination of the influence of modern European Christian intellectual currents on the United States, the author notes that World War I had a much greater impact on the continent than it did in America. Notes.

1113 Bachhuber, Claire M. "The German-Catholic Elite: Contributions of a Catholic Intellectual and Cultural Elite of German-American Background in Early Twentieth-Century

St. Louis." Ph.D. dissertation, St. Louis University, 1984.

The author presents the intellectual and cultural contributions of seven Catholic citizens of St. Louis to refute the claim that Catholics have not been prominent in these areas. DAI 45:2231-A.

1114 Brandon, Betty J. "A Wilsonian Progressive—Alexander Jeffrey McKelway." *Journal of Presbyterian History* 48 (1970): 2–17.

A leading Presbyterian activist and editor, McKelway urged Wilson and the Democrats to back welfare and labor reform. His influence was apparent in the 1916 party platform, and he campaigned effectively for the president's reelection. Notes.

1115 Britsch, R. Lanier. "The Closing of the Early Japan Mission." *Brigham Young University Studies* 15 (1975): 171–90.

The Mormon church closed its first mission to Japan after a quarter century of frustration marked by an inability to attract converts. Notes.

1116 Campbell, Debra. "A Catholic Salvation Army: David Goldstein, Pioneer Lay Evangelist." *Church History* 52 (1983): 322–32.

A converted Jewish socialist, Goldstein preached Catholicism in the streets and was cofounder of the Catholic Truth Guild in 1917.

1117 Carey, Robert B. "The Passing of the Parish Minister as a Learned Professional." Ph.D. dissertation, Columbia University, 1984.

The parish minister, once respected as a pastor-scholar, had become, by 1920, a "religious generalist." The nature of parish work itself had changed, as had church bureaucracies and seminary education. DAI 46:244-A.

1118 Carter, James E. "The Fraternal Address of Southern Baptists." *Baptist History and Heritage* 12 (1977): 211–18.

The 1919 "Fraternal Address of Southern Baptists," written chiefly by Dr. E. Y. Mullins, called for opening lines of communications between Baptist groups worldwide for the purpose of greater cooperation. Widely disregarded, it still stood as an important statement of the Baptist faith. Notes.

1119 Davis, R. D. "Billy Sunday: Preacher-Showman." *Southern Speech Journal* 32 (1966): 83–97.

While Billy Sunday was a great showman, his style did not advance the cause of evangelical Christianity. Notes.

1120 Dawson, Jan C. "The Religion of Democracy in Early Twentieth-Century America." *Journal of Church and State* 27 (1985): 47–63.

World War I and the Bolshevik Revolution changed the way many religious thinkers thought about the relationship between church and democracy. Notes.

1121 Doherty, Herbert J., Jr. "Alexander J. McKelway: Preacher to Progressive." *Journal of Southern History* 24 (1958): 177–90.

A former editor of a Presbyterian magazine in North Carolina, McKelway helped lead a nationwide fight for laws protecting child laborers and lent support to Wilson in politics. Notes.

1122 Dorn, Jacob H. *Washington Gladden: Prophet of the Social Gospel.* Columbus: Ohio State University Press, 1967.

Popularizer of the social gospel liberal theology and a lifelong Republican, Gladden endorsed Wilson in 1916, after the president had carefully courted him. Notes, bibliography, index.

1123 Dougherty, Patrick T. "Catholic Opinion and United States Recognition Policy." Ph.D. dissertation, University of Missouri, 1963.

Wilson used nonrecognition in Latin America and Moscow as a moral and diplomatic tool. The Vatican viewed recognition as simply a way of maintaining contact with the world, but American Catholics tended toward Wilson's attitude. DAI 24:4773.

1124 Dwyer, James A. "*Der Christliche Apologete*: German Prophet to America, 1914–1918." *Methodist History* 15 (1977): 75–94.

Der Christliche Apologete, the official publication of German Methodists in the United States, called for American neutrality after 1914. American entry into the war brought editorial changes under pressure from other Methodist groups. Notes.

1125 Eighmy, John L. "Religious Liberalism in the South during the Progressive Era." *Church History* 38 (1969): 359–72.

Conservatives lost control of southern Protestantism during the Progressive era, as church leaders of the New South embraced the social gospel. Notes.

1126 Feldman, Egal. "The Social Gospel and the Jews." *American Jewish Historical Quarterly* 58 (1969): 308–29.

During the Progressive era, Jews and liberal Christians worked together under the aegis of the social gospel, although centuries of anti-Semitism could not be undone in a few short years.

1127 Fish, John O. "Southern Methodism in the Progressive Era: A Social History." Ph.D. dissertation, University of Georgia, 1969.

Southern Methodists agreed that more work needed to be done in cities but disagreed over strategy, with some advocating revivalism, while others saw social work as the answer. Women were the most Progressive force in the church, but campaigns for prohibition and racial segregation diverted attention from more positive causes. DAI 30:2938-A.

1128 Flynt, Wayne. "Southern Baptists and Reform: 1890–1920." *Baptist History and Heritage* 7 (1972): 211–24.

Many Southern Baptists supported Progressive reforms, although they eschewed the demands of blacks and unions.

1129 Fones-Wolf, Kenneth A. "Trade Union Gospel: Protestantism and Labor in Philadelphia, 1865–1915." Ph.D. dissertation, Temple University, 1985.

Protestant rhetoric and Victorian morality were important in trade union struggles. DAI 47:1034-A.

1130 Frommer, Morris. "The American Jewish Congress: A History, 1914–1950." Ph.D. dissertation, Ohio State University, 1978.

The American Jewish Congress strove to protect the rights of Jews in Russia and Eastern Europe. Their lobbying efforts at the Paris Peace Conference resulted in guarantees of Jewish rights by the newly created states and the League of Nations. DAI 39:1058-A.

1131 Gaffey, James P. *Francis Clement Kelley and the American Catholic Dream.* 2 vols. Bensenville, IL: Heritage Foundation, 1980.

Leader of the home mission movement in the American West, Kelley became embroiled in international politics after World War I. Notes, bibliography, index.

1132 Giffin, Frederick C. "Billy Sunday: The Evangelist as 'Patriot.' " *Social Science* 48 (1973): 216–21.

Always a superpatriot, Sunday was a zealous supporter of American participation in World War I, dividing his time among preaching, encouraging enlistments and the sale of war bonds, and denouncing the enemy.

1133 Handy, Robert T. "Charles L. Thompson—Presbyterian Architect of

Cooperative Protestantism." *Journal of the Presbyterian Historical Society* 33 (1955): 207–28.

Thompson ministered to Presbyterian flocks in cities from Juneau to New York and was active during the Progressive era in the Federal Council of Churches of Christ, the Presbyterian Board of Home Missions, and the Home Missions Council.

1134 Harvey, Charles E. "John D. Rockefeller, Jr. and the Interchurch World Movement of 1919–1920: A Different Angle on the Ecumenical Movement." *Church History* 51 (1982): 198–209.

The younger Rockefeller gave his and his father's money to the Interchurch World Movement, because he was excited by the prospect of church unity. Notes.

1135 Hunt, James D. "The Social Gospel as a Way of Life: A Biography of H. C. Ledyard, Universalist Minister and Labor Leader, 1880–1950." *Journal of the Universalist Historical Society* 5 (1964): 31–63.

A Universalist minister, Ledyard embraced Christian socialism during the Progressive era and practiced pacifism during World War I. Following the conflict he became a labor organizer. Notes.

1136 Hutchison, William R. *The Modernist Impulse in American Protestantism.* Cambridge, MA: Harvard University Press, 1976.

Fundamentalism and neo-orthodoxy were in conflict with liberal Progressivism, also called modernism, during the Progressive era. The author explores the fundamentalist and humanist reactions to the key tenets of liberal theology. Appendix, notes, bibliography, index.

1137 King, K. J. "The American Negro as Missionary to East Africa: A Critical Aspect of African Evangelism." *African Historical Studies* 3 (1970): 3–22.

Few blacks did missionary work in Africa before 1917, because this was opposed by white church groups and philanthropic foundations. Although black missionaries were active in Africa briefly during the war, opposition mounted again, so that even missionaries of the Tuskegee school were unacceptable. Notes.

1138 Lamb, Blaine P. "Jewish Pioneers in Arizona, 1850–1920." Ph.D. dissertation, Arizona State University, 1982.

Jewish pioneers in Arizona generally undertook the same occupations as other pioneers and were easily accepted and assimilated.

However, Jews became prominent as developers of commercial banking and were able to form stable communities. The overt practice of Judaism increased and became more formalized by 1920. DAI 43:1265-A.

1139 Lankford, John. "Methodism 'Over the Top': The Joint Centenary Movement, 1917–1925." *Methodist History* 2 (1963): 27–37.

To celebrate the Methodist Missionary Society's centennial, the church raised money to carry out ambitious plans for worldwide programs.

1140 Lavey, Patrick B. "William J. Kerby, John A. Ryan, and the Awakening of the Twentieth-Century American Catholic Social Conscience, 1899–1919." Ph.D. dissertation, University of Illinois, Urbana-Champaign, 1986.

William J. Kerby and John A. Ryan are credited with bringing Progressive-era social consciousness to the Catholic church. Social problems are national in scope, they claimed, and should be addressed by national charities. DAI 47:2711-A.

1141 Lefever, Harry G. "The Involvement of the Men and Religion Forward Movement in the Cause of Labor Justice, Atlanta, Georgia, 1912–1916." *Labor History* 14 (1973): 521–35.

The working class received the attention of concerned southern liberal Christians touched by the social gospel. Notes.

1142 McAlpin, William B. "Presbyterians and the Relation of Church and State." *Journal of the Presbyterian Historical Society* 32 (1954): 187–202.

The Presbyterian church has taken official stands on important government issues throughout its history including support for separation of church and state, condemnation of the failure to join the League of Nations, and identification with Wilson's policies during World War I. Notes.

1143 McAvoy, Thomas T. "The Catholic Minority after the Americanist Controversy, 1899–1917: A Survey." *Review of Politics* 21 (1959): 53–82.

The 1899 papal condemnation of Americanism, or modernism, inside the church led to Catholic clergymen concentrating their efforts on Americanizing immigrants, at least until 1917. Notes.

1144 McDonnell, James R., and Aiken, John R. "Walter Rauchenbusch and Labor Reform: A Social Gospeler's Approach." *Labor History* 11 (1970): 131–50.

The social gospel had little practical advice to offer to the labor movement and misunderstood the needs of unions. Notes.

1145 McKeown, Elizabeth. "The National Bishops' Conference: An Analysis of Its Origins." *Catholic Historical Review* 66 (1980): 565–83.

The Reverend John J. Burke used the wartime atmosphere to further the cause of a national episcopal conference. Special interest politics was seen by his group as a way to enhance its presence at the seat of secular power. Opposition from the Vatican and from American Catholic leaders thwarted this movement.

1146 McLoughlin, William G., Jr. *Billy Sunday Was His Real Name*. Chicago: University of Chicago Press, 1955.

Billy Sunday was a baseball player who became an evangelist and attracted an astoundingly large following with his patriotic and fundamentalist message. The author explores the cultural conditions that made people receptive to Sunday between 1908 and 1918. Notes, bibliography, index.

1147 ———. "Billy Sunday and the Working Girl of 1915." *Journal of Presbyterian History* 54 (1976): 376–84.

In Sunday's services held for women only, he warned young women not to be lured by the temptations of evil. They should stay home, he said, reflecting traditional evangelical ideas.

1148 McShane, Joseph M. *"Sufficiently Radical": Catholicism, Progressivism, and the Bishop's Program of 1919*. Washington, DC: Catholic University of America Press, 1986.

Catholic bishops endorsed a cautious brand of Progressivism as a means of coming to grips with modern society. Notes, bibliography, index.

1149 Martin, Patricia S. "Hidden Work: Baptist Women in Texas, 1880–1920." Ph.D. dissertation, Rice University, 1982.

Baptist women, largely lower and middle class, believed in submitting to men in the home and as their church leaders. However, they were also able to find support in their religion for developing spheres of competence and minor power, particularly in missionary work. The influence of religion on domestic and political life is examined. DAI 43:527-A.

1150 Meyer, Carl S. "Some Aspects of the Observance of the Reformation Quadricentennial

by America's Lutherans." *Concordia Historical Institute Quarterly* 41 (1968): 14–35.

The 1917 quadricentennial of the Reformation brought about a reunion movement among several Lutheran factions and the use of public relations to make the public aware of the anniversary. Notes.

1151 Miller, Donald H. "A History of Hadassah, 1912–1935." Ed.D. dissertation, New York University, 1968.

The largest women's Zionist organization, Hadassah, focused on the health, education, and welfare aspects of building Jewish Palestine. Conflicts with the Zionist Organization of America, its parent body, led Hadassah to become financially and administratively semi-independent by 1921. DAI 29:2649-A.

1152 Ownby, Ted. "Evangelicalism and Male Culture: Recreation and Religion in the Rural South, 1865–1920." Ph.D. dissertation, Johns Hopkins University, 1986.

Southern men faced two contradictory ideals of behavior: the chaste, evangelical home and the competitive, masculine recreational group. As it became more difficult to separate these two arenas, southern evangelicals began to pass laws against recreational abuses, including swearing. DAI 47:4495-A.

1153 Pearson, Ralph L. "Internationalizing the Social Gospel: The Federal Council of Churches and European Protestantism, 1914–1925." *History Magazine of the Protestant Episcopal Church* 52 (1983): 275–92.

The Federal Council of Churches hoped to internationalize the social gospel. The hope that the war would provide an opportunity for such work was soon dashed, and the council concentrated on rebuilding destroyed churches and working for internationalism. Notes.

1154 Piper, John F., Jr. "Father John J. Burke, C.S.P. and the Turning Point in American Catholic History." *Records of the American Catholic Historical Society* 92 (1981): 101–13.

Burke worked successfully to create an officially recognized national Catholic agency through a series of conferences and councils. Notes.

1155 Rosenberg, Ann E. "The Influence of Freudian and Post-Freudian Theory on Religion in America as Reflected in Religious Journals, 1900–1965." Ph.D. dissertation, Columbia University, 1978.

Sigmund Freud's preoccupation with sex made religious leaders wary of psychology. Neo-Freudianism was more acceptable. DAI 39: 6300-A.

1156 Shapiro, Robert D. "A Reform Rabbi in the Progressive Era: The Early Career of Stephen S. Wise." Ph.D. dissertation, Harvard University, 1984.

Rabbi Stephen Wise was a well-known Progressive reformer in the Wilson era. During the war he changed direction, championing Zionism. DAI 45:2235-A.

1157 Sinclair, Karen K. "The Church Peace Union: Visions of Peace in Troubled Times." Ph.D. dissertation, University of Akron, 1987.

The Church Peace Union, established by Andrew Carnegie in 1914, was an interfaith organization that sought peace through propagating a belief in the unity of all mankind. Not actually pacifist, the union accepted the necessity of World War I. DAI 47:4174-A.

1158 Slawson, Douglas J. "The Attitudes and Activities of American Catholics regarding the Proposals to Establish a Federal Department of Education between World War I and the Great Depression." Ph.D. dissertation, Catholic University of America, 1981.

The desirability of a federal-level department of education was augmented by the lack of coordinated mobilization of support for World War I through the schools. The Catholic church successfully opposed federalization, ostensibly because it feared loss of freedom in education, but also because increased funding for public schools threatened Catholic schools. DAI 42:824-A.

1159 Sledge, Robert W. "A History of the Methodist Episcopal Church, South, 1914–1939." Ph.D. dissertation, University of Texas, Austin, 1972.

The Progressive movement challenged the conservative leadership of the Methodist Episcopal church by 1918. The differences between southern Methodist Progressives and conservatives split the movement, but they were not irreconcilable. DAI 33:3560-A.

1160 Smith, Gary S. "Calvinism and Culture in America, 1870–1915." Ph.D. dissertation, Johns Hopkins University, 1981.

Calvinists were thoroughly opposed to the evolving philosophies and science that opened the way for increased secularization of all areas of life, from government to social customs.

God's word should be given ultimate power, even in corporations, according to Calvinist theologians. DAI 42:825-A.

1161 Soden, Dale E. "Mark Allison Mathews: Seattle's Southern Preacher." Ph.D. dissertation, University of Washington, 1980.

A Presbyterian minister in Seattle for forty years, Mathews became a frequent correspondent of President Wilson. Mathews mixed in Pacific Northwest politics and became a zealous supporter of Wilson's war policies. DAI 41:4815-A.

1162 Staggers, Kermit L. "Reuben A. Torrey: American Fundamentalist, 1856–1928." Ph.D. dissertation, Claremont Graduate School, 1986.

Torrey, along with many nineteenth-century thinkers, believed that truth was solid, unchanging, and accessible to man. The Bible was, for him, a primary source of that absolute truth. Although active conversion of people to Christianity was his life's work, he took time to write and preach against U.S. involvement in World War I, claiming that patriotism was an enemy of Christian brotherhood. DAI 47:1036-A.

1163 Swanson, Merwin. "The 'Country Life Movement' and the American Churches." *Church History* 46 (1977): 358–73.

The Progressive-era country life movement tried to restore the old sense of community in rural areas. Rural churches created community centers as a means to this end. Notes.

1164 Szasz, Ferene M. "The Progressive Clergy and the Kingdom of God." *Mid-America* 55 (1973): 3–20.

Liberals and conservatives alike preached the social gospel during the Progressive era. Protestant ministers wholeheartedly supported the idea of scientific professionalism as well. Notes.

1165 Thompson, James J., Jr. "Southern Baptists and Post-War Disillusionment, 1918–1920." *Foundations* 21 (1978): 113–22.

Attitudes of Southern Baptists in 1918 to 1920 indicate that disillusion with the outcome of the war and the peace treaty was far from universal. Notes.

1166 Warnock, Henry H. "Moderate Racial Thought and Attitudes of Southern Baptists and Methodists, 1900–1921." Ph.D. dissertation, Northwestern University, 1963.

Southern Baptists and Methodists believed that blacks were essentially inferior to whites, and they sought parallel societies rather than integration. However, they supported black education, general welfare, and voting rights. DAI 24:3724.

1167 Webster, John C. B. "Presbyterian Missionaries and Gandhian Politics, 1919–1922." *Journal of Presbyterian History* 62 (1984): 246–57.

Presbyterian missionaries were forced to become involved in the politics of India after Mahatma Gandhi launched the movement for independence. Notes.

1168 White, Larry. "Margaret W. Rowen: Prophetess of Reform and Doom." *Adventist Heritage* 6 (1979): 28–40.

An Adventist, Margaret Rowen claimed to have had a series of divine visions beginning in 1916 and forged several documents to prove her claims to church leadership.

SPORTS

1169 Alexander, Charles C. *Ty Cobb*. New York: Oxford University Press, 1984.

Although he was not the most gifted of ball players, Cobb was the greatest baseball star of the Progressive era. A mean-spirited, racist southerner, Cobb was also an ardent supporter of Wilson. Photographs, notes, bibliography, index.

1170 Asinof, Eliot. *Eight Men Out*. New York: Holt, Rinehart and Winston, 1963.

The author sketches the lives of each of the eight Chicago White Sox who were permanently suspended for throwing the 1919 World Series. The economics and the image of baseball in 1919 are explored.

1171 Cox, James A. "Was 'The Gipper' Really for Real?" *Smithsonian* 16 (1985): 130–50.

The life of Notre Dame football star George Gipp, who became a hero from 1916 to 1920, is discussed along with the later movie in which he was portrayed by Ronald Reagan.

1172 Finfer, Lawrence A. "Leisure as Social Work in the Urban Community: The Progressive Recreation Movement, 1890–1920." Ph.D. dissertation, Michigan State University, 1974.

In many ways, the recreation movement mirrored the larger Progressive movement within which it operated. Progressives argued that supervised recreation for young people could counter negative influences in poor homes and neighborhoods. Nighttime social centers in public schools were promoted as democracy in action, but their real function was long-term management of social conflicts. DAI 36:478-A.

1173 Gilmore, Al-Tony. *Bad Nigger! The National Impact of Jack Johnson*. Port Washington, NY: Kennikat, 1975.

This black boxing champion was widely hated for his greatness and for his marriages to white women. Many blacks loved him for the very same reasons. Photographs, notes, bibliography, index.

1174 ———. "Jack Johnson, the Man and His Times." *Journal of Popular Culture* 6 (1972): 496–506.

Heavyweight boxing champion from 1908 to 1915, Jack Johnson became the most famous black man in the world. His marriages to white women and his pride angered white Americans. Notes.

1175 ———. "Jack Johnson and White Women: The National Impact, 1912–1913." *Journal of Negro History* 58 (1973): 18–38.

Whites and blacks alike condemn Jack Johnson for his liaisons with white women. Notes.

1176 Lehr, Robert Edward. "The American Olympic Committee, 1896–1940: From Chaos to Order." Ph.D. dissertation, Pennsylvania State University, 1986.

The U.S. Olympic Committee was formalized as the official American Olympic games organization in 1921, in response to various changes in leadership and degree of participation and a controversy over the 1920 games. DAI 47:829-A.

1177 Lewis, Guy. "World War I and the Emergence of Sport for the Masses." *Maryland Historian* 4 (1973): 109–22.

The government used sports to occupy the spare time of soldiers during World War I, an official sanction which led to sport's "golden age" in the coming decade. Notes.

1178 Lucas, John. "American Preparations for the First Post World War Olympic Games, 1919–1920." *Journal of Sport History* 10 (1983): 30–44.

Without funds or transport for American athletes going to the postwar Olympics in Antwerp, the American Olympic Committee secured an army transport ship, accommodations the athletes rebelled against. The United States won the most medals at the games, but not as many as in 1912. Notes.

1179 Murdock, Eugene C. "The Tragedy of Ban Johnson." *Journal of Sports History* 1 (1974): 26–40.

Founder and longtime president of the American League, Ban Johnson became the most powerful man in major league baseball after becoming the unofficial chairman of the national commission. His power began to slip in 1920, when Judge Landis was appointed commissioner. Notes.

1180 Riess, Steven A. "Baseball Myths, Baseball Reality, and the Social Function of Baseball in Progressive America." *Stadion* [West Germany] 3 (1977): 273–311.

Baseball was popular during the Progressive era, because it suggested the countryside, social integration, and democracy. In fact, this urban-based sport began in Britain. Notes.

1181 ———. "Professional Baseball and Social Mobility." *Journal of Interdisciplinary History* 11 (1980): 235–50.

It is a myth that professional baseball provided upward mobility during the Progressive era. Most ballplayers were educated, middle class, and native to the United States. Immigrants and the lower classes did not have the chance to develop their skills, so they were underrepresented in the game. Notes.

1182 ———. "Race and Ethnicity in American Baseball, 1900–1919." *Journal of Ethnic Studies* 4 (1977): 39–55.

Big-league baseball was dominated by the Irish and German working class during the Progressive era, with a few Jews and Eastern Europeans (especially Czechs and Bohemians) also appearing on team rosters. Discrimination, low pay, and parental disapproval kept many of the post-1880 immigrants from playing. Many American Indians became stars, but blacks were excluded until the late 1940s. Notes.

1183 ———. *Touching Base: Professional Baseball and American Culture in the Progressive Era.* Westport, CT: Greenwood, 1980.

The author correlates professional baseball with Progressive-era cultural ideology. The popular conception of the sport as transcending class was inaccurate; working-class people generally had no time for baseball during the week, and play was typically forbidden on Sundays. Poor and rural players were rarely able to

use baseball skills to better themselves, and most fans were white and middle class. Notes, bibliography, index.

1184 Ritter, Lawrence. *The Glory of Their Times.* New York: Macmillan, 1966.

Progressive-era baseball stars recall the game and the times in a series of interviews. Photographs.

1185 Roberts, Randy. *Papa Jack: Jack Johnson and the Era of White Hopes.* New York: Free Press, 1983.

Jack Johnson, the first black heavyweight champion, fought racist expectations in both his controlled public performances and his disorderly private life. Notes, bibliography, index.

1186 Seymour, Harold. *Baseball.* Vol. 2, *The Golden Age.* New York: Oxford University Press, 1960.

Seymour discusses the evolution of baseball as recreation, as a business, and as a national symbol. The operations of various ball clubs, memorable personalities, and important events such as the 1919 Black Sox scandal are covered. Bibliography, index.

1187 Smith, Dean. "The Black Sox Scandal." *American History Illustrated* 11 (1977): 16–24.

Eight members of the Chicago White Sox conspired to throw the 1919 World Series to the decidedly inferior Cincinnati Reds.

1188 Voigt, David Q. *America through Baseball.* Chicago: Nelson-Hall, 1976.

Topics covered include the Black Sox scandal, baseball as a mirror of American life, and baseball in a changing society. Notes, index.

1189 ———. *American Baseball.* Vol. 2, *From the Commissioners to Continental Expansion.* Norman: University of Oklahoma Press, 1970.

Voigt covers all angles, including the cultural, economic, and recreational aspects of baseball. The "deadball dynasties," the consequences of a livelier ball, and the Black Sox scandal are detailed. Notes, appendix, bibliography, index.

1190 ———. "The Chicago Black Sox and the Myth of Baseball's Single Sin." *Journal of the Illinois State Historical Society* 62 (1969): 293–306.

The throwing of the 1919 World Series by the Chicago White Sox was not an isolated incident, just the most sensationalized incidence of crookedness in the national pastime.

Science and Technology

See also Chapter 7, *The Progressive Movement.*

1191 Abrahams, Harold J. "The Ritchey-Chrétien Aplanatic Telescope: Letters from George Willis Ritchey to Elihu Thomson." *Proceedings of the American Philosophical Society* 116 (1972): 486–501.
The correspondence of George W. Ritchey during the Progressive era reveals much about developments in the building of large reflecting telescopes. Notes.

1192 Alexander, Charles C. "Prophet of American Racism: Madison Grant and the Nordic Myth." *Phylon* 23 (1962): 73–90.
Director of the New York Zoological Society, Grant advocated scientific racism. His *The Passing of the Great Race* (1916) warned that the great Nordic race was being destroyed by mixing with inferior races. Notes.

1193 Archer, Gleason L. *History of Radio to 1926.* New York: American Historical Society, 1938.
World War I accelerated the development of radio by both an infusion of money and a bypassing of patent infringement. The Radio Corporation of America was formed after the war to allow cooperation in sales and technical improvements among the large corporations, including General Electric and Westinghouse, that held patents. Commercial radio caught the public's fancy in the 1920s.

1194 Bradley, J. Chester, and Lambrecht, Frank L. "Bug Men and Botanists in Arizona." *Journal of Arizona History* 18 (1977): 469–84.
A group of Cornell biologists and botanists traveled over six thousand miles collecting specimens in 1917.

1195 Bruce, Darryl. "Lashley's Shift from Bacteriology to Neuropsychology, 1910–1917, and the Influence of Jennings, Watson, and Franz." *Journal of the History of the Behavioral Sciences* 22 (1986): 27–44.
The research during the Progressive era of Karl S. Lashley into the way the brain learns is detailed.

1196 Cambrosio, Alberto. "Psychology at the Factory: Control and Selection of American Workers in the 1910's" (in French). *Mouvement Social* [France] (1980): 37–65.
The World War I period witnessed increased use of psychological testing of personnel, which was designed to transform factory work.

1197 Carlson, Elof A. "The Drosophila Group: The Transition from the Mendelian Unit to the Individual Gene." *Journal of the History of Biology* 7 (1974): 31–48.
Thomas Morgan's seminar at Columbia University developed far-reaching theories on the individual gene. These theories were published in "The Mechanism of Mendelian Heredity" in 1915. Notes.

1198 Crelinsten, Jeffrey. "William Wallace Campbell and the 'Einstein Problem': An Observational Astronomer Confronts the Theory of Relativity." *Historical Studies in the Physical Sciences* 14 (1983): 1–91.
William W. Campbell of the Lick Observatory worked to confirm Einstein's theory of relativity by observing the bending of starlight by the sun's gravity. Notes.

1199 Desimone, Alfred A., Jr. "Ancestors or Aberrants: Studies in the History of American Paleoanthropology, 1915–1940." Ph.D. dissertation, University of Massachusetts, 1986.
Scientists sought to reject Neanderthal and other intermediate hominid species as true ancestors of man. The writings of five experts on evolution are examined. DAI 47:1033-A.

1200 Haber, Samuel. *Efficiency and Uplift: Scientific Management in the Progressive Era, 1890–1920.* Chicago: University of Chicago Press, 1964.
Scientific management spread from the factory to the political arena, becoming a Progressive plan for social control run by expert professionals for the good of all. Notes, bibliography, index.

1201 Heywood, Charles W. "Scientists and Society in the United States, 1900–1940: Changing Concepts of Social Responsibility." Ph.D. dissertation, University of Pennsylvania, 1954.
Before World War I, scientists communicated to the public their great faith in science as a tool to improve all areas of life. During the war, weapons-related research was given a tremendous boost, cooperation among

scientists increased, and the credibility of science was firmly established. After the war, the widespread crash of idealism led to questions about the roles and responsibilities of scientists and about society's capacity to adapt to rapid technological change. DAI 14:1375.

1202 Hufbauer, Karl. "Astronomers Take Up the Stellar Energy Problem, 1917–1920." *Historical Studies in the Physical Sciences* 11 (1981): 277–303.

Arthur S. Eddington and Harlow Shapley hypothesized in 1917 and 1918 that stars lived longer than had been previously thought. Using Henry Russell's idea to combine astronomical observations with theories, Eddington worked to refine his theory. Notes.

1203 Hughes, Thomas P. "The Lasting Influence of World War I upon the Development of Electric Power in the United States." In *XIVth International Congress of the History of Science, Proceedings No. 4*. Tokyo and Kyoto: Science Council of Japan, 1975, pp. 255–66.

Government and business worked as partners in Alabama, Massachusetts, and Pennsylvania to build electrical generating stations in the years 1918–1920.

1204 Jones, Daniel P. "The Role of Chemists in Research on War Gases in the United States during World War I." Ph.D. dissertation, University of Wisconsin, 1969.

American University was the site of the largest government research project of the war, which investigated the war gases being used in Europe. The research division developed several new gases and paved the way for peacetime chemical warfare research. DAI 30:5384-A.

1205 Kakar, Sudhir. *Frederick Taylor: A Study in Personality and Innovation*. Cambridge, MA: MIT Press, 1970.

Kakar analyzes the historical, cultural, and family influences on Frederick Taylor's personality and his inner motivation. Taylor, prophet of scientific management, died in 1915. Notes, index.

1206 Kingsland, Sharon. "Abbot Thayer and the Protective Coloration Debate." *Journal of the History of Biology* 11 (1979): 223–44.

Controversy raged between 1909 and 1918 in scientific circles over protective coloration, with neither side of the controversy using an argument based on genetics. Notes.

1207 Layton, Edwin T., Jr. *The Revolt of the Engineers: Social Responsibility and the*

American Engineering Profession. Cleveland: Case Western Reserve University Press, 1971.

During the Progressive era, engineers worked to professionalize themselves and to apply their knowledge to social problems. Professional goals lost out to the needs of big business. Notes, bibliography, index.

1208 Missner, Marshall. "Why Einstein Became Famous in America." *Social Studies of Science* [Great Britain] 15 (1985): 267–91.

Despite suspicions about him, Albert Einstein became famous because his theory of relativity stimulated the American imagination and because the American Jewish community rallied around him.

1209 Oppenheimer, Jane M. "Ross Harrison's Contributions to Experimental Embryology." *Bulletin of the History of Medicine* 40 (1966): 525–43.

In developing methods of culturing tissues and grafting embryos, Harrison was a great scientist who used logic and a methodical approach. Notes.

1210 Schettino, Edvige. "Alfred Locke Parson's Ring Electron Model." *Physis* [Italy] 26 (1984): 361–71.

Magnetic attraction was the basis of a theory on the chemical bonding of hydrogen molecules proposed in 1915 by Alfred L. Parson, an American chemist.

1211 Seely, Bruce E. "Highway Engineers as Policy Makers: The Bureau of Public Roads, 1893–1944." Ph.D. dissertation, University of Delaware, 1982.

Engineers in the Federal Bureau of Public Roads were a central though sometimes inconspicuous force in all aspects of road-building including researching, funding, establishing standards, planning, and executing. DAI 43:2427-A.

1212 Shearer, Benjamin F. "The Positivist Ideal in the United States: The Origins and Reforms of the New Machine." Ph.D. dissertation, St. Louis University, 1978.

The New Machine was a group advocating antidemocratic social theory based on the positivism of Auguste Comte. Founded in 1916, the New Machine attracted engineers, scientific managers, professors, journalists, and clergymen who were interested in applying science to social problems. As a result of American entry into the war, the society accomplished little. DAI 39:1790-A.

1213 Whittemore, Gilbert F., Jr. "World War I, Poison Gas Research, and the Ideals of American Chemists." *Social Studies of Science* 5 (1975): 135–63.

Even the horrors of World War I did not prevent the American Chemical Society from championing research into poison gas.

Environment

1214 Abbott, Carl. "The Active Force: Enos A. Mills and the National Park Movement." *Colorado Magazine* 56 (1979): 56–73.

A writer and innkeeper, Mills played an important role in the founding of Rocky Mountain National Park, although his prickly personality made it difficult for other environmentalists to work with him for long. Notes.

1215 Albright, Horace M., and Cahn, Robert. *The Birth of the National Park Service: The Founding Years, 1913–33.* Salt Lake City: Howe, 1985.

An early official with the National Park Service, Albright discusses his conservationism during the Wilson years. Photographs, index.

1216 Bates, J. Leonard. "Fulfilling American Democracy: The Conservation Movement, 1907–1921." *Mississippi Valley Historical Review* 44 (1957): 29–57.

While conservationists in the Progressive era crusaded to curtail needless waste of natural resources, they also were motivated by a desire to further democracy, curtail exploitation, and preserve what was left of the wilderness. Notes.

1217 ———. *The Origins of Teapot Dome: Progressives, Parties, and Petroleum, 1909–1921.* Urbana: University of Illinois Press, 1963.

The long-range causes of the Teapot Dome scandal of President Harding's administration were grounded in the military need for petroleum, the war, practices of the oil industry, and politics. Notes, bibliography, index.

1218 Chapman, David L. "An Administrative History of the Texas Forest Service, 1915–1975." Ph.D. dissertation, Texas A & M University, 1981.

Pushed through by W. Goodrich Jones, the Texas Forest Service was created in 1915. It is one of only four state forest services directed by a university (Texas A & M). The influences of its various directors are examined. DAI 42:3271-A.

1219 Clepper, Henry. "The Forest Service Backlashed." *Forest History* 11 (1968): 6–15.

The Forest Service came under fire from government agencies that wanted to control it and from mine owners, cattlemen, and land speculators who wanted to do away with it during the period 1910–1920.

1220 Hays, Samuel P. *Conservation and the Gospel of Efficiency: The Progressive Conservation Movement, 1890–1920.* Cambridge, MA: Harvard University Press, 1959.

Large corporations often favored conservation of natural resources in the early days, when this coincided with their long-term economic interests. On the other hand, small businesses without the means for long-term planning were severely threatened by conservation measures, and they vehemently resisted. Notes, bibliography, index.

1221 Ingersoll, Fern. "Pioneering in Southwest Forestry." *Forest History* 17 (1973): 4–11.

Arthur Ringland's work in the Forest Service is chronicled from 1909 to 1915, when he was stationed at the Fort Valley Ranger School. Notes.

1222 Leverette, William E., Jr. "Nature and Nostalgia: John Burroughs's Alternative to Modern America." *Proceedings of the South Carolina Historical Association* (1984): 32–42.

John Burroughs's back-to-nature movement appealed to Americans who regarded him as a sort of folk hero. Notes.

1223 Livesay, Harold C., and Porter, Glenn. "William Savery and the Wonderful Parsons Smoke-Eating Machine." *Delaware History* 14 (1971): 161–76.

William Savery pushed for adoption of the Parsons system of smoke abatement in steam engines, but the effort failed in 1914, when it became evident that railroads were not interested in the fuel-efficient "smoke-eating machine." Notes.

1224 McCarthy, G. Michael. "Colorado Progressives and Conservation." *Mid-America* 57 (1975): 213–26.

Eastern and western Progressives had very different ideas about conservation of natural resources, a factor which inhibited the movement's effectiveness. Notes.

1225 Maunder, Elwood R., ed. "Memoirs of a Forester." *Forest History* 10 (1967): 6–12ff.

An employee of the Forest Service, a teacher at the University of California at Berkeley, and an organizer of the timber valuation section of the Bureau of Internal Revenue, David T. Mason went on to become a wealthy consultant in Oregon.

1226 Merchant, Carolyn. "Women of the Progressive Conservation Movement." *Environmental Review* 8 (1984): 57–85.

Many women's groups, even the conservative Daughters of the American Revolution, were drawn into the Progressive crusade for environmental conservation.

1227 Mogren, Paul A. "The Development of a Philosophy of Land Reservation on General Land Office, United States Forest Service, and National Park Service Lands: 1787 to 1947." Ph.D. dissertation, University of Utah, 1980.

The National Park Service was established in 1916, but tensions between those who wanted to exploit, partially exploit, or wholeheartedly preserve forest lands persisted. DAI 41:4814-A.

1228 Nelson, Paula. "After the West Was Won: Homesteaders and Town-Builders in Western South Dakota, 1900–1917." Ph.D. dissertation, University of Iowa, 1984.

They were originally drawn to settle in South Dakota by the hope of material prosperity, and the drought of 1910–1911 tempered the goals of the settlers who elected to stay. Endurance, self-reliance, and irony became vital and lasting character traits. DAI 46:506-A.

1229 O'Connell, James C. "Technology and Pollution: Chicago's Water Policy, 1833–1930." Ph.D. dissertation, University of Chicago, 1980.

By the time of Wilson's presidency, Chicago had managed to mostly separate sewage from drinking water, and had begun to use chlorination, but industrial waste had not yet been effectively curtailed. DAI 41:1188-A.

1230 Ogden, Gerald R. "Forestry for a Nation: The Making of a National Forest Policy under the Weeks and Clark-McNary Acts, 1900–1924." Ph.D. dissertation, University of New Mexico, 1980.

The government failed to supply adequate fire protection, intelligent management, or protection from profit-oriented lumbermen for national forests. Both beauty-loving conservationists and the lumber industry forced passage of the Weeks bill in 1900 and the Clark-McNary act of 1924. DAI 41:2261-A.

1231 Scarpino, Philip V. *Great River: An Environmental History of the Upper Mississippi, 1890–1950*. Columbia: University of Missouri Press, 1985.

Industrial progress along the upper Mississippi caused increasing environmental damage that eventually began to distress inhabitants of the river region. The Keokuk, Iowa, hydroelectric project of 1913 is used as an example of changing attitudes toward progress and environmentalism. Notes, bibliography, index.

1232 Swain, Donald C. "The Founding of the National Park Service." *American West* 6 (1969): 6–9.

Nature lovers and conservationists advocating rational use of natural resources delayed the passage of the National Park Service act until 1916, when their views were finally reconciled.

1233 Vose, Clement E. "State against Nation: The Conservation Case of *Missouri v. Holland*." *Prologue* 16 (1984): 233–47.

Migratory bird treaties of 1916 and 1918 were held to be legal in the 1920 Supreme Court case *Missouri v. Holland*, in which Justice Oliver Wendell Holmes ruled that national treaties superseded state laws. Notes.

1234 Woodbury, Robert L. "William Kent: Progressive Gadfly, 1864–1928." Ph.D. dissertation, Yale University, 1967.

Independent Republican Congressman William Kent of California served as an adviser to Wilson, particularly on natural resource management. He was a skilled communicator who brought sophisticated Progressive thought to politicians. In 1916, he tried to rally Bull Moose Progressives behind Wilson. During the war, he persisted with his Progressive agenda, even though the rest of the nation was losing interest in reform. DAI 28:185-A.

6

Domestic Affairs: Minorities, Women, and Immigration

The Wilson years were times of trial for American minority groups. Women worked to improve their lot through trade unions and by fighting for female suffrage, a long struggle climaxed by passage of the Nineteenth Amendment. Immigrants continued to pour into the country, arousing nativism and stimulating the Progressive impulse to "Americanize" the newcomers.

Blacks lost ground in their struggle for civil rights during the Wilson administration, largely because of the attitudes and actions of the president and his southern Progressive allies. See Earl W. Crosby, "Progressive Segregation in the Wilson Administration" (#1240). There are a number of works on the race riots of the period, among them Robert V. Haynes, *A Night of Violence: The Houston Riot of 1917* (#1248); Elliott M. Rudwick, *Race Riot at East St. Louis, July 2, 1917* (#1257); and William M. Tuttle, Jr., *Race Riot: Chicago in the Red Summer of 1919* (#1260). On the rebirth of the KKK, see Kenneth T. Jackson, *The Ku Klux Klan in the City, 1915–1930* (#1249). Leonard Dinnerstein, *The Leo Frank Case* (#1242), examines the anti-Semitism behind the lynching of Leo Frank.

The Wilson years marked the end of Booker T. Washington's long career. See Louis R. Harlan, *Booker T. Washington: The Wizard of Tuskegee, 1901–1915* (#1277). There are a number of works on the black leader W. E. B. DuBois, among them Francis Broderick, *W. E. B. DuBois: Negro Leader in a Time of Crisis* (#1270). The origins of the Marcus Garvey movement are documented by Robert A. Hill et al., eds., *The Marcus Garvey and Universal Negro Improvement Association Papers* (#1279). For the struggles of the civil rights movement, see Charles F. Kellogg, *NAACP: A History of the National Association for the Advancement of Colored People, 1909–1920* (#1282), and Nancy J. Weiss, *The National Urban League, 1910–1940* (#1302). Florette Henri, *Black Migration: Movement North, 1900–1920* (#1322), examines the mass movement to the urban North by blacks.

Many works on women during Wilson's tenure have been published in recent years. The Progressive crusade against prostitution is examined by Mark T. Connelly, *The Response to Prostitution in the Progressive Era* (#1374), and by Ruth Rosen, *The Lost Sisterhood: Prostitution in America, 1900–1918* (#1411). The successful drive for women's suffrage is analyzed in Robert B. Fowler, *Carrie Catt: Feminist Politician* (#1433); Aileen S. Kraditor, *The Ideas of the Woman Suffrage Movement, 1890–1920* (#1468); and Christine A. Lunardini, *From Equal Suffrage to Equal Rights: Alice Paul and the National Woman's Party, 1910–1928* (#1470). For radical women, see Rosalynn F. Baxandall, *Words on Fire: The Life and Writing of Elizabeth Gurley Flynn* (#1440); Philip S. Foner and Sally M. Miller, eds., *Kate Richards O'Hare: Selected Writings and Speeches* (#1444); and Alice Wexler, *Emma Goldman: An Intimate Life* (#1451).

Of the many works on immigrants and nativism, the standard is still John Higham, *Strangers in the Land: Patterns of American*

Nativism, 1860–1925 (#1515). See also Paul McBride, *Culture Clash: Immigrants and Reformers, 1880–1920* (#1524). The Zionist movement is examined by Yonathan Shapiro, *Leadership of the American Zionist Organization, 1897–1930* (#1557), and by Melvin I. Urofsky, *American Zionism from Herzl to the Holocaust* (#1558).

Minority Groups

1235 Alexander, Charles C. "Kleagles and Cash: The Ku Klux Klan as a Business Organization, 1915–1930." *Business History Review* 39 (1965): 348–67.

The business side of the KKK is examined, including an analysis of Klan leaders, some of whom were in it strictly for the money. Notes.

1236 Allen, Howard W.; Clausen, Aage R.; and Clubb, Jerome M. "Political Reform and Negro Rights in the Senate, 1909–1915." *Journal of Southern History* 37 (1971): 191–212.

A study of the roll call votes of the 61st, 62d, and 63d congresses reveals a willingness to trade the rights of blacks for Progressive reforms. Although there were 'advanced' Progressives who cared about civil rights, none of them were in the Senate. Notes.

1237 Blumenthal, Henry. "Woodrow Wilson and the Race Question." *Journal of Negro History* 48 (1963): 1–21.

Wilson's presidency was a step backward for black civil rights. The president was a racist who believed that black people could only improve their lot very gradually through education and economic advancement. Civil rights did not have a place on the Wilson agenda. Notes.

1238 Bouwman, Robert E. "Race Suicide, Some Aspects of Race Paranoia in the Progressive Era." Ph.D. dissertation, Emory University, 1975.

The declining birthrate among old-stock Americans led to concern about "race suicide." The large volume of literature produced on this subject during the Progressive era is analyzed. DAI 36:4706.

1239 Cohen, William. "Riots, Racism, and Hysteria: The Response of Federal Investigative

Officials to the Race Riots of 1919." *Massachusetts Review* 13 (1972): 373–400.

Government reports on the race riots of 1919 reflected the racism of the era. The Justice Department collected documents to serve as justification for using the army to thwart black subversives. Notes.

1240 Crosby, Earl W. "Progressive Segregation in the Wilson Administration." *Potomac Review* 6 (1973): 41–57.

Southern Progressive Democrats who gained political power during Wilson's tenure moved to further segregate the races.

1241 Culley, John J. "Muted Trumpets: Four Efforts to Better Southern Race Relations, 1900–1919." Ph.D. dissertation, University of Virginia, 1967.

The Montgomery (Alabama) conference advocated honest elections, law and order, and separate but truly equal public facilities to better the lot of blacks. The Southern Sociological Congress, founded in 1912, was a biracial, paternalistic group that sought parallel societies. The University Commission on Southern Race Questions strove to enlighten southern college students, while the Southern Publicity Committee released positive news about black progress to counteract the racist stance typically adopted by southern newspapers. DAI 28:3585-A.

1242 Dinnerstein, Leonard. *The Leo Frank Case.* New York: Columbia University Press, 1968.

The Leo Frank case had several important repercussions, among them the rebirth of the Ku Klux Klan and the creation of the B'nai B'rith Anti-Defamation League. Photographs, notes, bibliography, index.

1243 ———. "Leo M. Frank and the American Jewish Community." *American Jewish Archives* 20 (1968): 107–26.

After a trial marked by anti-Semitism, Frank was convicted of murder. Jewish groups worked on his behalf, but a mob lynched him after his death sentence was commuted to life in prison. Notes.

1244 Ferrell, Claudine L. "Nightmare and Dream: Antilynching in Congress, 1917–1922." Ph.D. dissertation, Rice University, 1983.

The NAACP, with the support of many congressmen, unsuccessfully sought passage of an antilynching bill. Their argument for the bill was based on the Fourteenth Amendment's guarantee of equal protection, as well as on humanitarian reasons. It was chiefly southern Democratic congressmen who opposed the bill as an infringement of states' rights and who ultimately staged a filibuster to prevent passage. DAI 44:556-A.

1245 Friedman, Lawrence J. "In Search of Uncle Tom: Racial Attitudes of the Southern Leadership, 1865–1920." Ph.D. dissertation, University of California, Los Angeles, 1967.

The author analyzes the racial attitudes of six leaders, including Woodrow Wilson. Most favored segregation, and all wanted to preserve "racial purity." However, the effect of racial separation was to encourage black independence rather than to restore the "Uncle Tom" behavior for which the southern leaders had hoped. DAI 28:2173-A.

1246 Glazier, Kenneth M. "W. E. B. DuBois' Impressions of Woodrow Wilson." *Journal of Negro History* 58 (1973): 452–59.

In response to a scholar's query about Wilson, DuBois wrote a brief essay about his quest for black civil rights and about the president's racism.

1247 Grant, Donald L. *The Anti-Lynching Movement: 1883–1932.* San Francisco: R & E Research, 1975.

Antilynching laws did not interest Progressives, because they thought of their reforms as being for whites only. Notes, bibliography, index.

1248 Haynes, Robert V. *A Night of Violence: The Houston Riot of 1917.* Baton Rouge: Louisiana State University Press, 1976.

Members of the black Twenty-fourth Infantry attacked white Houstonians after suffering extreme racism, killing twenty-four in three hours of rioting. Nineteen of the black doughboys were hanged, and many others received long prison sentences. Notes, bibliography, index.

1249 Jackson, Kenneth T. *The Ku Klux Klan in the City, 1915–1930.* New York: Oxford University Press, 1967.

Many KKK members came from urban areas, especially in the Midwest. Concern about immigration restriction, prohibition, and imposing Protestant fundamentalist values on the country were more important to most members than were racial issues. Notes, bibliography, index.

1250 Kluger, Pearl. "Progressive Presidents and Black Americans." Ph.D. dissertation, Columbia University, 1974.

Blacks were disappointed by Wilson's segregationist policies, after he had made vague promises to treat blacks fairly. He made token gestures favoring blacks during the war, but he cared little about black civil rights even as he fought to make the world safe for democracy. DAI 37:3854-A.

1251 Meier, August. "The Rise of Segregation in the Federal Bureaucracy, 1900–1930." *Phylon* 28 (1967): 178–84.

Republicans share the blame with Democrats for the increasing segregation of federal agencies during the Progressive period. While Warren Harding promised black leaders during the 1920 election campaign that he would end this segregation, he did nothing. Notes.

1252 Osborn, George C. "The Problem of the Negro in Government, 1913." *Historian* 23 (1961): 330–47.

Blacks lost ground in the area of federal employment during Wilson's presidency in spite of efforts by the NAACP, the National Negro Press Association, and their supporters. Notes.

1253 ———. "Woodrow Wilson Appoints a Negro Judge." *Journal of Southern History* 24 (1958): 481–93.

Wilson reappointed a black Republican judge in the District of Columbia, even though southerners opposed the move. The president was applauded by northern Republicans and Democrats. Notes.

1254 Oxman, Daniel K. "California Reactions to the Leo Frank Case." *Western States Jewish Historical Quarterly* 10 (1978): 216–24.

During Frank's trial for the murder of a young girl, during the appeal process, and after his tragic lynching, California newspapers vehemently accused the authorities and the citizens of Georgia of perpetrating injustice. Notes.

1255 Rice, Arnold S. "The Southern Wing of the Ku Klux Klan in American Politics, 1915–1928." Ph.D. dissertation, Indiana University, 1959.

The Ku Klux Klan exercised its power by either electing its own people or enlisting the support of those already in office. Widespread public antagonism as well as legal prohibitions finally forced the Klan underground. DAI 20:4090.

1256 Rice, Roger L. "Residential Segregation by Law, 1910–1917." *Journal of Southern History* 34 (1968): 179–99.

Laws mandating residential segregation were passed in several southern cities during the Progressive era. The NAACP fought these laws through the courts and finally obtained a ruling from the Supreme Court that declared them unconstitutional. Notes.

1257 Rudwick, Elliott M. *Race Riot at East St. Louis, July 2, 1917.* Carbondale, IL: World, 1964.

The origins and consequences of the bloody racial violence in wartime St. Louis are examined and found to follow the pattern of riots in other cities to which blacks flocked during their great migration. Notes, bibliography, index.

1258 Sosna, Morton. "The South in the Saddle: Racial Politics during the Wilson Years." *Wisconsin Magazine of History* 54 (1970): 30–49.

Race relations suffered during the Wilson years as a result of the increased political clout of southern Democrats.

1259 Steinfield, Melvin. *Our Racist Presidents: From Washington to Nixon.* San Ramon, CA: Consensus, 1972.

Chapter 7 outlines Wilson's segregationist views and includes coverage of the *Chicago Defender's* account of a meeting Wilson held with black leaders in which he protested the "tone" of one spokesman's remarks.

1260 Tuttle, William M., Jr. *Race Riot: Chicago in the Red Summer of 1919.* New York: Atheneum, 1970.

Chicago's racial tensions exploded in 1919 after the drowning of a black youth. The social background of the race riot is explored in detail. Photographs, notes, bibliography, index.

1261 ———. " 'Red Summer': 1919." *American History Illustrated* 6 (1971): 32–41.

As coined by black intellectual James Weldon Johnson, "Red Summer" came to mean a series of race riots throughout the country that happened during the antiradical Red Scare. Postwar fear and anxiety touched off the twin waves of bloody repression.

1262 ———. "Views of a Negro during 'The Red Summer' of 1919—A Document." *Journal of Negro History* 51 (1966): 209–18.

A letter written by a black war veteran, Stanley Norvell, in the wake of the Chicago race riots of 1919 explains that blacks were expressing their frustration about continued discrimination and segregation.

1263 Waskow, Arthur I. "The 1919 Race Riots: A Study in the Connections between Conflict and Violence." Ph.D. dissertation, University of Wisconsin, 1963.

By 1920, Americans had, for the first time, accepted government as the only legitimate practitioner of violence. However, the escalation of the 1919 race riots into physical conflict was blamed on local police, awakening controversy about violence. The term "new Negro" was coined to identify a black man who would fight back, and suggestions for dealing with him ranged from guaranteeing him full equality to suppressing him by any means. DAI 24:2453.

1264 Weiss, Nancy J. "The Negro and the New Freedom: Fighting Wilsonian Segregation." *Political Science Quarterly* 84 (1969): 61–79.

While Wilson received significant political support from blacks in 1912, his administration moved quickly to complete racial segregation in federal facilities. Black protest was too disorganized and too restrained to be effective. Notes.

1265 Williams, Lee E., and Williams, Lee E., II. *Anatomy of Four Race Riots: Racial Conflict in Knoxville, Elaine (Arkansas), Tulsa and Chicago, 1919–1921.* Jackson: University and College Press of Mississippi, 1972.

Race riots in the four areas under study were all the result of whites trying to preserve the status quo in race relations. Specific acts of violence against blacks happened for different reasons in each area. Notes, appendix, bibliography, index.

1266 Williams, Lee E., II. "Racism and Race Riots, 1919." Ph.D. dissertation, Mississippi State University, 1975.

Race riots in 1919 in Washington, DC, Omaha, and Charleston pitted white civilians and military personnel against blacks. While blacks realized that the war for democracy had not applied to them at home, they were determined to be pushed no further by whites. DAI 36:4720-A.

1267 Wolgemuth, Kathleen L. "Woodrow Wilson and Federal Segregation." *Journal of Negro History* 44 (1959): 158–73.

Although northern blacks supported Wilson in 1912, he instituted reforms that furthered the cause of segregation. His attitudes contributed to racial violence and inspired racist legislation. Notes.

1268 ———. "Woodrow Wilson's Appointment Policy and Negroes." *Journal of Southern History* 24 (1958): 457–71.

Blacks and radical Democrats hoped that Wilson would work against racism, but they soon found that he was a racist himself. Notes.

LEADERS AND ORGANIZATIONS

1269 Aptheker, Bettina. "W. E. B. DuBois and the Struggle for Women's Rights: 1910–1920." *San Jose Studies* 1 (1975): 7–16.

DuBois devoted much of his writing to the oppression of women, especially to that of black women, who were doubly oppressed.

1270 Broderick, Francis L. *W. E. B. DuBois: Negro Leader in a Time of Crisis*. Stanford: Stanford University Press, 1959.

While DuBois was critical of the moderation of Booker T. Washington, he made his own entente with Progressives. Notes, index.

1271 Calista, Donald J. "Booker T. Washington: Another Look." *Journal of Negro History* 49 (1964): 240–55.

Washington's moderation is examined in light of the years in which he lived, times when blacks saw prospects for improvement disappearing. In his last years, Washington attacked segregation. He never stopped hoping for eventual equality between the races. Notes.

1272 Contee, Clarence G. "W. E. B. DuBois and African Nationalism: 1914–1945." Ph.D. dissertation, American University, 1969.

In an era of colonialism, DuBois was outspoken in his call for African freedom. A gradualist, DuBois reasoned that if Africans gained their liberty, blacks in America would also see some benefits. DAI 31:1183-A.

1273 Diggs, Irene. "DuBois and Children." *Phylon* 37 (1976): 370–99.

DuBois paid considerable attention to children's literature in his magazine, *The Crisis*. For a time, from 1919 to 1921, he put out a monthly magazine exclusively for black children. Notes.

1274 Eisenberg, Bernard. "Only for the Bourgeois? James Weldon Johnson and the NAACP, 1916–1930." *Phylon* 43 (1982): 110–24.

During James Weldon Johnson's tenure as secretary of the NAACP, the organization paid closer attention to black workers.

1275 Elkins, W. F. "Marcus Garvey, the *Negro World*, and the British West Indies, 1919–1920." *Science and Society* 36 (1972): 63–77.

After World War I, British authorities became alarmed by Marcus Garvey's black nationalist propaganda, which found its way into Africa and the West Indies. Garvey also gained a significant following in Latin America including the canal zone, temporary home to thousands of Afro-West Indians. Notes.

1276 Enck, Henry S. "Tuskegee Institute and Northern White Philanthropy: A Case Study in Fund Raising, 1900–1915." *Journal of Negro History* 65 (1980): 336–48.

Northern philanthropists were targeted by Booker T. Washington as the most likely source of funds for his Tuskegee Institute. Elaborate fund-raising campaigns brought in money and spread the message about Washington's "self-help" campaign for blacks, but the institute was never on firm financial ground. Notes.

1277 Harlan, Louis R. *Booker T. Washington: The Wizard of Tuskegee, 1901–1915*. New York: Oxford University Press, 1983.

Volume II of this definitive biography examines Washington as an educator who trained blacks for careers in business, farming, and education. Photographs, notes, index.

1278 Hellwig, David J. "Black Leaders and United States Immigration Policy, 1917–1929." *Journal of Negro History* 66 (1981): 110–27.

Some blacks believed that the war could bring about an improvement in their lot, but only if the never-ending flow of immigrants was cut back. This explains why many black leaders gave their support to immigration restriction proposals during this period.

1279 Hill, Robert A.; Tolbert, Emory J.; Rudisell, Carol A.; and Forczek, Deborah, eds. *The Marcus Garvey and Universal Negro Improvement Association Papers*. Berkeley: University of California Press, 1983–.

The first three years of Marcus Garvey's UNIA are covered in Volume I. Volume II covers the association's activities from August 1919 to August 1920. Photographs, appendixes, notes, index.

1280 Hixon, William B., Jr. "Moorfield Storey and the Struggle for Equality." *Journal of American History* 55 (1968): 533–54.

A former secretary to Senator Charles Sumner, Storey went on to cofound the National Association for the Advancement of Colored People. As NAACP counsel, he fought against racist laws and spoke out on behalf of black rights. Notes.

1281 Jack, Robert L. *History of the National Association for the Advancement of Colored People.* Boston: Meador, 1943.

Created during the Progressive era by a coalition of concerned blacks and whites, the NAACP fought racism and violence and campaigned for black education and political rights.

1282 Kellogg, Charles F. *NAACP: A History of the National Association for the Advancement of Colored People, 1909–1920.* Baltimore, MD: Johns Hopkins University Press, 1967.

The Progressive-era struggles of the NAACP are chronicled, including the civil rights organization's clash with the Wilson administration over increasing discrimination in government appointments and policies. Photographs, appendix, notes, bibliography.

1283 Lamon, Lester C. "W. T. Andrews Explains the Causes of Black Migration from the South." *Journal of Negro History* 63 (1978): 365–72.

Speaking before the South Carolina Negro Race Conference in 1917, W. T. Andrews analyzed the social, political, and economic reasons for the black exodus from the South. Notes.

1284 Levy, Eugene. *James Weldon Johnson: Black Leader, Black Voice.* Chicago: University of Chicago Press, 1973.

Johnson's *Autobiography of an Ex-Colored Man* foreshadowed the Harlem renaissance. He played an important role in the NAACP during the Wilson years. Photographs, notes, bibliography, index.

1285 Lively, Adam. "Continuity and Radicalism in American Black Nationalist Thought, 1914–1929." *Journal of American Studies* 18 (1984): 207–35.

The period under discussion was a transitional one, when intellectuals were absorbing new ideas such as socialism while reassessing older ideological beliefs such as Afro-American Christianity. A few hoped to synthesize the old and the new. Notes.

1286 Lunardini, Christine A. "Standing Firm: William Monroe Trotter's Meetings with Woodrow Wilson." *Journal of Negro History* 64 (1979): 244–64.

Trotter met with Wilson twice to voice his concern over the president's apparent breaking of his word not to further segregate the federal government. Notes.

1287 McGruder, Larry. "Kelly Miller: The Life and Thoughts of a Black Intellectual, 1863–1939." Ph.D. dissertation, Miami University, 1984.

Miller was a prolific writer and a prominent figure in the fight against racism. He stressed that higher education for blacks was essential to their elevation in society, he comprehensively analyzed the causes of black oppression, and he criticized the racial policies of the presidents who came to power in his lifetime. DAI 46:506-A.

1288 Marable, W. Manning. "Booker T. Washington and African Nationalism." *Phylon* 35 (1974): 398–406.

Washington influenced a generation of black activists in South Africa who took his message of pride and solidarity to heart. Notes.

1289 Marszalek, John F. "The Black Leader in 1919—South Carolina as a Test Case." *Phylon* 36 (1975): 249–59.

The typical black leader in South Carolina in 1919 was middle-aged and black-educated, lived in an area with a large black population, preached for a living, cared little for politics, and endorsed an accommodationist philosophy heavily influenced by Booker T. Washington.

1290 Mathews, Carl S. "After Booker T. Washington: The Search for a New Negro Leadership, 1915–1925." Ph.D. dissertation, University of Virginia, 1971.

When W. E. B. DuBois refused to step into the role of paramount black leader, several others vied for the position, including former Washington protégés Emmett Jay Scott and Robert Russa Moton as well as the NAACP's James Weldon Johnson. When black patriotism failed to improve social and economic conditions, many turned to Marcus Garvey. DAI 32:4531-A.

1291 ———. "The Decline of the Tuskegee Machine, 1915–1925: The Abdication of Political Power." *South Atlantic Quarterly* 75 (1976): 460–69.

Following the death of Booker T. Washington in 1915 his secretary, Emmett Jay Scott, hoped to become the head of Tuskegee Institute, which Washington had built into a formidible political machine. A majority of whites on the board of directors, though, chose someone else, and the machine declined in influence. Notes.

1292 ———. "Marcus Garvey Writes from Jamaica on the Mulatto Escape Hatch." *Journal of Negro History* 59 (1974): 170–76.

In this letter written in 1916, Garvey discusses racism in Jamaica and criticizes W. E. B. DuBois for overlooking Jamaican blacks, speculating that this oversight had to do with DuBois's light black skin color.

1293 Meier, August, and Rudwick, Elliott. "The Rise of the Black Secretariat in the NAACP, 1909–1935." *Crisis* 84 (1977):58–69.

During the Progressive era, whites on the board of the NAACP set policy for the organization. It was only after 1919 that power slowly began to pass to the black secretariat.

1294 Miller, M. Sammy. "Woodrow Wilson and the Black Judge." *Crisis* 84 (1977): 81–86.

Judge Robert H. Terrell of Washington, DC, received high marks for his performance on the bench, but his reappointment was jeopardized by Wilson's racism. After a period in limbo, this black judge was reappointed.

1295 Miller, Robert M. "The Protestant Churches and Lynching, 1919–1939." *Journal of Negro History* 42 (1957): 118–31.

Protestant churches were more concerned about the lynching of blacks than is commonly thought. Notes.

1296 Pamphile, Leon D. "The NAACP and the Occupation of Haiti." *Phylon* 47 (1986): 91–100.

James Weldon Johnson of the NAACP examined the American occupation of Haiti, which Wilson had undertaken in 1915. Johnson became critical of the occupation after finding that the chief result had not been peace, but rather a new movement of unrest and American seizure of Haitian customs. During the 1920 presidential campaign, Warren Harding made Haiti an issue. Notes.

1297 Scally, Anthony. "Woodson and the Genesis of A.S.N.L.H." *Negro History Bulletin* 40 (1977): 653–55.

The work of black historian Carter Woodson is examined, including the founding of the Association for the Study of Negro Life and History.

1298 Shipley, W. Maurice. "Reaching Back to Glory: Comparative Sketches in the 'Dreams' of W. B. Yeats and W. E. B. DuBois." *Crisis* 83 (1976): 195–201.

Yeats and DuBois each attempted, in his own way, to influence his people with creative art born of resistance to repression.

1299 Stowe, William M., Jr. "Damned Funny: The Tragedy of Bert Williams." *Journal of Popular Culture* 10 (1976): 5–13.

A popular comedian in minstrel shows during the Progressive era, Williams's act reflected the racial ideology of Booker T. Washington. Notes.

1300 Stueck, William. "Progressivism and the Negro: White Liberals and the Early NAACP." *Historian* 38 (1975): 58–78.

Whites who helped to lead the NAACP during the Progressive era were from the upper and middle classes but were quite diverse in other ways. Notes.

1301 Taylor, Brennen. "UNIA and American Communism in Conflict, 1917–1928: An Historical Analysis in Negro Social Welfare." Ph.D. dissertation, University of Pittsburgh, 1984.

The Universal Negro Improvement Association and the American Communist Party both developed programs for the benefit of blacks. Some of the programs were harmonious, while some sprang from conflicting ideologies; all are found here to have helped. Psychological ties with Africa developed, as did a sense of the contributions of blacks to American history. Both groups had productive health, education, and welfare programs. DAI 45:2274-A.

1302 Weiss, Nancy J. *The National Urban League, 1910–1940.* New York: Oxford University Press, 1974.

The National Urban League worked to improve the lives of urban blacks with welfare services including aid by social workers. While many people were helped, the league's Progressive beliefs prevented it from challenging the racism that kept blacks at the bottom of society. Tables, notes, bibliography, index.

1303 Wells, Ida B. *The Autobiography of Ida B. Wells.* Edited by Alfreda M. Duster. Chicago: University of Chicago Press, 1970.

A founder of the NAACP, Wells details her crusade for black civil rights during the Progressive era. Notes, bibliography, index.

BLACKS

1304 Austin, Gerlyn E. "The Advent of the Negro Actor on the Legitimate Stage in America." *Journal of Negro Education* 35 (1966): 237–45.

Black actors did not play leading roles on the legitimate stage until the 1917 production of *Three Plays for a Negro Theatre*, by Ridgely Torrence. Notes.

1305 Beardsley, Edward H. "The American Scientist as Social Activist: Franz Boas, Burt G. Wilder and the Cause of Racial Justice." *Isis* 64 (1973): 50–66.

Not all scientists were racist during the Progressive era. Boas, who taught anthropology at Columbia, and Wilder, a professor of anatomy at Cornell, fought against discrimination. Notes.

1306 Bittle, William E., and Geis, Gilbert L. "Alfred Charles Sam and an African Return: A Case Study in Negro Despair." *Phylon* 23 (1962): 178–96.

A native of the Gold Coast, Sam convinced blacks from Oklahoma, Kansas, Texas, and Arkansas to follow him back to Africa to start new lives free from the poverty and racism of America. While few survived the journey, Sam gave his followers hope for a time. Notes.

1307 Broderick, Francis L. "DuBois and the Democratic Party, 1908–1916." *Negro History Bulletin* 21 (1957): 41–44.

While DuBois supported Wilson in 1912, he became disillusioned very quickly and backed Charles Evans Hughes in 1916 and Warren Harding in 1920.

1308 Burdick, Norman R. "The 'Coatesville Address': Crossroad of Rhetoric and Poetry." *Western Journal of Speech Communication* 42 (1978): 73–82.

In observation of the first anniversary of the brutal murder of a black man by a mob in Coatesville, Pennsylvania, John Jay Chapman delivered an inspiring speech, which the author analyzes.

1309 Clark, Herbert L. "The Public Career of James Carroll Napier: Businessman, Politician, and Crusader for Racial Justice, 1845–1940." Ph.D. dissertation, Middle Tennessee State University, 1980.

Born into slavery, Napier became a lawyer and a loyal Republican. He resigned his appointment as register of the U.S. Treasury when Woodrow Wilson approved a segregation order mandating that whites and blacks use separate rest rooms in the Treasury Department. DAI 41: 1171-A.

1310 Contee, Clarence G. "DuBois, the NAACP, and the Pan-African Congress of 1919." *Journal of Negro History* 57 (1972): 13–28.

After World War I, DuBois held a Pan-African congress in Paris with help from the NAACP. While the gathering enhanced DuBois's political prestige in the Afro-American community, not much was accomplished. Notes.

1311 Cripps, Thomas R. "The Unformed Image: The Negro in the Movies before *Birth of a Nation*." *Maryland Historian* 2 (1971): 13–26.

Some early films portrayed blacks sympathetically but *Birth of a Nation* and the move of the motion picture industry from the East to Hollywood caused blacks to be restricted to minor roles. Southerners refused to accept blacks in heroic parts, while the NAACP saw to it that blacks were not used as villains. Notes.

1312 Diner, Steven J. "Chicago Social Workers and Blacks in the Progressive Era." *Social Service Review* 44 (1970): 393–410.

Social workers in Chicago made an effort to explore the special problems of impoverished blacks living in a racist society. Notes.

1313 Dittmer, John. *Black Georgia in the Progressive Era, 1900–1920.* Urbana: University of Illinois Press, 1977.

Blacks soon discovered that the Progressive movement in Georgia was not meant to help them. Black social, business, and educational activities are among the topics covered. Notes, bibliography, index.

1314 Enck, Henry S. "Black Self-Help in the Progressive Era: The 'Northern Campaigns' of

Smaller Southern Black Industrial Schools, 1900–1915." *Journal of Negro History* 61 (1976): 73–87.

In an effort to enlist northern white financial help for southern black industrial schools, the smaller institutions banded together, thus incurring the wrath of Booker T. Washington. Out of these early fund-raising campaigns came the United Negro College Fund. Notes.

1315 Fuklermarullo, Sam. "The Migration of Blacks to the North: 1911–1918." *Journal of Black Studies* 15 (1985): 291–306.

Blacks migrated to the North for the opportunities they hoped to find, and because the black press encouraged them to do so. The typical migrant was unskilled and married and had children.

1316 Glasrud, Bruce A. "Black Texans, 1900–1930: A History." Ph.D. dissertation, Texas Technical College, 1969.

Black Texans were victimized by racial violence and segregation during the Progressive era. They were politically powerless, and behaving submissively was their only defense against the racial majority. DAI 30:3398-A.

1317 Gottlieb, Peter. *Making Their Own Way: Southern Blacks' Migration to Pittsburgh, 1916–30*. Urbana: University of Illinois Press, 1987.

Blacks migrated to Pittsburgh as rural peasants and quickly became part of the marginal urban working class. Blacks' southern ways helped them to cope with modern city life. Notes, bibliography, index.

1318 Grantham, Dewey W., Jr. "The Progressive Movement of the Negro." *South Atlantic Quarterly* 54 (1955): 461–77.

The Progressives' lack of interest in civil rights helped to radicalize blacks and lead them to reject the accommodationism of Booker T. Washington. Notes.

1319 Heinl, Nancy G. "Col. Charles Young: Pointman." *Crisis* 84 (1977): 173–79.

A West Point graduate, Young became the first black man ever to reach the regular army rank of colonel, in 1917. Poor health forced him to retire as a brigadier after the war.

1320 Hellwig, David J. "Afro-American Reactions to the Japanese and the Anti-Japanese Movement, 1906–1924." *Phylon* 38 (1977): 93–104.

Many blacks agreed that immigration ought to be restricted, provided that no one racial group was singled out. Notes.

1321 Hemmingway, Theodore. "Prelude to Change: Black Carolinians in the War Years, 1914–1920." *Journal of Negro History* 65 (1980): 212–27.

World War I ushered in many changes for the black underclass in North and South Carolina. Increased chances for education, greater mobility, and more economic opportunities came about despite a white backlash. Notes.

1322 Henri, Florette. *Black Migration: Movement North, 1900–1920*. Garden City, NY: Anchor Doubleday, 1975.

Blacks should be considered as a special case, because they were not just another immigrant group. The "black scare" of 1919 was the culmination of decades of racism in the North. Notes, bibliography, index.

1323 Higgs, Robert. "The Boll Weevil, the Cotton Economy, and Black Migration, 1910–1930." *Agricultural History* 50 (1976): 335–50.

There was more to the great exodus of blacks from the South than the massive infestation of cotton crops by the boll weevil. The opportunity for factory work in the North was the magnet that drew blacks out of Dixie. Notes.

1324 James, Milton M. "Leslie Pinckney Hill." *Negro History Bulletin* 24 (1961): 135–38.

An educator and a poet, Hill guided Cheyney Training School of Teachers through the Pennsylvania accreditation process so that blacks could become fully certified teachers.

1325 Kogut, Alvin B. "The Negro and the Charity Organization Society in the Progressive Era." *Social Science Review* 44 (1970): 11–21.

The Charity Organization Society publicized the problems of black people, but aided them only in limited ways. Notes.

1326 Leab, Daniel J. " 'All-Colored'—But Not Much Different: Films Made for Negro Ghetto Audiences, 1913–1928." *Phylon* 36 (1975): 321–39.

Blacks in films never overcame the problem of racism during the silent era, because black filmmakers could not obtain the technical or management skills they needed from the white establishment. Notes.

1327 ———. "The Gamut from A to B: The Image of the Black in Pre-1915 Movies." *Political Science Quarterly* 88 (1973): 53–70.

Minstrel shows and vaudeville influenced the racist stereotyping of blacks in early films. Blacks were portrayed as ignorant beasts, happy flunkies, inveterate dancers, comical idiots, or villains. Notes.

1328 Levy, Eugene. "Ragtime and Race Pride: The Career of James Weldon Johnson." *Journal of Popular Culture* 1 (1968): 357–70.

Johnson encouraged blacks to take pride in themselves and to gain an appreciation of their unique art forms, including ragtime music.

1329 Lewis, David L. "Parallels and Divergencies: Assimilationist Strategies of Afro-American and Jewish Elites from 1910 to the Early 1930s." *Journal of American History* 71 (1984): 543–64.

Rich German Jews and the elite among northern blacks worked together in the battle against nativism and racism. The new assimilationist strategies, which turned out to be of more benefit to Jews than to blacks, were necessary because of the new flood of Jewish immigrants from Eastern Europe and the great exodus of blacks from the South. Notes.

1330 Marks, Carole. "Black Workers and the Great Migration North." *Phylon* 46 (1985): 148–61.

The great migration of blacks from the South in 1916–1918 occurred primarily among urban blacks, not rural ones as is commonly thought. Notes.

1331 ———. "Lines of Communication, Recruitment Mechanisms, and the Great Migration of 1916–1918." *Social Problems* 31 (1983): 73–83.

A network of communications that influenced many blacks to leave the deep South included enticement by labor agents, letters from kin and friends, black newspapers, and service organizations.

1332 Meier, August. "The Negro and the Democratic Party, 1875–1915." *Phylon* 17 (1956): 173–91.

Black leaders sought accommodation with the Democratic party on a number of occasions, because the Republicans were either indifferent or hostile to them. While many blacks supported Wilson, they soon became disillusioned with him.

1333 Miller, Robert M. "The Attitudes of American Protestantism toward the Negro." *Journal of Negro History* 41 (1956): 215–40.

The Christian creed had little to do with the actions of Protestant churches when it came to blacks. Most contented themselves with the notion that racial segregation in churches was wrong in theory. Notes.

1334 Moses, Wilson J. "Black Nationalism, 1895–1915: Afro-American Bourgeois Culture before the Great War." Ph.D. dissertation, Brown University, 1975.

Black intellectuals responded to the segregationist policies of the Progressive era with black nationalism, a defensive ethnic chauvinism. DAI 37:550-A.

1335 Osofsky, Gilbert. *Harlem: The Making of a Ghetto, Negro New York, 1890–1930.* New York: Harper and Row, 1966.

Harlem became a black ghetto during the Progressive era, as thousands of blacks migrated to New York from the South in search of a better life. Photographs, notes, bibliography, index.

1336 Reid, George W. "The Post-Congressional Career of George H. White, 1901–1918." *Journal of Negro History* 61 (1976): 362–73.

This former North Carolina congressman practiced law in Washington and in Philadelphia during the Progressive era. He also founded a black-owned bank, dealt in real estate, and established a black community in Whitesboro, New Jersey. Notes.

1337 Roy, Jessie H. "Colored Judges: Judge Robert H. Terrell." *Negro History Bulletin* 28 (1965): 158–62.

Only the third black man to graduate from Harvard Law School, Terrell served as a judge on the Municipal Court of Washington during four presidential administrations, including Wilson's.

1338 Scheiber, Jane L., and Scheiber, Harry N. "The Wilson Administration and the Wartime Mobilization of Black Americans, 1917–1918." *Labor History* 10 (1969): 433–58.

Wartime expediency led Wilson to treat blacks much more favorably in order to mobilize their labor. While the president made no promises, many blacks were under the impression that their war work would lead to social and economic justice for blacks in the future. Notes.

1339 Sherman, Richard B. "Republicans and Negroes: The Lessons of Normalcy." *Phylon* 27 (1966): 63–79.

Official and unofficial attitudes of the Republican party toward blacks during the Wilson years and the 1920s are examined. Notes.

1340 Spear, Allan H. *Black Chicago: The Making of a Negro Ghetto, 1890–1920*. Chicago: University of Chicago Press, 1967.

Racial discrimination and the continuing migration of blacks from the rural South to Chicago and other northern cities contributed to the development of large, all-black neighborhoods. In addition, blacks were becoming more interested in developing self-sufficient communities as an alternative to struggling against white discrimination. Photographs, tables, notes, bibliography, index.

1341 Turpin-Parham, Shirley. "A History of Black Public Education in Philadelphia, Pennsylvania, 1864 to 1914." Ph.D. dissertation, Temple University, 1986.

The cultural circumstances that relegated black children to poor-quality schools are examined. DAI 47:2920-A.

1342 Yancy, Dorothy Cowser. "Professor James Emman Kwegyir Aggrey's Personality." *Negro History Bulletin* 40 (1977): 722–24.

While Aggrey agreed with Booker T. Washington's philosophy of race relations, he also emphasized the importance of African culture. Notes.

1343 Yellin, Jean Fagan. "DuBois *Crisis* and Women's Suffrage." Massachusetts Review 14 (1973): 365–75.

DuBois supported suffrage in the NAACP's *Crisis* magazine. He hoped that blacks and women would unite in an alliance of the oppressed, but he gave up on the idea after the passage of the Nineteenth Amendment. Notes.

NATIVE AMERICANS

1344 Geier, Philip O., III. "A Peculiar Status: A History of Oneida Indian Treaties and Claims: Jurisdictional Conflict within the American Government, 1775–1920." Ph.D. dissertation, Syracuse University, 1980.

The Oneidas' problems with unfair treatment by whites were complicated by the federal government's failure to make treaties with the Oneidas, so that New York State had to deal with them instead. The Oneidas were also troubled by internal conflicts. DAI 41:2734-A.

1345 Hertzberg, Hazel W. *The Search for an American Indian Identity: Modern Pan-Indian Movements*. Syracuse: Syracuse University Press, 1971.

Native American elites and Christian reformers lent their support to pan-Indianism during the Progressive era. The Indian religious movement began in Oklahoma and spread throughout the country, but strong opposition developed to this cult, which centered itself on the use of peyote. Photographs, notes, bibliography, index.

1346 Holm, Thomas M. "Indians and Progressives: From Vanishing Policy to the Indian New Deal." Ph.D. dissertation, University of Oklahoma, 1978.

Native Americans retained their philosophies and cultures during the Progressive era, as white artists and social scientists finally saw the need to preserve rather than wreck what was distinctly Indian. DAI 39:6915-A.

1347 Hoxie, Frederick E. "Beyond Savagery: The Campaign to Assimilate the American Indians." Ph.D. dissertation, Brandeis University, 1977.

Once Native Americans had been conquered militarily, they were treated as a special minority group to be civilized and assimilated. By 1920, however, the white elite had concluded that this goal was impossible, and the government reverted to a policy of segregation. DAI 38:2997-A.

1348 Iverson, Peter. *Carlos Montezuma and the Changing World of American Indians*. Albuquerque: University of New Mexico Press, 1982.

A captured Yavapai Indian who became a medical doctor, Montezuma became an activist who fought against the Bureau of Indian Affairs to protect the rights of the Native Americans of Arizona. Photographs, notes, bibliography, index.

1349 Kelly, Lawrence C. *The Navajo Indians and Federal Indian Policy, 1900–1935*. Tucson: University of Arizona Press, 1968.

Navaho Indians expanded their land holdings, but the discovery of oil led to bitter conflicts with politicians and oilmen. Notes, bibliography, index.

1350 ———. "The Navajos and Federal Policy, 1913–1935." Ph.D. dissertation, University of New Mexico, 1961.

In 1913 and again in 1918, Congress passed laws to prevent Navahos from expanding their domain to include public lands in New Mexico and Arizona. The worst government abuses of Navaho rights began in the 1920s, when the discovery of oil increased the value of reservation land. DAI 22:2773.

1351 McDonnell, Janet. "Competency Commissions and Indian Land Policy." *South Dakota History* 11 (1980): 21–34.

Between 1913 and 1920, several commissions were established to evaluate the competence of various tribes to support and govern themselves. The government's expressed intention was to encourage Indian independence, but most Indians who had title to their land were forced or persuaded to sell, and so they became paupers.

1352 ———. "The Disintegration of the Indian Estate: Indian Land Policy, 1913–1929." Ph.D. dissertation, Marquette University, 1980.

Cato Sells, who was commissioner of Indian affairs for most of Wilson's presidency, appears to have been well-intentioned toward Indians, but he allowed millions of acres of Indian land to pass into white hands. Operating under the Dawes act of 1887, with the ultimate goal of assimilating Indians, Sells did not provide Indians with either the funds or the education to use their lands appropriately, and this forced many to sell. DAI 41:4141-A.

1353 Meyer, Melissa L. "Tradition and the Market: The Social Relations of the White Earth Anishinaabeg, 1889–1920." Ph.D. dissertation, University of Minnesota, 1985.

The Nelson act of 1889 allowed exploitation of White Earth Reservation lands. Traditional and capitalistic Anishinaabegs developed conflicts. Eventually, it became impossible for them to meet subsistence needs in traditional ways, and they were forced to either leave the reservation or depend on seasonal labor or government money. DAI 46:3137-A.

1354 Putney, Diane T. "Fighting the Scourge: American Indian Morbidity and Federal Policy, 1897–1928." Ph.D. dissertation, Marquette University, 1980.

Federal commissioners were largely ineffective in their attempts to alleviate major Indian health problems such as tuberculosis, infant mortality, and trachoma, an eye disease.

Although the rate of tuberculosis declined between 1915 and 1920, coincident with federal efforts to improve sanitation, it appears that the Indians' turn toward farming and the consequent change in their lifestyle was the major factor. The various federal health programs were more effective in the schools than they were on the reservations. DAI 41:4143-A.

HISPANIC AMERICANS AND ASIAN AMERICANS

See also *Immigration,* below.

1355 Castillo, Pedro G. "The Making of a Mexican Barrio: Los Angeles, 1890–1920." Ph.D. dissertation, University of California, Santa Barbara, 1979.

Mexicans flocked to Los Angeles to take factory jobs, although they were discriminated against so that they remained at the bottom of the socioeconomic ladder. Segregated in barrios, Mexican Americans developed their own culture and society in their urban villages. DAI 40:5557-A.

1356 Griswold del Castillo, Richard. "The Mexican Revolution and the Spanish-Language Press in the Borderlands." *Journalism History* 4 (1977): 42–47.

From 1911 to 1917, editors of the Spanish-language press analyzed the Mexican Revolution for Hispanic Americans, who identified with events in Mexico more than did other ethnic groups.

1357 Lamb, Blaine P. "The Convenient Villain: The Early Cinematic Views of the Mexican American." *Journal of the West* 14 (1975): 75–81.

American films of the early 1900s reinforced the racial stereotypes of Mexicans prevalent in the Southwest. Notes.

1358 Meier, Matt S., and Rivera, Feliciano, eds. *Readings on La Raza: The Twentieth Century.* New York: Hill and Wang, 1974.

This survey of Mexican Americans in the twentieth century includes material on the Wilson presidency, during which thousands of Mexicans fled to America from the revolution and for jobs. Bibliography, index.

1359 Oehling, Richard A. "Hollywood and the Image of the Oriental, 1910–1950: Part I." *Film and History* 8 (1978): 33–41.

This covers the period from 1910 to the 1920s, when Hollywood presented a relentlessly negative stereotype of Oriental people in films.

1360 Romo, Ricardo. *East Los Angeles: History of a Barrio*. Austin: University of Texas Press, 1983.

The formative years (1900–1930) of the Mexican-American barrio in Los Angeles are examined. A chapter on the "Brown Scare" (1913–1918) analyzes the nativist fears engendered by the mass migration of Mexicans into the Southwest. Notes, index.

1361 ———. "Responses to Mexican Immigration." *Aztlan* 6 (1976): 173–94.

Mexican immigrants played an important part in the development of the Southwest and the Midwest. Revolution in Mexico, the World War, and recruitment of workers by agricultural concerns all contributed to the mass migration to the United States that began in 1910. Notes.

1362 Zamora, Emilio. "Mexican Labor Activity in South Texas, 1900–1920." Ph.D. dissertation, University of Texas, Austin, 1983.

Mexican labor organizations were mostly isolated from larger, predominantly Anglo federations. Mexican culture usually remained intact, and it was perceived as threatening for sometimes contradictory reasons, including potential strikebreaking and possible revolutionary radicalism. Although the Socialist party showed interest in the Mexican laborers, it never really followed through on it. DAI 44:1183-A.

Women

See also Chapter 4, *Women Workers*, Chapter 5, *Health Issues*, and Chapter 11, *The Home Front, Women*.

1363 Abelson, Elaine S. " 'When Ladies Go A-Thieving': The Department Store, Shoplifting and the Contradictions of Consumerism." Ph.D. dissertation, New York University, 1986.

When store owners learned to advertise and to promote maximum demand for their merchandise, they inadvertently but inevitably created shoplifting. Mostly middle-class women, the shoplifters were excused as victims of uncontrollable kleptomania. DAI 47:1457-A.

1364 Addams, Jane. *The Second Twenty Years at Hull House*. New York: Macmillan, 1930.

Addams's second twenty years at the settlement house in Chicago coincided with her work in the Progressive movement and her increasing preoccupation with the peace issue.

1365 Aiken, Katherine G. "The National Florence Crittenton Mission, 1883–1925: A Case Study in Progressive Reform." Ph.D. dissertation, Washington State University, 1980.

The National Florence Crittenton Mission worked to rehabilitate prostitutes through the inculcation of middle-class values. It also fought against white slavery and did war work at army training camps. DAI 41:2256-A.

1366 Anderson, Eric. "Prostitution and Social Justice: Chicago, 1910–1915." *Social Science Review* 48 (1974): 203–28.

Business leaders and moralists combined forces in a drive to close down Chicago's notorious red-light district. Notes.

1367 Antler, Joyce. "The Educated Woman and Professionalization: The Struggle for a New Feminine Identity, 1890–1920." Ph.D. dissertation, State University of New York, Stony Brook, 1977.

Higher education did not prepare women well for decision making and career fulfillment. Career women suffered from an inner conflict, since the whole thrust of their education was toward domesticity. DAI 38:4320-A.

1368 Athey, Louis L. "Florence Kelley and the Quest for Negro Equality." *Journal of Negro History* 54 (1971): 249–61.

Although she was among the founders of the NAACP, Kelley never gave the campaign for racial equality top priority, preferring instead to work for the rights of women and children. Notes.

1369 Benjamin, Ludy T., Jr. "The Pioneering Work of Leta Hollingsworth in the Psychology of Women." *Nebraska History* 56 (1975): 493–507.

Leta Hollingsworth attacked leading psychologists of the day whose thought was grounded in the assumption that women were naturally inferior. A prolific author, she received a Ph.D. in 1916.

1370 Benson, Stella, and Brandon, William, eds. "Stella Benson: Letters to Laura Hutton,

1915–1919." *Massachusetts Review* 25 (1984): 225–46.

British novelist Stella Benson's letters to a friend are reprinted. They include her comments on the American scene, as she viewed it during her travels.

1371 Board, John C. "The Lady from Montana." *Montana* 17 (1967): 2–17.

Jeannette Rankin ran for Congress in 1916 after gaining political experience in the suffrage movement. The first woman elected to Congress, she voted against declaring war on Germany.

1372 Camhi, Jane J. "Women against Women: American Antisuffragism 1880–1920." Ph.D. dissertation, Tufts University, 1973.

Women in the antisuffrage movement became proficient in the art of political lobbying, a practice they engaged in to shelter other women from the corrupting influence of politics. Antisuffragism succeeded in dragging out the struggle for the vote by several years. DAI 35:3625-A.

1373 Campbell, Barbara K. *The Liberated Woman of 1914: Prominent Women in the Progressive Era.* Ann Arbor: University of Michigan Research Press, 1976.

That the period under study was the most progressive one for women in American history until recent times is evidenced by the lives and work of prominent female activists. Women gained greater equality without making their careers the most important part of their lives. Notes, bibliography, index.

1374 Connelly, Mark T. *The Response to Prostitution in the Progressive Era.* Chapel Hill: University of North Carolina Press, 1980.

Pervasive, widespread feelings of anxiety and shifting moral values made prostitution a national issue during the Progressive era. Urban vice commissions battled the problem, while many tales about white slavery appeared in the press. The medical profession debated the connections between venereal disease and prostitution. Prostitution was symbolic of what had gone wrong with modern urban America. Notes, bibliography, index.

1375 Conovan, Mary S. "Women's Ministries in the Episcopal Church, 1850–1920." Ph.D. dissertation, Columbia University, 1985.

Although women's groups were essential to the Episcopal church's support for missionaries and social service activities, a general convention in 1920 firmly excluded women from participation in basic policy decisions. DAI 46:2420-A.

1376 Conway, Jill. "Jane Addams: An American Heroine." *Daedalus* 93 (1964): 761–80.

Addams was a heroine to women of the Progressive era because of her effective activism and personal courage. Notes.

1377 Cook, Blanche W. "Female Support Networks and Political Activism: Lillian Wald, Crystal Eastman, Emma Goldman." In Nancy F. Cott and Elizabeth H. Pleck, eds. *A Heritage of Her Own: Toward a New Social History of American Women.* New York: Simon and Schuster, 1979, pp. 412–44.

Wald, Eastman, Goldman, and Jane Addams offered women a wide range of role model choices and affinities at a time when women were programmed to make shrines of their homes. These role models in turn received strength from female networks. Notes.

1378 Curti, Merle. "Jane Addams on Human Nature." *Journal of the History of Ideas* 22 (1961): 240–53.

Addams's contributions to the feminist and suffrage movements, to social welfare, and to the international peace campaigns are measured. Notes.

1379 Daniels, Adelaide W. *Recollections of a Cabinet Minister's Wife.* Raleigh: Mitchell, 1945.

Daniels remembers the social life of Washington during Wilson's terms. Photographs.

1380 Davis, Allen F. *American Heroine: The Life and Legend of Jane Addams.* New York: Oxford University Press, 1973.

Addams embodied many of the attitudes toward reform that changed during her prime years. Order and efficiency interested her less than did peace, justice, and a renewed sense of community. Notes, bibliography, index.

1381 Essa Gallaway, Sara. "Pioneering the Woman's Club Movement: The Story of Caroline Maria Severance in Los Angeles." Ph.D. dissertation, Carnegie-Mellon University, 1985.

Caroline Maria Severance was a feminist who used her traditional domestic role as a platform for political activities and establishing women's clubs. DAI 46:1719-A.

1382 Farrell, John C. *Beloved Lady: A History of Jane Addams' Ideas on Reform and Peace.* Baltimore, MD: Johns Hopkins University Press, 1967.

Addams came to see that reform and peace could not be separated, because without peace there could be no justice. Notes, bibliography, index.

1383 Fastenau, Maureen K. "Maternal Government: The Social Settlement Houses and the Politicization of Women's Sphere, 1889–1920." Ph.D. dissertation, Duke University, 1982.

Settlement houses grew out of women's need to influence the world beyond their own homes and to make women's priorities, particularly human welfare, also the priorities of government. Although the settlement houses helped women to redefine themselves and their possibilities in the world, they had little effect on the priorities of the nation's leaders. DAI 44: 556-A.

1384 Fitzpatrick, Ellen F. "Academics and Activists: Women Social Scientists and the Impulse for Reform, 1892–1920." Ph.D. dissertation, Brandeis University, 1981.

Among the first women graduate students of the University of Chicago were many who made careers of social activism. More rational, scientific, and professional than most reformers, they rigorously analyzed and wrote on social problems, successfully integrating academic and practical life. Crime, problems of immigrants, and labor were among the issues they addressed. DAI 42:2818-A.

1385 Geidel, Peter. "The National Woman's Party and the Origins of the Equal Rights Amendment." *Historian* 42 (1980): 557–82.

The National Woman's party succeeded in lobbying an equal rights bill to passage in Wisconsin but failed in other states and at the national level, in part because the social feminists refused to support the campaign. The failure of the ERA and the party's lack of an official magazine contributed to the NWP's decline. Notes.

1386 Goldmark, Josephine C. *Impatient Crusader.* Urbana: University of Illinois Press, 1953.

Florence Kelley is the subject of this friendly biography, which covers her work in the National Consumers League and her crusades to better the lot of women and children.

1387 Gordon, Linda. *Woman's Body, Woman's Right: A Social History of Birth Control in America.* New York: Grossman, 1976.

The birth control issue passed through an intermediary phase during the Wilson years, as radicals incorporated it into their agenda as a means of revolutionizing social relations. Photographs, notes, index.

1388 Grabowski, John J. *A Social Settlement in a Neighborhood in Transition: Hiram House, Cleveland, Ohio, 1896–1926.* Cleveland: Case Western Reserve University Press, 1977.

As far as the Jewish, Italian, and black residents of the Hiram House neighborhood were concerned, this Progressive settlement house failed to meet their needs. WASP social workers preferred counseling to genuine social reform. Notes, bibliography, index.

1389 Gullett, Gayle. "City Mothers, City Daughters, and Dance Hall Girls: The Limits of Female Political Power in San Francisco, 1913." In Barbara J. Harris and JoAnn K. McNamara, eds. *Women and the Structure of Society.* Durham, NC: Duke University Press, 1984, pp. 149–59.

California clubwomen were able to recall a judge who had been notoriously lenient in cases of sexual assault. They also fought to close down San Francisco's Barbary Coast vice district. Notes.

1390 Harris, Katherine L. H. "Women and Families on Northeastern Colorado Homesteads, 1873–1920." Ph.D. dissertation, University of Colorado, Boulder, 1983.

The isolation of the frontier rewarded innovation, independence, and egalitarianism in men. The author finds that similar traits emerged in women. Single women often filed land claims, while married women saw themselves as equal partners to their husbands. DAI 45:277-A.

1391 Hendrickson, Rick. "Mother's Day and the Mother's Day Shrine: A History." *Upper Ohio Valley Historical Review* 13 (1984): 2–4.

The origins of Woodrow Wilson's official proclamation of Mother's Day as a holiday are discussed.

1392 Hummel, Michael D. "The Attitudes of Edward Bok and the *Ladies' Home Journal* toward Woman's Role in Society, 1889–1919." Ph.D. dissertation, North Texas State University, 1982.

Ladies' Home Journal editor Edward Bok held strictly Victorian ideas about women. Nevertheless, he grudgingly allowed the *Journal* to reflect evolving attitudes toward women, particularly between 1910 and 1919. DAI 43:2425-A.

1393 Hundley, Norris C., Jr. "Katherine Philips Edson and the Fight for the Minimum Wage, 1912–1923." *Pacific Historical Review* 29 (1960): 271–85.

Edson's work for the Bureau of Labor Statistics in California led to the consideration of minimum wage laws for children and women and to the creation of a state commission. Notes.

1394 Hynes, Terry. "Magazine Portrayal of Women, 1911–1930." *Journalism Monographs* 72 (1981): 1–56.

Leading American magazines are examined to discover the connection between popular images of women and female emancipation.

1395 Jensen, Richard, and Campbell, Barbara. "How to Handle a Liberated Woman." *Historical Methods Newsletter* 5 (1972): 109–13.

In the course of preparing for the 1914 *Women's Who's Who in America*, the editors circulated thousands of questionnaires to discover what women thought about important social and political issues. Notes.

1396 Katz, Esther. "Grace Hoadley Dodge: Women and the Emerging Metropolis, 1856–1914." Ph.D. dissertation, New York University, 1980.

Grace Hoadley Dodge's underlying concern was for young women facing the temptations, insecurity, and corruption of the burgeoning cities. In finding solutions, she became involved with vocational education and with various urban clubs, notably the Young Women's Christian Association, that could provide a healthy focus. DAI 41:5221-A.

1397 Kennedy, David M. *Birth Control in America: The Career of Margaret Sanger*. New Haven, CT: Yale University Press, 1970.

While Sanger made a significant contribution to the birth control movement, it was well under way before she became an activist. Notes, bibliography, index.

1398 Kennedy, Susan Estabrook. "Poverty, Respectability, and Ability to Work." *International Journal of Women's Studies* [Canada] 2 (1979): 401–18.

Progressives used a variety of tools in their campaign to help working-class women, including sociological studies, investigative reporting, settlement houses, trade unionism, and protective legislation.

1399 Kobrin, Francis E. "The American Midwife Controversy: A Crisis of Professionalization." *Bulletin of the History of Medicine* 40 (1966): 350–63.

In order to win over the public and carve out a place for themselves in the medical establishment, obstetricians attacked the methods of midwives. Notes.

1400 Lagemann, Ellen C. *A Generation of Women: Education in the Lives of Progressive Reformers*. Cambridge, MA: Harvard University Press, 1979.

The educational backgrounds of five Progressive women are analyzed. While they came from different backgrounds, all developed a sense of high self-esteem early in their lives as well as a female consciousness that bridged class divisions. Photographs, notes, bibliography, index.

1401 Levine, Daniel. *Jane Addams and the Liberal Tradition*. Madison: State Historical Society of Wisconsin, 1971.

Addams's leadership of the settlement house movement, her Progressive activism, and her role in the peace movement are examined. Her work embodied what was best in the reform movement. Photographs, notes, bibliography, index.

1402 Lindig, Carmen M. "The Woman's Movement in Louisiana: 1879–1920." Ph.D. dissertation, North Texas State University, 1982.

Women's organizations, from church groups to suffragettes, empowered Louisiana women to enlarge their possibilities in the world. DAI 43:2425-A.

1403 Linn, James W. *Jane Addams*. New York: D. Appleton-Century, 1935.

Addams's nephew presents the story of her personal life. Photographs, index.

1404 McGovern, James R. "The American Woman's Pre-World War I Freedom in Manners and Morals." *Journal of American History* 55 (1968): 315–33.

The period of new freedoms for teenage girls and women did not start with the flappers of the 1920s; rather, it began a decade earlier as a result of changes in the urban scene, new household laborsaving devices, and the widespread use of automobiles. Notes.

1405 Mackey, Thomas C. "Red Lights Out: A Legal History of Prostitution, Disorderly Houses, and Vice Districts." Ph.D. dissertation, Rice University, 1984.

Progressive-era reformists attacked prostitution and disorderly houses (houses used for bawdy purposes), and states passed red-light abatement acts. In practice, however, many cities allowed vice in carefully limited areas. DAI 45:1188-A.

1406 Maxwell, William J. "Frances Kellor in the Progressive Era: A Case Study in the Professionalization of Reform." Ph.D. dissertation, Columbia University, 1968.

Frances Kellor worked in various capacities as a professional reformer, focusing on the problems of immigrants. She also wrote on the need for scientifically trained, consistent, efficient (and therefore paid) reformers. DAI 29:3561-A.

1407 Mehr, Linda H. "Down off the Pedestal: Some Modern Heroines in Popular Culture, 1890–1917." Ph.D. dissertation, University of California, Los Angeles, 1973.

The mass media reflected the changing social situation of women during the Progressive era. Modern heroines analyzed here include the Gibson girl, movie stars, serial queens, and Mary Pickford. Men were chiefly responsible for creating these heroines who wanted control over their lives but accepted marriage as inevitable. DAI 34:7161-A.

1408 Meyerowitz, Joanne J. "Holding Their Own: Working Women Apart from Family in Chicago, 1880–1930." Ph.D. dissertation, Stanford University, 1983.

A significant portion of young urban workers (20 percent in 1900) were women who lived away from their families. Their emotional, social, and economic survival strategies are examined. Various social analysts, who at first saw these women as victims of industrialization, eventually applauded them as individualists. DAI 44:557-A.

1409 Mottus, Jane E. "New York Nightingales: The Emergence of the Nursing Profession at Bellevue and New York Hospital, 1850–1920." Ph.D. dissertation, New York University, 1980.

By 1920 nursing had become a profession with standards for training and licensing. National organizations and journals existed for nurses, who were mostly well-educated, middle-class women. DAI 41:773-A.

1410 O'Neill, William L. "Feminism as a Radical Ideology." In Alfred F. Young, ed. *Dissent: Explorations in the History of American Radicalism.* DeKalb: Northern Illinois University Press, 1968, pp. 273–300.

"The woman movement," as its participants called it, comprised three groups: the social feminists, suffragists, and extreme feminists. Feminism cannot expect to have a female version of Lenin emerge until a female Marx has developed a significant body of theory. Notes.

1411 Rosen, Ruth. *The Lost Sisterhood: Prostitution in America, 1900–1918.* Baltimore, MD: Johns Hopkins University Press, 1981.

Progressives failed in their crusade to stop prostitution—they only made things more difficult for the "lost sisters," who often went into prostitution voluntarily to make more money. Photographs, notes, bibliography, index.

1412 Ruoff, John C. "Southern Womanhood, 1865–1920: An Intellectual and Cultural Study." Ph.D. dissertation, University of Illinois, Urbana-Champaign, 1976.

The image of southern womanhood in the works of southern writers is studied to explore how the South grappled with its transformation into an urban, middle-class society. DAI 37:3133-A.

1413 Schott, Linda K. "Women against War: Pacifism, Feminism, and Social Justice in the United States, 1915–1941." Ph.D. dissertation, Stanford University, 1985.

Believing that female pacifists had essentially different priorities from the existing, male-dominated pacifist organizations, American women formed the Woman's Peace Party in 1915. The group came to espouse a philosophy based on equality and mutual nurturance among all people. DAI 47:638-A.

1414 ———. "The Woman's Peace Party and the Moral Basis of Women's Pacifism." *Frontiers* 8 (1985): 18–24.

The Woman's Peace party stood for feminist pacifism, which was absolute, as well as equal rights for women.

1415 Scott, Anne F. "Jane Addams and the City." *Virginia Quarterly Review* 43 (1967): 53–62.

Jane Addams's practical experience as the head of the settlement house movement made her a pioneer of urban reform.

1416 Sherrick, Rebecca L. "Private Visions, Public Lives: The Hull-House Women in the Progressive Era." Ph.D. dissertation, Northwestern University, 1980.

Seven leaders of Hull House are profiled as examples of Progressive-era women who had a great sense of social responsibility. They hoped to blur the boundaries between the spheres of men and women and extend the values of the home into the workplace and the marketplace. DAI 41: 2740-A.

1417 ———. "Their Fathers' Daughters: The Autobiographies of Jane Addams and Florence Kelley." *American Studies* 27 (1986): 39–53.

In their autobiographies, both of these outstanding reformers devote much attention to the influence of their fathers. Both seem to accept basic Victorian tenets about women, even though they left them far behind in their own lives. Notes.

1418 Sloan, L. Alene. "Some Aspects of the Woman Suffrage Movement in Indiana." Ph.D. dissertation, Ball State University, 1982.

The leaders, the organizations, and the efforts of the Indiana suffrage movement are comprehensively examined, including the local effects of the national movement and the effects of other Indiana women's reform activities on the suffrage movement. DAI 43:902-A.

1419 Springer, Barbara A. "Ladylike Reformers: Indiana Women and Progressive Reform, 1900–1920." Ph.D. dissertation, Indiana University, 1985.

Women learned to organize, lobby, and gain public support for Progressive social and political change including child labor laws, women's suffrage, housing regulations, and temperance. Old-school businesses and politicians and dissension within the women's movement were barriers to success. DAI 46: 3845-A.

1420 Stevenson, Janet. "Lola Maverick Lloyd: 'I Must Do Something for Peace.' " *Chicago History* 9 (1980): 47–57.

Lloyd was a feminist converted to pacifism in 1914 who worked diligently for peace through international organizations.

1421 Stinson, Robert. "Ida M. Tarbell and Ambiguities of Feminism." *Pennsylvania Magazine of History and Biography* 101 (1977): 217–39.

A liberated woman herself, Tarbell believed that even working women should not attempt to change their feminine ways. Notes.

1422 Szopa, Anne. "Images of Women in Muncie Newspapers: 1895–1915." Ph.D. dissertation, Ball State University, 1986.

There were distinct differences among the images of prostitutes and other women in the three time periods studied. In 1915, prostitutes were perceived as victims of circumstances, and wealthier women appeared to be active news makers. DAI 47:3857-A.

1423 Wallace, Teresa A. "Frieda Segelke Miller: Reformer and Labor Law Administrator, 1889–1973." Ph.D. dissertation, Boston University, 1983.

During the Wilson administration Miller, educated as an economist, worked with the Philadelphia Women's Trade Union League. DAI 44:1553-A.

1424 Willis, Gwendolen B. "Olympia Brown." *Universalist Historical Society Journal* 4 (1963): 1–76.

The first woman to graduate from a theology school, Olympia Brown recounts her struggles in this autobiography edited by her daughter. Included is an account of her fight for women's suffrage in Wisconsin during the Wilson years.

1425 Wolfe, Allis R. "Women, Consumerism, and the National Consumers' League in the Progressive Era, 1900–1923." *Labor History* 16 (1976): 378–92.

The National Consumers' League came about as a result of women's growing awareness of their power as consumers. The league was concerned primarily with corporate ethics and women's issues. Notes.

1426 Wunsch, James L. "Prostitution and Public Policy: From Regulation to Suppression, 1858–1920." Ph.D. dissertation, University of Chicago, 1976.

In Victorian-era St. Louis and New York prostitution was regulated, because it was regarded as a necessary evil. The belief that prostitutes were feebleminded, combined with fears of venereal disease and white slavery, led the Progressives to stamp out the bawdy house at a time when prostitutes were turning to private rooms to conduct their business. DAI 37:5996-A.

FEMINISM

1427 Abrahams, Edward. "Randolph Bourne on Feminism and Feminists." *Historian* 43 (1981): 365–77.

Bourne believed that the liberation of women was essential for the transformation of society, but he became critical of the feminist movement, largely for personal reasons. Bourne's physical disfigurements affected his relations with the opposite sex. Notes.

1428 Cheney, Lynne. "How Alice Paul Became the Most Militant Feminist of Them All." *Smithsonian* 3 (1972): 94–100.

The rise to prominence of Alice Paul, leader of the militant wing of the suffragettes, is chronicled from World War I through her fight for the ERA in the 1920s.

1429 Daniels, Doris G. "Lillian D. Wald: The Progressive Woman and Feminism." Ph.D. dissertation, City University of New York, 1977.

Feminist Lillian D. Wald helped to found the Women's Trade Union League and specialized in bringing middle-class support to the cause of working women. She fought equally hard for suffrage and for world peace. DAI 37:7268-A.

1430 Ernst, Joy S., and Hill, Claibourne M. "Feminism." *Foundations* 19 (1976): 24–32.

A thumbnail biography of Hill is included with this reprint of his lecture to the Berkeley, California, Outlook Club in 1914 on the women's movement in general and on feminist gains in Colorado. Notes.

1431 Faderman, Lillian. "Lesbian Magazine Fiction in the Early Twentieth Century." *Journal of Popular Culture* 11 (1978): 800–817.

Lesbianism was a common theme in popular magazines during the Progressive period. It was tolerated because it was believed that women were not by nature sensual and that they would marry once the right man had been found.

1432 Ford, Linda G. "American Militants: An Analysis of the National Woman's Party, 1912–1919." Ph.D. dissertation, Syracuse University, 1984.

The consequences of the National Woman's party's militancy included numerous arrests during the hysteria of the war years, exclusion from more moderate suffrage groups, and, probably, the eventual success of the suffrage movement. DAI 45:3435-A.

1433 Fowler, Robert B. *Carrie Catt: Feminist Politician.* Boston: Northeastern University Press, 1986.

A leading organizer of the successful drive for women's suffrage, Catt was a powerful and contradictory figure who combined feminism with pragmatic politics. Notes, bibliography, index.

1434 Johnson, Abby A. "The Personal Magazine: Margaret C. Anderson and the *Little Review*, 1914–1929." *South Atlantic Quarterly* 75 (1976): 351–63.

As editor of the *Little Review*, Anderson featured articles on women's issues, peace, censorship, and avant-garde art. The serialization of James Joyce's *Ulysses* touched off years of legal problems. Notes.

1435 O'Neill, William L. *Everyone Was Brave: The Rise and Fall of Feminism in America.* Chicago: Quadrangle, 1969.

Some feminists concentrated on women's rights, while others worked to reform society as a whole. While the campaign for suffrage was successful ultimately, it did not improve the lot of women in general. Notes, index.

1436 Schmidt, Cynthia A. "Socialist-Feminism: Max Eastman, Floyd Dell and Crystal Eastman." Ph.D. dissertation, Marquette University, 1983.

Max Eastman, Floyd Dell, and Crystal Eastman synthesized socialism and radical feminism because they believed that women would have to be given the vote before socialism could be implemented. Socialism could not succeed without feminism, and feminism was not possible under capitalism. DAI 44:1182-A.

1437 Sochen, June. *The New Woman in Greenwich Village, 1910–1920.* New York: Quadrangle, 1972.

The Greenwich Village feminists were college-educated, middle-class, predominantly married women with professional careers. They believed in full economic and social equality for women, and they fought for widespread dissemination of birth control information. Initially, they found support from various organizations in the Village, but the socialist-pacifist stand many took toward the war alienated people, and the feminist group had disintegrated by 1920. Notes, bibliography, index.

RADICAL WOMEN

See also Chapter 8, *Anarchism, Syndicalism, Socialism,* and *Communism.*

1438 Basen, Neil K. "Kate Richards O'Hare: The 'First Lady' of American Socialism, 1901–1917." *Labor History* 21 (1980): 165–99.

One of the most popular leaders of the Socialist party, Kate Richards O'Hare espoused a brand of "common sense" socialism that had much in common with the socialism of Victor Berger and Morris Hillquit. Notes.

1439 Baxandall, Rosalynn F. "Elizabeth Gurley Flynn: The Early Years." *Radical America* 9 (1975): 97–115.

Flynn's early life as a feminist and her conversion to communism are discussed.

1440 ———. *Words on Fire: The Life and Writing of Elizabeth Gurley Flynn.* New Brunswick, NJ: Rutgers University Press, 1987.

The author provides a lengthy introduction and conclusion to this collection of the longtime Communist activist Flynn's writings on women. Photographs.

1441 Camp, Helen C. " 'Gurley': A Biography of Elizabeth Gurley Flynn, 1890–1964." Ph.D. dissertation, Columbia University, 1980.

Flynn was a dynamic activist who eventually became prominent in the American Communist party. A leader in several Wobbly strikes early in her career, she fell out of favor with the Industrial Workers of the World's general secretary, William Haywood, in 1916. Arrested with other Wobblies for opposing World War I, charges against her were dropped because her disagreement with Haywood had kept her inactive. From 1918 to 1924 she helped to defend radicals accused of Communist activities. DAI 43:1650-A.

1442 Degler, Carl N. "Charlotte Perkins Gilman on the Theory and Practice of Feminism." *American Quarterly* 8 (1956): 21–39.

Gilman tried to prove how the suppression of women affected society in general and argued that less-restricted women could make the country happier and more productive. Notes.

1443 Drinnon, Richard. *Rebel in Paradise: A Biography of Emma Goldman.* Chicago: University of Chicago Press, 1961.

A political bogey to most people, Goldman was a multidimensional person who was interested in the arts, sexuality, birth control, and civil liberties. Photographs, notes, bibliography, index.

1444 Foner, Philip S., and Miller, Sally M., eds. *Kate Richards O'Hare: Selected Writings and Speeches.* Baton Rouge: Louisiana State University Press, 1982.

A brief biography of this leading female socialist of the Progressive era is included along with her writings on socialism and World War I and her letters from prison, written while she was serving a sentence for speaking out against Wilson's war policies. Notes, index.

1445 Jones, Mary H. *The Correspondence of Mother Jones.* Edited by Edward M. Steel. Pittsburgh: University of Pittsburgh Press, 1985.

The correspondence of the aged labor leader Mother Jones is reprinted. It includes several letters about strikes and imprisoned workers during the Wilson years.

1446 Miller, Sally M. "Other Socialists: Native-Born and Immigrant Women in the Socialist Party of America." *Labor History* 24 (1983): 84–102.

While women played a significant role in the Socialist party, the men were reluctant to treat them as equals. Leading female party members profiled here include Kate Richards O'Hare, May Woods Simons, Lena Morrow Lewis, Theresa Serber Malkiel, Meta Stern Lilienthal, and Antoinette Konikow. Notes.

1447 Ogle, Stephanie F. "Anna Louise Strong: Progressive and Propagandist." Ph.D. dissertation, University of Washington, 1981.

Anna Louise Strong's activities during Wilson's presidency included leadership in the child welfare movement and involvement in the Seattle general strike of 1919. DAI 42:5223-A.

1448 Sharp, Kathleen A. "Rose Pastor Stokes: Radical Champion of the American Working Class, 1879–1933." Ph.D. dissertation, Duke University, 1979.

Rose Pastor Stokes was a Socialist party organizer, a labor agitator, a writer, and a birth control advocate during the Progressive era. Her arrest during World War I and the Bolshevik Revolution pushed her leftward into the Communist party. DAI 40:2230-A.

1449 Tamarkin, Stanley R. "Rose Pastor Stokes: The Portrait of a Radical Woman, 1905–1919." Ph.D. dissertation, Yale University, 1983.

The life of Rose Pastor Stokes, whose marriage transformed her from a poor factory worker into a millionaire socialist, is examined in terms of her inner drives. During the Wilson administration she spoke extensively for the Intercollegiate Socialist Society, and she was convicted in 1918 of violating the wartime Espionage Act. DAI 45:612-A.

1450 Wexler, Alice. "The Early Life of Emma Goldman." *Psychohistory Review* 8 (1980): 7–21.

Early influences on Goldman include ambivalent feelings about her father, an interest in female martyrs, and her Russian roots. It is possible that her childhood family relations account for her conversion to anarchism. Notes.

1451 ———. *Emma Goldman: An Intimate Life.* New York: Pantheon, 1984.

Goldman was an elitist who nevertheless fought for the rights of workers and willingly advocated violence to achieve anarchist ends, although she recognized the moral dilemma of using bad means to achieve good ends. Photographs, notes, bibliography, index.

1452 Zickefoose, Sandra. "Women and the Socialist Party of America, 1900–1915." *UCLA History Journal* 1 (1980): 26–41.

While the Socialist party was ahead of the Democrats and the Republicans on women's issues, many male comrades were traditionalists in matters of sex. When the party's fortunes began to decline, women's programs were among the first to be cut. Notes.

The Suffrage Movement

See also Chapter 7, *Nineteenth Amendment.*

1453 Bosmajian, Haig A. "The Abrogation of the Suffragists' First Amendment Rights." *Western Speech* 38 (1974): 218–32.

During Wilson's first term the drive for women's suffrage was stymied, in part because many communities restricted women's rights.

1454 Buenker, John D. "The Urban Political Machine and Woman Suffrage: A Study in Political Adaptability." *Historian* 33 (1971): 264–79.

The reactionary urban political machines of the nineteenth century responded positively to many Progressive reforms, including women's suffrage. Notes.

1455 Buhle, Mari Jo, and Buhle, Paul, eds. *The Concise History of Woman Suffrage.* Urbana: University of Illinois Press, 1978.

Selections are presented from the writings of Elizabeth Cady Stanton, Susan B. Anthony, Frances Gage, and Ida Husted Harper as well as documents from National American Woman Suffrage Association (NAWSA) conventions, the League of Women Voters, and

the suffrage campaigns of the Wilson years. Index.

1456 Caruso, Virginia A. P. "A History of Woman Suffrage in Michigan." Ph.D. dissertation, Michigan State University, 1986.

The sixty-five year struggle for suffrage in Michigan was characterized by cooperation among different suffrage groups, by persistence, and by increasingly skillful organization and agitation. DAI 47:4492-A.

1457 Claus, Ruth F. "Militancy in the English and American Woman Suffrage Movements." Ph.D. dissertation, Yale University, 1975.

The English suffrage movement employed violent tactics to demonstrate that its members were capable of more than traditional feminine passivity. The American suffrage movement did not commit illegal acts, because leaders such as Alice Paul and Harriet Stanton Blatch believed in their ability to legally change the political system. DAI 36:8230-A.

1458 Coulter, Thomas C. "A History of Woman Suffrage in Nebraska, 1856–1920." Ph.D. dissertation, Ohio State University, 1967.

The Nebraska suffrage movement intensified during the Wilson years and culminated in ratification of the federal suffrage amendment in 1919 and passage of a state suffrage law in 1920. DAI 28:4985-A.

1459 Flexner, Eleanor. *Century of Struggle: The Woman's Rights Movement in the United States.* Cambridge, MA: Harvard University Press, 1959.

Part Three surveys the twentieth-century suffrage movement and how it finally convinced men that women deserve the right to vote. Bibliography, notes, index.

1460 Glazer, Penina M. "Organizing for Freedom." *Massachusetts Review* 13 (1972): 29–44.

The women's suffrage movement had a radical wing, which advocated women's rights as a means to wholesale societal changes, although the majority of suffragettes did not want to change the system. Notes.

1461 Gluck, Sherna, ed. *From Parlor to Prison: Five American Suffragists Talk about Their Lives.* New York: Vintage, 1976.

The oral histories of five women who were active in the suffrage movement are included, along with contemporary newspaper and magazine articles and a chronology. Photographs, bibliography.

1462 Gordon, Felice D. "After Winning: The New Jersey Suffragists, 1910–1947." Ph.D. dissertation, Rutgers University, 1982.

Leaders of the largest New Jersey suffrage organizations are studied to assess how the movement affected them. The author divides the suffragettes into those who believed in the need for full equality of power for women and those who wanted women to maintain their traditional social roles after winning the vote. DAI 43:3397-A.

1463 Graham, Sally H. "Woodrow Wilson, Alice Paul, and the Woman Suffrage Movement." *Political Science Quarterly* 98 (1984): 665–79.

Woodrow Wilson changed his stance on women's suffrage in 1918 as a matter of practical politics. Alice Paul and her National Woman's party bested the president by embarrassing him politically and playing on the contradiction of his crusade to make the world safe for democracy while denying the vote to women at home. Notes.

1464 Hay, Melba P. "Madeline McDowell Breckinridge: Kentucky Suffragist and Progressive Reformer." Ph.D. dissertation, University of Kentucky, 1980.

Madeline McDowell Breckinridge was a leader of welfare reform in Kentucky and, later, of the suffrage movement. She began by working through women's clubs at the turn of the century and became convinced that women's suffrage was essential to the success of other Progressive reforms. She also helped found, in 1917, a Kentucky sanitorium for tuberculosis, a disease from which she suffered. DAI 41:2736-A.

1465 Hensley, Frances S. "Change and Continuity in the American Women's Movement, 1848–1930." Ph.D. dissertation, Ohio State University, 1981.

Although different issues have been emphasized in different phases of the women's movement (suffrage, for example, was the focus between 1869 and 1920), there have consistently been two distinct factions. The majority of women activists in this period were relatively moderate and stressed traditional women's concerns for human welfare, but there was always a radical minority pushing for full equality. DAI 42:4554-A.

1466 Jablonsky, Thomas J. "Duty, Nature, and Stability: The Female Anti-Suffragists in the United States, 1894–1920." Ph.D. dissertation, University of Southern California, 1978.

Emphasizing duty, nature, and stability, conservative women formed antisuffragette associations, although many of their members supported Progressive causes and the League of Nations. DAI 39:4446-A.

1467 Katz, David H. "Carrie Chapman Catt and the Struggle for Peace." Ph.D. dissertation, Syracuse University, 1973.

This longtime women's suffrage activist asked her sisters to support the American war effort for the sake of the suffrage movement. Once the war was over, she resumed her interest in the struggle for peace. DAI 34:6550-A.

1468 Kraditor, Aileen S. *The Ideas of the Woman Suffrage Movement, 1890–1920.* New York: Columbia University Press, 1965.

The new generation of women who took over the suffrage movement during the Progressive era was more conservative than the old, and also more racist and nativist. They wanted the vote for their own benefit and not for the benefit of society as a whole. Notes, bibliography, index.

1469 Louis, James P. "Sue Shelton White and the Woman Suffrage Movement in Tennessee, 1913–20." *Tennessee Historical Quarterly* 22 (1963): 170–90.

A feminist and an advocate of suffrage, White worked closely with the American Woman Suffrage Association and the National Woman's party. She was a key figure in the suffrage movement in Tennessee, a crucial state which approved the Nineteenth Amendment by a slim margin. Notes.

1470 Lunardini, Christine A. *From Equal Suffrage to Equal Rights: Alice Paul and the National Woman's Party, 1910–1928.* New York: New York University Press, 1986.

A new generation of women's rights activists, led by Alice Paul, breathed new life into the suffrage movement through mass demonstrations, lobbying, publicity, and picketing. Yet these new suffragists also created severe tensions within the women's movement. Notes, bibliography, index.

1471 McFarland, Charles K., and Neal, Nevin E. "The Reluctant Reformer: Woodrow Wilson and Woman Suffrage, 1913–1920." *Rocky Mountain Social Science Journal* 11 (1974): 33–43.

Wilson reversed himself on the suffrage issue during World War I, agreeing to support this democratic reform at home, while he fought to make the world safe for democracy abroad.

1472 Mahoney, Joseph F. "Woman Suffrage and the Urban Masses." *New Jersey History* 87 (1969): 151–72.

A study of the referendum on women's suffrage held in New Jersey in 1915 reveals that urban political bosses had no more control over immigrants than they did over native-born voters. Notes.

1473 Mambretti, Catherine C. "The Burden of the Ballot." *American Heritage* 30 (1978): 24–25.

Groups and individuals opposed to women's suffrage made a variety of arguments against extending the franchise, including the emotionalism of women, possible negative effects on the family, and states' rights.

1474 Morgan, David. *Suffragists and Democrats: The Politics of Woman Suffrage in America*. East Lansing: Michigan State University Press, 1972.

The final years of the suffrage movement, from 1916 to 1920, are studied with special attention paid to the role Democrats played in implementing the Nineteenth Amendment. Notes, bibliography, index.

1475 Porter, Melba D. "Madeline McDowell Breckinridge: Her Role in the Kentucky Woman Suffrage Movement, 1908–1920." *Register of the Kentucky Historical Society* 72 (1974): 342–63.

Breckinridge led the fight for women's suffrage in Kentucky, exhibiting genuine talents in public speaking, administration, and organization. Notes.

1476 Prescott, Grace E. "The Woman Suffrage Movement in Memphis: Its Place in the State, Sectional and National Movements." *West Tennessee Historical Society Papers* 18 (1964): 87–106.

Women were active in Memphis on behalf of suffrage for half a century prior to the passage of the Nineteenth Amendment. Notes.

1477 Rausch, Eileen R. " 'Let Ohio Women Vote': The Years to Victory, 1900–1920." Ph.D. dissertation, University of Notre Dame, 1985.

Although the relationship between the Ohio woman's suffrage organization and the national campaign was often strained, the

national movement owed much of its strength to state organizations. DAI 45:3199-A.

1478 Schaffer, Ronald. "The Problem of Consciousness in the Woman Suffrage Movement: A California Perspective." *Pacific Historical Review* 45 (1976): 469–93.

California suffragettes were successful because they networked their cause into the Progressive mainstream. Notes.

1479 Scott, Anne F., and Scott, Andrew M. *One Half the People: The Fight for Woman Suffrage*. Philadelphia: Lippincott, 1975.

An overview of the suffrage movement is presented, along with documents. A chapter on the education of Woodrow Wilson about women's issues is included. Bibliography.

1480 Stephens, Barbara J. "May Wright Sewall (1844–1920)." Ph.D. dissertation, Ball State University, 1977.

Long an activist in education, peace, and women's rights, Sewall's writings and speeches made her one of the most influential women of her time. DAI 38:6275-A.

1481 Stevenson, Louise L. "Women Anti-Suffragists in the 1915 Massachusetts Campaign." *New England Quarterly* 52 (1979): 80–93.

Women played an important role in the antisuffrage campaign. To give women the vote, they argued, was to risk destruction of the home and to give in to the forces of socialism. Notes.

1482 Sumners, Bill. "Southern Baptists and Women's Right to Vote, 1910–1920." *Baptist History and Heritage* 12 (1977): 45–51.

Southern Baptists were badly split on the issue of women's suffrage. The southern lady might be tarnished by politics, argued opponents, who also wondered about the impact of the female vote on government and politics. Many others approved of women's suffrage, if for no other reason than that they believed that women would vote for prohibition. Notes.

1483 Swarts, Valerie R. "The Function of Natural Law Warrants in the Rhetorical Discourse of Women's Suffrage, 1848–1920." Ph.D. dissertation, University of Iowa, 1984.

The natural order or God-given rights have been cited throughout history by those dissatisfied with human laws. Suffragettes philosophized that, as intelligent members of the human race who were responsible to themselves, they had a natural right to the vote. DAI 46: 300-A.

1484 Taber, Ronald W. "Sacagawea and the Suffragettes." *Pacific Northwest Quarterly* 58 (1967): 7–13.

Western suffragettes made Lewis and Clark's Indian guide, Sacagawea, a symbol of female heroism as part of their drive for the vote.

1485 Taylor, A. Elizabeth. "The Woman Suffrage Movement in Mississippi, 1890–1920." *Journal of Mississippi History* 30 (1968): 1–34.

Women's suffrage made only slow progress in Mississippi, although some men were willing to accept it to counter the potential black vote. Notes.

1486 ———. *The Woman Suffrage Movement in Tennessee.* New York: Bookman, 1957.

The politics of suffrage in Tennessee are chronicled through the successful fight to ratify the Nineteenth Amendment. Notes, bibliography, index.

1487 Trecker, Janice L. "The Suffrage Prisoners." *American Scholar* 41 (1972): 409–23.

Suffragettes pushed the Wilson administration hard in 1917. Picketing the White House, women activists became prisoners as they waited for the president to change his mind. Notes.

1488 Yellin, Carol Lynn. "Countdown in Tennessee, 1920." *American Heritage* 30 (1978): 12–23ff.

The struggle over ratification of the Nineteenth Amendment was especially fierce in Tennessee, since only one more state had to vote for suffrage for the amendment to pass. Following a lively debate, the amendment passed.

1489 Zacharis, John C. "Emmeline Pankhurst: An English Suffragette Influences America." *Speech Monographs* 8 (1971): 198–206.

Lecture tours by this British suffragette leader aided the American suffrage movement significantly. The year after her 1913 visit the House of Representatives began to pay serious attention to giving women the vote. Notes.

Immigration

See also Chapter 4, *Immigrants and Labor,* Chapter 8, *The Red Scare,* Chapter 11, *Civil Liberties,* and Chapter 12, *Paris Peace Conference, Public Opinion and the Press.*

1490 Altschuler, Glenn C. *Race, Ethnicity, and Class in American Social Thought.* Arlington Heights, IL: Harlan Davidson, 1982.

Although this period was a grim one for blacks, some groundwork was laid for the later assault on racism. The author compares and contrasts Progressive ideas on ethnicity and class with those of the nineteenth century. Bibliography, index.

1491 Betten, Neil. "Polish American Steelworkers: Americanization through Industry and Labor." *Polish American Studies* 33 (1976): 31–42.

United States Steel made sure that immigrant workers were thoroughly Americanized. Along the way, though, the company also exposed workers to unionization and work stoppages. Notes.

1492 Benkart, Paula K. "The Hungarian Government, the American Magyar Churches, and Immigrant Ties to the Homeland, 1903–1917." *Church History* 52 (1983): 312–21.

Hungarian immigrants kept close ties with their homeland through the Hungarian Royal Prime Ministry, which kept watch over religious, educational, and publishing activities. American entry into the war ended the program. Notes.

1493 Best, Gary Dean. "Jacob H. Schiff's Galveston Movement: An Experiment in Immigrant Deflection, 1907–1914." *American Jewish Archives* 30 (1978): 43–79.

Financier Jacob Schiff developed an elaborate scheme to populate the interior of the United States and Canada with Jewish immigrants. Galveston, Texas, was to be the starting point for the plan.

1494 Betten, Neil. "The Origins of Ethnic Radicalism in Northern Minnesota, 1900–1920." *International Migration Review* 4 (1970): 44–56.

A heritage of radicalism and brutal living conditions in northern Minnesota combined to radicalize the politics of immigrant Finns. Notes.

1495 Bicha, Karel D. "Hunkies: Stereotyping the Slavic Immigrants, 1890–1920." *Journal of American Ethnic History* 2 (1982): 16–38.

Americans were quick to stereotype the "hunkies" as dirty, drunken, dull-of-wit exploiters of women and children who nevertheless partially redeemed themselves through self-sufficiency. Notes.

1496 Bloom, Florence Teicher. "Struggling and Surviving: The Life Style of European Immigrant Breadwinning Mothers in American Industrial Cities, 1900–1930." *Women's Studies International Forum* 8 (1985): 609–20.

The quality of life did not improve much for working immigrant women, because they received low wages and were expected to carry out their traditional household duties as well.

1497 Buc, B. S. "The Role of Emigrants in Slovak Nationalism." *Slovakia* 9 (1959): 32–46.

Recent Slovak immigrants were largely responsible for the promotion of Slovak nationalism, bringing about the "Pittsburgh pact" between the Slovak League of America and T. G. Masaryk.

1498 Cândea, Virgil. "The Contribution of Romanian-Americans to the Unification of Romania in 1918." *Southeastern Europe* 6 (1979): 87–93.

Romanian Americans lobbied the U.S. government successfully and contributed much-needed social assistance at a crucial time in Romanian history. Notes.

1499 Carlson, Robert A. "Americanization as an Early Twentieth-Century Adult Education Movement." *History of Education Quarterly* 10 (1970): 440–64.

Recognized authorities on education dismissed the idea that immigrants had a right to preserve their own cultures. Instead, they advocated molding the immigrant to fit American mores. Notes.

1500 Carroll, Francis M. *American Aspirations and the Irish Question, 1910–23.* New York: St. Martin's, 1978.

American support for the Irish cause made possible a far more powerful kind of nationalism in Ireland than would otherwise have been the case. Appendix, notes, bibliography, index.

1501 Christian, Henry A. "Louis Adamic and the American Dream." *Journal of General Education* 27 (1975): 113–23.

Adamic came to America just before World War I and became an expert on immigrant life and minorities. Notes.

1502 Čizmić, Ivan. "The Volunteer Movement of Yugoslav Emigrants in the United States during World War I." *Historijski Zbornik* [Yugoslavia] 23 (1970): 21–43.

Few Slavs living in the United States during World War I joined the Habsburg armies, despite the empire's propaganda. Efforts by foreign Yugoslav committees and by the government of Serbia met with some success, although only about ten thousand of the emigrants volunteered. An American campaign to form Slavic legions was undertaken too late in the war to have much effect.

1503 Dadà, Adriana. "Italo-American Radicals and the Italian Society" (in Italian). *Italia Contemporanea* [Italy] (1982): 131–40.

Italian-American radicals preferred the Industrial Workers of the World (IWW) to the American Federation of Labor and, consequently, suffered persecution for their opposition to World War I. Notes.

1504 Detjen, David W. *The Germans in Missouri, 1900–1918: Prohibition, Neutrality, and Assimilation.* Columbia: University of Missouri Press, 1985.

German Americans in Missouri vocally supported their fatherland during the period of American neutrality, but their social and cultural alliances wilted during the war in the face of persecution. Notes, bibliography, index.

1505 Eisele, J. Christopher. "John Dewey and the Immigrants." *History of Education Quarterly* 15 (1975): 67–86.

In this revisionist account, Dewey is portrayed as having tried to allow for ethnic differences instead of insisting on the total Americanization of immigrants.

1506 Ewen, Elizabeth W. "Immigrant Women in the Land of Dollars, 1890–1920." Ph.D. dissertation, State University of New York, Stony Brook, 1979.

Jewish and Italian immigrant women in New York City managed their domestic spheres while working as home finishers in the garment industry. Traditional expectations changed under pressure from the modern urban environment. DAI 40:4715-A.

1507 Fasce, Ferdinando. "Inside and Outside the Ethnic Community: Oral Witnesses of Italian Immigrants in the United States in the Early 20th Century" (in Italian). *Movimento Operaio e Socialista* [Italy] 4 (1981): 33–48.

Two retired Italian workers are interviewed. Their experiences as immigrants in the United States during the Progressive period are discussed, including their participation in labor unions, the IWW, and socialist activities. Notes.

1508 Feldman, Egal. "Prostitution, the Alien Woman and the Progressive Imagination, 1910–1915." *American Quarterly* 19 (1967): 192–206.

Rural nativists blamed the widespread prostitution of the era on urban life, European influence, and the Jews. Progressive social reformers, many of them women, worked to clear the reputation of female immigrants and to change the system that led to the downfall of so many newcomers. Notes.

1509 Friedman, Reena Sigman. " 'Send Me My Husband Who Is in New York City': Husband Desertion in the American Jewish Immigrant Community, 1900–1926." *Jewish Social Studies* 44 (1982): 1–18.

Using the records of the National Desertion Bureau, the author questions the assertion that Jewish immigrant families were unaffected by settling in the United States and by Americanization. Notes.

1510 Gelb, Steven A. "Henry H. Goddard and the Immigrants, 1910–1917: The Studies and Their Social Context." *Journal of the History of the Behavioral Sciences* 22 (1986): 324–32.

Between 1912 and 1917 psychologist Henry H. Goddard came almost full circle in his beliefs about "feebleminded" immigrants. At first he insisted that public concern about mental and physical degenerates included in the current wave of immigrants from Europe was alarmist, but he joined the chorus of nativism himself five years later.

1511 Giese, James R. "Tuberculosis and the Growth of Denver's Eastern European Jewish Community: The Accommodation of an Immigrant Group to a Medium-Sized Western City, 1900–1920." Ph.D. dissertation, University of Colorado, Boulder, 1979.

East European Jewish immigrants in Denver had many adjustments to make. Many of them came to Denver because they suffered from consumption. DAI 40:2223-A.

1512 Gleason, Philip. *The Conservative Reformers: German-American Catholics and the Social Order.* Notre Dame, IN: University of Notre Dame Press, 1968.

Although it was quite conservative, the Roman Catholic *Central-Verein* fought for social justice during the Progressive era. Notes, bibliography, index.

1513 Goldstein, Judith. "Ethnic Politics: The American Jewish Committee as Lobbyist, 1915–1917." *American Jewish Historical Quarterly* 65 (1975): 36–58.

Moved by the plight of Russian Jews, who were persecuted in periodic pogroms, the American Jewish Committee lobbied Congress and President Wilson to put pressure on Russia and to modify literacy tests for immigrants.

1514 Hadda, Janet. "The Influence of America on Yiddish Literature" (in Yiddish). *Yivo Bleter* 44 (1973): 248–55.

Between 1912 and 1926 the New York journal *Shriften* provided an outlet for Yiddish writers reflecting on their impressions of America.

1515 Higham, John. *Strangers in the Land: Patterns of American Nativism, 1860–1925.* New York: Atheneum, 1963.

In this general history of American antiforeign sentiment, the author traces the cyclical nature of nativist feelings and the stresses that foster them. Notes, bibliographic essay, index.

1516 Houchins, Lee, and Houchins, Chang-su. "The Korean Experience in America, 1903–1924." *Pacific Historical Review* 43 (1974): 548–75.

Like other immigrant groups, Koreans wanted to make money while keeping their ethnic identity. Notes.

1517 Huff, Robert A. "Frederick C. Howe, Progressive." Ph.D. dissertation, University of Rochester, 1967.

Frederick Howe was a second-rank Progressive dedicated to increased public ownership and a single tax. Turning to social service as an alternative to his family's evangelicalism, Howe shared with other Progressives a sense of optimism before World War I and a bitter disillusionment afterward, disillusionment with both himself and the state of society. He resigned from his position as immigration commissioner in 1919. DAI 28: 175-A.

1518 Ichioka, Yuji. "Amerika Nadeshiko: Japanese Immigrant Women in the United States,

1900–1924." *Pacific Historical Review* 49 (1980): 339–57.

More than half of the married Japanese women who immigrated to the United States during this period were picture brides who had never met their spouses prior to their arrival in America. Leaders of the Japanese-American communities worked hard to keep these women subordinate. Notes.

1519 ———. "Japanese Associations and the Japanese Government: A Special Relationship, 1909–1926." *Pacific Historical Review* 46 (1977): 409–37.

Japanese-American voluntary associations had unusually close ties to the government of Japan, due to the Gentlemen's Agreement of 1907. Notes.

1520 Karni, Michael G., and Ollilia, Douglas J., Jr. *For the Common Good: Finnish Immigrants and the Radical Response to Industrial America.* Superior, WI: Tyamies Society, 1977.

Several essays on the Finnish radical labor movement during the Progressive years are presented.

1521 Kostiainen, Auvo. "Working People's College: An American Immigrant Institution." *Scandinavian Journal of History* [Sweden] 5 (1980): 295–309.

The Finns were one of the most active ethnic groups in the U.S. labor movement. This was reflected in Work People's College of Smithville, Minnesota, an institution with socialist leanings that helped immigrants to adjust to American life. Notes.

1522 Leonard, Henry B. "The Immigrants' Protective League of Chicago, 1908–1921." *Journal of the Illinois State Historical Society* 66 (1973): 271–84.

While the Immigrants' Protective League did not accomplish much, leaders like Jane Addams did at least call attention to the problems faced by urban newcomers. Notes.

1523 McBride, Paul W. "The Cultural Cold War: Immigrants and the Quest for Cultural Monism, 1890–1917." Ph.D. dissertation, University of Georgia, 1972.

Fear of immigrants and of the mongrelization of American culture was widespread among nativists and urban reformers. Cultural pluralism was unacceptable to even the most liberal of Progressives, who wanted immigrants to be Americanized at all costs. DAI 33:3549-A.

1524 ———. *Culture Clash: Immigrants and Reformers, 1880–1920.* San Francisco: R & E Research, 1975.

Progressive reformers and businessmen shared an interest in Americanizing immigrants through welfare and educational programs.

1525 ———. "Peter Roberts and the YMCA Americanization Program, 1907–World War I." *Pennsylvania History* 44 (1977): 145–62.

As an official with the YMCA, Roberts developed a more subtle approach to Americanizing immigrants through the teaching of English. Several patriotic organizations objected to the Roberts method, and the new militarism of the First World War put an end to it. Notes.

1526 McClymer, John F. "The Federal Government and the Americanization Movement, 1915–24." *Prologue* 10 (1978): 23–41.

Government at all levels, including the federal government, cooperated with private agencies in the drive to produce conservative, Americanized immigrants. While government agencies sponsored programs that overlapped and sometimes conflicted with one another, there was fundamental agreement on the need for Americanization. Notes.

1527 Meagher, Timothy J. " 'The Lord Is Not Dead': Cultural and Social Change among the Irish in Worcester, Massachusetts." Ph.D. dissertation, Brown University, 1982.

Although the Irish first arrived in Worcester in the first half of the nineteenth century, each succeeding generation continued the process of cultural adaptation. Changes in rites and rituals, ideals of behavior, and the degree of separateness as a subculture between 1880 and 1920 illustrate this ongoing adjustment. DAI 43:677-A.

1528 Michalski, Thomas A. "A Social History of Yugoslav Immigrants in Tonopah and White Pine County, Nevada, 1860–1920." Ph.D. dissertation, State University of New York, Buffalo, 1983.

Immigrants to the West were less able to transplant cultural institutions from their homelands. The particular experience of Yugoslavs in Nevada is examined. DAI 44: 3782-A.

1529 Mondello, Salvatore. "The Magazine *Charities* and the Italian Immigrants, 1903–14." *Journalism Quarterly* 44 (1967): 91–98.

A magazine speaking for social workers, *Charities* sympathized with Italian immigrants yet felt frustrated by their seeming indifference to Progressive .reforms. The writers of the magazine, like the social workers, did not fully understand the obstacles immigrants faced. Notes.

1530 Netea, Vasile. "Rumanians in America up to 1918" (in French). In *Nouvelle Études d'Histoire.* Bucharest: Editura Academiei, 1975, pp. 259–67.

By the time of the First World War, there were over 150,000 emigrants from Romania in the United States, most of them recent arrivals. Romania urged its emigrants to influence the Wilson administration on such matters as Romania's claims to Transylvania. Notes.

1531 Palmer, Susan L. "Building Ethnic Communities in a Small City: Romanians and Mexicans in Aurora, Illinois, 1900–1940." Ph.D. dissertation, Northern Illinois University, 1986.

In spite of different cultural backgrounds, different reasons for immigration, and different times of arrival, Mexican and Romanian immigrants to Aurora had similar problems with establishing themselves in their new community. Romanians, however, were a more cohesive group than were the Mexicans. Big-city immigrants were able to transplant more cultural institutions than were these small-town groups. DAI 47:4173-A.

1532 Procko, Bohdan P. "American Ukrainian Catholic Church: Humanitarian and Patriotic Activities." *Ukrainian Quarterly* 23 (1967): 161–69.

Political and philanthropic activities of the Washington-based Ukrainian National Alliance are summarized. Notes.

1533 Sanchez Korrol, Virginia E. "Settlement Patterns and Community Development among Puerto Ricans in New York City, 1917–1948." Ph.D. dissertation, State University of New York, Stony Brook, 1981.

Using oral history and first-person accounts, as well as various written materials, the author reconstructs the conditions that impelled Puerto Ricans to emigrate. Personal, political, and economic motives are described. The evolution of the Puerto Rican subculture in New York is explored. DAI 42:1764-A.

1534 Solomon, Barbara M. *Ancestors and Immigrants: A Changing New England Tradition.* Cambridge, MA: Harvard University Press, 1956.

New England's upper crust responded to the new immigration from Europe with racism and demands for a quota system. Notes, bibliography, index.

1535 Stipanovich, Joseph P. " 'In Unity Is Strength': Immigrant Workers and Immigrant Intellectuals in Progressive America: A History of the South Slav Social Democratic Movement, 1900–1918." Ph.D. dissertation, University of Minnesota, 1978.

Slovene, Croat, and Serb immigrants organized socialist movements during the Progressive era that were distinct from the Socialist party, which was dominated by native-born Americans. The South Slav movements created distinctive social and economic programs instead of relying primarily on participation in the electoral process. DAI 39:3783-A.

1536 Sullivan, Margaret J. "Hyphenism in St. Louis, 1900–1921: The View from the Outside." Ph.D. dissertation, St. Louis University, 1968.

German Americans, Irish Americans and German-Jewish Americans were the three largest immigrant groups in St. Louis. Each group maintained certain concerns for its homeland, and each responded differently to World War I. By 1920, sympathy for "hyphenated Americans" had eroded. The study elucidates how outsiders viewed the immigrants. DAI 29:2658-A.

1537 Szajkowski, Zosa. "The Consul and the Immigrant: A Case of Bureaucratic Bias." *Jewish Social Studies* 36 (1974): 3–18.

After World War I, restrictions were put on immigration from Germany and Eastern Europe. Anti-Semitism in the American diplomatic corps made it especially difficult for Jews to enter the United States. Notes.

1538 Vassady, Béla, Jr. "The 'Homeland Cause' as Stimulant to Ethnic Unity: The Hungarian-American Response to Károlyi's 1914 American Tour." *Journal of American Ethnic History* 2 (1982): 39–64.

Count Michael Károlyi's tour of the United States caused some factionalism among Hungarians, but in the long run it unified them. Notes.

1539 Wacker, R. Fred. "Assimilation and Cultural Pluralism in American Social Thought." *Phylon* 40 (1979): 325–33.

In the period from 1910 to 1920, most Americans believed that immigrants had to be assimilated into the mainstream. A minority, the most visible among which were Jewish New York intellectuals, argued that the country was big enough to permit cultural pluralism. Notes.

1540 Wefald, Jon. *A Voice of Protest: Norwegians in American Politics, 1890–1917.* Northfield, MN: Norwegian-American Historical Association, 1971.

Old-world values held by Norwegians led them to participate in left-wing politics aimed at curbing the injustices of capitalism. Notes, bibliography, index.

1541 Weinberg, Daniel E. "The Ethnic Technician and the Foreign-Born: Another Look at Americanization Ideology and Goals." *Societas* 7 (1977): 209–27.

To Americanize immigrants, the Foreign Language Information Service used a more sophisticated methodology than was prescribed by the backward-looking nostalgia then in vogue. Notes.

1542 Yu, Connie Young. "Rediscovered Voices: Chinese Immigrants and Angel Island." *Amerasia Journal* 4 (1977): 123–39.

Angel Island, just off San Francisco, was the immigration station that processed most Chinese entering the United States. The screening process was rigid and degrading, and most immigrants were turned away. Notes.

1543 Yu Renqiu. "Chinese American Contributions to the Educational Development of Toisan, 1910–1940." *Amerasia Journal* 10 (1983): 47–72.

Many Chinese immigrants sent part of their hard-earned pay back to China. Top priority was given to the construction of schools, which was seen as the key to the modernization of China. Notes.

1544 Zanger, Jules. "On Not Making It in America." *American Studies* 17 (1976): 39–48.

Turning their backs on part of their Jewishness (and on their mothers) was often the price Jewish immigrants had to pay if they were to become assimilated fully into the American system. Notes.

1545 Zatko, James J. "Slovaks in the U.S.A." *Slovakia* 19 (1966): 41–62.

While Slovak nationalism and continuing interest in European Slovakia prevented this ethnic group from becoming completely assimilated, Slovakian institutions did not survive the effects of American industrialization. Notes.

1546 Zeidel, Robert F. "The Literacy Test for Immigrants: A Question of Progress." Ph.D. dissertation, Marquette University, 1986.

First proposed in 1890 as a way to restrict immigration, the literacy test required immigrants to prove that they could read and write. By the Wilson era, restrictionists had shifted from reactionary to Progressive arguments, claiming that less immigration would help solve social problems. In 1917, the literacy test bill was finally passed despite Wilson's veto. DAI 47:4498-A.

ZIONISM

See also Chapter 7, *Supreme Court Justices, Louis Brandeis,* and Chapter 9, *Middle East.*

1547 Berlin, George L. "The Brandeis-Weizmann Dispute." *American Jewish Historical Quarterly* 60 (1970): 37–68.

After World War I, Supreme Court Justice Louis Brandeis clashed with Zionist leader Chaim Weizmann over how to proceed with the building of a Jewish homeland in Palestine under a British mandate. Notes.

1548 Friesel, Evyatar. "Jacob H. Schiff Becomes a Zionist: A Chapter in American-Jewish Self-Definition, 1907–1917." *Studies in Zionism* [Israel] 1 (1982): 55–92.

Although the powerful Schiff came to support a Jewish cultural/religious presence in the Holy Land, he refused to lend his support to a national homeland. Notes.

1549 Geoll, Yohai. "Aliya in the Zionism of an American Oleh: Judah L. Magnes." *American Jewish Historical Quarterly* 65 (1975): 99–120.

Magnes was an American Jew who became an early Zionist leader. Notes.

1550 Kislov, A. K. "The White House and the Zionist Lobby" (in Russian). *Voprosy Istorii* [USSR] (1973): 48–61.

The author examines the methods of the Zionist lobby and its effects on the White House, beginning with Wilson's presidency. The Zionists could only win assistance to the extent that their international interests conformed to American imperialist interests.

1551 Kutscher, Carol B. "The Early Years of Hadassah, 1912–1921." Ph.D. dissertation, Brandeis University, 1976.

The women's Zionist organization Hadassah was led by Henrietta Szold to a position of preeminence among American Jewish women's organizations. DAI 37:3091-A.

1552 Levitas, Irving. "Reform Jews and Zionism." *American Jewish Archives* 14 (1962): 3–19.

In 1919 an anti-Zionist petition was presented to President Wilson, a move that many Reform Jews refused to sanction.

1553 Lipstadt, Deborah E. "The Zionist Career of Louis Lipsky, 1900–1921." Ph.D. dissertation, Brandeis University, 1977.

Chairman of the Federation of American Zionists, Lipsky was free with his criticism of Jewish groups that he perceived as holding back the Zionist cause. His quarrels with Louis Brandeis over tactics threatened to split the movement. DAI 37:7921-A.

1554 Rischin, Moses. "The Early Attitude of the American Jewish Committee to Zionism (1906–1922)." *Publication of the American Jewish Historical Society* 49 (1960): 188–201.

Zionism held little interest for the American Jewish Committee in the prewar era, but the Balfour declaration led to most members endorsing Palestine as a Jewish homeland.

1555 Rudavsky, David. "Louis D. Brandeis at the London International Zionist Conference of 1920." *Yivo Annals of Jewish Social Science* 15 (1974): 145–65.

At the London conference of 1920, Brandeis took on Chaim Weizmann on several important Zionist questions, including the matter of financial responsibilities. Notes.

1556 Schmidt, Sarah L. "Horace M. Kallen and the Americanization of Zionism." Ph.D. dissertation, University of Maryland, 1973.

The period 1914–1921 was the high-water mark of Zionism in the United States before the establishment of Israel. Movement leader Louis Brandeis wanted to make the Jewish homeland a model of democracy and Progressivism. The social philosopher Horace Kallen was responsible for many ideas about how to build support for the cause. DAI 35:1029-A.

1557 Shapiro, Yonathan. *Leadership of the American Zionist Organization, 1897–1930.* Urbana: University of Illinois Press, 1971.

American Zionism was different from that in Europe, because it focused on the dream of a Jewish homeland in Palestine rather than on developing a separate Jewish identity. Notes, bibliography, index.

1558 Urofsky, Melvin I. *American Zionism from Herzl to the Holocaust.* Garden City, NY: Anchor, 1976.

Zionism held little interest for American Jews before 1914, but a new group of Jews Americanized the idea during World War I. Notes, bibliography, index.

1559 ———. *A Voice that Spoke for Justice: The Life and Times of Stephen S. Wise.* Albany: State University of New York Press, 1982.

An egocentric rabbi, Wise became a national Jewish leader while fighting against injustice and modernizing Judaism. Photographs, notes, bibliography, index.

Domestic Affairs:
Politics, Progressives, the Press,
and Administrative and Legal

Wilson's New Freedom pushed the Progressive movement in a different direction before this driving political force of the early twentieth century burned itself out. Constitutional and legal reforms were prominent, as three amendments became law during Wilson's tenure, and the Supreme Court heard cases with important implications for the future.

The literature on the Progressive movement is extensive. Among the many excellent and diverse overviews are John W. Chambers II, *The Tyranny of Change: America in the Progressive Era, 1900–1917* (#1593); Robert Crunden, *Ministers of Reform: The Progressives' Achievement in American Civilization, 1889–1920* (#1597); Arthur A. Ekrich, Jr., *Progressivism in America: A Study of the Era from Theodore Roosevelt to Woodrow Wilson* (#1602); Peter Filene, "An Obituary for 'The Progressive Movement' " (#1605); Richard Hofstadter, *The Age of Reform: From Bryan to F.D.R.* (#1618); David M. Kennedy, "Overview: The Progressive Era" (#1627); William E. Leuchtenburg, *The Perils of Prosperity, 1914–32* (#1634); Arthur S. Link and Richard L. McCormick, *Progressivism* (#1636); David W. Noble, *The Progressive Mind* (#1645); and William L. O'Neill, *The Progressive Years: America Comes of Age* (#1647). In addition to the many biographies and monographs on Wilson's New Freedom program cited in Chapters 1 and 2, see articles by Dewey W. Grantham, Jr., "Southern Congressional Leaders and the New Freedom, 1913–1917" (#1685); Arthur S. Link,

"The South and the 'New Freedom': An Interpretation" (#1694); and Melvin I. Urofsky, "Wilson, Brandeis and the Trust Issue, 1912–1914" (#1702).

The presidential campaign of 1912 featured three political giants of twentieth-century American history—Wilson, Theodore Roosevelt, and Eugene V. Debs—four if one counts William Howard Taft, the sitting president. For Wilson's part in the campaign, see John W. Davidson, "Wilson in the Campaign of 1912" (#1823), and an account by the embittered William F. McCombs, *Making Woodrow Wilson President* (#1849). The best work on the president's reelection is S. D. Lovell, *The Presidential Election of 1916* (#1886). The standard account of the 1920 election, which Wilson hoped would vindicate him, is still Wesley M. Bagby, *The Road to Normalcy: The Presidential Campaign and Election of 1920* (#1895).

Preparedness was one of the most highly charged political controversies of the Wilson period, with Democrats and Republicans vying to shape the campaign to prepare the United States for war even as Wilson steered a course of biased neutrality. See John Garry Clifford, *The Citizen Soldiers: The Plattsburg Training Camp Movement, 1913–1920* (#1926); John C. Edwards, *Patriots in Pinstripe: Men of the National Security League* (#1928); John P. Finnegan, *Against the Specter of a Dragon: The Campaign for American Military Preparedness, 1914–1918* (#1930); and Michael D. Pearlman,

To Make Democracy Safe for America: Patricians and Preparedness in the Progressive Era (#1934).

Journalists and publishers were important shapers of public opinion during the Wilson presidency. Among the biographies of leading media figures are: Robert C. Bannister, Jr., *Ray Stannard Baker: The Mind and Thought of a Progressive* (#1938); John E. Semonche, *Ray Stannard Baker: A Quest for Democracy in Modern America, 1870–1918* (#1979); Ronald Steel, *Walter Lippmann and the American Century* (#1985); and W. A. Swanberg, *Citizen Hearst* (#1991). On the influential liberal journal *New Republic*, see Charles Forcey, *The Crossroads of Liberalism: Croly, Weyl, Lippmann, and the Progressive Era, 1900–1925* (#1954).

As part of the drive to create lasting reforms, Progressives campaigned for constitutional amendments creating a federal income tax, prohibition, and women's suffrage. Among the many works on the Eighteenth Amendment, see Norman H. Clark, *Deliver Us from Evil: An Interpretation of American Prohibition* (#2025), and James H. Timberlake, *Prohibition and the Progressive Movement, 1900–1920* (#2033). Wilson's role in the passage of the suffrage amendment is examined in Christine A. Lunardini and Thomas J. Knock, "Woodrow Wilson and Woman Suffrage: A New Look" (#2037).

The Supreme Court handed down many important decisions that affected business, conservationism, women, free speech, and labor. See Alexander M. Bickel and Benno C. Schmidt, Jr., *The Judiciary and Responsible Government, 1910–1921* (#2040), and John E. Semonche, *Charting the Future: The Supreme Court Responds to a Changing Society, 1890–1920* (#2045). Wilson's most important appointment to the Supreme Court, Louis Brandeis, is the subject of a number of works, among them A. L. Todd, *Justice on Trial: The Case of Louis D. Brandeis* (#2065), and two books by Melvin I. Urofsky, *Louis D. Brandeis and the Progressive Tradition* (#2067) and *A Mind of One Piece: Brandeis and American Reform* (#2068).

National Politics

1560 Allen, Howard W., and Clubb, Jerome. "Progressive Reform and the Political System." *Pacific Northwest Quarterly* 65 (1974): 130–45.

In the Senate, Progressive legislation was supported by Democrats and insurgent Republicans and opposed by the old-line GOP.

1561 Boller, Paul F., Jr. *Presidential Campaigns.* New York: Oxford University Press, 1984.

Chapters 32 to 34 cover the 1912, 1916, and 1920 presidential campaigns briefly. Notes, index.

1562 Clubb, Jerome M. "Party Loyalty in the Progressive Years: The Senate, 1909–1915." *Journal of Politics* 29 (1967): 567–84.

Roll call votes are analyzed to see which senators voted against their party line on major issues. Democrats kept good party unity, while Progressivism splintered the GOP. Notes.

1563 Drescher, Nuala M. "The Opposition to Prohibition, 1900–1919. A Social and Institutional Study." Ph.D. dissertation, University of Delaware, 1964.

Roman Catholics, the United States Brewers' Association, German Americans, and unions involved in liquor-related work were among those who opposed prohibition. The anti-Germanism of World War I was a boon to prohibitionists. Imminent passage of the Eighteenth Amendment aroused a broader base of opposition. DAI 25:3532.

1564 Gould, Lewis L. *Reform and Regulation: American Politics, 1900–1916.* New York: Wiley, 1978.

During the Progressive era the Democratic party became an advocate of strong central government, while the Republicans shifted to the political right. Notes, bibliography, index.

1565 Hays, Samuel P. "The Social Analysis of American Political History, 1880–1920." *Political Science Quarterly* 80 (1965): 373–94.

Progressive reformers drew their energy from many sources and interest groups in their drive for economic and political modernization. Notes.

1566 Holt, James. *Congressional Insurgents and the Party System, 1909–1916.* Cambridge, MA: Harvard University Press, 1967.

The Progressive Republicans, who played such an important role in reform activity in Congress, were professional politicians who moved significantly to the left as a result of the Progressive mood. Notes, bibliography, index.

1567 Link, Arthur S. "Woodrow Wilson and the Democratic Party." In Arthur S. Link. *The Higher Realism of Woodrow Wilson and Other*

Essays. Nashville: Vanderbilt University Press, 1971, pp. 60–71.

Wilson gained mastery over the Democratic party during his first term through leadership and patronage, rebuilding the national party apparatus from the ground up. His control of the party enabled him to effect domestic reforms and maintain control of foreign affairs during the period of American neutrality. Notes.

1568 McKnight, Gerald D. "Republican Leadership and the Mexican Question, 1913–1916: A Failed Bid for Party Resurgence." *Mid-America* 62 (1980): 105–22.

The divided response of Republicans to the Panama Canal toll controversy undercut the GOP's attempt to use Wilson's Mexican policy against the Democrats. Notes.

CONSERVATISM

1569 McBride, Ralph L. "Conservatism in the Mountain West: Western Senators and Conservative Influences in the Consideration of National Progressive Legislation, 1906–1914." Ph.D. dissertation, Brigham Young University, 1976.

Political battle lines formed between conservatives and Progressives over the Underwood tariff bill of 1913 and the Clayton antitrust bill of 1914. The role of right-wing western mountain-state senators in these debates is discussed to assess their unique brand of conservatism. DAI 37:6705-A.

1570 Strong, Dennis F. "Conservative Social Thought in the Progressive Era." Ph.D. dissertation, University of Washington, 1959.

This study is based on the writings of twenty conservatives who were prominent between 1895 and 1917. Theodore Dreiser, Elihu Root, and Oliver Wendell Holmes, Jr., are included. DAI 20:2262.

LIBERALISM

1571 Bourke, Francis P. "Culture and the Status of Politics, 1909–1917: Studies in the Social Criticism of Herbert Croly, Walter Lippmann, Randolph Bourne and Van Wyck Brooks." Ph.D. dissertation, University of Wisconsin, 1967.

Randolph Bourne contended, at the time of World War I, that intellectuals sacrificed values and a broad viewpoint when they got caught in the excitement of political action. With this assessment in mind, the author analyzes the major works of social criticism of this period. DAI 28:580-A.

1572 ———. "The Status of Politics 1909–1919: *The New Republic*, Randolph Bourne and Van Wyck Brooks." *Journal of American Studies* [Great Britain] 8 (1974): 171–202.

Many Progressive reformers and liberals reacted negatively to the war in Europe, because they believed that war meant trouble for the liberal tradition in the United States. Notes.

1573 Crockatt, Richard. "American Liberalism and the Atlantic World, 1916–17." *Journal of American Studies* [Great Britain] 11 (1977): 123–43.

American liberals tended toward neutrality during World War I—at least until they saw that the Germans might win. After that, they argued that Germany would have to be beaten to save European democracy. Notes.

1574 Farrell, John C. "John Dewey and World War I: Armageddon Tests a Liberal's Faith." *Perspectives in American History* 9 (1975): 299–340.

The war tested Dewey's faith, and it was found wanting. While he supported the war as a way to spread the American system and topple the old order, the imperfect peace drove him to advocate isolationism as a way to remain untainted by that same old order. Notes.

1575 Hugh-Jones, E. M. *Woodrow Wilson and American Liberalism.* London: English Universities Press, 1947.

Wilson embodied American liberalism and its unique attachment to individualism and equality. Wilson was more of a Jeffersonian than a Hamiltonian, because he believed in both capitalism and individual liberty. Bibliography, index.

1576 Huthmacher, J. Joseph. "Urban Liberalism and the Age of Reform." *Mississippi Valley Historical Review* 49 (1962): 231–41.

There was more to the Progressive movement than just the urban middle class. Representatives of the lower urban classes also participated actively, sometimes collaborating effectively with their upper-class colleagues. Notes.

1577 Lubove, Roy. "Frederick C. Howe and the Quest for Community." *Historian* 39 (1977): 270–91.

Howe's thought is studied for what it reveals about the Progressive and liberal mind. Although the values of small-town America and evangelical Christianity inspired reformers such as Howe, the movement was extremely complex. Most Progressives were interested at some level in bringing back the lost sense of community. Notes.

1578 Madison, Charles A. *Leaders and Liberals in 20th Century America*. New York: Unger, 1961.

The author devotes chapters to Wilson, Robert La Follette, Louis Brandeis, and other Progressive leaders. Wilson is seen as a tragic figure, the most productive of Progressive presidents whose wartime antiradicalism can only be explained "as the behavior of a man overcome by messianic fanaticism." Bibliography, index.

1579 Mann, Arthur, ed. *The Progressive Era: Liberal Renaissance or Liberal Failure?* New York: Holt, Rinehart and Winston, 1963.

Thirteen essays representing the best scholarship of the post-World War II period on the Progressive movement are reprinted. Notes, bibliography.

1580 Norris, John M. "The Influence of British Nineteenth Century Liberalism." ·*World Affairs Quarterly* 28 (1957): 219–28.

Wilson was heavily influenced by nineteenth-century liberalism. While these beliefs dovetailed with Progressivism, his liberalism made him a moderate Progressive until 1916.

1581 Riccio, Barry D. "Walter Lippmann: Intellectual Odyssey of a Liberal." Ph.D. dissertation, University of California, Berkeley, 1985.

While Lippmann began as a socialist and ended as a conservative, he was always interested in the liberal political order. His ideas are compared and contrasted with those of John Dewey to discover the divisions within liberal thought. DAI 46:2790-A.

The Progressive Movement

See also Chapter 3, *Executive Branch* and *Congressional and Political Leaders,* Chapter 9,

Congress and Foreign Policy, and below, *New Freedom, State and Local Politics,* and *Elections.*

1582 Abrams, Richard M. *The Burdens of Progress, 1900–29*. Glenview, IL: Scott, Foresman, 1978.

While the Progressive movement was responsible for many social and political reforms, it failed to stem the tide of corporate ascendancy and special interests. It was too timid and ambiguous to succeed in the end. Bibliography, index.

1583 ————. "The Failure of Progressivism." In Richard Abrams and Lawrence Levine, eds. *The Shaping of Twentieth Century America*. Boston: Little, Brown, 1971, pp. 207–24.

Progressives struggled to maintain old values and moral assumptions in the face of change. Having failed to do so, they turned their attention to the crusade of World War I. Notes.

1584 Beede, Benjamin R. "Foreign Influences on American Progressivism." *Historian* 45 (1983): 529–49.

Scholars have not given enough attention to European influences on such American Progressive social legislation as workers' compensation and regulatory laws. Clearly, foreign influences were felt in the years before World War I. Notes.

1585 Bernstein, Barton J., and Leib, Franklin A. "Progressive Republican Senators and American Imperialism, 1898–1916: A Reappraisal." *Mid-America* 50 (1968): 163–205.

The attitudes and actions of Progressive Republican senators are used to challenge historian William E. Leuchtenburg's assertion that Progressivism and imperialism were intertwined. Progressive Republicans accepted Theodore Roosevelt's leadership in foreign affairs, but after 1911 they criticized American imperialism and opposed American participation in the world war. Notes.

1586 Bremner, Robert H. *From the Depths: The Discovery of Poverty in the United States*. New York: New York University Press, 1956.

Included in this survey of American perceptions of poverty is a discussion of charity and social workers during the Progressive era and how they sought to apply scientific methods to their work. Notes, bibliography, index.

1587 Brownlee, W. Elliot. "Wilson and Financing the Modern State: The Revenue Act of

1916." *Proceedings of the American Philosophical Society* 129 (1985): 173–205.

The Revenue Act of 1916 made the government dependent on money raised by the federal income tax. The act turned out to be more progressive than those who were charged with interpreting it. Notes.

1588 Buenker, John D. "The Progressive Era: A Search for a Synthesis." *Mid-America* 51 (1969): 175–93.

While historians have developed several sophisticated interpretations of the Progressive era, the author believes that a more pluralistic approach is needed to emphasize that many groups were responsible for this reform movement. Economic conflicts were no more important than the geographic and cultural divisions between competing groups that were fused temporarily for pragmatic reasons. Notes.

1589 Buenker, John D.; Burnham, John C.; and Crunden, Robert M. *Progressivism.* Cambridge, MA: Schenkman, 1977.

The authors agree that there was a Progressive movement, dismissing Peter Filene's assertion to the contrary, but they find much to criticize in their other colleagues' essays as well. Notes, bibliography.

1590 Cassidy, Keith M. "American Concepts of Leadership and Authority: The Progressive Era." Ph.D. dissertation, University of Toronto, 1974.

Progressives did not agree about the nature of leadership and authority. Their ideas were based on traditional values as well as on more modern bureaucratic and scientific currents. DAI 36:1714-A.

1591 Chamberlain, John. *Farewell to Reform: The Rise, Life and Decay of the Progressive Mind in America.* New York: John Day, 1932.

In this early study of the social and intellectual origins and the consequences of Progressivism, the author finds that the movement was often timid, ineffective, and reactionary. Like Theodore Roosevelt, Wilson mistakenly equated liberalism with morality. Index.

1592 Chambers, Clarke A. *Seedtime of Reform: American Social Service and Social Action, 1918–1933.* Minneapolis: University of Minnesota Press, 1963.

Many voluntary welfare agencies had their roots in the Progressive era, including the National Consumers League, the Women's Trade Union League, the American Association for Labor Legislation, and the National Child Labor Committee. Notes, bibliography, index.

1593 Chambers, John W., II. *The Tyranny of Change: America in the Progressive Era, 1900–1917.* New York: St. Martin's Press, 1980.

The Progressive era witnessed the first full-scale effort to come to grips with the rapidly emerging, multicultural, urban, industrial society. Wilson is seen as "the scholar as prime minister." Bibliography, index.

1594 Coben, Stanley, ed. *Reform, War, and Reaction, 1912–1932.* Columbia: University of South Carolina Press, 1973.

Key documents presented here shed light on the Progressives, World War I, and the Red Scare. Index.

1595 Colburn, David R., and Pozzetta, George E., eds. *Reform and Reformers in the Progressive Era.* Westport, CT: Greenwood, 1983.

Eight essays examine the activists and activism of the Progressive era in a volume honoring historian George Mowry. Notes, bibliography, index.

1596 Cooper, John M., Jr. "Progressivism and American Foreign Policy: A Reconsideration." *Mid-America* 51 (1969): 269–77.

Progressives are divided into three groups with different views on foreign affairs: imperialists (Theodore Roosevelt and Albert Beveridge) who saw aggressive expansion as a necessary part of domestic reform, anti-imperialists (William Jennings Bryan and other rural Democrats), and liberal internationalists (Wilson). On the eve of American entry into the war, most Democrats were either anti-imperialists or liberal internationalists. Notes.

1597 Crunden, Robert. *Ministers of Reform: The Progressives' Achievement in American Civilization, 1889–1920.* New York: Basic, 1982.

Shared moral values shaped the Progressive vision of the spiritual reformation of the country. Among those profiled are Wilson, John Dewey, Frank Lloyd Wright, Charles Ives, and Frederick Jackson Turner. Article X of the League Covenant, the last great Progressive reform, died in an atmosphere of disease, misunderstanding, and bitterness. Notes, index.

1598 DeYoung, Mary. "Help, I'm Being Held Captive! The White Slave Fairy Tale of the Progressive Era." *Journal of American Culture* 6 (1983): 96–99.

For all the attention paid to white slavery during the Progressive era, few cases actually turned up. The issue is important for what it says about Progressive concerns.

1599 Dowell, Peter W. "Van Wyck Brooks and the Progressive Frame of Mind." *Midcontinent American Studies Journal* 11 (1970): 30–44.

Brooks's writings during the Wilson presidency mirrored his generation's intellectual passion. His fusion of Progressive reformism and concern for the fine arts made his work appealing to this new generation. Notes.

1600 Ebner, Michael H., and Tobin, Eugene M., eds. *The Age of Urban Reform: New Perspectives on the Progressive Era.* Port Washington, NY: Kennikat, 1977.

Ten essays discuss urban Progressivism, from New York to Houston to Seattle. Notes, bibliography, index.

1601 Effross, Harris I. "The Political Philosophy of Herbert Croly." Ph.D. dissertation, Rutgers University, 1959.

Although Croly was thought of as a Progressive philosopher, he in fact disagreed with important aspects of the Progressive party's platform. As editor of the *New Republic*, he criticized the increasing power of government during and after World War I. DAI 20:2362.

1602 Ekrich, Arthur A., Jr. *Progressivism in America: A Study of the Era from Theodore Roosevelt to Woodrow Wilson.* New York: New Viewpoints, 1974.

An overview of the Progressive movement is presented, with final chapters on the New Freedom and World War I. Progressives had much in common with the social democrats and socialists of Europe, and they borrowed freely from European ideas. Bibliography, index.

1603 Fairbanks, Robert Bruce. "Better Housing Movements and the City: Definitions of and Responses to Cincinnati's Low Cost Housing Problem, 1910–1954." Ph.D. dissertation, University of Cincinnati, 1981.

During the Wilson years, the focus of housing reform changed. Before 1910, unsanitary and overcrowded conditions were the major concern. After 1920, it was thought that large-scale projects for community development and low-cost housing were the solution. DAI 42:3718-A.

1604 Fetner, Gerald L. "Counsel to the Situation: The Lawyer as Social Engineer, 1900–1945." Ph.D. dissertation, Brown University, 1973.

A new group of lawyers came to maturity during the Progressive era and redefined the needs of their profession in order to more effectively initiate community change. DAI 42:2817-A.

1605 Filene, Peter G. "An Obituary for 'The Progressive Movement.' " *American Quarterly* 22 (1970): 20–34.

The Progressive movement did not exist as such; rather, it is best understood as a series of shifting local, regional, state, and federal coalitions rallying around various issues. Notes.

1606 Fuller, Wayne E. "The Rural Roots of the Progressive Leaders." *Agricultural History* 42 (1968): 1–13.

Most Progressives identified with rural America, not with the urban scene as is commonly thought. Progressives hoped to preserve rural values in an increasingly industrial and urban society.

1607 Goldman, Eric F. *Rendezvous with Destiny: A History of Modern American Reform.* New York: Knopf, 1952.

This lively survey of reform movements from the end of Reconstruction to President Truman's Fair Deal discusses the New Freedom as the product of Wilson's presidential leadership that obliterated Theodore Roosevelt's New Nationalism. Notes, bibliography, index.

1608 Gould, Lewis L., ed. *The Progressive Era.* Syracuse: Syracuse University Press, 1974.

Several essays explore the Progressive movement, including its origins, thought, politics, diplomacy, and legacies. Notes, index.

1609 Graebner, William. "Federalism in the Progressive Era: A Structural Interpretation of Reform." *Journal of American History* 64 (1977): 331–57.

Often reluctant to legislate at the federal level, Progressives relied instead on uniform acts by the states that would provide social protection without risking the tyranny of a greatly strengthened national government. The idea of uniformity among states' laws worked best in the period from 1908 to 1914. Notes.

1610 Grantham, Dewey W., Jr. "The Progressive Era and the Reform Tradition." *Mid-America* 46 (1964): 227–51.

The Progressive movement provided fertile ground for many social ideas. While some of their reforms had unintended consequences, and some of their ideas were naive, much of Progressive thought has held up well over the years. Notes.

1611 Greenberg, Estelle F. "Pioneers of Professional Social Work: A Case Study in Professionalization, 1908–1919." Ph.D. dissertation, New York University, 1969.

Social work attained professional status during the Progressive era. This institutional expression of the Progressive spirit resulted from the belief that family social work by professionals could improve the urban-industrial world. DAI 30:3398-A.

1612 Greer, Thomas H. *American Social Reform Movements: Their Pattern since 1865.* New York: Prentice-Hall, 1949.

Chapters on the Progressive movement and World War I are included in this survey, which integrates key documents into the text. Notes, bibliography, index.

1613 Griffen, Clyde. "The Progressive Ethos." In Stanley Coben and Lorman Ratner, eds. *The Development of an American Culture.* Englewood Cliffs, NJ: Prentice-Hall, 1970, pp. 120–49.

The fervent Christianity of many Progressive reformers led them to see important social and political issues in moral terms. Notes.

1614 Grittner, Frederick K. "White Slavery: Myth, Ideology, and American Law." Ph.D. dissertation, University of Minnesota, 1986.

The practice of coercing young women into prostitution was never widespread. The intense response to this statistically insignificant crime implies that it expressed underlying concerns about sexuality, morality, and race. The Mann Act, created in response to the white slave panic, was used to enforce prevailing moral standards. DAI 47:3855-A.

1615 Havig, Alan R. "The Poverty of Insurgency: The Movement to Progressivize the Republican Party, 1916–1924." Ph.D. dissertation, University of Missouri, 1966.

When the Progressive party dissolved in 1916, a small but powerful group wanted to Progressivize the Republican party instead of merely returning to the fold. Theodore Roosevelt's death in 1919 seriously weakened this movement. DAI 27:3398-A.

1616 Hillje, John W. "New York Progressives and the War Revenue Act of 1917." *New York History* 53 (1972): 437–59.

Evidence that Progressivism remained alive during the war can be found in the drive by the American Committee on War Finance to use taxation to distribute wealth more evenly. Notes.

1617 Hobson, Wayne K. "Professionals, Progressives and Bureaucratization: A Reassessment." *Historian* 39 (1977): 639–58.

While historians Samuel P. Hays and Robert Wiebe contend that professionals in the Progressive period were elitist technocrats, that generalization does not always hold. It is important that the special circumstances of each profession be analyzed. Notes.

1618 Hofstadter, Richard. *The Age of Reform: From Bryan to F.D.R.* New York: Knopf, 1956.

The Progressives were motivated by status anxiety. They felt that great corporations and urban corruption threatened the American way of life. Notes, index.

1619 Hood, James L. "The Collapse of Zion: Rural Progressivism in Nelson and Washington Counties, Kentucky." Ph.D. dissertation, University of Kentucky, 1980.

Supreme confidence, deep religious faith, and the sense of a proud past and a better future characterized early Progressivism in rural Kentucky. However, rapid industrialization undermined the movement's stability and sureness, and by the end of World War I optimism had turned into suspicion and fear, which were reflected in increasingly prevalent reactionary political beliefs. DAI 41:2736-A.

1620 Howe, Frederick C. *The Confessions of a Reformer.* New York: Scribner's, 1925.

The Progressive-era reformer Howe details his life and work and remembers Woodrow Wilson, whom he first met at Johns Hopkins University, as a powerful, baffled, and lonely man. Index.

1621 Huber, Frances A. "The Progressive Career of Ben B. Lindsey, 1900–1920." Ph.D. dissertation, University of Michigan, 1963.

Lindsey, who supported Roosevelt in the 1912 election, is remembered for his efforts to rehabilitate rather than punish juvenile offenders. DAI 24:1998.

1622 Jaenicke, Douglas W. "Herbert Croly, Progressive Ideology, and the FTC Act." *Political Science Quarterly* 93 (1978): 471–93.

Analyzing the implementation of the Federal Trade Commission Act in terms of Progressive ideology, it becomes apparent that it was not a triumph for the forces of either small business or big business. Notes.

1623 Josephson, Mathew. *The President Makers: The Culture of Politics and Leadership in an Age of Enlightenment, 1896–1919.* New York: Harcourt, Brace, 1940.

The author judges the New Freedom to have been "a year or two of miracles," and he regards Wilsonian wartime idealism as the "final expression of the historic principles of liberalism." At Paris, Wilson's apparent strength masked weakness and indecision in a series of colossal blunders. Bibliography, index.

1624 Kantor, Harvey. "Benjamin Marsh and the Fight over Population Congestion." *Journal of the American Institute of Planners* 40 (1974): 422–29.

Social worker Benjamin Marsh was a pioneer in city planning during the Progressive era, arguing that the extreme overcrowding of the urban poor should be combated for the good of society.

1625 Kaplan, Sidney. "Social Engineers as Saviors: Effects of World War I on Some American Liberals." *Journal of the History of Ideas* 17 (1956): 347–69.

The war left its mark on the ideas of John Dewey, Randolph Bourne, Walter Lippmann, and Herbert Croly, making them less optimistic about the human condition. Notes.

1626 Karl, Barry D. *The Uneasy State: The United States from 1915 to 1945.* Chicago: University of Chicago Press, 1983.

In an essay on militant Progressivism, the movement is portrayed as having imposed regulatory limits on economic, social, and political behaviors until wartime nationalism sidetracked reform. Index.

1627 Kennedy, David M. "Overview: The Progressive Era." *Historian* 37 (1975): 453–68.

Too many historians have looked to the Progressive era as the wellspring of modern society, but it was more of a transition period than anything else. Notes.

1628 ———. *Progressivism: The Critical Issues.* Boston: Little, Brown, 1971.

This reader consists of reprinted scholarly essays and excerpts from the writings of Progressives including Wilson. Notes, bibliography.

1629 Kirby, Jack T. "Clarence Poe's Vision of Segregated 'Great Rural Civilization.' " *South Atlantic Quarterly* 68 (1969): 27–38.

Poe was a spokesman for rural southern Progressivism, which advocated racial segregation as a way to reform society. Visits to South Africa convinced Poe that total segregation was warranted. Notes.

1630 Kirschner, Don S. *The Paradox of Professionalism: Reform and Public Service in Urban America, 1900–1940.* Westport, CT: Greenwood, 1986.

While Progressive reformers believed in social control over the poor, they were also motivated by a sincere desire to bring a sense of community back to urban life. Notes, bibliography, index.

1631 Kreader, J. Lee. "Isaac Max Rubinow: Pioneering Specialist in Social Insurance." *Social Service Review* 50 (1976): 402–25.

Rubinow devoted much of his time and energy to fighting for social insurance in the United States during the Progressive era.

1632 Lee, R. Alton. "The Eradication of Phossy Jaw: A Unique Development of Federal Police Power." *Historian* 29 (1966): 1–21.

The White Phosphorous Match Act of 1912 used the power of taxation to eradicate the disease phossy jaw. This law showed the Progressives at their best. Notes.

1633 Leff, Mark H. "Consensus for Reform: The Mothers' Pension Movement in the Progressive Era." *Social Service Review* 47 (1973): 397–429.

Americans were unique in their attitudes coupling great concern for indigent fatherless children with loathing for any sort of public aid to indigent adult males. In the period 1911–1921, support for mothers' pensions gathered momentum. Notes.

1634 Leuchtenburg, William E. *The Perils of Prosperity, 1914–32.* Chicago: University of Chicago Press, 1958.

Wilson is seen as "the Victorian statesman incarnate" in this social, political, and economic overview of the time when the country was transformed from a rural and decentralized nation into an urban and industrialized one. Bibliography, index.

1635 Levine, Daniel. *Varieties of Reform Thought.* Madison: State Historical Society of Wisconsin, 1964.

The complexities of the Progressive movement are examined by focusing on the work of Jane Addams, Samuel Gompers, Albert Beveridge, Robert La Follette, and others. These reformers were not concerned about the decline in status of the middle class. Notes, bibliography, index.

1636 Link, Arthur S., and McCormick, Richard L. *Progressivism.* Arlington Heights, IL: Harlan Davidson, 1983.

Progressives used modern methods of reform, often with success, but their programs did not always accomplish what had been expected. The Progressives never came to grips with the divisions and conflicts in American society. Bibliography, index.

1637 Lubove, Roy. "The Progressives and the Prostitute." *Historian* 24 (1962): 308–30.

The Progressive drive against commercialized prostitution was an important effort to conserve human resources. Prostitution was attacked as an illicit business which thrived on ignorance and poverty. Notes.

1638 ———. "The Twentieth Century City: The Progressive as Municipal Reformer." *Mid-America* 41 (1959): 195–209.

During the Progressive period, many demanded a new, moral, and scientific politics. The urban reform movement failed, because Progressives assumed that people could put aside their differences for the sake of a higher good. Notes.

1639 ———. "Workmen's Compensation and the Prerogatives of Voluntarism." *Labor History* 8 (1967): 254–79.

Workmen's compensation was deemed acceptable, because it rested on the base of voluntarism, but it also rallied groups determined to halt further attempts to create social insurance programs. Notes.

1640 McGovern, James R. "David Graham Phillips and the Virility Impulse." *New England Quarterly* 39 (1966): 334–55.

Although Phillips was assassinated in 1911, this article contains useful material on the psychological elements that contributed to the Progressive obsession with virility. Notes.

1641 Mann, Arthur, ed. *The Progressive Era.* 2d ed. Hinsdale, IL: Dryden, 1975.

Sixteen scholarly articles on various aspects of Progressivism are reprinted. Notes, bibliography.

1642 May, Martha E. "Home Life: Progressive Social Reformers' Prescriptions for Social Stability, 1890–1920." Ph.D. dissertation, State University of New York, Binghamton, 1984.

As the philosophies of Progressive-era reformers developed, a clearly defined ideal working-class family emerged as a solution to numerous urban problems. Regulations to protect families, such as child labor laws, were urged, and the stable family unit was used more and more as a model for economic and social analysis. DAI 45:1188-A.

1643 Neuchterlein, James A. "The Dream of Scientific Liberalism: The *New Republic* and American Progressive Thought, 1914–1920." *Review of Politics* 42 (1980): 167–90.

The central controversy of Progressivism, moralism versus scientific analysis, was fought in the pages of the *New Republic* during the Wilson years. World War I brought a lack of faith in scientific liberalism and a lessening of intellectual analysis. Notes.

1644 Noble, David W. *The Paradox of Progressive Thought.* Minneapolis: University of Minnesota Press, 1958.

The many contradictions of leading Progressive intellectuals and activists are examined in detail. Notes, index.

1645 ———. *The Progressive Mind.* Chicago: Rand McNally, 1970.

The Progressives wrestled with a number of paradoxical ideas in their search for cures for the ills of the modern age, notably rural values in an urban society, the closing of the frontier, racism, the nature of federal power, and imperialism. Notes, bibliography, index.

1646 O'Neill, William L. *Divorce in the Progressive Era.* New Haven, CT: Yale University Press, 1967.

Progressives and liberals often opposed divorce, because it symbolized modern morality and weakened the male-dominated traditional family unit. Notes, bibliography, index.

1647 ———. *The Progressive Years: America Comes of Age.* New York: Dodd, Mead, 1975.

Modern America began during the Progressive era with the rise of bureaucracy, the domination of business, and the limited welfare state. Bibliography, index.

1648 Ong, Bruce N. "Constitutional and Political Change: James Madison, Thomas

Jefferson, and Progressive Reinterpretations (Aristotle, Herbert Croly, Walter Weyl, J. Allen Smith, Woodrow Wilson)." Ph.D. dissertation, University of Virginia, 1985.

Progressive-era theorists of constitutionalism, Woodrow Wilson among them, engaged in 'Aristotelian sedition' to loosen the bounds of power and pursue major reforms in politics and government. DAI 47: 645-A.

1649 Pease, Otis A. "Urban Reformers in the Progressive Era." *Pacific Northwest Quarterly* 62 (1971): 49–58.

In this general discussion of urban Progressivism, the author notes that some writers view the Progressives as reformists who failed to deliver significant change, while others believe that the movement laid the foundation for the New Deal.

1650 ———, ed. *The Progressive Years: The Spirit and Achievement of American Reform*. New York: Braziller, 1962.

The words of Progressive-era figures, including Wilson, illuminate the fight against poverty, labor in a middle-class society, the Progressive vision, and Progressive foreign policy. Bibliography.

1651 Rosenthal, Marguerite. "The Children's Bureau and the Juvenile Court: Delinquency Policy, 1912–1940." *Social Service Review* 60 (1986): 303–18.

During this period the U.S. Children's Bureau changed from enthusiastic advocacy of the juvenile court system to a realization that the system often did more harm than good.

1652 Ross, Edward A. *Seventy Years of It*. New York: D. Appleton-Century, 1936.

A leading advocate of Wisconsin Progressivism discusses the era. He had Wilson as a professor at Johns Hopkins and subsequently devoted himself to living up to Wilson's high standards of thought and English usage. Photographs, appendix, index.

1653 Rowland, Mary S. "Managerial Progressivism in Kansas, 1916–1930." Ph.D. dissertation, University of Kansas, 1980.

Between 1916 and 1930, there was a tremendous increase in both centralization and professionalization of governmental services. Business experienced similar changes. The trend toward centralization is discussed in terms of individual governors and different departments in Kansas, including the highway department, the Board of Health, and social services. Resultant

problems in banking are discussed. DAI 41: 2261-A.

1654 Schapsmeier, Frederick H. "The Political Philosophy of Walter Lippmann: A Half Century of Thought and Commentary." Ph.D. dissertation, University of Southern California, 1965.

Walter Lippmann joined the editorial staff of the *New Republic* in 1914, and he continued to be an influential political commentator for fifty years. Although he served in several official capacities during the Wilson administration, including participation in the Paris Peace Conference, he opposed the Treaty of Versailles. DAI 26:343.

1655 Scott, Andrew M. "The Progressive Era in Perspective." *Journal of Politics* 21 (1959): 685–701.

The Industrial Revolution created enormous social, political, economic, religious, and ethical problems. The Progressive movement was dedicated to rethinking and reconstructing American life. Notes.

1656 Scott, Anne F. "A Progressive Wind from the South, 1906–1913." *Journal of Southern History* 29 (1963): 53–70.

The Progressive wind did blow from the South before Wilson's presidency, especially on agrarian issues. This laid the groundwork for southerners to play an increasingly important role in passing Progressive legislation under Wilson. Notes.

1657 Seager, Robert, II. "The Progressives and American Foreign Policy, 1898–1917: An Analysis of the Attitudes of the Leaders of the Progressive Movement toward External Affairs." Ph.D. dissertation, Ohio State University, 1956.

Most Progressives had great faith in American capitalism, law, and morality, which they believed should be encouraged in and occasionally even forced on the rest of the world. A small group of Progressives headed by William Jennings Bryan and Robert La Follette held different views, but they were unable to gain a significant following. DAI 17:1322.

1658 Shapiro, Edward S. "Progressivism and Violence." *North Dakota Quarterly* 46 (1978): 47–54.

For all their differences, Progressives shared both a fear that the country was being torn apart by modernism and a faith that they could heal the damage. Notes.

1659 Shapiro, Stanley. "The Twilight of Reform: Advanced Progressives after the Armistice." *Historian* 33 (1971): 349–64.

American participation in the war halted the Progressive movement only temporarily. Many "advanced" Progressives continued to move to the left politically until 1920. Notes.

1660 Smilor, Raymond W. "Cacophony at 34th and 6th: The Noise Problem in America, 1900–1930." *American Studies* 18 (1977): 23–38.

Progressives mounted antinoise campaigns as part of their drive to reform the urban environment, forming societies to lobby politicians and to create quiet zones. Notes.

1661 Sponholtz, Lloyd. "The Initiative and Referendum: Direct Democracy in Perspective, 1898–1920." *American Studies* 14 (1973): 43–64.

The Progressives understood that laws were often most useful to special interest groups and that initiatives and referendums could be useful tools for direct democracy. Notes.

1662 Stevens, Edward W., Jr. "Social Centers, Politics, and Social Efficiency in the Progressive Era." *History of Education Quarterly* 12 (1972): 16–33.

The Progressives sacrificed democracy in education, because they gave social engineering a higher priority. Notes.

1663 Thompson, John E. "Radical Ideological Responses to the Closing of the Frontier in Oklahoma, 1889 to 1923." Ph.D. dissertation, Rutgers University, 1982.

During Wilson's tenure, Oklahoma's radical heritage first expressed itself in socialism, which aroused violent opposition, then, beginning in 1916, as populism. Oklahoma radicalism had a complex relationship with Oklahoma's status as one of the last frontier states, where rapid capitalist exploitation of natural resources occurred. DAI 43:1269-A.

1664 Thornburn, Neil. "A Progressive and the First World War: Frederick C. Howe." *Mid-America* 51 (1969): 108–18.

The Progressive Howe was disillusioned by the slaughter of World War I. His moral convictions shaken, he could no longer support the Progressive movement with the same enthusiasm. Notes.

1665 Tobin, Eugene M. "The Political Economy of George L. Record: A Progressive Alternative to Socialism." *Historian* 39 (1977): 702–16.

Record believed that monopolies had to be broken up for the good of the country. His advocacy of a single tax and nationalization of the railroads made him more radical than most Progressives, but less radical than the socialists. Notes.

1666 Trattner, Walter I. *Homer Folks: Pioneer in Social Welfare.* New York: Columbia University Press, 1968.

Homer Folks spent a lifetime fighting for the well-being of children. Wilson courted him as part of his plan to gain the support of social workers and used his expertise in the fight against tuberculosis during World War I. Notes, bibliography, index.

1667 ———. "Progressivism and World War I: A Re-Appraisal." *Mid-America* 44 (1962): 131–45.

Progressives did not necessarily favor American intervention in the European war. By 1914 the movement was so diverse and broadbased that it makes more sense for historians to think in terms of American rather than Progressive attitudes. Notes.

1668 Unger, Debi, and Unger, Irwin. *The Vulnerable Years: The United States, 1896–1917.* Hinsdale, IL: Dryden, 1977.

Progressive attitudes and actions culminated with Wilson's Fourteen Points and the League of Nations, the finest expressions of the Progressive spirit. Index.

1669 Watson, Richard L., Jr. *The Development of National Power: The United States, 1900–1919.* Boston: Houghton Mifflin, 1976.

Progressive reform and World War I both concentrated power in the hands of the federal government. The period brought no radical social or political changes, but institutions and practices were greatly affected. Bibliography, index.

1670 Weinberg, Julius. "E. A. Ross: The Progressive as Nativist." *Wisconsin Magazine of History* 50 (1967): 242–53.

Ross hoped to turn the clock back to the idealized Iowa of his youth by controlling immigrants with legal restrictions, prohibition, and eugenics. Notes.

1671 Wiebe, Robert H. *The Search for Order, 1877–1920.* New York: Hill and Wang, 1967.

The backbone of the Progressive movement was the new urban professional class, which hoped to use government to cope with industrialization through centralized administration and professional management. Bibliography, index.

1672 Wilson, William H. "J. Horace McFarland and the City Beautiful Movement." *Journal of Urban History* 7 (1981): 315–34.

The first experiment in national urban planning, the "city beautiful" movement of the Progressive era, attempted to improve the quality of life by making urban areas more pleasing to the eye. Notes.

1673 Wrigley, Steven W. "The Triumph of Provincialism: Public Life in Georgia, 1898–1917." Ph.D. dissertation, Northwestern University, 1986.

The temper of the times is examined through public documents such as newspapers and manuscripts. Georgia's rural elite managed to hold on to its local political power despite challenges from the diverse and growing urban areas. DAI 47:3171-A.

1674 Yellowitz, Irwin. "The Origins of Unemployment Reform in the United States." *Labor History* 9 (1968): 338–60.

A small group of social Progressives fought for welfare laws, but they were isolated from mainstream Progressives, who were interested primarily in the reform of business and politics. Notes.

New Freedom

See also Chapter 1, *Autobiographical and Biographical Materials*, Chapter 2, *Wilson Presidency*, and above and below, *The Progressive Movement*, *Elections*, and *Louis Brandeis*.

1675 Abrams, Richard M. "Woodrow Wilson and the Southern Congressmen, 1913–1916." *Journal of Southern History* 22 (1956): 417–37.

Many of the bills passed during Wilson's first term depart from his New Freedom principles. Looking at the voting records of southerners in Congress, the author contends that Dixie congressmen were not as radical as is generally believed nor was Wilson as conservative. Notes.

1676 Blaisdell, Thomas C., Jr. *The Federal Trade Commission: An Experiment in the Control of Business.* New York: Columbia University Press, 1932.

The origins of the FTC are discussed in this work, which is critical of this experiment in government control. Notes, index.

1677 Burdick, Frank. "Woodrow Wilson and the Underwood Tariff." *Mid-America* 50 (1968): 272–90.

Wilson fulfilled a rather unrealistic campaign promise about tariff reform, and the resulting reforms ended up hurting domestic competitors of large corporations. Notes.

1678 Chandler, Lester V. "Wilson's Monetary Reform." In Earl Latham, ed. *The Philosophy and Policies of Woodrow Wilson.* Chicago: University of Chicago Press, 1958, pp. 123–31.

Wilson's Federal Reserve act and the resulting system embody his gradualist approach to monetary reform. This important start toward monetary and banking reform took into consideration the existing financial system. Notes.

1679 Davidson, John W. "The Response of the South to Woodrow Wilson's New Freedom, 1912–1914." Ph.D. dissertation, Yale University, 1954.

The South was generally supportive of Wilson's efforts to reduce the power of big business in government and to increase competition. Reaction to the Underwood tariff reduction bill, the Federal Reserve bill, and the Clayton antitrust bill illustrate the South's position. DAI 25:3532.

1680 Davis, G. Cullom. "The Transformation of the Federal Trade Commission, 1914–1929." *Mississippi Valley Historical Review* 49 (1962): 437–55.

The FTC began as a watchdog over business, but Republican commissioners transformed the agency after Wilson left office. Notes.

1681 Davis, George C., Jr. "The Federal Trade Commission: Promise and Practice in Regulating Business, 1900–1929." Ph.D. dissertation, University of Illinois, 1969.

The capstone of Wilson's New Freedom, the Federal Trade Commission, began with great support, because reformers regarded it as a tool for battling big business, business perceived it to be a friendly arbitrator, and economists thought it was the embodiment of good public administration. By 1920, the Wilson administration had turned businessmen against the FTC. DAI 30:1103-A.

1682 Dimock, Marshall E. "Wilson the Domestic Reformer." In Earl Latham, ed. *The Philosophy and Policies of Woodrow Wilson.* Chicago: University of Chicago Press, 1958, pp. 228–43.

Wilson's training in history, economics, and political science, his moral philosophy, and his personal traits all contributed to his great success as a domestic reformer. He was an intellectual who understood the minds and aspirations of the common man. Notes.

1683 Eulau, Heinz. "Wilsonian Idealist: Walter Lippmann Goes to War." *Antioch Review* 14 (1954): 87–108.

Lippmann's wartime experiences and his frustration with the Treaty of Versailles turned him against Wilsonian idealism.

1684 Garrison, Elisha E. *Roosevelt, Wilson and the Federal Reserve Law.* Boston: Christopher, 1931.

The author discusses his part in the development and writing of the Federal Reserve law.

1685 Grantham, Dewey W., Jr. "Southern Congressional Leaders and the New Freedom, 1913–1917." *Journal of Southern History* 13 (1947): 439–55.

Southern congressional leaders of the Democratic party, such as Oscar Underwood and Carter Glass, played a vital role in pushing through the president's New Freedom legislation.

1686 Henderson, Gerald C. *The Federal Trade Commission: A Study in Administrative Law and Procedure.* New Haven, CT: Yale University Press, 1924.

The Wilson administration's attempt to regulate business through the Federal Trade Commission is examined in the opening pages of this administrative study. Notes, appendix, index.

1687 Howard, Vincent W. "Woodrow Wilson, the Press, and Presidential Leadership: Another Look at the Passage of the Underwood Tariff, 1913." *Centennial Review* 24 (1980): 167–84.

Wilson dramatized the passage of the Underwood tariff to give his new administration an image of strength and decisiveness. The tariff itself was not particularly newsworthy, but the press cooperated in making the signing a national event.

1688 Kenkel, Joseph F. "The Tariff Commission Movement: The Search for a Nonpartisan Solution of the Tariff Question." Ph.D. dissertation, University of Maryland, 1962.

Although Wilson was initially opposed to a tariff commission, business interests and the complications of World War I convinced him to establish one in 1916. DAI 23:2892.

1689 Klebaner, Benjamin J. "Potential Competition and the American Anti-trust Legislation of 1914." *Business History Review* 38 (1964): 163–85.

Progressives hoped to restore competition as a way of regulating trusts through the Clayton antitrust act and the Federal Trade Commission act. Notes.

1690 Kozenko, B. D. "Woodrow Wilson: Bourgeois Reformer" (in Russian). *Voprosky Istorii* [USSR] 4 (1979): 133–47.

Wilson's reforms were more petit bourgeois than Progressive, and they did not reflect any comprehension of class struggle. His democratic, positive ideas were hampered by his vanity.

1691 Krukones, Michael G. "Predicting Presidential Performance through Political Campaigns." *Presidential Studies Quarterly* 10 (1980): 527–43.

Between 1912 and 1972, presidents kept 70 to 80 percent of their campaign promises as reported by the national press during their election campaigns.

1692 Kutler, Stanley I. "Labor, the Clayton Act, and the Supreme Court." *Labor History* 3 (1962): 19–38.

The Clayton antitrust act was extremely ambiguous, so much so that it did labor little good notwithstanding Samuel Gompers's declaration that it was as important to workers as the Magna Charta. Notes.

1693 Laughlin, J. Laurence. *The Federal Reserve Act: Its Origins and Problems.* New York: Macmillan, 1933.

While the sworn enemies of bankers managed to shape certain provisions of the Federal Reserve act to their advantage, it was Woodrow Wilson who saw that the time had come for responsible banking reform. Appendix, index.

1694 Link, Arthur S. "The South and the 'New Freedom': An Interpretation." In Arthur S. Link. *The Higher Realism of Woodrow Wilson and Other Essays*. Nashville: Vanderbilt University Press, 1971, pp. 298–308.

Wilson's original conception of the New Freedom as a way to implement laissez-faire philosophy did not last long. Southern agrarians helped to move the administration toward a positive program of federal action.

1695 McCulley, Richard T. "The Origins of the Federal Reserve Act of 1913: Banks and Politics during the Progressive Era, 1897–1913." Ph.D. dissertation, University of Texas, Austin, 1980.

With finance capitalism in full bloom during the Progressive era, Wall Street revived the Hamiltonian idea of a partnership between business and government through a central banking system, a vision that led to the Federal Reserve act. DAI 42:1284-A.

1696 Miller, John P. "Woodrow Wilson's Contribution to Antitrust Policy." In Earl Latham, ed. *The Philosophy and Policies of Woodrow Wilson*. Chicago: University of Chicago Press, 1958, pp. 132–43.

Wilson's antitrust policy made a distinct contribution to the art of political economy. His was a positive policy of competition, rather than one of laissez-faire or of mere regulation of monopolies.

1697 Moore, Thomas L., III. "The Establishment of a 'New Freedom' Policy: The Federal Trade Commission, 1912–1918." Ph.D. dissertation, University of Alabama, 1980.

During his 1912 campaign, Wilson argued for a neoclassical antitrust policy to promote competition and lower prices. However, Louis Brandeis favored antitrust legislation to protect small companies. The incompatibility of these approaches was circumvented by the creation of the Federal Trade Commission, which was empowered to prevent unfair competition. It was not until 1917 that proponents of neoclassicism dominated the FTC and began to enact their policies. DAI 41:3695-A.

1698 Murray, Robert K. "Public Opinion, Labor, and the Clayton Act." *Historian* 21 (1959): 255–70.

Eager to be liberated from the Sherman antitrust act, organized labor twisted the meaning of the Clayton act in ways that proved to be unwarranted. Notes.

1699 Seager, Henry R., and Bulick, Charles A. *Trust and Corporation Problems*. New York: Harper, 1929.

The establishment of the Federal Trade Commission and the Clayton antitrust act proved to be the culmination of a long fight for effective antitrust action. Notes, bibliography, index.

1700 Seltzer, Alan L. "Woodrow Wilson as 'Corporate Liberal': Toward a Reconsideration of Left Revisionist Historiography." *Western Political Quarterly* 30 (1977): 183–212.

Left revisionists doubt Wilson's commitment to tough antitrust measures, but analysis of his foreign trade and domestic policies contradicts this interpretation.

1701 Toradash, Martin. "Woodrow Wilson and the Tariff Question: The Importance of the Underwood Act in His Reform Program." Ph.D. dissertation, New York University, 1966.

Wilson was consistent on the tariff issue from his college days to his time in the White House. Passage of the Underwood act was the president's first legislative victory, and it provided the New Freedom with momentum toward greater achievements. DAI 27:2489-A.

1702 Urofsky, Melvin I. "Wilson, Brandeis and the Trust Issue, 1912–1914." *Mid-America* 49 (1967): 3–28.

Brandeis's role as chief architect of Wilson's New Freedom is examined critically in light of the trust issue. Notes.

1703 West, Robert C. *Banking Reform and the Federal Reserve, 1863–1923*. Ithaca, NY: Cornell University Press, 1977.

The history of banking reform from the Civil War to the passage of the Federal Reserve act is covered along with the theories behind Progressive attempts to regulate the monetary system. Notes, bibliography, index.

1704 Willis, Henry P., and Steiner, William H. *The Federal Reserve System*. New York: Ronald, 1923.

This early, massive history of the Federal Reserve system finds that the Progressive reform had "little constructive ability" but served the nation well during the crucial period of wartime financing. Appendix, index.

State and Local Politics

See also *Elections,* below.

1705 Agan, Thomas R. "The New Hampshire Progressive Movement." Ph.D. dissertation, State University of New York, Albany, 1975.

New Hampshire's Progressive movement collapsed in the wake of the Theodore Roosevelt-William Howard Taft split, although economic woes, political dissension, and ennui all helped to end the reform period. DAI 36: 7585-A.

1706 Allen, Howard W. "Geography and Politics: Voting on Reform Issues in the United States Senate, 1911–1916." *Journal of Southern History* 27 (1961): 216–28.

The Progressive movement drew support from the East and the South, but, at least in the Senate, the greatest area of support for reform came from west of the Mississippi. Notes.

1707 Alsobrook, David E. "Alabama's Port City: Mobile during the Progressive Era, 1896–1917." Ph.D. dissertation, Auburn University, 1983.

As it was in some other Deep South cities, Progressivism in Mobile was dominated by middle-class businessmen, so that more effort went to commercial rather than social welfare improvements. DAI 44:263-A.

1708 Anders, Evan M. *Boss Rule in South Texas: The Progressive Era.* Austin: University of Texas Press, 1982.

Democratic party political rings in southern Texas counties used patronage and mobilized Mexican-American laborers to fight off Progressive reformers. They also used such extralegal tactics as voting fraud, physical intimidation, and embezzlement. Notes, bibliography, index.

1709 Beach, Frank L. "The Transformation of California, 1900–1920: The Effects of the Westward Movement on California's Growth and Development in the Progressive Period." Ph.D. dissertation, University of California, Berkeley, 1963.

California's urban population quintupled between 1900 and 1920, forcing dramatic social and political accommodations. Rapid growth, innovative solutions, and an eclectic population have characterized California throughout the twentieth century. DAI 24:5351.

1710 Bernard, Richard M., and Rice, Bradley R. "Political Environment and the Adoption of Progressive Municipal Reform." *Journal of Urban History* 1 (1975): 149–74.

Urban political reforms tended to be more successful during the Progressive era in smaller cities with high socioeconomic status and without ethnic minorities. Notes.

1711 Blackford, Mansel G. "Reform Politics in Seattle during the Progressive Era, 1902–1916." *Pacific Northwest Quarterly* 59 (1968): 177–85.

The working class was badly split in Seattle. Skilled, property-owning, native, and old immigrants identified with middle-class reforms, and unskilled, landless, newer immigrants embraced radicalism. Notes.

1712 Buenker, John D. "The Mahatma and Progressive Reform: Martin Lomasney as Lawmaker, 1911–1917." *New England Quarterly* 44 (1971): 397–419.

Ward boss Martin Lomasney was popular among his constituents, because he supported the causes of labor, welfare, and regulation while opposing prohibition and women's suffrage. Notes.

1713 ———. *Urban Liberalism and Progressive Reform.* New York: Scribner's, 1973.

Urban Democrats in New York, New Jersey, Connecticut, Rhode Island, Massachusetts, Ohio, and Illinois played crucial roles in the reform process. They were pragmatists rather than moralists. Photographs, notes, bibliography, index.

1714 Burckel, Nicholas C. "Progressive Governors in the Border States: Reform Governors of Missouri, Kentucky, West Virginia and Maryland, 1900–1918." Ph.D. dissertation, University of Wisconsin, 1971.

Progressive governors of the border states fought government corruption, tried to make government more responsive to the people, and pushed for social reforms and the regulation of corporations. Progressivism dominated the border states during this period. DAI 32:3195-A.

1715 Burts, Robert M. *Richard Irvine Manning and the Progressive Movement in South Carolina.* Columbia: University of South Carolina Press, 1974.

South Carolina's wartime governor was not a great politician, but he was courageous, idealistic, and the most progressive chief executive in the history of the state. Photographs, notes, bibliography, index.

1716 Calbert, Jack L. "James Edward and Miriam Amanda Ferguson: The 'Ma' and 'Pa' of Texas Politics." Ph.D. dissertation, Indiana University, 1968.

James Ferguson was elected governor of Texas in 1914 and was impeached in 1917 after a prolonged battle with the University of Texas and his apparent mishandling of state funds. Still powerful in Texas politics, Ferguson saw his wife elected governor in 1924 and again in 1932. DAI 29:3068-A.

1717   Carney, George O. "Oklahoma's United States House Delegation and Progressivism, 1901–1917." Ph.D. dissertation, Oklahoma State University, 1972.

The thirteen congressmen from Oklahoma from 1901 to 1917 played an important part in the forty-four Progressive issues brought before the House that the author selected for study. DAI 33:6818-A.

1718   Casdorph, Paul D. *Republicans, Negroes, and Progressives in the South, 1912–1916*. University: University of Alabama Press, 1981.

The struggle between Taft and Roosevelt for control of the Republican party loosened the allegiance of blacks to the GOP, paving the way for their shift to the Democratic party. Notes, bibliography, index.

1719   Chrislock, Carl H. *The Progressive Era in Minnesota, 1899–1918*. St. Paul: Minnesota Historical Society, 1971.

Minnesota's dynamic Progressive movement foundered on the rocks of World War I and the Nonpartisan League. Photographs, notes, index.

1720   Clark, Norman H. "The 'Hell-Soaked Institution' and the Washington Prohibition Initiative of 1914." *Pacific Northwest Quarterly* 56 (1965): 1–16.

The prohibitionists in Washington were driven by an evangelical instinct to bring back the good old days of rural America, and they made arguments based on race, economics, class consciousness, and sexuality. Notes.

1721   Cravens, Hamilton. "The Emergence of the Farmer-Labor Party in Washington Politics, 1919–1920." *Pacific Northwest Quarterly* 57 (1966): 148–57.

Farmers and unionists were united temporarily in the postwar period by political and economic discontent. Notes.

1722   Crowder, David L. "Moses Alexander, Idaho's Jewish Governor, 1914–1918." Ph.D. dissertation, University of Utah, 1972.

Rising from his status as a poor Jewish immigrant, Governor Alexander led the successful fight for prohibition in Idaho, fought the Industrial Workers of the World, and sent the National Guard to the Mexican border. DAI 33:1104-A.

1723   Dahlberg, Jane S. *The New York Bureau of Municipal Research: Pioneer in Government Administration*. New York: New York University Press, 1966.

The bureau provided formal training in public administration in the hope that education would bring about better government. Notes, bibliography.

1724   Deaton, Thomas M. "Atlanta during the Progressive Era." Ph.D. dissertation, University of Georgia, 1969.

Atlanta had become a prosperous urban area by the early 1900s. Progressive reformers were active in city politics during the Wilson years, but big business played the most prominent role in the reform movement. DAI 30:5372-A.

1725   Del Vecchio, Richard J. "Indiana Politics during the Progressive Era, 1912–1916." Ph.D. dissertation, University of Notre Dame, 1973.

In Indiana the 1912 and 1916 elections were fought along the same lines as the 1896 William Jennings Bryan-William McKinley campaign had been. The split between stalwarts and Progressives in the GOP had little to do with lost status, as historian Richard Hofstadter suggests. World War I also had little to do with the end of the Progressive movement. DAI 34:1815-A.

1726   Disbrow, Donald W. "Reform in Philadelphia under Mayor Blankenburg, 1912–1916." *Pennsylvania History* 27 (1960): 379–96.

Old-line Republicans dominated Philadelphia for years, with the exception of four years spent under the leadership of Democrat Rudolph Blankenburg. Notes.

1727   Dressner, Richard B., and Altschuler, Glenn C. "Sentiment and Statistics in the Progressive Era: The Debate on Capital Punishment in New York." *New York History* 56 (1975): 191–209.

The New York state constitutional convention of 1915 decided to keep the death penalty for certain crimes, not because they had evidence that it deterred crime, but for emotional reasons. Notes.

1728 Duffy, John J. "Charleston Politics in the Progressive Era." Ph.D. dissertation, University of South Carolina, 1963.

Charleston's Progressive-era dilemmas included unsatisfactory railroad service, public purchase of utilities, and general problems with funding and constructing public works. Mayoral elections were bitterly and sometimes dishonestly fought. DAI 25:429.

1729 Engelmann, Larry. "Dry Renaissance: The Local Option Years, 1889–1917." *Michigan History* 59 (1975): 69–90.

The prohibition movement succeeded in Michigan, because moderates came to believe that it would have a positive effect on society. Only the fanatical wing of the crusade saw prohibition primarily in moral terms. Notes.

1730 Felt, Jeremy P. *Hostages of Fortune: Child Labor Reform in New York State.* Syracuse: Syracuse University Press, 1965.

The New York Child Labor Committee fought long and hard on behalf of exploited children during the Progressive era. Photographs, notes, bibliography, index.

1731 Fischer, Joel. "Urban Transportation: Home Rule and the Independent Subway System in New York City, 1917–1925." Ph.D. dissertation, St. John's University, 1978.

Three separate subway lines competed against one another in Progressive-era New York City, as private, civic, and governmental groups jockeyed for control of the transit system. DAI 39:5101-A.

1732 Flanagan, Maureen A. "Charter Reform in Chicago, 1890–1915." Ph.D. dissertation, Loyola University of Chicago, 1981.

Charter reform failed in Chicago in 1914, as it had in 1907 and in 1908, seemingly due to lack of consensus about the best power structure for the city. The failure of charter reform has affected Chicago's political and economic development. DAI 41:4811-A.

1733 Foster, Mark. "Frank Hague of Jersey City: 'The Boss' as Reformer." *New Jersey History* 86 (1968): 106–17.

Hague was a practical politician who selectively supported Progressivism, until he became mayor. Notes.

1734 Franklin, Jimmie L. *Born Sober: Prohibition in Oklahoma, 1907–1959.* Norman: University of Oklahoma Press, 1971.

Prohibition in Oklahoma was different in that it was a part of the original state constitution, but, as elsewhere, many people flouted the law.

1735 Frognoli, Raymond R. "The Transformation of Reform: The Detroit Citizens League, 1912–1933." Ph.D. dissertation, University of Michigan, 1976.

Auto magnate Henry M. Leland founded the Detroit Citizens League to battle the political influence of saloons. The league was largely responsible for Detroit's 1918 charter reform. DAI 37:3851-A.

1736 Fuller, Wayne E. "The Ohio Railroad Experiment, 1913–1916." *Ohio History* 74 (1965): 13–28.

National, state, and county governments all chipped in to pay for the paving of the former National Road in Ohio, an experience that Congress used when it framed the federal highway act of 1916. Notes.

1737 Gieske, Millard L. *Minnesota Farmer-Laborism: The Third Party Alternative.* Minneapolis: University of Minnesota Press, 1979.

The origin of the Farmer-Labor party after World War I is discussed in the opening chapters. Notes, bibliography, index.

1738 Glaab, Charles N. "The Failure of North Dakota Progressivism." *Mid-America* 39 (1957): 195–209.

Progressivism failed in North Dakota, because it was an urban movement without a farm program of substance. Notes.

1739 Gould, Lewis L. "Progressives and Prohibitionists: Texas Democratic Politics, 1911–1921." *Southwestern Historical Quarterly* 75 (1971): 5–18.

Texas prohibitionists used the issue to vent their anger at immigrants and at the changes brought about by urbanization and industrialization. They believed that they were preserving rural values and improving the quality of life. Notes.

1740 ———. *Progressives and Prohibitionists: Texas Democrats in the Wilson Era.* Austin: University of Texas Press, 1973.

Texas Democrats were divided over the prohibition issue, a schism which diverted them from the problems of how to deal with big business and with farm and urban problems. Notes, bibliography, index.

1741 Grantham, Dewey W. *Southern Progressivism: The Reconciliation of Progress and Tradition*. Knoxville: University of Tennessee Press, 1983.

The urban middle class provided the leadership for southern Progressivism. To preserve the best of the past while ensuring stability, Progressives crusaded for child labor laws, prohibition of alcohol, teaching of evolution, and reform of education. Photographs, notes, bibliography, index.

1742 Greenbaum, Fred. *Fighting Progressive: A Biography of Edward P. Costigan*. Washington, DC: Public Affairs, 1971.

Costigan was typical of the middle-class reformers of the Progressive era. His work in Colorado politics, prohibition, and economic reforms is detailed. Index.

1743 Griffith, Ernest S. *A History of American City Government: The Progressive Years and Their Aftermath, 1900–1920*. New York: Praeger, 1974.

Urban Progressives were practical men and women who wanted city government to be honest, cost effective, and humane. Notes, bibliography, index.

1744 Gusfield, Joseph R. *Symbolic Crusade: Status Politics and the American Temperance Movement*. Urbana: University of Illinois Press, 1963.

Advocates of temperance were acting to preserve the dominance and prestige of their lifestyle and to force others to accept it. Notes, index.

1745 Haas, Paul A. "Sin in Wisconsin: The Teasdale Vice Committee of 1913." *Wisconsin Magazine of History* 49 (1966): 138–51.

The Teasdale commission blamed prostitution on the widespread availability of alcoholic beverages and called for stricter enforcement of the law. Notes.

1746 Hamilton, Charles G. "Mississippi Politics in the Progressive Era, 1904–1920." Ph.D. dissertation, Vanderbilt University, 1958.

Rural resentment of conservatives and strong leadership propelled Mississippi to enact a multitude of Progressive reforms. DAI 19:1066.

1747 Hohner, Robert A. "Prohibition Comes to Virginia: The Referendum of 1914." *Virginia Magazine of History and Biography* 75 (1967): 473–88.

The Anti-Saloon League and the Women's Christian Temperance Union combined forces to convince the voters to accept prohibition. Notes.

1748 Hoy, Suellen M. "Samuel M. Ralston: Progressive Governor, 1913–1917." Ph.D. dissertation, Indiana University, 1975.

A moderate Progressive Democrat, Ralston fought for a variety of reforms, most of which had been advocated by his defeated opponent, Albert J. Beveridge. DAI 36:3020-A.

1749 Huthmacher, J. Joseph. "Charles Evans Hughes and Charles Francis Murphy: The Metamorphosis of Progressivism." *New York History* 46 (1965): 25–40.

New York City Democrats supported Progressive legislation in such a way as to suggest that it was distinctly different from middle-class Progressivism, emphasizing social welfare issues. Notes.

1750 Isaac, Paul E. *Prohibition and Politics: Turbulent Decades in Tennessee, 1885–1920*. Knoxville: University of Tennessee Press, 1965.

Prohibition came to Tennessee through the combined efforts of Protestant churches, the Anti-Saloon League, and Progressives. Notes, bibliography, index.

1751 Janick, Herbert, Jr. "The Progressive Party and the Election of 1912 in Connecticut." *Connecticut Historical Society Bulletin* 30 (1965): 65–72.

Roosevelt's Progressive party grew quickly in the nutmeg state during the summer of 1912. Conservative amateurs provided leadership for the movement, which faltered in the fall elections and had all but died by 1916.

1752 Jones, Alton D. "Progressivism in Georgia, 1898–1918." Ed.D. dissertation, Emory University, 1963.

Progressives accomplished less in Georgia than they did in other states, due to Georgia's racism, philosophy of individualism, and lack of coordinated and capable Progressive leadership. DAI 25:432.

1753 Kaufman, Burton I. "Virginia Politics and the Wilson Movement, 1910–1914." *Virginia Magazine of History and Biography* 77 (1969): 3–21.

Two factions of Democrats fought for control of the Virginia party throughout the Progressive era. While Wilson sympathized with the antiorganization faction initially, he gave most patronage to the forces of Senator Thomas S. Martin after the 1912 election. Notes.

1754 Kaylor, Earl C. "The Prohibition Movement in Pennsylvania, 1865–1920." Ph.D. dissertation, Pennsylvania State University, 1963.

Prohibition never found enthusiastic support in Pennsylvania, partly due to the opposition of Roman Catholic and immigrant factions. DAI 25:1876.

1755 Kirby, Jack T. "Alcohol and Irony: The Campaign of Westmoreland Davis for Governor, 1909–1917." *Virginia Magazine of History and Biography* 73 (1965): 259–79.

An attorney, a farmer, and a publisher, Davis won the governor's race in Virginia by skirting the prohibition issue, while his two opponents divided the dry vote between them. Notes.

1756 ———. *Westmoreland Davis: Virginia Planter-Politician, 1859–1942.* Charlottesville: University Press of Virginia, 1968.

Davis was the wartime governor of Virginia. He led the Progressive farm bloc and fought against Democratic political machines. Notes, bibliography, index.

1757 Kurland, Gerald. "Seth Low: A Study in the Progressive Mind." Ph.D. dissertation, City University of New York, 1968.

Born in 1850, by the Wilson years Progressive Seth Low sought to improve labor's standard of living, and, toward the same end, to regulate big business. The author concludes that Progressives were more liberal than is commonly believed. DAI 29:1496-A.

1758 La Forte, Robert S. *Leaders of Reform: Progressive Republicans in Kansas, 1900–1916.* Lawrence: University Press of Kansas, 1974.

Progressive Republicans failed to attract support from the urban working class because of their positions on prohibition and on economic issues. Their accomplishments were not nearly as significant as they thought they would be. Notes, bibliography, index.

1759 Lanahan, Anna M. "Brooklyn's Political Life, 1898–1916." Ph.D. dissertation, St. John's University, 1977.

The people and politicians of Progressive-era Brooklyn resented the drive to centralize authority and hated moral legislation

regulating their rights to drink alcohol, watch baseball on Sunday, and gamble. DAI 38:4329-A.

1760 Ledbetter, Calvin R., Jr. "The Constitutional Convention of 1917–1918." *Arkansas Historical Quarterly* 34 (1975): 3–40.

The public was interested in neither the work nor the accomplishments of Arkansas's sixth constitutional convention, because it coincided with World War I. Notes.

1761 Lubove, Roy. *The Progressives and the Slums: Tenement House Reform in New York City, 1890–1917.* Pittsburgh: University of Pittsburgh Press, 1962.

The Progressives took it on faith that slum reform would remove all of the social ills facing the poor. Public housing might have been more constructive than was reform of building codes. Photographs, notes, appendix, bibliography, index.

1762 McClung, John B. "Texas Rangers along the Rio Grande, 1910–1919." Ph.D. dissertation, Texas Christian University, 1981.

The chaotic years of the Mexican Revolution and, later, World War I fostered rough, persistent, and desperate lawlessness along the Rio Grande between 1910 and 1919. The Texas Rangers responded with harsh forcefulness that they knew was necessary, but for which they were later criticized. Over time, the Rangers moderated their tactics. DAI 42:1762-A.

1763 Mahoney, Joseph F. "New Jersey Politics after Wilson: Progressivism in Decline." Ph.D. dissertation, Columbia University, 1964.

The Progressive party in New Jersey lacked both leadership and a clear-cut agenda after 1912. By 1916, most Progressives had merged with the Republicans. DAI 26:1615.

1764 Margulies, Herbert F. *The Decline of the Progressive Movement in Wisconsin, 1890–1920.* Madison: State Historical Society of Wisconsin, 1968.

Robert La Follette lost control of the Progressive movement in Wisconsin in 1912, and thereafter reformers engaged in bitter disputes over personalities, prohibition, and foreign policy. Notes, bibliography, index.

1765 Melvin, Patricia M. "Neighborhood in the 'Organic' City: The Social Unit Plan and the First Community Organization Movement, 1900–1920." Ph.D. dissertation, University of Cincinnati, 1978.

As cities expanded, people started to think in terms of neighborhoods. Groups formed to organize these new neighborhoods and to coordinate policies with the city. Wilbur C. Phillips worked to develop organizational models of neighborhoods in New York, Milwaukee, and Cincinnati. DAI 39:5681-A.

1766 Mitchell, J. Paul. "Progressivism in Denver: The Municipal Reform Movement, 1904–1916." Ph.D. dissertation, University of Denver, 1966.

After a long fight against Denver's Mayor Robert W. Speer, a coalition party of reformers ousted him in 1912. The newly elected reformers were too diverse to govern effectively, and Speer was reelected in 1916. However, the reformers did achieve their basic goals—the city's political life was regenerated, corruption was cleaned up, and in 1918 Denver purchased its own water system. DAI 27:4198-A.

1767 Morris, Stuart. "The Wisconsin Idea and Business Progressivism." *Journal of American Studies* 4 (1970): 39–60.

Schools in public administration in Wisconsin and Pennsylvania did not make a notable difference in the quality of government during the Progressive era. Notes.

1768 Mowry, George E. "The California Progressive and His Rationale: A Study in Middle Class Politics." In C. Vann Woodward, ed. *The Comparative Approach to American History.* New York: Basic, 1968, pp. 271–84.

The Progressives were not the only liberal reformers in the early twentieth century, for similar movements took place in Western Europe at the same time. Notes.

1769 ———. *The California Progressives.* Berkeley: University of California Press, 1951.

The typical California Progressive leader was young, male, born in the Midwest, college-educated, middle-class, and Protestant. The Progressive movement supplied an honest alternative to the corrupt labor party and the crooked corporate-controlled government. Notes, bibliography, index.

1770 Moyers, David M. "Arkansas Progressivism: The Legislative Record." Ph.D. dissertation, University of Arkansas, 1986.

Arkansas was a full participant in the national Progressive movement between 1900 and 1917. Conservation measures, regulation of certain businesses, and educational and election reforms were all enacted. DAI 47:2291-A.

1771 Muraskin, Jack D. "Missouri Politics during the Progressive Era, 1896–1916." Ph.D. dissertation, University of California, Berkeley, 1969.

Missouri politics mirrored Progressive ambiguities. The St. Louis business elite played a prominent role in the conflict of contending interest groups. DAI 30:4920-A.

1772 Nelli, Humbert S. "John Powers and the Italians: Politics in a Chicago Ward, 1896–1921." *Journal of American History* 67 (1970): 67–84.

The settlement house movement of Chicago was too middle-class and moralistic in its approach to politics to be effective against John Powers. Italians favored Powers, who could deliver jobs and other benefits to them. Notes.

1773 O'Connor, Robert E. "William Barnes, Jr.: A Conservative Encounters the Progressive Era." Ph.D. dissertation, State University of New York, Albany, 1971.

The conservative Republican boss of Albany, New York, fought Theodore Roosevelt for years before 1912, the year Barnes was able to salvage the nomination for President Taft. The successful battle against Roosevelt drained his power and ruined him in the end. DAI 33:2866-A.

1774 Palermo, Patrick F. "The Midwestern Republican Tradition: From Party to Insurgency." *Capitol Studies* 5 (1977): 43–56.

Republican insurgents hoped to defend the values of small-town America, which were threatened by changes wrought by industrialism and urbanization. Notes.

1775 Paterson, Thomas G. "California Progressives and Foreign Policy." *California Historical Society Quarterly* 47 (1968): 329–42.

The Progressive movement was too large to have any unified attitude toward foreign policy. California Progressives were split on the preparedness issue and on the appropriate American response to the Mexican Revolution. Notes.

1776 Patton, Thomas W. "An Urban Congressional Delegation in an Age of Reform: The New York County Democratic Delegation to the House of Representatives, 1901–1917." Ed.D. dissertation, New York University, 1978.

Progressive-era New York county delegates to the House either did not care about reforms or opposed them. Their main concern was with the economic and political impact of Progressive legislation on New York City. DAI 39:7486-A.

1777 Pendergrass, Lee F. "Urban Reform and Voluntary Association: A Case Study of the Seattle Municipal League, 1910–1929." Ph.D. dissertation, University of Washington, 1972.

The Seattle Municipal League was an urban reform association that prospered in its work during the prewar period of economic stability. It was fractured badly by World War I, the Red Scare, and the postwar economic turbulence. DAI 33:5101-A.

1778 Pickering, John R. "Blueprint of Power: The Public Career of Robert Speer in Denver, 1878–1918." Ph.D. dissertation, University of Denver, 1978.

The mayor of Denver for much of the Progressive era, Robert Speer is an example of a political boss who used his power to coordinate various interest groups at a time of unparalleled growth. He was a complex personality, at once practical and idealistic. DAI 39:6920-A.

1779 Pulley, Raymond H. *Old Virginia Restored: An Interpretation of the Progressive Impulse, 1870–1930*. Charlottesville: University Press of Virginia, 1968.

In Virginia, Progressivism grew out of reaction rather than a desire to modernize, so it gave a high priority to purifying politics and the electorate. Notes, bibliography, index.

1780 Quandt, Jean B. "Community in Urban America, 1890–1917: Reformers, City Planners, and Greenwich Villagers." *Societas* 6 (1976): 255–74.

City planners and settlement house workers met with opposition from artists and intellectuals who found their sense of community too stifling and unnatural.

1781 Renner, C. K. "Prohibition Comes to Missouri, 1910–1919." *Missouri Historical Review* 62 (1968): 363–97.

Although Missouri voters turned down prohibition four times at the polls, opponents of liquor used World War I to their advantage, arguing that prohibition would be a blow against Germans. Notes.

1782 Rice, Bradley. *Progressive Cities: The Commission Government Movement in America, 1901–1920*. Austin: University of Texas Press, 1977.

The Galveston plan of commission-style city government was implemented by several small and medium-sized cities before World War I, when the city manager idea became popular. Notes, bibliography, index.

1783 Rickard, Louise E. "The Politics of Reform in Omaha, 1918–1921." *Nebraska History* 53 (1972): 419–45.

Omaha reformers divided into moralist and structural camps, a dichotomy which resulted in failure to get much done. Notes.

1784 Ritchie, Donald A. "The Gary Committee, Businessmen, Progressives, and Unemployment in New York City, 1914–1915." *New York Historical Quarterly* 57 (1973): 327–47.

The business and social workers who served on the Gary committee helped only a fraction of the unemployed that they might have helped, as city funds earmarked for this purpose went unspent. Notes.

1785 Robinson, James H. "Progressivism and Legitimacy in New York, 1897–1917: A Case Study of a Third-Party Movement." Ph.D. dissertation, New York University, 1982.

When major parties fail to address the concerns of large groups of people, third-party movements step in to fill the void. Such was the case in New York, where the Progressives worked to reform local and state government to make it more responsive to modern needs. DAI 43:538-A.

1786 Rodabaugh, Karl. "Congressman Henry D. Clayton and the Dothan Post Office Fight: Patronage and Politics in the Progressive Era." *Alabama Review* 33 (1980): 125–49.

Alabama's Postmaster Byron T. Dothan's support of Theodore Roosevelt at the 1912 Republican convention cost him his job, as neither William Howard Taft nor Wilson wanted a Roosevelt man in this important civil service post. Notes.

1787 Rogin, Michael P. "Progressives and the California Electorate." *Journal of American History* 55 (1968): 297–314.

Although Hiram Johnson was first elected by middle-class Californians who had been born in the South, his emphasis on legislation benefiting the poor and working classes attracted laborers, ethnic groups, and those born in the North. Notes.

1788 Romanofsky, Peter. "The Public Is Aroused: The Missouri Children's Code Commission, 1915–1919." *Missouri Historical Review* 68 (1974): 204–22.

The Missouri Children's Code Commission was a broadbased citizens' coalition, not just an organization of social workers and teachers, which explains why it had widespread support. Notes.

1789 Rosenberg, Arnold S. "The Rise of John Adams Kingsbury." *Pacific Northwest Quarterly* 63 (1972): 55–62.

Kingsbury was active in the Progressive party and served as commissioner of public charities in New York during Wilson's first term.

1790 Rowley, William D. "Francis G. Newlands: A Westerner's Search for a Progressive and White America." *Nevada Historical Quarterly* 17 (1974): 68–79.

Land reclamation, expanded use of government, and further institutionalization of racism formed the basis of Newlands's vision of Progressive America. Notes.

1791 Saltvig, Robert D. "The Progressive Movement in Washington." Ph.D. dissertation, University of Washington, 1966.

Although the Progressive movement in Washington state reflected the national movement in most ways, Washington Progressivism was boosted by a unique link between labor, farmers, and the middle class, a holdover from the state's strong Populism. This coalition dissolved shortly after the war. DAI 27:4201-A.

1792 Schick, Thomas. *The New York State Constitutional Convention of 1915 and the Modern State Governor*. New York: National Municipal League, 1978.

The New York convention of 1915 strengthened the office of the governor through a variety of reforms. Notes, bibliography, index.

1793 Schiesl, Martin J. *The Politics of Efficiency: Municipal Administration and Reform in America, 1880–1920*. Berkeley: University of California Press, 1977.

Older urban reformers wanted to reorganize government so that better people would be elected, while younger reformers hoped to use city government to effect other changes. City government was made more efficient during the Progressive era at the price of removing it from popular influences. Notes, bibliography, index.

1794 Sherman, Richard B. "The Status Revolution and Massachusetts Progressive Leadership." *Political Science Quarterly* 78 (1963): 59–65.

Historian Richard Hofstadter's concept of status revolution does not hold up particularly well when applied to fifty leaders of the Progressive party in Massachusetts in 1912–13.

1795 Shover, John L. "The Progressives and the Working Class Vote in California." *Labor History* 10 (1969): 584–601.

Labor leaders were strong allies of Hiram Johnson and the Progressive movement in California, especially after 1914. Notes.

1796 Starr, Dennis J. "The Nature and Uses of Economic, Political and Social Power in Trenton, New Jersey, 1890–1917." Ph.D. dissertation, Rutgers University, 1979.

A small, cohesive upper class controlled Trenton's economy, system of higher education, and city politics. They shaped the values of workers through churches, schools, libraries, recreational facilities, and the YMCA. Instability developed in spite of these efforts, because the elite understood nothing about the working class. DAI 40:423-A.

1797 Steelman, Joseph F. "The Progressive Democratic Convention of 1914 in North Carolina." *North Carolina Historical Review* 46 (1969): 83–104.

In 1914, Progressive Democrats could not convince party regulars to accept their liberal agenda, although the party accepted much of it in subsequent years. Notes.

1798 Straetz, Ralph A. "The Progressive Movement in Illinois, 1910–1916." Ph.D. dissertation, University of Illinois, 1951.

Many Progressives believed in nonpartisan political action and therefore resisted forming an official party. Once established, however, the Illinois Progressive party belied this ideological purity by its preoccupation with the personalities of its own and its opposition's leaders instead of with nonpartisan ideals. DAI 12:99.

1799 Sweeney, Raymond S. "Progressivism in Maryland, 1900–1917." Ph.D. dissertation, University of North Carolina, Chapel Hill, 1971.

The Progressive movement in Maryland was far from unified. This ever-shifting informal coalition was responsible for a variety of reforms, as people accepted the need for a more powerful government. DAI 32:6910-A.

1800 Tager, Jack. "Progressives, Conservatives and the Theory of the Status Revolution." *Mid-America* 48 (1966): 162–75.

To test the status revolution theory, the Progressive movement in Toledo, Ohio, from 1905 to 1913 is examined. No differences can be discerned between Progressives and proponents of the status quo. Toledo's middle class was badly divided on most issues. Notes.

1801 Teaford, Jon C. "State Administrative Agencies and the Cities, 1890–1920." *American Journal of Legal History* 25 (1981): 225–48.

Urban reformers were more interested in restricting state legislative power and enhancing the power of state bureaucrats charged with overseeing urban affairs than they were in "home rule." Notes.

1802 Tindall, George B. *The Emergence of the New South, 1913–1945.* Baton Rouge: Louisiana State University Press, 1967.

Racism and the one-party political system do not sufficiently explain southern sectionalism during the period under study, for battle lines were often drawn over agrarian issues, civil rights, religion, and unionism. Photographs, notes, bibliography, index.

1803 Tobin, Eugene M. "Mark Fagan and the Politics of Urban Reform: Jersey City, 1900–1917." Ph.D. dissertation, Brandeis University, 1972.

Mark Fagan, mayor of Jersey City, led the urban reform movement, but quickly became frustrated by powerful and well-entrenched absentee landlords, railroads, and utilities. In the end, Progressive reformers failed to transform Jersey City. DAI 33:3564-A.

1804 ———. "The Progressive as Single Taxer: Mark Fagan and the Jersey City Experience, 1900–1917." *American Journal of Economics and Sociology* 33 (1974): 287–97.

Mark Fagan embraced single-tax reform to get elected and to fight conservatives.

1805 Vandermeer, Philip R. "A Social Analysis of Indiana Politics and Politicians, 1896–1920." Ph.D. dissertation, University of Illinois, Urbana-Champaign, 1976.

Democrats gained ground in Indiana as a result of a backlash against Republican-sponsored morality laws. Much of the political conflict had a religious basis. DAI 37:6711.

1806 Wade, Louise C. *Graham Taylor: Pioneer for Social Justice, 1851–1938.* Chicago: University of Chicago Press, 1964.

Taylor mixed reform with religion in his quest for social justice during the Progressive era in Chicago. Photographs, notes, bibliography, index.

1807 Warner, Hoyt L. *Progressivism in Ohio, 1897–1917.* Columbus: Ohio State University Press, 1964.

Progressivism spread across Ohio from bases in Cleveland, Toledo, and Columbus, reaching its high water mark during James Cox's administration. Progressive reformers made a difference, because they were honest, and they improved government. Notes, bibliography, index.

1808 Weiss, Nancy J. *Charles Francis Murphy, 1858–1924: Respectability and Responsibility in Tammany Politics.* Northampton, MA: Smith College, 1968.

Murphy worked to enact Progressive reforms but was not shy about using the tactics of bossism when they suited his purpose. Notes, bibliography.

1809 Wesser, Robert F. *A Response to Progressivism: The Democratic Party and New York Politics, 1902–1918.* New York: New York University Press, 1986.

The New Freedom and Wilson's wartime excesses hurt the Democratic party in New York. Al Smith triumphed in 1918 by putting distance between the state party and the national organization. Notes, bibliography, index.

1810 West, Elliott. "Cleansing the Queen City: Prohibition and Urban Reform in Denver." *Arizona and the West* 14 (1972): 331–46.

Denver Progressives sometimes cooperated with prohibitionists, but urban Progressivism encompassed too many interest groups to give blanket support to the controversial antiliquor forces. Notes.

1811 Zolot, Herbert M. "The Issue of Good Government and James Michael Curley: Curley and the Boston Scene from 1897–1918." Ph.D. dissertation, State University of New York, Stony Brook, 1975.

Elected mayor of Boston in 1913, Curley ran into opposition from the local Good Government Association. The mayor fought back against the Progressives by stirring up ethnic tensions. DAI 36:1053-A.

Elections

See also Chapter 11, *The Home Front, Politics.*

1812 Kleppner, Paul, and Baker, Stephen C. "The Impact of Voter Registration Requirements on Electoral Turnout, 1900–16." *Journal of Political and Military Sociology* 8 (1980): 205–26.

"An age-cohort replacement process," especially among the sons of immigrants, was largely responsible for lower voter turnouts during the Progressive era.

1912

See also Chapter 1, *Autobiographical and Biographical Materials*, Chapter 3, *Theodore Roosevelt* and *William Howard Taft*, and *Louis Brandeis*, below.

1813 Abernethy, Lloyd M. "The Progressive Campaign in Pennsylvania, 1912." *Pennsylvania History* 29 (1962): 175–92.

William Flynn, a former Republican boss from Pittsburgh, was the organizer most responsible for Roosevelt's victory in Pennsylvania in 1912.

1814 Ander, O. Fritiof. "The Swedish-American Press in the Election of 1912." *Swedish Pioneer Historical Quarterly* 14 (1963): 103–26.

Swedish-American newspapers reveal that many Swedes deserted the Republican party, which they had supported since the time of Lincoln, largely to support Theodore Roosevelt. A significant number found Wilson's candidacy more attractive than that of William Howard Taft. Notes.

1815 Bayard, Charles J. "The Colorado Progressive Republican Split of 1912." *Colorado Magazine* 45 (1968): 61–78.

A schism in the Colorado Progressive movement developed between urbanites and small-city and rural residents, which spelled disaster at the polls in 1912.

1816 Billington, Monroe. "Thomas P. Gore and the Election of Woodrow Wilson." *Mid-America* 39 (1957): 180–91.

Thomas P. Gore played a more important role in Wilson's election than has been hitherto recognized. Notes.

1817 Burdick, Francis A. "Businessmen in Politics: The Case of the Election of 1912." Ph.D. dissertation, University of Iowa, 1971.

Revisionist historians have oversimplified the business response to Progressivism. Some businessmen favored regulation, but they were on the whole divided on the issue. In the election of 1912, they did not act as a unified elite. DAI 32:1432-A.

1818 Burke, James L. "Judson Harmon: The Dilemma of a Constructive Conservative." *Cincinnati Historical Society Bulletin* 31 (1973): 28–47.

The two-term governor of Ohio lost the 1912 presidential nomination to Wilson, because he was not Progressive enough, and because Democrats in the Ohio delegation rebelled against his leadership. Notes.

1819 Casdorph, Paul D. "Governor William E. Glasscock and Theodore Roosevelt's 1912 Bull Moose Candidacy." *West Virginia History* 28 (1966): 8–15.

West Virginia's Governor Glasscock was an early supporter of Theodore Roosevelt's candidacy in 1912, leading a united delegation into the Republican convention. But when Roosevelt walked out of the convention to form a third party, Glasscock declined to follow. Notes.

1820 Coletta, Paolo E. "Bryan at Baltimore, 1912: Wilson's Warwick?" *Nebraska History* 57 (1976): 201–25.

William Jennings Bryan's insistence on an open convention strengthened the hand of Progressives and weakened conservatives at the Baltimore convention, thus aiding Wilson's candidacy. Notes.

1821 Crews, Kenneth D. "Woodrow Wilson, Wisconsin, and the Election of 1912." *Presidential Studies Quarterly* 12 (1982): 369–76.

Wilson's victory in Wisconsin is explained as a combination of an effective grass-roots organization, a strong Progressive element within the Democratic party, and a failure of the Republicans to unite. Notes.

1822 Daniels, Josephus. *Editor in Politics.* Vol. II. Chapel Hill: University of North Carolina Press, 1941.

This autobiography contains material on Woodrow Wilson's 1912 campaign. Photographs, index.

1823 Davidson, John W. "Wilson in the Campaign of 1912." In Earl Latham, ed. *The Philosophy and Policies of Woodrow Wilson.* Chicago: University of Chicago Press, 1958, pp. 85–99.

A complete reading of Wilson's speeches is necessary to fully understand his 1912 presidential campaign. Scholars have taken his speeches out of context to fit their theses. Notes.

1824 Davis, Allen F. "The Social Workers and the Progressive Party, 1912–1916." *American Historical Review* 69 (1964): 671–88.

Social workers supported the Progressive party in great numbers in 1912, not because of Roosevelt or the New Nationalism, but for the party's social and industrial planks, which they had a hand in drafting. Notes.

1825 Donagher, Richard J. "The Urban Bull Moose: A Case Study of Philadelphia and Pittsburgh." Ph.D. dissertation, Fordham University, 1979.

Reformers and some Republican dissidents in Pennsylvania turned to Theodore Roosevelt to break the power of the Republican political machines. They seized control of the state Republican party only to surrender it when TR set up his third-party movement. Big business supported Taft, with the bulk of Bull Moose support coming from middle- and upper-class old-stock Americans. DAI 39:6912-A.

1826 Gable, John A. *The Bull Moose Years: Theodore Roosevelt and the Progressive Party.* Port Washington, NY: Kennikat, 1978.

This revised doctoral dissertation covers Roosevelt's political career from 1912 to 1916, when he took on the role of activist prophet for political and social reform. Illustrations, notes, index.

1827 Gatewood, Willard B., ed. "The President and the 'Deacon' in the Campaign of 1912: The Correspondence of William Howard Taft and James Calvin Hemphill, 1911–1912." *Ohio History* 74 (1965): 35–54.

Alienation from liberals in their several political parties drew President Taft and Hemphill together in a friendship which bloomed through a series of letters. Notes.

1828 Gores, Stan. "The Attempted Assassination of Teddy Roosevelt." *Wisconsin Magazine of History* 53 (1970): 269–77.

During the 1912 election campaign, a bartender named John Shrank attempted to assassinate Theodore Roosevelt.

1829 Gould, Lewis L. "Theodore Roosevelt, William Howard Taft, and the Disputed Delegates in 1912: Texas as a Test Case." *Southwestern Historical Quarterly* 80 (1976): 33–56.

In the battle for forty Texas delegates, Taft obtained thirty-one of them, because Taft's forces controlled the party machinery. An objective analysis reveals that Roosevelt deserved at least one half of the Texas contingent. Notes.

1830 Green, G. N. "Republican, Bull Moose, and Negroes in Florida, 1912." *Florida Historical Quarterly* 43 (1964): 153–64.

Even while they were struggling for every Republican vote they could muster, the supporters of Taft and Roosevelt gave little attention to blacks.

1831 Hahn, Harlan. "The Republican Party Convention of 1912 and the Role of Herbert S. Hadley in National Politics." *Missouri History Review* 59 (1965): 407–23.

If Hadley had supported Taft at the nominating convention, he might have had the vice presidency. When a Taft-Roosevelt deadlock developed, Hadley's name emerged as a compromise, a scheme which Taft could have lived with but not Roosevelt, who chose to walk out instead.

1832 Hennings, Robert E. "James D. Phelan and the Woodrow Wilson Anti-Oriental Statement of May 3, 1912." *California Historical Quarterly* 42 (1963): 291–300.

The anti-Oriental statement issued by the Wilson campaign was written by Phelan, a former mayor of San Francisco. It expressed sentiments commonly found in Democratic party circles.

1833 Hill, C. Warren. "Colorado Progressives and the Bull Moose Campaign." *Colorado Magazine* 43 (1966): 93–113.

The history of the Progressive party in Colorado is traced from 1910 until 1916, when the organization's leaders supported Republican regular Charles Evans Hughes. Notes.

1834 Hunter, George S. "The Bull Moose Movement in Arizona." *Arizona and the West* 10 (1968): 343–62.

Two businessmen, Dwight B. Head and John C. Greenway, headed the Bull Moose party in Arizona from 1912 to 1916. Notes.

1835 Janick, Herbert. "The Mind of the Connecticut Progressive." *Mid-America* 52 (1970): 83–101.

Leaders of the Progressive movement in Connecticut were wealthy and status-conscious men trying to cope with change in urban and industrial America. Notes.

1836 Johnson, Evans C. "The Underwood Forces and the Democratic Nomination of 1912." *Historian* 31 (1969): 173–93.

Many conservative Democrats did not want Wilson to be nominated in 1912. Some pinned their hopes on Oscar Underwood, but, like other regional candidates, he went down to defeat at the hands of Wilson after forty-six ballots. Notes.

1837 Katz, Irving. "Henry Lee Higginson vs. Louis Dembitz Brandeis: A Collision between Tradition and Reform." *New England Quarterly* 41 (1968): 67–81.

The conservative Higginson gave his reluctant support to Wilson in 1912, hoping the Democrat would be less Progressive than his rivals. He broke with his former friend Brandeis over antitrust activities and protested in vain when Wilson appointed Brandeis to the Supreme Court. Notes.

1838 Kelly, Frank K. *The Fight for the White House: The Story of 1912*. New York: Crowell, 1961.

The social and political history of the 1912 campaign is recounted. It boiled down to the political philosophy of Wilson versus that of Roosevelt. Bibliography, index.

1839 Lawson, Hughie G. "Candidates and Issues in 1912: A Re-examination of the New Nationalism and the New Freedom." Ph.D. dissertation, Tulane University, 1970.

The New Nationalism of Roosevelt and the New Freedom of Wilson were not so different as has been widely thought. Their differences on the trust issue were real but not very large. Both advocated strong social programs as well. DAI 31:2847-A.

1840 Lindstrom, Andrew F. "Lawrence Stringer: A Wilson Democrat." *Journal of the Illinois Historical Society* 66 (1973): 20–40.

Stringer delivered Illinois to Wilson at the Baltimore convention in 1912, but when he needed a favor in return the president balked. Notes.

1841 Link, Arthur S. "The Baltimore Convention of 1912." In Arthur S. Link. *The Higher Realism of Woodrow Wilson and Other Essays*. Nashville: Vanderbilt University Press, 1971, pp. 216–42.

Factional politics almost wrecked the Wilson candidacy in early 1912. Going into the convention as an underdog, Wilson won the nomination on the forty-sixth ballot. Without the support of politicians and bosses, whom Wilson hated, he would not have won. Notes.

1842 ———. "Democratic Politics and the Presidential Campaign of 1912 in Tennessee." In Arthur S. Link. *The Higher Realism of Woodrow Wilson and Other Essays*. Nashville: Vanderbilt University Press, 1971, pp. 172–99.

Democratic party politics in Tennessee were in a state of chaos in the years before 1912. Independents carried the day for Wilson in the presidential election, giving him a majority of votes and electing a Republican governor. Notes.

1843 ———. "The Negro as a Factor in the Campaign of 1912." In Arthur S. Link. *The Higher Realism of Woodrow Wilson and Other Essays*. Nashville: Vanderbilt University Press, 1971, pp. 256–71.

Wilson's managers were concerned enough about their candidate winning the presidential election to make a bid for black support in the North, although Wilson was careful not to make hard promises. Most blacks probably voted for Taft. Notes.

1844 ———. "Theodore Roosevelt and the South in 1912." In Arthur S. Link. *The Higher Realism of Woodrow Wilson and Other Essays*. Nashville: Vanderbilt University Press, 1971, pp. 243–55.

Roosevelt hoped to gain the presidency on a third-party ticket by winning the solidly Democratic South. But southern liberals preferred Wilson, seeing him as a true Progressive and Roosevelt as a demagogue. Southern conservatives regarded Wilson as more of a moderate than Roosevelt. Notes.

1845 ———. "The Underwood Presidential Movement of 1912." In Arthur S. Link. *The Higher Realism of Woodrow Wilson and Other Essays*. Nashville: Vanderbilt University Press, 1971, pp. 200–215.

A Jeffersonian Democrat, Oscar Underwood was the first southerner living in the South to be an active candidate for the Democratic presidential nomination. Wilson's managers were able to negotiate an alliance with Underwood which prevented Champ Clark from winning. Notes.

1846 ———. "The Wilson Movement in Texas, 1910–1912." In Arthur S. Link. *The Higher Realism of Woodrow Wilson and Other Essays*. Nashville: Vanderbilt University Press, 1971, pp. 155–71.

In the face of a conservative reaction in Texas, Progressives looked in 1910 to Wilson for leadership. Within two years Wilson men had taken control of the Democratic party, a sweeping victory which saved Wilson's national candidacy. Notes.

1847 Linkugel, Wil A., and Sellen, Robert W. "The Presidential Candidate in Behalf of Himself." *South Atlantic Quarterly* 75 (1976): 290–311.

From the first presidential election until Wilson's victory in 1912, parties and issues rather than personalities were the substance of campaigns. The growing importance of electronic media contributed to the shift.

1848 Lyons, Maurice F. *William F. McCombs: The President Maker.* Cincinnati: Bancroft, 1922.

This brief account explains McCombs's controversial role in winning the 1912 Democratic nomination for Woodrow Wilson. Illustrations.

1849 McCombs, William F. *Making Woodrow Wilson President.* Edited by Louis J. Lang. New York: Fairview, 1921.

In this fragmentary draft penned by McCombs just before his death, he denies that his break with Woodrow Wilson came over unauthorized promises to delegates. He claims that poverty prevented him from taking party and administration posts following the 1912 election. Photographs.

1850 McInery, Thomas J. "The Election of 1912 in New York State." Ph.D. dissertation, University of Denver, 1977.

New York state politics during the 1912 presidential election are examined in depth from the perspectives of national candidates Wilson, Taft, and Roosevelt, as well as those of the Democratic and Republican state bosses. DAI 38:4330-A.

1851 McWilliams, Tennant S. *Harris Taylor: The New Southerner as an American.* University: University of Alabama Press, 1978.

A Republican attorney, diplomat, and writer, Taylor supported Wilson in 1912 as a southerner and a Progressive. The president regarded Taylor as a plagiarist and as far too excitable for a diplomatic appointment. Notes, bibliography, index.

1852 Margulies, Herbert F. "La Follette, Roosevelt and the Republican Nomination of 1912." *Mid-America* 58 (1976): 54–76.

Robert La Follette had his eye on becoming the 1912 Republican presidential candidate long before Theodore Roosevelt re-entered the fray. Enraged by the Roosevelt bandwagon, La Follette accused the former president of perfidy. He hoped that Wilson would defeat Taft and Roosevelt so that he might lead the GOP. Notes.

1853 Moody, Eric N. "Nevada's Bull Moose Progressives: The Formation and Function of a State Political Party in 1912." *Nevada Historical Quarterly* 16 (1973): 157–79.

Ambition rather than principle was the prime motive for leaders of the Nevada Bull Moose movement in 1912.

1854 Morgan, H. Wayne. "Eugene Debs and the Socialist Campaign of 1912." *Mid-America* 39 (1957): 210–26.

The Socialist party made a respectable showing in the 1912 presidential election because of the personal popularity of Eugene V. Debs, and because the party understood how to appeal to a significant portion of the electorate. Notes.

1855 Mugleston, William F. "The 1912 Progressive Campaign in Georgia." *Georgia Historical Quarterly* 61 (1977): 233–45.

Georgians, like others south of the Mason-Dixon Line, mistrusted Roosevelt on the race issue and embraced Wilson as a fellow southerner. Notes.

1856 Parker, James R. "Beveridge and the Election of 1912: Progressive Idealist or Political Realist?" *Indiana Magazine of History* 63 (1967): 103–14.

Albert Beveridge broke with Taft and the regular Republicans in 1912, not out of Progressive idealism so much as for realistic political considerations. Notes.

1857 Pike, Albert H., Jr. "Jonathan Bourne, Jr., Progressive." Ph.D. dissertation, University of Oregon, 1957.

A faithful advocate of popular government and sometime senator from Oregon, Bourne supported Roosevelt in the 1912 election. DAI 17:2585.

1858 Pinchot, Amos R. E. *History of the Progressive Party, 1912–1916.* Edited by Helene M. Hooker. New York: New York University Press, 1958.

A Progressive party organizer discusses the personalities, ideas, and fate of the movement. Notes, appendix, bibliography, index.

1859 Pitkin, William A. "Issues in the Roosevelt-Taft Contest of 1912." *Mid-America* 34 (1952): 219–32.

After Roosevelt and his supporters walked out of the Republican party, there were few Progressives left in it, but the debate over reforms led to the expanded use of government to insure social justice.

1860 Potts, E. Daniel. "The Progressive Profile in Iowa." *Mid-America* 47 (1965): 257–68.

Progressives were younger and had less political experience than did conservatives in Iowa, but they were alike in other ways. Having captured control of the state Republican party, Progressives turned their backs on Roosevelt's candidacy. Notes.

1861 Rorvig, Paul. "Clash of the Giants: The 1912 Presidential Election." *American History Illustrated* 14 (1979): 12–15ff.

An overview is presented of this three-cornered election campaign featuring Wilson, Roosevelt, and Taft.

1862 Sarasohn, David. "The Democratic Surge, 1905–1912: Forging a Progressive Majority." Ph.D. dissertation, University of California, Los Angeles, 1976.

The Democratic party majority in the House put together a Progressive program which foreshadowed Wilson's New Freedom. The Roosevelt-Taft split did not elect Wilson; rather, he would have been elected anyway, since the party had made steady inroads during the early Progressive era. DAI 37:7274-A.

1863 Schambra, William A. "Elihu Root, the Constitution, and the Election of 1912." Ph.D. dissertation, Northern Illinois University, 1983.

Theodore Roosevelt's ideas for radical constitutional reforms cost him the support of Elihu Root during the 1912 election campaign. Root helped to deliver the Republican nomination to Taft, thus preserving the Constitution. DAI 45:1514-A.

1864 Scott, Robert C. "William McCombs and the 1912 Democratic Presidential Nomination of Woodrow Wilson." *Arkansas Historical Quarterly* 44 (1985): 246–59.

McCombs, who met Wilson while attending Princeton in the 1890s, ran his presidential campaign in 1912. Notes.

1865 Sparlin, Estal E. "Bryan and the 1912 Democratic Convention." *Mississippi Valley Historical Review* 22 (1936): 537–46.

When Bryan developed doubts about the Progressivism of Champ Clark, he switched his support to Woodrow Wilson.

1866 Steelman, Joseph F. "Richmond Pearson, Roosevelt Republicans, and the Campaign of 1912 in North Carolina." *North Carolina Historical Review* 43 (1966): 122–39.

Leader of the Roosevelt forces in North Carolina, Pearson was among the founders of the Progressive party. Like other southern Republicans, Pearson supported Roosevelt in spite of the New Nationalism, not because of it. Notes.

1867 Tobin, Richard L. "The Incredible Election of 1912." *Mankind* 1 (1968): 28–31ff.

The three-cornered race between Taft, Roosevelt, and Wilson is given a popular treatment.

1868 Trattner, Walter I. "Theodore Roosevelt, Social Workers, and the Election of 1912: A Note." *Mid-America* 50 (1968): 64–69.

Correspondence between two prominent social workers illustrates the decidedly mixed feelings held by the social work community toward Roosevelt. Notes.

1869 Walker, Don D. "The Taft Victory in Utah in 1912." *Utah Historical Quarterly* 32 (1964): 44–56.

Newspapers are used to document the three-cornered presidential race in which Taft triumphed—at least in Utah. Notes.

1870 Warner, Robert M. "Chase S. Osborn and the Presidential Campaign of 1912." *Mississippi Valley Historical Review* 46 (1959): 19–45.

Osborn, the Republican governor of Michigan, backed Roosevelt's bid for the presidential nomination, then switched to Wilson, only to end up campaigning for Roosevelt. Notes.

1871 Wilensky, Norman N. *Conservatives in the Progressive Era: The Taft Republicans of 1912.* Gainesville: University of Florida Press, 1965.

President Taft fought back hard against Roosevelt's attempt to take control of the Republican party machinery. The party split between conservatives and Progressives, primarily over ideological differences. Notes.

1916

See also Chapter 2, *Wilson Presidency,* and Chapter 3, *Charles Evans Hughes.*

1872 Brandon, Betty J. "A Wilsonian Progressive—Alexander Jeffrey McKelway." *Journal of Presbyterian History* 48 (1970): 2–17.

McKelway strongly supported Wilson's bid for reelection as did women, who could vote in western states. The president's promises of peace, prosperity, and further reforms rallied to his side those, like McKelway, who were interested in social justice. Notes.

1873 Claussen, E. Neal. " 'He Kept Us Out of War': Martin H. Glynn's Keynote." *Quarterly Journal of Speech* 52 (1966): 23–32.

Glynn was chairman and keynote speaker of the 1916 Democratic national convention. His address expressed a strong desire for continued neutrality toward the European war. His phrase "but we didn't go to war" became "he kept us out of war," a slogan which struck a popular chord with the electorate. Notes.

1874 Cuddy, Edward. "Irish-Americans and the 1916 Election: An Episode in Immigrant Adjustment." *American Quarterly* 21 (1969): 228–43.

Most Irish Americans remained loyal to Wilson in the 1916 election, although the president had given support to anticlerical forces in Mexico and remained on good terms with Britain. Wilson's many Irish political appointments, organized labor's support for his reelection, and the Catholic church's neutrality all help to explain Irish loyalty. Notes.

1875 Cuddy, Joseph E. "Irish-America and National Isolationism: 1914–1920." Ph.D. dissertation, State University of New York, Buffalo, 1965.

Irish Americans supported any U.S. foreign policy that would aid Ireland's quest for independence. Although they applauded Wilson's Fourteen Points, they were disappointed that the final treaty neglected the Irish question, and they rejected the League on similar grounds. The author emphasized that Irish Americans advocate anti-British internationalism as distinct from the administration's pro-British internationalism. DAI 26:5991.

1876 Currie, Harold W. "Allan L. Benson, Salesman of Socialism, 1902–1916." *Labor History* 11 (1970): 285–303.

As the Socialist party's presidential candidate in 1916, the little-known Benson's activities are surveyed. Benson was a moderate who advocated evolutionary socialism and pacifism. Notes.

1877 Eiselen, Malcolm R. "The Day That California Changed World History." *Pacific Historian* 10 (1966): 49–57.

Wilson retired on election night, 1916, convinced that he had lost to Charles Evans Hughes, but late returns from California reelected him president. The blunders that led to Hughes's defeat in California are detailed.

1878 Garraty, John A., ed. "T.R. on the Telephone." *American Heritage* 9 (1957): 99–108.

This edited transcript of telephone calls made by Roosevelt in early June 1916 reveals his keen interest in becoming either the Republican or the Progressive party nominee for president.

1879 Grant, Philip A., Jr. "William Jennings Bryan and the Presidential Election of 1916." *Nebraska History* 63 (1982): 531–42.

In spite of his resignation as secretary of state, Bryan worked hard for Wilson's reelection in 1916, an effort which proved to be especially effective in the Midwest.

1880 Havig, Alan R. "The Raymond Robins Case for Progressive Republicanism." *Journal of the Illinois State Historical Society* 64 (1971): 401–18.

During the tight 1916 campaign, both major parties wooed Progressives such as Robins, who had chaired the national convention. Robins eventually leaned toward Republican Charles Evans Hughes. Notes.

1881 ———. "Restive Haven for Progressives: Both Parties." *Review of Politics* 34 (1972): 223–34.

Roosevelt's Bull Moose party was a haven for Progressives of both parties until 1916, when men such as Edward P. Costigan rejoined the Democrats and others such as Raymond Robins chose the Republicans. Notes.

1882 Kerr, Thomas J., IV. "German-Americans and Neutrality in the 1916 Election." *Mid-America* 43 (1961): 95–105.

German efforts on behalf of the Central Powers during the 1916 election campaign backfired, discrediting German Americans and further alienating the Wilson administration from Germany. Notes.

1883 Leary, William M., Jr. "Woodrow Wilson, Irish Americans, and the Election of 1916." *Journal of American History* 54 (1967): 54–72.

Americans of Irish descent found much to dislike in Wilson, including his pro-British policies, his stance on the Roger Casement question, and his actions toward Mexico. But Wilson received more votes in the Irish wards of many big cities than did any other Democratic candidate between 1904 and 1924 owing, the author believes, to the president's Progressivism. Notes.

1884 Levi, Steven C. "The Most Expensive Meal in American History." *Journal of the West* 18 (1979): 62–73.

While campaigning for the presidency in California in August 1916, Republican candidate Charles Evans Hughes went to a banquet at an antiunion restaurant. This act alienated organized labor, which failed to support him at the polls in the state where the election was lost. Notes.

1885 Lichtman, Allan J. "Critical Election Theory and the Reality of American Presidential Politics, 1916–40." *American Historical Review* 81 (1976): 317–51.

Using models of electoral stability and change, the author analyzes voter alignments between 1916 and 1940 in all counties outside of the Confederate South. Notes.

1886 Lovell, S. D. *The Presidential Election of 1916*. Carbondale: Southern Illinois University Press, 1980.

Wilson's reelection in 1916 was a personal victory, since it was the president who decided on the strategy of appealing to Progressives and independents. He ran well ahead of most other Democrats on the ticket. Notes, bibliography, index.

1887 Meyer, Jonah N. "The Presidential Election of 1916 in the Middle West." Ph.D. dissertation, Princeton University, 1966.

Midwest sentiment ran strongly against involvement in the European war and in favor of Progressivism. Wilson was able to stand on his record of reforms and nonintervention in the 1916 election, while Hughes ran a largely negative campaign. The reactions and voting records of various groups of Midwesterners are analyzed. DAI 27:168-A.

1888 Olin, Spencer C., Jr. "Hiram Johnson, the California Progressives, and the Hughes Campaign of 1916." *Pacific Historical Review* 31 (1962): 403–12.

Johnson and his Progressive followers did not work hard for the Hughes campaign and did not protest when Wilson's camp charged that the Republican nominee was a machine politician. Notes.

1889 Prasad, Y. D. "The German-Americans and the Election of 1916." *Indian Journal of American Studies* [India] 11 (1981): 49–57.

German Americans took a drubbing at the polls in 1916. Their defense of themselves and of all things German was too shrill for many to bear, Wilson's condemnation of hyphenate Americans was effective, and Republicans did not woo the German Americans as they might have done. Notes.

1890 Roberts, George C. "Woodrow Wilson, John W. Kern and the 1916 Indiana Election: Defeat of a Senate Majority Leader." *Presidential Studies Quarterly* 10 (1980): 63–73.

Although Senate Majority Leader John W. Kern loyally supported the president's legislative agenda, he lost his bid for reelection in 1916. Notes.

1891 Sarasohn, David. "The Election of 1916: Realigning the Rockies." *Western Historical Quarterly* 11 (1980): 285–305.

Wilson's victory in the eight Rocky Mountain states in 1916 was not the result, as is often thought, of special circumstances, but rather of a fundamental political realignment in a region which continued to vote Democratic for years. Notes.

1892 Thomas, Phyllis H. "The Role of Mississippi in the Presidential Election of 1916." *Southern Quarterly* 4 (1966): 207–26.

In 1916 only Senator James K. Vardaman among the leaders of Mississippi's Democratic party opposed Wilson's renomination. In the November election, the president received over 90 percent of the vote. Notes.
d14

1893 White, G. Edward. "The Social Values of the Progressives: Some New Perspectives." *South Atlantic Quarterly* 70 (1971): 62–76.

Any movement as complex as the Progressive coalition is difficult to analyze, but certain social values can be identified: its peculiar notion of progress, righteous moralism, elitism, and belief in Anglo-Saxon superiority. Notes.

1920

See also Chapter 2, *Wilson Presidency*, and Chapter 12, *Paris Peace Conference*, especially *Public Opinion and the Press* and *Ratification Controversy*.

1894 Anderson, Fenwick. "Hail to the Editor-in-Chief: Cox vs. Harding, 1920." *Journalism History* 1 (1974): 46–49.

In 1920 both the Democratic and Republican presidential nominees were journalists. Neither of their old newspapers shied away from highly partisan coverage of the political campaign.

1895 Bagby, Wesley M. *The Road to Normalcy: The Presidential Campaign and Election of 1920.* Baltimore, MD: Johns Hopkins University Press, 1962.

There was little evidence of the once-dominant Progressive movement during the 1920 election campaign. In the wake of war, the Red Scare, strikes, and renewed militarism, the New Freedom seemed only a distant memory. Notes, index.

1896 ———. "The 'Smoke Filled Room' and the Nomination of Warren G. Harding." *Mississippi Valley Historical Review* 41 (1955): 657–74.

Harding's candidacy was not hatched in a smoke-filled room at the Blackstone Hotel in Chicago in 1920. There was little contact or combination among the forces working for his nomination, which came about largely because of his popularity among the delegates. Notes.

1897 ———. "Woodrow Wilson, a Third Term, and the Solemn Referendum." *American Historical Review* 60 (1955): 567–75.

Wilson rendered his supporters impotent at the 1920 Democratic convention by refusing to withdraw his name from consideration. Notes.

1898 Burchell, R. A. "Did the Irish and German Voters Desert the Democrats in 1920? A Tentative Answer." *Journal of American Studies* [Great Britain] 6 (1972): 153–64.

The answer is yes, based on a close study of the political behavior of these two key ethnic groups in the Democratic party. Republicans gained votes on various local issues and because of the postwar economic downturn, which voters blamed on the policies of Wilson. Notes.

1899 Cebula, James E. *James M. Cox, Journalist and Politician.* New York: Garland, 1975.

The wartime governor of Ohio captured the 1920 Democratic presidential nomination by forging a coalition of urban reformers, southerners, and internationalists. Notes, bibliography, index.

1900 Cinclair, Richard J. "Will H. Hays: Republican Politician." Ph.D. dissertation, Ball State University, 1969.

Will Hays took over the Republican party at a low ebb in its fortunes, in early 1918, after successfully uniting the Indiana GOP. Deeply patriotic and a smooth political operator, Hays played an important part in his party's success in the 1918 and 1920 elections. DAI 30:3876-A.

1901 Downes, Randolph C. "Negro Rights and White Backlash in the Campaign of 1920." *Ohio History* 75 (1966): 85–107.

Angling for northern black votes, Harding courted moderate black leaders and endorsed antilynching legislation. In Oklahoma, he argued against using force to attain equality, a strategy designed to please whites. Notes.

1902 ———, ed. "Some Correspondence between Warren G. Harding and William Allen White during the Presidential Campaign of 1920." *Northwest Ohio Quarterly* 37 (1965): 121–32.

Nine letters sent between newspaper editor William Allen White and Harding are reprinted, revealing that while both men were equally conservative White had many reservations about the GOP nominee.

1903 Giglio, James N. "The Political Career of Harry M. Daugherty." Ph.D. dissertation, Ohio State University, 1968.

An active Republican from 1881 until 1924, Harry Daugherty is remembered for supporting Harding in the 1920 presidential campaign. However, the relationship between the two men was not close. DAI 29:3071-A.

1904 Hachey, Thomas E., ed. "Confidential Dispatch to the British Foreign Office: A Journalist's Analysis of American Politics in 1920." *Wisconsin Magazine of History* 53 (1969): 121–27.

Journalist Sir Arthur Willert wrote confidentially to the British Foreign Office, analyzing the often baffling twists and turns in the 1920 election campaign.

1905 Margulies, Herbert F. "Irvine L. Lenroot and the Republican Vice-Presidential Nomination of 1920." *Wisconsin Magazine of History* 61 (1977): 21–31.

The Wisconsin Progressive was offered the second spot on the Harding ticket twice before the convention nominated Calvin Coolidge. If Harding had made the offers public, the delegates would probably have endorsed the move. Notes.

1906 Mazza, David L. "Homer S. Cummings and Progressive Politics from Bryan through Wilson, 1896–1925." Ph.D. dissertation, St. John's University, 1978.

Acting chairman of the Democratic national committee during the 1918 elections, Cummings became a confidant of Wilson during the president's last years. His political power peaked during the 1920 election. DAI 39:4449-A.

1907 Merritt, Richard L. "Woodrow Wilson and the 'Great and Solemn Referendum,' 1920." *Review of Politics* 27 (1965): 78–104.

Determined to turn the 1920 presidential campaign into an idealistic referendum on the Treaty of Versailles, Wilson turned the election instead into a final signal of his failure. Notes.

1908 Murray, Lawrence L. "General John J. Pershing's Bid for the Presidency in 1920." *Nebraska History* 53 (1972): 217–52.

Pershing had some support for his bid to become the GOP standard-bearer in 1920, but his almost-total political ineptitude quickly ended the campaign.

1909 Rhoads, James B. "The Campaign of the Socialist Party in the Election of 1920." Ph.D. dissertation, American University, 1965.

Even though he was in prison for violating the Espionage Act, Eugene Debs was the Socialist party's 1920 presidential candidate. Militant enough to please the party's left wing, if not the Communists, he was willing to campaign on the moderate platform that had carried the convention. He was a sympathetic figure, and the party's stand on many issues had broad appeal, but nonsocialists were unwilling to vote for a candidate with such drastic underlying conflicts with American society. DAI 26:1619.

1910 Rhodes, Benjamin D. "Harding v. Cox: The 'Ohio' Election of 1920 as Viewed from the British Embassy at Washington." *Northwest Ohio Quarterly* 55 (1982): 17–24.

British analysis of the 1920 election campaign is highlighted.

1911 Shapiro, Stanley. " 'Hand and Brain': The Farmer-Labor Party of 1920." *Labor History* 26 (1985): 405–22.

The formation of the Labor party is discussed along with its attempt to unite with farmers under the banner of Robert La Follette during the 1920 election. Notes.

1912 Swanson, Jeffrey L. "That Smoke-Filled Room: A Utahn's Role in the 1920 GOP Convention." *Utah Historical Quarterly* 45 (1977): 369–79.

Senator Reed Smoot of Utah played a key role at the 1920 GOP convention, pushing Elihu Root's compromise on the League of Nation's platform plank as well as supporting the nomination of Harding at the famed "smoke-filled room" meeting of insiders. Notes.

1913 Ward, Robert D., and Brogdan, Frederick W. "The Revolt against Wilson: Southern Leadership and the Democratic Caucus of 1920." *Alabama Historical Quarterly* 38 (1976): 144–57.

Many southerners revolted against Wilson over the issues of continuing universal military training and keeping a large standing army. Notes.

1914 Williams, Brian. "Petticoats in Politics: Cincinnati Women and the 1920 Election." *Cincinnati Historical Society Bulletin* 35 (1977): 43–70.

Despite an extensive organizational framework, Cincinnati women voted as individuals and had no particular impact on the 1920 election.

Peace Groups

See also Chapter 12, *Paris Peace Conference, General Accounts, League of Nations, Public Opinion and the Press,* and *Ratification Controversy.*

1915 Chatfield, Charles. "World War I and the Liberal Pacifist in the United States." *American Historical Review* 75 (1970): 1920–37.

The war radicalized liberal pacifists, making them more interested in politics and aggressive activism. Notes.

1916 Craig, John M. "Lucia True Ames Mead: American Publicist for Peace and Internationalism." Ph.D. dissertation, College of William and Mary, 1986.

Mead was a leading publicist in the American peace movement during the Progressive era. In a male-dominated movement, she was one of the few women who worked to organize at the grass-roots level. DAI 47:3541-A.

1917 DeBenedetti, Charles. *Origins of the Modern American Peace Movement, 1915–1929.* Millwood, NY: KTO, 1978.

The establishment of the League to Enforce Peace marked the beginning of the modern peace movement. Conservatives emphasized the need for international law, while liberals advocated an international political organization. Notes, bibliography, index.

1918 Filene, Peter G. "The World Peace Foundation and Progressivism: 1910–1918." *New England Quarterly* 36 (1963): 478–501.

The World Peace Foundation was typical of the American peace movement in its ideology and tactics. Notes.

1919 Hershey, Burnet. *The Odyssey of Henry Ford and the Great Peace Ship.* New York: Taplinger, 1967.

Hershey was a young journalist who covered Ford's peace mission on the *Oscar II*. He found it to be "a foolish pilgrimage" exposed by newsmen with cruelty and levity. Bibliography, index.

1920 Holtzclaw, Harold W. "The American War Referendum Movement, 1914–1941." Ph.D. dissertation, University of Denver, 1965.

Introduced to Congress in 1914, the war referendum would have required voter approval before war could be declared. Robert La Follette and William Jennings Bryan supported the referendum, which gained more attention as the United States entered World War I. However, the war referendum movement's greatest battles occurred in the years before World War II. DAI 26:3281.

1921 Kraft, Barbara S. "Peacemaking in the Progressive Era: A Prestigious and Proper Calling." *Maryland Historian* 1 (1970): 121–44.

Hundreds of organizations dedicated to world peace were active during the Progressive era. The spirit of these movements was reflected in America's idealistic war aims of 1917–18. Notes.

1922 Marchand, C. Roland. *The American Peace Movement and Social Reform, 1898–1918.* Princeton: Princeton University Press, 1973.

The war transformed the peace movement from an amalgam of elitist groups seeking stability into a radical coalition of reformers demanding basic changes in American foreign policy. Notes, bibliography, index.

1923 Martin, James P. "The American Peace Movement and the Progressive Era, 1910–1917." Ph.D. dissertation, Rice University, 1975.

The American peace movement shared many traits with the Progressives: optimism, interest in efficiency, belief in education, and faith in the American mission. Peace groups fought against the rising tide of militarism during the period of American neutrality until the war declaration, when most of them disappeared. DAI 36:2369-A.

1924 Patterson, David S. "Woodrow Wilson and the Mediation Movement, 1914–1917." *Historian* 33 (1971): 535–56.

Many pacifist and Progressive groups and individuals lobbied President Wilson to get him to mediate an end to the European war. Those who advocated such an effort showed a mixture of pragmatism and idealism in their thinking. Notes.

1925 Tuttle, Peter G. "The Ford Peace Ship: Volunteer Diplomacy in the Twentieth Century." Ph.D. dissertation, Yale University, 1958.

While Wilson was not interested in a plan put forward by the International Conference of Women for a peace conference, Henry Ford chartered a ship to take an American delegation to Europe. DAI 30:4928-A.

Preparedness

See also Chapter 11, *Mobilization.*

1926 Clifford, John Garry. *The Citizen Soldiers: The Plattsburg Training Camp Movement, 1913–1920.* Lexington: University Press of Kentucky, 1972.

War anxiety led to the creation of the Plattsburg, New York, training camp movement, a joint civilian-military project to train a citizen army. The young officer corps trained at these camps helped to smooth the way for wartime mobilization. Notes, bibliography, index.

1927 Cuff, Robert D. "Samuel Gompers, Leonard Wood and Military Preparedness." *Labor History* 12 (1971): 280–88.

An exchange of letters between labor leader Gompers and General Wood in 1915 reveal the AFL president's concern that the upper crust was dominating the preparedness summer training camp movement.

1928   Edwards, John C. *Patriots in Pinstripe: Men of the National Security League.* Washington, DC: University Press of America, 1982.

The motivations and activities of the leaders of the National Security League are detailed. These "warrior aristocrats" organized for military preparedness and to fight against social disintegration. Photographs, appendix, notes, bibliography, index.

1929   ———. "Playing the Patriot Game: The Story of the American Defense Society." *Studies in History and Society* 1 (1976): 54–72.

The American Defense Society was an organization composed primarily of Republicans who pushed hard for preparedness for the world war. Despite financial irregularities, the society prospered in its campaign for militarism along with an offshoot group, the Vigilantes. Notes.

1930   Finnegan, John P. *Against the Specter of a Dragon: The Campaign for American Military Preparedness, 1914–1918.* Westport, CT: Greenwood, 1975.

The preparedness movement successfully created the necessary preconditions for a full-scale war effort. Notes, bibliography, index.

1931   Herring, George C., Jr. "James Hay and the Preparedness Controversy, 1915–1916." *Journal of Southern History* 30 (1964): 383–404.

Virginia Congressman James Hay, chairman of the House Military Affairs Committee, found himself the target of strong criticism for opposing all-out preparedness. When it appeared that Wilson was losing badly on the issue, Hay came up with a successful compromise. Notes.

1932   Larson, Simeon. "The American Federation of Labor and the Preparedness Controversy." *Historian* 37 (1974): 67–81.

Samuel Gompers, president of the AFL, supported Wilson's preparedness program, but many in his union did not. Neither Gompers nor the government could budge them—until America entered the war in 1917. Notes.

1933   O'Hanlon, Timothy P. "School Sports as Social Training: The Case of Athletics and the Crisis of World War I." *Journal of Sport History* 9 (1982): 5–29.

As part of the preparedness campaign several states, among them New York and Wyoming, adopted programs for youngsters of physical fitness with a military flavor. Notes.

1934   Pearlman, Michael D. *To Make Democracy Safe for America: Patricians and Preparedness in the Progressive Era.* Urbana: University of Illinois Press, 1984.

Advocates of military preparedness hoped that the effort to get ready for war would also discipline each individual into a new sense of community, a goal which the Progressives had failed to attain by other means. Photographs, appendix, notes, bibliography, index.

1935   Scott, James B. *Robert Bacon: Life and Letters.* Garden City, NY: Doubleday, 1923.

The author presents a series of excerpts from the letters of Robert Bacon, president of the preparedness-minded National Security League, aide to General John J. Pershing, and protégé of Elihu Root.

1936   Sutton, Walter A. "Republican Progressive Senators and Preparedness, 1915–1916." *Mid-America* 52 (1970): 155–76.

Republican Progressive senators divided into two camps on the preparedness issue: a group headed by Robert La Follette, who opposed it on idealistic grounds, and those such as Miles Poindexter, who supported it out of patriotism. Most members of both groups shared a loathing for capitalists who stood to grow rich from the manufacture of instruments of death. Notes.

Public Opinion and the Press

1937   Baker, Ray Stannard. *American Chronicle.* New York: Scribner's, 1945.

The muckraking journalist and Wilson biographer chronicles his own life story, including his close friendship with the president and his observations on the Paris Peace Conference. Index.

1938   Bannister, Robert C., Jr. *Ray Stannard Baker: The Mind and Thought of a Progressive.* New Haven, CT: Yale University Press, 1966.

Like many Progressives, Baker was an imperialist who suffered from status anxiety. His works published under the name "David Grayson" illuminate his world view. Photographs, notes, bibliography, index.

1939 Blanchard, Margaret A. "The Fifth-Amendment Privilege of Newsman George Burdick." *Journalism Quarterly* 55 (1978): 39–46.

In 1914 journalist George Burdick declined to reveal to a grand jury his source for a series of articles on the improprieties of a Wilson customs appointee. After Burdick declined a presidential pardon designed to loosen his tongue, the Supreme Court overturned a lower court's ruling that such a pardon could not be refused. Notes.

1940 Boller, Paul F., Jr. "Purlings and Platitudes: Mencken's Americana." *Southwest Review* 50 (1965): 357–71.

Critic H. L. Mencken's opinions on such diverse subjects as blacks, the Eighteenth Amendment, and religion are gleaned from his columns that ran during the Wilson administration.

1941 Brown, Michael Gary. "All, All Alone: The Hebrew Press in America from 1914 to 1924." *American Jewish Historical Quarterly* 59 (1969): 139–78.

The World War I era helped Jewish-American communities to mature, because they had to provide for their own development. Of forty-two newspapers, three are singled out for their outstanding contributions to Jewish life. Notes.

1942 Campbell, Gregg M. "Walter Lippmann: An Intellectual and Biographical Analysis of *A Preface to Politics*." Ph.D. dissertation, University of Minnesota, 1967.

Lippmann's original goal of becoming an art critic changed to becoming a social critic during his Harvard years. His interest in socialism was grounded in humanitarianism. *A Preface to Politics* argued for political reform through cultural reform. DAI 30:5370-A.

1943 Candela, Joseph L., Jr. "Concern for Family Stability in American Opinion, 1880–1920." Ph.D. dissertation, University of Chicago, 1978.

Americans were well aware of the many pressures that threatened family stability. Reformers could not agree on an agenda to preserve the family, though, since either individualism or social order would have to be sacrificed. DAI 39:425-A.

1944 Card, James. "When Newsreels Stood Still." *American Heritage* 36 (1985): 48–53.

During the Progressive era, glass lantern slides were used to present current events at moving picture shows. A recently discovered set of such slides from 1912 is reproduced.

1945 Chalmers, David. "Ray Stannard Baker's Search for Reform." *Journal of the History of Ideas* 19 (1958): 422–34.

From 1900 to 1912 Baker's ideas were in a state of flux as he flitted from individualism to socialism to Christian collectivism. While he admired Theodore Roosevelt, Baker came to see Woodrow Wilson as his idol. Notes.

1946 Cobb, Lawrence W. "Patriotic Themes in American National Magazine Advertising, 1898–1945." Ph.D. dissertation, Emory University, 1978.

Advertisers used patriotic themes to sell products throughout this period, especially during wars. During World War I, advertisers emphasized preserving and spreading democracy through industrial organization. DAI 39:4443-A.

1947 Cornuelle, R. C., ed. "Remembrance of *The Times*: From the Papers of Garet Garrett." *American Scholar* 36 (1967): 429–45.

Excerpts from the diary of a journalist and editor include vignettes of *New York Times* publisher Adolph S. Ochs and reactions to tragedies at sea in 1915–16.

1948 Culley, Margaret. "Dorothy Dix: The Thirteenth Juror." *International Journal of Women's Studies* [Canada] 2 (1979): 349–57.

During the Progressive era, Dix gained notoriety for reporting on criminal cases that involved women.

1949 Ervin, Charles W. *Homegrown Liberal: The Autobiography of Charles W. Ervin*. Edited by Jean Gould. New York: Dodd, Mead, 1954.

A socialist journalist, Ervin discusses his stint as editor of the *New York Call* during World War I. Index.

1950 Fanning, Charles. "Mr. Dooley in Chicago: Finley Peter Dunne as Historian of the Irish in America." In David N. Doyle and Owen D. Edwards, eds. *America and Ireland, 1776–1976: The American Identity and the Irish Connection*. Westport, CT: Greenwood, 1980, pp. 151–64.

Finley Peter Dunne's much-loved alter ego, a Chicago bartender named Mr. Dooley, delivered amusing and incisive analysis of national politics in an Irish dialect throughout the Progressive era.

1951 Faulkner, Ronnie W. "Samuel A'Court Ashe: North Carolina Redeemer and Historian, 1840–1938." Ph.D. dissertation, University of South Carolina, 1983.

Ashe was an ardent Democrat who served on the Senate Finance Committee from 1908 to 1917. He devoted much of the latter part of his life to researching and writing about North Carolina history. DAI 45:918-A.

1952 Filler, Louis. "The Muckrakers: In Flower and in Failure." In Donald Sheehan and Harold C. Syrett, eds. *Essays in American Historiography: Papers Presented in Honor of Allan Nevins*. New York: Columbia University Press, 1960, pp. 251–70.

The muckrakers have been too harshly criticized, since they played a positive role in the battle against antidemocratic forces in the Progressive era.

1953 Fitzgerald, Richard A. "Radical Illustrators of *The Masses* and *Liberator*: A Study of the Conflict between Art and Politics." Ph.D. dissertation, University of California, Riverside, 1969.

The cartoons of Maurice Becker, K. R. Chamberlain, Robert Minor, John Sloan, and Art Young are analyzed. DAI 31:1725-A.

1954 Forcey, Charles. *The Crossroads of Liberalism: Croly, Weyl, Lippmann, and the Progressive Era, 1900–1925*. New York: Oxford University Press, 1961.

Three prominent political journalists associated with the *New Republic* shared an interest in the use of nationalism for the common good within the democratic system. Each saw the world war as the crossroads of liberalism. Notes, index.

1955 Geiger, Louis G. "Muckrakers—Then and Now." *Journalism Quarterly* 43 (1966): 469–76.

The muckrakers exhibited an innocent optimism that is difficult to understand today about the possibilities for people to solve their problems. This long-lost optimism is a necessary quality for successful reform movements.

1956 Givner, Joan. "Katherine Anne Porter, Journalist." *Southwest Review* 64 (1979): 309–22.

Porter had a brief career as a columnist and theater critic in Texas and Colorado during the Wilson years.

1957 Glasner, Philip D. "Pacific Northwest Press Reaction to Wilson's Mexican Diplomacy, 1913–1916." Ph.D. dissertation, University of Idaho, 1965.

Various journals indicate that the Pacific Northwest supported Wilson's early attempts to bring peace to Mexico but became increasingly hostile when he refused to take action against Victoriano Huerta or otherwise intervene. Expansionist sentiment was strong. The punitive expedition against Pancho Villa in 1916 and the looming European war finally stilled the criticism. Overall, the Pacific Northwest press viewed Wilson's Mexican policy as overly idealistic and vacillating. DAI 27:427-A.

1958 Graybar, Lloyd J. *Albert Shaw of the Review of Reviews: An Intellectual Biography*. Lexington: University Press of Kentucky, 1974.

Shaw was a key promoter of the expanded use of government proposed by Theodore Roosevelt's New Nationalism. Notes, bibliography, index.

1959 Harrison, John M. "Finley Peter Dunne and the Progressive Movement." *Journalism Quarterly* 44 (1967): 475–81.

While Dunne had much in common with the Progressives, including indignation over life's injustices, anger against the false values of the age, and sympathy for individuals victimized by civilization, he was too anarchist to be part of any movement. Notes.

1960 Johnson, Walter. *William Allen White's America*. New York: Holt, 1947.

One of the most famous newspaper editors of his day, White was an ardent Roosevelt Republican and Progressive. Notes, index.

1961 Kirkpatrick, Ivy E. "The Struggle for Industrial Democracy: Croly, Lippmann, and Weyl—1912–1917." Ph.D. dissertation, Texas Christian University, 1974.

The *New Republic* assumed leadership of the movement for industrial democracy after 1914, presenting radical proposals to middle-class Progressives. Herbert Croly, Walter Lippmann, and Walter Weyl supported Wilson in 1916, because the president pushed a prolabor agenda through Congress. DAI 35:2903-A.

1962 Knight, Oliver. "Scripps and His Adless Newspaper: *The Day Book.*" *Journalism Quarterly* 41 (1964): 51–64.

E. W. Scripps became convinced that the elimination of advertisements would lead to a truly free press, an idea he tried to demonstrate with an adless Chicago paper from 1911 to 1917. Notes.

1963 Koscher, William P. "The Springfield *Republican* in the Progressive Era: A Guardian of American Values." Ph.D. dissertation, University of Illinois, Urbana-Champaign, 1974.

A stable and responsible newspaper, the Springfield *Republican* reflected the reformism of patrician mugwumps, arguing for justice for the poor and against imperialism. DAI 35:7841-A.

1964 Krock, Arthur. *Memoirs: Sixty Years on the Firing Line.* New York: Funk and Wagnalls, 1968.

Krock remembers covering Wilson as governor of New Jersey, in the White House, and at the Paris Peace Conference. He concludes that Wilson was a "pragmatic radical." Appendix, index.

1965 Kuehl, Warren F. *Hamilton Holt: Journalist, Internationalist, Educator.* Gainesville: University of Florida Press, 1960.

The longtime publisher of *The Independent*, Hamilton Holt, used the magazine to support many Progressive causes, pacifism (and then preparedness), and Wilsonian internationalism. Photographs, notes, bibliography, index.

1966 Lewis, David L. "Henry Ford Meets the Press: An Encounter with the *Chicago Tribune.*" *Michigan History* 53 (1969): 275–91.

Ford's lawsuit against the *Tribune* resulted in a six-cent verdict in his favor and forever tarnished his image among educated people. The episode further embittered him toward the urban press. Notes.

1967 Littlefield, Roy E. "William Randolph Hearst: His Role in American Progressivism." Ph.D. dissertation, Catholic University of America, 1979.

Hearst used his newspaper empire to espouse Progressive reforms in the hope of capturing the movement. By the time Wilson became president, he realized that he had become too controversial to capture the White House himself, and so he concentrated his efforts on supporting other Progressives. DAI 40:4717-A.

1968 Lyon, Peter. *Success Story: The Life and Times of S. S. McClure.* Deland, FL: Everett, Edwards, 1967.

The life story of the muckraking writer and editor is presented by his grandson. Bibliography, index.

1969 Meredith, Howard L. "The Agrarian Reform Press in Oklahoma, 1889–1922." *Chronicles of Oklahoma* 50 (1971): 82–94.

Oklahoma's popular Socialist party had an active press which agitated for revolution and reform during the Progressive era. Notes.

1970 Noble, David W. "The *New Republic* and the Idea of Progress, 1914–1920." *Mississippi Valley Historical Review* 38 (1951): 387–402.

World War I stripped the liberals of the *New Republic* of the notion that mankind was progressing toward utopia. Notes.

1971 Older, Cara M. *William Randolph Hearst: America.* New York: D. Appleton-Century, 1936.

The wife of a California publisher paints a favorable portrait of Hearst as a publisher and a Progressive activist. Photographs, index.

1972 Palermo, Patrick F. *Lincoln Steffens.* Boston: Twayne, 1978.

Steffens was a great reporter who dug out stories to expose the corruption of his era. He was hardly objective, twisting the facts to influence his readership. Notes, bibliography, index.

1973 Reid-Bills, Mae. "Attitudes toward Public Opinion Held by Some Leaders of American Reform, 1880–1920." Ph.D. dissertation, University of Denver, 1977.

Reformers tended to become pessimistic about human nature after acquiring political experience, but most retained their faith in democracy as the best form of government yet devised. DAI 38:980-A.

1974 Rollins, Alfred B., Jr. "The Heart of Lincoln Steffens." *South Atlantic Quarterly* 59 (1960): 239–50.

Steffens was wildly inconsistent in his political philosophy as he wrestled with the "utopian equation." He blamed the system rather than the evildoers he exposed as a muckraking writer. Notes.

1975 Sarasohn, David. "Power without Glory: Hearst in the Progressive Era." *Journalism Quarterly* 53 (1976): 474–82.

Although powerful politically, Hearst never attained the leadership position he sought. Many politicians courted him, but he alienated as many as he made allies. Notes.

1976 Schultze, Quentin J. "Manufacturers' Views of National Consumer Advertising, 1910–1915." *Journalism Quarterly* 60 (1983): 10–15.

Manufacturers began to use national advertising to fight against competitors and wholesalers and to stabilize prices. Advertising helped many manufacturers, but the results were hardly spectacular. Notes.

1977 Seideman, David. *The New Republic: A Voice of Modern Liberalism.* New York: Praeger, 1986.

Created in 1914, the *New Republic* crusaded for social equality and national economic planning during the Wilson years, supporting most of Wilson's policies. Notes, bibliography, index.

1978 Semonche, John E. "The *American Magazine* of 1906–15: Principle vs. Profit." *Journalism Quarterly* 40 (1963): 36–44.

Founded by leading muckrakers following a break with S. S. McClure, the magazine ran many excellent articles but lost money. After the Crowell company bought out the magazine's founders, the muckraking stories were phased out. Notes.

1979 ———. *Ray Stannard Baker: A Quest for Democracy in Modern America, 1870–1918.* Chapel Hill: University of North Carolina Press, 1969.

Baker was a firm believer in democracy and in man's ability to correct injustices. In 1918 he turned from a successful career in journalism to the writing of history. Notes, bibliography, index.

1980 Seymour, Thaddeus, Jr. "A Progressive Partnership: Theodore Roosevelt and the Reform Press—Riis, Steffens, Baker, and White (Muckrakers)." Ph.D. dissertation, University of Wisconsin, 1985.

Once a Roosevelt disciple, muckraking journalist Ray Stannard Baker became an equally ardent supporter of Woodrow Wilson. DAI 46:3844-A.

1981 Shapiro, Herbert. "Steffens, Lippmann, and Reed: The Muckraker and His Protégés." *Pacific Northwest Quarterly* 62 (1971): 142–50.

Lincoln Steffens had a significant influence on Walter Lippmann and John Reed when the two were young, but, as each of them

matured, they grew apart from their mentor. Notes.

1982 Sheifer, Isobel C. "Ida M. Tarbell and Morality in Big Business: An Analysis of a Progressive Mind." Ph.D. dissertation, New York University, 1967.

Muckraker Ida M. Tarbell analyzed Progressive issues in terms of her own strong, Christian-democratic morality. DAI 28:4584-A.

1983 Sinclair, Upton. *Autobiography.* New York: Harcourt, Brace and World, 1962.

While concentrating on the private side of his life, Sinclair provides insights into the Progressive era and World War I. Index.

1984 Stark, John D. *Damned Upcountryman: William Watts Ball.* Durham, NC: Duke University Press, 1968.

An influential conservative South Carolina newspaper editor, Ball battled against women's suffrage and civil rights for blacks during the Wilson period. Notes, bibliography, index.

1985 Steel, Ronald. *Walter Lippmann and the American Century.* Boston: Little, Brown, 1980.

Lippmann's activities during the Wilson years are covered in this massive biography, including his initial enthusiasm for the "new diplomacy" and his subsequent disillusion. Photographs, notes, bibliography, index.

1986 Steffens, Joseph Lincoln. *The Autobiography of Lincoln Steffens.* New York: Harcourt, Brace, 1931.

A leading muckraker discusses the Progressive movement, World War I, the Bolshevik Revolution, and the Red Scare. Index.

1987 ———. *The Letters of Lincoln Steffens.* 2 vols. New York: Harcourt, Brace, 1938.

The first volume covers the Progressive era, World War I, and Steffens's radicalization. Index.

1988 Stein, Harry H. "Lincoln Steffens and the Mexican Revolution." *American Journal of Economics and Sociology* 34 (1975): 197–212.

The Mexican Revolution fascinated Steffens, and his writings, in turn, influenced many Progressives. Notes.

1989 Stockstill, Michael A. "Walter Lippmann: His Rise to Fame, 1899–1945." Ph.D. dissertation, Mississippi State University, 1970.

During the Progressive era, Lippmann was an activist influenced by socialism and pragmatism. Turning against socialism, he advised Theodore Roosevelt, found cultural interests in Greenwich Village, and helped to found the liberal *New Republic.* He switched his support to Woodrow Wilson, serving in the government and the military during the war. Disappointment with the Treaty of Versailles caused him to turn inward for a time. DAI 31:5340-A.

1990 Sullivan, Mark. *Our Times: 1900–1925.* 6 vols. New York: Scribner's, 1946.

A leading journalist looks back on the first quarter of the twentieth century in detail. Volumes IV and V cover the Wilson years.

1991 Swanberg, W. A. *Citizen Hearst.* New York: Scribner's, 1961.

William Randolph Hearst's publishing and political interests are detailed. Notes, appendix, bibliography, index.

1992 Tompkins, C. David. "Profile of a Progressive Editor." *Michigan History* 53 (1969): 144–57.

The editorials of Arthur Hendrick Vandenberg (*Grand Rapids Herald*) are studied to gain insights into the Progressive movement. Vandenberg was a moderate who became less interested in Progressive reforms following Wilson's election. His failure to understand the problems of urban America prevented him from seeing that many Progressive reforms could not work. Notes.

1993 Trattner, Walter I. "Progressivism on the International Scene: William Allen White and World War I." *Midwest Quarterly* 3 (1962): 133–47.

World War I had a profound impact on White, as he wrestled with the projection of his Progressivism onto the world scene. Notes.

1994 Villard, Oswald G. *Prophets True and False.* New York: Knopf, 1928.

The editor of *The Nation* presents journalistic portraits of public figures he observed including Wilson, Edward House, William Jennings Bryan, Robert Lansing, Henry Cabot Lodge, and others.

1995 Watterson, Henry. *Marse Henry: An Autobiography.* 2 vols. New York: Doran, 1919.

A southern publisher examines his involvement with Progressive reforms and discusses women and blacks of the era.

1996 White, William Allen. *Autobiography.* New York: Macmillan, 1946.

A newspaper editor and ardent follower of Theodore Roosevelt, White discusses the

Wilson administration, World War I, and the battle over the Treaty of Versailles. He finds that God gave Wilson a great vision, while the devil gave him an imperious heart. Photographs, index.

1997 Wreszin, Michael. *Oswald Garrison Villard: Pacifist at War.* Bloomington: University of Indiana Press, 1965.

A liberal publisher, Villard advocated Progressive reforms and fought for peace. Notes, bibliography, index.

Administrative and Legal

TERRITORIES

1998 Clark, Truman R. "Puerto Rico and the United States, 1917–1933: A Failure of Imperial Tutelage." Ph.D. dissertation, Bryn Mawr College, 1970.

The United States never successfully resolved whether to treat Puerto Rico as a foreign country or as part of America. While the Jones act of 1917 granted citizenship to Puerto Ricans, the act's self-government provisions were sabotaged by American politicians. DAI 31:6510-A.

1999 Curry, Roy W. "Woodrow Wilson and Philippine Policy." *Mississippi Valley Historical Review* 41 (1954): 435–52.

Wilson's policies helped to move the Philippines toward independence in spite of opposition from Republicans, dissidents, and some businessmen. Notes.

2000 Fors, Bonnie D. "The Jones Act for Puerto Rico." Ph.D. dissertation, Loyola University of Chicago, 1976.

The 1917 Jones act, which gave citizenship to Puerto Ricans, also was a step in the direction of self-government for the island. Still, the people of Puerto Rico were disappointed that the act did not go further toward granting them autonomy. DAI 36:7588-A.

2001 Lyu, Kingsley K. "Korean Nationalist Activities in Hawaii and the Continental United States, 1900–1945: Part I: 1900–1919." *Amerasia Journal* 4 (1977): 23–90.

Once American-educated Koreans took control of the Korean-American communities in the United States and Hawaii during the Progressive era, they began to prepare for liberating their homeland from Japanese occupation. Eventually control of the Korean independence movement fell to the unscrupulous Syngman Rhee. Notes.

2002 Shelton, Charlotte J. "William Atkinson Jones, 1849–1918: Independent Democracy in Gilded Age Virginia." Ph.D. dissertation, University of Virginia, 1980.

William Jones, the most influential northern Virginia democrat of his time, served on the House Insular Affairs Committee during the early years of Wilson's presidency. Believing that American imperialism violated the democratic principle of self-rule, he wrote the Organic Act (Jones act) of 1916, which provided for the Philippines' eventual independence. DAI 41:2262-A.

2003 Soberano, Rawlein G. "Proposals for the American Annexation of the Philippines: A Study of Dissenting Views (1900–1935)." Ph.D. dissertation, St. John's University, 1974.

While Wilson favored Philippine independence in theory, he bowed to congressional pressure to keep the archipelago. Republican presidents before and after Wilson insisted that the United States needed the Philippines. DAI 35:5320-A.

2004 Stanley, Peter W. *A Nation in the Making: The Philippines and the United States, 1899–1921*. Cambridge, MA: Harvard University Press, 1974.

American political tutelage of the Philippines represented the "imperialism of suasion." Reforms were stifled by the policy of training only the landed and professional elites. Notes, bibliography, index.

2005 Wong, Kwok Chu. "The Jones Bill 1912–16: A Reappraisal of Filipino Views on Independence." *Journal of Southeast Asian Studies* [Singapore] 13 (1982): 252–69.

The Jones bill of 1912, which promised Filipinos independence in eight years, was applauded at first by Philippine nationalists. Upon reflection, though, they preferred that American guarantees be written to safeguard the archipelago from Japan. Notes.

LEGAL

See also *The Progressive Movement,* above.

2006 Auerbach, Jerold S. "The Patrician as Libertarian: Zechariah Chafee, Jr., and Freedom of Speech." *New England Quarterly* 42 (1969): 511–31.

This Harvard Law School professor was outspoken in his insistence that freedom of speech should be absolute. Often branded as a radical, Chaffee was a political moderate who believed that the American system could withstand criticism even in times of war. Notes.

2007 Beckman, Marlene D. "The White Slave Traffic Act: Historical Impact of a Federal Crime Policy on Woman." *Women and Politics* 4 (1984):85–101.

Although Congress passed the Mann Act to combat the kidnapping of white women and their impressment into prostitution, it was used by authorities to punish people who engaged in noncommercial sexual relations.

2008 Griffith, Kathryn. *Judge Learned Hand and the Role of the Federal Judiciary.* Norman: University of Oklahoma Press, 1973.

Hand practiced judicial restraint in his long career in the federal district court system and on the Second Circuit Court. Notes, bibliography, table, index.

2009 Holl, Jack M. *Juvenile Reform in the Progressive Movement: William R. George and the Junior Republic Movement.* Ithaca, NY: Cornell University Press, 1971.

Immigrant children and juvenile delinquents practiced partial self-government in junior republics run by social workers. The movement typified Progressive attitudes toward the underclass. Photographs, notes, bibliography, index.

2010 Larsen, Charles. *The Good Fight: The Life and Times of Ben B. Lindsey.* Chicago: Quadrangle, 1972.

A lawyer and children's court judge, Lindsey was controversial for his advocacy of civil liberties and sexual freedom. Although he supported his friend Theodore Roosevelt's bid for the White House in 1912, he endorsed Woodrow Wilson in 1916. Photographs, notes, bibliography, index.

2011 MacDonald, Norbert. "The Diggs-Caminetti Case of 1913 and Subsequent Interpretation of the White Slave Trade Act." *Pacific Historian* 29 (1985): 30–39.

In 1913 two men were convicted of violating the White Slave Trade Act, because they had traveled to Reno, Nevada, with two unmarried women. The act and its enforcement are analyzed as an example of Progressive reform. Notes.

2012 Platt, Anthony M. *The Child Savers: The Invention of Delinquency.* Chicago: University of Chicago Press, 1969.

Progressives in Illinois and elsewhere led crusades to provide programs to rehabilitate juvenile delinquents as an alternative to treating them as adult criminals. Notes, bibliography, index.

2013 Salsgiver, Richard O. "Child Reform in Pittsburgh, 1890–1915: The Development of the Juvenile Court and the Allegheny County Industrial and Training School for Boys." D.A. dissertation, Carnegie-Mellon University, 1975.

The juvenile court movement was the product of two factions: those who favored inculcating delinquents with middle-class values in an institutional setting and others who wanted to send troubled youths to foster homes. By 1915 the Allegheny County school for boys had become a juvenile jail with little emphasis on reform. DAI 36:4717-A.

2014 Smemo, Irwin K. "Progressive Judge: The Public Career of Charles Fremont Amidon." Ph.D. dissertation, University of Minnesota, 1967.

A Roosevelt Progressive in 1912, Federal District Judge Charles Amidon upheld the First Amendment throughout the irrational war years and championed labor rights as well. DAI 28:2632-A.

2015 Smith, J. Malcolm, and Cotter, Cornelius P. "Freedom and Authority in the Amphibial State." *Midwest Journal of Political Science* 1 (1957): 40–59.

The year 1917 marked the beginning of the movement toward the "amphibial state," one more concerned with national security than with positive social goals.

2016 Stagner, Stephen. "The Recall of Judicial Decisions and the Due Process Debate." *American Journal of Legal History* 24 (1980): 257–72.

During his 1912 drive to become president, Theodore Roosevelt advocated the revision of state supreme court decisions and the recall of justices when they ruled against what a majority of the people wanted. The legal community was split over the idea, with the American Bar Association against it and many judges and lawyers for it as a way to circumvent misinterpretation of the Fourteenth Amendment. Notes.

2017 Stevens, John D., et al. "Criminal Libel as Seditious Libel, 1916–65." *Journalism Quarterly* 43 (1966): 110–13.

Thirty-one cases of criminal libel argued in state and federal courts are examined briefly, including a precedent-setting case from 1916. Notes.

2018 Tighe, Janet A. " 'Be It Ever So Little': Reforming the Insanity Defense in the Progressive Era." *Bulletin of the History of Medicine* 57 (1983): 395–411.

Professor Edwin Keedy and Superintendent William White of the Government Hospital for the Insane worked together to change the laws governing the insanity defense, a task made difficult by fundamental disagreement between the legal and psychiatric professions. Notes.

2019 White, John P. "Progressivism and the Judiciary: A Study of the Movement for Judicial Reform, 1901–1917." Ph.D. dissertation, University of Michigan, 1957.

Progressives wanted greater popular control of both judges and judicial decisions. Legislation to allow judicial recall passed in some states, but the movement had lost momentum by 1914, partly because the judiciary had become more supportive of Progressive reforms. DAI 18:1781.

2020 Wood, Stephen B. *Constitutional Politics in the Progressive Era: Child Labor and the Law.* Chicago: University of Chicago Press, 1968.

Child labor laws and court opinions are examined with special attention given to Congress, the National Child Labor Committee, and the judiciary. Notes, bibliography, index.

THE CONSTITUTION

Seventeenth Amendment
See also Chapter 4, *Economics, Government Policies.*

2021 Buenker, John D. "The Urban Political Machine and the Seventeenth Amendment." *Journal of American History* 56 (1969): 305–22.

Richard Hofstadter was wrong in his assertion that Progressives supported the direct election of senators as a way to break the power of urban political machines. Many urban machine chieftains supported such reform efforts out of idealism and to thwart state legislatures disproportionately filled by old-stock rural Republicans. Notes.

2022 Easterling, Larry J. "Senator Joseph L. Bristow and the Seventeenth Amendment." *Kansas Historical Quarterly* 41 (1975): 488–511.

Author of the original amendment resolution, Bristow played a vital role in the passage of the Seventeenth Amendment, although William E. Borah received most of the credit. Notes.

Eighteenth Amendment

See also *National Politics* and *State and Local Politics,* above.

2023 Buenker, John D. "The Illinois Legislature and Prohibition, 1907–1919." *Journal of the Illinois State Historical Society* 62 (1969): 363–84.

Prohibition was used by both "old-stock" and "new-stock" Americans, as the two sides clashed over cultural dominance.

2024 Carter, Paul A. "Prohibition and Democracy: The Noble Experiment Reassessed." *Wisconsin Magazine of History* 56 (1973): 189–201.

There was more to the prohibition movement than conservative fanaticism. The prohibitionists anticipated New Dealers and radicals in some of their arguments. The movement also taught women's groups valuable lessons. Notes.

2025 Clark, Norman H. *Deliver Us from Evil: An Interpretation of American Prohibition.* New York: Norton, 1976.

Although prohibition was supported by radicals and cranks, it was a logical response to a major threat to public health and welfare, and it led to some positive results. Bibliography, index.

2026 ———. *The Dry Years: Prohibition and Social Change in Washington.* Seattle: University of Washington Press, 1965.

The movement for prohibition in the state of Washington was an integral part of the Progressive crusade. Photographs, tables, notes, bibliography, index.

2027 Drescher, Nuala M. "Organized Labor and the Eighteenth Amendment." *Labor History* 8 (1967): 280–99.

A split within the ranks of organized labor and the weak leadership of Samuel Gompers on the issue of prohibition weakened the influence of the American Federation of Labor. Notes.

2028 Hogan, Charles M. "Wayne B. Wheeler: Single Issue Exponent." Ph.D. dissertation, University of Cincinnati, 1986.

After his Anti-Saloon League victories in Ohio, Wheeler involved himself in the legalities of the Eighteenth Amendment and perfected high-pressure lobbying techniques. DAI 47:3168-A.

2029 Hohner, Robert A. "The Prohibitionists: Who Were They?" *South Atlantic Quarterly* 68 (1969): 491–505.

Rank-and-file prohibitionists were not fanatics. Rather, they were Progressives who advocated prohibiting the manufacture, sale, and consumption of alcoholic beverages to defend their status in society. Notes.

2030 Kingsdale, Jon M. "The 'Poor Man's Club': Social Functions of the Urban Working-Class Saloon." *American Quarterly* 25 (1973): 472–89.

Prohibitionists and other reformers, such as the Progressives, despised saloons, because they were bastions of immigrant and working-class values. If they could be closed, immigrants and workers would gravitate toward the WASP ideal. Notes.

2031 Nethers, John L. " 'Driest of the Drys': Simeon D. Fess." *Ohio History* 79 (1970): 178–92.

A congressman and then a senator from Ohio, the conservative Fess was a consistent supporter of prohibition. Notes.

2032 Silverman, Joan L. " ' I'll Never Touch Another Drop': Images of Alcoholism and Temperance in American Popular Culture, 1874–1919." Ph.D. dissertation, New York University, 1979.

The literature of temperance is examined to discover popular attitudes toward drinking. Drunks were regarded either as good-natured but weak people or as morally defective, with the latter image gaining predominance during the Progressive-era drive for prohibition. DAI 40:2844-A.

2033 Timberlake, James H. *Prohibition and the Progressive Movement, 1900–1920.* Cambridge, MA: Harvard University Press, 1963.

Prohibitionists were natural allies of the Progressives, because both groups had faith in moral law, although urban and ethnic groups objected to prohibition as unwarranted interference with modern culture. Photographs, notes, index.

Nineteenth Amendment

See also Chapter 6, *Women* and *The Suffrage Movement*.

2034 Alpern, Sara, and Baum, Dale. "Female Ballots: The Impact of the Nineteenth Amendment." *Journal of Interdisciplinary History* 16 (1985): 43–67.

Suffrage leaders were disappointed that women neither seemed anxious to vote nor voted dissimilarly from men in 1920, the first national election in which they could participate. However, historians have not emphasized that this was a period of general apathy toward voting. Notes.

2035 Fry, Amelia. "Along the Suffrage Trail: From West to East for Freedom Now!" *American West* 6 (1969): 16–25.

Suffragettes collected over one-half million signatures on a petition at the Panama Pacific International Exposition in San Francisco in 1915. Sara Bard Field traveled by automobile over 3,000 miles, with attendant publicity all along the way, in order to present the petition to President Wilson.

2036 Johnson, Kenneth R. "Kate Gordon and the Woman-Suffrage Movement in the South." *Journal of Southern History* 38 (1972): 365–92.

A longtime advocate of women's suffrage, Gordon opposed the constitutional amendment because it infringed on states' rights. Notes.

2037 Lunardini, Christine A., and Knock, Thomas J. "Woodrow Wilson and Woman Suffrage: A New Look." *Political Science Quarterly* 95 (1980): 655–71.

Initially opposed to women's suffrage, Wilson eventually became a strong advocate.

SUPREME COURT

2038 Allen, Ann. "Women's Labor Laws and the Judiciary: Reaction to Progressive Philosophy." *Proceedings of the South Carolina Historical Association* (1985): 75–85.

Three important court decisions that affected women and labor are discussed including *Stettler v. O'Hara* (1914), in which the Supreme

Court upheld Oregon's Progressive minimum wage for women. Notes.

2039 Bates, J. Leonard. "The Midwest Decision, 1915: A Landmark in Conservation History." *Pacific Northwest Quarterly* 51 (1980): 26–34.

The 1915 Supreme Court case *United States v. Midwest Oil Company* set important precedents for government power over public lands.

2040 Bickel, Alexander M., and Schmidt, Benno C., Jr. *The Judiciary and Responsible Government, 1910–1921.* Vol. IX in Paul A. Freud and Stanley N. Katz, eds. *History of the Supreme Court of the United States.* New York: Macmillan, 1984.

Chapters covering the Wilson years include those on the fate of social legislation from 1914 to 1920, the heyday of Jim Crow, the Peonage cases, and black disfranchisement. Photographs, tables, notes, index.

2041 Carrott, Montgomery B. "Expansion of the Fourteenth Amendment to Include Freedom of Expression." *North Dakota Quarterly* 39 (1971): 5–20.

Freedom of expression cases seldom came before the Supreme Court prior to World War I. The war and the subsequent Red Scare forced the high court to abandon the old prior restraint doctrine and edge slowly toward the idea that freedom of expression was protected under the Fourteenth Amendment. Notes.

2042 Dalrymple, Candice. "Sexual Distinctions in the Law: Early Maximum Hour Decisions of the United States Supreme Court, 1905–1917." Ph.D. dissertation, University of Florida, 1979.

Women gained unequal constitutional rights in the workplace as a result of three key Supreme Court decisions, including *Bunting v. Oregon* (1917). DAI 40:4714-A.

2043 Handburg, Roger, Jr. "Decision-Making in a Natural Court, 1916–1921." *American Political Quarterly* 4 (1976): 357–78.

Judicial ideology during Wilson's second term is analyzed at a time when, in the face of increased government activism, the court began to reassess its own position.

2044 Leavitt, Donald C. "Attitude Change on the Supreme Court, 1910–1920." *Michigan Academician* 4 (1971): 53–65.

Guttman scales show little change in the attitudes of the justices who sat on the court during this ten-year period. The opinions of the more respected jurists had more influence than did the politics of the day. Notes.

2045 Semonche, John E. *Charting the Future: The Supreme Court Responds to a Changing Society, 1890–1920.* Westport, CT: Greenwood, 1978.

The court was more pragmatic than is commonly thought in responding to the demands of industrial America, although it consistently took an extremely conservative stance toward the rights of organized labor. Notes, bibliography, index.

2046 Wolfe, Christopher. "Woodrow Wilson: Interpreting the Constitution." *Review of Politics* 41 (1979): 121–42.

The Supreme Court was originally intended to uphold the popular will as expressed in the Constitution. However, Wilson's interpretation granted the court judicial legislative power.

SUPREME COURT JUSTICES

2047 Abraham, Henry J. *Justices and Presidents: A Political History of Appointments to the Supreme Court.* New York: Oxford University Press, 1974.

The judicial appointment process is an unpredictable one. Various factors that have gone into the selection process are discussed. Notes, bibliography, appendix.

2048 Friedman, Leon, and Israel, Fred L., eds. *The Justices of the United States Supreme Court, 1789–1978: Their Lives and Major Opinions.* 5 vols. New York: Chelsea House, 1980.

Essays on each of the Supreme Court justices, including those who served during the Wilson years, are presented along with coverage of important court opinions. Appendix, bibliography, index.

2049 Konefsky, Samuel J. *The Legacy of Holmes and Brandeis.* New York: Macmillan, 1956.

The liberal Louis Brandeis had a better grasp on how law should be adapted to meet the needs of modern America than did his older colleague on the Supreme Court, Oliver Wendell Holmes. Notes, index.

2050 Romine, Ronald H. "The 'Politics' of Supreme Court Nominations from Theodore

Roosevelt to Ronald Reagan: The Construction of a 'Politicization Index.' " Ph.D. dissertation, University of South Carolina, 1984.

Court nominations have become increasingly political throughout the twentieth century. Wilson's nomination of Louis Brandeis was the most political of the fifty-two studied. DAI 46:511-A.

Louis Brandeis

See also Chapter 6, *Zionism,* and *New Freedom* and *Elections, 1912,* above.

2051 Abrahams, Paul P. "Brandeis and Lamont on Finance Capitalism." *Business History Review* 47 (1973): 72–94.

In 1913, Louis Brandeis met with J. P. Morgan partner Thomas W. Lamont to discuss the Progressive reformer's public denunciation of the Money Trust. This verbatim transcript indicates that Lamont accepted that further economic reforms were necessary. Notes.

2052 Brandeis, Louis D. *Letters of Louis D. Brandeis.* Edited by Melvin I. Urofsky and David W. Levy. 5 vols. Albany: State University of New York Press, 1971–1978.

Volumes III (1913–1915) and IV (1916–1921) contain a wealth of material on the Wilson administration and the Supreme Court. Photographs, index.

2053 Freund, Paul A. "The Liberalism of Justice Brandeis." *American Jewish Archives* 10 (1958): 3-11.

Brandeis made a great contribution to society by combining legal craftsmanship with moral judgment.

2054 Gal, Allon. *Brandeis of Boston.* Cambridge, MA: Harvard University Press, 1980.

The work of Brandeis to 1914 is examined. His conversion to the Progressive cause and to Zionism came gradually, as he battled against large corporations and found the high principles that he used to guide his later public career. Notes, bibliography, index.

2055 ———. "Brandeis, Progressivism, and Zionism: A Study in the Interaction of Ideas and Social Background." Ph.D. dissertation, Brandeis University, 1976.

A business lawyer turned Progressive, Brandeis rallied Jews to the Wilson camp. His interest turned to Zionism, when he realized that a

Jewish state could serve as a unique "city on a hill" for mankind. DAI 37:1144-A.

2056 ———. "Brandeis's View on the Upbuilding to Palestine, 1914–1923." *Studies in Zionism* [Israel] (1982): 211–40.

Rather than rely on charity, Brandeis contended that a Jewish homeland needed a solid internal economic base, a view not shared by Chaim Weizmann. A critic of many Zionist activities and policies, Brandeis remained a firm supporter of the homeland idea. Notes.

2057 ———. "In Search of a New Zion: New Light on Brandeis' Road to Zionism." *American Jewish History* 68 (1978): 19–31.

Brandeis's conversion to Zionism came about after he worked with the Boston Jewish community on Progressive reforms, made contacts with Jews during a series of garment workers' strikes in New York, and associated with Palestinian Zionists. Notes.

2058 Geller, Stuart. "Why Did Louis Brandeis Choose Zionism?" *American Jewish Historical Quarterly* 62 (1973): 383–400.

Brandeis did not become a Zionist for opportunistic reasons. If he had done so to advance his career, he would have joined the American Jewish Committee rather than the rather unpopular group that he did join. Notes.

2059 Halpern, Ben. "Brandeis and the Origins of the Balfour Declaration." *Studies in Zionism* [Israel] (1983): 71–100.

Colonel Edward House rather than the British convinced Wilson to support the Balfour Declaration. Louis D. Brandeis's lack of action did not serve the Zionist cause well. Notes.

2060 ———. "Brandeis' Way to Zionism." *Midstream* 17 (1971): 3–13.

Brandeis's family played an important role in his conversion to Zionism, which did not take place until after he had become a distinguished public servant. Notes.

2061 Mason, Alpheus T. *Brandeis: A Free Man's Life.* New York: Viking, 1956.

Brandeis's work as a reformer and an architect of the New Freedom is analyzed. Notes, bibliography, index.

2062 Murphy, Bruce A. "Supreme Court Justices as Politicians: The Extrajudicial Activities of Justices Louis D. Brandeis and Felix Frankfurter." Ph.D. dissertation, University of Virginia, 1978.

Like many other justices, Brandeis and Frankfurter were involved in many political activities while they were on the bench. Brandeis continued to advise Woodrow Wilson after his appointment to the high court. DAI 43:3408-A.

2063 Schmidt, Sarah L. "The Zionist Conversion of Louis D. Brandeis." *Jewish Social Studies* 37 (1975): 18–34.

Horace Kallen is given credit for converting Brandeis from a belief in immigrant assimilation to Zionism after the two men had discussed the matter from 1912 to 1915.

2064 Shapiro, Yonathan. "American Jews in Politics: The Case of Louis D. Brandeis." *American Jewish Historical Quarterly* 55 (1965): 199–211.

While Wilson decided not to give Brandeis a cabinet position in 1913, he emerged as a key adviser. His efforts on behalf of Zionism and his image as a representative of Jews helped him to become a Supreme Court justice. Notes.

2065 Todd, A. L. *Justice on Trial: The Case of Louis D. Brandeis.* New York: McGraw-Hill, 1964.

Brandeis's views on social justice made his appointment to the Supreme Court a controversial one and resulted in an acrimonious struggle for his confirmation. Bibliography, index.

2066 Urofsky, Melvin I. "Louis D. Brandeis on Legal Education." *American Journal of Legal History* 22 (1978): 189–201.

Brandeis was a thorough and methodical legalist who was wise enough to be patient in his expectations of reform. Notes.

2067 ———. *Louis D. Brandeis and the Progressive Tradition.* Boston: Little, Brown, 1981.

Brandeis's Zionism grew out of his Progressive convictions. He was too high-minded to become mired in the divisive political squabbles of his time. Bibliography, index.

2068 ———. *A Mind of One Piece: Brandeis and American Reform.* New York: Scribner's, 1971.

Brandeis's morality was rooted in his New England upbringing. His "mind of one piece" brought the Progressive movement's many reform tendencies together. Notes, bibliography, index.

Oliver Wendell Holmes, Jr.

2069 Burton, David H. *Oliver Wendell Holmes, Jr.* Boston: Twayne, 1980.

The writings and decisions of Justice Holmes are examined in light of his legal realism. Notes, bibliography, index.

2070 Regan, Fred D. "Justice Oliver Wendell Holmes, Jr., Zechariah Chafee, Jr., and the Clear and Present Danger Test for Free Speech: The First Year, 1919." *Journal of American History* 58 (1971): 24–45.

Holmes's test for free speech was consistent with William Blackstone's notion of 'presumptive intent' to commit conspiracy. Chafee and others criticized the decision and urged the court to recognize the need for free speech. Notes.

Others

2071 Birkby, Robert H. "Teaching Congress How to Do Its Work: Mr. Justice McReynolds and Maritime Torts." *Congressional Studies* 8 (1981): 11–20.

Supreme Court Justice James McReynolds launched a campaign in 1917 to persuade Congress to pass an improved maritime benefits law for injured seamen and their survivors, an effort which bore fruit ten years later in the Longshoremen and Harbor Workers Compensation Act.

Domestic Affairs: Radicalism and the Red Scare

The Wilson years were marked by a rich diversity of radical political ideologies. Much has been written about the syndicalist Industrial Workers of the World. Begin with the contemporary work by Paul F. Brissenden, *The IWW: A Study of American Syndicalism* (#2079). See also Joseph R. Conlin, *Bread and Roses Too: Studies of the Wobblies* (#2085); Melvyn Dubofsky, *We Shall Be All: A History of the Industrial Workers of the World* (#2089); and Donald E. Winters, Jr., *The Soul of the Wobblies: The I.W.W., Religion, and American Culture in the Progressive Era, 1905–1917* (#2105). Melvyn Dubofsky, *"Big Bill" Haywood* (#2087), has written an excellent biography of the IWW leader.

The last years of the "golden age" of socialism are examined by James R. Green, *Grass-Roots Socialism: Radical Movements in the Southwest, 1895–1943* (#2138); David A. Shannon, *The Socialist Party of America: A History* (#2176); and James Weinstein, *The Decline of Socialism in America, 1912–1925* (#2186). For the lives of Socialist party leaders, see Sally M. Miller, *Victor Berger and the Promise of Constructive Socialism* (#2163); Norma F. Pratt, *Morris Hillquit: A Political History of an American Jewish Socialist* (#2169); and Nick Salvatore, *Eugene V. Debs: Citizen and Socialist* (#2174). The beginnings of American communism are analyzed by Theodore Draper, *The Roots of American Communism* (#2190), and by Irving Howe and Lewis Coser, *The American Communist Party: A Critical History (1919–1957)* (#2195).

The postwar Red Scare of 1919–20 was a cataclysmic event for the American Left, and it left deep scars on the American body politic. The standard work is Robert K. Murray, *Red Scare: A*

Study in National Hysteria, 1919–1920 (#2224). See also Peter H. Buckingham, *America Sees Red: Anticommunism in America, 1870s to 1980s* (#2207); Richard Polenberg, *Fighting Faiths: The Abrams Case, the Supreme Court, and Free Speech* (#2225); and William Preston, Jr., *Aliens and Dissenters: Federal Suppression of Radicals, 1903–1933* (#2227). For local studies of the Red Scare, see Robert L. Friedheim, *The Seattle General Strike* (#2239), and Julian F. Jaffe, *Crusade against Radicalism: New York during the Red Scare, 1914–1924* (#2240).

Radical Ideologies

ANARCHISM

See also Chapter 6, *Radical Women,* for material on Emma Goldman.

2072 Drinnon, Richard. "*The Blast*: An Introduction and an Appraisal." *Labor History* 11 (1970): 82–88.

The Blast was a radical publication edited before World War I by the noted anarchist Alexander Berkman.

2073 Marsh, Margaret. *Anarchist Women, 1870–1920.* Philadelphia: Temple University Press, 1981.

Anarchist women developed ideas that were different from those of anarchist men. Emma Goldman and other women active during the Progressive era are profiled. Appendix, notes, bibliography, index.

SYNDICALISM

See also Chapter 4, *Labor,* Chapter 9, *Civil Liberties,* and below, *The Red Scare.*

2074 Aubery, Pierre. "The IWW Rebels of American Syndicalism" (in French). *Revue d'Histoire Economique et Sociale* [France] 32 (1954): 413–36.

This work presents an overview of the creation and tactics of the Industrial Workers of the World, an organization that left its mark on unskilled laborers of the West.

2075 Barnes, Donald M. "The Everett Massacre: A Turning Point in I.W.W. History." *Organon* 1 (1969): 35–42.

The turning point for the IWW came after the acquittal of one of its members for his part in the Everett "massacre." IWW chief Bill Haywood became concerned about radical literature that had been introduced as evidence at the trial. After that, propaganda was toned down, recruitment procedures changed, and the IWW seemed less interested in fomenting revolution. Notes.

2076 ———. "The Ideology of the Industrial Workers of the World: 1905–1921." Ph.D. dissertation, Washington State University, 1962.

The ideology of the IWW was totalitarian in that it promised to solve all problems, and utopian in that it promised a just future. Preferring direct action to political action, the organization nevertheless came to endorse nonviolence and education as ways to achieve its goals. DAI 23:2887.

2077 Bell, Leland. "Radicalism and Race: The IWW and the Black Worker." *Journal of Human Relations* 19 (1971): 48–56.

The IWW's stance on race relations has been overlooked by historians. Racism, union leaders believed, was a result of capitalism. Wobblies advocated an immediate end to segregation and inequality. Notes.

2078 Bird, Stewart; Georgakas, Dan; and Shaffer, Deborah. *Solidarity Forever: An Oral History of the IWW.* Chicago: Lakeview, 1985.

IWW bindle stiffs, women, "timberbeasts," miners, dockworkers, and union officials are interviewed regarding their experiences. Photographs, notes, index.

2079 Brissenden, Paul F. *The IWW: A Study of American Syndicalism.* New York: Russell and Russell, 1919.

This early work remains an important comprehensive history of the IWW. The Wobblies were feared because of their demand that democracy be extended from political into economic life. Notes, bibliography, index.

2080 Bubka, Tony. "Time to Organize! The IWW Stickeretts." *American West* 5 (1968): 21–22ff.

As part of the propaganda war against the bosses, IWW organizer Ralph Chaplin employed stickeretts, adhesive-backed squares bearing Wobbly slogans. The government used Chaplin's invention to help convict him and other IWW leaders of antiwar activities.

2081 Carlson, Peter. *Roughneck: The Life and Times of Big Bill Haywood.* New York: Norton, 1983.

Haywood believed in direct economic action rather than political action to fight the capitalists, because politicians were often controlled by the ruling class. Notes, index.

2082 Carter, David A. "The Industrial Workers of the World and the Rhetoric of Song." *Quarterly Journal of Speech* 66 (1980): 365–74.

An investigation of the lyrics and the use of music by members of the IWW at union meetings and rallies reveals the importance of song in Wobbly ritual. These songs also helped to shape the union's image from both within and without.

2083 Clark, Norman H. "Everett, 1916, and After." *Pacific Northwest Quarterly* 57 (1966): 57–64.

The efforts of the IWW on behalf of workers that led to the tragic "Bloody Sunday" are chronicled. Notes.

2084 Conlin, Joseph R. *Big Bill Haywood and the Radical Union Movement.* Syracuse: Syracuse University Press, 1969.

Haywood has become famous as a colorful labor radical, but he was also a competent union administrator. Photographs, notes, bibliography, index.

2085 ———. *Bread and Roses Too: Studies of the Wobblies.* Westport, CT: Greenwood, 1969.

This series of essays analyzes the challenge to historians presented by the IWW, an organization which both moved with the American mainstream and bucked it. Notes, bibliography, index.

2086 ———, ed. *At the Point of Production: The Local History of the I.W.W.* Westport, CT: Greenwood, 1981.

Ten essays make the point that there were many IWWs, with different locals pursuing different strategies. Notes, bibliography, index.

2087 Dubofsky, Melvyn. *"Big Bill" Haywood.* New York: St. Martin's, 1987.

This brief, interpretive biography of the IWW leader finds Haywood to be enigmatic: he would counsel strikers to engage in passive resistance at times, while on other occasions he would resort to violent hyperbole. His life "defined the limits of dissent in a Capitalist democracy." Bibliography, appendixes, index.

2088 ———. "The Radicalism of the Dispossessed: William Haywood and the IWW." In Alfred F. Young, ed. *Dissent: Explorations in the History of American Radicalism.* DeKalb: Northern Illinois University Press, 1968, pp. 173–213.

Scholars have been too quick to dismiss Haywood and the IWW as merely colorful. The Wobblies' hatred for existing institutions and their failure to conceptualize practical alternatives led to internal anarchy and repression by the state. Notes.

2089 ———. *We Shall Be All: A History of the Industrial Workers of the World.* Chicago: Quadrangle, 1969.

The rapid economic growth of the West during the Industrial Revolution spawned violence and radicalism among workers. The war, government repression, and internal problems combined to doom the IWW. Notes, bibliography, index.

2090 Ebner, Michael H. "The Passaic Strike of 1912 and the Two I.W.W.s." *Labor History* 11 (1970): 452–66.

Two factions of the IWW, followers of Daniel DeLeon and the Bill Haywood-James P. Thompson group, fought to control the strike of immigrant laborers. The bickering weakened the strike effort and made some wary of the industrial union. Notes.

2091 Foner, Philip S. "The IWW and the Black Worker." *Journal of Negro History* 55 (1970): 45–64.

The IWW encouraged black workers to join their struggle, relying on the argument that discrimination would end with the fall of the wage system. Little headway was made, except among lumber workers and longshoremen. Notes.

2092 Golin, Steve. "Defeat Becomes Disaster: The Paterson Strike of 1913 and the Decline of the IWW." *Labor History* 24 (1983): 223–48.

Defeat became disaster when the Wobblies refused to admit that they had been bested by the capitalists in the Paterson silk workers' strike. Instead, the IWW itself became the target of criticism, and the union's subsequent reorganization turned out to be counterproductive. Notes.

2093 Hokanson, Nels. "Swedes and the I.W.W." *Swedish Pioneer Historical Quarterly* 23 (1972): 25–35.

While a majority of Swedes opposed radicalism, many joined the IWW in the Pacific Northwest. The most famous Swedish Wobbly was Joe Hill, born Joel Emanuel Hagglund. Notes.

2094 Johnson, Michael R. "The I.W.W. and Wilsonian Democracy." *Science and Society* 28 (1964): 257–74.

The rapid growth of the IWW after World War I attracted government repression which, in turn, served as a springboard for the Red Scare. Notes.

2095 McEnroe, Thomas H. "The Industrial Workers of the World: Theories, Organizational Problems, and Appeals, as Revealed Principally in the *Industrial Worker.*" Ph.D. dissertation, University of Minnesota, 1960.

The *Industrial Worker* originally functioned as an instrument of both self-criticism and propaganda. The practical functioning of this newspaper is analyzed along with its ideology. The inherent, destabilizing contradictions between Communist ideals and the problems of maintaining a large organization are emphasized. DAI 21:3507.

2096 Mal'kov, V. L. "Two Unpublished Letters by William D. Haywood" (in Russian). *Amerikanskii Ezhegodnik* [USSR] (1980): 301–11.

Haywood's first letter, written from jail in 1918, describes his background and ideology. The second letter, written from Moscow in 1921, details his life following his decision to flee to

Soviet Russia rather than serve a long prison term in the United States. Notes.

2097 Nishimoto, Koichi. "The American Labor Movement and Anarcho-Syndicalism" (in Japanese). *Rekishigaku Kenkyu* [Japan] (1969): 17–29.

An overview of the left wing of the American labor movement is provided, including analysis of the ideas of Daniel DeLeon, Eugene Debs, and Bill Haywood, cofounders of the IWW.

2098 Palmer, Bryan D. " 'Big Bill' Haywood's Defection to Russia and the IWW: Two Letters." *Labor History* 17 (1976): 271–78.

Haywood's escape to Soviet Russia hurt the IWW socially and financially. Notes.

2099 Renshaw, Patrick. *The Wobblies: The Story of Syndicalism in the United States.* Garden City, NY: Doubleday, 1967.

A British journalist surveys the Industrial Workers of the World, including their persecution during World War I and the Red Scare. Notes, bibliography, index.

2100 Seraile, William. "Ben Fletcher, I.W.W. Organizer." *Pennsylvania History* 46 (1979): 213–32.

Fletcher organized dockworkers on the East Coast for the IWW until World War I, when he was jailed for his opposition to the war. He was one of the most effective black labor organizers of the period. Notes.

2101 Tyler, Robert L. "The I.W.W. and the Brainworkers." *American Quarterly* 15 (1963): 41–51.

Understanding the need to include the growing technical class in their organization, the IWW actively recruited engineers, moderating IWW rhetoric in the process. The effort was not a success, and little would have been gained by those who might have joined. Notes.

2102 ———. "The I.W.W. and the West." *American Quarterly* 12 (1960): 175–87.

There was more to the IWW than the stereotype of the rugged frontier figure. Many members spoke little English and lived in eastern cities. Notes.

2103 ———. "The Rise and Fall of an American Radicalism: The I.W.W." *Historian* 19 (1956): 48–65.

The IWW began as a radical industrial union intended to supplant the American Federation of Labor, but it evolved into a western union for hoboes. Notes.

2104 Weisberger, Bernard. "Here Come the Wobblies!" *American Heritage* 18 (1967): 30–35ff.

The colorful history of the radical union is presented along with brief portraits of Wobbly leaders.

2105 Winters, Donald E., Jr. *The Soul of the Wobblies: The I.W.W., Religion, and American Culture in the Progressive Era, 1905–1917.* Westport, CT: Greenwood, 1985.

Religion played an important part in the lives and work of IWW members. Some saw themselves as latter-day prophets. Notes, appendixes, bibliography, index.

SOCIALISM

See also below, *The Red Scare*, Chapter 6, *Radical Women*, and Chapter 11, *The Home Front, Civil Liberties.*

2106 Aaron, Daniel. "*Good Morning* and 'Art' Young: An Introduction and Appraisal." *Labor History* 10 (1969): 100–104.

Radical writer and artist Art Young edited *Good Morning*, a leftist newspaper, during the Red Scare.

2107 Barkey, Frederick A. "The Socialist Party in West Virginia from 1898 to 1920: A Study in Working Class Radicalism." Ph.D. dissertation, University of Pittsburgh, 1971.

Native-born American laborers with unskilled or semiskilled jobs made up the backbone of the Socialist party in West Virginia. The mixture of Marxism and reformism appealed to workers. The party turned to direct action as a result of the bitter Cabin Creek-Paint Creek coal strike (1912–1914), a tactic which divided the movement. DAI 32:2019-A.

2108 Bassett, Michael E. "Municipal Reform and the Socialist Party, 1910–1914." *Australian Journal of Politics and History* [Australia] 19 (1973): 179–87.

Several cities elected Socialist mayors in 1910–11, at least in part because of corrupt incumbents. While these Socialists promoted reform, many had been defeated by 1914.

2109 ———. "The Socialist Party of America, 1912–1919: Years of Decline." Ph.D. dissertation, Duke University, 1964.

Socialist party membership fell from its peak of 136,000 in 1912 to 20,000 in 1920. Socialistic Democratic reforms appropriated some of the Socialist agenda, and the party's antiwar stance both alienated members and brought government harrassment. Pro-Bolshevik, activist Socialists polarized, split and weakened what remained of the party in 1919. DAI 28:2189-A.

2110 ———. "The Socialist Party Dilemma, 1912–1914." *Mid-America* 47 (1965): 243–56.

Internal bickering and money problems did not lead to the decline of the Socialist party so much as did the party's inability to make continuing inroads against the Democratic and Republican parties. Notes.

2111 Bell, Daniel. *Marxian Socialism in the United States*. Princeton: Princeton University Press, 1952.

Radicals never resolved the basic dilemma between ethics and politics. The Socialist party was "in the world, but not of it," setting goals without integrating itself into society. Bibliography, index.

2112 Bindler, Norman. "American Socialism and the First World War." Ph.D. dissertation, New York University, 1970.

From the outset of the war in Europe, the Socialist party opposed it. While the rank and file stood against American entry into the war, some of the party's leaders bolted to form a splinter group. Opposition to the war brought the wrath of the Wilson administration down on the party in 1917–1919. DAI 31:4663-A.

2113 Brommel, Bernard J. "Debs's Cooperative Commonwealth Plan for Workers." *Labor History* 12 (1971): 560–69.

Eugene Debs's plan to organize workers into a cooperative commune foundered on a split within the Socialist party and Debs's preoccupation with a strike by coal miners. Notes.

2114 ———. "The Pacifist Speechmaking of Eugene V. Debs." *Quarterly Journal of Speech* 52 (1966): 146–54.

Debs made many antiwar speeches between 1915 and 1922, the most famous of which was delivered at Canton, Ohio, in June 1916. Notes.

2115 Buenker, John D. "Illinois Socialists and Progressive Reform." *Journal of the Illinois State Historical Society* 63 (1970): 368–86.

Chicago socialists in the Illinois legislature sponsored and supported bills not unlike those of urban Progressives, although they differed with the liberals on war, prohibition, and public ownership of utilities and corporations. Notes.

2116 Buhle, Mary Jo. *Women and American Socialism, 1870–1920*. Urbana: University of Illinois Press, 1981.

Immigrant and native-born women socialists had very different ways of organizing and diverse world views. The role of women in the early days of the Socialist party is examined along with the Woman's National Committee, women and labor, suffrage, sexual liberation, and the breakdown of the party in the wake of World War I and the Red Scare. Photographs, notes, index.

2117 Buitenhuis, Peter. "Upton Sinclair and the Socialist Response to World War I." *Canadian Review of American Studies* [Canada] 14 (1983): 121–30.

Upton Sinclair broke with the Socialist party when it refused to support the war effort. To do his part for the war, Sinclair created a new magazine that showcased his and other prowar writings. Notes.

2118 Cantor, Milton. "The Radical Confrontation with Foreign Policy: War and Revolution, 1914–1920." In Alfred F. Young, ed. *Dissent: Explorations in the History of American Radicalism*. DeKalb: Northern Illinois University Press, 1968, pp. 215–49.

American radicals were insulated from foreign policy before World War I. The many schisms in the movement and the failure to find common ground on foreign policy made practical collaboration impossible. Notes.

2119 Cassidy, Keith M. "The American Left and the Problem of Leadership, 1900–1920." *South Atlantic Quarterly* 82 (1983): 386–97.

Different ideas about leadership are evident in the writings of Emma Goldman, Daniel DeLeon, and William English Walling. In the period 1900–1920, the American Left was identified with the democratic system, but it rarely based its policy on the opinion of the people. Notes.

2120 Conkin, Paul K. *Two Paths to Utopia: The Hutterites and the Llano Colony*. Lincoln: University of Nebraska Press, 1964.

The Hutterites and the Llano colony offer two examples of utopias that were very different from one another in form and structure. Notes, index.

2121 Conlin, Joseph R. "The I.W.W. and the Socialist Party." *Science and Society* 31 (1967): 22–36.

Reformist rather than radical, the Socialist party was fatally weakened by a schism between the Victor Berger wing and the radical wing. Notes.

2122 Cotkin, George. "The Socialist Popularization of Science in America, 1901 to the First World War." *History of Education Quarterly* 24 (1984): 201–14.

During the Progressive era, socialist intellectuals made the cause of science their own to strengthen their arguments for a cooperative commonwealth and to give the working class access to scientific information. Notes.

2123 Cotton, Carol. "Helen Keller's First Public Speech." *Alabama Historical Quarterly* 37 (1975): 68–72.

Keller made her speaking debut at a meeting of the Socialist party in 1913 at Montclair, New Jersey. Her background and the subject of her address are discussed. Notes.

2124 Critchlow, Donald T., ed. *Socialism in the Heartland: The Midwestern Experience, 1900–1925.* Notre Dame, IN: University of Notre Dame Press, 1986.

Essays drawn from doctoral dissertations and other scholarship detail a wide variety of socialist experiences in such places as Milwaukee, Indiana, Flint, Dayton, Minneapolis, and Illinois. Notes, index.

2125 Dubofsky, Melvyn. "Success and Failure of Socialism in New York City, 1900–1918: A Case Study." *Labor History* 9 (1968): 361–75.

The Socialist party allied successfully with the needle trades, but failed to expand its base of ethnic support beyond Jews and Germans. The political climate of the Progressive period and the party's internal contradictions also help to explain why support for socialism withered away. Notes.

2126 Duram, James C. "In Defense of Conscience: Norman Thomas as an Exponent of Christian Pacifism during World War I." *Journal of Presbyterian History* 52 (1974): 19–32.

During the years 1915 to 1918, the future leader of the Socialist party emerged as an outspoken libertarian who defended the rights of conscientious objectors in opposing the war.

2127 Foner, Philip S. "Reverend George Washington Woodbey: Early Twentieth Century Black Socialist." *Journal of Negro History* 61 (1976): 136–57.

A leader of the black socialist movement during the Progressive era, Woodbey was all but forgotten after 1915. Notes.

2128 Fox, Richard W. "The Paradox of 'Progressive' Socialism: The Case of Morris Hillquit, 1901–1914." *American Quarterly* 26 (1974): 127–40.

Hillquit's career embodies that of the Socialist party before World War I. His revolutionary ideals were weakened by his acceptance of the American political system and by his immigrant's craving to be considered a good American. Notes.

2129 Frankel, Jonathan. "The Jewish Socialists and the American Jewish Congress Movement." *Yivo Annals of Jewish Social Science* 16 (1976): 202–341.

In this history of the American Jewish Congress from 1914 to 1918, the author discusses the considerable influence of the socialist movement on American Jews and why so many socialist Jews favored Americanization rather than Jewish nationalism.

2130 Frieburger, William J. "The Lone Socialist Vote: A Political Study of Meyer London." Ph.D. dissertation, University of Cincinnati, 1980.

Meyer London was a middle-of-the-road socialist, and one of the few socialists ever elected to Congress. He enjoyed strong labor support. Socialists to the left and the right of him were angered by his stands on issues such as immigration and World War I. He lost his seat in 1918, when he opposed Zionism, but he won it back in 1920. DAI 41:1186-A.

2131 Gilbert, James B. "Collectivism and Charles Steinmetz." *Business History Review* 48 (1974): 520–40.

Steinmetz worked out a socialist framework based on the structure of the modern corporation and the goals of economic democracy. Notes.

2132 Ginger, Ray. *The Bending Cross: A Biography of Eugene Victor Debs.* New Brunswick, NJ: Rutgers University Press, 1949.

Debs believed that the common people were being crucified by capitalism, and he devoted his life to fighting for the oppressed. His inconsistencies can be traced to overlapping beliefs in Marxism and Christianity. Index.

2133 Glaser, William A. "Algie Martin Simons and Marxism in America." *Mississippi Valley Historical Review* 41 (1954): 419–34.

An organizer of the American Socialist party, Simons became the foremost authority on agriculture within the party. He broke with Debs and others in 1917 over the party's militant opposition to participation in the war effort. Notes.

2134 Gleberzon, William I. "Intellectuals and the American Socialist Party, 1901–1917." *Canadian Journal of History* 11 (1976): 43–68.

Many middle-class intellectuals were attracted to the Socialist party during the Progressive era but defected when the party refused to support the war effort of 1917–18. Notes.

2135 Goldberg, Gordon J. "Meyer London and the National Social Insurance Movement, 1914–1922." *American Jewish Quarterly* 65 (1975): 59–73.

Social insurance was advocated by socialists at a time when Progressives considered it too radical to be considered seriously, although Congressman Meyer London and others helped to convince some reformers that it would be necessary eventually. Notes.

2136 ———. "Meyer London: A Political Biography." Ph.D. dissertation, Lehigh University, 1971.

The Socialist party lawyer advocated evolutionary political methods and was elected to Congress in 1914, 1916, and 1920. He championed the cause of workers and urban immigrants while supporting the war and denouncing the Bolshevik Revolution. DAI 32:356-A.

2137 Gordon, Linda. "Are the Interests of Men and Women Identical?" *Signs* 1 (1976): 1011–18.

Unlike other political parties of the era, the Socialist party allowed women full participation and advocated suffrage and equal rights. Working-class feminist socialism did not succeed because of resistance from some male party members and because of the lack of common ground between the movement and the mostly middle-class suffragettes. Notes.

2138 Green, James R. *Grass-Roots Socialism: Radical Movements in the Southwest, 1895–1943*. Baton Rouge: Louisiana State University Press, 1978.

The Socialist party had strong organizations in Oklahoma, Texas, Louisiana, and Arkansas during the Progressive era. Old moralistic radicalism fused with twentieth-century socialism in this movement of workers and poor farmers. Photographs, notes, index.

2139 ———. "The 'Salesmen-Soldiers' of the 'Appeal' Army: A Profile of Rank-and-File Socialist Agitators." In Bruce M. Stave, ed. *Socialism and the Cities*. Port Washington, NY: Kennikat, 1975, pp. 13–40.

A study of 500 rank-and-file Socialist agitators reveals that they were mostly native white males or older, well-assimilated immigrants. While they failed to expand the Socialist party's base to include newer immigrants, blacks, and females, these salesmen-soldiers helped to radicalize farmers, artisans, and small businessmen. Notes.

2140 Haines, Randall A. "Walter Lanfersiek: Socialist from Cincinnati." *Cincinnati Historical Society Bulletin* 40 (1982): 124–44.

Walter B. Landell (born Walter Lanfersiek) was the national executive secretary of the Socialist party from 1913 to 1916. He was a vigorous advocate for labor.

2141 Harpham, Geoffrey. "Jack London and the Tradition of Superman Socialism." *American Studies* 16 (1975): 23–33.

Group individualism is how Jack London thought of socialism. A believer in racial purity, he argued that under socialism superior men would naturally become dominant. Notes.

2142 Hendrickson, Kenneth E., Jr. "George R. Lunn and the Socialist Era in Schenectady, New York, 1909–1916." *New York History* 47 (1966): 22–40.

A prominent pastor and mayor of Schenectady, Lunn popularized socialism for a time, but the local movement quickly fell apart under his leadership. Notes.

2143 ———. "The Pro-War Socialists, the Social Democratic League and the Ill-Fated Drive for Industrial Democracy in America, 1917–1920." *Labor History* 11 (1970): 304–22.

A portion of the Socialist party's right wing split off after the declaration of war, hoping to form a prowar party. Although the movement failed, many intellectuals were lost to the Socialist party permanently. Notes.

2144 ———. "Tribune of the People: George R. Lunn and the Rise and Fall of Christian Socialism in Schenectady." In Bruce M. Stave, ed.

Socialism and the Cities. Port Washington, NY: Kennikat, 1975, pp. 72–98.

The Reverend George R. Lunn led the Socialist party to victory in the election of 1911 in Schenectady, New York. Lunn proved to be a reformist, was thrown out of office in 1913, and was thrown out of the party shortly thereafter. Notes.

2145 Huston, Robert S. "A. M. Simons and the American Socialist Movement." Ph.D. dissertation, University of Wisconsin, 1965.

Simons worked as writer, editor, and analyst on various small socialist newspapers. During the Wilson years, he also worked on a Marxist analysis of farm economics and a Marxist version of U.S. history published as *Social Forces in American History*. Tiring of the apparent fruitlessness of much of his work, Simons became more conservative, accusing the socialists of treason for opposing World War I. DAI 25:5879.

2146 Johnson, Oakley. "Marxism and the Negro Freedom." *Journal of Human Relations* 13 (1965): 21–39.

While Marx left a sound framework for dealing with the race question, both the Socialist Labor party and the Socialist party failed to act on it. Notes.

2147 Kaltinick, Arnold. "Socialist Municipal Administration in Four American Cities (Milwaukee, Schenectady, New Castle, Pennsylvania, and Conneaut, Ohio), 1910–1916." Ph.D. dissertation, New York University, 1982.

The whole social milieu leading to the rise and fall of socialist municipal government is examined. The four cities selected for this study represent a wide range of populations and economic underpinnings. Socialist and Progressive administrators are compared and found to be similar in practice, but not in ideology. DAI 43:3685-A.

2148 Kaufman, Murray D. A. "The Image of Eugene V. Debs in the American Popular Mind: 1894–1926." D.A. dissertation, Carnegie-Mellon University, 1981.

Many people admired Debs, valuing his honesty and dedication, even though they disapproved of his ideas. The living embodiment of the popular Christian novel *In His Steps*, Debs became a moral leader possessed of divine grace. DAI 41:3695-A.

2149 Kraditor, Aileen S. *The Radical Persuasion, 1890–1917: Aspects of the Intellectual History and the Historiography of Three American Radical Organizations.* Baton Rouge: Louisiana State University Press, 1981.

This critical examination of the Socialist Labor party, the Socialist party of America, and the IWW finds inconsistencies between radical rhetoric and ideology. Radicals misunderstood the American worker. Notes, index.

2150 Kreuter, Kent. "The Vernacular History of A. M. Simons." *Journal of American Studies* [Great Britain] 2 (1968): 65–81.

During the Progressive era, the socialist Simons wrote a Marxist interpretation of American history that debunked capitalism and made a "collective hero" out of the working class. Notes.

2151 Kreuter, Kent, and Kreuter, Gretchen. *An American Dissenter: The Life of Algie Martin Simons, 1870–1950.* Lexington: University of Kentucky Press, 1969.

This social worker turned Socialist party activist moved steadily to the political right, joining in the repression of his former colleagues during World War I. Photographs, notes, bibliography, index.

2152 ———. "The Coming Nation: *The Masses'* Country Cousin." *American Quarterly* 19 (1967): 583–86.

The Coming Nation was the first socialist literary magazine, publishing works by such young writers as Sinclair Lewis and Walter Lippmann. After this Girard, Kansas, magazine folded, *The Masses* became a new outlet for literary radicalism. Notes.

2153 Laslett, John H. M. "End of an Alliance: Selected Correspondence between Socialist Party Secretary Adolph Germer, and U.S.W. of A. Leaders in World War I." *Labor History* 12 (1971): 570–95.

A series of letters shows how ideological differences weakened the socialist alliance during the war. Notes.

2154 Leinenweber, Charles. "The American Socialist Party and 'New' Immigrants." *Science and Society* 32 (1968): 1–25.

Because most party members were either native to America or came from Europe in an earlier wave of immigration, they showed some hesitance to recruit newcomers from southern and eastern Europe. Some foreign-language federations materialized late in the Progressive period, but the new immigrants never joined in great numbers. Notes.

2155 ————. "Socialists in the Streets: The New York City Socialist Party in the Working Class Neighborhoods, 1908–1918." *Science and Society* 41 (1977): 152–71.

There was more to the socialist movement than just politics, for ethnic and class traditions made socialism appealing to many members of the working class in New York. Notes.

2156 Leslie, W. Bruce. "Coming of Age in Urban America: The Socialist Alternative, 1901–1920." *Teachers College Record* 85 (1984): 459–76.

Socialists were just as interested in educational reform as the Progressives, but they lacked the political clout to push through legislation. Consequently, the Socialist party relied on providing the working class with such alternatives as socialist Sunday schools and youth groups. Notes.

2157 Lippmann, Walter. "On Municipal Socialism, 1913: An Analysis of Problems and Strategies." In Bruce M. Stave, ed. *Socialism and the Cities*. Port Washington, NY: Kennikat, 1975, pp. 184–96.

Reprinted is a letter from Walter Lippmann to the national office of the Socialist party on the nature of propaganda and political action. Lippmann sent this letter after resigning from his post as executive secretary to George Lunn, the socialist mayor of Schenectady.

2158 McNaught, Kenneth. "American Progressives and the Great Society." *Journal of American History* 53 (1966): 504–20.

Socialism was an important force during the Progressive era, respectable among intellectuals and popular with the working classes. The party foundered on the rocks of wartime patriotism and intolerance. Notes.

2159 Meredith, Howard L. "Agrarian Socialism and the Negro in Oklahoma, 1900–1918." *Labor History* 12 (1970): 277–84.

Oklahoma socialists included voting rights for blacks among their demands, and they received black support in return. Notes.

2160 ————. "A History of the Socialist Party in Oklahoma." Ph.D. dissertation, University of Oklahoma, 1970.

The Socialist party jumped into the void in Oklahoma caused by the failure of Populism. The most successful membership recruiter of all state Socialist parties, it was already weakened by

internal strife before the war. Wartime prosperity, syndicalism, and the Green Corn rebellion all contributed to its rapid decline during World War I. DAI 31:715-A.

2161 Miller, Sally M. "Milwaukee: Of Ethnicity and Labor." In Bruce M. Stave, ed. *Socialism and the Cities*. Port Washington, NY: Kennikat, 1975, pp. 41–71.

The Socialist party grew rapidly in Milwaukee during the Progressive era through a mixture of immediate reformist demands and radicalism. Milwaukee offered a unique opportunity for urban socialism, but the national party did not seem to be interested. Notes.

2162 ————. "The Socialist Party and the Negro, 1901–1920." *Journal of Negro History* 56 (1971): 220–29.

Socialists did little work among blacks, who they regarded primarily as oppressed workers rather than as victims of racism. Overthrowing capitalism interested blacks less than did attaining equality within the system. Notes.

2163 ————. *Victor Berger and the Promise of Constructive Socialism, 1910–1920*. Westport, CT: Greenwood, 1973.

A leader of the Socialist party, Berger was convicted under the Espionage Act for opposing the war, and he refused his seat in Congress. He was a moderate Marxist who chose to work for social justice within the system. Notes, bibliography, index.

2164 Morgan, H. Wayne. *Eugene V. Debs: Socialist for President*. Syracuse: Syracuse University Press, 1962.

Debs and the Socialist party played an important role during the Progressive era, attracting support from poor farmers and the working class and nudging the reform movement to the left. Notes, index.

2165 ————. "The Utopia of Eugene V. Debs." *American Quarterly* 11 (1959): 120–35.

Debs was more of a socialist evangelist than a theoretician. His version of revolutionary utopia did not reduce his humanitarian concern for workers. Notes.

2166 Peterson, Walfred H. "The Foreign Policy and Foreign Policy Theory of the American Socialist Party, 1901–1920." Ph.D. dissertation, University of Minnesota, 1957.

Early Socialists wrote little about foreign policy, claiming that reform was impossible under capitalism. However, beginning in 1914, Socialists began to advocate nonimperialist, democratic international peace. DAI 18:1479.

2167 ———. "The Foreign Policy of the Socialist Party of America before World War I." *Pacific Northwest Quarterly* 65 (1974): 176–83.

Serious analysis of American foreign policy did not interest Socialists, because they took for granted the inevitability of imperialism and war under capitalism. Little was said about foreign affairs until American participation in World War I. Notes.

2168 Pivert, Marceau. "A Great Revolutionary Socialist, Eugene V. Debs (1855–1926)" (in French). *Revue Socialiste* [France] (1956): 189–99.

Debs's ideas are examined to show that he was the greatest revolutionary leader produced in the New World.

2169 Pratt, Norma F. *Morris Hillquit: A Political History of an American Jewish Socialist.* Westport, CT: Greenwood, 1979.

Hillquit shaped the ideology of the Socialist party for thirty years, emphasizing evolution over revolution. A party centrist, he wanted nothing to do with the right-wing idea of making alliances with the middle class or the leftist inclination toward violence. Photographs, notes, bibliography, index.

2170 Quint, Howard H. "The Failure of Political Socialism in America." In Howard H. Quint, Milton Cantor, and Dean Albertson, eds. *Main Problems in American History.* Vol. II. Homewood, IL: Dorsey, 1976, pp. 174–202.

The author documents his contention that the socialists did not pay sufficient attention to immigrants and women and that socialism was a movement wracked by internal dissension. Bibliography.

2171 Reynolds, Robert D., Jr. "The Millionaire Socialists: J. G. Phelps Stokes and His Circle of Friends." Ph.D. dissertation, University of South Carolina, 1974.

The "millionaire socialists" were a group of well-heeled radicals who brought money and prestige to the Socialist party. After the declaration of war in 1917, most bolted to the Social Democratic League, which supported Wilson's war. DAI 35:2190-A.

2172 ———. "Pro-War Socialists: Intolerant or Bloodthirsty?" *Labor History* 17 (1976): 413–15.

Prowar socialists were intolerant of their former comrades during World War I, but they did not advocate executing them.

2173 Rosenstone, Robert A. *Romantic Revolutionary: A Biography of John Reed.* New York: Knopf, 1975.

A leading journalist and radical political activist, Reed rode with Pancho Villa, covered World War I, and watched the Bolshevik Revolution unfold during the Wilson years. Photographs, notes, bibliography, index.

2174 Salvatore, Nick. *Eugene V. Debs: Citizen and Socialist.* Urbana: University of Illinois Press, 1982.

Debs was not a larger-than-life hero, but rather a powerful critic of industrial capitalism whose thought and action were rooted in the American experience. Notes, bibliography, index.

2175 Scott, Mark. "The Little Blue Books in the War on Bigotry and Bunk." *Kansas History* 1 (1978): 155–76.

Emanuel Haldeman-Julius, who worked for the popular socialist paper *Appeal to Reason*, bought out the paper in 1919 and used the presses to reprint pocket-size books. He hoped that the working classes would use these dime books to improve themselves. Notes.

2176 Shannon, David A. *The Socialist Party of America: A History.* New York: Macmillan, 1955.

The Socialist party played a significant role during the Progressive era, electing officials in city and state-wide races. Eugene Debs was idolized by millions as both a socialist and an American. Militant opposition to the war, the Red Scare, and the splits caused by the Bolshevik Revolution wrecked the party. Notes, bibliography, index.

2177 Shepperson, Wilbur S., and Folkes, John G. *Retreat to Nevada: A Socialist Colony of World War I.* Reno: University of Nevada Press, 1966.

Members of the Llano del Rio Colony of Antelope Valley retreated to Nevada to avoid the war and to begin the experiment in socialist living anew, only to fail within a few years. Notes, bibliography, appendixes, index.

2178 Shore, Elliot. *Talkin' Socialism: J. A. Wayland and the Role of the Press in American Radicalism, 1890–1914.* Lawrence: University of Kansas Press, 1988.

Julius A. Wayland's importance as a socialist leader has been underestimated. His newspaper, *Appeal to Reason*, was widely read. Factors that weakened the socialist movement are also examined. Photographs, notes, bibliography, index.

2179 Stave, Bruce M., ed. *Socialism and the Cities.* Port Washington, NY: Kennikat, 1975.

Seven essays on the urban socialist movement during the Progressive era are presented along with Walter Lippmann's "On Municipal Socialism, 1913" (#2157). Notes, bibliography, index.

2180 Stevens, Errol W. "Heartland Socialism: The Socialist Party of America in Four Midwestern Communities, 1898–1920." Ph.D. dissertation, Indiana University, 1978.

Labor unions worked closely with the Socialist party in each of the four Midwest cities under study. The party was popular only in working-class neighborhoods surrounding factory districts, making it difficult to elect its candidates to city-wide office. Socialists concentrated on attainable goals and were honest when elected to office. DAI 39:3104-A.

2181 Stuart, Jack. "William English Walling and the Search for an American Socialist Theory." *Science and Society* 35 (1971): 193–208.

In his writings, Walling devoted far too much space to attacking other socialists and making an unconvincing case for capitalist collectivism as a bridge between capitalism and socialism. The author finds that Walling did not successfully relate ideas he borrowed from Herbert Spencer, Friedrich Nietzsche, and John Dewey to Marxism. Notes.

2182 ———. "William English Walling: A Study in Politics and Ideas." Ph.D. dissertation, Columbia University, 1968.

Revolutionary socialist William Walling was an important American theorist who correctly predicted an upswing in state-dominated welfare capitalism as the next major societal trend. During World War I, Walling established the Social Democratic League and became a staunch supporter of the Wilson administration. After the war, he worked with the AFL for labor rights. DAI 29:551-A.

2183 Teitelbaum, Kenneth, and Reese, William J. "American Socialist Pedagogy and Experimentation in the Progressive Era: The Socialist Sunday School." *History of Education Quarterly* 23 (1983): 429–54.

Socialist Sunday schools offered weekend education to children of the working class without the chauvinism and procapitalist bias of state schools, replacing these values with those of international socialism. The Red Scare put an end to this small Socialist party program. Notes.

2184 Von Mohrenschildt, Dmitri. "Reformers and Radicals in Pre-World War I America." *Russian Review* 17 (1958): 128–38.

Reformist and radical movements active during the Progressive era are surveyed.

2185 Webber, Christopher. "William Dwight Porter Bliss: Priest and Socialist." *History Magazine of the Protestant Episcopal Church* 28 (1959): 9–39.

Bliss's radicalism alienated many social Christians, but he did convince the Federal Council of Churches of Christ to endorse social Christianity.

2186 Weinstein, James. *The Decline of Socialism in America, 1912–1925.* New York: Vintage, 1969.

The Socialist party continued to prosper after the 1912 election through World War I, but the schisms caused by the Bolshevik Revolution and the Red Scare tore the party apart. Notes, bibliography, index.

2187 Whitfield, Stephen J. "Scott Nearing and the Ambiguity of American Radicalism." Ph.D. dissertation, Brandeis University, 1972.

Fired in 1915 from his teaching position at the University of Pennsylvania, Nearing was also forced to resign from Toledo University, in 1917, for denouncing preparedness. He rose to the forefront of the socialist antiwar movement in 1917–18 and was among the founders of the American Civil Liberties Union. DAI 33:3566-A.

COMMUNISM

See also below, *The Red Scare,* Chapter 6, *Radical Women,* and Chapter 11, *The Bolshevik Revolution.*

2188 Bo, Daniele. "On the Formation Process of the American Communist Party" (in Italian). *Movimento Operaio e Socialista* [Italy] 22 (1976): 51–86.

The Communist party grew out of the left wing of the Socialist Party over such issues as labor disputes and reaction to World War I. Militant socialists came together in early 1921 to form the American Communist party. Notes.

2189 Bykov, Vil'. "William Foster: Pages from His Life and Struggle" (in Russian). *Novaia i Noveishaia Istoriia* [USSR] (1973): 97–116.

A writer active in the Oregon Socialist party during the Progressive period, Foster became a labor organizer and eventually joined the Communist party in 1919. Notes.

2190 Draper, Theodore. *The Roots of American Communism.* New York: Viking, 1957.

American communism rose out the Socialist party's left wing following the Bolshevik Revolution. It appealed primarily to foreign-born workers. Notes, index.

2191 Evans, William B. " 'Revolutionist Thought' in the *Daily Worker*, 1919–1939." Ph.D. dissertation, University of Washington, 1965.

Chapter 1 covers the period from 1919 to 1921. The author finds a precise definition of 'revolutionist thought' difficult to arrive at, because it was constantly evolving, and because it was interdependent with revolutionist action. DAI 26:1002.

2192 Foner, Philip S. "Karl Liebknecht and the United States: A Documentary Study" (in German). *Jahrbuch für Wirtschaftsgeschichte* [East Germany] (1968): 11–75.

This German revolutionary leader, who made a speaking tour of the United States before World War I, is compared and contrasted with Eugene V. Debs. Liebknecht's writings were reprinted on occasion in American socialist papers. Notes.

2193 Furaev, V. K. "V. I. Lenin and the Consolidation of the Marxist Forces in the USA (1915–1922)" (in Russian). *Vestnik Leningradskogo Universiteta* [USSR] 14 (1970): 42–54.

Lenin followed the political situation in the United States and helped to educate American Marxists in practical politics. In 1919, Lenin dispatched Aleksandra M. Kollontai to give him a firsthand report on the United States. Notes.

2194 Hendrickson, Kenneth E. "The Public Career of Richard F. Pettigrew of South Dakota, 1848–1926." Ph.D. dissertation, University of Oklahoma, 1962.

Ambitious and energetic, Richard Pettigrew began his career as a conservative Republican, defected to the Democrats, then rejoined the Republicans so that he could support Theodore Roosevelt against Wilson in 1912. He became increasingly intrigued by left-wing politics, and by the end of World War I he had become a Communist. DAI 23:1333.

2195 Howe, Irving, and Coser, Lewis. *The American Communist Party: A Critical History (1919–1957).* Boston: Beacon, 1957.

The origins of the party in the aftermath of World War I and the Red Scare are discussed in the opening chapters. Notes, index.

2196 Ilkka, Richard J. "Rhetorical Dramatization in the Development of American Communism." *Quarterly Journal of Speech* 63 (1977): 413–27.

The Communist party was created after World War I amidst a barrage of rhetoric criticizing the Socialist party for being too moderate and praising the Bolshevik Revolution. Notes.

2197 Klehr, Harvey. "Leninist Theory in Search of America." *Polity* 9 (1976): 81–96.

An overview of Lenin's understanding and misunderstanding of American capital and labor is presented.

2198 Kostiainen, Auvo. *The Forging of Finnish-American Communism, 1917–1924.* Turku, Finland: Migration Institute, 1978.

The civil war in Finland and the Bolshevik Revolution both influenced Finnish Americans, who became Communists in large numbers. Appendixes, notes, bibliography, index.

2199 Krasnov, I. M. "The Rise of the Workers' Movement and the Founding of the Communist Party USA" (in Russian). *Voprosy Istorii* [USSR] (1981): 43–58.

The Communist party was not a foreign body in the United States. Rather, it was the agent of international Marxism-Leninism and the enemy of class collaboration.

2200 Millett, Stephen M. "Charles E. Ruthenberg: The Development of an American Communist, 1909–1927." *Ohio History* 81 (1972): 193–209.

Ruthenberg was a former Progressive who moved left to embrace first the Socialist party and then the Communist party. Thanks to friends in Moscow, Ruthenberg remained in a leadership position until his death. Notes.

2201 ———. "The Midwest Origins of the American Communist Party: The Leadership of

Charles E. Ruthenberg, 1919–1927." *Old Northwest* 1 (1975): 253–90.

Executive secretary of the Communist party, Ruthenberg gained ascendency by keeping the organization absolutely subservient to Moscow. Notes.

2202 Petrov, G. D. "Aleksandra Kollontai in the USA" (in Russian). *Novaia i Noveishaia Istoriia* [USSR] (1972): 128–42.

Exiled from czarist Russia because of her Leninist beliefs, Kollontai promoted Marxism-Leninism through speeches and publishing activities during two tours of the United States in 1915 and 1916. Notes.

2203 Shaffer, Ralph E. "Formation of the California Communist Labor Party." *Pacific Historical Review* 36 (1967): 59–78.

Following the Bolshevik Revolution, the Socialist party of California split, with one faction emerging as the Communist Labor party. Notes.

2204 Shapiro, Herbert. "Lincoln Steffens: The Evolution of an American Radical." Ph.D. dissertation, University of Rochester, 1964.

Lincoln Steffens was a thoughtful and intelligent journalist as well as a muckraker who used his influence to further causes he believed in. Increasingly leftist, he became interested in the process of revolution and was a strong supporter of Bolshevism. DAI 25:2953.

2205 Shopov, Petur. "Vladimir Ilyich Lenin and the United States of America" (in Bulgarian). *Istoricheski Pregled* [Bulgaria] 26 (1970): 179–94.

Lenin's influence on the American Left was apparent in the formation of the American Communist party. Lenin viewed America's actions during and after World War I as imperialism. Notes.

The Red Scare

GENERAL STUDIES

2206 Bowles, Dorothy. "Newspaper Support for Free Expression in Times of Alarm, 1920 and 1940." *Journalism Quarterly* 54 (1977): 271–79.

Most urban newspapers supported freedom of expression during the Red Scare.

2207 Buckingham, Peter H. *America Sees Red: Anti-Communism in America, 1870s to 1980s.* Claremont, CA: Regina, 1988.

Chapter 1 contains an overview of the Red Scare, including analysis of its origins, the Palmer raids, conservative reactions, and consequences. Part Two includes an extensive bibliography. Index.

2208 Burlingame, Roger. *The Sixth Column.* Philadelphia: Lippincott, 1962.

Assuming that anti-Communist crusades are always counterproductive (hence, a "sixth column"), the author includes a chapter on the Red Scare. Bibliography, index.

2209 Candeloro, Dominic. "Louis F. Post and the Red Scare of 1920." *Prologue* 11 (1979): 41–55.

The aged assistant secretary of labor played an important role in the Red Scare, standing up to A. Mitchell Palmer and J. Edgar Hoover on the issue of deporting alien anarchists when it became obvious to him that the rights of the accused were being violated in an atmosphere of hysteria. Notes.

2210 ———. "Louis Freeland Post: Carpetbagger, Singletaxer, Progressive." Ph.D. dissertation, University of Illinois, Urbana-Champaign, 1970.

The leader of the single-tax movement after the death of Henry George, Post was assistant secretary of labor from 1913 to 1921. His refusal to countenance the mass deportation of radicals during the Red Scare helped to checkmate the schemes of A. Mitchell Palmer and J. Edgar Hoover. DAI 31:6509-A.

2211 Cantelon, Philip L. "In Defense of America: Congressional Investigations of Communism in the United States, 1919–1935." Ph.D. dissertation, Indiana University, 1971.

The Red Scare brought the first appearance of the anti-Communist congressional investigation. The Overman committee chose to concentrate on the Bolshevik Revolution rather than on the activities of American Communists. DAI 32:6331-A.

2212 Chafee, Zechariah, Jr. *Free Speech in the United States.* Cambridge, MA: Harvard University Press, 1941.

Part One discusses freedom of speech in the wake of the Red Scare, including the wartime prosecutions, the Abrams case, postwar sedition laws, and the deportation of immigrants. Notes, appendix, index.

2213 ———. *Freedom of Speech*. New York: Harcourt, Brace, 1920.

A Harvard law professor and outspoken opponent of the Red Scare details the gross violations of American civil liberties that took place during that time of hysteria. Notes, bibliography, appendixes, index.

2214 Coben, Stanley. "A Study of Nativism: The American Red Scare of 1919–1920." *Political Science Quarterly* 79 (1964): 52–75.

The Red Scare is explained in terms of those who will respond to nativist appeals. At any given time, millions will follow demagogues into anti-Communist crusades. Notes.

2215 Damon, Allan L. "The Great Red Scare." *American Heritage* 19 (1968): 22–27ff.

In the wake of strikes, political violence, and racial incidents, Attorney General Palmer abandoned caution and took action together with young J. Edgar Hoover of the General Intelligence Division. The government's high-handed methods for dealing with suspected radicals created a backlash of feeling against Palmer.

2216 Fusfeld, Daniel R. *The Rise and Repression of Radical Labor USA—1877–1918*. Chicago: Charles Kerr, 1980.

Liberal reformers and conservative labor leaders worked together to repress labor radicalism. The Red Scare was a severe blow to the labor movement. Notes, bibliography, index.

2217 Gengarelly, William A. "Resistance Spokesmen: Opponents of the Red Scare, 1919–1921." Ph.D. dissertation, Boston University, 1972.

Resistance spokesmen were labor leaders, newspaper editors, clergymen, and lawyers opposed to the violence and hysteria of the Red Scare. They gravitated toward two organizations, the American Civil Liberties Union and the National Popular Government League. DAI 33:1649-A.

2218 ———. "Secretary of Labor William B. Wilson and the Red Scare, 1919–1920." *Pennsylvania History* 47 (1980): 311–30.

Wilson's subordinates, including Attorney General Palmer, worked together to circumvent the rights of enemy aliens accused of subversion. In 1920, when Wilson left town

briefly, Assistant Secretary of Labor Louis Post annulled over one thousand warrants of deportation, a move the secretary of labor eventually supported. Notes.

2219 Kostin, P. V. "The Unpublicized War against the Labor Movement (the American Secret Police in Action)" (in Russian). *Voprosy Istorii* [USSR] 10 (1967): 118–30.

During World War I and the Red Scare, government agencies curtailed the political rights of Americans and stifled the labor movement in the name of national security. Notes.

2220 Lamson, Peggy. *Roger Baldwin: Founder of the American Civil Liberties Union*. Boston: Houghton Mifflin, 1976.

This biography of Baldwin includes material on the Red Scare and on Baldwin's subsequent founding of the ACLU. Photographs, notes, bibliography, index.

2221 Lax, John, and Pencak, William. "Creating the American Legion." *South Atlantic Quarterly* 81 (1982): 43–55.

Fear engendered by the Bolshevik Revolution, the comradeship of wartime doughboys, and the special needs of war veterans were all key factors in the creation of the American Legion in 1919. Notes.

2222 Markmann, Charles L. *The Noblest Cry: A History of the American Civil Liberties Union*. New York: St. Martin's, 1965.

The opening chapters deal with the formation of the ACLU by concerned liberals after the massive violations of civil liberties during World War I and the Red Scare. Bibliography, appendix, index.

2223 Murray, Robert K. "The Outer World and the Inner Light: A Case Study." *Pennsylvania History* 36 (1969): 265–89.

The chief architect of the Red Scare, A. Mitchell Palmer had a Quaker background, a liberal record, and a reputation as a supporter of organized labor. Hesitant at first to exploit the public's fear, the "Fighting Quaker" and J. Edgar Hoover trampled on the civil liberties of those deemed "reds," although Palmer failed to parlay his work into election as president. Notes.

2224 ———. *Red Scare: A Study in National Hysteria, 1919–1920*. New York: McGraw-Hill, 1964.

The United States became engulfed in a Red Scare when fear supplanted faith and reason. The origins of the scare are detailed along with the effect of the Russian Revolution on America, strikes in Seattle and Boston, coal and steel strikes, and the Palmer raids. Notes, bibliography, index.

2225 Polenberg, Richard. *Fighting Faiths: The Abrams Case, the Supreme Court, and Free Speech.* New York: Viking, 1987.

Jacob Abrams was a Russian Jewish anarchist arrested and deported for protesting against the Allied intervention in the Russian Civil War. It was this case that led Justice Oliver Wendell Holmes to present his famous dissent expressing the view that the defendants posed no "clear and imminent danger" to the American system. Notes, bibliography, index.

2226 Powers, Richard G. *Secrecy and Power: The Life of J. Edgar Hoover.* New York: Free Press, 1987.

Hoover's ruthless ambition and political skill made him an important power beginning with the Red Scare of 1919–20. Photographs, notes, bibliography, index.

2227 Preston, William, Jr. *Aliens and Dissenters: Federal Suppression of Radicals, 1903–1933.* Cambridge, MA: Harvard University Press, 1963.

Nativist and antiradical upheaval were evident throughout the Progressive era and gained dominance during World War I. The Palmer raids and deportations of the Red Scare were sacrificial offerings to nativism and repression. Notes, bibliography, index.

2228 Prude, Jonathan. "Portrait of a Civil Libertarian: The Faith and Fear of Zechariah Chafee, Jr. " *Journal of American History* 60 (1973): 633–56.

The conservative Chafee devoted his life to fighting for free speech after the abuses of the Red Scare. Free speech, he argued, defused tension and brought about evolutionary change. Notes.

2229 Ragan, Fred D. "The *New Republic*: Red Hysteria and Civil Liberties." Ph.D. dissertation, University of Georgia, 1965.

The *New Republic* asserted that conservatism caused postwar hysteria by attempting to turn wartime anti-German passions against Bolsheviks and anarchists. Although the journal favored some repression of free speech when the war effort was threatened, it championed civil rights in most other cases. Generally, the *New Republic* furnished intelligent, compassionate, and even progressive

commentary during a period of hysteria and disillusionment. DAI 27:443-A.

2230 Smith, Donald L. *Zechariah Chafee, Jr.: Defender of Liberty and Law.* Cambridge, MA: Harvard University Press, 1986.

A law professor at Harvard, Chafee was an outspoken opponent of the Red Scare. He was forced to defend his right to speak out at the famous Harvard Club trial. Photographs, notes, index.

2231 Szajkowski, Zosa. "Double Jeopardy—The Abrams Case of 1919." *American Jewish Archives* 23 (1971): 6–32.

Several Russian Jews, including Jacob Abrams, were prosecuted under the Espionage Act. After the Supreme Court upheld the convictions, they were deported to Soviet Russia. Notes.

2232 ———. *Jews, Wars, and Communism.* 2 vols. New York: KTAV, 1974.

After World War I, American Jews assumed a position of leadership among Jews worldwide. Volume II contains material on the effect of the Red Scare on Jewish leftists. Notes, bibliography, index.

2233 Warth, Robert D. "The Palmer Raids." *South Atlantic Quarterly* 48 (1949): 1–23.

The Palmer raids against alien and native radicals during the Red Scare were the worst abuse of executive power against individual liberties in American history. Notes.

2234 Williams, David. "The Bureau of Investigation and Its Critics, 1919–1921: The Origins of Federal Political Surveillance." *Journal of American History* 68 (1981): 560–79.

Government spying on political dissenters began during World War I and escalated in the subsequent Red Scare. J. Edgar Hoover, head of the General Intelligence Division, learned during this period that Congress and the chief executive would support covert operations against radicals. Notes.

LOCAL AND REGIONAL STUDIES

2235 Colburn, David R. "Governor Alfred E. Smith and the Red Scare, 1919–20." *Political Science Quarterly* 88 (1973): 423–44.

New York's Governor Smith played an important role in stopping the Red Scare by advocating continued reform efforts and civil liberties for all. Notes.

2236 Cook, Philip L. "Red Scare in Denver." *Colorado Magazine* 43 (1966): 308–26.

Postwar frustrations, yellow journalism, and political demagoguery touched off the Red Scare in Denver. The scare climaxed in August 1920 during a violent strike by streetcar and electric railway workers, but it faded thereafter. Notes.

2237 Flynt, Wayne. "Florida Labor and Political 'Radicalism,' 1919–1920." *Labor History* 9 (1968): 73–90.

Work stoppages by cigar makers, miners, firemen, and others combined with the efforts of blacks to become unionized alarmed the general public during the Red Scare in Florida. Notes.

2238 ———. "Organized Labor, Reform and Alabama Politics, 1920." *Alabama Review* 23 (1970): 163–80.

The atmosphere of hysterical antiradicalism and antilaborism made it impossible for the United Mine Workers to elect officials who would represent their interests in Alabama. Notes.

2239 Friedheim, Robert L. *The Seattle General Strike*. Seattle: University of Washington Press, 1964.

Seattle's rapid growth during the war created a special brand of labor radicals who were determined to demonstrate their power and to keep what they had gained during the wartime boom. Photographs, notes, bibliography, index.

2240 Jaffe, Julian F. *Crusade against Radicalism: New York during the Red Scare, 1914–1924*. Port Washington, NY: Kennikat, 1972.

The Red Scare in New York had its origins in World War I. Large numbers of immigrants and radicals made the scare more intense and longer lasting in New York than it was elsewhere. The New York experience was repulsive enough to the American people to bring about a reaction against it. Notes, bibliography, index.

2241 Josephson, Harold. "The Dynamics of Repression: New York during the Red Scare." *Mid-America* 59 (1977): 131–46.

Conservatives used the Red Scare to fight radicalism and labor unions. The scare also brought the besieged radicals together and provided them with inspiring martyrs. Notes.

2242 Koss, Frederick M. "The Boston Police Strike of 1919." Ph.D. dissertation, Boston University Graduate School, 1966.

After years of fruitless attempts to win adequate wages and decent working conditions, the Boston police, encouraged by the AFL, formed a union. The union's legality was immediately questioned, a trial board was convened, and a committee was appointed to resolve the problem. No agreement emerged, and the policemen went on strike. Governor Calvin Coolidge stepped in and insisted on discharging all union police, giving them no hope of rehiring. The postwar press and public approved of this harsh solution. DAI 27:1321-A.

2243 Lovin, Hugh T. "The Red Scare in Idaho, 1916–1918." *Idaho Yesterdays* 17 (1973): 2–13.

Vigilantes and the state violated the civil liberties of radicals during the Red Scare, but mostly in nonviolent and apparently legal ways.

2244 McClelland, John M., Jr. "Terror on Tower Avenue." *Pacific Northwest Quarterly* 57 (1966): 65–72.

Events surrounding the Centralia massacre of November 1919 are reexamined, including the gun battle between the IWW and local vigilantes and the subsequent murder trials. Notes.

2245 Murray, Robert K. "Communism and the Great Steel Strike of 1919." *Mississippi Valley Historical Review* 38 (1951): 445–66.

The hysteria of the Red Scare was so great that it turned the public against the steel strikers and made industrial unionism impossible until after passage of the Wagner Act. Notes.

2246 O'Connor, Harvey. *Revolution in Seattle: A Memoir*. New York: Monthly Review, 1964.

An unreconstructed socialist details his part in the Seattle general strike during the Red Scare, a time when the American Left was briefly unified in the heady days following the Bolshevik Revolution. Notes, appendixes, index.

2247 Russell, Francis. "The Strike that Made a President." *American Heritage* 14 (1963): 44–47ff.

Massachusetts's Governor Calvin Coolidge gained national prominence from his actions during the Boston police strike. He parlayed this performance into the Republican vice-presidential nomination in 1920.

2248   Sale, Roger. "Seattle's Crisis, 1914–1919." *American Studies* 14 (1973): 29–48.

A special set of factors made Seattle especially vulnerable to the Red Scare, among them its newness, isolation, militant radicalism, and excessive moralism. Notes.

2249   Sanbonmatsu, Akira. "Darrow and Rorke's Use of Burkeian Identification Strategies in *New York vs Gitlow* (1920)." *Speech Monographs* 38 (1971): 36–48.

In defense of Benjamin Gitlow, a Communist publisher and political leader, Clarence Darrow used the identification theory of Kenneth Burke to sway the jury. Notes.

2250   Taft, Philip. "Mayor Short and the I.W.W. Agricultural Workers." *Labor History* 7 (1966): 173–77.

Mayor Wallace Short of Sioux City, Iowa, faced down hostile locals when the IWW held a mass convention in his city in April 1919.

2251   Williams, David. "Sowing the Wind: The Deportation Raids of 1920 in New Hampshire." *Historic New Hampshire* 34 (1979): 1–31.

The Palmer raids of 1920 netted 260 suspected alien radicals in New Hampshire. Those arrested were systematically deprived of their constitutional rights. The role of Weston Anderson (a native of New Hampshire) in securing the release of the accused radicals is examined. Notes.

9

Foreign Affairs:
General and Bilateral

Wilson began his presidency with the hope that he could bring a new sense of justice to American foreign policy, in contrast to the illiberalism of his immediate predecessors. The impulse to help Western hemispheric peoples of color behave more like Americans led to military interventions and other interference in the internal affairs of other nations. Increasingly, though, the president became preoccupied with Europe, where the great powers were engaged in what was then called "The Great War."

A thoughtful essay written a generation ago by William E. Leuchtenburg, "Progressivism and Imperialism: The Progressive Movement and American Foreign Policy" (#2253), is a good place to begin an examination of the links between Progressive domestic reform and foreign policy. The basic documents are reproduced in U.S. Department of State, *Foreign Relations of the United States, 1913–1921* (#2262). Among the most useful general interpretations of Wilsonian foreign policy are Sidney Bell, *Righteous Conquest: Woodrow Wilson and the Evolution of the New Diplomacy* (#2264); Frederick S. Calhoun, *Power and Principle: Armed Intervention in Wilsonian Foreign Policy* (#2267); Lloyd Gardner, *A Covenant with Power: America and World Order from Wilson to Reagan* (#2272) and "A Progressive Foreign Policy, 1900–1921" (#2273); Arthur S. Link, *Woodrow Wilson: Revolution, War, and Peace* (#2283); and Harley Notter, *The Origins of the Foreign Policy of Woodrow Wilson* (#2289). Wilson's shaping of public opinion in support of his policies is examined by Robert C. Hilderbrand, *Power and the People: Executive Management of Public Opinion in Foreign Affairs, 1897–1921* (#2308).

For general background on Wilson's Asia policy, see the still useful works by Roy W.

Curry, *Woodrow Wilson and Far Eastern Policy, 1913–1921* (#2312), and A. Whitney Griswold, *The Far Eastern Policy of the United States* (#2313). The American response to the upheaval in China is examined by Warren I. Cohen, "America and the May Fourth Movement: The Response to Chinese Nationalism, 1917–1921" (#2317); Daniel M. Crane and Thomas A. Breslin, *An Ordinary Relationship: American Opposition to Republican Revolution in China* (#2318); Jerry Israel, *Progressivism and the Open Door: America and China, 1905–1921* (#2325); Li Tien-yi, *Woodrow Wilson's China Policy, 1913–1917* (#2327); and Noel Pugach, "Making the Open Door Work: Paul S. Reinsch in China, 1913–1919" (#2333). The best overview on the growing friction between Japan and the United States during the Wilson years is Burton Beers, *Vain Endeavor: Robert Lansing's Attempts to End the American-Japanese Rivalry* (#2338).

Paternalism and interventionism dominated Caribbean policy. Differing interpretations may be found in Purvis M. Carter, *Congressional and Public Reaction to Wilson's Caribbean Policy, 1913–1917* (#2350), and Dana G. Munro, *Intervention and Dollar Diplomacy in the Caribbean, 1900–1921* (#2353). On Cuba, see George W. Baker, Jr., "The Wilson Administration and Cuba, 1913–1921" (#2355), and Leo J. Meyer, "The United States and the Cuban Revolution of 1917" (#2357). David Healy, *Gunboat Diplomacy in the Wilson Era: The U.S. Navy in Haiti, 1915–1916* (#2364), finds that strategic and financial considerations mixed with racism to shape policy toward Haiti, while Hans Schmidt, *The United States Occupation of Haiti, 1915–1934* (#2369), examines the realities of American colonialism.

Wilson's brand of Pan-Americanism is the subject of a monograph by Mark T. Gilderhus, *Pan American Visions: Woodrow Wilson in the Western Hemisphere, 1913–1921* (#2380). Interventionism is examined by Lester D. Langley, *The Banana Wars: An Inner History of American Empire, 1900–1934* (#2385). Postwar policy is covered in Joseph C. Tulchin, *The Aftermath of War: World War I and U.S. Policy toward Latin America* (#2394).

Historians have studied the president's attitudes and actions toward Mexico very closely. Overviews are provided by Mark T. Gilderhus, *Diplomacy and Revolution: U.S.-Mexican Relations under Wilson and Carranza* (#2423); P. Edward Haley, *Revolution and Intervention: The Diplomacy of Taft and Wilson in Mexico, 1910–1917* (#2433); Larry D. Hill, *Emissaries to a Revolution: Woodrow Wilson's Executive Agents in Mexico, 1910–1917* (#2440); Robert Freeman Smith, *The United States and Revolutionary Nationalism in Mexico, 1916–1932* (#2474); and Berta Ulloa Ortiz, *La Revolución Intervenida: Relaciones Diplomáticas entre México y Estados Unidos, 1910–1914* (#2482). International rivalry in Mexico during this period is examined by Peter Calvert, *The Mexican Revolution, 1910–1914: The Diplomacy of Anglo-American Conflict* (#2408), and Friedrich Katz, *The Secret War in Mexico: Europe, the United States and the Mexican Revolution* (#2448).

Wilson's determination to force the ouster of General Victoriano Huerta led to the intervention at Veracruz in 1914, one of the most controversial episodes in Wilson's presidency. Begin with Robert E. Quirk, *An Affair of Honor: Woodrow Wilson and the Occupation of Veracruz* (#2464). See also Kendrick A. Clements, "Woodrow Wilson's Mexican Policy, 1913–1915" (#2412); Kenneth J. Grieb, *The United States and Huerta* (#2431); Michael C. Meyer, "The Arms of the *Ypiranga*" (#2457); and Louis M. Teitelbaum, *Woodrow Wilson and the Mexican Revolution (1913–1916): A History of United States-Mexican Relations from the Murder of Madero until Villa's Provocation across the Border* (#2477). On Villa's raid and the subsequent American punitive expedition, see Clarence C. Clendenen, *The United States and Pancho Villa: A Study in Unconventional Diplomacy* (#2414), and a number of works cited in Chapter 3. The 1919 crisis is examined by Manuel A. Machado, Jr. and James T. Judge, "Tempest in a Teapot? The Mexican-United States Intervention Crisis of 1919" (#2456), and by Clifford W. Trow, "Woodrow Wilson and the Mexican Interventionist Movement of 1919" (#2479).

America's interest in the Middle East grew during the Wilson period as a result of increasing dependence on oil, Turkey's participation in World War I, and Zionist agitation for a Jewish homeland. See John A. DeNovo, *American Interests and Policies in the Middle East, 1900–1939* (#2493); Laurence Evans, *United States Policy and the Partition of Turkey, 1914–1924* (#2495); Harry N. Howard, *Turkey, the Straits and U.S. Policy* (#2500); and Roger R. Trask, *The United States Response to Turkish Nationalism and Reform, 1914–1939* (#2504). On the Balfour Declaration, see Charles I. Goldblatt, "The Impact of the Balfour Declaration in America" (#2496), and Richard N. Lebow, "Woodrow Wilson and the Balfour Declaration" (#2502).

For works that concentrate on relations between the United States and France, see the opening chapters in Henry Blumenthal, *Illusion and Reality in Franco-American Diplomacy, 1914–1945* (#2507), and Melvyn P. Leffler, *The Elusive Quest: America's Pursuit of European Stability and French Security, 1919–1933* (#2508). Many of the points of friction between the United States and Britain during the first two years of Wilson's tenure are noted in a doctoral dissertation by Phillip S. Kaplan, "The Crisis in Anglo-American Relations of 1913–1914" (#2522), but Michael J. Hogan, *Informal Entente: The Private Structure of Cooperation in Anglo-American Economic Diplomacy, 1918–1928* (#2519), emphasizes that cooperation rather than conflict was the rule after World War I. Italian-American relations are examined in a doctoral dissertation by John W. Gould, "Italy and the United States, 1914–1918: Background to Confrontation" (#2536).

Foreign Affairs: General

GENERAL ACCOUNTS

See also *Bibliographies: Foreign Affairs,* in Chapter 13.

2252 Dallek, Robert. *The American Style of Foreign Policy: Cultural Politics and Foreign Affairs.* New York: Mentor, 1983.

The author includes a chapter on Wilson's foreign policy, which reflected an intensification of the Progressive mood. Americans became interested in saving foreign peoples from themselves. Notes, index.

2253 Leuchtenburg, William E. "Progressivism and Imperialism: The Progressive Movement and American Foreign Policy, 1898–1916." *Mississippi Valley Historical Review* 39 (1952): 483–504.

Progressive domestic reform and imperialism overseas were motivated by the same impulses. One of the most debated of scholarly articles, this is still important reading. Notes.

2254 Link, Arthur S., and Leary, William M., Jr., eds. *The Diplomacy of World Power: The United States, 1889–1920.* New York: St. Martin's, 1970.

Key documents from the period when America became a world power are presented, including documents on Wilson and Latin America, the Far East, the Great War, and peacemaking. Bibliography.

2255 Livermore, Seward W. " 'Deserving Democrats': The Foreign Service under Woodrow Wilson." *South Atlantic Quarterly* 69 (1970): 144–60.

Secretary of State William Jennings Bryan and southern Democrats wanted to reward their followers with diplomatic jobs and Wilson obliged them—to the detriment of American foreign policy. Notes.

2256 Marina, William F. "Opponents of Empire: An Interpretation of American Anti-Imperialism, 1898–1921." Ph.D. dissertation, University of Denver, 1968.

Anti-imperialists were reduced to a tiny band of activists during the Progressive era. Their only accomplishment was the congressional passage of the Jones act of 1916 pledging eventual independence to the Philippines. DAI 30:662-A.

2257 Markowitz, Gerald E. "Progressive Imperialism: Consensus and Conflict in the Progressive Movement on Foreign Policy, 1898–1917." Ph.D. dissertation, University of Wisconsin, 1971.

Progressives were interested in foreign affairs, and they regarded the United States as a perfect model for the underdeveloped to follow. World peace was necessary for American commercial expansion, so Progressives supported peace efforts and international organizations such as the League of Nations. DAI 32:2036-A.

2258 Murphy, Donald J. "Professors, Publicists, and Pan Americanism, 1905–1917: A Study in the Origins of the Use of 'Experts' in Shaping American Foreign Policy." Ph.D. dissertation, University of Wisconsin, 1970.

In 1905, Secretary of State Elihu Root brought together a group of academics to promote a new Pan-Americanism designed to open new markets to the south. Wilson's acceptance of South American mediation in the dispute with Mexico revived intellectual interest in helping the government. DAI 31:5992-A.

2259 O'Brien, Dennis J. "The Oil Crisis and the Foreign Policy of the Wilson Administration." Ph.D. dissertation, University of Missouri, Columbia, 1974.

Oilmen and the State Department cooperated on oil policy during and after World War I, as the strategic importance of petroleum became apparent. Cooperation on strategy during the crisis with Mexico set important precedents in what became a new era of international and multinational petroleum diplomacy. DAI 36: 489-A.

2260 Shimura, Kosuke. "An Aspect of Progressivism in America: In Relation to Imperialism" (in Japanese). *Seiyo-shigaku* [Japan] 38 (1958): 109–27.

Progressivism and imperialism both came to the fore in the United States after the turn of the century. Progressives accepted imperialism, because they already saw themselves as a national elite, and because they were influenced by the intellectual currents of Social Darwinism and nativism.

2261 Tarlton, Charles D. "Internationalism, War, and Politics in American Thought, 1898–1920." Ph.D. dissertation, University of California, Los Angeles, 1964.

The author identifies three styles of early internationalist thought: utopian, deterministic, and pragmatic internationalism. While the first two styles were more popular, it was only the third, pragmatic internationalism, that allowed sufficient flexibility to deal with the complexity of the real world. DAI 25:598.

2262 U.S. Department of State. *Foreign Relations of the United States.* Annual volumes, 1913–1921, and supplements. Washington, DC: Government Printing Office, 1920–1947.

Annual volumes and special supplements published by the Department of State are an important source for basic documents in American foreign relations. The diplomacy of the Wilson administration is documented in the following volumes, listed by year covered, subtitle if any, number of volumes if more than one, and publication date: 1913 (1920); 1914 (1922); 1914 supplement, the World War (1931); 1915 (1924); 1916 (1925); 1917 supplement 1, the World War (1931); 1918 (1930); 1918 Russia, 3 vols. (1931); 1919, 2 vols. (1934); 1919 Russia (1937); 1919 The Paris Peace Conference, 13 vols. (1942–1947); 1920, 3 vols. (1936); 1921, 2 vols. (1936); The Lansing Papers, 1914–1920, 2 vols. (1939–40).

2263 Varg, Paul A. "The United States a World Power, 1900–1917: Myth or Reality?" In John Braeman, Robert H. Bremner, and David Brody, eds. *Twentieth-Century American Foreign Policy.* Columbus: Ohio State University Press, 1971, pp. 207–40.

American policies toward China and Cuba are contrasted to illustrate that the country was just becoming aware of its new status as a great power. Notes.

WILSON AND FOREIGN AFFAIRS

See also Chapter 1, *Autobiographical and Biographical Materials,* Chapter 2, *Wilson Presidency,* Chapter 10, and Chapter 12.

2264 Bell, Sidney. *Righteous Conquest: Woodrow Wilson and the Evolution of the New Diplomacy.* Port Washington, NY: Kennikat, 1972.

In this analysis of the interaction between Wilson's thought and diplomatic practice prior to America's entry into the World War, the author hypothesizes that Wilson tried to create a new order to make the world a place fit for American growth. Notes, bibliography, index.

2265 Buehrig, Edward H., ed. *Wilson's Foreign Policy in Perspective.* Gloucester, MA: Peter Smith, 1970.

Lectures by leading scholars on Wilsonian foreign policy marking the 1956 centennial of Wilson's birth are reprinted. Topics include the role of Colonel House, collective security, the Far East, Latin America, and a British view of Wilson's foreign policy.

2266 Burns, Richard Dean, and Urquidi, Donald. "Woodrow Wilson and Disarmament: Ideas vs. Realities." *Aerospace History* 18 (1971): 186–94.

Disarmament was given a low priority at the Paris Peace Conference, and Wilson never

thought out the problem completely, but he pioneered in developing a commitment to disarm. Notes.

2267 Calhoun, Frederick S. *Power and Principle: Armed Intervention in Wilsonian Foreign Policy.* Kent, OH: Kent State University Press, 1986.

More than any other president, Wilson defined how foreign interventions could be used to support foreign policy. His seven armed interventions left models for dealing with revolutions and international aggression and showed how convenient a method force was. In the end, though, Wilson realized that force offered few lasting benefits. Notes, bibliography, index.

2268 Dobson, John M. *America's Ascent: The United States becomes a Great Power, 1880–1914.* DeKalb: Northern Illinois University Press, 1978.

American expansionism was fueled by economic necessity, missionary zeal, and moralism. A concluding chapter deals with Wilson, who was unable to reconcile divergent impulses of altruism and national selfishness. Notes, bibliography, index.

2269 Ford, Harold P. "Centennial Thoughts about Wilsonian Diplomacy." *Christianity and Crisis* 16 (1956): 176–78.

Wilson's approach to diplomacy was a black-and-white one, with world problems reduced to simple symbols and the president overconfident about his ability to grasp problems and manipulate public opinion.

2270 Gandi, Vera. "The Limits of Wilsonian Internationalism" (in Italian). *Communità* [Italy] 35 (1981): 96–152.

Wilson's idealism and his more practical ideas for a new world order are discussed along with his transformation from a British-style liberal into a proponent of the New Freedom.

2271 Gardner, Lloyd C. "American Foreign Policy 1900–1921: A Second Look at the Realist Critique of American Diplomacy." In Barton J. Bernstein, ed. *Towards a New Past: Dissenting Essays in American History.* New York: Pantheon, 1968, pp. 202–31.

This radical critique of the realists regards Wilson as the most imperialist-minded of the Progressive presidents, whose vision of world peace rested on antiradicalism. Notes.

2272 ———. *A Covenant with Power: America and World Order from Wilson to Reagan.* New York: Oxford University Press, 1984.

Wilson made a covenant to serve liberal capitalism in the world against the forces of war and revolution. He embraced preparedness, hoping to use it for his own liberal purposes, for the war threatened American political institutions on several fronts. Bibliography, index.

2273 ———. "A Progressive Foreign Policy, 1900–1921." In William A. Williams, ed. *From Colony to Empire: Essays in the History of American Foreign Relations*. New York: Wiley, 1972, pp. 203–51.

This overview of Progressive foreign policy from the New Left perspective finds Wilson to be the high priest of the liberal faith, who made fashionable once again the argument that America was the world's savior while he was busily engaged in seeking new economic advantages overseas. Notes.

2274 ———. *Wilson and Revolutions: 1913–1921*. Philadelphia: Lippincott, 1976.

Part One is an extended essay discussing Wilson's reactions to the Mexican Revolution, the overthrow of the czar of Russia, the Bolsheviks' rise to power, and intervention in the Russian civil war. Part Two reproduces key source documents. Notes, bibliography.

2275 Gelfand, Lawrence E. "The Mystique of Wilsonian Statecraft." *Diplomatic History* 7 (1983): 87–101.

From the outset of his presidency, Wilson was determined to be his own secretary of state. To prevent future wars, he proposed freedom of the seas, nationhood based on ethnic self-determination, and a League of Nations based on collective security. Central to the debate over his foreign policies is whether they failed because of basic fallacies or because of the way in which they were managed. Notes.

2276 Glen, Johnson M. "Human Rights and United States Foreign Policy." *India Quarterly* [India] 35 (1978): 471–90.

Wilson was the first president to use human rights as a guiding principle in foreign policy, with far-reaching effects to the present day.

2277 Graham, Otis L., Jr. *The Great Campaign: Reform and War in America, 1900–1928*. Englewood Cliffs, NJ: Prentice-Hall, 1971.

Part Three discusses Wilson, who should have used his power more effectively to keep the United States out of World War I and concentrated instead on continued domestic reform. Photographs, notes, bibliography, index.

2278 Herman, Sondra R. *Eleven against War: Studies in American Internationalist Thought, 1898–1921*. Stanford, CA: Hoover Institution Press, 1969.

Wilson is among the eleven intellectuals and statesmen discussed. The president united internationalists by giving them common interests and an inspiring set of ideals. Notes, bibliography, index.

2279 Huthmacher, J. Joseph, and Susman, Warren I., eds. *Wilson's Diplomacy: An International Symposium*. Cambridge, MA: Schenkman, 1973.

Arthur Link, Jean-Baptiste Duroselle, Ernst Fraenkel, and H. G. Nicholas contribute essays on Wilson's foreign policy seen from different national perspectives. A rejoinder section following the articles allows participants to comment on one another's work. Notes.

2280 Kihl, Mary A. "A Failure in Ambassadorial Diplomacy." *Journal of American History* 57 (1970): 636–53.

By late 1916, Anglo-American diplomatic communications were breaking down, because the American ambassador to London, Walter Hines Page, was too pro-British for a president determined to remain neutral, while the British ambassador, Cecil Spring-Rice, was disliked by Wilson's right-hand man, Colonel Edward M. House. Notes.

2281 Langer, William L. "Woodrow Wilson: His Education in World Affairs." *Confluence* 5 (1956): 183–94.

Wilson knew little about foreign affairs before he became president, so he learned mostly by hard experience. He learned that the Allies wanted no guidance from him and were far more interested in their secret treaty arrangements than in the president's own peace ideas. Wilson also discovered the perils of relying on public opinion and the need for more education among the people.

2282 Link, Arthur S. " 'Wilson the Diplomatist' in Retrospect." In Dewey W. Grantham, ed. *The Higher Realism of Woodrow Wilson and Other Essays*. Nashville: Vanderbilt University Press, 1971, pp. 72–87.

The world has honored Wilson most for his failures, but his achievements were many. He reaffirmed the American tradition of helpfulness toward nations struggling for democracy, vindicated the right of self-determination, strengthened the principle of peaceful settlement of disputes, and left a strong foundation of peace through cooperation. Notes.

2283 ———. *Woodrow Wilson: Revolution, War, and Peace*. Arlington Heights, IL: Harlan Davidson, 1979.

This revised edition of *Wilson the Diplomatist* (Baltimore, MD: Johns Hopkins University Press, 1957) represents a more mature understanding of Wilson's foreign policy based on twenty more years of research and the work of a new generation of scholars. Topics include an overview of the president's diplomacy, neutrality, the decision for war, the peace program, and the fight for the League of Nations. Bibliography, index.

2284 ———, ed. *Woodrow Wilson and a Revolutionary World*. Chapel Hill: University of North Carolina Press, 1982.

Papers from a 1979 Princeton University symposium on various aspects of Wilsonian foreign policy are presented by Lloyd Gardner, Betty Miller Unterberger, Inga Floto, Kurt Wimer, and others. Notes, index.

2285 Manning, Clarence. "Woodrow Wilson and American Foreign Policy." *Ukrainian Quarterly* 12 (1956): 332–39.

Theodore Roosevelt and Henry Cabot Lodge, ideological opponents of Wilson, had a better grasp of world politics than did the president. The League was more important to Wilson than anything, even peace. Notes.

2286 Martin, Laurence. "Necessity and Principle: Woodrow Wilson's Views." *Review of Politics* 22 (1960): 96–114.

Wilson tried to transcend the balance of power with a balance of satisfaction to keep the peace. He hoped that war would become an ineffective method of satisfying national aspirations and that moral satisfaction would result. Notes.

2287 Moynihan, Daniel P. "Morality and American Foreign Policy: Was Woodrow Wilson Right?" *Foreign Service Journal* 51 (1974): 8–12ff.

Wilson was right in his determination to make American foreign policy moral.

2288 Ninkovich, Frank. "Ideology, the Open Door, and Foreign Policy." *Diplomatic History* 6 (1982): 185–208.

The ideology behind the Open Door is identified as nineteenth-century liberalism, a pacifist, nonpolitical approach to expanding trade and culture throughout the world. Many proponents of the Open Door, such as Wilson, advocated the use of force when necessary. Notes.

2289 Notter, Harley. *The Origins of the Foreign Policy of Woodrow Wilson*. Baltimore, MD: Johns Hopkins Press, 1937.

All the essential elements of Wilson's foreign policy were formulated before he became president. Part One covers prepresidential backgrounds, and Part Two discusses Wilson's foreign policy from 1913 to 1917. Notes, bibliography, index.

2290 Osgood, Robert E. "Woodrow Wilson, Collective Security, and the Lessons of History." *Confluence* 5 (1957): 341–54.

American membership in the United Nations is a partial vindication of Wilson. Collective security as he envisioned it, though, is far from the modern reality.

2291 Safford, Jeffrey J. *Wilsonian Maritime Diplomacy, 1913–1921*. New Brunswick, NJ: Rutgers University Press, 1978.

The Wilson administration understood the need for a strong merchant marine to help insure a stable domestic political economy and carry out United States foreign policy. Notes, bibliography, index.

2292 Schmickle, William E. "For the Proper Use of Victory: Diplomacy and the Imperatives of Vision in the Foreign Policy of Woodrow Wilson, 1916–1919." Ph.D. dissertation, Duke University, 1979.

Wilson held a high moral vision of a reformed postwar order. Diplomatic inexperience corrupted his program, while his pride led him to commit further errors. Pure theory and idealism proved to be poor substitutes for practicality. DAI 40:2253-A.

2293 Schmid, Karl. "Some Observations on Certain Principles of Woodrow Wilson." *Confluence* 5 (1956): 264–76.

Wilson clung too much to lofty principles, although his aims and goals (including the rule of law, freedom for all peoples, collective security, and a lasting peace) were valid and attainable.

2294 Seymour, Charles. "Woodrow Wilson in Perspective." *Foreign Affairs* 34 (1955): 175–86.

Wilson should be remembered not so much for creating the League of Nations as for his attempts to foster freedom and international justice.

2295 Sheikholislam, Ali. "Open Diplomacy and Registration of Treaties." Ph.D. dissertation, New York University, 1959.

World War I exposed a number of secret treaties between nations, eliciting considerable public protest. Wilson's 1918 peace plan proposed that only "open covenants openly arrived at" should be valid, a condition that was widely accepted and incorporated into the League of Nations. DAI 20:4159.

2296 Thompson, J. A. "Woodrow Wilson and World War I: A Reappraisal." *Journal of American Studies* [Great Britain] 19 (1985): 325–48.

Wilson was realistic in his approach to the war and to the peace that followed, but he became unpopular when he could not tie them to continuing economic growth and future American security. Notes.

2297 Van Alstyne, Richard W. "World War I and Its Aftermath." *Current History* 35 (1958): 193–98.

Wilson's foreign policy went through two distinct phases, beginning with neutrality and evolving into taking control of a crusade for world righteousness. Notes.

2298 Walden, Daniel. "Race and Imperialism: The Achilles Heel of the Progressives." *Science and Society* 31 (1967): 222–32.

Self-appointed conveyers of the white Anglo-Saxon Protestant tradition, the Progressives were imperialists abroad and used racial segregation at home to further their colonialist ideology. Notes.

CONGRESS AND FOREIGN POLICY

See also Chapter 3, *Congressional and Political Leaders,* and Chapter 12, *Paris Peace Conference and Ratification Controversy.*

2299 Adams, John W. "The Influences Affecting Naval Shipbuilding Legislation, 1910–1916." *Naval War College Review* 22 (1969): 41–70.

Isolationism and an economic downturn made Congress reluctant to support naval requests for a substantial shipbuilding program. The German threat finally moved Congress to action.

2300 Allen, Howard W. "Republican Reformers and Foreign Policy, 1913–1917." *Mid-America* 44 (1962): 222–29.

Progressive Republican senators seldom voted as a bloc on foreign policy issues during Wilson's first term, because they held a wide variety of opinions and were responding to different constituencies.

2301 Butler, Harold T. "Partisan Positions on Isolationism vs. Internationalism, 1918–1933." Ph.D. dissertation, Syracuse University, 1963.

The Republican party appeared to be more isolationist than the Democrats in 1919–20, but this was more a reflection of short-term political tactics than deep-seated ideology. DAI 25:5885.

2302 Grinder, Robert D. "Progressives, Conservatives and Imperialism: Another Look at the Senate Republicans, 1913–1917." *North Dakota Quarterly* 41 (1973): 28–39.

Consistent in their thinking about domestic as well as foreign matters, conservative senators tended to be more imperialist than were Progressives.

2303 Ryley, Thomas W. *A Little Group of Willful Men: A Study of Congressional-Presidential Authority.* Port Washington, NY: Kennikat, 1975.

This is a study of the Senate group that opposed American entry into the World War. Notes, bibliography, index.

2304 Sutton, Walter A. "The Command of Gold—Progressive Republican Senators and Foreign Policy, 1912–1917." Ph.D. dissertation, University of Texas, 1964.

Progressive Republicans in the Senate believed that America was the greatest nation on earth in its final process of perfection. Most were isolationists who equated an aggressive foreign policy with narrow economic interests. Their varied positions on Latin American as well as European relations are analyzed. DAI 25:443.

PUBLIC OPINION AND FOREIGN AFFAIRS

See also Chapter 7, *Public Opinion and the Press,* and Chapter 12, *Paris Peace Conference, Public Opinion and the Press.*

2305 Blassingame, John W. "The Press and American Intervention in Haiti and the

Dominican Republic, 1904–1920." *Caribbean Studies* 9 (1969): 27–43.

Most journalists supported the right and the need to intervene in Caribbean countries during the Progressive era and only changed to noninterventionism in 1920. Notes.

2306 Buckley, John P. *The New York Irish: Their View of American Foreign Policy, 1914–1921*. New York: Arno, 1976.

A hardcore of Irish professionals alienated the majority of New York Irish with their demands for Irish independence during World War I. They picked up majority support for their views after the war and played a large role in defeating the Treaty of Versailles because it ignored the Irish question.

2307 Gerson, Louis L. *The Hyphenate in Recent American Politics and Diplomacy*. Lawrence: University of Kansas Press, 1964.

Part Two discusses the influence of immigrant groups on Wilson's thinking about neutrality, the war, and the peace settlement. Notes, appendix, index.

2308 Hilderbrand, Robert C. *Power and the People: Executive Management of Public Opinion in Foreign Affairs, 1897–1921*. Chapel Hill: University of North Carolina Press, 1981.

Presidents in this period gave closer attention to the press and public opinion. Wilson used a public relations campaign to win support for his Mexico policy and created the Committee on Public Information to publicize his war and peace aims. His attempt to rally public support for the Treaty of Versailles had little effect on the Senate. Notes, bibliography, index.

2309 Startt, James D. "Early Press Reaction to Wilson's League Proposal." *Journalism Quarterly* 39 (1962): 301–8.

The newspapers of William Randolph Hearst criticized the League idea from the outset. Papers in the South and Far West generally favored the idea, while editorial opinion in the East and Midwest was split. Notes.

2310 Tarlton, Charles D. "The Styles of American International Thought: Mahan, Bryan, and Lippmann." *World Politics* 17 (1965): 584–614.

Three different types of political philosophy translated into three divergent world views. Alfred T. Mahan was at once pessimistic and realistic, William Jennings Bryan was idealistic and moralistic, and Walter Lippmann was scientific and pragmatic. Notes.

Foreign Affairs: Bilateral Relations

AFRICA

See also Chapter 6, *Minority Groups, Leaders and Organizations,* and *Blacks.*

2311 Coger, Dalvan M. "American District Commissioners on the Liberian Frontier." *Liberian Studies Journal* 10 (1984): 24–38.

To make up for Liberia's loss of trade with Germany after 1914, the Wilson administration dangled a loan and American administrators before President D. B. King, who thwarted the deal because it would have violated Liberian sovereignty. Notes.

ASIA

See also Chapter 6, *Immigration,* and Chapter 10, *Wartime Relations, Asia.*

2312 Curry, Roy W. *Woodrow Wilson and Far Eastern Policy, 1913–1921.* New York: Bookman, 1957.

Wilson was president at a time of momentous change in the Far East. His methods were flexible within his framework of traditional American principles. Notes, bibliography, index.

2313 Griswold, A. Whitney. *The Far Eastern Policy of the United States.* New York: Harcourt, Brace and World, 1938.

Chapters 5, 6, and 7 of this classic account cover Wilson's Far East policies. Three key factors interacted to shape the president's outlook on the Orient: the precedents of his predecessors, his own "war-inspired gospel," and the influences of China and Britain. Notes, appendix, bibliography, index.

China
See also Chapter 3, *Paul S. Reinsch.*

2314 Berger, Henry W. "Warren Austin in China, 1916–1917." *Vermont History* 40 (1972): 246–61.

An international lawyer, Warren Austin, negotiated agreements between American companies and the Chinese government in 1916 and 1917, an experience that left him pessimistic about the possibilities for close economic relations with China. Notes.

2315 Brewer, Karen L. "From Philanthropy to Reform: The American Red Cross in China, 1906–1930." Ph.D. dissertation, Case Western Reserve University, 1983.

The Red Cross, in association with the U.S. government, undertook many public health, engineering, and famine relief projects in China. Red Cross policy was influenced by political developments. DAI 44:2553-A.

2316 Chih Yü-ju. "Goodnow's Mission to China." *Tsing Hua Journal of Chinese Studies* [Taiwan] 13 (1981): 197–220.

A public administration scholar, Frank J. Goodnow, advised the Chinese government on the making of its constitution between 1913 and 1917. While he had some influence, he was too ignorant of China, too idealistic, and too conservative to be of great service. Notes.

2317 Cohen, Warren I. "America and the May Fourth Movement: The Response to Chinese Nationalism, 1917–1921." *Pacific Historical Review* 35 (1966): 83–100.

The American failure to understand the new Chinese nationalism led to a great reluctance to help guide the May Fourth Movement. Notes.

2318 Crane, Daniel M., and Breslin, Thomas A. *An Ordinary Relationship: American Opposition to Republican Revolution in China.* Miami: Florida International University Press, 1986.

William Howard Taft's dollar diplomacy and Wilson's missionary diplomacy in China from 1909 to 1916 is examined. American policy was neutral in theory, but in fact favored established regimes regardless of their politics. China proved not to be a special case. Notes, bibliography, index.

2319 Davis, Clarence B. "Financing Imperialism: British and American Bankers as Vectors of Imperial Expansion in China, 1908–1920." *Business History Review* 56 (1982): 236–64.

Anglo-American bankers and policymakers wanted to make China dependent on the West but not at the expense of its political and territorial integrity. Notes.

2320 ———. "Limits of Effacement: Britain and the Problem of American Cooperation and Competition in China, 1915–1917." *Pacific Historical Review* 48 (1979): 47–63.

Preoccupied with the European war but unwilling to see Japan and the United States make great inroads in China, Britain tried to play the Japanese and the Americans against one another. Notes.

2321 Dayer, Roberta A. "Struggle for China: The Anglo-American Relationship, 1917–1925." Ph.D. dissertation, State University of New York, Buffalo, 1972.

Thomas W. Lamont, a partner in J. P. Morgan and Company, influenced Wilson's China policy, which was designed to cooperate with the great powers to preserve the status quo while making sure that Britain did not regain its prewar hold over the Chinese market. DAI 35:1590-A.

2322 Ellison, Duane C. "The United States and China, 1913–1921: A Study of the Strategy and Tactics of the Open Door Policy." Ph.D. dissertation, George Washington University, 1974.

Seeking to gain economic hegemony in China, the Wilson administration relied on its ability to compete against the other great powers between 1913 and 1919. At the end of the war, the United States reverted to a cooperative policy, using a banking consortium and control over China's mass media to gain influence. DAI 35:1590-A.

2323 George, Brian T. "The Open Door and the Rise of Chinese Nationalism: American Policy and China, 1917–1928." Ph.D. dissertation, University of New Mexico, 1977.

To preserve the Open Door in China, America launched a policy of formal cooperation with Japan and the Allies. When the Japanese-American condominium failed, the two countries started down the road to Pearl Harbor. DAI 38:3650-A.

2324 Huskey, James Layton. "Americans in Shanghai: Community Formation and Response to Revolution, 1919–1928." Ph.D. dissertation, University of North Carolina, Chapel Hill, 1985.

While most Americans living in Shanghai maintained a separate, colonial lifestyle, a few were more open to Chinese thought and culture. DAI 47:289-A.

2325 Israel, Jerry. *Progressivism and the Open Door: America and China, 1905–1921.* Pittsburgh: University of Pittsburgh Press, 1971.

The arrogant impulse to Americanize China was an extension of domestic reforms to foreign affairs, an effort that could not succeed because Americans did not understand China. The only thing unique about the Open Door was that Americans thought it was unique. Notes, bibliography, index.

2326 Keenan, Barry C. "John Dewey in China: His Visit and the Reception of His Ideas, 1917–1927." Ph.D. dissertation, Claremont Graduate School, 1969.

Dewey's arrival in China in 1919 coincided with the May Fourth Movement, a time when rebellious students welcomed his ideas. His gradualism proved impossible under the chaotic circumstances of the period. DAI 30:5385-A.

2327 Li Tien-yi. *Woodrow Wilson's China Policy, 1913–1917*. Kansas City: University of Kansas Press, 1952.

Wilson's answer to dollar diplomacy and the administration's anger over wartime encroachments by Japan are examined.

2328 Matsuda, Takeshi. "Woodrow Wilson's Dollar Diplomacy in the Far East: The New Chinese Consortium, 1917–1921." Ph.D. dissertation, University of Wisconsin, Madison, 1979.

Through the new Chinese consortium, Wilson used bankers to implement foreign policy. The consortium led to greater Anglo-American cooperation in China while restraining Japan. It did not help China to regain its lost sovereignty. DAI 40:3490-A.

2329 Metallo, Michael V. "American Missionaries, Sun Yat-sen, and the Chinese Revolution." *Pacific Historical Review* 47 (1978): 261–82.

American missionaries hailed the 1911 Chinese revolution and hoped that the Chinese would pattern their new society after the United States. At the behest of businessmen and American diplomats Taft withheld recognition, but Wilson recognized the government in May 1913, just when the missionaries were concluding that Sun Yat-sen was too radical. Notes.

2330 ———. "The United States and Sun Yat-sen, 1911–1925." Ph.D. dissertation, New York University, 1974.

Although Sun Yat-sen was both Christian and pro-American, Washington preferred that Yüan Shih-k'ai become the leader of the new China, a stance which was influenced by American missionaries. DAI 35:4395-A.

2331 Munson, Vivian L. "American Merchants of Capital in China: The Second Chinese Banking Consortium." Ph.D. dissertation, University of Wisconsin, 1968.

To bolster American influence in China, a second Chinese banking consortium was organized among American, Japanese, French, and British bankers. The consortium was not a success, as Americans did not wish to invest in China. DAI 30:252-A.

2332 Pugach, Noel. "Embarrassed Monarchist: Frank J. Goodnow and Constitutional Development in China, 1913–1915." *Pacific Historical Review* 42 (1973): 499–517.

Frank J. Goodnow's outspoken advocacy of monarchy for China following the revolution of 1911 was embarrassing to the Wilson administration, which supported republican concepts. Notes.

2333 ———. "Making the Open Door Work: Paul S. Reinsch in China, 1913–1919." *Pacific Historical Review* 38 (1969): 157–75.

Wilson's minister to China, Paul Reinsch, promoted closer Sino-American economic relations to strengthen the Open Door policy. Fearful American businessmen, Chinese political instability, and the encroachments of Japan limited the minister's maneuvering room. Notes.

2334 ———. "Standard Oil and Petroleum Development in Early Republican China." *Business History Review* 45 (1971): 452–73.

In 1914, Standard Oil of New York proposed, with the Wilson administration's blessing, a partnership with the Chinese government to explore for oil in North China. Chinese politics, pressure from other great powers, personality clashes, and Standard Oil's poor management practices doomed the project to failure. Notes.

2335 Trani, Eugene P. "Woodrow Wilson, China, and the Missionaries, 1913–1921." *Journal of Presbyterian History* 49 (1971): 328–51.

What Wilson knew about China came from missionaries at Princeton. He approved of the 1911 revolution as a vehicle for democracy and Christianity, and he sent an ambassador to China who would be supportive of those values. The president continued to listen to the missionaries throughout his two terms in office. Notes.

2336 Whitaker, Urban G., Jr. "Americans and Chinese Political Problems, 1912–1923." Ph.D. dissertation, University of Washington, 1954.

In 1912, China was actively seeking Western technological and political knowledge. Missionary schools, Chinese students in the United States, business associations, and American journalism were important points of contact. Advisers suggested that China approach democracy through economic development and education, but in practice education remained authoritarian and focused on science and politics. DAI 14:2116.

Japan

2337 Asada, Sadao. "Japan and the United States, 1915–1925." Ph.D. dissertation, Yale University, 1963.

Although this study focuses on the Washington conference of 1921–22, its opening chapters contain material on Wilson's growing concern about Japan. DAI 27:158-A.

2338 Beers, Burton. *Vain Endeavor: Robert Lansing's Attempts to End the American-Japanese Rivalry.* Durham, NC: Duke University Press, 1962.

Lansing understood Japan better than did Wilson, who needlessly antagonized the Japanese and turned his back on two opportunities to reach agreements that would have served American interests well. Notes, bibliographic essay, index.

2339 Fulton, Lloyd G. "Japanese-American Relations, 1918–1922: Attempts to Nail Down the Swinging Open Door." Ph.D. dissertation, Michigan State University, 1975.

The Wilson administration fought against potential Japanese imperialism through such diplomatic devices as mandates, a joint military program in Siberia, and a new China consortium. Americans also hoped that Japanese liberalism would blossom, leading to closer relations. DAI 36:3923-A.

2340 Hosoya, Chihiro. "The United States and Japan's Twenty-One Demands in 1915" (in Japanese). *Hitotsu-bashi Ronsó* [Japan] 43 (1960): 28–50.

Under William Jennings Bryan the United States appeased Japan, but under the influence of Wilson that policy began to change. The note of 11 May 1915 expressed this new policy with a threat to withdraw recognition of Japan's special interest in China.

2341 Ichioka, Yuji. "An Instance of Private Japanese Diplomacy: Suzuki Bunji, Organized American Labor, and Japanese Immigrant Workers, 1915–1916." *Amerasia Journal* 10 (1983): 1–22.

Japanese labor leader Suzuki Bunji visited the United States in 1915 and again in 1916 to champion the cause of Japanese immigrant labor to American unionists. Notes.

2342 Kawabe, Nobuo. "Japanese Business in the United States before World War II: The Case of Mitsubishi Shoji Kaisha, the San Francisco and Seattle Branches." Ph.D. dissertation, Ohio State University, 1980.

Mitsubishi Trading Company was an enormous firm with greatly diversified product lines and branches worldwide. The interplay between its Japanese headquarters and U.S. offices reveals the adaptability of the firm, the nature of the economies of the two countries between 1918 and 1942, and the two countries' management styles. DAI 41:1733-A.

2343 Lyman, Donald R. "The United States and Japan, 1913–1921." Ph.D. dissertation, University of North Carolina, Chapel Hill, 1976.

Wilson's shift from a passive Far Eastern policy to an active one in 1918–19 confused Japan and ensured American failure. DAI 38:949-A.

2344 Okabe, Hiroji. "The Significance of the Lansing-Ishii Agreement" (in Japanese). *Rekishi-gaku Kenkyu* [Japan] 75 (1954): 11–20.

The 1917 exchange of memoranda between Secretary of State Robert Lansing and Ambassador Kikujiro Ishii was a logical culmination of relations since the turn of the century and of a policy that chiefly benefited monopoly capital.

2345 Osipova, P. E. "American-Japanese Struggle for Micronesia in 1919–22" (in Russian). *Voprosy Istorii* [USSR] 9 (1955): 95–101.

After World War I, Japan and the United States struggled for control of Micronesia, a conflict which led to bad relations between the two powers.

2346 Prescott, Francis C. "The Lansing-Ishii Agreement." Ph.D. dissertation, Yale University, 1949.

Under the pressure of World War I, Secretary of State Robert Lansing recognized Japan's special interests in China, while Viscount Kikujiro Ishii of Japan affirmed support for the Open Door and the essential integrity of China. This agreement enabled Japan and America to cooperate during the war, but it was not strong enough to boost Japanese efforts to dominate China. DAI 27:734-A.

2347 Thompson, Richard A. "The Yellow Peril, 1890–1924." Ph.D. dissertation, University of Wisconsin, 1957.

The huge population of Oriental countries, Oriental industrialization, and Oriental immigrants perceived as too culturally different to ever assimilate were all considered part of the Yellow Peril. Beginning in 1905, Sino-Japanese imperialism was a major focus of American fears. DAI 17:2589.

CARIBBEAN

General

2348 Baker, George W., Jr. "The Caribbean Policy of Woodrow Wilson, 1913–1917." Ph.D. dissertation, University of Colorado, 1961.

Wilson delegated much of the responsibility for handling Caribbean problems to his secretaries of state, William Jennings Bryan from 1913 to 1915, then Robert Lansing. Diplomatic paternalism, often couched in idealistic terms, dominated policy. Lansing was frank about his primary concern for American self-interest and security, and he was often practical and successful. DAI 22:3170.

2349 Callcott, Wilfrid H. *The Caribbean Policy of the United States, 1890–1920.* Baltimore, MD: Johns Hopkins Press, 1942.

There is little room for criticism in this account, which justifies the Spanish-American war and subsequent Caribbean interventions. Wilson is viewed as an idealist in foreign affairs. Notes, bibliography, index.

2350 Carter, Purvis M. *Congressional and Public Reaction to Wilson's Caribbean Policy, 1913–1917.* New York: Vantage, 1977.

In spite of his promise to cultivate the friendship of Caribbean nations, Wilson intervened in Haiti, the Dominican Republic, and Nicaragua. Newspapers and most members of Congress supported the interventions, and even the few dissenting voices agreed with the need to preserve order in the region.

2351 Doerries, Reinhard R. "American Foreign Policy in the Caribbean Prior to World War I" (in German). *Jahrbüch für Amerikastudien* [West Germany] 18 (1973): 62–77.

Americans had long been interested in the Caribbean, and the Progressives were no exception. German meddling in Latin America, especially in Mexico, made American policymakers feel threatened. Notes.

2352 Millett, Richard, and Gaddy, G. Dale. "Administering the Protectorates: The U.S. Occupation of Haiti and the Dominican Republic." *Revista Interamericana* 6 (1976): 383–402.

The United States was a colonial power without a colonial office. Rather, colonial administration was handled by the military, which lacked the training necessary for the job and made the occupations of Haiti and the Dominican Republic especially difficult. Notes.

2353 Munro, Dana G. *Intervention and Dollar Diplomacy in the Caribbean, 1900–1921.* Princeton: Princeton University Press, 1964.

A former foreign service officer argues that American intervention in the Caribbean was less economic than political, because regional stability had a higher priority than trade in the region. Notes, index.

2354 Thomas, Gerald E. "William D. Leahy and America's Imperial Years, 1893–1917." Ph.D. dissertation, Yale University, 1973.

Chapter 6 deals with this naval officer's participation in the American interventions in Nicaragua, Haiti, and the Dominican Republic. He was torn between his humanitarian impulses and his conviction that American imperialism was necessary and proper. DAI 34:7172-A.

Cuba

2355 Baker, George W., Jr. "The Wilson Administration and Cuba, 1913-1921." *Mid-America* 46 (1964): 48–63.

Wilsonian idealism did not apply to Cuba, where Secretary of State Robert Lansing used the "big stick" to encourage political stability. Notes.

2356 Hoernel, David. "Large Corporations and the Big Stick Policy in Cuba and Mexico" (in Spanish). *Historia Mexicana* [Mexico] 30 (1980): 209–46.

Theodore Roosevelt and William Howard Taft were very concerned with the financial ramifications of their Latin American policy, but Wilson did not cater to U.S. businesses with interests in Mexico and Cuba.

2357 Meyer, Leo J. "The United States and the Cuban Revolution of 1917." *Hispanic American Historical Review* 10 (1930): 138–66.

A threat posed by Alberto Zayas's liberal revolutionaries to American economic interests led Washington to reaffirm its support for the government in power with a military contingent.

2358 Pérez, Louis A., Jr. "Capital, Bureaucrats, and Policy: The Economic Contours of United States-Cuban Relations, 1916–1921." *Inter-American Economic Affairs* 29 (1975): 65–80.

American diplomats developed a close relationship with the Americans who controlled the Cuban sugar industry.

2359 ———. "The Platt Amendment and Dysfunctional Politics in Cuba: The Electoral Crises of 1916–1917." *West Georgia College Studies in the Social Sciences* 17 (1978): 49–60.

Mario Menocal's 1916 reelection bid set off a struggle within Cuba's political elite during which both sides tried to use the threat of American intervention for their own purposes.

Dominican Republic

2360 Calder, Bruce J. "Caudillos and Gauilleros versus the United States Marines: Guerrilla Insurgency during the Dominican Intervention, 1916–1924." *Hispanic American Historical Review* 58 (1978): 649–75.

Peasants in the eastern portion of the Dominican Republic waged a guerrilla war against the U.S. occupiers. They were not bandits, as the government claimed, but peasants fighting for principles and for their way of life. Notes.

2361 ———. "Some Aspects of the United States Occupation of the Dominican Republic, 1916–1924." Ph.D. dissertation, University of Texas, Austin, 1974.

Officially, Wilson intervened in the Dominican Republic to preserve order, but paternalism, interest in the Dominican economy, and concern about the security of the Panama Canal were also on his mind. With little guidance from Washington, the military occupiers formulated their own policy. DAI 36:6890-A.

2362 Juárez, J. R. "United States Withdrawal from Santo Domingo." *Hispanic American Historical Review* 42 (1962): 152–90.

The American occupation of Santo Domingo came to an end, because it had become a partisan issue in the 1920 election campaign,

because it no longer made sense from a strategic viewpoint, and because American public opinion was turning against it. Notes.

2363 Sutton, Walter A. "The Wilson Administration and a Scandal in Santo Domingo." *Presidential Studies Quarterly* 12 (1982): 552–60.

In 1914, James M. Sullivan, American minister to Santo Domingo, became involved in a bank fraud and in selling favors. After investigating the charges, Wilson forced his minister's resignation, but the scandal drew little public interest. Notes.

Haiti

See also Chapter 6, *Minority Groups, Leaders and Organizations.*

2364 Healy, David. *Gunboat Diplomacy in the Wilson Era: The U.S. Navy in Haiti, 1915–1916.* Madison: University of Wisconsin Press, 1976.

American gunboat diplomacy in Haiti was influenced by Caribbean strategic and financial concerns and by racism. The administration made the situation worse by giving the American occupation force wide latitude over policy. Notes, bibliography, index.

2365 Logan, Rayford W. "James Weldon Johnson and Haiti." *Phylon* 32 (1971): 396–402.

A critic of the American occupation of Haiti, Johnson wrote that the action there was motivated by economics and not humanitarian reasons. He exposed American cruelty and racism, too, but had little impact on policy. Notes.

2366 Lutskov, N. D. "The U.S. Occupation of Haiti (1915–1934)" (in Russian). *Novaia i Noveishaia Istoriia* [USSR] (1976): 66–79.

The origins of Wilson's order to occupy Haiti and Haitian resistance to the Americans are examined.

2367 Plummer, Brenda G. "Black and White in the Caribbean: Haitian-American Relations, 1902–1934." Ph.D. dissertation, Cornell University, 1981.

The literature of native Haitian intellectuals and State Department documents are principal sources for this study. Haiti's economic dependence made it vulnerable to foreign influence and occupation. America kept Haiti off-balance by undermining local leadership and perpetuating the ignorant underclass status of the majority of Haitians. DAI 42:1763-A.

2368 Posner, Walter H. "American Marines in Haiti, 1915–1922." *The Americas* 20 (1963): 231–66.

Financial problems and an unstable political system led Wilson to occupy Haiti in 1915. American officials took control of finances, rewrote the constitution, and put down peasant rebellions. Notes.

2369 Schmidt, Hans. *The United States Occupation of Haiti, 1915–1934.* New Brunswick, NJ: Rutgers University Press, 1971.

Economic factors played a role in the 1915 occupation of Haiti, but the American move should be placed in the context of long-term expansionism and short-term concern over German influence in the region. Racist colonial realities distorted liberal democratic missionary impulses once the Americans had occupied Haiti. Photographs, notes, bibliography, index.

2370 Venzon, Anne C. "The Papers of General Smedley Darlington Butler, USMC, 1915–1918." Ph.D. dissertation, Princeton University, 1982.

This study organizes General Butler's papers into a first-person account of the American occupation of Haiti. America's mostly successful efforts to implement construction and public health projects pleased the Haitian masses but antagonized the elite, who wanted to maintain their own exploitative control. DAI 42:4909-A.

LATIN AMERICA

See also Chapter 10, *Wartime Relations, Latin America.*

General

2371 Baker, George W., Jr. "Ideals and Realities in the Wilson Administration's Relations with Honduras." *The Americas* 21 (1965): 3–19.

Ideals and realities mixed together in United States-Honduran relations during the Wilson years. After a cordial beginning, relations became strained, until a forced overthrow of the government in 1919 led to the hiring of an American financial adviser. Notes.

2372 ———. "The Woodrow Wilson Administration and El Salvadoran Relations, 1913–1921." *Social Studies* 56 (1965): 97–103.

The Pan-American pact did not bring about better relations between the United States and El Salvador. Wilson regarded El Salvador as too insignificant to deal with himself, and his subordinates took a harder line than the president might have.

2373 ———. "The Woodrow Wilson Administration and Guatemalan Relations." *Historian* 27 (1965): 155–69.

Wilson left American policy toward Guatemala to his secretaries of state. A mixture of philosophical noninterference and practical indifference led to the toleration of a dictatorship. Notes.

2374 ———. "The Woodrow Wilson Administration and Nicaragua, 1913–1921." *The Americas* 22 (1966): 339–76.

In spite of his criticisms of big stick diplomacy, Wilson proved to be an interventionist bent on imposing political and economic stability on countries such as Nicaragua. Notes.

2375 ———. "Woodrow Wilson's Use of the Non-Recognition Policy in Costa Rica." *The Americas* 22 (1965): 3–21.

After a coup by General Federico Tinoco in Costa Rica in 1917, Wilson refused to extend diplomatic recognition. Once an elected successor took office, recognition was granted, although the author questions just how much Wilson's policy helped the Costa Rican people. Notes.

2376 Baylen, J. O. "American Intervention in Nicaragua, 1909–33: An Appraisal of Objectives and Results." *Southwestern Social Science Quarterly* 35 (1954): 128–54.

The American willingness to intervene in Nicaragua is explained in terms of concern over the security of the Canal Zone and for the lives and property of Americans living in the region. Notes.

2377 Coletta, Paolo E. "William Jennings Bryan and the United States-Colombia Impasse." *Hispanic American Historical Review* 47 (1967): 486–501.

Bryan worked, as secretary of state, to settle a dispute with Colombia dating back to when Roosevelt helped the Panamanians to gain independence. The Senate held up the treaty until after Roosevelt's death. Notes.

2378 Dinwoodle, David H. "Expedient Diplomacy: The United States and Guatemala, 1898–1920." Ph.D. dissertation, University of Colorado, 1966.

American-Guatemalan relations reveal the nature of the U.S. presence in the region. Secretary of State Robert Lansing's policies, as well as those of his Progressive predecessors, were aimed at preserving American security and control. Although they were somewhat successful at stabilizing Guatemala, Americans had to work with a tyrannical Guatemalan president, Manuel Cabrera, thus alienating Cabrera's enemies. DAI 28:1369-A.

2379 Gilderhus, Mark T. "Pan-American Initiatives: The Wilson Presidency and Regional Integration, 1914–1917." *Diplomatic History* 4 (1980): 409–23.

Before becoming preoccupied with World War I, Wilson worked toward the goal of regional integration with Latin America, visualizing a system of trade and investment linked to a multilateral security pact. While some trade agreements were secured, the wary Latin Americans discouraged Wilson's other ideas. Notes.

2380 ———. *Pan American Visions: Woodrow Wilson in the Western Hemisphere, 1913–1921.* Tucson: University of Arizona Press, 1986.

Wilson used his Pan-American policy as a model for his world view, envisioning a system based on free trade and the Open Door. The United States used the war to gain economic dominance in Latin America. Notes, bibliography, index.

2381 Hudson, Manley O. "The Central American Court of Justice." *American Journal of International Law* 26 (1932): 759–86.

The rise and fall of this experiment in regional collective security during the Wilson years is chronicled. Notes.

2382 Knott, Alexander W. "The Pan-American Policy of Woodrow Wilson, 1913–1921." Ph.D. dissertation, University of Colorado, 1968.

Wilson was committed to Pan-Americanism, accepting the mediation of the ABC powers (Argentina, Brazil, and Chile) in his dispute with Mexico. During the periods of neutrality and then involvement in the European war, the administration worked to promote economic solidarity and hemispheric security. DAI 29:3953-A.

2383 Krenn, Michael L. *U.S. Policy toward Economic Nationalism in Latin America, 1917–1929.* Wilmington: Scholarly Resources, 1990.

U.S. interactions with Colombia, Venezuela, and Brazil illustrate the nature of, perceptions of, and conflicts over economic nationalism in Latin America. DAI 46:2052-A.

2384 Lael, Richard L. "Struggle for Ratification: Wilson, Lodge, and the Thomson-Urrutia Treaty." *Diplomatic History* 2 (1978): 81–102.

The Wilson administration brought an end to ten years of hostility between the United States and Colombia with a conciliatory treaty. Seeing the implied criticism of his friend Theodore Roosevelt's policies, Henry Cabot Lodge blocked ratification for seven years. Notes.

2385 Langley, Lester D. *The Banana Wars: An Inner History of American Empire, 1900–1934.* Lexington: University Press of Kentucky, 1983.

America's many military interventions in Cuba, Nicaragua, Mexico, Haiti, and the Dominican Republic resulted from perceived threats to American lives, property, and national security rather than from economic motives. Photographs, notes, bibliography, index.

2386 Mock, James R. "The Creel Committee in Latin America." *Hispanic American Historical Review* 22 (1942): 262–79.

The Creel committee engaged in an effective anti-German propaganda campaign during the war.

2387 Murillo-Jiménez, Hugo. "Wilson and Tinoco: The United States and the Policy of Non-Recognition in Costa Rica, 1917–1919." Ph.D. dissertation, University of California, San Diego, 1978.

Wilson refused to recognize the Federico Tinoco government, because it had overthrown a legitimate regime, even though the new government had the support of American corporations doing business in Costa Rica. Nonrecognition brought about internal strife, and, after the threat of intervention, Tinoco withdrew. DAI 39:1062-A.

2388 Newton, Wesley P. "Aviation in the Relations of the United States and Latin America, 1916-1929." Ph.D. dissertation, University of Alabama, 1964.

Since Latin America had virtually no aircraft industry of its own in the early days of aviation, it was a target for both airborne military pressures and rival marketers of airplanes. Private U.S. planes were used in the Mexican Revolution, and military planes were part of John J. Pershing's expedition to Mexico in 1916. DAI 25:4110.

2389 Roberts, Derrel. "Mobile and the Visit by Woodrow Wilson." *Alabama Historical Quarterly* 27 (1966): 81–90.

In 1913 the president visited Mobile, Alabama, where he gave an address outlining his rather idealistic view of United States-Latin American relations.

2390 Rosenberg, Emily. "The Politics of President Wilson in Central America: The Struggle against Economic Instability" (in Spanish). *Revista de Historia* [Costa Rica] 5 (1980): 33–58.

Like his Republican predecessors, Wilson used dollar diplomacy and direct military intervention in Latin America to keep the region stable and primed for American hegemony.

2391 Sealander, Judith. "In the Shadow of Good Neighbor Diplomacy: The Women's Bureau and Latin America." *Prologue* 11 (1979): 236–50.

Feminist Mary Cannon toured Latin America as a representative of the Women's Bureau of the Labor Department, which was established in 1920. While publicly promoting goodwill, she privately encouraged labor reforms favoring women.

2392 Seidel, Robert N. "Progressive Pan Americanism: Development and United States Policy toward South America, 1906–1931." Ph.D. dissertation, Cornell University, 1973.

To expand trade, investments, and access to sources of raw materials in South America, internationalist Progressives such as Elihu Root, William G. McAdoo, Charles Evans Hughes, and Herbert Hoover supported Progressive Pan-Americanism, which entailed significant government involvement in the economic affairs of the Southern Hemisphere. DAI 34:1224-A.

2393 Small, Melvin. "The United States and the German 'Threat' to the Hemisphere, 1905–1914." *The Americas* 28 (1972): 252–70.

While Germany never presented a threat to American political interests in Latin America, a growing German presence appeared ominous— and served as an additional justification for the U.S. declaration of war. Notes.

2394 Tulchin, Joseph S. *The Aftermath of War: World War I and U.S. Policy toward Latin America.* New York: New York University Press, 1971.

The experience of World War I determined U.S. policy toward Latin America for years after the war. American policymakers developed an antipathy to protectorates, but they still reserved the right to intervene on behalf of clients. Notes, bibliographic essay, index.

2395 Vivian, James F. "Wilson, Bryan, and the American Delegation to the Abortive Fifth Pan American Conference, 1914." *Nebraska History* 59 (1978): 56–69.

In the wake of World War I, the Fifth Pan American Conference was canceled late in 1914. The president's choice of delegates is examined along with what their positions might have been.

2396 Wright, Theodore P., Jr. "Honduras: A Case Study of United States Support of Free Elections in Central America." *Hispanic American Historical Review* 40 (1960): 212–23.

In 1919 and 1923 the United States tried to force democracy on Honduras, with the result that a politician calling for free elections became the new dictator, a story that should make Americans think twice before promoting democracy where its prerequisites have not been met. Notes.

Mexico

See also Chapter 3, *Henry Lane Wilson* and *John J. Pershing,* and Chapter 10, *The Zimmermann Note.*

2397 Anderson, William W. "The Nature of the Mexican Revolution as Viewed from the United States, 1910–1917." Ph.D. dissertation, University of Texas, 1967.

America's incompatible trends toward idealistic reform and self-serving economic expansion resulted in a divided and often confused attitude toward the Mexican Revolution. The public wanted simplistic explanations, such as that the rebelling peons were justified and the revolution was for the best, or the opposite, that the revolution was unjust. DAI 28:1751-A.

2398 Aoki, Yoshio. "The Mexican Revolution and the American Punitive Expedition" (in Japanese). *Shirin* [Japan] 60 (1977): 533–62.

Details of the negotiations for the withdrawal of American troops sent across the border after Pancho Villa are examined along with Venustiano Carranza's economic policies designed to free Mexico from economic dependence on the United States. Notes.

2399 Archer, Jules. "Woodrow Wilson's Dirty Little War." *Mankind* 1 (1968): 44–55.

Wilson began his presidency determined to break with past imperialist policies. The Mexican Revolution led to a deterioration in relations, though, and the president intervened in

Veracruz and later in northern Mexico, although war was never declared.

2400 Astorino, Samuel J. "Senator Albert B. Fall and Wilson's Last Crisis with Mexico." *Duquesne Review* 13 (1968): 3–17.

When Carranza carried out provisions of the Mexican constitution that threatened the interests of American oil companies, Wilson insisted on nonintervention, while Senator Albert B. Fall led the forces determined to stop the Mexican government. Notes.

2401 Baecker, Thomas. "The Arms of the *Ypiranga*: The German Side." *The Americas* 30 (1973): 1–17.

The anti-German reaction in the United States following the detention of the German ship *Ypiranga* was unfounded. Although the ship was carrying arms to the Victoriana Huerta regime, Germany only provided the transportation. Notes.

2402 Baldridge, Donald C. "Mexican Petroleum and United States-Mexican Relations, 1919–1923." Ph.D. dissertation, University of Arizona, 1971.

While Wilson used American diplomacy on behalf of oil companies facing expropriation in Mexico, he refused to mount another military invasion. The petroleum lobby almost caused a war between Mexico and the United States in 1919 when Wilson was incapacitated. After the overthrow of Carranza, Wilson refused to recognize the new government until it promised that American interests would be protected. DAI 32:1429-A.

2403 Balmaseda-Nápoles, Francisco A. "Mexico and the United States, 1912–1917: A Study of Selected Writings of Isidro Fabela." Ph.D. dissertation, Case Western Reserve University, 1974.

The writings of Isidro Fabela, a Mexican diplomat, jurist, and writer, are examined for what they say about Mexican-American relations during the Wilson administration. DAI 35:355-A.

2404 Barnhill, John H. "The Punitive Mission against Pancho Villa: The Forced Motorization of the American Army." *Military History of Texas and the Southwest* 14 (1978): 135–46.

While the punitive expedition never caught up with Villa, it did become motorized, a first for the U.S. Army.

2405 Braddy, Haldeen. *Pancho Villa at Columbus: The Raid of 1916*. El Paso: Texas Western Press, 1965.

Villa's raid came about as a result of his political frustration and his need for plunder to finance his operations. Notes.

2406 ———. *Pershing's Mission in Mexico*. El Paso: Texas Western Press, 1966.

General John J. Pershing did not withdraw until he was certain that Villa would not strike across the border again. The expedition was a tough experience that forged a General of the Armies and created a cadre that lasted through two world wars. Notes.

2407 Busey, J. L. "Don Victoriano and the Yankee Press" (in Spanish). *Historia Mexicana* [Mexico] 4 (1955): 582–94.

In this survey of American newspaper editorials on Mexican President Huerta, the author finds a surprising number of favorable opinions, due in large part to the reports of American businessmen.

2408 Calvert, Peter. *The Mexican Revolution, 1910–1914: The Diplomacy of Anglo-American Conflict*. Cambridge: Cambridge University Press, 1968.

Anglo-American friction and accommodation over Mexico are examined. Wilson's nonrecognition policy was a new form of dollar diplomacy, using financial starvation to influence a foreign power. Notes, bibliography, index.

2409 Christopulos, Diana K. "American Radicals and the Mexican Revolution, 1900–1925." Ph.D. dissertation, State University of New York, Binghamton, 1980.

American socialists argued against intervention in the Mexican and other foreign revolutions, and they influenced Wilson's 1916 decision to avoid full-scale war with Mexico. Socialists broadly agreed that American intervention protected capitalist investment at the expense of American workers. Also, socialists endorsed the Mexican people's right to find their own solutions. Some American leftists went to Mexico to join the revolution. DAI 41:2732-A.

2410 Clements, Kendrick A. "Emissary from a Revolution: Luis Cabrera and Woodrow Wilson." *The Americas* 35(1979): 353–71.

Carranza dispatched the capable Luis Cabrera to Washington as a special agent in charge of convincing the Americans to lift the arms embargo and to help the constitutionalist forces without Mexico giving up sovereignty in return. Notes.

2411 ———. " 'A Kindness to Carranza': William Jennings Bryan, International Harvester, and Intervention in Yucatán." *Nebraska History* 57 (1976): 479–90.

While Bryan had denounced International Harvester as a trust in his younger days, as secretary of state he went along with a proposed intervention in Yucatán that would have helped the corporate giant, a good example of Bryan's moral imperialism.

2412 ———. "Woodrow Wilson's Mexican Policy, 1913–15." *Diplomatic History* 4 (1980): 113–36.

Wilson did not want to force liberal capitalism on Mexico; rather, he wanted to see Mexico become truly independent and, preferably, run under democratic conditions. Notes.

2413 Clendenen, Clarence C. *Blood on the Border: The United States Army and the Mexican Irregulars*. London: Macmillan, 1969.

The American response to Mexican irregulars raiding across the border from 1850 to 1930 is covered, including heightened concern during the Wilson years.

2414 ———. *The United States and Pancho Villa: A Study in Unconventional Diplomacy*. Ithaca, NY: Cornell University Press, 1961.

Villa's political and military exploits are detailed, including the raid on Columbus, New Mexico, which provoked Wilson into sending a punitive expedition after him. The expedition was a success in that Villa never raided across the border again. Notes, bibliography, index.

2415 Coker, William S. "British Mediation in the Wilson-Huerta Conflict" (in Spanish). *Historia Mexicana* [Mexico] 18 (1968): 244–57.

In late 1913 the British attempted to mediate the crisis touched off by Wilson's pressure campaign against what he considered to be the illegal government of General Huerta. The British effort failed when the president rejected its compromises. Notes.

2416 ———. "Naval Diplomacy during the Mexican Revolution: An Episode in the Career of Admiral Frank Friday Fletcher." *North Dakota Quarterly* 40 (1972): 51–64.

Fletcher, commander of the U.S. naval force off Mexico, and his British counterpart were expected to cooperate in the production of the lives and property of both nations' citizens, a task made easy because the British were eager to please the United States. Notes.

2417 ———. "United States-British Diplomacy over Mexico, 1913." Ph.D. dissertation, University of Oklahoma, 1965.

Victoriano Huerta assumed the Mexican presidency under suspicious circumstances, and Wilson refused to recognize him as the legitimate head of government. America requested Huerta's resignation and pressured other nations to do the same, threatening direct intervention. Britain's response to the situation in Mexico had been more pragmatic from the beginning, and this brought Britain and America into conflict. Britain unsuccessfully attempted to engineer various compromises. DAI 26:1611.

2418 Cumberland, Charles C. "Huerta, Carranza, and the Occupation of Veracruz" (in Spanish). *Historia Mexicana* [Mexico] 6 (1957): 534–47.

Huerta's government was strengthened for a time by Wilson's landing of troops at Veracruz, since this rallied patriotic Mexicans to his cause. Carranza wisely issued bellicose anti-American statements and took power when Huerta faltered.

2419 Edwards, Warrick R., III. "United States-Mexican Relations, 1913–1916: Revolution, Oil, and Intervention." Ph.D. dissertation, Louisiana State University, 1971.

Wilson followed a policy of unprecedented interference in the internal affairs of Mexico in order to force Huerta from power. By late 1915 he had reluctantly extended de facto recognition to the Carranza regime, although armed intervention was inevitable in the prevailing climate of mistrust and hatred. DAI 32:3916-A.

2420 Forster, Merlin H. "U.S. Intervention in Mexico: The 1914 Occupation of Vera Cruz." *Military Review* 57 (1977): 88–96.

While the occupation was a success from a military standpoint, the moralistic reasons for the intervention were less sound. Notes.

2421 Furman, Necah S. "*Vida Nueva*: A Reflection of Villista Diplomacy, 1914–1915." *New Mexico Historical Review* 53 (1978): 171–92.

Villa's newspaper *Vida Nueva* is examined for its anti-Americanism which did not become evident until late 1915, when the United

States recognized the Carranza government. Notes.

2422 Gerlach, Allen. "Conditions along the Border—1915: The Plan de San Diego." *New Mexico Historical Review* 43 (1968): 195–212.

The Plan of San Diego, calling for an uprising of Mexicans and Mexican-Americans, was hatched by Germans and followers of General Huerta. Notes.

2423 Gilderhus, Mark T. *Diplomacy and Revolution: U.S.-Mexican Relations under Wilson and Carranza.* Tucson: University of Arizona Press, 1977.

Wilson and Carranza neither understood one another nor shared common objectives. The Mexican leader wanted to preserve national pride above all, while Wilson wanted the revolution to create a liberal capitalist nation like the United States. Notes, bibliography, index.

2424 ———. "The United States and Carranza, 1917: The Question of *De Jure* Recognition." *The Americas* 29 (1972): 214–31.

The decision to recognize Carranza was an expedient. The Department of State hoped de jure recognition would lead to an agreement on American property in Mexico. Above all, the president wanted to end the distraction from the war in Europe. The diversion was avoided, but Carranza refused to bend on the matter of property rights. Notes.

2425 ———. "Wilson, Carranza, and the Monroe Doctrine: A Question in Regional Organization." *Diplomatic History* 7 (1983): 103–15.

Wilson hoped to unite the hemisphere behind an inflated version of the Monroe Doctrine, but Latin nations led by Mexico balked, feeling that the Americans were already too dominant and too ready to intervene unilaterally when it suited their interests. Notes.

2426 Glaser, David. "1919: William Jenkins, Robert Lansing, and the Mexican Interlude." *Southwestern Historical Quarterly* 74 (1971): 337–56.

Mexican revolutionaries kidnapped the American consular agent, Jenkins, to discredit the Carranza regime. With Wilson ill, Secretary of State Robert Lansing and Senator Albert Fall almost carried off a military invasion before the president intervened to stop them. Notes.

2427 Grieb, Kenneth J. "The Benton Case and the Diplomacy of the Revolution" (in Spanish).

Historia Mexicana [Mexico] 19 (1969): 282–301.

Villa's execution of a British citizen created a diplomatic uproar, but Great Britain was too preoccupied with the European war to pay much attention to the incident. Notes.

2428 ———. "The Lind Mission to Mexico." *Caribbean Studies* 7 (1968): 24–43.

Wilson foolishly chose, for a special mission designed to resolve the crisis with Huerta, a well-intentioned diplomatic amateur, John Lind. Mexican officials duped Lind, but Wilson continued to rely on his advice. Notes.

2429 ———. "Reginald del Valle: A California Diplomat's Sojourn in Mexico." *California Historical Society Quarterly* 47 (1968): 315–28.

In May 1913, Secretary of State Bryan sent former California State Senator del Valle to Mexico, because the Wilson administration did not trust Ambassador Henry Lane Wilson. His report, which favored recognition of the Huerta government, fell on deaf ears since Wilson had already decided against recognition. Notes.

2430 ———. "Standard Oil and the Financing of the Mexican Revolution." *California Historical Quarterly* 50 (1971): 59–71.

Because what it was doing might be considered illegal, Standard Oil covered its tracks well, but it probably lent at least indirect aid to Mexican revolutionaries in the hope of future dividends. Notes.

2431 ———. *The United States and Huerta.* Lincoln: University of Nebraska Press, 1969.

Wilson's refusal to recognize Huerta as the legitimate ruler of Mexico set an important precedent in U.S. foreign policy. Photographs, notes, bibliography, index.

2432 Hager, William M. "The Plan of San Diego: Unrest on the Texas Border in 1915." *Arizona and the West* 5 (1963): 327–36.

The ambitious Plan of San Diego called for the reconquest of the Southwest (to be followed by its reannexation by Mexico) and the establishment of a Midwestern buffer zone. In reality it was a justification for border raids and part of a plan to force American recognition of Carranza. Notes.

2433 Haley, P. Edward. *Revolution and Intervention: The Diplomacy of Taft and Wilson in Mexico, 1910–1917.* Cambridge, MA: MIT Press, 1970.

After Porfirio Díaz had made Mexico safe for American investments for many years, the instability of the Mexican Revolution came as a shock to many north of the border, creating political and diplomatic problems for Wilson, who came into office determined not to intervene and ended up doing so anyway. Notes, bibliography, index.

2434 Hall, Linda B. "The Mexican Revolution and the Crisis in Naco, 1914–1915." *Journal of the West* 16 (1977): 27–35.

The forces of Villa and José Maytorena battled for control of Naco, Mexico, in 1914–15 with the result that Americans on the other side of the border were killed and their property damaged. Wilson avoided the temptation to intervene, and the crisis ended when both Mexican armies were routed by Alvaro Obregón.

2435 Harper, James W. "The El Paso-Juárez Conference of 1916." *Arizona and the West* 20 (1978): 231–44.

The May 1916 conference reduced tensions on the Mexican-American border and bought the United States time to deal with the more serious U-boat crisis, although basic questions were not resolved. Notes.

2436 ——. "Hugh Lenox Scott and the Diplomacy of the United States toward the Mexican Revolution" (in Spanish). *Historia Mexicana* [Mexico] 27 (1978): 427–45.

Wilson's man in Mexico, Hugh Lenox Scott, supported Pancho Villa as a pro-American moderate. When Carranza emerged as the military victor, Scott remained opposed to American intervention.

2437 Harris, Charles H., III, and Sadler, Louis R. "The Plan of San Diego and the Mexican-United States War Crisis of 1916: A Reexamination." *Hispanic American Historical Review* 58 (1978): 381–408.

To force the withdrawal of American troops from Mexico and diplomatic recognition of his government, Carranza launched an offensive announced by the Plan of San Diego in which the southwestern United States would break away and become independent. Germany was not involved with the Plan of San Diego. Notes.

2438 Harrison, Benjamin T. "Chandler Anderson and Business Interests in Mexico, 1913–1920: When Economic Interests Failed to Alter U.S. Foreign Policy." *Inter-American Economic Affairs* 33 (1979): 3–23.

An international lawyer who represented several American businesses in Mexico, Anderson did not obtain Wilson's support for aggressive steps to protect American commercial interests south of the border. Notes.

2439 Henderson, Paul V. N. "Woodrow Wilson, Victoriano Huerta, and the Recognition Issue in Mexico." *The Americas* 41 (1984): 151–76.

To unseat Huerta, President Wilson attempted a return to the eighteenth-century view of legitimacy rejected by Thomas Jefferson. This diplomatic campaign was the first use by the United States "of public international law for imperialistic ends in Latin America." Notes.

2440 Hill, Larry D. *Emissaries to a Revolution: Woodrow Wilson's Executive Agents in Mexico, 1910–1917.* Baton Rouge: Louisiana State University Press, 1973.

Wilson used at least ten different executive agents to confer with the Mexican government and with important Mexican political factions during his presidency. Notes, bibliography, index.

2441 ——. "The Progressive Politician as a Diplomat: The Case of John Lind in Mexico." *The Americas* 27 (1971): 355–72.

A special agent of President Wilson, Lind was dispatched to Mexico to hasten Huerta's departure. The Progressive Lind saw the same evils in Mexico as he had battled in America: corrupt politicians and greedy industrialists. He thought democracy and an enlightened elite could make things right, but only if the United States would take control of the Mexican Revolution. Notes.

2442 Hinckley, Ted C. "Wilson, Huerta, and the Twenty-One Gun Salute." *Historian* 22 (1960): 197–206.

In detailing the Tampico incident of 1914, the author blames the chauvinism and misunderstandings of both Wilson and Huerta for what could have been a tragic episode. Notes.

2443 Holcombe, Harold E. "United States Arms Control and the Mexican Revolution, 1910–1924." Ph.D. dissertation, University of Alabama, 1968.

Because Mexico had no munitions factories, the United States was able to affect the Mexican Revolution by limiting the export of arms. Wilson, for example, maintained an arms embargo to thwart Huerta in 1914, while allowing weapons to be smuggled to Huerta's enemies. During and after World War I, arms control was more difficult. DAI 29:1494-A.

2444 Hundley, Norris, Jr. *Dividing the Waters: A Century of Controversy between the United States and Mexico*. Berkeley: University of California Press, 1966.

Not until World War II did the United States and Mexico settle their differences over water rights in the border regions. Material on the Wilson years is included. Notes, bibliography, index.

2445 Johnson, Robert B. "The Punitive Expedition: A Military, Diplomatic, and Political History of Pershing's Chase after Pancho Villa, 1916–1917." Ph.D. dissertation, University of Southern California, 1964.

General Pershing was sent into Mexico to bring Pancho Villa to justice. The troubled Mexican government saw the invasion as a threat, and eventually it mounted an attack against Pershing, bringing Mexico and America to the brink of war. A joint commission was established to solve problems, but it made little headway. Eventually Pershing and his men were called home to prepare for America's increasingly likely entry into World War I. DAI 25:3537.

2446 Kahle, Louis G. "Robert Lansing and the Recognition of Venustiano Carranza." *Hispanic American Historical Review* 38 (1958): 353–72.

Lansing advocated diplomatic recognition of Carranza as the legal ruler of Mexico to end a major diversion in U.S. foreign policy, as the government had more important problems to deal with in Europe. Notes.

2447 Katz, Friedrich. "Pancho Villa and the Attack on Columbus, New Mexico." *American Historical Review* 83 (1978): 101–30.

Villa attacked across the border in anger over a possible Carranza-Wilson conspiracy to make Mexico a protectorate. Without government sanction, Leon Canova of the State Department had discussed such a pact with American businessmen and Mexican conservatives. Notes.

2448 ———. *The Secret War in Mexico: Europe, the United States and the Mexican Revolution*. Chicago: University of Chicago Press, 1981.

The Wilson administration gave top priority to the protection of American business interests and to countering the more radical tendencies of the Mexican Revolution. By 1920 the United States enjoyed greater economic power in Mexico than it had before the revolutionary upheaval.

2449 Kestenbaum, Justin L. "The Question of Intervention in Mexico, 1913–1917." Ph.D. dissertation, Northwestern University, 1963.

Most Americans strongly opposed armed intervention in the Mexican Revolution and supported Wilson's use of diplomatic and economic pressure to influence events in Mexico. Geography and America's economic relationship with Mexico made strict nonintervention impossible. DAI 25:434.

2450 Knoblauch, Jess. "Lord Cowdray's Interests in Mexico, 1889–1919." Ph.D. dissertation, Arizona State University, 1985.

Weetman D. Pearson (later Viscount Cowdray) was maligned by commercial rivals who sought to cover their own political interference in Mexican affairs. The Wilson administration was prejudiced against Pearson by the slander of his enemies. DAI 46:3839-A.

2451 Langston, Edward L. "The Impact of Prohibition on the Mexican-United States Border: The El Paso-Ciudad Juarez Case." Ph.D. dissertation, Texas Tech University, 1974.

In 1918 the wide-open border town of El Paso cleaned itself up under pressure from the War Department. Saloons, bordellos, liquor stores, and gambling houses simply moved a few hundred yards south, across the border into Mexico, creating a whole new set of problems. DAI 35:2178-A.

2452 Lopez de Roux, Maria E. "Mexican-North American Relations (1917–18)" (in Spanish). *Historia Mexicana* [Mexico] 14 (1965): 445–68.

The Carranza Doctrine, developed as a reaction against American interference in the affairs of Mexico, called for national self-determination, nonintervention, and equality among nations. Notes.

2453 Lutzker, Michael A. "Can the Peace Movement Prevent War? The U.S.-Mexican Crisis of April 1914." In Solomon Weeks, ed. *Doves and Diplomats: Foreign Offices and Peace Movements in Europe and America in the 20th Century*. Westport, CT: Greenwood, 1978, pp. 127–53.

Wilson's effective presidential leadership played a more important role than did the peace movement in molding public opinion about the crisis with Mexico. Notes.

2454 Lyon, Jessie C. "Diplomatic Relations between the United States, Mexico and Japan: 1913–1917." Ph.D. dissertation, Claremont Graduate School, 1975.

Japan actively opposed Wilson's Mexican policy in retaliation for American opposition to Japanese encroachments on China, a policy that heightened American distrust of Japan. DAI 36:3045-A.

2455 Machado, Manuel A., Jr. "The Mexican Revolution and the Destruction of the Mexican Cattle Industry." *Southwestern Historical Quarterly* 79 (1975): 1–20.

Mexican revolutionaries regarded cattle both as food and as a commodity that could be bartered for arms. The U.S. government skewed beef imports to aid some factions at the expense of others, while the Mexican government did not want cattle shipped at all for fear of helping its enemies. Notes.

2456 Machado, Manuel A., Jr., and Judge, James T. "Tempest in a Teapot? The Mexican-United States Intervention Crisis of 1919." *Southwestern Historical Quarterly* 74 (1970): 1–23.

The United States was brought to the verge of intervention in 1919 in Mexico because of Carranza's inability to protect American lives and property. Although the State Department and many members of Congress formed a war party, the president prevailed by urging moderation. Notes.

2457 Meyer, Michael C. "The Arms of the *Ypiranga*." *Hispanic American Historical Review* 50 (1970): 543–56.

German agents purchased arms in the United States for resale in Mexico, and Wilson used the *Ypiranga* shipment as a pretext for moving against the Huerta regime. Notes.

2458 ———. "Villa, Sommerfeld, Columbus, and the Germans" (in Spanish). *Historica Mexicana* [Mexico] 28 (1979): 546–66.

A German agent named Felix Sommerfeld urged Villa to raid Columbus to touch off a Mexican-American war. Only indirect evidence has been found to support this thesis. Notes.

2459 Mumme, Stephen P. "The Battle of Naco: Factionalism and Conflict in Sonora, 1914–1915." *Arizona and the West* 21 (1979): 157–86.

The siege of Naco, in which revolutionaries surrounded this Mexican border town, finally came to an end as a result of American mediation in 1915, although hostilities resumed in Sonora subsequently. Notes.

2460 Paulsen, George E. "Reaping the Whirlwind in Chihuahua: The Destruction of the Minas de Corralitos, 1911–1917." *New Mexico Historical Review* 58 (1983): 253–70.

The American-managed mining operations of northwest Chihuahua were wrecked during the revolution, but owner Edwin D. Morgan never pressed for compensation, because he could not document his claimed losses and may have been involved in fraud. Notes.

2461 Pletcher, David M. "An American Mining Company in the Mexican Revolution of 1911–1920." *Journal of Modern History* 20 (1948): 19–26.

The revolution harmed the interests of the Chicago Exploration Company, an American mining enterprise.

2462 Prisco, Salvatore, III. "John Barrett's Plan to Mediate the Mexican Revolution." *The Americas* 27 (1971): 413–25.

As the director-general of the Pan American Union, Barrett favored mediating the crisis between Huerta and Wilson through a multilateral commission, a suggestion the president turned down flat. Notes.

2463 Pyron, Darden A. "Mexico as an Issue in American Politics, 1911–1916." Ph.D. dissertation, University of Virginia, 1975.

Many politicians attempted to exploit the Mexican Revolution for their own ends. Democrats and Republicans alike sniped at Wilson over his policies, while Progressive Republicans and conservatives used the issue to kiss and make up. Wilson shrewdly used Mexico to foil Republican criticisms. DAI 36:4680-A.

2464 Quirk, Robert E. *An Affair of Honor: Woodrow Wilson and the Occupation of Veracruz.* Lexington: University of Kentucky Press, 1962.

The occupation of Veracruz illustrates that Wilson's instinct to recognize only moral governments was impossible in practice. He reluctantly accepted the fact that Latin Americans could no longer be treated like children. Notes, bibliography, index.

2465 Rausch, G. J., Jr. "Exile and Death of Victoriano Huerta." *Hispanic American Historical Review* 42 (1962): 133–51.

After his overthrow in 1914, Huerta went into exile in the United States, where he faced charges of violating neutrality laws at the time of his death in 1916. Notes.

2466 Richmond, Douglas W. "Mexican Immigration and Border Strategy during the Revolution, 1910–1920." *New Mexico Historical Review* 57 (1982): 269–88.

To help solve a basic problem in Mexican-American relations, President Carranza discussed working conditions and business interests on both sides of the border with representatives from the American national and state governments. Notes.

2467 Roberts, Richard C. "The Utah National Guard on the Mexican Border in 1916." *Utah Historical Quarterly* 46 (1978): 262–81.

Utah National Guardsmen called to duty by Wilson to protect the border against Villa's forces gained experience that became important when the United States entered the European war. Notes.

2468 Rocha, Rodolfo. "The Influence of the Mexican Revolution on the Mexico-Texas Border, 1910–1916." Ph.D. dissertation, Texas Tech University, 1981.

During the Mexican Revolution, the border towns on the Mexican side were attacked several times. On the Texas side, towns housed refugees, sold guns and ammunition, and remained on alert for attacks. The revolution offered hope to Mexican-Americans who had been exploited for generations by rich Anglos and Mexicans and by the Texas Rangers. While a few Anglos suffered property damage from border raids, Mexican-Americans were more often the victims of Anglo reprisals. DAI 42:1758-A.

2469 Rosenberg, Emily S. "Economic Pressures in Anglo-American Diplomacy in Mexico, 1917–1918." *Journal of Inter-American Studies and World Affairs* 17 (1975): 123–52.

Americans used money and food in an attempt to moderate the course of the Mexican Revolution in 1917–18, a tactic that failed as Mexico looked to Great Britain and Latin America for alternative economic arrangements. Notes.

2470 Ryan, Paul B. "Ten Days at Veracruz." *US Naval Institute Proceedings* 98 (1972): 64–73.

This account of the American landing at Veracruz in April 1914 focuses on the battleship *New Jersey* and its landing battalion.

2471 Sandos, James A. "German Involvement in Northern Mexico, 1915–1916: A New Look at the Columbus Raid." *Hispanic-American Historical Review* 50 (1970): 70–88.

Villa's massacre of sixteen Americans on a Mexican train and his subsequent raid on Columbus, New Mexico, were for very different purposes. A German agent may have convinced Villa to attack the American town to start a war between the United States and Mexico, a move which would have benefited Villa as well as Germany. Notes.

2472 ——. "The Mexican Revolution and the United States, 1915–1917: The Impact of Conflict in the Tamaulipas-Texas Frontier upon the Emergence of Revolutionary Government in Mexico." Ph.D. dissertation, University of California, 1978.

Frontier unrest along the Texas-Mexico border influenced Wilson to implement a selective embargo and discourage foreign loans. The president's policies may have prolonged the Mexican civil war by as much as four years. DAI 42:3269-A.

2473 Sessions, Tommie G. "American Reformers and the Mexican Revolution: Progressives and Woodrow Wilson's Policy in Mexico, 1913–1917." Ph.D. dissertation, American University, 1974.

Most Progressives supported Wilson's Mexico policies, including his limited interventions, although some wanted him to be more aggressive and others favored nonintervention. Progressives failed to understand why the Mexicans did not want to be like them. DAI 35:2193-A.

2474 Smith, Robert Freeman. *The United States and Revolutionary Nationalism in Mexico, 1916–1932.* Chicago: University of Chicago Press, 1972.

The author examines the reactions of Americans, especially businessmen, to the first socioeconomic revolution in the Western Hemisphere, concluding that attempts to control underdeveloped countries bring about not solutions but only bad feelings and complications. Notes, bibliography, index.

2475 Sonnichsen, C. L. "Pancho Villa and the Cananea Copper Company." *Journal of Arizona History* 20 (1979): 87–100.

Desperate for money and supplies, Villa bargained with the Cananea Copper Company in late 1915. Villa received American money and Mexican gold, and in return he released some company employees he had detained. Notes.

2476 Tate, Michael L. "Pershing's Punitive Expedition: Pursuer of Bandits or Presidential Panacea?" *The Americas* 32 (1975): 46–71.

Wilson's decision to order General Pershing into Mexico is put into the larger perspective of Wilson's Latin American policy and seen as counterproductive, since it quickened the Mexican march toward nationalization of American oil assets.

2477 Teitelbaum, Louis M. *Woodrow Wilson and the Mexican Revolution (1913–1916): A History of United States-Mexican Relations from the Murder of Madero until Villa's Provocation across the Border.* New York: Exposition, 1967.

Although Wilson comes in for his share of criticism, the author concludes that less cool heads might have led the United States into a second Mexican-American war.

2478 Trow, Clifford W. " 'Tired of Waiting': Senator Albert B. Fall's Alternative to Woodrow Wilson's Mexican Policies, 1920–1921." *New Mexico Historical Review* 57 (1982): 159–82.

As the Republican chairman of a special Senate subcommittee set up to keep watch on the Mexican Revolution, Senator Albert B. Fall emerged as the leading critic of President Wilson's "watchful waiting." Notes.

2479 ———. "Woodrow Wilson and the Mexican Interventionist Movement of 1919." *Journal of American History* 58 (1971): 46–72.

Senator Fall's resolution of 3 December 1919 calling on the president to no longer recognize the Carranza government and to cut diplomatic relations was part of a scheme to bring about military intervention and a protectorate over Mexico. Supporters included big oil companies and Secretary of State Lansing. Wilson's opposition scotched the movement. Notes.

2480 Turchen, Lesta V. "The Oil Expropriation Controversy, 1917–1942, in United States-Mexican Relations." Ph.D. dissertation, Purdue University, 1972.

The Mexican constitution of 1917 and President Carranza's oil decrees of 1918 and 1919 threatened the interests of American oil companies. President Wilson protested Mexico's attempt to take control of its petroleum but did not intervene. DAI 33:5108-A.

2481 Ulloa Ortiz, Berta. "Carranza and United States Armament" (in Spanish). *Historia Mexicana* [Mexico] 17 (1967): 253–62.

Wilson's embargo on arms shipments to Mexico was designed to hurt the Huerta government. American officials and representatives of Carranza's forces agreed early in 1914 to lift the embargo. Notes.

2482 ———. *La Revolución Intervenida: Relaciones Diplomáticas entre México y Estados Unidos, 1910–1914* (The intervening revolution: diplomatic relations between Mexico and the United States, 1910–1914). Mexico City: El Colegio de Mexico, 1971.

The Tampico incident was a minor matter that Wilson used as an excuse to intervene against a government of which he disapproved. Notes, bibliography, index.

2483 Wharfield, H. B. "The Affair at Carrizal." *Montana* 18 (1968): 24–39.

While Pershing's punitive expedition of 1916 never met up with Villa, the general did order a detachment of black cavalrymen to the Carranzista stronghold of Carrizal, where a fierce battle ensued. The author speculates that Pershing hoped to outrage American public opinion to the point where a full-scale invasion of Mexico would follow. Notes.

2484 White, E. Bruce. "The Muddied Waters of Columbus, New Mexico." *The Americas* 32 (1975): 72–98.

Events leading up to Villa's 9 March 1916 raid on Columbus, New Mexico, are discussed.

2485 Williams, Vernon L. "Lieutenant George S. Patton, Jr., and the American Army: On the Texas Frontier in Mexico, 1915–1916." *Military History of Texas and the Southwest* 17 (1982): 1–76.

Patton's involvement with the punitive expedition into Mexico in 1915–16 is detailed. Notes.

2486 Wolfe, Margaret Ripley. "The Border Service of the Tennessee National Guard, 1916–1917." *Tennessee Historical Quarterly* 32 (1973): 374–88.

The history of the Tennessee National Guard during the Progressive era is recounted, especially its service along the Mexican border in 1916–17.

2487 Woods, Kenneth F. "Samuel Guy Inman and Intervention in Mexico." *Southern California Quarterly* 46 (1964): 351–70.

This Protestant missionary leader worked to prevent American intervention in the Mexican Revolution, writing a book on the subject in 1919 and testifying before Congress.

Panama

2488 Baker, George W., Jr. "The Wilson Administration and Panama, 1913–1921." *Journal of InterAmerican Studies* 8 (1966): 279–93.

Wilson paid close attention to events in Panama and proved himself to be no different than his Republican predecessors in his willingness to play big brother.

2489 Block, Robert H. "Southern Congressmen and Wilson's Call for Repeal of the Panama Canal Toll Exemption." *Southern Studies* 17 (1978): 91–100.

In 1913, President Wilson relied on southern Democrats in his bid to repeal an exemption for American ships using the Panama Canal that Congress had passed a year earlier. Southerners more than northerners supported the president out of party loyalty. Notes.

2490 Coker, William S. "The Panama Canal Tolls Controversy: A Different Perspective." *Journal of American History* 55 (1968): 555–64.

Wilson wanted, on moral grounds, a clause in the Panama Canal Act exempting American coastal trade from canal tolls, while Bryan hoped that the repeal would set a good example for the peaceful resolution of disputes. Notes.

MIDDLE EAST

See also *Zionism,* in Chapter 6.

2491 Bryson, Thomas A. "Admiral Mark Lambert Bristol: An Open Door Diplomat in Turkey." *International Journal of Middle East Studies* 5 (1974): 450–67.

This unsentimental admiral had little use for Armenia, preferring to treat with the Turks to gain an Open Door in the Near East. Notes.

2492 Daniel, Robert. "The Armenian Question and American-Turkish Relations, 1914–1927." *Mississippi Valley Historical Review* 46 (1959): 252–75.

The mistreatment of Armenians, a Christian minority in the Ottoman Empire, proved to be a major impediment to the restoration of Turkish-American diplomatic relations after World War I. Turkish nationalism and the American stereotype of the "Terrible Turk" complicated matters further. Notes.

2493 DeNovo, John A. *American Interests and Policies in the Middle East, 1900–1939.* Minneapolis: University of Minnesota Press, 1963.

Surveying American diplomatic, economic, and cultural activities in the Near and Middle East, the author examines Wilson's "radical departure from traditional policy"—and his hasty retreat from responsibility following the defeat of the Treaty of Versailles. Notes, bibliography, index.

2494 Einstein, Lewis. *A Diplomat Looks Back.* Edited by Lawrence Gelfand. New Haven, CT: Yale University Press, 1968.

A veteran diplomat, Einstein served in Turkey and Bulgaria during the Wilson years and offers here a candid assessment of American policies. Wilson leaned heavily on the advice of missionaries in the Near East. Bibliography, index.

2495 Evans, Laurence. *United States Policy and the Partition of Turkey, 1914–1924.* Baltimore, MD: Johns Hopkins University Press, 1965.

The two outstanding factors in American policy toward the Middle East during this period, the author notes, were: 1) that the United States could influence events in that region only by coercing other powers, and 2) that policy "was conducted almost entirely at one remove from its object." Notes, bibliography, index.

2496 Goldblatt, Charles I. "The Impact of the Balfour Declaration in America." *American Jewish Historical Quarterly* 57 (1968): 455–515.

The 1917 Balfour Declaration promising a Jewish homeland in Palestine, American comments about it in religious publications, and the comments of elected officials are analyzed.

2497 Grabill, Joseph L. "Cleveland H. Dodge, Woodrow Wilson and the Near East." *Journal of Presbyterian History* 48 (1970): 249–64.

Wilson's friend Dodge worked to get the administration to support a system of U.S. mandates in what had been the Ottoman Empire. It was at Dodge's urging that Wilson refrained from declaring war on Turkey. The Senate's failure to accept a mandate for Armenia did not stop Dodge from championing the rights of Middle Eastern peoples. Notes.

2498 ———. *Protestant Diplomacy and the Near East: Missionary Influence on American*

Policy, 1810–1927. Minneapolis: University of Minnesota Press, 1971.

Missionaries and philanthropists played a key role in America's Near Eastern policy. Following the slaughter of Armenians by the Turks in 1915, these groups crusaded for—and almost obtained—an American mandate over Asia Minor. Notes, bibliographic essay, index.

2499 Halpern, Ben. "Brandeis and the Origins of the Balfour Declaration." *Studies in Zionism* [Israel] 7 (1983): 71–100.

Louis Brandeis's inaction hurt the Zionist cause at a time when Wilson's endorsement was much sought after. Notes.

2500 Howard, Harry N. *Turkey, the Straits and U.S. Policy*. Baltimore, MD: Johns Hopkins University Press, 1974.

After surveying the foundations of American policy toward the Turkish straits prior to World War I, the author traces the growing interest in that strategic waterway, including Wilson's determination to play an active role in the Near East. Notes, bibliography, index.

2501 Laffey, Robert M. "United States Policy toward and Relations with Syria, 1914 to 1949." Ph.D. dissertation, University of Notre Dame, 1981.

Included in this study of Syrian-American relations is material on Wilson's attitudes and actions toward the Middle East. Wilson laid much of the groundwork for America's interwar policies. DAI 42:1271-A.

2502 Lebow, Richard N. "Woodrow Wilson and the Balfour Declaration." *Journal of Modern History* 40 (1968): 501–23.

Wilson gave secret official sanction to the declaration supporting a Jewish homeland because of concern that Germany might endorse the homeland proposal and for strategic reasons. Notes.

2503 Raphalides, Samuel J. "The United States and the Question of the Greco-Turkish War, 1919–1922." *Byzantine and Modern Greek Studies* [Great Britain] 8 (1982): 171–89.

While the Wilson and Harding administrations expressed humanitarian concerns about the Greco-Turkish war of 1919–1922, both avoided becoming involved, except for providing minimal aid to refugees. Notes.

2504 Trask, Roger R. *The United States Response to Turkish Nationalism and Reform,*

1914–1939. Minneapolis: University of Minnesota Press, 1971.

The groundwork for post-World War II Turkish-American cooperation was laid after World War I, when the United States tried to become a "good neighbor" to the increasingly nationalistic Turks. Notes, bibliography, index.

2505 Van de Bilt, Eduardus Franciscus. "Proximity and Distance: American Travellers to the Middle East, 1819–1918." Ph.D. dissertation, Cornell University, 1985.

Writings of journalists, missionaries, and other travelers reveal the prejudices and openness with which Americans responded to the exotic Middle East. DAI 46:2791-A.

2506 Yeselson, Abraham. "United States-Persian Diplomatic Relations, 1883–1921." Ph.D. dissertation, Brown University, 1954.

The United States tried to remain unentangled in Persian affairs, and American missionaries and advisers went to Persia at their own risk. After the war, the United States refused Persia's request for representation at the peace talks, although private financial relief was provided. Britain began to compete with America for Persian oil. DAI 14:2390.

EUROPE

France

See also Chapter 10, *Wilsonian Diplomacy* and *Wartime Relations, Entente,* and Chapter 12.

2507 Blumenthal, Henry. *Illusion and Reality in Franco-American Diplomacy, 1914–1945*. Baton Rouge: Louisiana University Press, 1986.

The clash between Wilson's idealism and Georges Clemenceau's realism harmed Franco-American relations and led to the lost peace. Notes, bibliography, index.

2508 Leffler, Melvyn P. *The Elusive Quest: America's Pursuit of European Stability and French Security, 1919–1933*. Chapel Hill: University of North Carolina Press, 1979.

While Wilson and his Republican successors retreated from political involvement with Europe, they understood that prosperity at home depended on the economic security of Europe. Notes, bibliography, index.

2509 McDougall, Walter A. *France's Rhineland Diplomacy, 1914–1924: The Last Bid* *for a Balance of Power in Europe*. Princeton: Princeton University Press, 1978.

France was consistent in its prime objective of gaining extensive guarantees against Germany. To this end, France regarded Wilsonian internationalism as an opportunity to gain the support of the Anglo-Saxon powers. Notes, bibliography, index.

2510 Renouvin, Pierre. "The Fate of the American Assistance Pact with France in 1919" (in French). *Annales d'Etudes Internationales* [Switzerland] 1 (1970): 9–22.

Wilson's promise of armed aid should France be attacked foundered on the rocks of the Senate. Following the defeat of the Treaty of Versailles, the Franco-American pact never was brought to the floor for a vote. Notes.

2511 Sharp, William G. *The War Memoirs of William Graves Sharp, American Ambassador to France, 1914–1919*. Edited by Warrington Dawson. London: Constable, 1931.

A wealthy former congressman from Ohio and one of many "deserving Democrats" appointed by Wilson to important diplomatic positions discusses Franco-American relations during the Great War.

Germany

See also Chapter 3, *James W. Gerard,* Chapter 6, *Immigration,* Chapter 10, *Wartime Relations, Others* and *Armistice,* and Chapter 12.

2512 Barthold, Theodore R. "Assignment to Berlin: The Embassy of James W. Gerard, 1913–1917." Ph.D. dissertation, Temple University, 1981.

A political appointee, Gerard rose to the challenge following the outbreak of war in Europe, although his reports to Washington were often of poor quality. Gerard's efforts suffered as a result of Wilson's holding all serious talks in Washington and using Colonel Edward House to convey messages to Berlin. DAI 42:2258-A.

2513 Dallas, Jerry W. "Anglo-American Attitudes toward the German Revolution, November 1918–June 1919." Ph.D. dissertation, Emory University, 1972.

Anglo-American attitudes toward the postwar German revolution were shaped by anti-German and anti-Bolshevik feelings. Consequently policymakers feared that German leftists would bring about communism and so supported the right wing, but since they distrusted all Germans they also fretted that Germany had not changed enough. DAI 33:1633-A.

2514 Fraenkel, Ernst. "The German Image of Wilson" (in German). *Jahrbüch für Amerikastudien* [West Germany] 5 (1960): 66–120.

For years German politicians, journalists, and historians blamed Wilson for the harsh peace imposed by the victors, and these feelings contributed to the rise of fascism.

2515 Hirsch, Felix. "Stresemann, Ballin and the United States." *Vierteljahrshefte für Zeitgeschichte* [West Germany] 3 (1955): 20–35.

Gustav Stresemann's perceptions of the United States are surveyed along with an examination of his friendship with American steamship magnate Albert Ballin, which the wily German used to keep open an informal line of communications between the two countries during and after World War I. Notes.

2516 Lowinsky, Benjamin D. "The Enigma of U.S. Policy toward Germany: American Perceptions and Foreign Policy Objectives regarding Germany between 1917 and 1924." Ph.D. dissertation, York University, 1984.

The punitive peace established after World War I set Germany on an unstable financial and political course. DAI 45:2629-A.

2517 Small, Melvin. "The American Image of Germany, 1906–1914." Ph.D. dissertation, University of Michigan, 1965.

Until Germany invaded Belgium in 1914, most Americans held a neutral opinion of Germany, influenced more by popular literature and feature articles than by actual events. On the other hand, most government officials had minor grievances against Germany. A few minority groups, including German Americans and Scandinavian Americans, were solidly pro-German. DAI 26:7288.

Great Britain and Its Dominions

See also Chapter 3, *Edward M. House* and *Walter Hines Page,* Chapter 10, *Wilsonian Diplomacy* and *Wartime Relations, Entente,* and Chapter 12.

2518 Boothe, Leon E. "A Fettered Envoy: Lord Grey's Mission to the United States, 1919–1920." *Review of Politics* 33 (1971): 78–94.

The primary purpose of Lord Grey's special mission to the United States of 1919–20 was to show British goodwill. He gained Wilson's enmity by trying to mediate the dispute about the Versailles Treaty between the president and Henry Cabot Lodge. Notes.

2519 Hogan, Michael J. *Informal Entente: The Private Structure of Cooperation in Anglo-American Economic Diplomacy, 1918–1928.* Columbia: University of Missouri Press, 1977.

Cooperation rather than conflict dominated Anglo-American economic relations in the decade after the Great War. Notes, bibliography, index.

2520 Jensen, Joan M. "The 'Hindu Conspiracy': A Reassessment." *Pacific Historical Review* 48 (1979): 65–83.

British claims of a conspiracy between Indian nationalists and Germany to free British India were believed by American government officials, who halted Hindu nationalist activities in the United States in 1918. Notes.

2521 Jha, Manoranjan. "Britain and the Pro-India Activities in the U.S.A." *Political Science Review* [India] 12 (1973): 1-34.

Indian groups in the United States who worked for the cause of independence after World War I were the targets of a British pressure campaign.

2522 Kaplan, Phillip S. "The Crisis in Anglo-American Relations of 1913–1914." Ph.D. dissertation, Johns Hopkins University, 1966.

Britain and America competed for South American oil, argued over Panama Canal tolls, and disagreed about the Mexican Revolution during Wilson's first two years as president. DAI 27:2990-A.

2523 Klachko, Mary. "Anglo-American Naval Competition, 1918–1922." Ph.D. dissertation, Columbia University, 1962.

During World War I, the United States began to threaten Britain's naval supremacy. Despite much diplomatic maneuvering, Britain was forced to accept naval equality with the United States. DAI 23:4737.

2524 Klein, Ira. "Whitehall, Washington, and the Anglo-Japanese Alliance, 1919–1921." *Pacific Historical Review* 41 (1972): 460–83.

The British Foreign Office favored the abrogation of the Anglo-Japanese alliance to foster closer relations with the United States and hoped for a new tripartite agreement to curb Japanese expansion without offending Japan. Notes.

2525 Link, Arthur S. "The Cotton Crisis, the South, and Anglo-American Diplomacy." In Arthur S. Link. *The Higher Realism of Woodrow*

Wilson and Other Essays. Nashville: Vanderbilt University Press, 1971.

The cotton market collapsed in late 1914 as fear of oversupply spread in the wake of the European war. Although the crisis passed within a year, it left southerners with anti-British feelings. Notes.

2526 Meaney, Neville K. "The American Attitude towards the British Empire from 1919 to 1922: A Study in the Diplomatic Relations of the English-Speaking Nations." Ph.D. dissertation, Duke University, 1959.

America remained largely ignorant of the implications of Britain's Imperial Conference of 1917. At the peace conference, Wilson and House saw that Britain was releasing the reins of empire, and so they accepted a total of six votes in the League of Nations for British dominions. Many Americans were opposed to this apparent imbalance. DAI 20:653.

2527 Murdoch, Floyd M. "For the Birds: Backgrounds of the Anglo-American Bird Treaty of 1916." Ph.D. dissertation, American University, 1975.

After several court rulings struck down the constitutionality of federal laws protecting birds, the United States signed the Migratory Bird Treaty with Britain in 1916 to add teeth to legislation already passed. DAI 36:2373-A.

2528 Pugach, Noel H. "Anglo-American Aircraft Competition and the China Arms Embargo, 1919–1921." *Diplomatic History* 2 (1978): 351–71.

The end of the war created a large surplus of combat aircraft, which led the United States and the other Allies to look to China, where civil war was raging. In spite of an embargo on arms sales to China, the British negotiated a large contract with the Chinese government thanks to adroit diplomacy and American indifference. Notes.

2529 Sarbaugh, Timothy. "British War Policies in Ireland, 1914–1918: The California Irish-American Reaction." *San Jose Studies* 9 (1983): 24–33.

British actions in Ireland during World War I outraged many Irish Americans in California. A broad-based movement to promote Irish republicanism was the chief result.

2530 Schmidt, Earl R. "American Relations with South Asia, 1900–1940." Ph.D. dissertation, University of Pennsylvania, 1955.

Missionaries in India profoundly affected American-Indian relations. Various events in India are analyzed in an attempt to discover the sources of Indian suspiciousness of American motives. DAI 15:2281.

2531 Singh, Diwakar P. "American Official Attitudes towards the Indian Nationalist Movement, 1905–1929." Ph.D. dissertation, University of Hawaii, 1964.

America was generally supportive of India's striving for democratic self-rule, but it disapproved of occasional outbreaks of terrorism. DAI 25:2954.

2532 Smith, Douglas L. "Viscount Grey's 'Special Mission' and Postwar Anglo-American Relations." *Southern Quarterly* 11 (1973): 257–74.

The appointment of Viscount Edward Grey as special ambassador to the United States in August 1919 to settle Anglo-American differences over war debts, mandates, naval power, the League, and German reparations was a success in that some problems were solved and others were at least clarified. Notes.

2533 Spinelli, Lawrence. *Dry Diplomacy: The United States, Great Britain and Prohibition.* Wilmington, DE: Scholarly Resources, 1989.

Prohibition caused conflicts with Great Britain over the sale of liquor on foreign ships in U.S. waters and the sale and transfer of British liquor to American ships just beyond U.S. territory. These disputes caused a more general and serious mistrust.

2534 Williams, Joyce G. "Colonel House and Sir Edward Grey: A Study in Anglo-American Diplomacy." Ph.D. dissertation, Indiana University, 1971.

Britain's Foreign Secretary Sir Edward Grey cultivated the friendship of Colonel Edward House to keep their two countries on good terms during World War I. House, in turn, influenced his friend, President Wilson. DAI 32:2581-A.

Italy

See also Chapter 6, *Immigration,* Chapter 10, *Wartime Relations, Entente,* and Chapter 12.

2535 Gaines, Anne-Rosewell J. "Political Reward and Recognition: Woodrow Wilson Appoints Thomas Nelson Page Ambassador to Italy." *Virginia Magazine of History and Biography* 39 (1981): 328–40.

A friend of Wilson from the president's academic days, this wealthy Progressive writer served in his political post throughout the war years. Notes.

2536 Gould, John W. "Italy and the United States, 1914–1918: Background to Confrontation." Ph.D. dissertation, Yale University, 1969.

Italian foreign policymakers blundered badly during the war by ignoring the new and important American factor. Wilson paid little attention to Italy and refused to recognize the existence of secret treaties that promised territory to Italy. Unlike Wilson, who knew what he wanted at the peace conference, the Italians were badly divided among themselves. DAI 31:1190-A.

2537 Tobia, Bruno. "The Italian Socialist Party and the Policy of Woodrow Wilson, 1916–19" (in Italian). *Storia Contemporanea* [Italy] 5 (1974): 275–303.

Italy's Socialist party opposed World War I from start to finish. While they applauded Wilson's Fourteen Points, the actual peace settlement disappointed them. Notes.

Poland

See also Chapter 6, *Immigration,* and Chapter 12, *Self-Determination.*

2538 Bienkowski-Biskupski, Mieczyslaw B. "The United States and the Rebirth of Poland, 1914–1918." Ph.D. dissertation, Yale University, 1981.

Millions of Polish immigrants infected the American public with an intense interest in the rebirth of Poland. Polish suffering during the war also made Americans sympathetic to the cause. DAI 45:1181-A.

2539 Landau, Zbigniew. "Some Controversial Problems in the Polish-American Relationship during the Years 1918–20" (in Polish). *Kwartalnik Historyczny* [Poland] 65 (1958): 1093–1108.

Stalinist historians have long claimed that America wanted to make Poland into an anti-Soviet base of operations as early as 1918–1920. In fact, though, America showed little interest in Poland until the middle 1920s.

2540 Urbanski, Adam. "Americanism and the Polish-American Press, 1916–1925." Ph.D. dissertation, University of Rochester, 1974.

The Polish-language press in the United States supported the American war effort primarily for the sake of the rebirth of Poland. DAI 36:500-A.

2541 Zake, Louis J. "The National Department and the Polish American Community, 1916–1923." *Polish American Studies* 38 (1981): 16–25.

An umbrella committee formed to lobby for Poland's independence, this department quickly fell apart once Poland had been reformulated. Notes.

Russia

See also Chapter 11, *The Bolshevik Revolution*, and Chapter 12, *Russian Question*.

2542 Dazhina, I. M., and Tsivlina, R., eds. "American Diaries of A. M. Kollontai, 1915–1916" (in Russian). *Istoricheski Arkhiv* [USSR] (1962): 128–59.

Included in these excerpts from a Russian Marxist's diaries are her impressions of America and letters to Lenin and his wife.

2543 Fike, Claude E. "Aspects of the New American Recognition Policy toward Russia following World War I." *Southern Quarterly* 4 (1965): 1–16.

In early 1919, the Soviet Russian government sent an ambassador to the United States, but Wilson would not acknowledge him, as the administration still recognized the minister sent by the long-since deposed Aleksandr Kerensky regime. Notes.

2544 Fithian, Floyd J. "Soviet-American Economic Relations, 1918–1933: American Business in Russia during the Period of Nonrecognition." Ph.D. dissertation, University of Nebraska, 1964.

When Russia outlawed private ownership, U.S. companies lost all their Russian holdings. Wilson offered no government protection to businessmen who traded with the USSR, although America did try to use economic pressure to discourage the development of communism. DAI 25:2943.

2545 Horak, Stephan M. "The United States in Lenin's Image." *Ukrainian Quarterly* 23 (1967): 226–37.

Lenin's perceptions of the social and political conditions in the United States and its diplomacy are discussed. Notes.

2546 Kostiainen, Auvo. "Santeri Nuorteva and the Origins of Soviet-American Relations."

American Studies in Scandinavia [Norway] 15 (1983): 1–13.

Santeri Nuorteva became the representative of the Finnish Red Revolutionary government to the United States. When his cause collapsed, he turned to promoting the Bolshevik Revolution until the Red Scare, when he journeyed to the Soviet Union. Notes.

2547 Libbey, James K. *Alexander Gumberg and Soviet-American Relations, 1917–1933.* Lexington: University of Kentucky Press, 1977.

A confidant of Raymond Robins, Gumberg dedicated his life to improving Soviet-American relations for the benefit of both countries. Gumberg became "a conveyor belt" between the two powers at a time when normal relations did not exist. Notes, bibliographic essay, index.

2548 ———. "The American-Russian Chamber of Commerce." *Diplomatic History* 9 (1985): 233–48.

The American-Russian Chamber of Commerce was founded early in 1916 in response to increased wartime trade between the two nations. The Bolshevik Revolution and Russia's subsequent pullout from the war enraged the chamber, which became inactive in 1920. Notes.

2549 Owen, Gail L. "Dollar Diplomacy in Default: The Economics of Russian-American Relations, 1910–1917." *History Journal* 13 (1970): 251–72.

Russian-American trade relations boomed between 1914 and 1917 as a result of billions of dollars in credit advanced to the czarist regime. The Bolshevik Revolution put a quick end to this short-lived boom. Notes.

2550 Parks, Jimmy D. "Culture, Conflict and Coexistence: American-Soviet Cultural Relations, 1917–1958." Ph.D. dissertation, University of Oklahoma, 1980.

Given the antagonistic political relationship between America and the Soviet Union, the two countries enjoyed surprisingly good cultural interchanges. DAI 41:3234-A.

2551 Propas, Frederic L. "The State Department, Bureaucratic Politics and Soviet-American Relations, 1918–1938." Ph.D. dissertation, University of California, Los Angeles, 1982.

American policy toward Bolshevism was always colored by hostility. The State Department and bureaucratic politics were major forces in shaping Soviet-American relations. DAI 43:1267-A.

2552 Savitt, Robert P. "To Fill a Void: Soviet 'Diplomatic' Representation in the U.S. Prior to Recognition." Ph.D. dissertation, Georgetown University, 1983.

The travails of unrecognized representatives from Soviet Russia are discussed, including the mission of Ludwig C. A. K. Martens, who came to America in early 1919 and left two years later, when the government threatened to deport him. DAI 45:270-A.

2553 Singerman, Robert. "The American Career of the *Protocols of the Elders of Zion.*" *American Jewish History* 71 (1981): 48–78.

A propagandist representing the czar of Russia tried to link the Russian Revolution to an international conspiracy of Jews by publishing the spurious *Protocols of the Elders of Zion* in the United States, a campaign which attracted little interest except that of Henry Ford. Notes.

2554 Williams, Rowan A. "Reporting from Petrograd, 1914–1915." *East European Quarterly* 14 (1980): 335–44.

Reports on the state of the Russian army early in the war were written by Lieutenant Sherman Miles, a U.S. military attaché. Notes.

Others

See also Chapter 10, *Wartime Relations, Other,* and Chapter 12, *Self-Determination.*

2555 Cassimatis, Louis P. "Greek-American Relations, 1917–1929." Ph.D. dissertation, Kent State University, 1978.

The United States became involved in Greece by participating in the 1918 loan to the Eleuthérios Venizélos regime following the ouster of King Constantine. DAI 39:5662-A.

2556 Davis, Gerald H. "The Diplomatic Relations between the United States and Austria-Hungary, 1913–1917." Ph.D. dissertation, Vanderbilt University, 1958.

U.S. relations with Austria-Hungary were polite until World War I. While it was neutral, America tried to represent Austria-Hungary's interests to the Allies, and Austria-Hungary urged America to stop delivering Allied

weapons. The escalation of submarine warfare soured relations. The United States was eventually forced to declare war on Austria-Hungary "not because of any essential conflict of interests, but because of a military technicality." DAI 19:3288.

2557 Jackson, Shirley F. "The United States and Spain, 1898–1918." Ph.D. dissertation, Florida State University, 1967.

After humiliating Spain in the war of 1898, the United States made token gestures of friendship early in the Progressive era. After 1914, the two powers increased their trade with one another as the two leading neutrals. After American intervention, diplomatic relations became even closer. DAI 30:657-A.

2558 Krizman, Bogdan. "Activities of Archibald Coolidge's American Mission in the South Slav Lands of Former Austria-Hungary, 1919" (in Serbo-Croation). *Istorijski Glasnik* [Yugoslavia] 1 (1962): 111–46.

Coolidge was an agent of the U.S. government. He operated out of Zagreb.

2559 Paikert, Geza C. "Southeastern Europe and the United States" (in German). *Südostoforschungen* [West Germany] 15 (1956): 526–39.

Southeastern Europe has never been of much interest to Americans except during the world wars. This lack of interest contributed to the collapse of the Versailles-created governments in the 1930s.

2560 Stanciu, Ion. "Relations between the United States and Romania during Romanian Neutrality, 1914–16" (in Romanian). *Revue de Istorie* [Romania] 29 (1976): 921–34.

Increased trade between the United States and Romania early in World War I was a result of both countries remaining neutral.

2561 Vopicka, Charles J. *Secrets of the Balkans: Seven Years of a Diplomat's Life in the Storm Center of Europe.* Chicago: Rand-McNally, 1921.

Wilson's minister to Romania, Serbia, and Bulgaria remembers his service in Eastern Europe, although the "secrets" mentioned here are mere gossip about royal personalities.

President Wilson reads his war message to Congress, 2 April 1917. *Library of Congress.*

10

Foreign Affairs: The Origins and Diplomacy of World War I

The outbreak of war in Europe raised a series of great challenges for Wilsonian diplomacy. Historians have long debated the origins of American intervention in April 1917 after almost three years of perilous neutrality during which the president asked Americans to remain impartial. Did events change Wilson's policies or was it the other way around? For general background on the origins of the war, see Walter Carp, *The Politics of War: The Story of Two Wars Which Altered Forever the Political Life of the American Republic (1890–1920)* (#2562); Denna F. Fleming, *The Origins and Legacies of World War I* (#2564); and Barbara W. Tuchman, *The Proud Tower: A Portrait of the World before the War, 1890–1914* (#2566).

The best general works on American neutrality are John M. Cooper, Jr., *The Vanity of Power: American Isolationism and the First World War, 1914–1917* (#2575); Ross Gregory, *The Origins of American Intervention in the First World War* (#2581); and Daniel Smith, *Robert Lansing and American Neutrality, 1914–1917* (#2594). Revisionist works of the late 1920s and 1930s that emphasize economics and British propaganda as deciding factors include Harry Elmer Barnes, *The Genesis of the World War: An Introduction to the Problem of War Guilt* (#2567); C. Hartley Grattan, *Why We Fought* (#2580); Walter Millis, *Road to War: America, 1914–1917* (#2587); Horace C. Peterson, *Propaganda for War: The Campaign against American Neutrality* (#2592); and Charles C. Tansill, *America Goes to War* (#2599). Proponents of the "submarine school" who view the German U-boat warfare against Allied shipping as the primary cause of American involvement include Alice M.

Morrissey, *The American Defense of Neutral Rights, 1914–1917* (#2588), and Charles Seymour, *American Neutrality, 1914–1917: Essays on the Causes of American Intervention in the World War* (#2669).

Wilson's diplomacy is analyzed in Patrick Devlin, *Too Proud to Fight: Woodrow Wilson's Neutrality* (#2608); Arthur S. Link, "Wilson and the Ordeal of Neutrality" (#2615) as well as Volumes III, IV, and V of *Wilson* (#0186, #0187, and #0189) and *Woodrow Wilson: Revolution, War, and Peace* (#2283); and Ernest R. May, *World War and American Isolation* (#2616). For works dealing with maritime rights, see Karl E. Birnbaum, *Peace Moves and U-boat Warfare: Germany's Policy toward the United States, April 18, 1916–January 9, 1917* (#2625); John W. Coogan, *The End of Neutrality: The United States, Britain, and Maritime Rights, 1899–1915* (#2626); and Gaddis Smith, *Britain's Clandestine Submarines, 1914–1915* (#2638). The sinking of the *Lusitania* is examined by Thomas A. Bailey and Paul B. Ryan, *The "Lusitania" Disaster: An Episode in Modern Warfare and Diplomacy* (#2641), and Colin Simpson, *The "Lusitania"* (#2645), who disagree over whether or not the sinking was a British conspiracy to draw America into the war. The best general work on the Zimmermann Note is still Barbara Tuchman, *The Zimmermann Telegram* (#2653).

A controversy has arisen over what Wilson did or did not say to journalist Frank Cobb on the eve of America's entry into the war. See John L. Heaton, *Cobb of "The World": A Leader in Liberalism* (#2661), for the journalist's version of the meeting recounted several years after the fact. The main combatants are Jerold S. Auerbach, "Woodrow Wilson's 'Prediction' to Frank Cobb: Words Historians Should Doubt Ever Got Spoken" (#2654), and Arthur S. Link, "That Cobb Interview" (#2665). Wilson's decision for war is analyzed in Melvin Small, *Was War Necessary? National Security and U.S. Entry into War* (#2670).

Wartime diplomacy is the subject of a superb work by Arno J. Mayer, *Wilson vs. Lenin: Political Origins of the New Diplomacy, 1917–1918* (#2675). See also Arthur S. Link, "Wilson and Peace Moves" (#2674); Carl Parrini, *Heir to Empire: United States Economic Diplomacy, 1916–1923* (#2707); and Charles Seymour, *American Diplomacy during the World War* (#2676). For relations with Asian nations, see Ernest R. May, "American Policy and Japan's Entrance into World War I" (#2680), and a doctoral dissertation by Madeleine Chi Sung-chun, "The Chinese Question during the First World War" (#2678). On Latin America, see the dissertation by Emily S. Rosenberg, "World War I and the Growth of United States Preponderance in Latin America" (#2686). Kathleen Burk, *Britain, America and the Sinews of War, 1914–1918* (#2688); Wilton B. Fowler, *British-American Relations, 1917–1918: The Role of Sir William Wiseman* (#2693); and Joyce G. Williams, *Colonel House and Sir Edward Grey: A Study in Anglo-American Diplomacy* (#2718), cover various aspects of Anglo-American wartime relations. Benson L. Grayson, *Russian-American Relations in World War I* (#2696), does the same for relations with pre-Bolshevik Russia. On France and the United States, see Louis A. R. Yates, *United States and French Security, 1917–1921* (#2719). The diplomacy of the Armistice is examined by Harry R. Rudin, *Armistice, 1918* (#2738), and by Arthur Walworth, *America's Moment: 1918, American Diplomacy at the End of World War I* (#2740).

Origins

2562 Carp, Walter. *The Politics of War: The Story of Two Wars Which Altered Forever the Political Life of the American Republic (1890–1920)*. New York: Harper and Row, 1979.

While the period from 1890 to 1920 has been most often called the age of reform, it was also the age of war. Connections are made between domestic politics and the increasingly ambitious American foreign policy of this period. The second half of the book deals with the origins and consequences of American involvement in World War I. Notes, bibliography, index.

2563 Cooper, John Milton, Jr. "World War I: European Origins and American Intervention." *Virginia Quarterly Review* 56 (1980): 1–18.

The breakdown of diplomacy and internal affairs in Europe were responsible for the European war. The sinking of the *Lusitania* angered Americans who had thought of themselves as innocent and far away from the fray. German resumption of U-boat warfare in early 1917 led to American involvement.

2564 Fleming, Denna F. *The Origins and Legacies of World War I*. London: Allen and Unwin, 1969.

The long-term and short-term causes of the war are discussed along with an analysis of why American neutrality and the League of Nations failed. Notes, index.

2565 Stromberg, Roland. "On Cherchez le Financier: Comments on the Economic Interpretation of World War I." *History Teacher* 10 (1977): 435–43.

The economic interpretation of the origins of World War I is dismissed as being too old and too simple to be believable. Notes.

2566 Tuchman, Barbara W. *The Proud Tower: A Portrait of the World before the War, 1890–1914*. New York: Macmillan, 1966.

This volume contains several essays that contain useful background material on the origins of World War I. Photographs, notes, bibliography, index.

American Neutrality

GENERAL

2567 Barnes, Harry Elmer. *The Genesis of the World War: An Introduction to the Problem of War Guilt*. New York: Knopf, 1926.

German-American trade rivalry caused growing antagonisms between 1870 and 1914, and British war propaganda made the situation worse. Wilson had decided to help the Allies by late 1915. The resumption of U-boat warfare played into the hands of the administration and strongly pro-Allied American business and financial interests. Notes, bibliography, index.

2568 Bernstorff, Johann H. von. *Memoirs of Count Bernstorff.* Translated by Eric Sutton. New York: Random House, 1936.

The German ambassador to Washington discusses the period of neutrality and America's slow tilt toward the Allies.

2569 ———. *My Three Years in America.* New York: Scribner's, 1920.

Ambassador Bernstorff describes his diplomatic service in America before the war in self-serving terms.

2570 Block, Robert H. "Southern Opinion of Woodrow Wilson's Foreign Policies, 1913–1917." Ph.D. dissertation, Duke University, 1968.

Most southerners supported the president's foreign policies because he was a southern Democrat and they were patriotic. They were more supportive of his Mexican policies than of his handling of neutrality, which some suspected was influenced by northern capitalists. DAI 30:238-A.

2571 Chambers, John W., II, ed. *The Eagle and the Dove: The American Peace Movement and United States Foreign Policy, 1900–1922.* New York: Garland, 1976.

Several short pieces illustrating the ideas of the peace movement during the period of American neutrality are included. Bibliography.

2572 Child, Clifton J. *The German-Americans in Politics, 1914–1917.* Madison: University of Wisconsin Press, 1939.

During American neutrality, German Americans stood together in large enough numbers to make their viewpoints known. The work of the National German-American Alliance is analyzed. Notes, bibliography, index.

2573 Cook, Blanche W. "Woodrow Wilson and the Antimilitarists, 1914–1917." Ph.D. dissertation, Johns Hopkins University, 1970.

The American Union against Militarism was founded in 1915 to preserve the American liberal system through neutrality. The group supported Wilson's policies, having a naive faith in his promises. DAI 31:2298-A.

2574 Cooper, John Milton, Jr. "The Command of Gold Reversed: American Loans to Britain, 1915–1917." *Pacific Historical Review* 45 (1976): 209–30.

Recently released documents strengthen the case for the crucial role played by economic considerations in relations between the United States and the Allies during the period of American neutrality and in the decision to intervene. The Allies wanted America's "ultimate weapon," the command of finances, on their side. Notes.

2575 ———. *The Vanity of Power: American Isolationism and the First World War, 1914–1917.* Westport, CT: Greenwood, 1969.

Many thinking people saw isolationism as the only way to preserve American interests and ideals. An isolationist movement emerged as Congress debated the merits of preparedness and the arming of American ships. Even Wilson shared the fear of many isolationists that the war would wreck liberal reforms. Notes, bibliography.

2576 Cuddy, Edward. "Pro-Germanism and American Catholicism, 1914–1917." *Catholic Historical Review* 54 (1968): 427–54.

Catholics responded to the European war in diverse fashions. The church's neutrality and long-standing mission to unite various ethnic groups tended to offset pro-German feelings held by German and Irish Americans.

2577 Dayer, Roberta A. "Strange Bedfellows: J. P. Morgan & Co., Whitehall, and the Wilson Administration." *Business History* [Great Britain] 18 (1976): 127–51.

While it was attempting to remain neutral, the Wilson administration did not trust Morgan's activities on behalf of Britain. After April 1917, though, the U.S. government developed a cozy relationship with the banking house. Notes.

2578 Esslinger, Dean R. "American, German and Irish Attitudes toward Neutrality, 1914–1917: A Study of Catholic Minorities." *Catholic Historical Review* 53 (1967): 194–216.

National ancestry had more to do with ethnic opposition to American entrance into the war than did religious faith. Irish and German Americans favored the Central Powers, while other Catholics in the United States were split in their sentiments.

2579 Fowler, James H., II. "Creating an Atmosphere of Suppression, 1914–1917." *Chronicles of Oklahoma* 59 (1981): 202–23.

The period of American neutrality was marked increasingly by intolerance of dissenting opinions. Wilson's words were used by vigilantes to justify suppression of free speech. Notes.

2580 Grattan, C. Hartley. *Why We Fought.* Edited by Keith L. Nelson. Indianapolis: Bobbs-Merrill, 1969.

This republication of an early revisionist work blames British propaganda and economic factors for propelling Wilson into the war. Bibliography, index.

2581 Gregory, Ross. *The Origins of American Intervention in the First World War.* New York: Norton, 1971.

During the period of American neutrality, Wilson promoted economic policies that benefited the Allies, policies that led Germany to renew its submarine warfare and the president to declare war on Germany. Wilson led the country into war to protect American honor, rights, and general interests. Notes, appendix, bibliography, index.

2582 Harbaugh, William H. "Wilson, Roosevelt, and Intervention, 1914–1917: A Study of Domestic Influences on the Formulation of American Foreign Policy." Ph.D. dissertation, Northwestern University, 1954.

Wilson did not adequately inform the American people of their responsibilities during the period of neutrality, while Theodore Roosevelt and the internationalists compromised themselves on defense and rejected internationalism, thus also failing to contribute fully. DAI 14:1693.

2583 Hirst, David W. "German Propaganda in the United States, 1914–1917." Ph.D. dissertation, Northwestern University, 1962.

Led by German Ambassador Johann von Bernstorff, Germans and German sympathizers were able to keep Germany's point of view before the public throughout the war. Some propagandists also acted as espionage agents. DAI 23:3334.

2584 Kerr, Thomas J., IV. "Diplomacy and Conspiracy: German Involvement in U.S. Internal Affairs." In Milton Plesur, ed. *An American Historian: Essays to Honor Selig Adler.* Buffalo: State University of New York Press, 1980, pp. 107–15.

Germans were heavily involved in conspiracies to violate American neutrality, including sabotage and the blocking of munitions shipments to the Allies.

2585 Lovoll, Odd S. "North Dakota's Norwegian-Language Press Views World War I,

1914–1917." *North Dakota Quarterly* 39 (1971): 73–84.

Comprising more than 20 percent of North Dakota's population, Norwegian Americans expressed sympathy toward the plight of persecuted German Americans. It was also noted by the Norwegian-language press that several powers in Europe shared the guilt in starting the war. The papers urged the government to take a more evenhanded approach to neutrality. Notes.

2586 McCorkle, James L., Jr. "Mississippi from Neutrality to War (1914–1917)." *Journal of Mississippi History* 43 (1981): 85–125.

Mississippians worked hard to preserve their European markets during the period of American neutrality. Preparedness was debated sharply in a state represented by James K. Vardaman, an outspoken opponent of intervention. Notes.

2587 Millis, Walter. *Road to War: America, 1914–1917.* Boston: Houghton Mifflin, 1935.

The racial, economic, political, and social currents of American life during the period of neutrality are detailed. Wilson and Colonel Edward House are portrayed as virtuous men full of faults, embodiments of American innocence about Old World hatreds. Photographs, index.

2588 Morrissey, Alice M. *The American Defense of Neutral Rights, 1914–1917.* Cambridge, MA: Harvard University Press, 1939.

While administration sympathies and American prosperity were tilted toward the Allies, brutal submarine warfare led to the end of neutrality. Notes, bibliography, index.

2589 Nouailhat, Yves-Henri. *France et Etats-Unis: Août 1914–Avril 1917* (France and the United States: August 1914–April 1917). Paris: Publications de la Sorbonne, 1979.

During the period of American neutrality, France needed American goods and credit, even if this meant increased dependence on the United States. Franco-American relations were generally good, with many Americans sympathetic to the French cause. Notes, bibliography, index.

2590 ———. "A French Loan in the United States in July 1916: The Loan of the 'American Foreign Securities Company' " (in French). *Revue d'Histoire Moderne et Contemporaine* [France] 14 (1967): 356–74.

Six months of intensive negotiations were rewarded with the July 1916 American loan to France. By that time bankers were jittery about the future strength of France and a possible war with Mexico, while the Wilson administration was concerned about growing ties between American capital and the French government. Notes.

2591 O'Keefe, Thomas M. "*America*, the *Ave Maria* and the *Catholic World* Respond to the First World War, 1914–1917." *Records of the American Catholic Historical Society* 94 (1983): 101–15.

While *Catholic World* was consistently anti-German during the period of American neutrality, the other two leading American Catholic journals were mild in their strictures against the Central Powers, owing to the attitudes of many American Catholics. Notes.

2592 Peterson, Horace C. *Propaganda for War: The Campaign against American Neutrality, 1914–1917.* Norman: University of Oklahoma Press, 1939.

Slick British propaganda convinced many Americans of the need to intervene on the side of their Anglo-Saxon kinsmen. British arguments became American arguments as the war was advertised as a simple conflict of good versus evil. Photographs, notes, appendix, bibliography, index.

2593 Rappaport, Armin. *The British Press and Wilsonian Neutrality.* Stanford, CA: Stanford University Press, 1951.

The English and Scottish press wanted the United States to be more anti-German, although neutrality was not openly criticized until the war settled into a long stalemate. By 1916 the press showed signs of impatience with Wilson's reluctance to declare war. Notes, appendix, index.

2594 Smith, Daniel M. *Robert Lansing and American Neutrality, 1914–1917.* Berkeley: University of California Press, 1958.

Robert Lansing concluded long before Wilson did that the United States and Germany were on a collision course and that America and Britain could make common cause for mutual benefit. Lansing influenced the president through suggestion and quiet but persuasive arguments. Notes, bibliography, index.

2595 ———. "Robert Lansing and the Formulation of American Neutrality Policies, 1914–1915." *Mississippi Valley Historical Review* 43 (1956): 59–81.

As a counselor to the State Department, the pro-Allied Lansing helped to shape the American concept of neutrality, which was

inconsistent in demanding that belligerents obey international law. Notes.

2596 Squires, James D. *British Propaganda at Home and in the United States from 1914 to 1917.* Cambridge, MA: Harvard University Press, 1935.

The British used propaganda as a potent instrument of warfare. While it was not the only cause of American entry, it was an important factor. A checklist of British propaganda sent to the United States is included. Notes, bibliography, index.

2597 Sutton, Walter A. "Bryan, La Follette, Norris: Three Western Politicians." *Journal of the West* 8 (1969): 613–30.

William Jennings Bryan, George Norris, and Robert La Follette all fought to keep the United States out of the European war as the crisis brewed in 1917, supporting American neutral rights. During the war they were regarded as traitors, although in the post-1920 period people saw them as heroes.

2598 Swisher, Carl B. "The Control of War Preparations in the United States." *American Political Science Review* 34 (1940): 1085–1103.

The security of the nation was more important than the right of Congress to take total control of preparedness for war during the period late in American neutrality.

2599 Tansill, Charles C. *America Goes to War.* Boston: Little, Brown, 1938.

In this book written at the height of the isolationist movement in the 1930s, Wilson is portrayed as having declared war because of his pro-British advisers, House and Lansing, and because of a long background of suspicion and mistrust of Germany. Notes, bibliography, index.

2600 Thompson, J. A. "American Progressive Publicists and the First World War, 1914–1917." *Journal of American History* 58 (1971): 364–83.

While the reactions of Progressive politicians to the European war between 1914 and 1917 were complex and mixed, former muckrakers and Progressives writing in the popular press were united in their beliefs that an international body of peace should result from the war and that the conflict might advance the cause of social reform at home. Notes.

2601 Unterberger, Betty M. "The Arrest of Alice Masaryk." *Slavic Review* 33 (1974): 91–106.

Widespread publicity given to Austria-Hungary's arrest of Alice Masaryk for high treason created popular anger toward the Habsburg regime in 1915–16.

2602 Van Alstyne, Richard W. "Private American Loans to the Allies, 1914–1916." *Pacific Historical Review* 2 (1933): 180–93.

American private bank loans to the Allies during the period of neutrality bolstered the war effort and helped to tilt the United States away from the Central Powers. Notes.

2603 Ward, Larry W. " 'Official' European War Films in Neutral America, 1914–1917." *Indiana Social Studies Quarterly* 34 (1981): 57–68.

Both sides in the European war used motion pictures to dramatically tell their side of the story. The Wilson administration adopted many ideas for its own program of official films after April 1917.

2604 Wilkins, Robert P. "Tory Isolationist: Porter J. McCumber and World War I, 1914–1917." *North Dakota History* 34 (1967): 192–207.

North Dakota's Senator McCumber worked to prevent U.S. involvement in the European war, but he should not be considered a Progressive isolationist. Notes.

2605 Wittenberg, Ernest. "The Thrifty Spy on the Sixth Avenue El." *American Heritage* 17 (1965): 60–64ff.

In mid-1915 a German lawyer working for Captain Franz von Papen, a German military attaché, lost his briefcase on the El (elevated railway). The contents, picked up by the Secret Service, provided hard evidence that the Germans were violating American neutrality.

WILSONIAN DIPLOMACY

See also Chapter 1, *Autobiographical and Biographical Materials,* Chapter 2, *Wilson Presidency,* and Chapter 9, *Wilson and Foreign Affairs.*

2606 Coletta, Paolo E. "A Question of Alternatives: Wilson, Bryan, Lansing, and America's Intervention in World War I." *Nebraska History* 63 (1982): 33–57.

The events of early 1917 leading up to American intervention in the European war are analyzed from the perspective of William Jennings Bryan, Wilson's first secretary of state.

2607 Cooper, John Milton. "The British Response to the House-Grey Memorandum: New Evidence and New Questions." *Journal of American History* 59 (1973): 958–71.

New evidence indicates that the British cabinet's War Committee as a whole, rather than just Sir Edward Grey, stands accountable for rejecting American mediation to end the European war in 1916. Notes.

2608 Devlin, Patrick. *Too Proud to Fight: Woodrow Wilson's Neutrality.* New York: Oxford University Press, 1975.

After presenting a brief sketch of Wilson's life and work to 1914 in the opening chapters, the author discusses the diplomacy of American neutrality. Wilson did not trust either side and decided to enter the war only when the Germans turned on America. Notes, bibliography, index.

2609 Doerries, Reinhard R. "Imperial Berlin and Washington: New Light on Germany's Foreign Policy and America's Entry into World War I." *Central European History* 11 (1978): 23–49.

Germany refused to heed Wilson's offers of mediation long after the conflict had entered into a vicious stalemate. The failure of German diplomacy contributed to the United States joining the Allied cause. Notes.

2610 Fusco, Jeremiah N. "Diplomatic Relations between Italy and the United States, 1913–1917." Ph.D. dissertation, George Washington University, 1969.

Italian-American relations had become strained during the Progressive era over the matter of immigration. Diplomatic bonds deteriorated further in 1915–1917, as Italy joined the Allies and the United States remained neutral. Italy opposed Wilson's peace efforts because it sought a peace based on a division of the spoils. Wilson's wartime idealism and the declaration of war against Austria-Hungary brought about cordial relations. DAI 30:1495-A.

2611 Grey, Sir Edward. *Twenty-Five Years, 1892–1916.* 2 vols. New York: Stokes, 1925.

Volume II of the British foreign minister's memoirs contains much information on America and the war during the neutrality period, negotiations with Colonel Edward House, and Grey's friendship with Theodore Roosevelt. Photographs, appendixes, index.

2612 Jensen, Billie B. "House, Wilson and American Neutrality, 1914–1917." Ph.D. dissertation, University of Colorado, 1962.

Edward Mandell House was a trusted friend of Wilson's, as well as a foreign policy adviser. House undertook three peace missions to Europe which, while unsuccessful, convinced him (and through him Wilson) of the importance of the European war to America's future. House also influenced Wilson's choices for various foreign service appointments. DAI 23:2108.

2613 Kernek, Sterling. "The British Government's Reactions to President Wilson's 'Peace' Note of December 1916." *History Journal* 13 (1970): 721–66.

Wilson's peace note angered the British, who countered it with the outcry that it would bring about peace without victory. Privately, the proposal frightened British leaders and made them suspect that Wilson only desired power. Notes.

2614 Link, Arthur S. "President Wilson and his English Critics: Survey and Interpretation." In Arthur S. Link. *The Higher Realism of Woodrow Wilson and Other Essays*. Nashville: Vanderbilt University Press, 1971, pp. 110–26.

During the period of American neutrality, the British came to regard Wilson as a parochial moralist who should have been aiding the Allies. At the peace conference British leaders did not take Wilson seriously, continuing to misunderstand him. Notes.

2615 ———. "Wilson and the Ordeal of Neutrality." In Arthur S. Link. *The Higher Realism of Woodrow Wilson and Other Essays*. Nashville: Vanderbilt University Press, 1971, pp. 88–98.

Public opinion limited Wilson's options as he attempted to steer a neutral course between the warring powers of Europe.

2616 May, Ernest R. *World War and American Isolation, 1914–1917*. Cambridge, MA: Harvard University Press, 1959.

In dealing with Britain and Germany during the period of neutrality, Wilson concerned himself with immediate nationalist interests, but he risked them on occasion to pursue his dream of peace. In the end Wilson decided to enter the war because he feared the sacrifice of America's prestige and moral influence if he did not stand up to the German challenge. Notes, bibliography, index.

2617 Seymour, Charles. "The House-Bernstorff Conversations in Perspective." In A. O. Sarkissian, ed. *Studies in Diplomatic History and Historiography in Honour of G. P. Gooch, C.H.* London: Longmans, 1961, pp. 90–106.

The House-Bernstorff discussions were an important factor in postponing war between the United States and Germany.

2618 Small, Melvin. "Woodrow Wilson and U.S. Intervention in World War I." In John M. Carroll and George C. Herring, eds. *Modern American Diplomacy*. Wilmington, DE: Scholarly Resources, 1986.

At first, Wilson followed a truly neutral course, but eventually he bowed to economic interests in permitting American credits and loans to Britain. He also allowed arms trade to belligerents and interpreted neutrality in a way that was favorable to the Allies. Bibliography.

2619 West, Rachel. *The Department of State on the Eve of the First World War*. Athens: University of Georgia Press, 1979.

The State Department was unprepared for World War I in almost every way. Wilson and Bryan had undercut Republican attempts to professionalize the diplomatic corps. Notes, bibliography, index.

2620 Woodward, David R. "Great Britain and President Wilson's Efforts to End World War I in 1916." *Maryland Historian* 1 (1970): 45–58.

War hysteria in Britain forced the government there to reject Wilson's proposal, but the British also mistrusted the American president. Sir Edward Grey, the only member of the War Cabinet to favor the proposal, papered over what could have been a serious Anglo-American diplomatic rift. Notes.

2621 Živojinović, Dragan R. "Pope Benedict XV's Peace Efforts (1914–1917)." In Richard Bosworth and Gianfranco Cresciani, eds. *Altro Polo: A Volume of Italian Studies*. Sydney: University of Sydney Press, 1971, pp. 71–104.

Pope Benedict's peace proposals were mistrusted by all the belligerents. Neither Wilson nor the Germans were interested in cooperating with the Holy See for peace. Notes.

MARITIME ISSUES

See also Chapter 11, *Navy*.

2622 Allin, Lawrence C. "Ill-Timed Initiative: The Ship Purchase Bill of 1915." *American Neptune* 33 (1973): 178–98.

Designed to prevent American trade from being hurt by lack of ships, the ship purchase bill of 1915 was torpedoed by a

Congress apprehensive over belligerent action against American shipping. Notes.

2623 Bailey, Thomas A. "The United States and the Blacklist during the Great War." *Journal of Modern History* 6 (1934): 14–35.

Britain blacklisted neutrals, including American firms that did business with the enemy, a policy which strained Anglo-American relations. Notes.

2624 Billington, Monroe. "The Gore Resolution of 1916." *Mid-America* 47 (1965): 89–98.

Senator Thomas Gore amended his own resolution designed to keep Americans off belligerent ships to say that war would follow the German sinking of any ship on which an American was traveling. This effort to embarrass the president was voted down. Notes.

2625 Birnbaum, Karl E. *Peace Moves and U-boat Warfare: Germany's Policy toward the United States, April 18, 1916–January 9, 1917*. Stockholm: Almquist and Wiksell, 1958.

Germany misread American intentions and gambled on renewed U-boat warfare instead of peace after months of wavering indecision. Paul von Hindenburg and Erich von Ludendorff failed to see that American entry would boost sagging Allied morale. Notes, appendix, bibliography, index.

2626 Coogan, John W. *The End of Neutrality: The United States, Britain, and Maritime Rights, 1899–1915*. Ithaca, NY: Cornell University Press, 1981.

Historians who begin their accounts of the neutral rights controversy with the outbreak of war distort the issue. A viable system of international law did exist in 1914, but by placing Anglo-American friendship above the preservation of neutrality Wilson allowed this legal order to crumble. Notes, bibliography, index.

2627 Davis, Gerald H. "The *Ancona* Affair: A Case of Preventive Diplomacy." *Journal of Modern History* 38 (1966): 267–77.

The November 1915 sinking of an Italian ship resulted in the death of Americans on board, touching off a crisis with Austria-Hungary. While the Austrians accepted responsibility for the incident, it was a German U-boat that committed the act. Notes.

2628 ———. "The *Petrolite* Incident: A World War I Case Study on the Limitations of Warfare." *Historian* 29 (1967): 238–48.

A dispute between Austria-Hungary and the United States arose when a German U-boat flying Austrian colors fired on an American oil tanker. Notes.

2629 Graham, Malbone W., Jr. *The Controversy between the United States and the Allied Governments Respecting Neutral Rights and Commerce during the Period of American Neutrality, 1914–1917*. Austin: University of Texas Press, 1923.

This early scholarly monograph describes legal problems arising from neutrality, including mail seizures, the Declaration of London, armed merchant ships, contraband, transfer of registry, and the blockade. Notes, appendixes, bibliography, index.

2630 Gregory, Ross. "A New Look at the Case of the *Dacia*." *Journal of American History* 5 (1968): 292–96.

The seizure of the German ship *Dacia*, which had been switched to American registry, has long been seen as a British operation, although France actually precipitated the conflict. Evidence indicates that Britain had nothing to do with it.

2631 Hall, Phyllis. "German Raiders at Hampton Roads." *Virginia Cavalcade* 35 (1986): 122–35.

In 1915 two former German luxury liners converted to service as raiders were interned at Hampton Roads, Virginia. Following American entry into the war, they were made into American troop carriers.

2632 Long, Wellington. "The Cruise of the *U-53*." *U.S. Naval Institute Proceedings* 92 (1966): 86–95.

In October and November 1916 the German submarine *U-53* cruised off the eastern coast of the United States to sink Allied ships and to pay a call on an American navy base to discourage American entry into the war.

2633 Lowitt, Richard. "The Armed-Ship Bill Controversy: A Legislative View." *Mid-America* 46 (1964): 38–47.

Party lines were blurred during the passionate debate over the Armed-Ship Bill in the Senate. While Wilson had a majority on his side, a "little group of willful men" did not wish to surrender congressional power on an issue that might plunge the United States into the European war. Notes.

2634 McDiarmid, Alice M. "The Neutrality Board and Armed Merchantmen, 1914–1917." *American Journal of International Law* 69 (1975): 374–81.

The Neutrality Board investigated the rights and responsibilities of nonbelligerents, concluding that merchant ships had the right to protect themselves by force of arms. Notes.

2635 McDonald, Timothy G. "The Gore-McLemore Resolutions: Democratic Revolt against Wilson's Submarine Policy." *Historian* 26 (1963): 50–74.

Democrats in Congress were far from unanimous in supporting the president's submarine policy. Their attempts to thwart Wilson were stymied by the tabling of their resolutions. Notes.

2636 Sevage, Carlton. *Policy of the United States toward Maritime Commerce in War.* 2 vols. Washington, DC: Government Printing Office, 1934.

Volume II contains a wealth of material on the neutrality period and on wartime policies.

2637 Siney, Marion C. *Allied Blockade of Germany, 1914–1916.* Ann Arbor: University of Michigan Press, 1957.

The Allies were determined to choke off neutral trade with Germany, even at the risk of offending the United States. Germany saw no alternative but to renew U-boat warfare. Notes, bibliography, index.

2638 Smith, Gaddis. *Britain's Clandestine Submarines, 1914–1915.* New Haven, CT: Yale University Press, 1964.

Bethlehem Steel was allowed to build submarines for Britain even though this raised disturbing questions about American neutrality. The episode suggests a genuine triangle of cooperation among the United States, Canada, and Britain. Notes, bibliography, index.

2639 ———. "The Clandestine Submarines of 1914–15: An Essay in the History of the North American Triangle." *Canadian Historical Association Annual Report* (1963): 194–203.

To skirt the Department of State's interpretation of neutrality, Bethlehem Steel secretly built ten submarines in Canada for the British. Even the prime minister of Canada was not told at first.

2640 Sutton, Walter A. "Progressive Republican Senators and the Submarine Crisis, 1915–1916." *Mid-America* 47 (1965): 75–88.

Progressives tended to split into two camps on the neutrality issue, with nationalists such as William Borah and Miles Poindexter countered by isolationists such as George Norris and Robert La Follette, the latter group associating internationalism with narrow economic interests.

THE *LUSITANIA* SINKING

See also Chapter 9, *Great Britain and Its Dominions.*

2641 Bailey, Thomas A., and Ryan, Paul B. *The "Lusitania" Disaster: An Episode in Modern Warfare and Diplomacy.* New York: Free Press, 1975.

The sinking of the *Lusitania* had important repercussions for American neutrality but was not the result of a British conspiracy. While the Germans were legally justified in sinking the ship, the sinking proved to be counterproductive. Photographs, notes, bibliography, index.

2642 Handlin, Oscar. "A Liner, a U-boat . . . and History." *American Heritage* 6 (1955): 40–45, 105.

The *Lusitania* tragedy forced Wilson to proceed on the assumption that German U-boat warfare was an aggressive act of war.

2643 Lewis, Brenda R. "*Lusitania*." *British Heritage* [Great Britain] 2 (1981): 46–55.

Launched in 1906 and sunk by a German U-boat in 1915, the British luxury liner's history is detailed.

2644 Mooney, Christopher. "Moral Consensus and Law." *Thought* 51 (1976): 231–54.

Rallying public opinion behind his stance on the sinking of the *Lusitania* by Germany, Wilson attempted to inaugurate a moral crusade against modern U-boat warfare, as this new phenomenon was not covered under international law. Thus Wilson insisted that Americans had the right to travel on any foreign ship while neglecting to mention that the *Lusitania* had been carrying ammunition.

2645 Simpson, Colin. *The "Lusitania."* Boston: Little, Brown, 1973.

The German view that the British conspired to outrage the world and bring the United States into the war with the sinking of the *Lusitania* is validated. A case is made that the luxury liner carried a cargo of weapons. Notes, bibliography, index.

THE ZIMMERMANN NOTE

See also Chapter 9, *Mexico* and *Germany*.

2646 Bridges, Lamar W. "Zimmermann Telegram: Reaction of Southern, Southwestern Newspapers." *Journalism Quarterly* 46 (1969): 81–86.

Reaction to the Zimmermann Note proposing a German-Mexican alliance in the event that the United States joined the Allied cause created anger in southern and southwest newspapers while unifying the people and giving a boost to the preparedness movement. Notes.

2647 Burdick, Charles B. "A House on Navidad Street: The Celebrated Zimmermann Note on the Texas Border." *Arizona and the West* 8 (1966): 19–34.

A morals charge lodged in San Antonio led to details of an Austro-German plot to use a Mexican base for operations against the United States in the event of war. The American government seized this information to substantiate the conspiracy outlined in the Zimmermann Note, but it turned out that the story was not true. Notes.

2648 Katz, Friedrich. "Germany and Francisco Villa" (in Spanish). *Historia Mexicana* [Mexico] 12 (1962): 88–102.

Germany covertly encouraged Pancho Villa to attack the United States because such an attack might divert the Americans from the war in Europe, although this encouragement was not official policy but rather the work of German secret service agents. When the border incidents proved insufficient for their purposes, the Germans turned to Venustiano Carranza and the Zimmermann Note to make further trouble. Notes.

2649 Meyer, Michael C. "The Mexican-German Conspiracy of 1915." *Americas* 23 (1966): 76–89.

Germany gave supporters of the ousted Mexican president, Victoriano Huerta, promises of future aid if the general would lead a separatist movement in the southwest, but American authorities foiled the plot. Notes.

2650 Munch, Francis J. "Villa's Columbus Raid: Practical Politics or German Design?" *New Mexico Historical Review* 44 (1969): 189–214.

Villa's raid came about as a result of both the situation on the Mexican-American border and a conspiracy of Germans and Mexicans. Notes.

2651 Sandos, James A. "German Involvement in Northern Mexico, 1915–1916: A New Look at the Columbus Raids." *Hispanic American Historical Review* 50 (1970): 70–88.

German-born Felix Sommerfeld, a friend of Francisco Madero, may have used Villa's personal physician to influence the raid on Columbus in order to promote another Mexican-American war and weaken the United States. Notes.

2652 Smith, Dean. "The Zimmermann Telegram, 1917." *American History Illustrated* 13 (1978): 28–37.

The British interception of the Zimmermann Note touched off a crisis in German-American relations that eventually led to American entry into the European war.

2653 Tuchman, Barbara. *The Zimmermann Telegram*. New York: Viking, 1958.

The British interception of the Zimmermann Note assured that it would be brought to the attention of the Wilson administration. It played an important role in the American decision to intervene in the European war. Notes, bibliography, index.

Intervention

See also Chapter 1, *Autobiographical and Biographical Materials,* and Chapter 2, *Wilson Presidency.*

2654 Auerbach, Jerold S. "Woodrow Wilson's 'Prediction' to Frank Cobb: Words Historians Should Doubt Ever Got Spoken." *Journal of American History* 54 (1967): 608–17.

Wilson probably did not warn Frank Cobb on 2 April 1917 that civil liberties would be endangered by American entry into the European war. Evidence for the alleged interview came secondhand seven years later.

2655 Avery, Laurence G. "Maxwell Anderson's Report on Frank Cobb's Interview with Woodrow Wilson: Documentary Source." *North Dakota Quarterly* 45 (1981): 13–15.

Wilson discusses the Allies and their chances for winning the war in this manuscript of a 1917 interview with Frank Cobb. The exchange supposedly took place just before Wilson asked Congress to declare war. Notes.

2656 Birdsall, Paul. "Neutrality and Economic Pressures, 1914–1917." *Science and Society* 3 (1939): 217–28.

The American decision to intervene on the side of the Allies was the result of a gradual erosion of neutrality caused by loans and trade. Notes.

2657 Buchanan, A. Russell. "American Editors Examine American War Aims and Plans in April, 1917." *Pacific Historical Review* 9 (1940): 253–65.

Public opinion, as reflected in newspaper editorials, reveals anti-German feelings and many ideas as to how the war should be fought.

2658 Cohen, Warren I., ed. *Intervention, 1917: Why America Fought*. Boston: Heath, 1966.

Excerpts are presented from previously published works by left revisionists, proponents of the submarine theory, and those concerned primarily with American nationalist interests.

2659 Dalton, Brian J. "Wilson's Prediction to Cobb: Notes on the Auerbach-Link Debate." *Historian* 32 (1970): 545–63.

The controversy between Arthur S. Link and Jerold S. Auerbach over the secondhand account of Wilson's interview with journalist Frank Cobb just before the declaration of war is analyzed. The conclusion here is that the interview did not take place. Notes.

2660 Dupuy, Ernest R. *Five Days to War: April 2–6, 1917*. Harrisburg, PA: Stackpole, 1967.

A journalist recreates the last days of peace with pictures and a narrative. Photographs.

2661 Heaton, John L. *Cobb of "The World": A Leader in Liberalism*. New York: Dutton, 1924.

The author recounts Cobb's famous (and controversial) interview with Wilson on the eve of war in which the president revealed his agony over the decision for war.

2662 Ivie, Robert L. "Presidential Motives for War." *Quarterly Journal of Speech* 60 (1974): 337–45.

Presidents use particular vocabularies and images to justify war. The vocabularies of Wilson and six other presidents are analyzed.

2663 Johnson, Timothy D. "Anti-War Sentiment and Representative John Lawson Burnett of Alabama." *Alabama Review* 39 (1986): 187–95.

This congressman from Alabama voted against declaring war in April 1917, because he thought that the voters back home wanted it that way. Notes.

2664 Leopold, Richard W. "The Problem of American Intervention, 1917: An Historical Retrospect." *World Politics* 2 (1950): 405–25.

Surveying the literature on intervention, the author finds it wanting, because several important factors have not been researched.

2665 Link, Arthur S. "That Cobb Interview." *Journal of American History* 72 (1985): 7–17.

Cobb's famous interview with Wilson, which actually took place on 19 March 1917, reflects a president in the agonized throes of decision. He feared that American entry into the war might further destabilize Europe. Notes.

2666 May, Ernest R. "Wilson (1917–1918)." In Ernest R. May, ed. *The Ultimate Decision: The President as Commander in Chief*. New York: Braziller, 1960, pp. 109–31.

Wilson's idea of his role as commander in chief of American armed forces was unique in that he endeavored to avoid that role. During the period of American neutrality he made it clear that, should the United States join the Allies, his aims and aspirations would be different from theirs because he sought a peace to make the world safe for democracy. Illustrations, bibliography, index.

2667 ———, ed. *The Coming of War, 1917*. Chicago: Rand McNally, 1963.

Documents are used to illuminate the end of neutrality. Topics include the submarine issue, German and American perspectives, Wilson's appeals for peace and the decision for war.

2668 Newell, William D. "The Problem of American Entry into Twentieth Century World War: A Study in Conflicting Historiography." Ph.D. dissertation, University of Idaho, 1982.

After World War I, a group of historians claimed that Wilson was anything but neutral and that he used the German submarine policy as an excuse for war. "Submarinists" argue that the German policy of renewed attacks on American shipping justified a war declaration. A national security school of historians contend that Wilson went to war because he understood that a German victory would hurt the United States. DAI 43:1642-A.

2669 Seymour, Charles. *American Neutrality, 1914–1917: Essays on the Causes of American*

Intervention in the World War. New Haven, CT: Yale University Press, 1935.

Writing at a time when conspiracy theories were gaining attention, the author makes a case for the renewed German submarine campaign in the Atlantic as the prime reason for Wilson's decision to intervene. The U-boat was Germany's only effective means to strike at the backbone of the Allies, Great Britain. Notes, index.

2670 Small, Melvin. *Was War Necessary? National Security and U.S. Entry into War*. Beverly Hills, CA: Sage, 1980.

Postwar disillusionment can be traced to the manner in which the United States entered the war and the general misunderstanding of what the real issues were in Europe. Wilson went to war to uphold American prestige in the world. Bibliography, appendix.

2671 Spencer, Samuel R., Jr. *Decision for War, 1917*. Ridge, NH: Smith, 1953.

The sinking of the *Laconia* and the Zimmermann telegram were key factors in turning the American people against Germany. Notes, illustrations.

2672 Vandermeer, Philip R. "Congressional Decisionmaking and World War I: A Case Study of Illinois Congressional Opponents." *Congressional Studies* 8 (1981): 59–79.

Six congressmen from Illinois who opposed Wilson's war declaration against the Central Powers did so for a variety of reasons, among them ethnic and party loyalties and concern about what the war would do to the Progressive reform movement.

Wartime Relations

See also Chapter 9, *Foreign Affairs: Bilateral Relations*, under various individual nations.

GENERAL

2673 Bell, Walter F. "American Embassies in Belligerent Europe, 1914–1918." Ph.D. dissertation, University of Iowa, 1983.

Wilson's diplomats in Europe, many of whom were political appointees, became more important than the president could have imagined because of the world war. The effectiveness of the

ambassadors and administrative matters are analyzed. DAI 44:2222.

2674 Link, Arthur S. "Wilson and Peace Moves." In Arthur S. Link, *The Higher Realism of Woodrow Wilson and Other Essays*. Nashville: Vanderbilt University Press, 1971, pp. 99–109.

Wilson took control of the peace movement, inspiring the world with a vision of peace with justice while forcing the warring powers to make peace on the basis of liberal principles.

2675 Mayer, Arno J. *Wilson vs. Lenin: Political Origins of the New Diplomacy, 1917–1918*. New Haven, CT: Yale University Press, 1959.

The new diplomacy originated as part of a wartime debate between the political Right and Left over war aims, with the latter hoping that nonannexationist war aims would help to change the status quo. Concentrating on the period between March 1917 and January 1918, the author uses Lenin's April Theses and Wilson's Fourteen Points as symbols of the new ideological era in global politics. Notes, bibliography, index.

2676 Seymour, Charles. *American Diplomacy during the World War*. Baltimore, MD: Johns Hopkins University Press, 1934.

Allied interference with American trade, the role of German submarines, Wilson's efforts to mediate peace, American entry into the war, and the diplomacy of the wartime alliance and Armistice are among the topics covered. Notes, bibliography, index.

ASIA

2677 Alvarez, David J. "The Department of State and the Abortive Papal Mission to China, August 1918." *Catholic Historical Review* 62 (1976): 455–63.

To counter German influence in Siberia, the Department of State pressured the Chinese not to accept a Germanophile papal nuncio. The department worked with France to block other papal diplomats as well, a move designed to boost Allied power in China to counterbalance Japan's growing interests.

2678 Chi Sung-chun, Madeleine. "The Chinese Question during the First World War." Ph.D. dissertation, Fordham University, 1968.

During the war, Japan energetically exploited the temporary inattention of America and Europe by advancing militarily and politically in China. Warlords and revolutionaries had both weakened China, opening the way for foreign intervention. If such intervention had come from the West rather than from Japan, China's fate would have been different. DAI 29:538-A.

2679 Holdcamper, Forrest R. "Thirty 'Easterns' and Others: Ships Built in Japan for the United States, 1919–1920." *American Neptune* 23 (1963): 270–76.

Japan chartered ships to the United States and built thirty vessels for the Americans in return for steel. Constructed under the supervision of an American shipbuilder and a U.S. war agency, the ships proved to be well built.

2680 May, Ernest R. "American Policy and Japan's Entrance into World War I." *Mississippi Valley Historical Review* 40 (1953): 279–90.

The bungling diplomacy of William Jennings Bryan and the State Department made it easier for Japan to make wartime gains while the Allies were preoccupied.

2681 Safford, Jeffrey J. "Experiment in Containment: The United States Steel Embargo and Japan, 1917–1918." *Pacific Historical Review* 39 (1970): 439–51.

The American government tried to thwart Japanese aspirations for territory in the Pacific with an embargo on steel. But the embargo only further convinced Japan of its need for territory to avoid being subject to such pressures in the future. Notes.

LATIN AMERICA

2682 Harris, Charles H., III. "Witzke Affair: German Intrigue on the Mexican Border, 1917–1918." *Military Review* 59 (1979): 36–50.

German efforts to penetrate the United States through Mexico failed miserably in 1917, because two of the three agents sent to do the job were counterspies. American intelligence agents in Mexico kept other Germans out during the war. Notes.

2683 Healy, David. "Admiral William B. Caperton and United States Naval Diplomacy in South America, 1917–1919." *Journal of Latin American Studies* [Great Britain] 8 (1976): 297–323.

Although he was genuinely popular with South Americans, Admiral Caperton failed to commit Uruguay and Argentina to declare war on

the Central Powers. Meanwhile, Brazil acceded to American pressures at a time when American naval officers were replacing the British as advisers. Notes.

2684 Martin, Percy A. *Latin America and the War*. Baltimore, MD: Johns Hopkins University Press, 1925.

This expanded version of several lectures covers Latin America country-by-country during the war. Notes, index.

2685 Rosenberg, Emily S. "World War I and 'Continental Solidarity.' " *The Americas* 31 (1975): 313–34.

The war produced two rival political blocs: United States-Brazil and Mexico-Argentina. The Brazilians saw their alliance with the Americans as a way to become preeminent. American military and economic power doomed the Mexican-Argentinian bid for increased power in Latin America. The United States and Brazil both benefited from their cooperation. Notes.

2686 ———. "World War I and the Growth of United States Preponderance in Latin America." Ph.D. dissertation, State University of New York, Stony Brook, 1973.

The war gave American officials a new appreciation of the importance of Latin America. The government supported American businessmen wherever they helped to keep order. Stability and further economic penetration became the administration's highest priorities. American influence spread rapidly throughout Latin America during the war. DAI 34:256-A.

ENTENTE

2687 Ara, Angelo. "The United States between Italy and Austria from the American Declaration of War against Austria-Hungary to the Peace Conference" (in Italian). *Storia e Politica* [Italy] 12 (1973): 476–89.

America's dismissal of Italy as a factor in the war was a mistake, at least as regards the boundaries of the Austro-Hungarian empire. Notes.

2688 Burk, Kathleen. *Britain, America and the Sinews of War, 1914–1918*. Boston: George Allen and Unwin, 1985.

This revised thesis, written under A. J. P. Taylor, covers the political, diplomatic, and economic issues between declining Britain and rising America. The British were economically dependent on America during the war, a situation American leaders used to political advantage. Notes, bibliography, index.

2689 ———. "The Diplomacy of Finance: British Financial Missions to the United States, 1914–1918." *History Journal* [Great Britain] 22 (1979): 351–72.

Anglo-American economic relations during the war are scrutinized. The war strengthened the U.S. economic position and weakened the British to the point that the British became dependent on the Americans. Notes.

2690 Dignan, Don K. "The Hindu Conspiracy in Anglo-American Relations during World War I." *Pacific Historical Review* 40 (1971): 57–76.

Germany financed Indian independence movements to undermine the British. American sympathy for the Hindus made the Wilson administration reluctant to take action, although eventually 105 persons were indicted on violations of American neutrality laws. Notes.

2691 Farrar, Marjorie M. "Toward a Complete Blockade: The American Adherence to France's Objectives of Economic War, April-August 1917" (in French). *Revue d'Histoire Diplomatique* [France] 89 (1975): 127–43.

The Wilson administration slapped an embargo on exports to European neutrals in August 1917, thereby supporting France's view of economic warfare instead of Britain's. Notes.

2692 Feist, Joe M. "Theirs Not to Reason Why: The Case of the Russian Railway Service Corps." *Military Affairs* 42 (1978): 1–6.

A call for help from the Russian provisional government led to the creation of the Russian Railway Service Corps, which served in Vladivostok in 1918–19. Notes.

2693 Fowler, Wilton B. *British-American Relations, 1917–1918: The Role of Sir William Wiseman*. Princeton: Princeton University Press, 1969.

This British Army captain, who ran intelligence operations in the United States, caught Colonel Edward House's attention and became one of the few Britishers trusted by Wilson. He played an important role in diplomacy as a liaison between his government and the Americans. Photographs, notes, appendix.

2694 Goedeken, Edward A. "A Banker at War: The World War I Experiences of Charles Gates Dawes." *Illinois Historical Journal* 78 (1985): 195–206.

Rising to the position of general purchasing agent, Dawes used central control to coordinate the supplying of Allied armies. He battled against waste and high costs while creating several bureaus to streamline requests. Notes.

2695 ———. "Charles Dawes and the Military Board of Allied Supply." *Military Affairs* 50 (1986): 1–6.

Coordination of the various national armies was the key to winning the war, and Dawes was given the power to make the Military Board of Allied Supply into an important agency for requisitioning supplies. Notes.

2696 Grayson, Benson L. *Russian-American Relations in World War I*. New York: Ungar, 1979.

Russian-American relations are examined from the beginning of World War I in Europe to the Wilson administration's recognition of the short-lived provisional government in 1917. Notes, bibliography, index.

2697 Herzstein, Daphne S. "The Diplomacy of Allied Credit Advanced to Russia in World War I." Ph.D. dissertation, New York University, 1972.

The Allies granted credit to the czarist regime, with misgivings, to keep the war in the East going. In 1916 the Russian government decided that after the war it would distance itself from the Allies to avoid economic exploitation. The provisional government cooperated more closely with the Allies than did the czarist regime. Bolshevik repudiation of the huge wartime debt deepened Allied hostility. DAI 33:6273-A.

2698 Lesouef, Pierre. "Marshal Joffre's Mission to the United States at the Time of the US Entry into the War" (in French). *Revue Historique des Armées* [France] (1984): 18–26.

Marshal Joseph Joffre came to the United States after the American declaration of war to help coordinate Allied logistics. His effectiveness helped to win the war.

2699 Lloyd George, David. *War Memoirs*. 6 vols. London: Nicholson and Watson, 1933–1936.

These volumes contain much information on military relations among the Allies and between Britain and the United States.

Lloyd George finds that Wilson was "not cut out for a great War Minister." Index.

2700 Lyddon, W. G. *British War Missions to the United States, 1914–1918*. London: Oxford University Press, 1938.

British activities in the United States during the period of neutrality, the Balfour mission, and wartime diplomacy are covered. Index.

2701 Manning, Clarence A. "The Ukrainians and the United States in World War I." *Ukrainian Quarterly* 13 (1957): 346–54.

Ukrainians in the United States overcame poverty, political weakness, and Russian propaganda as they organized themselves into a lobbying group at the Paris Peace Conference and arranged for relief overseas. Notes.

2702 Martin, Laurence W. "Woodrow Wilson's Appeals to the People of Europe: British Radical Influence on the President's Strategy." *Political Science Quarterly* 74 (1959): 498–516.

British radicals (liberals) encouraged President Wilson's belief that the people of Europe wanted an idealistic peace settlement, not a vindictive one. Notes.

2703 Marwick, Arthur. *War and Social Change in the Twentieth Century: A Comparative Study of Britain, France, Germany, Russia and the United States*. New York: Macmillan, 1974.

Chapter 3 discusses the uneasy alliance during the war between the Entente and the United States. Photographs, notes, bibliography, index.

2704 Nies, John L. "Franco-American Relations, 1917–1918." Ph.D. dissertation, University of Nebraska, Lincoln, 1973.

Franco-American relations between American entry into the war and the Armistice were marked by conflicts over wartime objectives, peace policies, resource allocation, military strategy, personalities, and bureaucratic organizations. Only fear of the common enemy kept the two powers working together. DAI 34:2528-A.

2705 Nigro, Louis J., Jr. "Propaganda, Politics, and the New Diplomacy: The Impact of Wilsonian Propaganda on Politics and Public Opinion in Italy, 1917–1919." Ph.D. dissertation, Vanderbilt University, 1979.

Wilson sold his idea of the new diplomacy in other countries through the use of propaganda. Italy's poor showing in the war and public disillusion with the crusade made the Americans especially anxious to propagandize

there. Efforts by the Committee on Public Information and other organizations made Wilson popular in Italy. DAI 40:3464-A.

2706 Nouailhat, Yves-Henri. "French, British, and Americans and the Problem of the Reorganization of International Commerce, 1914–1918" (in French). *Relations Internationales* [France] (1977): 95–114.

Looking beyond the war, France led a movement to plan for long-term economic discrimination against German trade in 1916, but Anglo-American opposition scotched the project.

2707 Parrini, Carl P. *Heir to Empire: United States Economic Diplomacy, 1916–1923*. Pittsburgh: University of Pittsburgh Press, 1969.

By 1916, American political and business leaders hoped to use the Open Door to market goods and services more effectively. The Allied Paris Economic Conference of 1916 formulated an anti-American scheme based on state capitalism and neomercantilism, thus setting off an urgent race for postwar economic advantage. Notes, bibliography, index.

2708 Parsons, Edward B. *Wilsonian Diplomacy: Allied-American Rivalries in War and Peace*. St. Louis: Forum, 1978.

Wilson abandoned peace proposals formulated during the period of American neutrality once the war had been won and it was time to make the peace. Notes, bibliography, index.

2709 Rosenberg, Emily S. "Anglo-American Economic Rivalry in Brazil during World War I." *Diplomatic History* 2 (1978): 131–52.

Britain's preoccupation with the war weakened its economic grip on Brazil, and Americans took the opportunity to gain significant influence. Notes.

2710 Rothwell, Victor H. *British War Aims and Peace Diplomacy, 1914–1919*. Oxford: Clarendon, 1971.

The paramount British fear was that Wilson would implement sanctions to protect American neutrality. The government knew that the president distrusted British war aims designed primarily to benefit the British Empire. Notes, bibliography, index.

2711 Rowland, Peter. *David Lloyd George: A Biography*. New York: Macmillan, 1975.

Lloyd George was a masterful if flawed politician and diplomat who juggled the roles of reformer, war leader, and statesman to benefit the

British national interest. Notes, bibliography, index.

2712 Schwartz, Donald R. "From Rapprochement to Appeasement: Domestic Determinants of Anglo-American Relations under Lloyd George and Wilson." Ph.D. dissertation, New York University, 1977.

Britain and America clashed during and after World War I in a number of areas, because the British were greatly weakened and the Americans were correspondingly strengthened by the conflict. The British appeased the Americans, because they were in no financial position to do otherwise. DAI 38:7493-A.

2713 Smith, Gaddis. "Nation and Empire: Canadian Diplomacy during the First World War." Ph.D. dissertation, Yale University, 1960.

Canada came into the war determined to demonstrate its loyalty to the British Empire while becoming more self-reliant and industrialized. After April 1917 the Canadian government worked for close relations with the United States. DAI 30:1511-A.

2714 Snell, John L. "Wilson on Germany and the Fourteen Points: Document." *Journal of Modern History* 26 (1954): 364–69.

Notes taken by the chief of British intelligence of a conversation with Woodrow Wilson on 16 October 1918 reveal the president's thoughts on the defeated Central Powers, the Fourteen Points, and Russia.

2715 Stevenson, David. "French War Aims and the American Challenge, 1914–1918." *History Journal* [Great Britain] 22 (1979): 877–94.

Before American entry into the war, France opposed Wilson's attempted mediation on the grounds that a just peace would not secure the French against Germany. American power ended up frustrating French war aims anyway. Notes.

2716 White, Dorothy S. "Franco-American Relations in 1917–1918: War Aims and Peace Prospects." Ph.D. dissertation, University of Pennsylvania, 1954.

France's covert goal of controlling the Rhineland was at odds with Wilson's peace proposals. When the Allied plans came to light, French socialists criticized their government's imperialism. America and France had very different ideas about the peace. DAI 14:820.

2717 Wiegland, Wayne A. "British Propaganda in American Public Libraries, 1914–

1917." *Journal of Library History* 18 (1983): 237–54.

The British ran a slick and comprehensive propaganda campaign on behalf of their military cause during the period of American neutrality. Its effect on the American public needs more research. Notes.

2718 Williams, Joyce G. *Colonel House and Sir Edward Grey: A Study in Anglo-American Diplomacy.* Lanham, MD: University Press, 1984.

Wilson's confidant, Colonel House, and Britain's foreign secretary, Sir Edward Grey, worked as friends and diplomats to avoid a showdown between their countries over violations of American neutral rights. Notes, bibliography, index.

2719 Yates, Louis A. R. *United States and French Security, 1917–1921.* New York: Twayne, 1957.

French attitudes on security against Germany were inconsistent with those of Lloyd George and Wilson. The Guarantee Treaties promised a revolutionary solution to the French problem, but American rejection of the security arrangements doomed the enterprise. Notes, appendix, bibliography, index.

OTHERS

2720 Bailey, Thomas A. *The Policy of the United States toward Neutrals: 1917–1918.* Baltimore, MD: Johns Hopkins University Press, 1942.

Having suffered through the travails of being a neutral power in time of war itself from 1914 to 1917, the United States was fairly consistent in respecting neutral rights following its April 1917 declaration of war. Nonetheless, with the stakes so desperately high, American violation of neutral rights became inevitable. Notes, bibliography, index.

2721 Barton, James L. *The Story of Near East Relief, 1915–1930: An Interpretation.* New York: Macmillan, 1930.

Near East Relief was strictly a humanitarian operation, claims the author, a leading participant in the organization, which was not without its political influence. Appendixes.

2722 David, William M. "The Development of United States Policy toward the Baltic States,

1917–1922." Ph.D. dissertation, Columbia University, 1962.

Latvia, Lithuania, and Estonia requested U.S. aid in maintaining their independence and exercising their right of self-determination. Although the Wilson administration was sympathetic in principle, relations with Russia and Germany took precedence over the problems of these smaller nations. DAI 23:1765.

2723 Gates, Caleb F. *Not to Me Only*. Princeton: Princeton University Press, 1940.

American missionaries and educators carried on with their work during the war and lobbied for protection of their interests during the peace settlement.

2724 Hitchins, Keith. "Woodrow Wilson and the Union of Transylvania with Romania" (in Romanian). *Revue Roumaine d'Histoire* [Romania] 18 (1979): 803–10.

Wilson was at first more concerned with pacifying Austria than with the right of the Romanians of Transylvania to self-determination, but he gradually reversed his stance. The American Preparatory Commission, Romanian propaganda, and Vasile Stoica all influenced U.S. policy.

2725 Keserich, Charles. "George D. Herron, The United States and Peacemaking with Bulgaria, 1918–1919." *East European Quarterly* 14 (1980): 39–58.

A true believer in the Wilsonian quest for peace, Herron failed to talk the Bulgarians out of their alliance with the Germans. After the Armistice, he spoke out on behalf of Bulgaria as the Allies redrew the boundaries of Eastern Europe. Notes.

2726 Mehl, Joseph M., Jr. "Intelligence Reporting by American Observers from the European Neutrals, 1917–1919: Select Cases." Ph.D. dissertation, American University, 1962.

Intelligence gathering was coordinated by the Committee on Public Information and involved military officers and academics. The stability of foreign governments was a major concern. Information gathering and information synthesis were not well coordinated, and the results did not significantly affect diplomatic strategy. DAI 22:4337.

2727 Petkov, Petko. "The American Protestant Missionaries and Bulgaria (1917–1918)" (in Bulgarian). *Istoricheski Pregled* [Bulgaria] 37 (1981): 75–87.

American missionaries interceded with the Wilson administration to prevent an American declaration of war on Bulgaria. Bulgaria might have been treated more harshly without the missionary lobbying. Notes.

2728 Snell, John L. "Wilson's Peace Program and German Socialism, January-March 1918." *Mississippi Valley Historical Review* 38 (1951): 187–214.

Wilson waged a high-level propaganda campaign aimed at preventing German socialists from supporting international Bolshevism, although the Germans did not trust him enough to take direct action. Notes.

2729 Živojinović, Dragan R. *The United States and the Vatican Policies, 1914–1918*. Boulder: Colorado Associated University Press, 1978.

The United States and the Vatican both pretended to be neutral while each favored a different side. During American involvement in the war, the Vatican's advocacy of the status quo antebellum met with Wilson's contempt. By the end of the war, the Vatican had begun to recognize the changed political circumstances. Notes, bibliography, index.

2730 ———. "The Vatican, Woodrow Wilson, and the Dissolution of the Hapsburg Monarchy, 1914–1918." *East European Quarterly* 3 (1969): 31–70.

Fear of postwar anarchy in Eastern Europe motivated the Vatican to try to save the Austro-Hungarian empire. While Wilson would have none of it, he handled the Vatican gently, because he thought it might be useful at some later time in the peace talks. Notes.

Armistice

2731 Briggs, Mitchell P. *George D. Herron and the European Settlement*. Stanford, CA: Stanford University Press, 1932.

This eccentric defrocked minister acted as a liaison between Wilson and the Germans as the two powers discussed terms of the Armistice and the peace. The author concludes that the peace settlement was completely unaffected by Herron's labors. Notes, bibliography, index.

2732 Cutchins, John A. *An Amateur Diplomat in the World War*. Richmond, VA: Garrelt and Massie, 1938.

The author discusses his wartime military service, including his membership on the Armistice commission. Photographs, index.

2733 Lowry, Bullett. "Pershing and the Armistice." *Journal of American History* 55 (1968): 281–91.

Pershing's letter of 30 October 1918 to the Allied Supreme War Council, long seen as a criticism of Wilson's desire for a mild peace, was just that, but it had little effect on the subsequent Armistice dictated by France.

2734 Lowry, Francis B. "The Generals, the Armistice, and the Treaty of Versailles, 1919." Ph.D. dissertation, Duke University, 1963.

The Armistice with Germany was largely the work of U.S. and Allied generals, but their input at the peace talks was effectively limited to strictly military matters. Field generals were dominated by "political" generals, and there was considerable disagreement between individuals. DAI 24:4161.

2735 Nelson, Keith L. *Victors Divided: America and the Allies in Germany, 1918–1923*. Berkeley: University of California Press, 1975.

Although the United States did not intend to occupy Germany after the Armistice, its army remained there for five years. Wilson saw that such a force could preserve German unity, act as a brake on the Allies, and ensure German obedience. Notes, bibliography, index.

2736 ———. "What Colonel House Over-looked in the Armistice." *Mid-America* 51 (1969): 75–91.

In discussing the prospects for a peace based on the Fourteen Points, Colonel Edward House did not fully understand that the French, and the British hoped to use their military position to attain political goals. House's pre-Armistice diplomacy made Wilson's work at Paris more difficult.

2737 Noring, Nina J. "American Coalition Diplomacy and the Armistice, 1918–1919." Ph.D. dissertation, University of Iowa, 1972.

Wilson was careful to cooperate fully with the Allies on the German Armistice. National interest predominated over coalition unity after that as Americans realized that, while they were junior partners in the alliance, they held all of the high economic cards. DAI 33:6848-A.

2738 Rudin, Harry R. *Armistice, 1918*. New Haven, CT: Yale University Press, 1944.

If anyone stabbed Germany in the back, it was General Erich von Ludendorff, not the new German regime. People were overjoyed at the news of the Armistice, not realizing that it was easier to end the war than to make peace. Notes, appendix, index.

2739 Schwabe, Klaus. "American and German Secret Diplomacy and the Problem of Peace by Consultation, 1918" (in German). *Vierteljahrshefte für Zeitgeschichte* [West Germany] 19 (1971): 1–32.

The German foreign office opened secret talks with the Americans about a peace based on Wilson's Fourteen Points. Notes.

2740 Walworth, Arthur. *America's Moment: 1918, American Diplomacy at the End of World War I*. New York: Norton, 1977.

America's moment to lead the world into a new era of lasting peace arrived in 1918 as Wilson arranged for the Armistice. But forces were already at work that would turn the triumph into tragedy within a short time. Notes, appendix, bibliography, index.

11

World War I at Home and Abroad

American participation in World War I changed the world. Although the United States had become the mightiest of industrial nations by the turn of the century, the American people were unwilling to accept concomitant global responsibilities, clinging instead to traditional isolationism. The American moment arrived in 1917–18 as two million troops landed in the Old World to break the deadly military standoff between alliances of empires. The country lapsed back temporarily into prewar "normalcy" following Wilson's failure to bring about the millennium at the Paris Peace Conference, but the lessons learned during the war were to be put to the test within a generation when the world was again engulfed in mass bloodletting.

For an overview of America and the war, begin with Robert H. Ferrell, *Woodrow Wilson and World War I* (#2745); David M. Kennedy, *Over Here: The First World War and American Society* (#2750); and Daniel Smith, *The Great Departure: The United States and World War I, 1914–1920* (#2764). There are a number of excellent works on the mobilization of American society, among them, William J. Breen, *Uncle Sam at Home: Civilian Mobilization, Wartime Federalism, and the Council of National Defense, 1917–1919* (#2770); Valerie J. Conner, *The National War Labor Board: Stability, Social Justice, and the Voluntary State in World War I* (#2774); Robert D. Cuff, *The War Industries Board: Business-Government Relations during World War I* (#2779); and Charles Gilbert, *American Financing of World War I* (#2786). The subject of labor and the war is examined by Frank Grubbs, Jr., *The Struggle for Labor Loyalty:*

Gompers, the A.F. of L., and the Pacifists, 1917–1920 (#2788), and by Simeon Larson, *Labor and Foreign Policy: Gompers, the AFL, and the First World War, 1914–1918* (#2798). For firsthand accounts of mobilization, see G. B. Clarkson, *Industrial America in World War* (#2773), and Francis W. O'Brien, ed., *The Hoover-Wilson Wartime Correspondence, September 24, 1914 to November 11, 1918* (#2801).

Propaganda played a vital part in mobilization and in the twisting of the Progressive faith in an informed electorate. The best general work is Stephen Vaughn, *Holding Fast the Inner Lines: Democracy, Nationalism, and the Committee on Public Information* (#2839). The effects of propaganda on education are explored by George T. Blakey, *Historians on the Homefront: American Propagandists for the Great War* (#2816), and by Carol S. Gruber, *Mars and Minerva: World War I and the Uses of Higher Learning in America* (#2821).

Wilson may or may not have observed just prior to intervention that "Once lead this people into war and they'll forget there ever was such a thing as tolerance" (see Chapter 10), but there can be little doubt that the civil liberties of dissenters were violated with impunity during the war. See Donald Johnson, *The Challenge to American Freedom: World War I and the Rise of the American Civil Liberties Union* (#2874); Paul L. Murphy, *World War I and the Origins of Civil Liberties in the United States* (#2892); and H. C. Peterson and Gilbert C. Fite, *Opponents of War, 1917–1918* (#2898). The persecution of German Americans is examined by Frederick C. Luebke, *Bonds of Loyalty: German-Americans and World War I* (#2885). James Weinstein, "The

President Wilson and his war advisers, 1918. Front row, l. to r.: Assistant Secretary of War Benedict Crowell, Secretary of the Treasury William G. McAdoo, the president, Secretary of the Navy Josephus Daniels, Chairman Bernard Baruch of the War Industries Board. Back row, l. to r.: Food Commissioner Herbert Hoover, Chairman Edward N. Hurley of the Shipping Board, Chairman Vance McCormick of the War Trade Board, Fuel Commissioner Harry A. Garfield. *U.S. War Department photo courtesy of the Herbert Hoover Presidential Library.*

Anti-War Sentiment and the Socialist Party, 1917–1918" (#2915), analyzes the party's militant opposition to the war.

Government intolerance of dissidents is the subject of works by Donald O. Johnson, "Wilson, Burleson and Censorship in the First World War" (#2924); Harry N. Scheiber, *The Wilson Administration and Civil Liberties, 1917–1921* (#2928); and Philip Taft, "The Federal Trials of the IWW" (#2930). Joan M. Jensen, *The Price of Vigilance* (#2939), looks at the unholy alliance between the Wilson administration and the superpatriot American Protective League. See also Robert D. Ward, "The Origins and Activities of the National Security League, 1914–1919" (#2943).

While Wilson grandly declared that "politics is adjourned" for the duration of the war, bipartisanship was quickly forgotten. See a doctoral dissertation by Richard K. Horner, "The House at War: The House of Representatives during World War I, 1917–1919" (#2950); Seward W. Livermore, *Politics Is Adjourned: Wilson and the War Congress, 1916–1918* (#2951); and Richard L. Watson, Jr., "A Testing Time for Southern Congressional Leadership: The War Crisis of 1917–1918" (#2959).

The war offered women the opportunity to break new ground in employment, although government and business were reluctant at first to use women in war work. Two excellent works on this subject are Maurine W. Greenwald, *Women, War, and Work: The Impact of World War I on Women Workers in the United States* (#2990), and Barbara J. Steinson, *American Women's Activism in World War I* (#2995). On black women, see William J. Breen, "Black Women and the Great War: Mobilization and Reform in the South" (#2987).

America won the war but was woefully unprepared to readjust to peacetime conditions. See David Burner, "1919: Prelude to Normalcy" (#2999); William K. Klingaman, *1919: The Year Our World Began* (#3004); James R. Mock and Evangeline Thurber, *Report on Demobilization* (#3007); Burl Noggle, *Into the Twenties: The United States from Armistice to Normalcy* (#3008); and the opening chapters of Geoffrey Perrett, *America in the Twenties: A History* (#3010).

Thousands of books, articles, and dissertations have been written on the military dimension of the war. Excellent starting points are offered by Edward M. Coffman, *The War to End All Wars: The American Military Experience in World War I* (#3021), and Harvey A. DeWeerd, *President Wilson Fights His War: World War I and American Intervention* (#3025). The diplomacy of the military alliance is examined by David F.

Trask, *The United States in the Supreme War Council: American War Aims and Inter-Allied Strategy, 1917–1918* (#3040). Documents from the American Expeditionary Force can be found in U.S. Department of the Army, *United States Army in the World War, 1917–1919* (#3078). Primary sources on the air service are in Maurer Maurer, ed., *The U.S. Air Service in World War I* (#3048). For an overview of the army's officer corps, see Timothy K. Nenninger, *The Leavenworth Schools and the Old Army: Education, Professionalism, and the Officer Corps of the United States Army, 1881–1918* (#3064). Frederick S. Harrod, *Manning the New Navy: The Development of a Modern Naval Enlisted Force, 1899–1940* (#3083), analyzes changing patterns of naval enlistments. Black officers are examined by Gerald W. Patton, *War and Race: The Black Officer in the American Military, 1915–1941* (#3067). Overviews of the navy in World War I include W. R. Braisted, *The United States Navy in the Pacific, 1909–1922* (#3080), and David F. Trask, *Captains and Cabinets: Anglo-American Naval Relations, 1917–1918* (#3089).

The Bolshevik Revolution in Russia attracted great interest and concern in wartime America. For analysis of American reactions, see N. Gordon Levin, Jr., *Woodrow Wilson and World Politics: America's Response to War and Revolution* (#3118), and Arno J. Mayer, *Wilson vs. Lenin: Political Origins of the New Diplomacy, 1917–1918* (#2675). See also Chapter 1 of Edward M. Bennett, *Recognition of Russia: An American Foreign Policy Dilemma* (#3092); Peter G. Filene, *Americans and the Soviet Experiment, 1917–1933* (#3101); Linda R. Killen, *The Russian Bureau: A Case Study in Wilsonian Diplomacy* (#3115); Christopher Lasch, *American Liberals and the Russian Revolution* (#3117); and Leonid I. Strakhovsky, *American Opinion about Russia, 1917–1920* (#3134). Diplomatic analysis of the Revolution is contained in U.S. Department of State, *Papers Relating to the Foreign Relations of the United States, Russia, 1918* (#3135).

American participation in the Allied intervention in the Russian civil war has been examined by a number of historians with differing perspectives on Wilson's motives. For overviews, see John Bradley, *Allied Intervention in Russia* (#3142); Robert J. Maddox, *The Unknown War with Russia: Wilson's Siberian Adventure* (#3161); and Leonid Strakhovsky, *Intervention at Archangel: The Story of Allied Intervention and Russian Counter-Revolution in North Russia, 1918–1920* (#3168). George F. Kennan, *Soviet-American Relations, 1917–1920* (#3155), and Christopher Lasch, "American Intervention in Siberia: A Reinterpretation"

(#3157), argue that concern about Germany moved Wilson to join the Allied scheme. Betty M. Unterberger, "Woodrow Wilson and the Bolsheviks: The 'Acid Test' of Soviet-American Relations" (#3173) and *America's Siberian Expedition* (#3172), finds that Wilson reluctantly agreed to send troops to uphold self-determination and check Japan. For the anti-Bolshevik interpretation, see William A. Williams, "American Intervention in Russia, 1917–1920" (#3176 and #3177).

The Home Front

GENERAL

2741 Churchill, Allen. *Over Here!: An Informal Re-creation of the Home Front in World War I.* New York: Dodd, Mead, 1968.

This popular account of life on the home front concludes that, although the war accelerated certain economic and political freedoms, it led only to disillusion and cynicism. Photographs, bibliography, index.

2742 Cywar, Alan. "John Dewey in World War I: Patriotism and International Progressivism." *American Quarterly* 21 (1969): 578–94.

Dewey tended toward pacifism, but in an atmosphere of wartime propaganda and irrationality he deviated from his long-held tenets of rationalism. Notes.

2743 Danbom, David B. "For the Period of the War: Thorstein Veblen, Wartime Exigency, and Social Change." *Mid-America* 62 (1980): 91–104.

Veblen was harshly criticized by fellow radicals for his support of the war. His expectations for the peace were realistic, and he took a job in the U.S. Food Administration to see the effects of government-sponsored social change. Notes.

2744 Ellis, Edward R. *Echoes of Distant Thunder: Life in the United States, 1914–1918.* New York: Coward, McCann and Geoghegan, 1975.

Based on secondary sources, this narrative history begins with Wilson's inauguration and ends with the Red Scare. Americans were caught off balance by the

outbreak of war, the author concludes, and when they became involved they lost their emotional balance. Bibliography, index.

2745 Ferrell, Robert H. *Woodrow Wilson and World War I, 1917–1921.* New York: Harper and Row, 1985.

This overview of the war effort covers the end of neutrality, mobilization, the Allied Expeditionary Force, the peace conference, readjustment, civil liberties, and the election of 1920. The war taught Americans how to perform within an alliance, and lessons were learned from the failings of mobilization and from military organization, economic readjustment, and the violations of political freedoms. Photographs, notes, bibliography, index.

2746 Geiger, Clarence J. "Peace in War: American Social Thought and the First World War." Ph.D. dissertation, Ohio State University, 1972.

The outbreak of war in 1914 did not destroy the optimism of liberal intellectuals: they regarded it merely as a bump on the road to progress. The only lesson they learned was that war was not an effective instrument of social reform. DAI 33:4300-A.

2747 Grubbs, Frank L., Jr. "Organized Labor and the League to Enforce Peace." *Labor History* 14 (1973): 247–58.

After America entered the war, the League to Enforce Peace and the American Federation of Labor each tried to use the other to increase its own influence, thereby promoting right-wing internationalism in both groups. Notes.

2748 Herwig, Holger H., and Heyman, Neil M. *Biographical Dictionary of World War I.* Westport, CT: Greenwood, 1982.

An extensive historical introduction to the war is included in this dictionary of civilian and military personalities. Appendix, bibliography, index.

2749 Kennan, George F. *American Diplomacy, 1900–1950.* Chicago: University of Chicago Press, 1951.

The dean of the realist approach to American foreign policy discusses the origins and consequences of World War I in Chapter 4.

2750 Kennedy, David M. *Over Here: The First World War and American Society.* New York: Oxford University Press, 1980.

Using the war period as a window on early twentieth-century America, the author surveys the war's impact on economics, politics, diplomacy, culture, and society as a whole. Notes, bibliography, index.

2751 Kevles, Daniel J. "Federal Legislation for Engineering Experiment Stations: The Episode of World War I." *Technology and Culture* 12 (1971): 182–89.

Three competing factions fought over legislation to fund public engineering experiment stations during World War I, with the result that legislation passed. Notes.

2752 ———. "George Ellery Hale, the First World War, and the Advancement of Science in America." *Isis* 59 (1968): 427–37.

This affluent astronomer worked to enhance pure science during the war. The National Research Council, which he helped to found, did not work as effectively as a clearinghouse for scientific work as he had hoped, but the Rockefeller fellowship program helped the cause of American science. Notes.

2753 Knoles, George H. "American Intellectuals and World War I." *Pacific Northwest Quarterly* 59 (1968): 203–15.

The responses of intellectuals to the war were diverse. Some believed that war was barbarism, some race suicide, and others high adventure.

2754 Link, Arthur S., ed. *The Impact of World War I.* New York: Harper and Row, 1969.

This collection presents short articles excerpted from previously published material on the theme of World War I as a watershed in American history. Bibliography.

2755 McMahan, Russell S., Jr. "The Protestant Churches during World War I: The Home Front, 1917, 1918." Ph.D. dissertation, St. Louis University, 1968.

In general, Protestant churches actively supported the war effort, helping with food conservation, fund-raising, conscription, and the welfare of military men. During the war, the churches also kept many social issues alive, such as prohibition, free speech, labor reform, and compassionate race relations. DAI 29:2648-A.

2756 O'Toole, William J. "A Prototype of Public Housing Policy: The USHC." *Journal of the American Institute of Planners* 34 (1968): 140–52.

Reformers and businessmen worked together during the war in response to the housing problem. Although the U.S. Housing Corporation was created in 1918, most of those concerned did not want federal housing programs to become permanent.

2757 Paxson, Frederick L. *American Democracy and the World War.* 3 vols. Boston: Houghton Mifflin, 1936.

Details about wartime America are included in this study of America from 1913 to 1923. The author emphasizes the flexibility of democracy during the crisis period. Bibliography, index.

2758 Piper, John F., Jr. "Robert E. Speer: Christian Statesman in War and Peace." *Journal of Presbyterian History* 47 (1969): 201–25.

Speer eschewed chauvinism and racism in his work as chairman of the General Wartime Commission of Churches. Although he supported the war, he was also concerned about the ill effects of superpatriotism. Notes.

2759 ———. "The American Churches in World War I." *Journal of the American Academy of Religion* 38 (1970): 147–55.

The war secularized American churches, which were becoming more concerned than ever with present-day problems. Protestants and Catholics both founded councils and commissions to contribute to the war effort. Notes.

2760 Reimen, Jacqueline. "1917–1918: America's Warring Intellectuals" (in French). *Revue Française d'Études Américaines* [France] 11 (1986): 309–24.

The response of intellectuals to American entry into the war was complex, as each had to wrestle with his or her own political behavior and with the repercussions for society as a whole.

2761 Scheidt, David L. "Some Effects of World War I on the General Synod and General Council." *Concordia Historical Institute Quarterly* 43 (1970): 83–92.

Confronted by slanders about all things German, the Lutheran General Synod and General Council suffered during the war. Lutherans became Americanized under great pressure in spite of their instinct to preserve their German ethnic heritage.

2762 Seymour, Charles. *Woodrow Wilson and the World War.* New Haven, CT: Yale University Press, 1921.

While Wilson was responsible for many domestic reforms, he will be remembered chiefly for his foreign policy, which fell into three phases (neutrality, war, and peace). Each phase brought out distinct aspects of his character. Bibliography, index.

2763 Shearer, Benjamin F. "An Experiment in Military and Civilian Education: The Students' Army Training Corps at the University of Illinois." *Journal of the Illinois State Historical Society* 72 (1979): 213–24.

The Students' Army Training Corps at the University of Illinois dominated campus activities in 1918 to the point that the army had more power on campus than the president and the faculty. Notes.

2764 Smith, Daniel. *The Great Departure: The United States and World War I, 1914–1920.* New York: Wiley, 1965.

The United States entered the war for several reasons, among them neutral rights, self-interest, and a desire to secure a better postwar world. Although Wilson was always mindful of the national interest, his idealistic pronouncements made the American people fearful of taking on the responsibilities of the world. Notes, bibliography, index.

2765 Stallings, Laurence. "The War to End War." *American Heritage* 10 (1959): 4-17ff.

The special mood of idealism among those going "over there" and among the folks staying on the homefront is examined.

2766 Trask, David F. *World War I at Home: Readings on American Life, 1914–1920.* New York: Wiley, 1970.

Contemporary magazine articles are grouped together by topic to give readers the flavor of American life during the periods of American neutrality and belligerency. Bibliography.

2767 Watts, Phyllis A. "Casework above the Poverty Line: The Influence of Home Service in World War I on Social Work." *Social Service Review* 38 (1964): 303–15.

Soldiers far from home and their families received help from the Home Service, an offshoot of the Red Cross created in 1918. Since its clientele was above the poverty line, the emphasis of the Home Service was on psychological needs. Notes.

2768 Wynn, Neil A. *From Progressivism to Prosperity: World War I and American Society.* New York: Holmes and Meier, 1986.

The war accelerated changes already in progress as production, efficiency, and standardization all increased. The war also

brought new concerns, new ideas, and new people into the limelight. Notes, bibliography, index.

MOBILIZATION

See also Chapter 1, *Autobiographical and Biographical Materials,* Chapter 2, *Wilson Presidency,* and Chapter 3, *Executive Branch.*

2769 Beaver, Daniel R. "Newton D. Baker and the Genesis of the War Industries Board." *Journal of American History* 52 (1965): 43–58.

While Baker played an important part in shaping the board's policies early in its history, he quickly made himself unpopular with Republicans and Democrats alike. Notes.

2770 Breen, William J. *Uncle Sam at Home: Civilian Mobilization, Wartime Federalism, and the Council of National Defense, 1917–1919.* Westport, CT: Greenwood, 1984.

Wartime government agencies whipped up support for the crusade against the Central Powers. The Council of National Defense became a liaison between state and national agencies, with federal authorities retaining effective power. Photographs, notes, bibliography, index.

2771 Bustard, Bruce I. "The Human Factor: Labor Administration and Industrial Manpower Mobilization during the First World War." Ph.D. dissertation, University of Iowa, 1984.

This comprehensive study includes early twentieth-century and Progressive-era labor relations as the background for the labor-management "partnerships" and the antiregulatory approach to boosting productivity during the war. The problem of meeting wartime needs was addressed by unions and by government and business leaders, and the relationships between these groups and their generally intelligent solutions are the main topic. The war's effects on welfare, housing, and postwar business are also examined. DAI 45:2972-A.

2772 Byrne, Kevin B. "The United States Railroad Administration, 1917–1920." Ph.D. dissertation, Duke University, 1974.

The American railroad system was unified through private and federal efforts by the end of 1917. The U.S. Railroad Administration, run primarily by railroad executives, carried out its mandate successfully. DAI 35:5288-A.

2773 Clarkson, G. B. *Industrial America in World War.* Boston: Houghton Mifflin, 1923.

The official historian of the War Industries Board discusses the American mobilization effort of 1917–18.

2774 Conner, Valerie J. *The National War Labor Board: Stability, Social Justice, and the Voluntary State in World War I*. Chapel Hill: University of North Carolina Press, 1983.

Wilson created the National War Labor Board as part of the reorganization of war mobilization machinery. This "Supreme Court of labor relations" centralized government wartime labor policies, setting valuable precedents and serving the nation well. Notes, bibliography, index.

2775 Cuff, Robert D. "A 'Dollar-a-Year Man' in Government: George N. Peek and the War Industries Board." *Business History Review* 41 (1967): 404–20.

Vice President Peek, of Deere and Company, became the industrial representative of the War Industries Board. Business and government forged a new partnership through such men, whose government salaries were one dollar per year. Notes.

2776 ———. "The Dollar-a-Year Men of the Great War." *Princeton University Library Chronicle* 30 (1969): 10–24.

Businessmen played an important role in organizing the economic mobilization for war in 1917–18, running such wartime agencies as the War Industries Board.

2777 ———. "Harry Garfield, the Fuel Administration, and the Search for a Cooperative Order during World War I." *American Quarterly* 30 (1978): 39–53.

Garfield, son of the assassinated president, headed the Fuel Administration during the war, seeing an opportunity to erect a Progressive corporate order. While he gained the trust of the coal industry and brought about cooperation between labor and management, he failed to convince Americans of the need to institutionalize the changes made during the wartime emergency. Notes.

2778 ———. "Herbert Hoover, the Ideology of Voluntarism and War Organization during the Great War." *Journal of American History* 64 (1977): 358–72.

Voluntarism was widespread during the war because of American idealism and the perception that power had to be centralized without adding to the government's permanent powers. Notes.

2779 ———. *The War Industries Board: Business-Government Relations during World War I*. Baltimore, MD: Johns Hopkins University Press, 1973.

While the board brought business under government regulation, the system worked by compromise. Effective authority often rested with administrators who had strong ties to the business community. Notes, bibliography, index.

2780 ———. "We Band of Brothers—Woodrow Wilson's War Managers." *Canadian Review of American Studies* 5 (1974): 135–48.

Wilson's War Council, created in 1918, was more careful than its predecessor not to abuse government powers in the drive to organize the country for war. Notes.

2781 ———. "Woodrow Wilson and Business-Government Relations during World War I." *Review of Politics* 31 (1969): 385–407.

In 1914, Wilson moved to gain the support of business in the event that America went to war. By the time American entry came in 1917 an intimate relationship had developed, and the president seemed willing to overlook the potential for abuse of power in such an alliance of powerful interests. Notes.

2782 Cuff, Robert D., and Urofsky, Melvin I. "The Steel Industry and Price-Fixing during World War I." *Business History Review* 44 (1970): 291–306.

Bargaining and hostility marked the negotiations between the Wilson administration and the steel industry over a proposed price-fixing arrangement. The administration wanted to coordinate production without excessive interference with private industry. Notes.

2783 Danbom, David B. "The Agricultural Extension System and the First World War." *Historian* 41 (1979): 315–31.

The Department of Agriculture was charged with mobilizing farmers for the war effort, a task made difficult by the individualism of the American farmer. In addition to their regular duties, county agents did propaganda work, sold Liberty bonds, and organized fundraising campaigns. Higher prices for farm goods may have been most responsible for increased yields. Notes.

2784 Davis, Allen F. "Welfare, Reform and World War I." *American Quarterly* 19 (1967): 516–33.

Wartime mobilization provided important precedents later used by New Dealers. Progressive reform continued during the war in the form of social welfare laws, public housing, and social insurance, as well as efforts on behalf of women and blacks. Notes.

2785 Fickle, James E. "Defense Mobilization in the Southern Pine Industry: The Experience of World War I." *Journal of Forest History* 22 (1978): 206–23.

The southern pine industry was mobilized for war through patriotic appeals and government planning. Problems with pricing, labor, and some lumbermen led to strained relations with the government. Notes.

2786 Gilbert, Charles. *American Financing of World War I*. Westport, CT: Greenwood, 1970.

The financing of World War I was typical in that it marked the triumph of expediency over sound economic policy, as the government tried to pay for the war without touching off a taxpayers' rebellion. Tables, notes, bibliography, index.

2787 Godfrey, Aaron A. *Government Operation of the Railroads: Its Necessity, Success, and Consequences, 1918–1920*. Austin: Jenkins, 1974.

The government was forced to take over the railroads during the war, because Progressive reforms had weakened the nation's railways. Government operations did no one any good, as workers were exploited and the railroads lost money. Photographs, notes, bibliography.

2788 Grubbs, Frank L., Jr. *The Struggle for Labor Loyalty: Gompers, the A.F. of L., and the Pacifists, 1917–1920*. Durham, NC: Duke University Press, 1968.

Samuel Gompers created the American Alliance for Labor and Democracy to rally labor behind the war effort. Wilson's longtime support of the AFL and Gompers's hopes for a powerful new place in the postwar world were key motivating factors. Notes, bibliography, index.

2789 Hall, Tom G. "Wilson and the Food Crisis: Agricultural Price Control during World War I." *Agricultural History* 47 (1973): 25–46.

Price controls on wheat imposed during the war were designed to prevent strikes and to provide profit incentives to farmers. The American farmer discovered that government intervention could benefit them without imposing unacceptable demands. Notes.

2790 Hessen, Robert. "Charles Schwab and the Shipbuilding Crisis of 1918." *Pennsylvania History* 38 (1971): 389–99.

To speed up the production of desperately needed ships, Wilson made Charles Schwab the head of the Emergency Fleet Corporation, an appointment which proved successful. Schwab made excellent use of personnel, used the promise of profits well, and got rid of the wasteful cost-plus system. Notes.

2791 Himmelberg, Robert F. "The War Industries Board and the Antitrust Question in November 1918." *Journal of American History* 52 (1965): 59–74.

Businessmen on the War Industries Board tried to further their interests at the end of the war by pushing for modifications of antitrust policies and continued price protection, schemes which the president rejected. Notes.

2792 Johnson, James P. "The Wilsonians as War Managers: Coal and the 1917–18 Winter Crisis." *Prologue* 9 (1977): 193–208.

The Fuel Administration bungled the job of coal allocations through excessive hostility toward producers. In early 1918 all manufacturing was halted for two weeks in the East in order to clear up transportation problems and save fuel, a move which did not solve the basic problems. Notes.

2793 Kaufman, Burton I. "Wilson's 'War Bureaucracy' and Foreign Trade Expansion." *Prologue* 6 (1974): 19–31.

Wartime government centralization of the economy and increased coordination in the United States were influenced by developments in Europe. Notes.

2794 Kerr, K. Austin. "Decision for Federal Control: Wilson, McAdoo, and the Railroads, 1917." *Journal of American History* 54 (1967): 550–60.

Wilson and McAdoo decided that the government should take over the railroads during the war for the sake of efficiency, because rates, operations, and the various interests of individual railroads could best be coordinated from Washington.

2795 Koistinen, Paul A. "The 'Industrial-Military Complex' in Historical Perspective: The Inter-War Years." *Journal of American History* 56 (1970): 819–39.

Businessmen staffed wartime agencies as part of the economic mobilization effort, which created the foundation for the "industrial-military complex." Initial difficulty in working with the War Department was overcome by Bernard Baruch in 1918. Notes.

2796 ———. "The 'Industrial Military Complex' in Historical Perspective: World War I."

Business History Review 41 (1967): 378–403.

The government relied heavily on businessmen to organize wartime mobilization, thus laying the foundation for what would become, after World War II, the military-industrial complex. Notes.

2797 Lael, Richard L., and Killen, Linda. "The Pressure of Shortage: Platinum Policy and the Wilson Administration during World War I." *Business History Review* 56 (1982): 545–58.

Although platinum was vital to the war effort, the Wilson administration did not want to interfere with the free market, so few controls governed its acquisition and use. Notes.

2798 Larson, Simeon. *Labor and Foreign Policy: Gompers, the AFL, and the First World War, 1914–1918.* Cranbury, NJ: Fairleigh Dickinson University Press, 1975.

Like most Americans, Samuel Gompers gave little thought to foreign policy before the Great War, espousing a vague pacifism. The war in Europe converted him into an advocate of preparedness, and he delivered the AFL to Wilson after American entry in 1917. Notes, bibliography, index.

2799 Mullendore, William C. *History of the United States Food Administration.* Stanford: Stanford University Press, 1941.

The work of the wartime Food Administration is detailed in this official account, with much of the credit going to its director, Herbert Hoover.

2800 Nash, Gerald D. "Experiments in Industrial Mobilization: WIB and NRA." *Mid-America* 45 (1963): 157–74.

Franklin Roosevelt modeled the National Recovery Administration (1933) after the War Industries Board (1917). The two agencies for economic mobilization are described. Notes.

2801 O'Brien, Francis W., ed. *The Hoover-Wilson Wartime Correspondence, September 24, 1914 to November 11, 1918.* Ames: Iowa State University Press, 1974.

The Hoover-Wilson letters reveal the many problems involved in the work of the Food Administration and the president's efforts to assist Hoover as well as the influence the two leaders had upon one another. Bibliography, index.

2802 Ohl, John K. "General Hugh S. Johnson and the War Industries Board." *Military Review* 55 (1975): 35–48.

As a member of both the War Industries Board and the War Department general staff, Johnson was in a position to further the integration of the military-industrial complex. He worked especially hard to convince military men that they should accept businessmen as partners in the war effort. Notes.

2803 ———. "The Navy, the War Industries Board, and the Industrial Mobilization for War, 1917–1918." *Military Affairs* 40 (1976): 17–22.

At first the navy mistrusted the business-dominated War Industries Board, but by 1918 it was working harmoniously with it. Notes.

2804 Polishbrook, Sheila S. "The American Federation of Labor, Zionism, and the First World War." *American Jewish Quarterly* 65 (1976): 228–44.

Wilson recognized organized labor as a legitimate interest group during the war in return for its support. In spite of opposition from proponents of pacifism and socialism, Samuel Gompers pushed through the AFL an endorsement for a Jewish homeland. Notes.

2805 Safford, Jeffrey J. "Edward Hurley and American Shipping Policy: An Elaboration on Wilsonian Diplomacy, 1918–1919." *Historian* 35 (1973): 568–86.

Hurley, chairman of the U.S. Shipping Board and of the president's War Council, regarded the peace as an opportunity to build a world based on market capitalism to make the world safe for further American economic expansion. Notes.

2806 Scott, Emmett Jay. *Scott's Official History of the American Negro in the World War.* New York: Arno, 1969.

Scott, special assistant for Negro affairs to the secretary of war, was controversial among blacks because of his conservative approach to race relations. He discusses racial problems in the military, black soldiers in Europe, the black civilian contribution to the war effort, and what blacks gained from their service. Photographs, appendix.

2807 Sherfy, Marcella M. "The National Park Service and the First World War." *Journal of Forest History* 22 (1978): 203–5.

During the war, both the government and the public were willing to subjugate anything to the war effort. Fortunately, Stephen T. Mather and Horace M. Albright, director and assistant director of the National Park Service, ably and energetically protected the parks and their funding, partly through encouraging visitors.

2808 Stricker, Frank. "Jobs and Inflation: Lessons from the World War I Era." *Southwest Economy and Society* 6 (1984): 28–46.

The wartime economy is examined, with special attention given to the issues of inflation, jobs, wages, and work conditions.

2809 ———. "The Wages of Inflation: Worker's Earnings in the World War One Era." *Mid-America* 63 (1981): 93–105.

World War I was financed chiefly by the pay cuts and reduced consumption of public workers and others on low salaries. On the whole, though, wage earners made more money than they did in the pre-1917 period. Notes.

2810 Surface, Frank M., and Bland, Raymond L. *American Food in the World War and Reconstruction Period*. Stanford: Stanford University Press, 1931.

Statistical data on American food relief is detailed, along with a brief narrative. Tables, index.

2811 Thurston, William N. "Management-Leadership in the United States Shipping Board, 1917–1918." *American Neptune* 32 (1972): 155–70.

Originally a regulatory body with power over private merchant ships, the board soon switched to supervising the building of a massive new merchant fleet. Notes.

2812 Webb, William J. "The United States Wooden Steamship Program during World War I." *American Neptune* 35 (1975): 275–88.

The Emergency Fleet Corporation was desperate enough for ships that it authorized the building of many wooden and wood-and-steel ships during the war, vessels quickly scrapped after the Armistice. Notes.

2813 Wicker, Elmus R. *Federal Reserve Monetary Policy, 1917–1933*. New York: Random House, 1966.

The opening chapters focus on wartime monetary policies of the Federal Reserve Board and the Department of Treasury.

2814 Yardley, Herbert O. *The American Black Chamber*. London: Faber and Faber, 1931.

The director of the State Department's code room discusses his operation's role in winning the war.

2815 Young, Arthur P. *Books for Sammies: The American Library Association and World War I*. Pittsburgh: Beta Phi Mu, 1981.

Members of the American Library Association became caught up in wartime mobilization, collecting millions of books for American soldiers while using the opportunity to demonstrate their professionalism. Photographs, appendixes, notes, bibliography, index.

PROPAGANDA

See also Chapter 3, *George Creel*.

2816 Blakey, George T. *Historians on the Homefront: American Propagandists for the Great War*. Lexington: University Press of Kentucky, 1970.

Historians thought that they could serve both their profession and their country during the war, but they soon compromised themselves by becoming propagandists. In the long run the national interest is not served when the guardians of the past lead the retreat from scholarship.

2817 Bonadio, Felice A. "The Failure of German Propaganda in the United States, 1914–1917." *Mid-America* 41 (1959): 40–57.

Germans charged with propagandizing Americans never understood the power of the melting pot to assimilate immigrants. Notes.

2818 Breen, William J. "Mobilization and Cooperative Federalism: The Connecticut State Council of Defense, 1917–1919." *Historian* 1 (1979): 58–84.

The Connecticut State Council of Defense was a sophisticated and wide-ranging program designed to put the state on a wartime footing. Historians have underestimated the effectiveness of such state ventures in cooperative federalism. Notes.

2819 Buitenhuis, Peter. "The Selling of the Great War." *Canadian Review of American Studies* 7 (1976): 139–50.

The Committee on Public Information quickly became a propaganda agency during the war. While it mobilized public opinion successfully, the committee's propaganda contributed to the cynicism and disillusionment of the postwar period. Notes.

2820 Cornebise, Alfred E. *War as Advertised: The Four Minute Men and America's Crusade, 1917–1918*. Philadelphia: American Philosophical Society, 1984.

Thousands of volunteers mobilized the homefront with four-minute speeches on behalf of the war effort. Photographs, notes, bibliography, index.

2821 Gruber, Carol S. *Mars and Minerva: World War I and the Uses of Higher Learning in America*. Baton Rouge: Louisiana State University Press, 1975.

Historians and other academics are condemned here for using their disciplines for propaganda purposes. Militarized higher education, cheap propaganda, and the lack of academic freedom served the government rather than the truth. Notes, bibliography, index.

2822 Hollihan, Thomas A. "Propagandizing in the Interest of War: A Rhetorical Study of the Committee on Public Information." *Southern Speech Communication Journal* 49 (1984): 241–57.

The Committee on Public Information's propaganda techniques are discussed along with the issue of censorship in this study of wartime government rhetoric. Notes.

2823 Isenberg, Michael T. "The Mirror of Democracy: Reflections of the War Films of World War I, 1917–1919." *Journal of Popular Culture* 9 (1976): 878–85.

American films reflect the challenge that the war posed to American ideals. Movies were critical of those who refused to go to war and fostered a romantic image of democracy. Notes.

2824 Josephson, Harold. "History for Victory: The National Board for Historical Service." *Mid-America* 52 (1970): 205–24.

The National Board for Historical Service, founded by prominent historians, gave top priority to the use of scholarship to meet patriotic needs and worked to that end with the Committee on Public Information. The board had few critics and became increasingly reckless with historical truth as the war went on.

2825 Lasswell, Harold D. *Propaganda Techniques in the World War*. London: Keegan Paul, 1938.

The art of propaganda bloomed during the war as nations manipulated public opinion to weaken the enemy and strengthen national security.

2826 Marks, Barry A. "The Idea of Propaganda in America." Ph.D. dissertation, University of Minnesota, 1957.

The American public first became aware of propaganda as a tool by Germans during World

War I. Only later was the use of propaganda by the Allies and Americans even acknowledged. The author discusses the impact of propaganda on our self-concept, philosophy, and education. DAI 19:788.

2827 Mitchell, Charles R. "New Message to America: James W. Gerard's *Beware* and World War I Propaganda." *Journal of Popular Film* 4 (1975): 275–95.

Many anti-German films were produced after American entry into the war, most notably the 1919 movie *Beware*, based on the observations of the former ambassador to Germany.

2828 Mock, James R., and Larson, Cedric. *Words that Won the War: The Story of the Committee on Public Information, 1917–1919*. Princeton: Princeton University Press, 1939.

The committee's propaganda work extended into education, factories, and motion pictures, with special attention given to ethnic groups suspected of divided loyalties. Written at a time when another world war seemed likely, the author reaffirms the belief that publicity and propaganda have a legitimate place in "totalitarian democracy." Notes, index.

2829 Mould, David H. *American Newsfilm, 1914–1919: The Underexposed War*. New York: Garland, 1983.

This published master's thesis discusses the fragmented and frequently distorted picture Americans received from wartime newsreels. Many scenes were faked or re-created. Notes, bibliography.

2830 Pope, Daniel. "The Advertising Industry and World War I." *Public History* 2 (1980): 4–25.

World War I transformed the American advertising industry, preparing it for an enhanced role in American life in the 1920s.

2831 Read, James M. *Atrocity Propaganda, 1914–1919*. New Haven, CT: Yale University Press, 1941.

Atrocity propaganda effectively motivated people to make greater efforts in wartime, but it tied the hands of the peacemakers, putting them under great pressure to pursue a punitive settlement. Bibliography, index.

2832 Roetter, Charles. *The Art of Psychological Warfare, 1914–1945*. New York: Stein and Day, 1974.

The Allies used propaganda and psychological warfare to court the United States and to help them win World War I. Photographs, index.

2833 Rubin, Bernard. "Propaganda and Ideological Conflicts, 1917–1945: The Need for Psychological Peacefare." *Contemporary Review* 200 (1961): 630–36.

British propaganda in the United States before 1917 helped make Americans lean toward the Allied cause.

2834 Sanders, M. L. "Wellington House and British Propaganda during the First World War." *Historical Journal* 18 (1975): 119–46.

The British were masterful propagandists who successfully countered clumsy German fabrications with their own manipulations of public opinion.

2835 Shover, Michele J. "Roles and Images of Women in World War I Propaganda." *Politics and Science* 5 (1975): 469–86.

Women became the central figures in poster propaganda designed to motivate the civilian and military populations to make greater sacrifices. Notes.

2836 Tyler, Robert L. "The United States Government as Union Organizer: The Loyal Legion of Loggers and Lumbermen." *Mississippi Valley Historical Review* 47 (1960): 434–51.

During the war, the Wilson administration created the Loyal Legion to undercut the radical IWW, a strategy that earned members higher wages and better working conditions for a short time. Notes.

2837 Vaughn, Stephen. "Arthur Bullard and the Creation of the Committee on Public Information." *New Jersey History* 97 (1979): 45–63.

More than anyone else, Arthur Bullard was responsible for creating the Committee on Public Information. His prewar writings on the importance of wartime propaganda came to the attention of Colonel Edward House and the president. As a result of the committee's work, civil liberties were endangered for the sake of an ideal vision. Notes.

2838 ———. "First Amendment Liberties and the Committee on Public Information." *American Journal of Legal History* 23 (1979): 95–119.

The committee was involved in much more than public information, for it propagandized the public and censored critics of the war as well. Notes.

2839 ———. *Holding Fast the Inner Lines: Democracy, Nationalism, and the Committee on Public Information.* Chapel Hill: University of North Carolina Press, 1980.

Progressive reformers flocked to the Committee on Public Information during the war, mixing liberalism with their anti-German propaganda. Notes, bibliography, index.

2840 ———. "Prologue to *Public Opinion*: Walter Lippmann's Work in Military Intelligence." *Prologue* 15 (1983): 151–63.

Lippmann's elitism stems from his wartime service in France as an intelligence officer whose job was to question prisoners of war to determine what kinds of propaganda might be most effective. Notes.

2841 ———. " 'To Create a Nation of Noble Men': Public Education, National Unity, and the *National School Service*, 1918–1919." *Historian* 41 (1979): 429–49.

The government bulletin *National School Service* was both propaganda and reformist literature that discussed citizenship in a democracy at war. Notes.

2842 Ventry, Lance T. "The Impact of the United States Committee on Public Information on Italian Participation in the First World War." Ph.D. dissertation, Catholic University of America, 1968.

The ambassador to Italy and the Italian commissioner of the Committee on Public Information disagreed over the best way to propagandize Italy out of its territorial aspirations, a division which had an effect on the Italian state. DAI 30:1123-A.

2843 Ward, Larry W. *The Motion Picture Goes to War: The U.S. Government Film Effort during World War I.* Ann Arbor, MI: UMI Research Press, 1985.

George Creel created the Division of Films within the Committee on Public Information to exploit movies for information and propaganda. This effort was more important to the film industry than it was to the government, since it meant official recognition for the medium of motion pictures. Notes, bibliography, index.

CIVIL LIBERTIES

See also Chapter 4, *Agricultural Discontent*, Chapter 6, *Women*, and Chapter 8, *Radical Ideologies, Anarchism, Syndicalism, Socialism*, and *Communism*.

General

2844 Abrams, Ray H. *Preachers Present Arms: A Study of Wartime Attitudes and Activities of the Churches and the Clergy in the United States, 1914–1918*. Philadelphia: Round Table, 1933.

A majority of the American clergy became caught up in the wartime hysteria, standing behind the government's repression of dissenters. A courageous minority refused to violate their religious principles and suffered as a consequence.

2845 Allen, Leola. "Anti-German Sentiment in Iowa during World War I." *Annals of Iowa* 42 (1974): 418–29.

The large German-American population of Iowa was the target of harassment during the war. Members of this ethnic group had to prove their loyalty by buying Liberty bonds, by not speaking German, by explaining themselves before kangaroo courts, and by participating in patriotic rallies. Notes.

2846 Baldwin, Roger. "Recollections of a Life in Civil Liberties—Part I." *Civil Liberties Review* 2 (1975): 39–72.

Founder of the American Civil Liberties Union, Baldwin discusses the events of the Wilson years that made him a civil libertarian.

2847 Barbeau, Art. "Thy Brothers' Keeper." *Journal of the West Virginia Historical Association* 2 (1978): 25–40.

The YMCA discriminated against blacks in its efforts to establish medical and social services for soldiers during the war. The Salvation Army and the Knights of Columbus had better records in civil rights.

2848 Bromberg, Alan B. "Free Speech at Mr. Jefferson's University: The Case of Professor Leon Whipple." *Virginia Magazine of History and Biography* 88 (1980): 3–20.

This journalism professor was fired from his position at the University of Virginia for abusing freedom of speech after he called for American withdrawal from the war. His firing was not in keeping with the principles of the university's founder, Thomas Jefferson. Notes.

2849 Brommel, Bernard J. "Kate Richards O'Hare: A Midwestern Pacifist's Fight for Free Speech." *North Dakota Quarterly* 44 (1976): 5–19.

As a result of a local political battle, O'Hare was arrested for delivering a speech she had already given many times. She was sentenced to five years in federal prison for violating the Espionage Act. Notes.

2850 Cantor, Milton. "The Radical Confrontation with Foreign Policy: War and Revolution, 1914–1920." In Alfred F. Young, ed., *Dissent: Explorations in the History of American Radicalism*. DeKalb: Northern Illinois University Press, 1968, pp. 215–49.

American radicalism was smashed during the war as a result of its own blunders, the appeal of Wilsonian idealism, and the Bolshevik Revolution. Notes.

2851 Chambers, John W., II. "Conscripting for Colossus: The Adoption of the Draft in the United States in World War I." Ph.D. dissertation, Columbia University, 1973.

Voluntarism was scrapped in favor of selective service during World War I to improve efficiency. This reflected the markedly centralized economy and the increased power of the federal government. The Progressive belief in universal military training made the draft acceptable to many, although others had to be convinced. DAI 34:3290-A.

2852 Chrislock, Carl H. *Ethnicity Challenged: The Upper Midwest Norwegian-American Experience in World War I*. Northfield, MN: Norwegian-American Historical Association, 1981.

The war hastened the Americanization of Norwegians, as immigrant groups were harassed for clinging to their old cultural ways. Photographs, notes, index.

2853 Cook, Blanche W. "Democracy in Wartime: Antimilitarism in England and the United States, 1914–1918." *American Studies* [Lawrence, KS] 13 (1972): 51–68.

Wartime England and America both witnessed political repression and the rise of groups determined to preserve civil liberties. Notes.

2854 Decker, Joe F. "Progressive Reaction to Selective Service in World War I." Ph.D. dissertation, University of Georgia, 1969.

The Selective Service Act of 1917 was controversial among Progressives. Some supported it out of loyalty to Wilson, others saw it as advancing reform, and a few opposed it. DAI 30:5372-A.

2855 Derr, Nancy. "The Babel Proclamation." *Palimpsest* 60 (1979): 98–115.

This proclamation by Iowa's Governor William L. Harding banned all things German from public life.

2856 Dobbert, G. A. "The Ordeal of Gotthard Deutsch." *American Jewish Archives* 20 (1968): 129–55.

Deutsch, historian and president of Hebrew Union College of Cincinnati, was charged in 1917 with not supporting the war effort with sufficient enthusiasm. While the college board vindicated him after a prolonged wrangle, his persecution created hard feelings. Notes.

2857 Dorsett, Lyle W. "The Ordeal of Colorado's Germans during World War I." *Colorado Magazine* 51 (1974): 277–93.

German nationals living in Colorado during the war suffered at the hands of patriots and vigilantes.

2858 Dubay, Robert W. "The Opposition to Selective Service, 1916–1918." *Southern Quarterly* 7 (1969): 301–22.

A wide variety of groups and individuals opposed selective service. Among them were minorities, unions, political groups, and private citizens. Notes.

2859 Durham, James C. "In Defense of Conscience: Norman Thomas as an Exponent of Christian Pacifism during World War I." *Journal of Presbyterian History* 52 (1974): 19–32.

Unlike the many Christian pacifists who wilted under the pressure of public opinion during World War I, Thomas stubbornly defended the right to be a conscientious objector to conscription. Notes.

2860 Fernandez, Ronald. "Getting Germans to Fight Germans: The Americanizers of World War I." *Journal of Ethnic Studies* 9 (1981): 53–68.

Many of the eight million German Americans living in the United States in 1917 were subject to extreme pressure to become Americanized overnight. They are a classic example of the wrong group in the wrong place at the wrong moment. Notes.

2861 Fishbein, Leslie. "Federal Suppression of Left-Wing Dissidence in World War I." *Potomac Review* 6 (1974): 47–68.

The wartime government campaign against socialists and syndicalists resulted in thousands of arrests.

2862 Fowler, James H., II. "Tar and Feather Patriotism: The Suppression of Dissent in Oklahoma during World War I." *Chronicles of Oklahoma* 56 (1978): 409–30.

German Americans and radicals were the targets of patriotic vigilante committees who used boycotts, forced loyalty oaths, and violence against those suspected of harboring un-American tendencies. Notes.

2863 Giffin, Frederick C. *Six Who Protested: Radical Opposition to the First World War.* Port Washington, NY: Kennikat, 1977.

Six leading leftists who actively opposed the war effort are examined. Their struggle is viewed as a failure because of its utter futility. Notes, bibliography, index.

2864 Glidden, William B. "Casualties of Caution: Alien Enemies in America, 1917–1919." Ph.D. dissertation, University of Illinois, Urbana-Champaign, 1970.

Millions of German and Austro-Hungarian aliens were subject to summary federal powers including restrictions on travel, confiscation of firearms, and forced registration with local authorities. Harassment of these groups was severe, especially for some 2,300 men and women who were put in army internment camps. DAI 31:6496-A.

2865 Gunns, Albert F. "Civil Liberties and Crisis: The Status of Civil Liberties in the Pacific Northwest, 1917–1940." Ph.D. dissertation, University of Washington, 1971.

Federal, state, and local authorities persecuted antiwar dissenters during the war in the Pacific Northwest with the help of vigilantes. Most of those jailed did not constitute any threat to the war effort. DAI 32:2602-A.

2866 Gutfeld, Arnon. *Montana's Agony: Years of War and Hysteria, 1917–1921.* Gainesville: University Presses of Florida, 1979.

Economically, Montana was a colonial state during the Progressive era. During the war, the government and conservative mining interests persecuted reformist farmers, Progressives, and labor leaders to preserve the status quo. Notes, bibliography, index.

2867 ———. "The Murder of Frank Little: Radical Labor Agitation in Butte, Montana, 1917." *Labor History* 10 (1969): 177–92.

The murder of IWW leader Frank Little in Montana touched off a campaign of legal and extralegal repression against labor radicalism. Notes.

2868 Hickey, Donald R. "The Prager Affair: A Study in Wartime Hysteria." *Journal of the Illinois State Historical Society* 62 (1969): 117–34.

Robert Prager was lynched on the outskirts of an Illinois mining town in April 1918 in an atmosphere of hysteria engendered by a labor dispute and by the fears of a German-American community under siege.

2869 Holli, Melvin G. "Teuton vs. Slav: The Great War Sinks Chicago's German *Kultur.*" *Ethnicity* 8 (1981): 406–51.

German-American cultural activities were sacrificed to the war effort in Chicago, because all things German were regarded as anathema. Notes.

2870 Howlett, Charles F. "Academic Freedom versus Loyalty at Columbia University during World War I: A Case Study." *War and Society* 2 (1984): 43–53.

Columbia University tried to limit free speech on campus during the war. Several faculty members were fired for protesting university policies, including some teachers who supported the war effort. Notes.

2871 Hubbell, John T. "A Question of Academic Freedom: The William A. Schaper Case." *Midwest Quarterly* 17 (1976): 111–21.

Schaper was fired from his job as a professor of political science at the University of Minnesota for his opposition to the war, an example of how academic freedom is jeopardized in times of hysteria.

2872 Hummasti, P. George. "World War I and the Finns of Astoria, Oregon: The Effects of the War on an Immigrant Community." *International Migration Review* 11 (1977): 334–49.

Finnish-American socialists in Astoria, Oregon, were persecuted during the war for their political beliefs.

2873 Jenson, Carol E. "Agrarian Pioneer in Civil Liberties: The Nonpartisan League in Minnesota during World War I." Ph.D. dissertation, University of Minnesota, 1968.

Although the Wilson administration did not consider the Nonpartisan League to be subversive, the state of Minnesota insisted that it was disloyal. The Republican state government used the loyalty issue to defeat the League politically. DAI 30:657-A.

2874 Johnson, Donald. *The Challenge to American Freedom: World War I and the Rise of the American Civil Liberties Union.* Lexington: University of Kentucky Press, 1963.

The American Civil Liberties Union was created to counter the wholesale violations of the civil liberties of people who opposed the war effort. Notes, bibliography, index.

2875 Johnson, Neil M. "The Patriotism and Anti-Prussianism of the Lutheran Church-Missouri Synod, 1914–1918." *Concordia Historical Institute Quarterly* 39 (1966): 99–118.

Lutherans responded to unprecedented attacks on all persons and things German by becoming superpatriots and thoroughly Americanizing their culture.

2876 Joost, Nicholas. "Culture vs. Power: Randolph Bourne, John Dewey, and *The Dial.*" *Midwest Quarterly* 9 (1968): 245–59.

Writing in the Chicago literary magazine *The Dial*, Randolph Bourne advocated pacifist transnationalism during World War I. John Dewey, meanwhile, called on Americans to support the policies of the Wilson administration.

2877 Jordan, David W. "Edward A. Steiner and the Struggle for Toleration during World War I." *Annals of Iowa* 46 (1983): 523–42.

This Austrian American and longtime professor of religion at Grinnell College was attacked for suggesting that Christians should love their enemies. Notes.

2878 Juhnke, James C. "Mob Violence and Kansas Mennonites in 1918." *Kansas Historical Quarterly* 43 (1977): 334–50.

When pacifist Mennonites refused to demonstrate their patriotism by buying Liberty bonds, vigilantes turned to violence in central Kansas. Notes.

2879 Keller, Phyllis. "German-America and the First World War." Ph.D. dissertation, University of Pennsylvania, 1969.

During the period of American neutrality, leaders of the German-American community tried unsuccessfully to organize a political power bloc. After American entry into the war, the extreme pressures put on German Americans hastened their assimilation as they turned their backs on ethnic nationalism. DAI 30:4896-A.

2880 Kohrman, Allan. "Respectable Pacifists: Quaker Response to World War I." *Quaker History* 75 (1986): 35–53.

The Quaker church created the American Friends Service Committee to place drafted members in alternative service jobs. A majority of those drafted opted to accept military service, and the Quakers as a whole supported the war effort. Notes.

2881 Kozenko, Boris D. " 'Total Democracy' in the United States, 1914–18" (in Russian). *Voprosy Istorii* [USSR] (1983): 106–18.

A Soviet historian looks at the American human rights record during World War I, detailing the reign of terror against leftists, blacks, and pacifists. Notes.

2882 Lee, Art. "Hometown Hysteria: Bemidji at the Start of World War I." *Minnesota History* 49 (1984): 65–75.

The lumber town of Bemidji, Minnesota, became extremely patriotic during the war. Socialists faced verbal and physical attacks, and the IWW was chased out of town after a mysterious mill fire. Notes.

2883 Lindquist, John H. "A Sociological Interpretation of the Bisbee Deportation." *Pacific Historical Review* 37 (1968): 401–22.

A strike of copper miners called by the IWW in June 1917 led to the forced deportation of 1,200 strikers and sympathizers to Hermanas, New Mexico, an action applauded by many. Notes.

2884 Lovin, Hugh T. "Moses Alexander and the Idaho Lumber Strike of 1917: The Wartime Ordeal of a Progressive." *Pacific Northwest Quarterly* 66 (1975): 115–22.

Governor Alexander defended the rights of labor, including the IWW, against vigilantes and lumber interests in wartime Idaho.

2885 Luebke, Frederick C. *Bonds of Loyalty: German-Americans and World War I.* DeKalb: Northern Illinois University Press, 1974.

The persecution of German Americans during the war is put in perspective as the nadir of a long struggle of an ethnic minority that opposed Progressive reforms such as prohibition, women's suffrage, immigration restriction, and mandatory education designed to Americanize them. Notes, bibliography, index.

2886 ———. "Superpatriotism in World War I: The Experience of a Lutheran Pastor." *Concordia History Institute Quarterly* 41 (1968): 3–11.

A pastor of a German Lutheran church in rural Nebraska, Herman Studier, was hounded by superpatriots for his pro-German views.

2887 McBride, James D. "Henry S. McCluskey: Workingman's Advocate." Ph.D. dissertation, Arizona State University, 1982.

This study includes a section on McCluskey's efforts on behalf of the Western Federation of Miners during Wilson's presidency. DAI 43:527-A.

2888 MacKinnon, Jan, and MacKinnon, Steve. "Agnes Smedley's 'Cell Mates.' " *Signs* 3 (1977): 531–39.

Jailed in New York in 1918 for inciting revolution in British India and for violating local birth control laws, Smedley eventually won release and wrote about her ordeal. Notes.

2889 Mander, Mary S. "The Journalist as Cynic." *Antioch Review* 38 (1980): 91–107.

Journalists became cynical once they experienced censorship and the other restrictions they were forced to endure during World War I.

2890 Mock, James R. *Censorship 1917.* Princeton: Princeton University Press, 1941.

During the war the First Amendment was set aside in the name of a higher cause. Wartime repression spilled over into the peace, stifling reconstruction. Bibliography, index.

2891 Morton, Michael. "No Time to Quibble: The Jones Family Conspiracy Trial of 1917." *Chronicles of Oklahoma* 59 (1981): 224–36.

"The Jones family" was the name given to seven men arrested for participating in the Green Corn rebellion, an uprising of tenant farmers who opposed the war. They were all convicted in an atmosphere of hysteria on little hard evidence. Notes.

2892 Murphy, Paul L. *World War I and the Origin of Civil Liberties in the United States.* New York: Norton, 1979.

Civil liberties emerged as an important public issue during World War I for the first time in American history, the author says. Through a series of "persuasive Americanism campaigns" and repressive laws the government assaulted civil liberties guaranteed by the Bill of Rights. Some used the war as an excuse to repress ethnocultural traits and leftist ideas they hated and feared. Notes, index.

2893 Nelson, Clifford L. *German-American Political Behavior in Nebraska and Wisconsin,*

1916–1920. Lincoln: University of Nebraska-Lincoln Publications, 1972.

German Americans in Wisconsin and Nebraska voted Democratic until 1916, when they turned on Wilson for his anti-German neutrality. Notes, bibliography.

2894 Nicholas, William E., III. "Academic Dissent in World War I, 1917–1918." Ph.D. dissertation, Tulane University, 1970.

Professors who expressed sympathy for pacifism or for Germany were subject to dismissal for disloyalty. The American Association of University Professors condoned the firings. DAI 31:4685-A.

2895 ———. "World War I and Academic Dissent in Texas." *Arizona and the West* 14 (1972): 215–30.

Most institutions of higher learning accepted the need for superpatriotism during the war, but a few individuals resisted. Some professors were fired from the University of Texas and from Rice University, while others were disciplined. Notes.

2896 Pankratz, Herbert. "The Suppression of Alleged Disloyalty in Kansas during World War I." *Kansas Historical Quarterly* 42 (1976): 277–307.

Most Kansans either lent their support or turned a blind eye to the persecution of wartime dissidents. Notes.

2897 Petersen, Peter L. "Language and Loyalty: Governor Harding and Iowa's Danish-Americans during World War I." *Annals of Iowa* 42 (1974): 405–17.

A May 1918 law forbidding the use of foreign languages in public met with resistance from Danish Americans in Iowa, who felt they had demonstrated their anti-Germanism sufficiently. Notes.

2898 Peterson, H. C., and Fite, Gilbert C. *Opponents of War, 1917–1918*. Seattle: University of Washington Press, 1957.

The authors examine the conflict between prowar elements and antiwar groups such as anarchists, the IWW, and socialists. The persecution of aliens, blacks, movie producers, teachers, publishers, and conscientious objectors is also covered. Illustrations, notes, bibliography, index.

2899 Piper, John F., Jr. *The American Churches in World War I*. Athens: Ohio University Press, 1985.

Church leaders accepted the war as a necessity and provided religious comfort to civilians and soldiers alike. While churches sometimes acquiesced in government repression, they also fought to protect their ministry. Notes, bibliography, index.

2900 Raff, Willis H. "Coercion and Freedom in a War Situation: A Critical Analysis of Minnesota Culture during World War One." Ph.D. dissertation, University of Minnesota, 1957.

In Minnesota, the drive for unanimity of opinion and effort in support of the war overwhelmed respect for individual freedoms. The Commission of Public Safety, representing both Democrats and Republicans and headed by Judge John McGee, threw professors, teachers, officials, and lawyers suspected of antiwar sentiments out of their jobs. Mob action against dissenters, even against those who merely failed to buy enough war bonds, was condoned. DAI 19:2593.

2901 Reader, Benjamin G. "The Montana Lumber Strike of 1917." *Pacific Historical Review* 36 (1967): 189–207.

Federal, state, and local authorities, vigilantes, and hostile newspaper editorials all helped to destroy the Industrial Workers of the World in Montana during World War I. Notes.

2902 Shapiro, Herbert. "The Herbert Bigelow Case: A Test of Free Speech in Wartime." *Ohio History* 81 (1972): 108–21.

This Progressive Cincinnati minister was investigated by the government and then whipped by a mob for his opposition to the war. The government made little effort to investigate the incident, feeling that unpopular speech did not merit protection. Notes.

2903 Shields, Sarah D. "The Treatment of Conscientious Objectors during World War I: Mennonites at Camp Funston." *Kansas History* 4 (1981): 255–69.

Mennonites were suspected of disloyalty because they spoke German and some supported Germany during the period of American neutrality. Once America went to war many Mennonites declared themselves conscientious objectors, a stance the government accommodated reluctantly and with extreme suspicion. Notes.

2904 Sprague, Lloyd D. "The Suppression of Dissent during the Civil War and World War I." Ph.D. dissertation, Syracuse University, 1959.

In contrast to the suppression of dissent during the Civil War, laws were passed and procedures followed to suppress opposition to World War I, making the process more palatable to the American public. DAI 20:3359.

2905 Stevens, John D. "Suppression of Expression in Wisconsin during World War I." Ph.D. dissertation, University of Wisconsin, 1967.

Ninety people, many of German ancestry, were tried in Wisconsin under federal laws, and another eighty-one were indicted under either the state sedition law or local laws against disorderly conduct. Newspapers further reported hundreds of acts against suspected dissenters, including tarring, yellow painting, and forced flag kissing. There was a strong correlation between a newspaper's editorial attitude toward civil liberties and the attitudes of its readership. DAI 28:5003-A.

2906 Stucky, Gregory J. "Fighting against War: The Mennonite *Vorwaerts* from 1914–1919." *Kansas Historical Quarterly* 38 (1972): 169–86.

The Mennonite *Vorwaerts* of Hillsboro, Kansas, edited by Abraham Schellenberg, switched from a Progressive, pro-German stance during the period of American neutrality to support for Mennonite pacifism after April 1917. The paper was censored by the government for its outspoken opinions. Notes.

2907 Swisher, Carl B. "Civil Liberties in Wartime." *Political Science Quarterly* 55 (1940): 321–47.

Laws passed during the war were designed originally to protect civil liberties rather than to give the government the power to crush legitimate dissent. Notes.

2908 Taft, Philip. "The Bisbee Deportation." *Labor History* 13 (1972): 3–40.

The rights of striking copper miners and sympathizers in Bisbee, Arizona, were violated when they were deported to New Mexico. Those responsible for the deportations were acquitted quickly by a state court. Notes.

2909 Teichroew, Allan, ed. "Military Surveillance of Mennonites in World War I." *Mennonite Quarterly Review* 53 (1979): 95–127.

A report by army intelligence on the pacifist Mennonites is presented as evidence of government spying on civilians during World War I.

2910 Tischauser, Leslie V. "The Burden of Ethnicity: The German Question in Chicago, 1914–1941." Ph.D. dissertation, University of Illinois, Chicago Circle, 1981.

There were no compelling issues to unite Chicago's German Americans, so, for the most part, they merged with the larger community. However, during World War I, identifiably German people were arrested and their institutions banned. After the war, a hard core of German Americans revived a semblance of ethnic identity, but they never attracted many followers. DAI 42:3277-A.

2911 Tolzmann, Don H. "The Survival of an Ethnic Community: The Cincinnati Germans, 1918 through 1932." Ph.D. dissertation, University of Cincinnati, 1983.

Anti-German sentiment engendered by World War I disrupted but did not destroy German cultural life in Cincinnati, where Germans constituted over one third of the population. DAI 44:2557-A.

2912 Vacha, J. E. "When Wagner Was Verboten: The Campaign against German Music in World War I." *New York History* 64 (1983): 171–88.

The New York Metropolitan Opera Company purged its program of German works and fired German and Austrian alien singers. Karl Muck, director of the Boston Symphony, was jailed and his wife deported. German operas were not heard again until the 1920s. Notes.

2913 Ventresco, Fiorello B. "Loyalty and Dissent: Italian Reservists in America during World War I." *Italian Americana* 4 (1978): 93–122.

Italian-American reservists suffered a crisis of loyalty when they were sent to Italy, where the Italian government wanted them to fight in its own military service.

2914 Wagner-Seavey, Sandra E. "The Effects of World War I on the German Community in Hawaii." *Hawaiian Journal of History* 14 (1980): 109–40.

By late 1917 an atmosphere of increasing hysteria put the tightly knit German community of Hawaii under extreme pressure to prove its American patriotism. A year later, little was left of this ethnic group in the islands. Notes.

2915 Weinstein, James. "The Anti-War Sentiment and the Socialist Party, 1917–1918." *Political Science Quarterly* 74 (1959): 215–39.

The Socialist party gained popularity during the war, because many people agreed with the party's militant opposition to American participation in the conflict. Notes.

2916 Willis, James F. "The Cleburne County Draft War." *Arkansas Historical Quarterly* 26 (1967): 24–39.

In mid-1918, Russellites (Jehovah's Witnesses) violently resisted the military draft in Cleburne County. Machine gun-toting National Guardsmen failed to capture the resisters, who eventually surrendered.

2917 Wrede, Steven. "The Americanization of Scott County." *Annals of Iowa* 44 (1979): 627–38.

A series of hearings and investigations by a local Council of National Defense pressured German Americans to become Americanized in Scott County, Iowa.

2918 Zellick, Anna. "Patriots on the Rampage: Mob Action in Lewistown, 1917–1918." *Montana* 31 (1981): 30–43.

Fear of German Americans, the Nonpartisan League, and the IWW led to arson, demonstrations, and the public burning of German books. Notes.

2919 Zimmerman, Norman A. "A Triumph for Orthodoxy: The University of Wisconsin during World War I." Ph.D. dissertation, University of Minnesota, 1971.

Before World War I, the University of Wisconsin had become the greatest public institution of higher learning in the country. An atmosphere of hysteria gripped the campus during the war, and conformity and orthodoxy were the rules of the day. DAI 32:3237-A.

2920 Zubok, L. I. "The Workers and Socialist Movement in the United States during the First World War" (in Russian). *Voprosy Istorii* [USSR] 7 (1955): 61–74.

The government and right-wing labor unions joined forces first to condemn and then to repress worker organizations that opposed the world war.

Government

2921 Bassett, Michael. "The American Socialist Party and the War, 1917–18." *Australian Journal of Politics and History* 11 (1965): 277–91.

The federal government was largely responsible for the breakup of the Socialist party in 1919, a process that began when the organization opposed World War I. Support for the Fourteen Points did not save the party.

2922 Cary, Lorin L. "The Bureau of Investigation and Radicalism in Toledo, Ohio: 1918–1920." *Labor History* 21 (1980): 430–40.

Reports from Bureau of Investigation agents in Toledo, Ohio, on the antiwar activities of the IWW and other radical groups are presented to illustrate the usefulness of the BI's files as a source for historians. Notes.

2923 Foner, Philip S. "United States of America vs. Wm. D. Haywood, et al.: The I.W.W. Indictment." *Labor History* 11 (1970): 500–530.

Bill Haywood's indictment by a Chicago grand jury in 1917 is reprinted, a vague document which fails to cite specific overt acts committed by Haywood and the IWW. Notes.

2924 Johnson, Donald O. "Wilson, Burleson and Censorship in the First World War." *Journal of Southern History* 28 (1962): 46–58.

The Espionage Act of 1917 gave Postmaster General Albert S. Burleson extraordinary powers of censorship which he used against government critics during and after World War I. Notes.

2925 Koppes, Clayton R. "The Kansas Trial of the I.W.W." *Labor History* 16 (1975): 338–58.

The IWW believed that the Kansas indictments were as crucial to their survival as the more publicized Chicago trials. Financial problems, the lack of a political defense, and an atmosphere of hatred all contributed to the union's downfall. Notes.

2926 Longaker, Richard P. *The Presidency and Individual Liberties*. Ithaca, NY: Cornell University Press, 1961.

Wilson's record on civil liberties is not a good one, because he bears the onus for the massive violation of rights during World War I and during the Red Scare. The president was too preoccupied by fighting to make the world safe for democracy to see what his policies were doing to democracy at home. Notes, index.

2927 Moore, William H. "Prisoners in the Promised Land: The Molokans in World War I." *Journal of Arizona History* 14 (1973): 281–302.

A minority Russian religious group, the Molokans moved to Phoenix to get away from the Great War. When they refused to register for the draft, the government arrested them as an example to other slackers. Notes.

2928 Scheiber, Harry N. *The Wilson Administration and Civil Liberties, 1917–1921*. Ithaca, NY: Cornell University Press, 1960.

This extended essay examines Wilson's increasing intolerance for dissent against his policies and increasing willingness to sanction the violation of civil liberties in the name of a higher cause.

2929 Selig, Michael. "United States v. Motion Picture Film *The Spirit of '76*: The Espionage Case of Producer Robert Goldstein." *Journal of Popular Film and Television* 10 (1983): 168–74.

Goldstein was convicted under the Espionage Act for producing a film on the American Revolution that showed the British in a bad light.

2930 Taft, Philip. "The Federal Trials of the IWW." *Labor History* 3 (1962): 57–91.

Mass trials of the IWW were held during the war in Chicago, Sacramento, and Wichita on charges of resisting the draft and sabotage. After the war Wilson refused to consider the Wobblies' release from prison, although Presidents Harding and then Coolidge let them out without pardons. Notes.

2931 Turner, Arthur W. "The Mayor, the Governor, and the People's Council: A Chapter in American Wartime Dissent." *Journal of the Illinois State Historical Society* 66 (1973): 124–43.

The People's Council, a pacifist organization founded by Louis Lochner, held a national meeting in Chicago in 1917, touching off a power struggle between Mayor Big Bill Thompson, who supported the group's right to convene, and Governor Frank Lowden, who wanted the delegates to be locked out. Notes.

2932 Wagaman, David G. "*Rausch Mit*: The I.W.W. in Nebraska during World War I." In Joseph R. Conlin, ed. *At the Point of Production: The Local History of the I.W.W.* Westport, CT: Greenwood, 1981, pp. 115–42.

Because farming dominated the Nebraska economy, organization was especially difficult there for the IWW. Government raids on the Wobbly offices in Omaha disrupted their activities. By 1920, the government and powerful economic interests had destroyed the organization. Notes.

2933 White, Earl B. "*The United States v. C. W. Anderson et al.*: The Wichita Case, 1917–1919." In Joseph R. Conlin, ed. *At the Point of Production: The Local History of the I.W.W.* Westport, CT: Greenwood, 1981, pp. 143–64.

Prewar centralization made the IWW a more disciplined and effective organization, but wartime hysteria ruined it. Several locals were raided in 1917 including the Wichita, Kansas,

hall where affiliated unions of farm and oil field workers also had offices. Notes.

2934 ———. "The Wichita Indictments and Trial of the Industrial Workers of the World, 1917–1919 and the Aftermath." Ph.D. dissertation, University of Colorado, Boulder, 1980.

Between 1917 and 1919 the federal government coordinated indictments of members of the IWW and affiliated groups in Texas, Oklahoma, Chicago, Sacramento, Omaha, and Wichita, charging them with violations of the Espionage and Selective Service acts. The Wichita defendants spent two years in jail before the trial that found twenty-eight of them guilty. Recently declassified Justice Department documents reveal that the government used the Wichita indictments to break an important oil field union. DAI 41:3697-A.

Superpatriots and Vigilantes

2935 Blum, John M. "Nativism, Anti-Radicalism, and the Foreign Scare, 1917–1920." *Midwest Journal* 3 (1950): 46–53.

Nativism and antiradicalism are inherent parts of the American character that surface to battle perceived threats to traditional institutions.

2936 Breen, William J. "The North Carolina Council of Defense during World War I, 1917–1918." *North Carolina Historical Review* 50 (1973): 1–31.

This statewide patriotic group traded support for government war policies in return for an upholding of the status quo.

2937 Cary, Lorin L. "The Wisconsin Loyalty Legion, 1917–1918." *Wisconsin Magazine of History* 53 (1969): 33–50.

The Loyalty Legion grew out of the wave of superpatriotism that swept across the United States in 1917, painting the issue of loyalty strictly in black-and-white terms.

2938 Edwards, John C. "Princeton's Passionate Patriot: McElroy's Committee on Patriotism through Education." *New Jersey History* 95 (1977): 207–26.

Director of the National Security League's Committee on Patriotism through Education, Robert McElroy organized a speakers program to rouse Americans to the task of winning the war. The committee waged war on minority groups with unpopular ideas. Notes.

2939 Jensen, Joan M. *The Price of Vigilance.* Chicago: Rand McNally, 1968.

The American Protective League was a voluntary patriotic group that attained quasi-legal status during the war. Since there were few German spies, the AFL turned its attention to antiwar dissidents, using autocratic methods to safeguard democracy. Photographs, bibliography, appendix, index.

2940 Lovin, Hugh T. "World War Vigilantes in Idaho, 1917–1918." *Idaho Yesterdays* 18 (1974): 2–11.

During the war, Idaho was the scene of vigorous vigilante action against Americans and aliens of German and Austrian extraction.

2941 Rippley, La Vern J. "Conflict in the Classroom: Anti-Germanism in Minnesota Schools, 1917–1919." *Minnesota History* 47 (1981): 170–83.

The Minnesota Commission of Public Safety became a patriotic watchdog in a state in which one fourth of the people were ethnically German. Textbooks were scrutinized for pro-German references, and the speaking of German in schools was strongly discouraged. Notes.

2942 Schwantes, Carlos A. "Making the World Unsafe for Democracy: Vigilantes, Grangers and the Walla Walla 'Outrage' of June, 1918." *Montana* 31 (1981): 18–29.

Walla Walla, Washington, vigilantes chased members of the Grange out of town in June 1918. This farm organization was suspected of supporting the Nonpartisan League and the IWW. Notes.

2943 Ward, Robert D. "The Origins and Activities of the National Security League, 1914–1919." *Mississippi Valley Historical Review* 47 (1960): 51–65.

Before the war, the league worked for preparedness, and especially for universal military training. Once America became involved in the war, the organization snooped into the private lives of teachers and propagandized against labor unions and socialists. Notes.

POLITICS

See also Chapter 3, *Congressional and Political Leaders,* under various personalities, and Chapter 7, *Elections.*

2944 Adler, Selig. "The Congressional Election of 1918." *South Atlantic Quarterly* 36 (1937): 447–65.

The public voted decisively against Wilson's leadership in 1918, indicating its desire to return to isolationism rather than to follow the president into the uncharted waters of the new diplomacy. Notes.

2945 Burner, David. *The Politics of Provincialism: The Democratic Party in Transition, 1918–1932.* New York: Norton, 1967.

The Democratic party is seen as the arena of confrontation between rural interests and nativists on the one hand and urban interests and immigrants on the other. Chapter 2 discusses the rise and fall of the Wilson coalition, which collapsed as a result of a reversal of political feelings as the war wound down. Notes, bibliography, index.

2946 Chern, Kenneth S. "The Politics of Patriotism: War, Ethnicity, and the New York Mayoral Campaign, 1917." *New York Historical Society Quarterly* 63 (1979): 290–313.

The 1917 New York mayoral election campaign was a bitter struggle won by a Tammany-supported conservative, John F. Hylan, who won because the incumbent had alienated many Irish and German Americans through patriotic appeals. Notes.

2947 Cuddy, Joseph E. *Irish-America and National Isolationism: 1914–1920.* New York: Arno, 1976.

Irish Americans turned against Wilson on the war issue, allying themselves with German Americans in opposition to the peace treaty and the League of Nations, splintering the Democratic coalition in the process.

2948 Cuff, Robert D. "The Politics of Labor Administration during World War I." *Labor History* 21 (1980): 546–69.

While the Department of Labor successfully resisted attempts by wartime agencies to usurp its powers, actual administrative control remained elusive. Notes.

2949 Hirschfeld, Charles. "National Progressivism and World War I." *Mid-America* 45 (1963): 139–56.

Nationalist Progressives saw the war as an opportunity to implement further reform. Wilson's war measures were regarded as furthering their agenda. Notes.

2950 Horner, Richard K. "The House at War: The House of Representatives during World War I, 1917–1919." Ph.D. dissertation, Louisiana State University, 1977.

The bipartisan coalition that supported American entry into the war faded away quickly. The influence of Progressivism was not great with the Republicans. Although they were more supportive of it than were the Democrats, concerns for region and party often played the dominant role in roll calls. DAI 38:2996-A.

2951 Livermore, Seward W. *Politics Is Adjourned: Wilson and the War Congress, 1916–1918.* Middletown, CT: Wesleyan University Press, 1966.

Wilson lost control over Congress in 1918 as a result of Democratic ineptitude and Republican shrewdness. The chairman of the Republican National Committee, Will Hays, brought the party back together under difficult circumstances and manipulated public opinion against Wilson masterfully. Notes, bibliography, index.

2952 ———. "The Section Issue in the 1918 Congressional Elections." *Mississippi Valley Historical Review* 35 (1948): 29–60.

Farm issues, rather than foreign policy, played a key role in the 1918 elections, when cotton and wheat farmers voted against Democrats as a protest against administration food policies. Notes.

2953 Lowitt, Richard. "Senator Norris and His 1918 Campaign." *Pacific Northwest Quarterly* 57 (1966): 113–19.

That Norris's opposition to American intervention did not stop his reelection in 1918 was due largely to his influential friends and to disarray among Nebraska Democrats.

2954 McGeary, M. Nelson. "Gifford Pinchot's Years of Frustration: 1917–1920." *Pennsylvania Magazine of History and Biography* 83 (1959): 327–42.

Teddy Roosevelt's former "fair-haired boy" found himself far from the center of political power during the war, working in the U.S. Food Administration.

2955 Newby, I. A. "States' Rights and Southern Congressmen during World War I." *Phylon* 24 (1963): 34–50.

By supporting the war effort in Washington, southern congressmen undermined states' rights even to the point of endorsing the suspension of Senate filibustering, a time-honored device for fostering white supremacy.

2956 Robertson, James O. "Progressives Elect Will H. Hays Republican National Chairman, 1918." *Indiana Magazine of History* 64 (1968): 173–90.

Hays's election to the chairmanship of the GOP came about as a result of an elaborate compromise that brought Progressives back into the party. His leadership helped Warren Harding to capture the White House in 1920. Notes.

2957 Seabrook, John H. "Bishop Manning and World War I." *History Magazine of the Protestant Episcopal Church* 36 (1967): 301–21.

Rector in Trinity Parish, New York City, Bishop Manning argued for preparedness and against pacifism. He supported the war, because he believed it would further American ideals. Notes.

2958 Shapiro, Stanley. "The Great War and Reform: Liberals and Labor, 1917–1919." *Labor History* 12 (1971): 323–44.

The great liberal reform campaign did not end with the war, as is commonly claimed, but came to a halt as a result of the bitter struggle over the Wilsonian peace program. Notes.

2959 Watson, Richard L., Jr. "A Testing Time for Southern Congressional Leadership: The War Crisis of 1917–1918." *Journal of Southern History* 44 (1978): 3–40.

Southern congressmen helped to mobilize the country for war, putting aside regional priorities for the sake of a larger cause. Notes.

2960 Wells, Merle W. "Fred T. Dubois and the Nonpartisan League in the Idaho Election of 1918." *Pacific Northwest Quarterly* 56 (1965): 17–29.

The conservative Dubois tried to use the left-wing Nonpartisan League to political advantage, but Senator William E. Borah proved to be even more astute at this political game.

2961 Williams, Michael. *American Catholics in the War: National Catholic War Council, 1917–1921.* New York: Macmillan, 1921.

The work of the National Catholic War Council is detailed, along with the work of such subcommittees as the Committee on Special War Activities and the Knights of Columbus Committee on War Activities.

2962 Wood, Barry R. "Holy Joe Folk's Last Crusade: The 1918 Election in Missouri." *Missouri Historical Review* 71 (1977): 284–314.

The Democratic party's divisions in Missouri over prohibition, war issues, and the actions of the Wilson administration led to Republican victories in the 1918 elections. Notes.

STATE AND LOCAL STUDIES

2963 Bigham, Darrel E. "Charles Leich and Company of Evansville: A Note on the Dilemma of German Americans during World War I." *Indiana Magazine of History* 70 (1974): 95–121.

Leich, an elderly citizen of Evansville of German birth, was stranded in Germany when war was declared in 1917. His sons fought a long battle to protect his property, one they did not win until 1922. Notes.

2964 Chrystal, William G. "Reinhold Niebuhr and the First World War." *Journal of Presbyterian History* 55 (1977): 285–98.

As a young pastor in Detroit, Niebuhr emphasized the need for national loyalty as he struggled with a realistic approach to the war. He compromised his pacifist instincts for the sake of establishing a basis for lasting peace. Notes.

2965 Demuth, David O. "An Arkansas County Mobilizes: Saline County, Arkansas, 1917–1918." *Arkansas Historical Quarterly* 36 (1977): 211–33.

Wartime patriotism motivated the residents of Saline County to volunteer for military service, to buy bonds, and to contribute to causes in excess of preset quotas. Notes.

2966 Derr, Nancy R. "Iowans during World War I: A Study of Change under Stress." Ph.D. dissertation, George Washington University, 1979.

German Americans, persecuted in Iowa during the war, were subject to kangaroo courts and violence. Nativists attacked Catholics, foreigners, and drinkers because they represented change, while Iowa reached its war bond quotas just hours after they were announced. DAI 40:2221-A.

2967 Dubofsky, Melvyn. "Organized Labor in New York City and the First World War, 1914–1918." *New York History* 42 (1961): 380–400.

Garment workers's unions and the AFL clashed during World War I over tactics and over such issues as participation in the war, the loss of civil liberties, and the Russian Revolution. Notes.

2968 Elm, Adelaide. "The University of Arizona: The War Years." *Arizona and the West* 27 (1985): 37–54.

Isolated and far from Washington, the University of Arizona slipped into the mainstream of American education as a result of its vigorous support for the war. Notes.

2969 Fraser, Bruce. "Yankees at War: Social Mobilization on the Connecticut Homefront, 1917–1918." Ph.D. dissertation, Columbia University, 1976.

Connecticut's old-line elite used the war to reassert their beliefs and values. Control of the Connecticut Council allowed them to watch over the Committee on Public Information's propaganda, while they pushed their own agenda. DAI 37:4557-A.

2970 Furer, Howard B. " 'Heaven, Hell, or Hoboken': The Effects of World War I on a New Jersey City." *New Jersey History* 92 (1974): 147–69.

Patriotism, food and housing shortages, and industrial expansion marked Hoboken's wartime experience.

2971 Gibbs, Christopher C. "The Lead Belt Riot and World War One." *Missouri Historical Review* 71 (1977): 396–418.

A riot in July 1917 in Missouri is analyzed as a response to sudden industrial change, abuses of corporate power, and involvement in the war. Notes.

2972 ———. "Missouri Farmers and World War I: Resistance to Mobilization." *Missouri Historical Society Bulletin* 35 (1978): 17–27.

Many Missouri farmers opposed the war, because they believed that their security was not threatened. Superpatriots and the government made matters worse by demanding that the farmers step up production and invest their profits in Liberty bonds. Farmers nevertheless made gains as a result of forced modernization. Notes.

2973 ———. "Patriots and Slackers: The Impact of World War One on Missouri." Ph.D. dissertation, University of Missouri, Columbia, 1980.

Many Missourians resisted American participation in World War I, because they thought that it would promote the power and centralization of government and the wealth of corporations, modern trends that they opposed. The Missouri Council of Defense, acting for the federal government, attempted to force war measures such as conscription, the sale of war bonds, food conservation, and postponement of strikes on Missourians, but support for the war effort remained weak. DAI 42:820-A.

2974 Kennett, Lee. "The Camp Wadsworth Affair." *South Atlantic Quarterly* 74 (1975): 197–211.

Camp Wadsworth in South Carolina was the scene of wartime racial tensions, as the presence of black troops training there led to fear and resentment. Notes.

2975 Lutter, Martin H. "Oklahoma and the World War, 1914–1917." Ph.D. dissertation, University of Oklahoma, 1961.

Like much of the South and the Midwest, Oklahoma strongly resisted both preparing for and entering into World War I but supported the war effort once it was begun. Anger over German submarine attacks hastened the shift in public opinion. The Green Corn rebellion, in which poor farmers and socialists united against the war and were jailed for their efforts, embarrassed the majority of Oklahomans and softened their attitude toward war. DAI 21:3439.

2976 Makarewicz, Joseph T. "The Impact of World War I on Pennsylvania Politics with Emphasis on the Election of 1920." Ph.D. dissertation, University of Pittsburgh, 1972.

To understand the collapse of the Democratic party in the 1920 election, it is necessary to examine the 1918 election, when voters vented their frustration at the many wartime regulations infringing on their freedoms. Pennsylvania Democrats argued bitterly over prohibition as well. Urban workers and immigrants turned against the party of Wilson as a result of the Red Scare. DAI 33:6846-A.

2977 Moore, John H. "Charleston in World War I: Seeds of Change." *South Carolina Historical Magazine* 86 (1985): 39–49.

Women and blacks made small gains in status in Charleston during the war, although Jim Crow laws remained untouched. Notes.

2978 Mormino, Gary R. "Over Here: St. Louis Italo-Americans and the First World War." *Missouri Historical Society Bulletin* 30 (1973): 44–53.

The war put pressure on all immigrant groups to become fully Americanized. Italian Americans became acculturated rapidly but suffered psychological damage as well. Notes.

2979 Ring, Daniel F. "Fighting for Their Hearts and Minds: William Howard Brett, the Cleveland Public Library, and World War I." *Journal of Library History* 18 (1983): 1–20.

This director of the public library in Cleveland took it upon himself to help mobilize the city for war. Notes.

2980 Schaffer, Daniel. "War Mobilization in Muscle Shoals, Alabama, 1917–1918." *Alabama Review* 39 (1986): 110–46.

The war led to a boom in Muscle Shoals, with the large nitrate manufacturing plants fueling rapid development. Notes.

2981 Scott, Clifford H. "Assimilation in a German-American Community: The Impact of World War I." *Northwest Ohio Quarterly* 52 (1980): 153–67.

At first the war intensified German patriotism among German Americans in Fort Wayne, Indiana, but they were soon Americanized under pressure from an intolerant majority.

2982 Still, William N., Jr. "Shipbuilding in North Carolina: The World War I Experience." *American Neptune* 41 (1981): 188–207.

During the war nine new shipyards went up in North Carolina after the industry had declined for years. The achievements and problems of these companies during their brief existence are examined. Notes.

2983 Taft, Philip. "The I.W.W. in the Grain Belt." *Labor History* 1 (1960): 53–67.

The syndicalist labor union met with disaster during World War I because it advocated sabotage against the war effort and other direct actions. Notes.

2984 Watne, Joel A. "Public Opinion toward Non-Conformists and Aliens during 1917, as Shown by the Fargo *Forum*." *North Dakota History* 34 (1967): 5–29.

The *Forum* became a firm supporter of the war effort, branding the Socialist party, the IWW, and "slackers" as traitors and urging extralegal action against them. Notes.

2985 Watson, Richard L., Jr. "Principle, Party, and Constituency: The North Carolina Congressional Delegation, 1917–1919." *North Carolina Historical Review* 56 (1979): 298–323.

The powerful North Carolina congressional delegation supported Wilson most of the time in the 1917–1919 session, although they sometimes dissented to suit the feelings of their constituents or out of political opportunism. Notes.

2986 Wolkerstorfer, John C. "Nativism in Minnesota in World War I: A Comparative Study of Brown, Ramsey, and Stearns Counties, 1914–1918." Ph.D. dissertation, University of Minnesota, 1973.

Control over education was used to destroy German culture in Minnesota during World War I. The Minnesota Commission of

Public Safety also attacked the Nonpartisan League, socialists, and labor unions. DAI 34:7176-A.

WOMEN

See also Chapter 4, *Women Workers*, and Chapter 6, *Women*.

2987 Breen, William J. "Black Women and the Great War: Mobilization and Reform in the South." *Journal of Southern History* 44 (1978): 421–40.

During the period of neutrality the government paid scant attention to the potential role of women in an all-out war effort. Late in the war, Alice Dunbar Nelson of the Woman's Committee helped to organize southern black women, although little headway was gained in the area of social reform. Notes.

2988 ———. "Southern Women in the War: The North Carolina Woman's Committee, 1917–1919." *North Carolina Historical Review* 55 (1978): 251–83.

The attitudes of men, a lack of funds, a lack of interest on the part of other women, and poorly defined goals were among the problems faced by the North Carolina Woman's Committee, which sought to place women in wartime service, boost food production, continue social services, help soldiers, and enlist black women in its program. Notes.

2989 Conner, Valerie J. " 'The Mothers of the Race' in World War I: The National War Labor Board and Women in Industry." *Labor History* 21 (1980): 31–54.

The National War Labor Board implemented Progressive policies for working women in wartime, laying groundwork for the principle of equal pay for equal work. The pervasive feeling that women were supposed to be mothers limited such reform efforts. Notes.

2990 Greenwald, Maurine W. *Women, War, and Work: The Impact of World War I on Women Workers in the United States.* Westport, CT: Greenwood, 1980.

The war accelerated trends toward segregation of the sexes in the workplace, but it also brought some men and women into direct competition and strife as well. The effects of the war on women's work are explored in three case studies: railroads, streetcars, and the telephone industry. Notes, bibliography, index.

2991 ———. "Women Workers and World War I: The American Railway Industry, a Case Study." *Journal of Social History* 9 (1975): 154–77.

Most women who took jobs with American railroads during the war did not break new ground, since their assigned positions had already been designated as women's work. Notes.

2992 Malan, Nancy E. "How 'Ya Gonna Keep 'Em Down? Women and World War I." *Prologue* 5 (1973): 209–39.

Some of the many ways in which women served the war effort are pictured.

2993 Martelet, Penny. "The Woman's Land Army, World War I." In Mabel E. Deutrich and Virginia C. Purdy, eds. *Clio Was a Woman: Studies in the History of American Women.* Washington, DC: Howard University Press, 1980, pp. 136–46.

The Woman's Land Army helped to place women in agricultural jobs during the war. The program was controversial, because it involved women in what was viewed as unfeminine work. Notes.

2994 Ruckman, Jo Ann. " 'Knit, Knit, and then Knit': The Women of Pocatello and the War Effort." *Idaho Yesterdays* 26 (1982): 26–36.

While women in Pocatello, Idaho, were told repeatedly that they should contribute to the Great War, in fact there was little for them to do except knit and conserve food. Notes.

2995 Steinson, Barbara J. *American Women's Activism in World War I.* New York: Garland, 1982.

Women were very active in the peace movement following the outbreak of war in Europe. Relief and preparedness work also attracted female volunteers. Women who joined government committees were frustrated by their lack of power. Notes, bibliography, index.

2996 ———. " 'The Mother Half of Humanity': American Women in the Peace and Preparedness Movements in World War I." In Carol R. Berkin and Clara M. Lovett, eds. *Women, War and Revolution.* New York: Holmes and Meier, 1980, pp. 259–84.

The activism of women during the war made them aware of their power and created a special feeling of female solidarity. Many women were motivated by nurturing ideals that limited how far they were willing to carry their campaigns.

2997 ———. "Sisters and Soldiers: American Women and the National Service Schools, 1916–1917." *Historian* 43 (1981): 225–39.

Years of activism smoothed the way for wartime women's groups such as the National Service Schools, which provided quasi-military training and boosted the spirits of participants. Notes.

READJUSTMENT

See also Chapter 4, *Business, General,* Chapter 8, *The Red Scare,* and Chapter 10, *Armistice.*

2998 Boylan, Bernard L. "Army Reorganization 1920: The Legislative Story." *Mid-America* 49 (1967): 115–28.

The National Defense Act of 1920 provided for a reorganization of the army that remained in effect for over twenty years, creating a small professional army appropriate for an isolationist power. Notes.

2999 Burner, David. "1919: Prelude to Normalcy." In John Braeman, Robert H. Bremner, and David Brody, eds. *Change and Continuity in Twentieth-Century America: The 1920's.* Athens: Ohio State University Press, 1968, pp. 3–31.

The optimism of the war years was shattered by inflation, strikes, racial antagonism, and a bitter debate over foreign policy. The postwar mood was such that a majority craved "normalcy." Notes.

3000 Conway, Theodore J. "The Great Demobilization: Personnel Demobilization of the American Expeditionary Force and the Emergency Army, 1918–1919: A Study in Civil-Military Relations." Ph.D. dissertation, Duke University, 1986.

After World War I ended on 11 November 1918, four million servicemen entered the civilian work force within seven months. Although the discharges themselves went smoothly, there was short-term social and economic chaos. The ideas and attitudes of the secretary of war, the chief of staff and other primary actors, as revealed in correspondence and other documents, are analyzed. DAI 47:3166-A.

3001 Girard, Jolyon P. "Congress and Presidential Military Policy: The Occupation of Germany, 1919–1923." *Mid-America* 56 (1974): 211–20.

Although it was unwilling to withdraw funding for American troops abroad after the war, Congress pressured Presidents Wilson and Harding to bring the men home as soon as possible.

3002 Hanrahan, John J. "The High Cost of Living Controversy, 1919–1920." Ph.D. dissertation, Fordham University, 1969.

The controversy over the high cost of living played a key part in the collapse of the coalition that had elected Wilson to the White House in 1912 and 1916. With the president totally preoccupied with foreign affairs, the administration dissolved into factionalism as people demanded relief from high consumer prices. DAI 30:5380-A.

3003 Hogan, Michael J. "The United States and the Problem of International Economic Control: American Attitudes toward European Reconstruction, 1918–1920." *Pacific Historical Review* 44 (1975): 84–103.

Wilson balked at international economic controls after the war, fearing that the Allies were intent on keeping Germany artificially weak and that such controls might inadvertently spread communism. His administration hoped for a hybrid of state capitalism and laissez-faire, with the League of Nations acting as an international economic referee for private business. Notes.

3004 Klingaman, William K. *1919: The Year Our World Began.* New York: St. Martin's, 1987.

The year 1919 brought disaster, discontent, and disillusionment. The atmosphere of everyday life is re-created here in detail. Notes, bibliography, index.

3005 Kornweibel, Theodore, Jr. "Apathy and Dissent: Black America's Negative Responses to World War I." *South Atlantic Quarterly* 80 (1981): 322–38.

While black leaders exhorted their race to give the war their all-out support, many refused on the grounds that it was a conflict of the rich and of whites. About half of the black population supported the war, one tenth actively opposed it, and the rest did not care. Notes.

3006 Margulies, Herbert F. "The Articles of War, 1920: The History of a Forgotten Reform." *Military Affairs* 43 (1979): 85–89.

The Articles of War sought to liberalize military law and court martial proceedings. Although the articles represented an improvement over the old codes, they still had serious shortcomings. Notes.

3007 Mock, James R., and Thurber, Evangeline. *Report on Demobilization*. Norman: University of Oklahoma Press, 1944.

Written at a time when Americans were thinking ahead to the post-World War II period, the authors detail the many failures of the demobilization of 1918–1920.

3008 Noggle, Burl. *Into the Twenties: The United States from Armistice to Normalcy*. Urbana: University of Illinois Press, 1974.

The yearning for normalcy began after the Armistice, as the nation stumbled through the traumas of demobilization, reconversion, race riots, strikes, and the Red Scare. Notes, bibliography, index.

3009 Olssen, Erik N. "Dissent from Normalcy: Progressives in Congress, 1918–1925." Ph.D. dissertation, Duke University, 1970.

The Red Scare and Wilson's failed economic policies created a new breed of Progressive who was more radical than the old and supported by marginal farmers and labor unions. DAI 31:2854-A.

3010 Perrett, Geoffrey. *America in the Twenties: A History*. New York: Simon and Schuster, 1982.

The opening chapters discuss the period between the Armistice and the end of Wilson's presidency, focusing on the flu pandemic, the Wilsonian peace, postwar strikes, racial violence, and the Red Scare. Notes, bibliography, index.

3011 Pyne, John M. "Woodrow Wilson's Abdication of Domestic and Party Leadership: Autumn 1918 to Autumn 1919." Ph.D. dissertation, University of Notre Dame, 1979.

Bitter partisanship in Washington during the war intensified Republican hatred of Wilson. The Republicans succeeded in polarizing the Democrats during the 1918 elections and swept to victory. Wilson's prolonged trips to France caused a political vacuum to form as the president virtually abdicated party leadership, with disastrous results for the Democrats. DAI 40:1652-A.

3012 Smythe, Donald. "Pershing after the Armistice, 1918–1919." *Missouri Historical Review* 79 (1984): 43–64.

General John Pershing remained in Europe after the Armistice, demanding that the doughboys remain fit through continued military training, although he eventually gave his men

time for recreation. The general quarreled with the French marshal Ferdinand Foch and the American colonel George Marshall, only to later develop friendships with both. Notes.

3013 Young, Arthur P. "Aftermath of a Crusade: World War I and the Enlarged Program of the American Library Association." *Library Quarterly* 50 (1980): 191–207.

The Library War Service of the American Library Association provided reading material for millions of doughboys during the war. In 1919, the association launched an enlarged program to revolutionize library services, an ambitious project that flopped in the aftermath of war.

The Military Dimension

GENERAL ACCOUNTS

3014 Baldwin, Fred D. "The Invisible Armor." *American Quarterly* 16 (1964): 432–44.

Government repression, the activities of private agencies, and the oversensitivity of the doughboys themselves kept most of them chaste during their tours of duty in Europe.

3015 Bane, Suda L., and Lutz, Ralph. *The Blockade of Germany after the Armistice, 1918–1919*. Stanford: Stanford University Press, 1942.

This collection of documents contains material on the food blockade, its expansion to the Baltic, and American efforts to modify it. Appendixes, index.

3016 Barbeau, Arthur E., and Henri, Florette. *The Unknown Soldiers: Black American Troops in World War I*. Philadelphia: Temple University Press, 1974.

Blacks made a major contribution to the war effort in the hope that this would awaken America to their plight. Notes, bibliography, index.

3017 Beardsley, Edward H. "Allied against Sin: American and British Responses to Venereal Disease in World War I." *Medical History* [Great Britain] 20 (1976): 189–202.

The Americans had more success than the British did in controlling venereal disease in their armed forces. The United States built clinics, issued prophylactics, and limited the opportunities to visit brothels.

3018 Chambers, John W., II. "Conscripting for Colossus: The Progressive Era and the Origin of the Modern Military Draft in the United States in World War I." In Peter Karsten, ed. *The Military in America: From the Colonial Era to the Present*. New York: Free Press, 1980, pp. 275–96.

The needs of the war and social values resulting from industrialization both shaped the system of military conscription developed in the period 1915–1917.

3019 Chase, Hal S. "Struggle for Equality: Fort Des Moines Training Camp for Colored Officers, 1917." *Phylon* 39 (1978): 297–310.

Some 1,250 black officers were trained at the Fort Des Moines facility during the four months that the program operated in 1917.

3020 Coffman, Edward M. "The American Military and Strategic Policy in World War I." In Barry Hunat and Adrian Preston, eds. *War Aims and Strategic Policy in the Great War, 1914–1918*. London: Croom Helm, 1977, pp. 67–84.

Wilson held the American military in limbo until April 1917 and then delegated most military powers to General John Pershing, who cooperated with the Allies only on his own terms. Notes.

3021 ———. *The War to End All Wars: The American Military Experience in World War I*. New York: Oxford University Press, 1968.

An excellent overview of the American war effort is presented including strategy, mobilization, logistics, and administration. Notes, bibliography, index.

3022 Cornebise, Alfred E. *The "Stars and Stripes": Doughboy Journalism in World War I*. Westport, CT: Greenwood, 1984.

The *Stars and Stripes* reflected the early excitement and fear of doughboys as well as the propaganda of the war effort. The paper praised ethnic and racial groups for their wartime contributions. Photographs, notes, bibliography, index.

3023 Crozier, Emmet. *American Reporters on the Western Front, 1914–1918*. New York: Oxford University Press, 1959.

American coverage of the war was limited by military censorship and lack of mobility.

3024 Dawes, Charles G. *A Journal of the Great War*. 2 vols. Boston: Houghton Mifflin, 1921.

The American Expeditionary Force's (AEF) general purchasing agent details how the Allies were provisioned and the many problems he encountered in supplying a multinational force.

3025 DeWeerd, Harvey A. *President Wilson Fights His War: World War I and American Intervention*. New York: Macmillan, 1968.

In this history of the American military contribution to the war, the author finds that the United States provided leadership, influence, and high morale to the flagging Allied cause. Wilson's unwillingness to envision participation in the crusade before late 1916 limited American achievements as did excessively high military goals. Notes, appendixes, bibliography, index.

3026 Goedeken, Edward A. "Charles G. Dawes in War and Peace, 1917–1922." Ph.D. dissertation, University of Kansas, 1984.

Charles Dawes (1865–1951) was a banker until World War I, when, in his fifties, his activities managing military purchases and supplies launched his new career in public service. A Republican, he was primarily active in finance-related work, but he also served as vice president and as ambassador to Great Britain. DAI 46:1069-A.

3027 Grenville, J. A. S. "Diplomacy and War Plans in the United States, 1890–1917." *Transactions of Royal Historical Society* [Great Britain] 8 (1961): 1–21.

In this survey of the interaction of American war planning, strategic planning, and diplomacy, the author discusses the defensive nature of prewar naval planning. A plan for military intervention in Europe was not drawn up until February 1917.

3028 Hankey, Maurice P. *The Supreme Command, 1914–1918*. 2 vols. London: Allen and Unwin, 1961.

A British diplomat who worked with the Supreme Command details its history and includes much material on the American latecomers.

3029 Jeffreys-Jones, Rhodri. *American Espionage: From Secret Service to CIA*. New York: Free Press, 1977.

This survey of American intelligence policy to 1947 includes material on Frank Polk's work to coordinate espionage through the Department of State during World War I. Notes, bibliography, index.

3030 Kemeny, Jim. "Professional Ideologies and Organizational Structures: Tanks and the Military." *Journal of Sociology* [Great Britain] 24 (1983): 223–40.

The tank had a significant impact on professional soldiers. Searching for the most effective way to use the weapon, the British and the Americans deployed tanks together with foot soldiers and cavalry, while the Germans put them into speedy panzer groups.

3031 Kevles, Daniel J. "Testing the Army's Intelligence: Psychologists and the Military in World War I." *Journal of American History* 55 (1968): 565–81.

Psychologist Robert M. Yerkes worked with the surgeon general to develop and implement an intelligence testing program for the army, testing 1.75 million men. Cultural bias and prejudice against those scoring low on the tests were among the project's problems. Resentful of outside interference, the army scrapped the program after the war. Notes.

3032 McKenna, Charles D. "The Forgotten Reform: Field Maneuvers in the Development of the United States Army." Ph.D. dissertation, Duke University, 1981.

An overlooked contribution of Elihu Root to army reform was the use of field maneuvers in training. The tremendous benefits in development of confidence and refinement of tactics made field maneuvers indispensable to army training by 1920. DAI 42:2821-A.

3033 Miller, Kelly. *Kelly Miller's History of the World War for Human Rights*. New York: Negro Universities Press, 1969.

This reprint of a work published in 1919 details the role of black soldiers in World War I. The author ends with an open letter to Wilson, pleading for social justice.

3034 Ohl, John K. "Hugh S. Johnson and the Draft, 1917–18." *Prologue* 8 (1976): 85–96.

Hugh Johnson did excellent work for General Enoch H. Crowder in organizing and then carrying out the draft, but he had to be supervised with care, because he did not get along well with other people.

3035 Parsons, Edward B. "Why the British Reduced the Flow of American Troops to Europe in August-October 1918." *Canadian Journal of History* 12 (1977): 173–91.

Confident that the war would soon be won, the British used their control over troop movements to reduce American economic and diplomatic power and enhance their own. Notes.

3036 Revoldt, Daryl L. "Raymond B. Fosdick: Reform, Internationalism, and the Rockefeller Foundation." Ph.D. dissertation, University of Akron, 1982.

This Progressive was named chairman of the Commission on Training Camp Activities in 1917 and charged with providing wholesome recreation to the armed forces. After supervising efforts to boost American morale in France, Fosdick became under secretary-general of the League of Nations, then resigned following the Senate's defeat of the Treaty of Versailles. DAI 42:3275-A.

3037 Shillinglaw, David L. *An American in the Army and YMCA, 1917–1920: The Diary of David Lee Shillinglaw*. Edited by Glen E. Holt. Chicago: University of Chicago Press, 1971.

Shillinglaw ran the construction department of the YMCA in wartime France, where he was forced to deal with what he regarded as old-world corruption. Photographs, notes, index.

3038 Speedy, John C., III. "From Mules to Motors: Development of Maintenance Doctrine for Motor Vehicles by the U.S. Army, 1896–1918." Ph.D. dissertation, Duke University, 1977.

The army struggled with the development of maintenance procedures for its motorized vehicles, but the Mexican punitive expedition of 1916 provided a testing ground on a small scale. Perennial shortages of spare parts plagued the AEF during World War I. DAI 38:5012-A.

3039 Tidwell, Cromwell. "Luke Lea and the American Legion." *Tennessee Historical Quarterly* 28 (1969): 70–83.

Luke Lea played a prominent role in the founding of the American Legion in 1919, helping to draft the organization's charter and shaping the nativist and red-baiting nature of the group. Notes.

3040 Trask, David F. *The United States in the Supreme War Council: American War Aims and Inter-Allied Strategy, 1917–1918*. Middletown, CT: Wesleyan University Press, 1961.

Wilson's vision of the postwar peace played a vital role in American war aims, tactics, and diplomacy with the Allies. Notes, bibliography, index.

3041 Vincent, C. Paul. *The Politics of Hunger: The Allied Blockade of Germany, 1915–1919*. Athens: Ohio State University Press, 1985.

Hunger, deformity, and death on a mass scale resulted from the Allied blockade of Germany, which continued after the war had ended as a political weapon against Germany. Bibliography, index.

3042 Watson, Griff. "A Profile of the Tennessee Serviceman of World War I." Ph.D. dissertation, Middle Tennessee State University, 1985.

Tennessee servicemen tended to be less educated and poorer than those from other states, because many were farmers and blacks. DAI 46:3845-A.

3043 White, Bruce. "The American Military and the Melting Pot in World War I." In Peter Karsten, ed. *The Military in America: From the Colonial Era to the Present.* New York: Free Press, 1980, pp. 301–12.

While it was argued that wartime military service would Americanize ethnic groups, segregated ethnic and racial battalions were the rule.

3044 Wilson, John B. "Army Readiness Planning, 1899–1917." *Military Review* 64 (1984): 60–73.

Between the end of the Spanish-American War and American entry into World War I, American battle plans were developed on the assumption that war would be fought in the United States. The structure of the infantry division had to be redesigned for the trench warfare of Europe. Notes.

AIR SERVICE

See Chapter 3, *Eddie Rickenbacker.*

3045 Finney, Robert T. "Early Air Corps Training and Tactics." *Military Affairs* 20 (1956): 154–61.

It was not until World War I that tactics were developed for using air power. A field officers' training school came into existence in 1920 at Langley Field, Virginia.

3046 Frank, Sam H. "American Air Service Observation in World War I." Ph.D. dissertation, University of Florida, 1961.

The American Air Service encountered numerous difficulties, both in producing aircraft and in training personnel. The author contends that both offensive and defensive air maneuvers

sprang from the use of aircraft for close observation of the enemy. DAI 22:4335.

3047 Greer, Thomas H. "Air Arm Doctrinal Roots, 1917–1918." *Military Affairs* 20 (1956): 202–16.

Airmen had to fight hard to break away from the Army Signal Corps during World War I. Controversy also developed over the proper tactical use of planes, until the victories of massed Allied squadrons settled the matter, at least for a time.

3048 Maurer, Maurer, ed. *The U.S. Air Service in World War I.* 4 vols. Washington, DC: Government Printing Office, 1978–79.

Included are the final report written in 1921 on the Air Service's activities, early concepts of military aviation, the battle of St. Mihiel, and lessons learned. Photographs, notes, index.

3049 Yoshino, Ronald W. "A Doctrine Destroyed: The American Fighter Offensive, 1917–1939." Ph.D. dissertation, Claremont Graduate School, 1985.

During World War I, America developed a successful offensive air strategy, flying and attacking far behind enemy lines. However, the defensive fighters were more visible and familiar during the war and came to dominate air tactic doctrine after the war, simply because the leader of the defensive team was active in air force education. By World War II the strategy of an aggressive air offense had been lost, weakening American effectiveness. DAI 46:3141-A.

ARMY

3050 Ball, Harry P. "A History of the U.S. Army War College: 1901–1940." Ph.D. dissertation, University of Virginia, 1983.

Before World War I, the Army War College struggled to become an effective agency for contingency planning, tactical development, and education. It ceased to exist during the war, for which it was unprepared, but became a successful officer education institution afterwards. DAI 45:2231-A.

3051 Barbeau, Arthur E. "The Black American Soldier in World War I." Ph.D. dissertation, University of Pittsburgh, 1970.

Serving under taxing circumstances, black soldiers acquitted themselves well during the war. DAI 31:2829-A.

3052 Blackburn, Forrest R. "The AEF under Foreign Flags." *Military Review* 48 (1968): 56–65.

As the American Expeditionary Force began to arrive in Europe in the spring of 1918, many divisions received French/British training or went into combat under foreign command, including several black regiments.

3053 Braim, Paul F. "The Test of Battle: The American Expeditionary Forces in the Meuse-Argonne Campaign, 26 September-11 November 1918." Ph.D. dissertation, University of Delaware, 1983.

In the greatest test up to that point in American history of a United States battle group, the inexperienced AEF showed spirit and ingenuity but took extra casualties as a result of the army's many deficiencies. DAI 44:1894-A.

3054 Brophy, Leo P. "The Origins of the Chemical Corps." *Military Affairs* 20 (1956): 217–26.

The Chemical Corps was created during World War I to develop, procure, and supply smoke and gas bombs for the armed forces.

3055 Cary, Norman M., Jr. *The Use of the Motor Vehicle in the United States Army, 1899–1939*. University of Georgia, 1980.

The Mexican punitive expedition of 1916 and World War I made motorization of the army imperative. The technical problems of adapting motor vehicles to army use were not as difficult as were the political problems, such as infighting, inadequate funding, and inappropriate congressional interference.

3056 Christides, Michelle A. "Women Veterans of the Great War." *Minerva: Quarterly Report on Women and the Military* 3 (1985): 103–27.

Women who served in France as U.S. Army switchboard operators are profiled.

3057 Giffin, William W. "Mobilization of Black Militiamen in World War I: Ohio's Ninth Battalion." *Historian* 40 (1978): 686–703.

The War Department had ill-defined policies concerning the training and use of black troops during the war. Ohio's Ninth Battalion was shipped from post to post, while Washington decided what to do with them, although they performed well once they finally got into battle.

3058 Hapak, Joseph T. "Recruiting a Polish Army in the United States, 1917–1919." Ph.D. dissertation, University of Kansas, 1985.

An Allied agreement led to the raising of a Polish army in the United States. Polish immigrants and prisoners of war from France and Italy made up a fighting force of some sixty thousand men. DAI 47:631-A.

3059 Heller, Charles E. "The Perils of Unpreparedness: The American Expeditionary Forces and Chemical Warfare." *Military Review* 65 (1985): 12–25.

One out of every four American casualties during the war came from poison gas, a tragedy which could have been prevented or at least diminished if the army had kept closer watch on new chemical warfare technology. Notes.

3060 James, Felix. "Robert Russa Moton and the Whispering Gallery after World War I." *Journal of Negro History* 62 (1977): 235–42.

President Wilson dispatched Moton to France to investigate rumors that black troops had not performed up to par. His mission exonerated blacks but failed to change many minds back home. Notes.

3061 Johnson, Elliott L. "The Military Experiences of General Hugh A. Drum from 1898–1918." Ph.D. dissertation, University of Wisconsin, Madison, 1975.

Drum assisted General John Pershing in organizing the AEF. Pershing made him chief of staff of the American First Army in 1918. DAI 36:5501-A.

3062 Lawrence, Joseph D. *Fighting Soldier: The AEF in 1918*. Edited by Robert H. Ferrell. Boulder: Colorado Associated University Press, 1985.

Lawrence became a second lieutenant during the final months of the war, seeing action during the Meuse-Argonne campaign. Photographs, notes, index.

3063 Lee, David D. *Sergeant York: An American Hero*. Lexington: University Press of Kentucky, 1985.

Winner of the Medal of Honor for his bravery in killing and capturing many Germans during the Meuse-Argonne offensive, Alvin C. York was poorly educated and cared little about his status as a war hero. Notes, bibliography, index.

3064 Nenninger, Timothy K. *The Leavenworth Schools and the Old Army: Education, Professionalism, and the Officer Corps of the United States Army, 1881–1918*. Westport, CT: Greenwood, 1978.

The Leavenworth schools trained most of the officers of World War I, providing men with unimaginative training in tactics and failing to come to grips with the effects of modern weaponry. Appendixes, notes, bibliography, index.

3065 Paquier, Pierre. "The Lafayette Squadron" (in French). *Revue d'Histoire de l'Armée* [France] 13 (1957): 103–13.

This volunteer American squadron fought under the French and then, after April 1917, as the 103d Pursuit Squadron, also called the Lafayette Squadron to signify Franco-American friendship.

3066 Pastore, Nicholas. "The Army Intelligence Tests and Walter Lippmann." *Journal of the History of the Behavioral Sciences* (1978): 316–27.

After World War I, a controversy developed over a mass of data accumulated from the intelligence testing of American soldiers.

3067 Patton, Gerald W. *War and Race: The Black Officer in the American Military, 1915–1941.* Westport, CT: Greenwood, 1981.

The army accepted black officers only with great reluctance and quickly pronounced them failures. The bulk of this work covers the World War I era. Appendixes, notes, bibliography, index.

3068 Pickett, Calder M. "A Paper for the Doughboys: *Stars and Stripes* in World War I." *Journalism Quarterly* 42 (1965): 60–68.

Lieutenant Guy Visknishki guided the *Stars and Stripes* through the war as the first newspaper written by soldiers for soldiers. Several staff members later became famous journalists, including Grantland Rice.

3069 Pliska, Stanley R. "The 'Polish-American Army,' 1917–1921." *Polish Review* 10 (1965): 46–59.

Some thirty thousand Polish Americans volunteered for service in the Allied Polish Legion during World War I. The campaign to organize this unit bolstered American support for a new Polish state.

3070 Rainey, James W. "Ambivalent Warfare: The Tactical Doctrine of the AEF in World War I." *Parameters* 13 (1983): 34–46.

The U.S. Army, which had always used highly mobile tactics in wide-open spaces, had trouble adjusting to trench warfare in the Great War. General Pershing never fully accepted the situation or the new weapons of land war such as machine guns, tanks, and heavy artillery. Notes.

3071 Smythe, Donald. "A.E.F. SNAFU at Sedan." *Prologue* 5 (1973): 135–49.

A terrible blunder by the American Expeditionary Force at the Battle of Sedan is explained. With the war rapidly coming to an end, officers became desperate for glory. Notes.

3072 ———. "AEF Strategy in France, 1917–1918." *Army Quarterly and Defence Journal* [Great Britain] 115 (1985): 192–203.

Only slowly trained and shipped off to Europe, the American Expeditionary Force found that its accomplishments along the Western Front were meager compared to those of the Allies.

3073 ———. "Pershing Goes 'Over There': The *Baltic* Trip." *American Neptune* 34 (1974): 262–77.

General Pershing and a token contingent of soldiers sailed to Europe in May to June 1917 as the first members of the Allied Expeditionary Force, making war plans as the ship steamed east. Notes.

3074 ———. "The Pershing-March Conflict in World War I." *Parameters* 11 (1981): 53–62.

As U.S. Army chief of staff, Major General Peyton C. March engaged in a running struggle for power with the head of the AEF in Europe, General Pershing. The two men battled over the promotion of officers, the control of supplies, and the size of the fighting force. Notes.

3075 ———. "St. Mihiel: The Birth of an American Army." *Parameters* 13 (1983): 47–57.

The American First Army's attack on the Germans at St. Mihiel was a success in spite of the Americans' lack of experience and proved Pershing's point that American troops should fight under American commanders. Notes.

3076 ———. "Venereal Disease: The AEF's Experience." *Prologue* 9 (1977): 65–74.

American doughboys did not acquire venereal disease in the same numbers as other combatants, thanks largely to the strenuous efforts of General Pershing.

3077 Spiers, Edward M. *Chemical Warfare.* Urbana: University of Illinois Press, 1986.

The opening chapters of this general history of chemical warfare deal with the use of gas in World War I. Appendixes, notes, bibliography, index.

3078 U.S. Department of the Army. *United States Army in the World War, 1917–1919.* 17 vols. Washington, DC: Government Printing Office, 1948.

This wide and representative selection of records on the American Expeditionary Force in the war covers such topics as organization, policies, training, operations, the Armistice, occupation, and final reports.

NAVY

3079 Blackford, Charles M. *Torpedoboat Sailor*. Annapolis: United States Naval Institute, 1968.

Blackford discusses his peacetime service in the Caribbean and his life as an enlisted man during the war aboard a destroyer. Photographs.

3080 Braisted, W. R. *The United States Navy in the Pacific, 1909–1922*. Austin: University of Texas Press, 1971.

Wartime naval policy in the Pacific is examined against a backdrop of larger foreign policy considerations. During the war, naval planners learned to think in global terms. Notes, bibliography, index.

3081 Coletta, Paolo E. *Admiral Bradley A. Fiske and the American Navy*. Lawrence: Regents Press of Kansas, 1979.

Fiske fought against the conservative naval establishment to create a staff structure capable of waging modern warfare. Notes, bibliography, index.

3082 DeNovo, John A. "Petroleum and the United States Navy before World War I." *Mississippi Valley Historical Review* 41 (1955): 641–56.

By the time World War I broke out, the United States was between complacency and anxiety about future supplies and prices of oil. While Congress created national petroleum reserves, little else was done to ensure steady supplies of petroleum products during times of emergency. Notes.

3083 Harrod, Frederick S. *Manning the New Navy: The Development of a Modern Naval Enlisted Force, 1899–1940*. Westport, CT: Greenwood, 1978.

In the years before World War I the navy moved away from an international force of enlisted men recruited in coastal areas to a native American force lured from small towns across the country. Photographs, notes, bibliography, index.

3084 Maurer, John H. "American Naval Concentration and the German Battle Fleet, 1900–1918." *Journal of Strategic Studies* [Great Britain] 6 (1983): 147–81.

From the turn of the century onward, American naval experts watched the German naval buildup in the North Sea carefully, regarding it as a threat to American national security. The destruction of Germany's fleet after the war freed the U.S. Navy to pursue a two-ocean policy. Notes.

3085 Schilling, Warner R. "Admirals and Foreign Policy, 1913–1919." Ph.D. dissertation, Yale University, 1954.

Influential naval officers believed that wars resulted from commercial conflicts and that the United States was therefore vulnerable to attack by any nation with a larger navy and incompatible trade ambitions. This philosophy and a concomitant push for increased naval power were virtually unchanged by World War I. DAI 26:2306.

3086 ———. "Civil-Naval Politics in World War I." *World Politics* 7 (1955): 572–91.

Cooperation and clashes between civilian and naval agencies of the government during World War I are detailed.

3087 Shulimson, Jack. "The First to Fight: Marine Corps Expansion, 1914–1918." *Prologue* 8 (1976): 4–16.

The marines grew by sevenfold during the war, thanks in part to the effective political lobbying of Commandant George Barnett, who appeased navy brass, kept the corp's integrity, and secured prime combat assignments.

3088 Sprout, Harold, and Sprout, Margaret. *Toward a New Order of Sea Power: American Naval Policy and the World Scene, 1918–1922*. Princeton: Princeton University Press, 1940.

Changing concepts of sea power as an instrument of national policy are discussed in light of the changed post-World War I order and the League of Nations.

3089 Trask, David F. *Captains and Cabinets: Anglo-American Naval Relations, 1917–1918*. Columbia: University of Missouri Press, 1973.

The two great sea powers cooperated in the war against Germany, but they were always mindful of their national interests in the coming postwar world. Notes, bibliography, index.

3090 Yerxa, Donald A. "The United States Navy and the Caribbean Sea, 1914–1919." Ph.D. dissertation, University of Maine, 1982.

The United States created a maritime empire in the Caribbean after the Spanish-American War, crowned by construction of the Panama Canal. This study encompasses the full scope of naval activity in the region, particularly the dual roles of defending against aggression from outside the hemisphere and maintaining stability within. DAI 44:847-A.

3091 Živojinović, Dragan R. "The Americans in the Adriatic, 1918–19" (in Serbo-Croatian). *Vojnoistorijski Glasnik* [Yugoslavia] 21 (1970): 105–62.

Italy and Yugoslavia might have gone to war at the end of World War I if the U.S. Navy had not stepped in to prevent it. Problems connected with the American armed presence at Dalmatia are also covered.

The Bolshevik Revolution

AMERICAN REACTIONS

See also Chapter 8, *The Red Scare.*

3092 Bennett, Edward M. *Recognition of Russia: An American Foreign Policy Dilemma.* Waltham, MA: Blaisdell, 1970.

Chapter 1 discusses the origins of nonrecognition, first applied to Mexico and then to Russia following the Bolshevik seizure of power. Nonrecognition became a harbinger of the return to isolationism. Notes, bibliography, index.

3093 Biskupski, M. B. "The Poles, the Root Mission, and the Russian Provisional Government, 1917." *Slavonic and East European Review* [Great Britain] 63 (1985): 56–68.

The Elihu Root commission's ignorance of the tangled web of Polish independence movements proved fortuitous, as Root conveyed his belief that the Poles were unified to Wilson, and that added to the power of Ignacy Paderewski. Notes.

3094 Buchin, V. T. "Eugene Debs on the Great October Socialist Revolution" (in Russian). *Novaia i Noveishaia Istoriia* [USSR] 11 (1967): 83–90.

Debs championed the Bolshevik Revolution, urging Americans to establish friendly ties with the new government. Notes.

3095 Davis, Donald E., and Trani, Eugene P. "An American in Russia: Russell M. Story and the

Bolshevik Revolution, 1917–1919." *Historian* 36 (1974): 704–21.

Story was a YMCA representative in Russia during the Bolshevik Revolution. His perceptions of the complex events he witnessed, although imperfect, were more accurate than most. Notes.

3096 ———. "The American YMCA and the Russian Revolution." *Slavic Review* 33 (1974): 469–91.

Americans organized YMCA chapters in Russia beginning in 1900. Following the Bolshevik Revolution, YMCA personnel worked with anti-Communists in Siberia. This proved to be its undoing, although the new government probably would have cast them out anyway. Notes.

3097 Davison, Joan D. "Raymond Robins and United States Foreign Policy toward Revolutionary Russia." Ph.D. dissertation, University of Notre Dame, 1984.

American policy toward Bolshevism in Russia was dictated by wartime considerations, not by concerns about ideology, as the Wilson administration treated the Leninists the same way it had treated the czarists and the provisional government. DAI 45:918-A.

3098 Dimushev, Georgi. "The Repercussions of the October Revolution among the Workers in the USA" (in Bulgarian). *Istoricheski Pregled* [Bulgaria] 33 (1977): 92–101.

The Bolshevik Revolution led to the formation of the American Communist party and to an atmosphere of alarm engendered by the United States government.

3099 Feist, Joe M., ed. "Railways and Politics: The Russian Diary of George Gibbs, 1917." *Wisconsin Magazine of History* 62 (1979): 179–99.

This member of the advisory commission to Russia recorded his impressions of the Russian Revolution in a diary while traveling between Vladivostok and Petrograd. Notes.

3100 ———, ed. "A Wisconsin Man in the Russian Railway Service Corps: Letters of Fayette W. Keeler, 1918–1919." *Wisconsin Magazine of History* 62 (1979): 217–44.

Keeler volunteered for service on the Russian railway system in 1918. His letters reveal impressions of the Russian Revolution, the Czech Legion, Allied intervention, and Japanese activities in Siberia. Notes.

3101 Filene, Peter G. *Americans and the Soviet Experiment, 1917–1933.* Cambridge, MA: Harvard University Press, 1967.

Americans were overjoyed by the overthrow of the czar in the March 1917 Revolution but were enraged when the Bolsheviks tossed out the provisional government a few months later, pulled out of the war, and instituted communism. Notes, bibliography, index.

3102 Francis, David Rowland. *Russia from the American Embassy, April 1916–November, 1918.* New York: Scribner's, 1921.

Ambassador Francis emphasizes the connections between bolshevism and Germany to justify American anti-Communist activities during World War I.

3103 Frank, J. A. "The Gestation of American Policy toward Revolutionary Russia" (in French). *Revue de l'Université d'Ottawa* [Canada] 40 (1970): 92–116.

The mission of Elihu Root to Russia had a great impact on American attitudes and actions toward the Bolshevik Revolution. Notes.

3104 Golovanov, N. I. "On the Role of the Imperialists of the United States and the Entente during the Advance of the Russian Army in June 1917" (in Russian). *Istorii SSSR* [USSR] 4 (1960): 126–37.

American and Entente leaders were more afraid of the Bolshevik Revolution than of the Germans. They developed a strategy designed to defeat the Central Powers and the Communists, but not enough support was given to the Russian army of the provisional government.

3105 Goodman, Melvin A. "The Diplomacy of Nonrecognition: Soviet-American Relations, 1917–1933." Ph.D. dissertation, Indiana University, 1972.

The origins of Wilson's nonrecognition of Russia are discussed. While the Soviets were eager to establish diplomatic and economic relations, the U.S. government refused, hoping that nonrecognition would be a moral sanction against bolshevism. DAI 33:5086-A.

3106 Grenier, Judson A. "A Minnesota Railroad Man in the Far East, 1917–1918." *Minnesota History* 38 (1963): 310–25.

Armed with commissions from the War Department, American civilian railroad workers went to wartime Russia to work on the Trans-Siberian Railway. One member, Peter Copeland, kept a diary on which this account is based.

3107 Gronskii, A. S., and Riss, O. V. "The Baltic Ports as an Object of the Expansion of Imperialists in 1918–1920" (in Russian). *Voprosy Istorii* [USSR] (1955): 92–98.

Anglo-American ruling circles hoped to use Baltic ports as advanced naval bases from which to seize control of the Russian economy.

3108 Gvishiani, L. A. "From the Early History of Soviet-American Relations—the Robins Mission" (in Russian). *Voprosy Istorii* [USSR] (1963): 210–17.

Raymond Robins failed to establish diplomatic relations between the United States and the new Bolshevik regime in 1918. Although public opinion supported him, his mission was thwarted by American ruling circles. Notes.

3109 Hodge, Larry G. "American Diplomacy towards Transcaucasia during the Russian Revolution, March 1917-March 1918." *New Review of East-European History* [Canada] 15 (1975): 20–38.

The American consul at Tiflis (Tbilisi) kept Washington informed of events in the region including the breakdown of the Russian army, the status of the Turks, and German intrigues with the Bolsheviks. Notes.

3110 Hopkins, C. Howard, and Long, John W. "American Jews and the Root Mission to Russia in 1917: Some New Evidence." *American Jewish History* 69 (1980): 342–54.

Wilson sent the Elihu Root mission to Russia in 1917 to show his solidarity with the provisional government and to help the Russians to stay in the war. There were no Jewish representatives on the committee, although several prominent Russian Jews were interviewed for their assessment of their situation. Notes.

3111 Ingram, Alton E. "The Root Mission to Russia, 1917." Ph.D. dissertation, Louisiana State University, 1970.

Americans were overjoyed with the Russian Revolution of March 1917, because they assumed that liberal capitalism would follow. The Root mission was dispatched to Russia in mid-1917 to investigate the new regime's stability and what would be needed to keep the eastern front operational. DAI 31: 4088-A.

3112 Ioffe, A. E. "Arms Supplies of the United States, England and France to Russia at the Time of the Provisional Government (1917)" (in Russian). *Istoricheski Arkiv* [USSR] (1955): 150–80.

Arms shipments to Russia were delayed and reduced following the overthrow of the czar, despite pleas from authorities of the provisional government.

3113 ———. "Root's Mission to Russia in 1917" (in Russian). *Voprosy Istorii* [USSR] (1958): 87–100.

While the Root mission pretended to be interested only in unselfish aid to the provisional government, its hidden agenda included protection of American imperialism and expansion of capitalist interests.

3114 Jeffreys-Jones, Rhodri. "W. Somerset Maugham: Anglo-American Agent in Revolutionary Russia." *American Quarterly* 28 (1976): 90–106.

Maugham was a very shrewd observer of events for the Americans during the Russian Revolution. He had a sound grasp of how the Allies could have used military intervention more favorably for the West.

3115 Killen, Linda R. *The Russian Bureau: A Case Study in Wilsonian Diplomacy.* Lexington: University Press of Kentucky, 1983.

Refusing to recognize the competing governments of Russia following the Bolshevik Revolution, Wilson and other Americans waited for a more democratic regime to rise, hoping to nudge the process along with aid from the Russian Bureau. The wartime agency provided too little, too late to make much difference. Notes, bibliography, index.

3116 ———. "The Search for a Democratic Russia: Bakhmetev and the United States." *Diplomatic History* 2 (1978): 237–56.

The Russian provisional government's ambassador, Boris Bakhmetev, was recognized by the Wilson administration long after his government had been swept away. Notes.

3117 Lasch, Christopher. *American Liberals and the Russian Revolution.* New York: Columbia University Press, 1962.

The Bolshevik Revolution raised troubling questions for liberals who believed in the slow, orderly, and inevitable spread of democracy. Belief in progress through revolution could only be continued if they deluded themselves into believing that the Bolsheviks were nonrevolutionary and pro-German. Notes, bibliography, index.

3118 Levin, N. Gordon, Jr. *Woodrow Wilson and World Politics: America's Response to War*

and Revolution. New York: Oxford University Press, 1968.

Wilson hoped that America would establish a position of world leadership through the creation of a new order based on liberal capitalism, not imperialism or revolutionary socialism. The ideological setting of the conflict between Wilson and Lenin is examined. Notes, bibliography, index.

3119 Libbey, James K. "Alexander Gumberg and Soviet-American Relations, 1917–1933." Ph.D. dissertation, University of Kentucky, 1976.

This Russian-born American citizen went back to Russia as a businessman sympathetic to the March 1917 Revolution. He became an intermediary between the Bolsheviks and the Wilson administration, working with Progressive politicians who favored recognition and liberal publications interested in the new Russia. DAI 37:1722-A.

3120 Listikov, S. V. "The Influence of Revolutionary Events in Russia on Struggles in the US Trade-Union Movement, 1917–19" (in Russian). *Voprosy Istorii* [USSR] (1984): 48–61.

The Russian Revolution affected the struggle between moderate trade unionists of the Samuel Gompers stripe and more radical industrial unionists. Notes.

3121 Lowenfish, Lee E. "American Radicals and Soviet Russia, 1917–1940." Ph.D. dissertation, University of Wisconsin, 1968.

American radicals at first celebrated the Bolshevik Revolution, but later they came to question certain developments in Russia. John Reed sent brilliant eyewitness reports on the revolution home to be published by Max Eastman in his journal, *Liberator*. Raymond Robins was a moderate Progressive who also wrote lyrical firsthand accounts of the revolution, though he favored recognition rather than imitation of the Bolsheviks. DAI 29:4430-A.

3122 McCoy, Pressley C. "An Analysis of the Debates on Recognition of the Union of Soviet Socialist Republics in the United States Senate, 1917–1934." Ph.D. dissertation, Northwestern University, 1954.

America officially recognized the USSR in 1933, but the issue was argued in the Senate in 1920–21. Concerns included the stability, power, and trustworthiness of the Russian government, trade issues, and the effect recognition would have on American relations with other countries. DAI 14:1786.

3123 Meiburger, Anne V. *Efforts of Raymond Robins toward the Recognition of Soviet Russia and the Outlawry of War, 1917–1933.* Washington, DC: Catholic University of America Press, 1958.

Robins worked on behalf of American recognition of Soviet Russia, because he believed that the two countries needed one another, and because he admired Lenin and much of his system. Notes, appendix, bibliography, index.

3124 Petrov, P. S. "America Reads Lenin, 1917–19" (in Russian). *Voprosy Istorii* [USSR] (1968): 55–68.

The life and teachings of Lenin were followed closely by many Americans during the period 1917–1919 through newspaper accounts and through the writings of Elizabeth Gurley Flynn and John Reed, among others. Lenin's works contributed to revolutionary excitement in the United States. Notes.

3125 Pidhainy, Oleh S., Scales, Loventrice A., and Pidhainy, Alexander S. "Silver and Billions: American Finances and the Bolshevik Revolution." *New Review of East European History* [Canada] 14 (1974): 1–47.

George F. Kennan was wrong when he insisted that the American government did not give anti-Bolshevik forces money. In fact, Aleksandr Kerensky's representative was given $1 billion in rubles and 100 tons of silver bars to help the White Russians. Notes.

3126 Popov, I. A. "Lenin's Contacts with Prominent Representatives of American Culture" (in Russian). *Voprosy Istorii* [USSR] (1982): 110–17.

Lenin had long been interested in America. Once in power, he met with John Reed, Louise Bryant, and other American radicals to discuss the potential for an American revolution. Notes.

3127 Radosh, Ronald. "John Spargo and Wilson's Russian Policy, 1920." *Journal of American History* 52 (1965): 548–65.

A socialist, Spargo supported Wilson's war policies and his posture toward Russia after the war. Spargo did not further the socialist cause as he had hoped; instead, he allowed himself to be duped. Notes.

3128 Robins, Elizabeth. *Raymond and I.* New York: Macmillan, 1956.

Actress and novelist Elizabeth Robins discusses her brother Raymond's role as unofficial ambassador to the Bolsheviks.

3129 St. John, Jacqueline D. "John F. Stevens: American Assistance to Russian and Siberian Railroads, 1917–1922." Ph.D. dissertation, University of Oklahoma, 1969.

John F. Stevens chaired three railway commissions for the purpose of rebuilding Russian railroads. The instability of the provisional government hampered the first commission's work. Following the Bolshevik Revolution, Stevens became a diplomat instead of an engineer. DAI 30:2953-A.

3130 Salzman, Neil V. "Reform and Revolution: The Life Experience of Raymond Robins." Ph.D. dissertation, New York University, 1976.

This Roosevelt Progressive went to Russia in 1917 as a member of the Red Cross mission. After the Bolshevik takeover, he devoted himself to the cause of Soviet-American cooperation. Although he failed in his mission, he was one of the few Americans who understood what the revolution meant to Russians. DAI 38:980-A.

3131 Schillinger, Elisabeth. "British and U.S. Newspaper Coverage of the Bolshevik Revolution." *Journalism Quarterly* 43 (1966): 10–16ff.

Anglo-American coverage of the Bolshevik Revolution was very poor, based on unreliable accounts emphasizing Lenin's shortcomings.

3132 Seal, Enoch, Jr. "Attitude of the United States toward the Russian Provisional Government March 15 to November 7, 1917." *Southern Quarterly* 4 (1966): 331–47.

American aid designed to keep the provisional government in the war arrived at a trickle, too late to do much good. Wilson and his ambassador did not understand either Russian history or the Bolshevik movement.

3133 Shelton, Brenda K. "President Wilson and the Russian Revolution." *University of Buffalo Studies* 23 (1957): 112–55.

Wilson had an idealized view of the Russian people, but his actions contradicted his beliefs. Notes.

3134 Strakhovsky, Leonid I. *American Opinion about Russia, 1917–1920.* Toronto: University of Toronto Press, 1961.

The public reacted negatively to bolshevism, not only because of its nature and methods but also out of a belief that it was a German plot. Notes, bibliography, index.

3135 U.S. Department of State. *Papers Relating to the Foreign Relations of the United States, Russia, 1918.* 3 vols. Washington, DC: Government Printing Office, 1931–32.

Topics covered include American observations on the March 1917 Revolution, the Prince Georgi Lvov and Kerensky governments, the Bolshevik Revolution, the Allied interventions, and economic matters. Index.

3136 Unterberger, Betty M. "The Russian Revolution and Wilson's Far Eastern Policy." *Russian Review* 16 (1957): 35–46.

The manner of American intervention was actually a compromise, but one that pleased virtually no one. Notes.

3137 Walsh, William J. "Secretary of State Robert Lansing and the Russian Revolutions of 1917." Ph.D. dissertation, Georgetown University, 1986.

Although he applauded the seemingly democratic Russian Revolution of March 1917, Robert Lansing was appalled by bolshevism and regarded it as dangerous both to the Allies and to Western civilization. He urged a policy of nonrecognition of the Bolshevik regime and encouragement of anti-Bolshevik groups within Russia. Although this eventually became official policy, Lansing had a poor relationship with Wilson, who initially adopted a more moderate stance. DAI 47:2715-A.

3138 Weeks, Charles J., Jr. "The Life and Career of Admiral Newton A. McCully, 1867–1951." Ph.D. dissertation, Georgia State University, 1975.

McCully served as a naval attaché in Petrograd from 1914 to 1917, commander of U.S. naval forces in northern Russia, and special agent for the Department of State in southern Russia after the war. The navy's "Russia expert" had a better understanding of the situation in Russia during the Wilson years than did most American observers. DAI 36:5501-A.

3139 Weeks, C. J., and Baylen, J. O. "Admiral James H. Glennon's Mission in Russia, June-July 1917." *New Review of East-European History* [Canada] 13 (1973): 14–31.

The Navy's representative on the Root mission, Admiral Glennon did not understand Russia, but his American ideals inspired Russian naval officials, at least temporarily. His suggestion that the American government aid the provisional regime was not based on reality. Notes.

3140 Williams, Wayne. "The Y.M.C.A., American Diplomacy, and the Ukrainian Republic." *The New Review* 12 (1972): 20–46.

Edward Heald, a YMCA secretary, thought he was an official government agent of diplomacy in the Ukraine, where he was stationed. His ignorance of Russia and his lack of training made him ineffective in any case. Notes.

ALLIED INTERVENTION

See also Chapter 12, *Russian Question.*

3141 Bereskin, A. V., and Mazev, V. I., eds. "On the Intervention of the United States against Soviet Russia (1919)" (in Russian). *Istoricheski Arkiv* [USSR] (1960): 3–28.

Documents from the Kolchak movement are used to show that the United States intervened in the Russian civil war to reestablish capitalism by putting Aleksandr Kolchak in power.

3142 Bradley, John. *Allied Intervention in Russia.* New York: Basic, 1968.

An overview of the disastrous Allied intervention in the Russian civil war is presented.

3143 Brinkley, George A., Jr. "Allied Intervention and the Volunteer Army in South Russia, 1917–1921." Ph.D. dissertation, Columbia University, 1964.

The Allies first responded to the Russian Revolution strictly in terms of its effect on the war with Germany. Later, as the claims of the Russian border states, the Bolsheviks, and the anti-Bolsheviks endlessly complicated the situation, the Allies were too depleted and preoccupied to implement a coherent response. In southern Russia, the anti-Bolshevik volunteer army had to endure both its own and the Allies' contradictions. DAI 26:2303.

3144 Dobson, Christopher, and Miller, John. *The Day They Almost Bombed Moscow: The Allied War in Russia, 1918–1920.* New York: Atheneum, 1986.

Two British journalists chronicle the military and intelligence operations of the Allied intervention. While the focus is on Britain, there is material on the American contingent. Bibliography, index.

3145 Dupuy, Richard E. *Perish by the Sword: The Czechoslovakian Anabasis and Our Supporting Campaigns in North Russia and*

Siberia, 1918–1920. Harrisburg, PA: Military Service Publishing, 1939.

State Department interference is blamed for the failure of the American interventions.

3146 Fry, Michael G. "Britain, the Allies, and the Problem of Russia, 1918–1919." *Canadian Journal of History* 2 (1967): 62–84.

The British were badly divided on the subject of intervention in the Russian civil war, and this factor contributed to the confusion of the Allied effort. Notes.

3147 Fursenko, A. A. "How the United States Prepared Its Intervention against Soviet Russia" (in Russian). *Voprosy Istorii* [USSR] (1986): 43–61.

The earliest evidence that the United States contemplated invading Soviet Russia is found in a naval intelligence memorandum of 31 October 1917. The American government was not interested so much in preventing the Russians from leaving the war as it was in helping counterrevolutionaries. Notes.

3148 Gaworek, Norbert H. "Allied Economic Warfare against Soviet Russia from November 1917 to March 1921." Ph.D. dissertation, University of Wisconsin, 1970.

To transform Bolshevik Russia into a democratic society willing to be exploited economically, the Allies blockaded Russia and sent a multinational military force to help anti-Bolshevik forces. Economic warfare failed, because the war-weary Allies could not agree on how to best employ it. DAI 31:5317-A.

3149 Goldhurst, Richard. "Steadying Efforts: The War at Archangel, 1918–1919." *Wisconsin Magazine of History* 62 (1979): 200–216.

An overview of the Allied operations in northern Russia is presented along with several photographs.

3150 Graves, William S. *America's Siberian Adventure, 1918–1920.* New York: Cape and Smith, 1931.

The author, who commanded the American force in Siberia, blames the Allies and the Department of State for sending troops into the Russian maelstrom.

3151 Guins, George C. "The Siberian Intervention, 1918–1920." *Russian Review* 28 (1969): 428–40.

The circumstances surrounding the sending of American troops into the Russian Far East are discussed. Notes.

3152 Haliday, E. M. "Where Ignorant Armies Clashed by Night." *American Heritage* 10 (1958): 26–29ff.

American troops sent to Russia during the civil war clashed with the Red Army on several occasions. Notes.

3153 Hayes, Harold B., III. "The Iron(ic) Horse from Nikolsk." *Military Review* 62 (1982): 18–28.

By mid-1918 chaos prevailed in Russia, a land with at least thirty governments claiming a share of power. Wilson sent ten thousand troops to Siberia, where they protected the Russians from the Japanese. Notes.

3154 Hopkins, George W. "The Politics of Food: United States and Soviet Hungary, March-August, 1919." *Mid-America* 55 (1973): 245–70.

Herbert Hoover's idea of stopping food shipments to Hungary was preferred by the Allies to the direct use of force. Béla Kun's Bolshevik regime fell as a result of the food boycott, his own agrarian policies, and military pressure from Romania. Notes.

3155 Kennan, George F. *Soviet-American Relations, 1917–1920.* 2 vols. Princeton: Princeton University Press, 1956.

By the time American forces arrived in Russia most of the reasons originally conceived for them to be there were no longer valid. The slender thread of communication between Washington and the Bolsheviks was sacrificed in this dubious endeavor. The hysteria of militancy, philosophical and intellectual shallowness, and dilettantism all played parts in the tragic blunder of intervention. Photographs, notes, appendixes, bibliography, index.

3156 ———. "Soviet Historiography and America's Role in the Intervention." *American Historical Review* 65 (1960): 302–22.

Soviet accounts of American intervention are of little use to Western scholars, because they are the work of polemicists who have no claim to objectivity. Notes.

3157 Lasch, Christopher. "American Intervention in Siberia: A Reinterpretation." *Political Science Quarterly* 77 (1962): 205–23.

American concern about Germany, rather than halting the spread of Bolshevism, was the primary motive for intervening in the Russian civil war. Notes.

3158 Long, John W. "American Intervention in Russia: The North Russian Expedition, 1918–19." *Diplomatic History* 6 (1982): 45–67.

Allied pressure led Wilson to participate in operations in northern Russia. After the war, the president withdrew the force. Notes.

3159 Luckett, Judith A. "The Siberian Intervention: Military Support of Foreign Policy." *Military Review* 64 (1984): 54–63.

The American intervention in Siberia (1918–1920) was the first time that the U.S. military had been used for purely diplomatic purposes. Notes.

3160 Maddox, Robert. "Doughboys in Siberia." *American History Illustrated* 12 (1977): 10–21.

American intervention in the Russian civil war only served to prolong the struggle.

3161 ———. *The Unknown War with Russia: Wilson's Siberian Adventure.* San Rafael, CA: Presidio, 1977.

Wilson's decision to intervene in the Russian civil war makes sense only in the larger context of his peace program, which was endangered by the Bolsheviks and by the uncertain outcome of the war. Notes, bibliography, index.

3162 Morley, James W. *The Japanese Thrust into Siberia, 1918.* New York: Columbia University Press, 1957.

The Japanese leadership was divided into anti-Western and pro-Western factions, as Japan sent troops into Siberia. Wilson's intervention acted as a brake on Japan's ambitions in Russia. Notes, bibliography, index.

3163 Naidel, M. I., and Sogomonov, Iu V. "On the History of U.S. Intervention in Transcaucasia in 1917–21" (in Russian). *Istoriia SSSR* [USSR] (1961): 28–46.

The United States, more than any other foreign power, was responsible for the Allied intervention. American plans for holding mandates over seized Russian territories are also discussed.

3164 O'Connor, Richard. "Yanks in Siberia." *American Heritage* 25 (1974): 10–17ff.

American military intervention in the Russian civil war is analyzed, including American aid to the White Army.

3165 Rhodes, Benjamin D. "The Anglo-American Railroad War at Archangel, 1918–1919." *Railroad History* (1984): 70–83.

Allied troops, including a contingent from the United States, were dispatched to Archangel to prevent the Bolsheviks from using a mountain of supplies stockpiled for use against Germany.

3166 Shao Ting-hsun. "The Struggle between American and Japanese Imperialists during Their Armed Intervention in the Russian Far East (1917–22)" (in Chinese). *Li-shih Yen-chiu* [China] 8 (1957): 35–61.

The United States and Japan vied with one another for access to the natural resources of Soviet Russia during their intervention in the Russian civil war.

3167 Shapiro, Sumner. "Intervention in Russia (1918–1919)." *US Naval Institute Proceedings* 99 (1973): 52–61.

American intervention in the Russian civil war was a military, political, and diplomatic disaster. Reports sent to Washington were confused and confusing.

3168 Strakhovsky, Leonid I. *Intervention at Archangel: The Story of Allied Intervention and Russian Counter-Revolution in North Russia, 1918–1920.* Princeton: Princeton University Press, 1944.

American intervention in northern Russia is detailed here as part of a larger story of Allied interference in the Russian civil war.

3169 Svetachev, M. I. "Siberia and the Far East in the Counterrevolutionary Plans of the Entente and the United States: November 1917-November 1918" (in Russian). *Istoricheskie Zapiski Akademmi Nauk SSSR* [USSR] (1979): 62–106.

The United States and the Entente powers intervened on the side of the White Russians during the Russian civil war. Western historians have underestimated the unremitting hostility of the Allies toward the Bolshevik Revolution. Notes.

3170 Ullman, Richard H. *Anglo-Soviet Relations, 1917–1921.* 2 vols. Princeton: Princeton University Press, 1961.

Preoccupied with the war against Germany and the coming peace, American policy toward Russia followed the British lead. Notes, bibliography, index.

3171 U.S. Department of State. *Papers Relating to the Foreign Relations of the United States, Russia, 1919.* Washington, DC: Government Printing Office, 1937.

Topics covered include the abortive Prinkipo conference, nonrecognition, and the Allied campaigns in Siberia and northern Russia. Index.

3172 Unterberger, Betty M. *America's Siberian Expedition, 1918–1920*. Durham, NC: Duke University Press, 1956.

Anti-imperialism and the Open Door were among Wilson's concerns when he reluctantly agreed to the intervention in Siberia. Notes, bibliography, index.

3173 ———. "Woodrow Wilson and the Bolsheviks: The 'Acid Test' of Soviet-American Relations." *Diplomatic History* 11 (1987): 71–90.

Wilson intervened in the Russian civil war to uphold the principle of self-determination for the Russian people. He tried to restrain the Allies without alienating them and succeeded at least in checking Japanese territorial ambitions. Notes.

3174 ———. "Woodrow Wilson and the Decision to Send American Troops to Siberia." *Pacific Historical Review* 24 (1955): 63–74.

Fear of a renewed German push against Russia as well as fear of Japanese designs against Siberia motivated Wilson to intervene in the Russian civil war. If the United States had not done so, Japan might have seized Siberia and northern Manchuria. Notes.

3175 White, John A. *The Siberian Intervention*. Princeton: Princeton University Press, 1950.

Wilson's concern about the Japanese desire to expand into Siberia was his prime motive for sending American troops there. Notes, bibliography, index.

3176 Williams, William A. "American Intervention in Russia, 1917–1920 (Part I)." *Studies on the Left* 3 (1963): 24–48.

Wilson was a moralist, but he also had a hardheaded concern for overseas economic expansion. Wilson followed an anti-Bolshevik strategy because Lenin challenged American beliefs, although American rhetoric was couched in anti-German terms. Notes.

3177 ———. "American Intervention in Russia, 1917–1920 (Part II)." *Studies on the Left* 4 (1964): 39–57.

Wilson and Robert Lansing rejected a French proposal to aid the Bolsheviks to keep them in the war. Wilson had moral qualms about military intervention, but his agreement to join the scheme was anti-Bolshevik in origins and purpose. Notes.

3178 Woodward, David R. "The British Government and Japanese Intervention in Russia during World War One." *Journal of Modern History* 46 (1974): 663–85.

Ullman's monograph (#3170) on Anglo-Soviet relations is no longer the last word on the subject in light of newly declassified documents. Notes.

3179 ———. "The West and the Containment of Russia, 1914–1923." Ph.D. dissertation, University of Georgia, 1965.

After the Bolshevik Revolution, the Allies turned on their former partner, Russia, launching an invasion to check possible Communist expansion. Britain and France were too war weary to do more than mount a token military effort and offer advice to Russia's neighbors. DAI 26:6685.

The Big Four at the Paris Peace Conference. l. to r.: David Lloyd George, Vittorio Orlando, Georges Clemenceau, Woodrow Wilson. *U.S. Signal Corps photo courtesy of the Herbert Hoover Presidential Library.*

12

The Peace Settlement

Woodrow Wilson went to Paris to bring about "peace without victory" and returned with a treaty which, while it was unsatisfactory in many respects, created a League of Nations and imposed generally fair territorial settlements. The problem, as Robert H. Ferrell has observed, was that "bitterness made peace unlikely." The victorious Entente had endured too many losses, human and monetary, to fully accept the liberal peace program that Wilson had in mind. The president made several mistakes, among them attending the conference in person, accepting Paris as the site of the talks, choosing a weak team of peace commissioners, overestimating American power, and underestimating the leaders of Britain and France. Wilson's inattention to domestic politics, his rapidly deteriorating health, and a concomitant decline in his judgment all contributed to the American rejection of the Versailles system, an event as tragic for the country as it was for the president.

The best work on American preparations for the peace conference remains Lawrence E. Gelfand, *The Inquiry: American Preparations for Peace* (#3181). Of special interest to historians is a doctoral dissertation by Jonathan M. Nielsen, "American Historians at the Versailles Peace Conference, 1919" (#3184).

For excellent overviews of the peace conference, see Lloyd E. Ambrosius, *Woodrow Wilson and the American Diplomatic Tradition* (#3190), and Arno Mayer, *Politics and Diplomacy of Peacemaking: Containment and Counterrevolution at Versailles, 1918–1919* (#3212). A different interpretation may be found in Arthur Walworth, *Wilson and His Peacemakers: American Diplomacy at the Paris Peace Conference* (#3230). Wilson's German policy is examined by Klaus Schwabe, *Woodrow Wilson, Revolutionary Germany, and Peacemaking, 1918–1919: Missionary Diplomacy and the*

Realities of Power (#3219), and Seth P. Tillman, *Anglo-American Relations at the Paris Peace Conference of 1919* (#3226), examines relations between the English-speaking empires. Some older works on the Paris Peace Conference remain worth reading. See Thomas A. Bailey, *Woodrow Wilson and the Lost Peace* (#3192), and Ray S. Baker, *Woodrow Wilson and World Settlement* (#3193).

Primary sources on the conference are abundant. U.S. Department of State, *Papers Relating to the Foreign Relations of the United States: The Paris Peace Conference, 1919* (#3228), contains a judicious selection of documents in thirteen volumes. The complete records are contained in U.S. Department of State, *General Records of the American Commission to Negotiate Peace, 1919–1931* (#3227), which runs to 563 rolls of microfilm. For the French records of the conference, see Paul Mantoux, *Paris Peace Conference: Proceedings of the Council of Four, March 24-April 18* (#3210), available both in English and in French. Important memoirs and collections of letters include C. H. Haskins and R. H. Lord, *Some Problems of the Paris Peace Conference* (#3206); Robert Lansing, *The Peace Negotiations: A Personal Narrative* (#3208); David H. Miller, *My Diary at the Conference at Paris* (#3213); Harold Nicolson, *Peacemaking, 1919: Being Reminiscences of the Paris Peace Conference* (#3215); Francis W. O'Brien, ed., *Two Peacemakers in Paris: The Hoover-Wilson Post-Armistice Letters, 1918–1920* (#3217); and Charles Seymour, *Letters from the Paris Peace Conference* (#3221). For the crucial role played by Colonel Edward House, see Inga Floto, *Colonel House in Paris: A Study of American Policy at the Paris Peace Conference* (#3204).

The reparations question is examined in the works of Robert E. Bunselmeyer, *The Cost of the War, 1914–1919: British Economic War*

Aims and the Origin of Reparation (#3235), and Philip M. Burnett, *Reparation at the Paris Peace Conference from the Standpoint of the American Delegation* (#3236). A blistering critique of the settlement is offered by John Maynard Keynes, *The Economic Consequences of the Peace* (#3239), and is rebutted by Étienne Mantoux, *The Carthaginian Peace: Or, the Economic Consequences of Mr. Keynes* (#3240).

On the origins of the League of Nations, see George W. Egerton, *Great Britain and the Creation of the League of Nations: Strategy, Politics, and International Organization, 1914–1919* (#3248); the old but still useful work by Denna F. Fleming, *The United States and the League of Nations, 1918–1920* (#3251); a dissertation by Thomas J. Knock, "Woodrow Wilson and the Origins of the League of Nations" (#3257); and Warren F. Kuehl, *Seeking World Order: The United States and International Organization to 1920* (#3258). For firsthand accounts, see Raymond B. Fosdick, *Letters on the League of Nations: From the Files of Raymond B. Fosdick* (#3253), and David Hunter Miller, *The Drafting of the Covenant* (#3262).

For an overview of the mandate system applied to Germany, see the doctoral dissertation by William S. Martin, Jr., "The Colonial Mandate Question at the Paris Peace Conference of 1919: The United States and the Disposition of the German Colonies in Africa and the Pacific" (#3291). The battles with France and Britain over African mandates are examined by a participant, George L. Beer, *African Questions at the Paris Peace Conference: With Papers on Egypt, Mesopotamia, and the Colonial Settlement* (#3275). Much has been written on the Armenian mandate controversy. See the doctoral dissertation by Thomas A. Bryson, "Woodrow Wilson, the Senate, Public Opinion and the Armenian Mandate, 1919–1920" (#3282), and James B. Gidney, *A Mandate for Armenia* (#3286).

American public opinion on the peace conference is surveyed in a doctoral dissertation by James D. Startt, "American Editorial Opinion of Woodrow Wilson and the Main Problems of Peacemaking in 1919" (#3308). Key ethnic groups are examined in Joseph P. O'Grady, ed., *The Immigrants' Influence on Wilson's Peace Policies* (#3305). See also Louis L. Gerson, *Woodrow Wilson and the Rebirth of Poland, 1914–1920: A Study in the Influence on American Policy of Minority Groups of Foreign Origin* (#3301). Liberal opinion is analyzed by Stuart I. Rochester, *American Liberal Disillusionment in the Wake of World War I* (#3306).

The failure of the conference to deal with the Russian question had far-reaching implications for the future. See Claude E. Fike, "The United States and Russian Territorial Problems, 1917–1920" (#3315), and John M. Thompson, *Russia, Bolshevism, and the Versailles Peace* (#3318).

Wilson's idea of national self-determination played an important role at the peace conference. Self-determination for Arab peoples is examined by Harry N. Howard, *The King-Crane Commission: An American Inquiry into the Middle East* (#3332), and *The Partition of Turkey: A Diplomatic History* (#3333). On Eastern Europe, see Victor S. Mamatey, *The United States and East Central Europe, 1914–1918: A Study in Wilsonian Diplomacy and Propaganda* (#3343). For the creation of Yugoslavia, consult Ivo J. Lederer, *Yugoslavia at the Paris Peace Conference: A Study in Frontier Making* (#3340), and Dragan R. Živojinović, *America, Italy, and the Birth of Yugoslavia (1917–1919)* (#3365).

For the struggle over ratification, see Thomas A. Bailey, *Woodrow Wilson and the Great Betrayal* (#3369); John C. Vinson, *Referendum for Isolation: The Defeat of Article Ten of the League of Nations Covenant* (#3394); and a number of doctoral dissertations, among them Kurt Wimer, "Executive-Legislative Tensions in the Making of the League of Nations" (#3396). The hard core of opposition to the Wilsonian peace is examined in Ralph Stone, *The Irreconcilables: The Fight against the League of Nations* (#3390).

Preparations

See Chapter 3, *Edward M. House.*

3180 Dockrill, M. L. "The Foreign Office and the 'Proposed Institute of International Affairs 1919.'" *International Affairs* 56 (1980): 665–72.

The British and American delegations to the peace conference created the Institute of International Affairs in 1919 as an unofficial vehicle for promoting the mission of the conference.

3181 Gelfand, Lawrence E. *The Inquiry: American Preparations for Peace, 1917–1919.* New Haven, CT: Yale University Press, 1963.

Within months of America's entry into the war, Wilson created "The Inquiry" to make specific recommendations for the American peace program. Wilson was a "sturdy nationalist" who understood the realities of international politics. Notes, appendix, bibliography, index.

3182 Hitchens, David L. "Peace, World Organization and the Editorial Philosophy of Hamilton Holt and *The Independent* Magazine." Ph.D. dissertation, University of Georgia, 1968.

Hamilton Holt, as owner and editor of *The Independent*, advocated an international peace league. His readership included Woodrow Wilson. Holt's magazine is compared with similar journals. DAI 29:3074-A.

3183 Hovannisian, Armen K. "The United States Inquiry and the Armenian Question, 1917–1919: The Archival Papers." *Armenian Revolution* 37 (1984): 146–63.

The U.S. "Inquiry" was created during the war to investigate political problems of probable interest to the forthcoming peace conference. This commission's papers reveal concern over Turkish genocide against the Armenians.

3184 Nielson, Jonathan M. "American Historians at the Versailles Peace Conference, 1919: The Scholar as Patriot and Diplomat." Ph.D. dissertation, University of California, Santa Barbara, 1986.

Professional historians faced ethical and intellectual conflicts as the government tried to enlist their help in prowar propaganda campaigns. Objectivity was an early victim. Historians made some contributions to the peace as members of the American delegation to Versailles. DAI 47:1859-A.

3185 Posey, John P. "David Hunter Miller and the Far Eastern Question at the Paris Peace Conference, 1919." *Southern Quarterly* 7 (1969): 373–92.

Miller's advice to Wilson on Far Eastern questions at the Paris conference carried weight, and he had a moderating influence on the Chinese delegation. Notes.

3186 Spustek, Irena. "The Problem of Poland's Western Boundaries during the Preparations for the Paris Peace Conference in Light of Materials of the US Inquiry" (in Polish). *Przeglad Historica* [Poland] 63 (1972): 651–67.

In 1917, Wilson appointed a special commission to inquire about Poland's western boundary for the coming peace conference. Commission documents indicate that the matter had been thoroughly investigated in advance of the postwar gathering. Notes.

3187 Startt, James D. "Wilson's Mission to Paris: The Making of a Decision." *Historian* 30 (1968): 599–616.

Wilson's decision to go to Paris to personally negotiate the peace was controversial from the start. He went because he believed that he had a unique moral obligation to the people of Europe. Notes.

3188 Wilson, John B. "Documents: The US Inquiry." *Armenian Review* 37 (1984): 164–202.

The U.S. "Inquiry" took depositions from missionaries who had witnessed Turkish mistreatment of Armenians.

Paris Peace Conference

GENERAL ACCOUNTS

See also Chapter 1, *Autobiographical and Biographical Materials*, Chapter 2, *Wilson Presidency*, Chapter 3, *Executive Branch, Diplomats* and *Military Officers*, Chapter 9, *Foreign Affairs: General*, and Chapter 10, *Armistice*.

3189 Albrecht-Carrié, René. *Italy at the Peace Conference*. New York: Columbia University Press, 1938.

Italy's ambitions at the peace conference created many problems for Wilson and the Allies, diverting their attention from larger matters. Key documents from the conference are included in an extended appendix. Notes, bibliography, index, appendix.

3190 Ambrosius, Lloyd E. *Woodrow Wilson and the American Diplomatic Tradition*. New York: Cambridge University Press, 1987.

Wilson failed to convert the new American involvement in internationalism into political reality. He regarded the League of Nations as a way to extend American power without sacrificing freedom of action. Although Republicans blocked the Treaty of Versailles, the president shared responsibility for its defeat, because he did not understand the modern world. Notes, bibliography, index.

3191 Artaud, Denise. "On the Interwar Period: Wilson at the Peace Conference, 1919" (in

French). *Revue d'Histoire de la Deuxième Guerre Mondiale* [France] 31 (1981): 97–107.

Wilson's refusal to deal realistically with the problem of Britain's huge war debt and American concern about British economic interests explain why the peace conference did not deal with the reconstruction of Europe. Notes.

3192 Bailey, Thomas A. *Woodrow Wilson and the Lost Peace.* New York: Macmillan, 1944.

Wilson faced many dilemmas during his noble campaign to remake the postwar world through the Fourteen Points and the Treaty of Versailles. Bibliographic notes, index.

3193 Baker, Ray S. *Woodrow Wilson and World Settlement.* 3 vols. Garden City, NY: Doubleday, Page, 1922.

Wilson gave his friend Baker access to his official papers so that he could write this account, which consists of two volumes of narrative and another volume of documents. Photographs.

3194 Benns, F. Lee. "The Two Paris Peace Conferences of the Twentieth Century." In Dwight E. Lee and George E. McReynolds, eds. *Essays in History and International Relations in Honor of George Blakeslee.* Worcester, MA: Clark University Press, 1949, pp. 153–70.

The conferences held in Paris at the end of the two world wars are compared and contrasted.

3195 Binkley, Robert C. *Selected Papers of Robert C. Binkley.* Edited by Max H. Fisch. Cambridge, MA: Harvard University Press, 1948.

Three articles written during the interwar period are reprinted under the heading of "The Peace that Failed." Appendix, bibliography, index.

3196 Birdsall, Paul. *Versailles Twenty Years After.* New York: Reynal and Hitchcock, 1941.

The Treaty of Versailles was a compromise, but Wilson did the best he could and cannot be held accountable for the subsequent breakdown of the peace, which the author blames on disillusioned liberals. Wilson was the only real statesman at Paris. Notes, bibliography, index.

3197 Bonsal, Stephen. *Unfinished Business.* Garden City, NY: Doubleday, Doran, 1944.

Colonel Bonsal, an interpreter for Wilson and Edward House at the peace conference, recorded his impressions in a diary.

3198 Burlingame, Roger, and Stevens, Alden. *Victory without Peace.* New York: Harcourt, Brace, 1944.

Wilson's fight for peace is given a popular treatment, written at a time when Americans were thinking again about winning a war and making peace. Notes, bibliography, index.

3199 Civitello, Maryann. "The State Department and Peacemaking, 1917–1920: Attitudes of State Department Officials toward Wilson's Peacemaking Efforts." Ph.D. dissertation, Fordham University, 1981.

By 1917, the State Department had become overburdened, and Wilson chose his friend and adviser Colonel House to draft an American peace program. The author analyzes the reactions of six major State Department officials to Wilson's foreign policy. Little resentment was expressed about Wilson's tendency to bypass the State Department, but differences over certain issues arose. Secretary of State Robert Lansing became bitterly critical of Wilson in Paris, and he and others favored a compromise with Congress at home. DAI 42:2260-A.

3200 Czernin, Ferdinand. *Versailles, 1919: The Forces, Events and Personalities that Shaped the Treaty.* New York: Capricorn, 1965.

The peace settlement is divided into six distinct phases: (1) the first five weeks, (2) the month of Wilson's absence, (3) the two weeks following Wilson's return, (4) the dark period, (5) three weeks of compromises, and (6) the final phase, when the belligerents came face to face. Notes.

3201 Dillon, E. J. *The Inside Story of the Peace Conference.* New York: Harper, 1920.

The greatest mistake made at the conference was tying the League of Nations charter to the Treaty of Versailles, because this created a sharp opposition to the whole peace settlement in the United States. The failure to deal with the Russian question also contributed to the failure to make a lasting settlement.

3202 Domanyckyj, Victor. "The National Problem and World War I." *Ukrainian Quarterly* 12 (1956): 298–312.

Wilson's ideas about peace and the future clashed at Paris with practitioners of the old diplomacy, those committed to preserving the old ways of solving national disputes. Wilson also had to confront bolshevism, which offered captive peoples an alternative means of attaining liberation. Notes.

3203 Ferrell, Robert H. "Woodrow Wilson and Open Diplomacy." In George L. Anderson, ed. *Issues and Conflicts: Studies in Twentieth Century American Diplomacy.* Lawrence: University of Kansas Press, 1959, pp. 193–209.

Wilson's advocacy of open diplomacy was timely, because people were tired of the old diplomacy, because he saw the need to launch a counteroffensive against bolshevism, and because it could serve the cause of national self-determination. Notes.

3204 Floto, Inga. *Colonel House in Paris: A Study of American Policy at the Paris Peace Conference, 1919.* Translated by Pauline B. Katborg. Copenhagen: Universitets Forlaget Aarhaus, 1973.

Colonel House was an extremely ambitious man whose first loyalty was not to Wilson or to the United States, but to himself. Notes, bibliography, index.

3205 Hankey, Maurice P. *The Supreme Court at the Paris Peace Conference of 1919: A Commentary.* London: Allen and Unwin, 1963.

A leading British diplomat and secretary to the Big Four offers shrewd insights into the procedures and organization of the Paris Peace Conference, which was the most memorable episode of his life. Appendix, index.

3206 Haskins, C. H., and Lord, R. H. *Some Problems of the Paris Peace Conference.* Cambridge, MA: Harvard University Press, 1920.

Two of Wilson's advisers at the peace conference examine the many flaws in the Treaty of Versailles, but they conclude that the general outcome was an immense gain for the cause of liberty.

3207 Hughes, H. Stuart. "Thirty-Five Years after Versailles." *New Leader* 37 (1954): 16–19.

In examining American peace policies following both world wars, it is clear that the United States has had a responsibility to participate in both the peacemaking and in efforts to solve subsequent problems concerning international peace.

3208 Lansing, Robert. *The Peace Negotiations: A Personal Narrative.* Boston: Houghton Mifflin, 1921.

Lansing presents his side of the story, arguing that he followed Wilson's guidance and obeyed his instructions loyally, if unwillingly. Photographs, appendix, index.

3209 Lentin, Antony. *Lloyd George, Woodrow Wilson and the Guilt of Germany: An Essay in the Pre-History of Appeasement.* Baton Rouge: Louisiana State University Press, 1984.

"A powerful undertow of disenchantment" was present among British delegates at the peace conference, a malaise that transformed the Treaty of Versailles from the Wilson peace to a Carthaginian peace in the minds of the British elite. Notes, bibliography, index.

3210 Mantoux, Paul. *Paris Peace Conference: Proceedings of the Council of Four, March 24-April 18.* Translated by John B. Whitton. Geneva: Librairie Droz, 1964.

The French secretary's minutes of the Council of Four meetings during a crucial period in the peace conference are an important source of information, because they contain information not found elsewhere. Readers of French should consult the original volumes, published in 1955. Index.

3211 Marston, Frank S. *The Peace Conference of 1919.* London: Oxford University Press, 1944.

Although it was published during World War II, this overview of the conference is still useful for its description of procedures and organization.

3212 Mayer, Arno. *Politics and Diplomacy of Peacemaking: Containment and Counterrevolution at Versailles, 1918–1919.* New York: Knopf, 1967.

An intense interplay of domestic and international politics took place at the peace conference to produce a right-wing resurgence in the victor nations. The peace treaties merely shifted the crisis of disorder, frustration, and exhaustion from the international to the internal arena. Notes, bibliography, index.

3213 Miller, David H. *My Diary at the Conference at Paris.* 21 vols. New York: Appeal, 1924.

Colonel House's legal adviser paints a detailed picture of the Paris conference in his diaries, and he supplements his observations with important documents. Index.

3214 Nelson, Harold. *Land and Power: British and Allied Policy on Germany's Frontiers, 1916–1919.* London: Routledge and Kegan Paul, 1963.

Britain cooperated with Wilson on the League, on mandates, and on territorial problems but hedged its diplomatic bets for fear that the United States would lapse back into isolationism. Notes, bibliography, index.

3215 Nicolson, Harold. *Peacemaking, 1919: Being Reminiscences of the Paris Peace Conference.* Boston: Houghton Mifflin, 1933.

The author laments that most accounts of the peace conference fail to capture "the element of confusion," an important factor in what this veteran diplomat calls his "study in fog." The book is divided between analysis and excerpts from the author's diary. Index.

3216 Noble, George B. *Policies and Opinions at Paris, 1919: Wilsonian Diplomacy, the Versailles Peace, and French Public Opinion.* New York: Macmillan, 1935.

Instability in international affairs persisted after World War I because the peacemakers used faulty procedures, misunderstood the dynamics of national and international politics, and were unable to shape history in the face of national passions. Notes, bibliography, index.

3217 O'Brien, Francis W., ed. *T w o Peacemakers in Paris: The Hoover-Wilson Post-Armistice Letters, 1918–1920.* College Station: Texas A & M University Press, 1978.

Wilson relied heavily on Hoover's advice at the peace conference. Hoover had much to say in his letters about bolshevism, the postwar blockade of Germany, hunger, and reparations. Index.

3218 Rozwenc, Edwin C., and Lyons, Thomas, eds. *Realism and Idealism in Wilson's Peace Program.* Lexington, MA: D. C. Heath, 1965.

Key documents are presented to illuminate Wilson's concept of peacemaking and the diplomacy of self-interest. Excerpts from scholarly works on the Wilsonian peace program are also included. Bibliography.

3219 Schwabe, Klaus. *Woodrow Wilson, Revolutionary Germany, and Peacemaking, 1918–1919: Missionary Diplomacy and the Realities of Power.* Translated by Rita and Robert Kimber. Chapel Hill: University of North Carolina Press, 1985.

Based on a work published in German in 1971, this book examines official and unofficial contacts between the governments of the United States and Germany from the last months of the war to the signing of the Treaty of Versailles. Both countries used missionary diplomacy to counter the forces of monarchy and bolshevism. Notes, bibliography, index.

3220 Seymour, Charles. *Geography, Justice, and Politics at the Peace Conference of 1919.* New York: American Geographical Society, 1951.

Geography and politics combined to shape the Treaty of Versailles in ways that have not been fully appreciated. Wilson's fight for justice against the forces of national self-interest was handicapped by his excessive faith in popular opinion.

3221 ———. *Letters from the Paris Peace Conference.* New Haven, CT: Yale University Press, 1965.

A member of The Inquiry, the author was named chief of the Austro-Hungarian Division of the American commission and wrote long letters to his family which reflect the views of both a conference insider and a historian. Index.

3222 Shotwell, James T. *At the Paris Peace Conference.* New York: Macmillan, 1937.

A member of The Inquiry, the author presents a contemporary record based on a diary and on notes taken at the time. Wilson was an aloof figure, while Colonel House was "the chief." Photographs, appendix, index.

3223 Smith, Gaddis. "The Alaska Panhandle at the Paris Peace Conference, 1919." *International Journal* 17 (1962): 25–29.

Although the scheme was never accepted, the trade of the Alaskan panhandle for British Honduras discussed by some illustrates an older mentality still at work in the North Atlantic triangle. Notes.

3224 Temperly, H. W. V., ed. *A History of the Peace Conference of Paris.* 6 vols. London: Frowde, Hodder and Stoughton, 1920.

Diplomats and historians provide commentary on the conference. Conference documents are also presented. Notes, appendixes, index.

3225 Thompson, Charles T. *The Peace Conference Day by Day.* New York: Brentano, 1920.

This early volume provides a chronological record of the conference from the perspective of an Associated Press reporter.

3226 Tillman, Seth P. *Anglo-American Relations at the Paris Peace Conference of 1919.* Princeton: Princeton University Press, 1961.

American and British delegates to the peace conference worked together in reasonable harmony where they had common objectives, although they had no coherent common strategy. Settling accounts with the vanquished powers proved to be the area of greatest difference between the English-speaking empires. Notes, bibliography, index.

3227 U.S. Department of State. *General Records of the American Commission to Negotiate Peace, 1918–1931*. Washington, DC: National Archives and Records Administration, n.d. Microfilm. M820, 563 rolls.

This microfilm edition is a comprehensive compilation of the papers of the American Commission to Negotiate Peace at the Paris Peace Conference.

3228 ———. *Papers Relating to the Foreign Relations of the United States: The Paris Peace Conference, 1919*. 13 vols. Washington, DC: Government Printing Office, 1942–1947.

Published as the Department of State contemplated the possibility of another peace conference, this collection includes most of the important documents. Index.

3229 Van Meter, Robert H., Jr. "The United States and European Recovery, 1918–1923: A Study of Public Policy and Private Finance." Ph.D. dissertation, University of Wisconsin, 1971.

Wilson hoped that private enterprise, rather than the government, would provide America's contribution to Europe's reconstruction, provided that the League of Nations did its job. DAI 32:6359-A.

3230 Walworth, Arthur. *Wilson and His Peacemakers: American Diplomacy at the Paris Peace Conference, 1919*. New York: Norton, 1986.

Meant to be a grand synthesis of Wilson's negotiations at Paris, this work finds that the president boldly challenged the great powers of Europe to live up to his spiritual revelations. Power politics and economic necessities intruded on his plans, thus producing an imperfect peace. Notes, appendix, bibliography, index.

3231 Widenor, William C. "The United States and the Versailles Peace Settlement." In John M. Carroll and George C. Herring, eds. *Modern American Diplomacy*. Wilmington, DE: Scholarly Resources, 1986, pp. 35–52.

Americans were as unprepared to make peace as they had been for war. The peace settlement created a new international order, but it was laced with fatal inconsistencies. Bibliography.

WAR DEBTS AND REPARATIONS

3232 Artaud, Denise. "The American Government and the Question of War Debts on the Eve of the Armistice, 1918–1920" (in French). *Revue d'Histoire Moderne et Contemporaine* [France] 20 (1973): 201–29.

Why did the Americans insist that the Allies repay their war debts? The most important of many factors were ignorance, financial imperialism, and public opinion. Notes.

3233 Baruch, Bernard M. *The Making of the Reparation and Economic Sections of the Treaty*. New York: Harper, 1920.

This key and influential figure in the American delegation discusses his part in the compromises over reparations and the economic settlement. Index.

3234 Bergmann, Carl. *The History of Reparations*. London: Ernest Benn, 1927.

Reparations are examined from the viewpoint of a German moderate. The opening chapters discuss Wilson's program and the peace settlement. Index.

3235 Bunselmeyer, Robert E. *The Cost of the War, 1914–1919: British Economic War Aims and the Origin of Reparation*. Hamden, CT: Shoe String, 1975.

The reparations settlement is reexamined in light of what the British hoped to accomplish and the staggering costs of the war. Notes, bibliography, index.

3236 Burnett, Philip M. *Reparation at the Paris Peace Conference from the Standpoint of the American Delegation*. 2 vols. New York: Columbia University Press, 1940.

The first part of Volume I contains a judicious history of the reparations problem, and the balance of the work reprints over 500 important documents. Bibliography, index.

3237 Carroll, John M. "The Making of the Dawes Plan, 1919–1924." Ph.D. dissertation, University of Kentucky, 1972.

While the focus is on Republican efforts to settle the reparations issue, Chapter 1 contains material on Wilson's economic foreign policy, emphasizing the president's determination to create a new world order based on the Open Door. The Republicans disagreed with Wilson over specifics, but they shared his basic outlook. DAI 34:3289-A.

3238 Fitzhardinge, L. F. "W. M. Hughes and the Treaty of Versailles, 1919." *Journal of Commonwealth Political Studies* [Great Britain] 5 (1967): 130–42.

The Australian representative to the peace conference came to Paris determined to check Japanese ambitions and to eliminate Germany as a Pacific power. His demand for an Australian mandate over Papua New Guinea led to bitter clashes with Wilson.

3239 Keynes, John Maynard. *The Economic Consequences of the Peace.* New York: Harcourt, Brace and Howe, 1920.

This famed British economist, who advised the British delegation, analyzes Wilson's role at the peace conference and predicts disastrous economic consequences as a result of high reparations and the failure to settle the question of war debts.

3240 Mantoux, Étienne. *The Carthaginian Peace: Or, the Economic Consequences of Mr. Keynes.* New York: Scribner's, 1952.

Keynes's severe critique (#3239) of the reparations settlement reached at the peace conference was wrong, because the settlement was not recriminatory. Wilson's only illusion was his faith in mankind. Notes, index.

3241 Moulton, Harold G., and Pasvolsky, Leo. *War Debts and World Prosperity.* Washington, DC: Brookings Institution, 1932.

In a synthesis of ten years of research, the authors analyze the complexities of World War I war debts and reparations. The origins of the war debts are discussed along with postwar debts negotiations and the history of reparations negotiations. Tables, appendixes, index.

3242 Pruessen, Ronald W. "John Foster Dulles and Reparations at the Paris Peace Conference, 1919: Early Patterns of Life." *Perspectives in American History* 8 (1974): 381–410.

Dulles's role as a legal adviser to the American delegation was his first important diplomatic assignment and made a profound impression on him. He helped to convince the Allies to reduce their crushing demands on Germany for reparations. Notes.

LEAGUE OF NATIONS

See Chapter 7, *Peace Groups.*

3243 Boothe, Leon E. "Anglo-American Pro-League Groups Lead Wilson, 1915–1920." *Mid-America* 51 (1969): 92–107.

Wilson's vagueness about the League of Nations during American neutrality and through the war retarded pro-League public opinion. The British government gained more public support by endorsing specifics.

3244 Burns, Richard Dean. "International Arms Inspection Policies between World Wars, 1919–1934." *Historian* 31 (1969): 583–603.

Allied differences over arms inspection policies began in 1919 and were never resolved to the satisfaction of all. Notes.

3245 Curry, George. "Woodrow Wilson, Jan Smuts, and the Versailles Settlement." *American Historical Review* 66 (1961): 968–86.

Wilson benefited greatly at Versailles from the political ideas of Jan Smuts, although Smuts's talent for finding compromise solutions placed Wilson's idealism in jeopardy on occasion, especially in regard to reparations. Notes.

3246 Dubin, Martin D. "The Carnegie Endowment for International Peace and the Advocacy of a League of Nations, 1914–1918." *Proceedings of the American Philosophical Society* 123 (1979): 344–68.

The Carnegie Endowment endeavored to convince the public of the need for a League of Nations based on the voluntary principles of the prewar Hague system. Headed by Elihu Root, Nicholas Murray Butler, and James Brown Scott, the endowment became the leading voice of conservative internationalism. Notes.

3247 ———. "Toward the Concept of Collective Security: The Bryce Group's 'Proposals for the Avoidance of War,' 1914–1917." *International Organization* 24 (1970): 288–318.

The ideas of Britain's Lord James Bryce and his group formed the basis for the League of Nations' collective security provisions. Notes.

3248 Egerton, George W. *Great Britain and the Creation of the League of Nations: Strategy, Politics, and International Organization, 1914–1919.* Chapel Hill: University of North Carolina Press, 1978.

British leaders wanted a League that would complement their world strategy of a Pax Anglo-Americana. Wilson, Lord Robert Cecil, and the League of Nations Union convinced a majority of Britons to support the world body. Notes, bibliography.

3249 Fitzgerald, Oscar P., IV. "The Supreme Economic Council and Germany: A Study of Inter-

Allied Cooperation after World War I." Ph.D. dissertation, Georgetown University, 1971.

The Supreme Economic Council, created in early 1919 at Wilson's suggestion, made arrangements to get food relief to Germany and took on the responsibility of setting economic policy in occupied Germany. After the signing of the Treaty of Versailles, Wilson withdrew American representatives. DAI 32:2598-A.

3250 Flanagan, John H., Jr. "The Disillusionment of a Progressive: U.S. Senator David I. Walsh and the League of Nations Issue, 1918–1920." *New England Quarterly* 41 (1968): 483–504.

The only Democrat elected to the Senate in 1918, Massachusetts's David Walsh broke with the president in October 1919, because he saw the League of Nations as an instrument of the status quo that would not further the cause of national self-determination. Notes.

3251 Fleming, Denna F. *The United States and the League of Nations, 1918–1920.* New York: Putnam's, 1932.

This early scholarly history of the League idea details its creation by Wilson and its rejection by the Senate. Photographs, notes, appendix.

3252 ———. "Woodrow Wilson and Collective Security Today." *Journal of Politics* 18 (1956): 611–24.

History repeated itself when many people repudiated the foreign policy of Franklin D. Roosevelt after his death, just as they did Woodrow Wilson's following the Treaty of Versailles. Notes.

3253 Fosdick, Raymond B. *Letters on the League of Nations: From the Files of Raymond B. Fosdick.* Princeton: Princeton University Press, 1966.

The creation of the League is detailed by the American who became the first under secretary-general of the world body, only to see his own country reject it. Index.

3254 Jeffreys-Jones, Rhodri. "Massachusetts Labour and the League of Nations Controversy in 1919." *Irish Historical Studies* 19 (1975): 396–416.

In Massachusetts, labor turned against the Treaty of Versailles because the hope that the League of Nations would restore economic prosperity no longer seemed important once the American economy rebounded in late 1919. Ethnic dissatisfaction had little to do with it. Notes.

3255 Joyce, James A. *Broken Star: The Story of the League of Nations.* Swansea, England: Christopher Davis, 1978.

The League was a revolutionary enterprise, and, while Wilson was its *deus ex machina*, his own country refused to accept his plans. Photographs, notes, bibliography.

3256 Kimmich, Christoph M. *Germany and the League of Nations.* Chicago: University of Chicago Press, 1976.

Chapter 1 discusses Wilson's role in the decision to exclude Germany from the League. Notes, bibliography.

3257 Knock, Thomas J. "Woodrow Wilson and the Origins of the League of Nations." Ph.D. dissertation, Princeton University, 1982.

Wilson's childhood, academic career, and Presbyterian background affected his concept of the League of Nations. Wilson's Pan-American pact, proposed in 1914, was a failed attempt to institute a model for collective security and cooperation among nations. The American peace movement and various internationalists also contributed to Wilson's ideas. Wilson's League of Nations was the culmination of years of experience, discussion, and thought. DAI 43:2766-A.

3258 Kuehl, Warren F. *Seeking World Order: The United States and International Organization to 1920.* Nashville: Vanderbilt University Press, 1969.

Many peace groups had long been interested in some form of international organization, and most rallied around the League of Nations idea. But as long as the United States remained outside of the world body, the League remained a hollow victory for internationalists. Notes, bibliography, index.

3259 Lauren, Paul G. "Human Rights in History: Diplomacy and Racial Equality at the Paris Peace Conference." *Diplomatic History* 2 (1978): 257–78.

Japan's campaign at the peace conference to include a statement on racial equality in the League Covenant met with opposition from Wilson, who nixed the proposal in spite of majority support from the League commission. Notes.

3260 Marburg, Theodore. *Development of the League of Nations Idea: Documents and Correspondence of Theodore Marburg.* 2 vols. Edited by John H. Latane. New York: Macmillan, 1932.

The writings of this leading internationalist, who presided over the foreign organization committee of the League to Enforce Peace, shed light on support for the League idea from 1915 through the war and the peace conference. Wilson is credited as the most potent exponent of an international organization. Notes, index.

3261 Marburg, Theodore, and Flack, Horace E., eds. *Taft Papers on League of Nations.* New York: Macmillan, 1920.

Former President William Howard Taft headed the League to Enforce Peace and endorsed Wilson's League idea.

3262 Miller, David Hunter. *The Drafting of the Covenant.* 2 vols. New York: Putnam's, 1928.

A member of the American delegation who helped to hammer out the Covenant details his work in Volume I and presents forty supporting documents in Volume II. Index.

3263 Mitchell, David. "Woodrow Wilson as 'World Savior.' " *History Today* [Great Britain] 26 (1976): 3–14.

The dark side of Wilson's moral idealism is discussed in this analysis of origins of the League of Nations.

3264 Northedge, F. S. *The League of Nations: Its Life and Times, 1920–1946.* New York: Holmes and Meier, 1986.

While Wilson's strategy of tying the League to the Treaty of Versailles successfully persuaded many to accept the world body, the League became a guardian of a peace settlement hated by the defeated, and it was disowned by the United States. Notes, bibliography, index.

3265 Raffo, Peter. "The Anglo-American Preliminary Negotiations for a League of Nations." *Journal of Contemporary History* [Great Britain] 9 (1974): 153–76.

The League of Nations owes its origin to Lord Robert Cecil, whose 1916 memorandum outlined the organization. The British and the Americans worked up their own League drafts in 1918. Wilson concentrated his energy on shaping the Covenant, leaving the British to formulate specifics. Notes.

3266 Schwabe, Klaus. "Woodrow Wilson and Germany's Membership in the League of Nations, 1918–19." *Central European History* 8 (1975): 3–22.

Wilson wanted Germany in the League of Nations, then changed his mind, and finally concluded that membership should be permitted after German disarmament. Notes.

3267 Scott, George. *The Rise and Fall of the League of Nations.* London: Hutchinson, 1973.

Wilson was a lofty, arrogant sermonizer, but without him there would not have been a League of Nations, although Jan Smuts and Lord Robert Cecil also deserve credit for its creation. Illustrations, appendix.

3268 Stromberg, Roland N. "The Riddle of Collective Security." In George L. Anderson, ed. *Issues and Conflicts: Studies in Twentieth Century American Diplomacy.* Lawrence: University of Kansas Press, 1959, pp. 147–70.

Wilson, Henry Cabot Lodge, and the American people have all been blamed for the American failure to embrace collective security during the World War I era. The author suggests that the elusive concept of collective security itself is a better villain. Notes.

3269 Veatch, Richard. *Canada and the League of Nations.* Toronto: University of Toronto Press, 1975.

Canadian membership in the League meant that Canada had to have its own foreign policy for the first time. Canadians were torn by a desire for continuing isolation and their need to take a place in the international state system. Notes, bibliography.

3270 Verma, Dina N. *India and the League of Nations.* Patra, India: Bharati Bhawan, 1968.

While Wilson admired India, he did not want it to be admitted to the League, lest the Philippines also demand entrance. He finally accepted the British formula. Appendixes, notes.

3271 Walters, Francis P. *A History of the League of Nations.* London: Oxford University Press, 1952.

The first seven chapters include material on the League's origins during the war and the translation of these ideas into the League Covenant. Appendix, index.

3272 Wimer, Kurt. "Woodrow Wilson's Plans to Enter the League of Nations through an Executive Agreement." *Western Political Quarterly* 112 (1958): 800–812.

Wilson tried but failed to lead the United States into the League of Nations through an executive agreement. Wilson's predecessor Theodore Roosevelt had much more success with this device for skirting the will of Congress. Notes.

3273 Witte, William D. "American Quaker Pacifism and the Peace Settlement of World War I." *Bulletin of the Friends Historical Association* 46 (1957): 84–98.

Many Quakers favored the idea of the League of Nations, but they worried that collective security violated their absolute commitment to nonviolence.

MANDATES

3274 Ballendorf, Dirk A. "Secrets without Substance: U.S. Intelligence in the Japanese Mandates, 1915–1935." *Journal of Pacific History* 19 (1984): 83–99.

For twenty years, U.S. naval intelligence kept a close watch on Japan's Pacific mandates, as control of these islands gave Japan the power to cut American supply lines to the Pacific. Notes.

3275 Beer, George L. *African Questions at the Paris Peace Conference: With Papers on Egypt, Mesopotamia, and the Colonial Settlement.* Edited by Louis H. Gray. New York: Macmillan, 1923.

An American expert on mandates at the peace conference discusses the battles with Britain and France over African mandates. Appendix.

3276 Brown, Philip M. "The Mandate over Armenia." *American Journal of International Law* 14 (1920): 396–406.

This contemporary article contains a judicious analysis of the Senate's rejection of the Armenian mandate, based on the fear that acceptance might constitute implicit recognition of the League of Nations.

3277 Bryson, Thomas A. "The Armenia-America Society: A Factor in American-Turkish Relations, 1919–1924." *Records of the American Catholic Historical Society* 82 (1971): 83–105.

The Armenia-America Society was formed to keep the Armenian homeland issue before the American people. The society succeeded in killing the Turkish-American Treaty of Lausanne. Notes.

3278 ———. "John Sharp Williams: An Advocate for the Armenian Mandate, 1919–1920." *Armenian Review* 26 (1973): 23–42.

This Mississippi Democrat emerged as a champion of an American mandate over Armenia, representing Armenian views to Wilson and to the Senate.

3279 ———. "Mark Lambert Bristol, U.S. Navy, Admiral-Diplomat: His Influence on the Armenian Mandate Question." *Armenian Review* 21 (1968): 3–22.

The outspoken Bristol, who headed the American naval task force in Near Eastern waters, influenced the Senate against taking on the Armenian mandate.

3280 ———. *Walter George Smith.* Washington, DC: Catholic University Press, 1977.

Smith represented Armenian interests at the peace conference, fighting for an American mandate as the only way to safeguard the rights of a much-persecuted Christian minority group. Notes, bibliography, index.

3281 ———. "Woodrow Wilson and the Armenian Mandate: A Reassessment." *Armenian Review* 21 (1968): 10–28.

Conflicting interpretations of Wilson's crusade for an American mandate over Armenia are discussed. Notes.

3282 ———. "Woodrow Wilson, the Senate, Public Opinion and the Armenian Mandate, 1919–1920." Ph.D. dissertation, University of Georgia, 1965.

After the war Armenia, which had aided the Allies against the Turks, sought American protection from Russia. The Senate eventually rejected the Armenian mandate for the same reason that it had rejected participation in the League of Nations—a reluctance to commit American troops to unrewarding and distant conflicts. DAI 26:2706.

3283 Burns, Richard Dean. "Inspection of the Mandates, 1919–1941." *Pacific Historical Review* 37 (1968): 445–62.

Formerly German-held islands in the Pacific, including several strategic sites, were given to Japan as mandates during the peace conference. Subsequently, Americans suspected that the Japanese were violating their promise not to fortify their mandates. Notes.

3284 Cardashian, Vahan. "A 1921 Memorandum to the President on Armenia." *Armenian Review* 26 (1973): 46–63.

This memorandum for President Wilson on the plight of Armenia is reprinted along with editorial comments.

3285 Evans, Luther H. "The Mandates System and the Administration of Territories under C Mandate." Ph.D. dissertation, Stanford University, 1927.

C-mandated territories, as established by the League Covenant, were allowed only limited self-regulation. The author assesses the status of the various C mandates in 1927, concluding, in general, that no administering country fully lived up to its obligation to promote "to the utmost the material and moral well-being and social progress" of the indigenous people. DAI 25:4240.

3286 Gidney, James B. *A Mandate for Armenia*. Kent, OH: Kent State University Press, 1967.

American attitudes and actions toward the Armenians are traced from wartime concern about "starving Armenians" at the mercy of the "Terrible Turk" to the failed drive for a mandate and the subsequent poisoning of Turkish-American relations. Notes, bibliography, index.

3287 Housepian, Marjorie. *The Smyrna Affair*. New York: Harcourt Brace Jovanovich, 1971.

The American Navy stood by while Turks massacred Armenians in Smyrna and advocated a pro-Turkish policy at the expense of the Armenian mandate. Notes, bibliography, index.

3288 Louis, William R. "African Origins of the Mandates Idea." *International Organization* 19 (1965): 20–36.

The mandates system was derived from the devices used to control African colonies embodied in the Berlin Act of 1885 and the Algeciras Act of 1906. The new system's major innovation was self-determination. Notes.

3289 ———. "The United States and the African Peace Settlement of 1919: The Pilgrimage of George Louis Beer." *Journal of African History* 4 (1963): 413–33.

As a U.S. delegate on colonial matters at Versailles, Beer made an important contribution to the rules governing mandates. His idea that the United States should take the Cameroons as a mandate was not accepted, and he was helpless to prevent Britain and France from repartitioning parts of Africa.

3290 Maga, Timothy P. "Prelude to War? The United States, Japan, and the Yap Crisis, 1918–22." *Diplomatic History* 9 (1985): 215–31.

Japan's seizure of the German-held island of Yap in 1914 touched off years of American concern capped by the settlement of the issue at the Washington Naval Conference of 1921. Notes.

3291 Martin, William S., Jr. "The Colonial Mandate Question at the Paris Peace Conference of 1919: The United States and the Disposition of the German Colonies in Africa and the Pacific." Ph.D. dissertation, University of Southern Mississippi, 1982.

Wilson urged the peacemakers to accept the mandate system to prevent outright annexation of African colonies and Japanese militarization of Pacific islands. The British were satisfied with the control granted them over African colonies, while the colonies could plan for eventual independence. DAI 43:2065-A.

3292 Stivers, William. "Woodrow Wilson and the Arab World: The Liberal Dilemma." *Colorado College Studies* (1984): 106–23.

Wilson's endorsement of British and French mandates in the Middle East at once denied his principle of self-determination and reaffirmed it, as colonial power over Arab peoples was to be limited.

3293 Westermann, William L. "The Armenian Problem and the Disruption of Turkey." In Edward M. House and Charles Seymour, eds. *What Really Happened at Paris: The Story of the Peace Conference*. New York: Scribner's, 1921.

Wilson and the American delegation studied the Armenian problem and proposed an American mandate over the Christian minority.

PUBLIC OPINION AND THE PRESS

See also Chapter 2, *Wilson and the Press*, Chapter 9, *Public Opinion and Foreign Affairs*, and Chapter 11, *Civil Liberties*.

3294 Abbott, Frank. "The Texas Press and the Covenant." *Red River Valley Historical Review* 4 (1979): 32–41.

Press comments in early 1919 from Texas on the Paris Peace Conference are analyzed.

3295 Adler, Selig. "The War-Guilt Question and American Disillusionment, 1918–1928." *Journal of Modern History* 23 (1951): 1–28.

The war guilt clause in the Versailles treaty contributed to American cynicism toward the problems of Europe. Notes.

3296 Bartlett, Ruhl J. *The League to Enforce Peace*. Chapel Hill: University of North Carolina Press, 1944.

The activities of the League to Enforce Peace are detailed, including initial enthusiasm over the League of Nations, the suggestion of several amendments to the League Covenant, and the organization's moral collapse in the face of political pressure. Notes, appendix, index.

3297 Duff, John B. "German-Americans and the Peace, 1918–1920." *American Jewish Historical Quarterly* 59 (1970): 424–59.

The reactions of German-American newspapers to the issues of peace are examined. By 1920, German Americans had deserted the Democratic party to vote for Warren Harding. Notes.

3298 ——. "The Politics of Revenge: The Ethnic Opposition to the Peace Policies of Woodrow Wilson." Ph.D. dissertation, Columbia University, 1964.

Italian, Irish, and German Americans strenuously fought the League of Nations. Although each group initially supported Wilson's Fourteen Points, each was disappointed by how the principles were applied. The Irish expected more support for Ireland's independence, Italians expected more territorial gains, and Germans expected a more generous peace. Resentment and revenge fueled their fight against the League. DAI 28:1369-A.

3299 ——. "The Versailles Treaty and the Irish-Americans." *Journal of American History* 55 (1968): 582–98.

While Irish Americans supported Wilson's idea of a peace based on the Fourteen Points, many came to oppose the League of Nations. The president snubbed influential Irish-American leaders and insisted that the League would deal fairly with the Irish question. Notes.

3300 Epstein, Matthew H. "A Study of the Editorial Opinions of the New York City Newspapers toward the League of Nations and the United States during the First Year of Life, 1919–1920 and 1945–1946." Ph.D. dissertation, New York University, 1954.

Editorials in 1919–20 from sixteen newspapers are studied for explicit statements about the League of Nations. About 50 percent were primarily opposed to the League, 44 percent were in favor, and 6 percent were varied. The author found that many editorials had only a fuzzy factual basis and that different papers reached opposite conclusions from the same facts. DAI 14:816.

3301 Gerson, Louis L. *Woodrow Wilson and the Rebirth of Poland, 1914–1920: A Study in the*

Influence on American Policy of Minority Groups of Foreign Origin. New Haven, CT: Yale University Press, 1953.

Polish Americans created effective pressure groups that influenced Wilson's decision to seek the reformation of Poland. Notes, bibliography, appendix, index.

3302 McCallum, R. B. *Public Opinion and the Lost Peace*. London: Oxford University Press, 1944.

The defection of the United States from the League of Nations was a great blow to the League. Wilson was obstinate and maladroit, but he understood that Article X was critical to the success of the League. Index.

3303 McCarthy, Dennis J. "The British-Americans and Wilson's Peacemaking." *Duquesne Review* 9 (1964): 115–36.

British Americans did not put direct pressure on the president and the Congress so much as they exerted indirect influence through a vast network of social contacts.

3304 Martin, Laurence W. *Peace without Victory: Woodrow Wilson and the British Liberals*. New Haven, CT: Yale University Press, 1958.

The antiwar faction of British liberals and some socialists hoped that Wilson would lead the peace movement following the American declaration of war and the Bolshevik Revolution. Notes, appendix, bibliography, index.

3305 O'Grady, Joseph P., ed. *The Immigrants' Influence on Wilson's Peace Policies*. Lexington: University of Kentucky Press, 1967.

Key ethnic groups are studied to determine their impact on Wilson's decisions at the Paris Peace Conference. Among those studied are Germans, Irish, Italians, British, Jews, and various East European immigrant groups. Notes, index.

3306 Rochester, Stuart I. *American Liberal Disillusionment in the Wake of World War I*. University Park: Pennsylvania State University Press, 1977.

The prewar liberal generation was provincial in its thinking, but World War I dimmed its illusions about peace and progress, and the Versailles settlement extinguished them as the old order quickly retrenched. Notes, index.

3307 Sierpowski, Stanislaw. "Support for the League of Nations, 1919–1926" (in French). *Acta Poloniac Historica* [Poland] (1983): 165–93.

League support came from peace groups seeking to avoid the horrors of war, officials looking for insurance against aggression, and internationalists hoping to transcend nationalism. Notes.

3308 Startt, James D. "American Editorial Opinion of Woodrow Wilson and the Main Problems of Peacemaking in 1919." Ph.D. dissertation, University of Maryland, 1965.

Wilson enjoyed the most support from the South and the far West, from labor and religious publications, and from Democratic, liberal, and independent journals. In general, the press supported the League until the first Senate vote on the issue; it then favored a modified League, but Wilson ignored the shift in opinion. Some vital aspects of the League question were overlooked by the press. DAI 27:172-A.

3309 ———. "The Uneasy Partnership: Wilson and the Press at Paris." *Mid-America* 52 (1970): 55–69.

Although the president gave scant attention to the press during the war, he attempted to court the Fourth Estate to gain a consensus for his peace policies, but the new partnership quickly became strained. Notes.

3310 ———. "Wilson's Trip to Paris: Profile of Press Response." *Journalism Quarterly* 46 (1969): 737–42.

Although most newspapers disapproved at first of the idea of the president traveling to Paris to attend the peace conference, his formal announcement brought forth a great show of support, with the anti-Wilson Hearst press silent on the matter. Notes.

3311 Zacharewicz, Mary M. "The Attitude of the Catholic Press toward the League of Nations, Part I." *Records of the American Catholic Historical Society* 67 (1956): 3–30.

Most Catholic newspapers surveyed here favored the League of Nations, so much so that Republicans used anti-Catholic prejudice against it.

3312 ———. "The Attitude of the Catholic Press toward the League of Nations, Part II." *Records of the American Catholic Historical Society* 67 (1956): 88–104.

Some Catholic periodicals opposed the League of Nations, although the cases made against the League do not hold up particularly well.

3313 ———. "The Attitude of the Catholic Press toward the League of Nations, Part III." *Records of the American Catholic Historical Society* 68 (1957): 46–50.

While a majority of Catholic periodicals favored the League of Nations, some expressed reservations because self-determination for Ireland had not been dealt with fairly.

RUSSIAN QUESTION

See also Chapter 9, *Foreign Affairs: General, General Accounts* and *Wilson and Foreign Affairs,* Chapter 10, *Wartime Relations,* and Chapter 11, *The Bolshevik Revolution.*

3314 Epstein, Fritz T. "Studies on the History of the 'Russian Question' at the Paris Peace Conference of 1919" (in German). *Jahrbücher für Geschichte Osteuropas* [West Germany] 7 (1959): 431–78.

The influence of the Russian political council is examined along with the influence of representatives of Russian ethnic minorities seeking autonomy, American policies, and ways in which the League of Nations might have been used to effect solutions of the "Russian question."

3315 Fike, Claude E. "The United States and Russian Territorial Problems, 1917–1920." *Historian* 24 (1962): 331–46.

Wilson was determined to be consistent about national self-determination, but the Bolshevik Revolution made it difficult to defend this proposition in regard to Russian ethnic territories. Notes.

3316 Kennan, George F. "Russia and the Versailles Conference." *American Scholar* 30 (1960): 13–42.

The failure of the Allies to deal with the Russian question at the peace conference had momentous implications for the Soviets' subsequent relations with the West.

3317 Smallwood, James. "Banquo's Ghost at the Paris Peace Conference: The United States and the Hungarian Question." *East European Quarterly* 12 (1978): 289–307.

While Wilson would have accepted the Communist government of Béla Kun in Hungary after World War I, the attitudes of his staff and the actions of the Allies made the point moot. Notes.

3318 Thompson, John M. *Russia, Bolshevism, and the Versailles Peace.* Princeton: Princeton University Press, 1966.

The inability of the Allies to deal with the Russian question at the peace conference embittered relations with the Soviets and increased hostility on both sides. The diplomats lacked both the power and the public backing to force their will on the Soviets. Notes, appendixes, bibliography, index.

SELF-DETERMINATION

See also Chapter 6, *Immigration,* Chapter 9, *Poland,* and Chapter 10, *Wartime Relations, Others.*

3319 Albee, Parker B., Jr. "American and Allied Policies at the Paris Peace Conference: The Drawing of the Polish-German Frontier." Ph.D. dissertation, Duke University, 1968.

The fundamental problem in drawing the German-Polish border was that Poland needed secure access to the sea, but the German-populated town of Danzig had the only logical port. The personalities, political philosophies, and diplomatic styles of the various peace conference leaders, particularly Wilson and Colonel Edward House, are revealed in their slow resolution of this conflict. DAI 29:1186-A.

3320 Beloff, Max. "Self-Determination Reconsidered." *Confluence* 5 (1956): 195–203.

Wilson was ahead of his time in seeing that national self-determination was an important element of keeping peace.

3321 Bryson, Thomas A. "Walter George Smith and the Armenian Question at the Paris Peace Conference, 1919." *Records of the American Catholic Historical Society* 81 (1970): 3–26.

After a tour of Armenia in 1919, Smith worked to get more relief supplies for the Turkish minority, helped with their repatriation, and convinced the British to ward off the Turks from outside Armenia. Notes.

3322 Buzanski, Peter M. "The Inter-Allied Investigation of the Greek Invasion of Smyrna, 1919." *Historian* 25 (1963): 325–43.

The Greek landing at Smyrna was investigated by an Allied commission, which included an American naval officer. Notes.

3323 Carroll, F. M. " 'All Standards of Human Conduct': The American Commission on Conditions in Ireland, 1920–21." *Éire-Ireland* 16 (1981): 59–74.

The American Commission on Conditions in Ireland gathered evidence on the Irish independence movement and proved to be a useful counterweight to British propaganda, although it was too late to have an effect on the deliberations at Paris. Notes.

3324 Chi, Madeleine. "China and Unequal Treaties at the Paris Peace Conference of 1919." *Asian Profile* [Hong Kong] 1 (1973): 49–61.

Wilson yielded on the question of Chinese territorial integrity in return for Allied support of the League, a trade-off which led to the Chinese refusal to sign the peace accords. Notes.

3325 Chin Wen-su. *Woodrow Wilson, Wellington Koo and the China Question at the Paris Peace Conference.* Leyden: Sythoff, 1959.

A former member of the Chinese diplomatic corps describes the Shantung settlement, which is viewed here as ill-considered because it led to "the Red deluge." Notes.

3326 Devasia, A. Thomas. "The United States and the Formation of Greater Romania, 1914–1918: A Study in Diplomacy and Propaganda." Ph.D. dissertation, Boston College, 1970.

Throughout most of the war, Wilson hoped to deal more leniently with Austria-Hungary, because he regarded Germany as the primary evil. Public opinion finally swayed the president in favor of a Greater Romania. DAI 31:6512-A.

3327 Drake, Edson J. "Bulgaria at the Paris Peace Conference: A Diplomatic History of the Treaty of Neuilly-sur-Seine." Ph.D. dissertation, Georgetown University, 1967.

Bulgaria had a just claim to much of the territory that the peace conference eventually assigned to other nations. The author concludes that the Treaty of Neuilly-sur-Seine violated many of Wilson's tenets. DAI 28:4087-A.

3328 Dulles, Foster Rhea. "Woodrow Wilson—A Contemporary Evaluation." *United Asia* [India] 9 (1957): 115–22.

Wilson and Jawaharlal Nehru are compared as champions of idealism, liberty, and national self-determination.

3329 Dumin, Frederick. "Self-Determination: The United States and Austria in 1919." *Research Studies* 40 (1972): 176–94.

Although uniting much of Germany and Austria would have followed the spirit of self-determination, there was never any real chance that the peace conference would approve such an *anschluss.* Notes.

3330 Frass-Ehrfeld, Claudia. "The Reports of the Miles Mission regarding the Final Carinthian

Border" (in German). *Carinthia* 1 [Austria] (1975): 255–66.

The Miles mission to Carinthia of 1919 was dispatched by the American delegation at the peace conference to investigate the ethnic makeup of the region. Notes.

3331 Helmreich, Paul C. *From Paris to Sèvres: The Partition of the Ottoman Empire at the Peace Conference, 1919–1920.* Columbus: Ohio State University Press, 1974.

While the Allies were determined to carve up the "sick man of Europe," the Americans argued for a Near Eastern settlement that would include the principle of national self-determination for the long-suffering minorities of the Ottoman Empire. Notes, appendix, bibliography, index.

3332 Howard, Harry N. *The King-Crane Commission: An American Inquiry into the Middle East.* Beirut: Khayats, 1963.

The peace conference empowered the King-Crane commission to investigate the special problem of peace in the Middle East. This commission's long-suppressed report was critical of a Zionist Palestine and a French mandate in Syria, while it endorsed British mandates and an American mandate for Armenia. Notes, bibliography, appendix, index.

3333 ———. *The Partition of Turkey: A Diplomatic History, 1913–1923.* Norman: University of Oklahoma Press, 1931.

The partition of Turkey and Turkish-American relations during the Wilson administration are discussed in a book that is still quite useful. Notes, bibliography, index.

3334 Kalvoda, Josef. "Masaryk in America in 1918" (in German). *Jahrbücher für Geschichte Osteuropas* [West Germany] 27 (1979): 85–99.

Tomás Masaryk's American visit was only one factor among many that led to the creation of Czechoslovakia. The Czech Legion's actions in Russia, Austria-Hungary's continuing support for Germany, and the work of Czech revolutionaries all were instrumental. Notes.

3335 Kernek, Sterling J. "Woodrow Wilson and National Self-Determination along Italy's Frontier: A Study of the Manipulation of Principles in the Pursuit of Political Interests." *Proceedings of the American Philosophical Society* 126 (1982): 243–300.

Wilson was prepared to compromise his principles for the sake of creating the League of Nations. His handling of Italian boundaries is an illustration of the pragmatic course he was

capable of pursuing for the sake of his larger goal. Notes.

3336 Knee, Stuart E. "The King-Crane Commission of 1919: The Articulation of Political Anti-Zionism." *American Jewish Archives* 29 (1977): 22–52.

Christian missionary ideals played a role in the anti-Zionist outlook of the King-Crane commission.

3337 Kusielewicz, Eugene. "New Light on the Curzon Line." *Polish Review* 1 (1956): 82–88.

A letter from diplomat Robert H. Lord to Norman Davis of the State Department shows the tentative nature of the Curzon line and that the Polish border line was an objective application of Wilson's Thirteenth Point. Notes.

3338 ———. "The Teschen Question at the Paris Peace Conference: A Re-Examination in the Light of Materials in the Archives of the United States." Ph.D. dissertation, Fordham University, 1963.

The Duchy of Teschen was an economically important center claimed by both Poland and the Czecho-Slovak states. Although a settlement was reached in 1920, the issue continued to disrupt relations between the two countries. The archives of the United States are used to construct a detailed and relatively objective account of the dispute. DAI 24:5362.

3339 ———. "Wilson and the Polish Cause at Paris." *Polish Review* 1 (1956): 64–79.

Wilson's Thirteenth Point makes it clear that the president strongly favored an independent Polish state. His opposition to the cession of Danzig to Poland and to a plebiscite in Silesia are more difficult to understand. Notes.

3340 Lederer, Ivo J. *Yugoslavia at the Paris Peace Conference: A Study in Frontier Making.* New Haven, CT: Yale University Press, 1963.

Yugoslav nationalists found a powerful ally in Woodrow Wilson for their fight with Italy over self-determination for the peoples of Istria and Fiume. Notes, bibliography, index.

3341 McCrum, Robert. "French Rhineland Policy at the Paris Peace Conference." *Historical Journal* 21 (1978): 623–48.

A French scheme to create an independent Rhineland met with opposition from the people in the area and from the other Allies, who preferred guarantees of France's national security. Notes.

3342 Malkasian, Mark. "The Disintegration of the Armenian Cause in the United States, 1918–1927." *International Journal of Middle East Studies* 16 (1984): 349–65.

Americans supported an independent Armenian homeland after World War I, but the movement collapsed as a result, among other things, of quarrels between rival movements and intervention by Soviet Russia in the proposed state. Notes.

3343 Mamatey, Victor S. *The United States and East Central Europe, 1914–1918: A Study in Wilsonian Diplomacy and Propaganda.* Princeton: Princeton University Press, 1957.

American attitudes and actions toward the breakup of the Habsburg Empire are examined. American and Soviet propaganda stimulated nationalism in the region, and the defeat of the Central Powers brought self-determination to East Central Europe. Notes, bibliography, index.

3344 Manijak, William. "Polish American Pressure Groups, Woodrow Wilson and the Thirteenth Point: The Significance of Polish Food Relief, the Polish Vote, and European Events in the Eventual Self-Determination for Poland." Ph.D. dissertation, Ball State University, 1975.

The influence of House and Jan Paderewski on Wilson, as well as strong support from Polish Americans, led the president to press for Polish self-determination at the Paris Peace Conference. DAI 37:1145-A.

3345 May, Arthur J. "H. A. Miller and the Mid-European Union of 1918." *American Slavic and East European Review* 16 (1977): 473–88.

The high tide of American support for national self-determination for the peoples of the Austro-Hungarian empire came with the short-lived Mid-European Union of 1918, headed by Herbert A. Miller.

3346 Mitchell, Kell. "The United States' Greek Policy at the Paris Peace Conference, June-December, 1919." *North Dakota Quarterly* 47 (1979): 30–44.

After Wilson returned to the United States upon signing the Treaty of Versailles, the American delegation stayed behind to work on the problem of Greek territories.

3347 Myers, Duane. "The United States and Austria, 1918–1919: The Problem of National Self-Determination." *Proceedings of the South Carolina Historical Association* (1975): 5–15.

At the Paris Peace Conference, Austrian Germans found that the principle of national self-determination did not apply to them. Wilson had little sympathy for them, preferring to concentrate on the claims of other ethnic groups. Notes.

3348 Noer, Thomas J. "The American Government and the Irish Question during World War I." *South Atlantic Quarterly* 72 (1973): 95–114.

During the period of American neutrality, some Irish Americans hoped that a German victory over Britain might free Ireland. During the war, they lobbied to have Irish independence considered as part of Wilson's plan for national self-determination, but British propaganda turned many Americans against the idea. When Wilson came back from Paris without having dealt with Ireland satisfactorily, Irish Americans deserted him. Notes.

3349 O'Grady, Joseph P. "Irish-Americans, Woodrow Wilson, and Self-Determination." *Records of the American Catholic Historical Society* 74 (1963): 159–73.

Wilson sympathized with the plight of the Irish, but he felt that he could not make an issue of the subject at the peace conference. Less-scrupulous politicians used the Irish question for partisan purposes.

3350 Pantev, Andrei. "The Border Line between Sympathy and Support: The United States and the Bulgarian Territorial Question at the Paris Peace Conference in 1919." *Southeastern Europe* 8 (1981): 171–97.

Only the American delegation sympathized with Bulgarian territorial aspirations at the peace conference. Missionaries who had worked in Bulgaria emerged as champions of a large Bulgaria as did those who saw this as a way to diminish Anglo-French economic penetration into Eastern Europe. Notes.

3351 ———. "The Plans of the United States to Define the Boundaries of Bulgaria during 1918–19" (in Bulgarian). *Istoricheski Pregled* [Bulgaria] 37 (1981): 33–49.

America supported Bulgaria's boundary claims, but career diplomats siding with the Allies carried the day, to the detriment of Bulgarians. Notes.

3352 Pliska, Stanley R. "The Polish American Community and the Rebirth of Poland." *Polish American Studies* 26 (1969): 41–60.

Polish Americans played an important part in the creation of a new Polish state. They helped to raise a Polish army for the Allies and conducted propaganda campaigns in the United States.

3353 Pomerance, Michla. "The United States and Self-Determination: Perspectives on the Wilsonian Conception." *American Journal of International Law* 70 (1976): 1–27.

Self-determination has been criticized from several different perspectives as either impractical or even imperialistic. The term is a vague one, which Wilson hoped the League of Nations would develop. Notes.

3354 Posey, John P. "David Hunter Miller and the Polish Minorities Treaty, 1919." *Southern Quarterly* 8 (1970): 163–76.

Miller had a strong influence on the Polish Minorities Treaty negotiated at the Paris Peace Conference, which guaranteed full civil rights to all peoples living in the new Polish state, an agreement which was largely disregarded. Notes.

3355 Prinz, Friedrich. "The USA and the Foundation of Czechoslovakia." *Central Europe Journal* [West Germany] 20 (1972): 171–85.

American attitudes toward the Czechs shifted between 1914 and 1918 from wanting to keep the Habsburg monarchy, to using the idea of self-determination as a propaganda weapon, to endorsement of a Czech nation.

3356 Sabki, Hisham. "Woodrow Wilson and Self-Determination in the Arab Middle East." *Journal of Political Studies* 4 (1979): 381–99.

Like other captive ethnic minorities, Arabs in the Ottoman Empire were affected by Wilson's talk of national self-determination—and disappointed by the subsequent peace settlement.

3357 Seymour, Charles. "Woodrow Wilson and Self-Determination in the Tyrol." *Virginia Quarterly Review* 38 (1962): 567–87.

Although he was a great believer in national self-determination, Wilson seemed indifferent to German-speaking Tyrol. Wilson most likely traded Tyrol for other points that he regarded as more important. Notes.

3358 Sullivan, Dennis M. "Eamon De Valéra and the Forces of Opposition in America, 1919–1920." *Éire-Ireland* 19 (1984): 98–115.

Eamon de Valéra visited the United States in 1919–20 to borrow money and seek recognition for Irish revolutionaries. Battling British countermeasures and enemies within the movement, he raised money and consciousness for the Irish cause. Notes.

3359 Van Alstyne, Richard W. "Woodrow Wilson and the Idea of the Nation State." *International Affairs* 37 (1961): 293–308.

The age of the liberal nation-state came to an end with World War I. The American nationalist Wilson tried and failed to end the total independence of nation-states. Notes.

3360 Walsh, James P. "De Valéra in the United States, 1919." *Records of the American Catholic Historical Society* 73 (1962): 91–107.

De Valéra was temperate in his criticisms of Wilson, unlike some other Irish religious and political leaders. His moderation may have swayed David Lloyd George into setting in motion freedom for Ireland.

3361 Ward, Alan J. "America and the Irish Problem, 1899–1921." *Irish Historical Studies* 16 (1968): 64–90.

Irish Americans were outraged when, after years of struggle, the Treaty of Versailles contained nothing on Irish independence.

3362 Witkowski, Peter A. "Roman Dmowski and the Thirteenth Point." Ph.D. dissertation, Indiana University, 1981.

Wilson's Thirteenth Point, which called for the re-creation of Poland, was influenced not only by Colonel House and Ignacy Jan Paderewski but also by Polish politician Roman Dmowski. Dmowski's political thought is analyzed in detail. DAI 42:3267-A.

3363 Wolfe, James H. "Woodrow Wilson and the Right of Self-Determination: The Problem of the Bohemian Border." *Bohemia* [West Germany] 8 (1967): 217–26.

While the president's Tenth Point pledged self-determination for the ethnic populations of Austria-Hungary, he did not want to uproot the Sudeten Germans, although this happened anyway. Self-determination along the Bohemian border proved impossible to implement. Notes.

3364 Zerby, Charles L. "John Dewey and the Polish Question: A Response to the Revisionist Historians." *History of Education Quarterly* 15 (1975): 17–30.

John Dewey's 1918 study of American policy toward Poland led to a critique of Wilson's implementation of self-determination for the Poles as anti-Semitic and undemocratic.

3365 Živojinović, Dragan R. *America, Italy, and the Birth of Yugoslavia (1917–1919).* New York: Columbia University Press, 1972.

Wilson was more flexible than is often realized in his dealings with the Italians over Yugoslavia during the peace conference. The Yugoslavs were careful to keep Wilson on their side, a strategy that paid off in the end. Notes, bibliography, index.

WORLD COURT

See also Chapter 3, *Elihu Root.*

3366 Curtis, George H. "The Wilson Administration, Elihu Root, and the Founding of the World Court." Ph.D. dissertation, Georgetown University, 1972.

Although Wilson did not wish to include a World Court in the peace settlement, his advisers and the British convinced him of the need for such an institution. Elihu Root's disapproval of the peace treaty made him balk at serving on the court's advisory committee. In 1920 he reversed his position, and his participation helped to get the World Court on its feet. DAI 35:999-A.

3367 Patterson, David S. "The United States and the Origins of the World Court." *Political Science Quarterly* 91 (1976): 259–77.

The war had an important impact on ideas about international law. Wilson opposed the idea of a world court but acceded to demands that it be created as part of the peacekeeping machinery. Notes.

RATIFICATION CONTROVERSY

See also Chapter 3, *Congressional and Political Leaders.*

3368 Ambrosius, Lloyd E. "Wilson, the Republicans, and French Security after World War I." *Journal of American History* 59 (1972): 341–52.

Republicans offered positive alternatives to the League during the treaty fight. Many wanted to keep the wartime coalition alive or guarantee the security of France as a means of keeping the peace. Notes.

3369 Bailey, Thomas A. *Woodrow Wilson and the Great Betrayal.* New York: Macmillan, 1945.

The "great betrayal" happened when the Senate refused to ratify the Treaty of Versailles and join the League of Nations. Because the United States had nothing to lose and everything to gain from joining the League, Wilson should have compromised with the Senate on their reservations. Bibliographic notes, index.

3370 ———. "Woodrow Wilson Wouldn't Yield." *American Heritage* 8 (1957): 21–25ff.

The struggle to ratify the Treaty of Versailles came down to a clash between Wilson and Henry Cabot Lodge, two men who refused to compromise.

3371 Boothe, Leon E. "Woodrow Wilson's Cold War: The President, the Public, and the League Fight, 1919–1920." Ph.D. dissertation, University of Illinois, Urbana-Champaign, 1966.

Wilson politicized the League issue by postponing, for partisan purposes, official involvement for so long that his ideas were not well formulated by the time of the peace conference. Alienation of the Republican senators, the president's illness, and his denunciations of those seeking political compromise all contributed to the defeat of a treaty that majorities in both parties favored. DAI 27:2112-A.

3372 Chan, Loren G. "Fighting for the League: President Wilson in Nevada, 1919." *Nevada Historical Quarterly* 22 (1979): 115–27.

Although Wilson was warmly received by Democrats when he stopped in Reno on his tour to drum up support for the League of Nations, Nevada's senators voted against him, and popular sentiment concerning the League vacillated.

3373 Chappell, Ben A. "The League of Nations Debate: A Lesson in Public Education." *Southern Quarterly* 2 (1964): 30–47.

While a majority of the American people favored joining the League of Nations in the spring of 1919, Senate Republicans wanted to attach reservations to the Treaty of Versailles. Efforts at compromise failed, and the 1920 general election became a referendum of sorts on foreign policy.

3374 Creel, George. *The War, the World, and Wilson.* New York: Harper, 1920.

Wilson's propaganda chief writes that at Paris the president fought the imperialists and beat them. The Treaty of Versailles was the greatest war settlement in human history, but the Republicans have turned the voice of America into a "polyglot screech."

3375 Egerton, George W. "Britain and the 'Great Betrayal': Anglo-American Relations and the Struggle for United States Ratification of the Treaty of Versailles." *History Journal* [Great Britain] 21 (1978): 885–911.

Viscount Edward Grey's inability to smooth over the struggle between Wilson and the Senate over the ratification of the Treaty of Versailles led him to publish a letter in *The Times* of London in early 1920 which made relations between the United States and Britain even worse. Notes.

3376 Fleming, Denna F. *The Treaty Veto of the American Senate.* New York: Putnam's, 1930.

The Senate's power over treaties and the pacts that have been rejected are discussed, including the fight over the League and the Treaty of Versailles. Notes, index.

3377 Freeman, Walden S. "Will H. Hays and the League of Nations." Ph.D. dissertation, Indiana University, 1967.

As chairman of the Republican National Committee, Will Hays fought to unify Republicans in support of an amended League of Nations. No consensus was reached despite popular support for some sort of League, and the issue died after the 1920 campaign. DAI 28: 3603-A.

3378 Hewes, James E., Jr. "Henry Cabot Lodge and the League of Nations." *Proceedings of the American Philosophical Society* 114 (1970): 245–55.

Lodge was neither inconsistent nor unreasonable about yielding national sovereignty to international organizations during his long career in the Senate. Notes.

3379 Hill, Thomas M. "The Senate Leadership and International Policy from Lodge to Vandenberg." Ph.D. dissertation, Washington University, 1970.

Chapter 2 examines the Senate leadership of Lodge in the contest with Wilson over the Versailles treaty. While the showdown with the president was partly personal and partly political, Lodge also believed that the Senate had a constitutional duty to uphold. DAI 31:1726-A.

3380 Holt, W. Stull. *Treaties Defeated by the Senate: A Study of the Struggle between President and Senate over the Conduct of Foreign Relations.* Baltimore, MD: Johns Hopkins University Press, 1933.

The Senate's rejection of the Treaty of Versailles is analyzed in Chapter 10 as part of the ongoing fight between government branches for control of foreign policy. Notes, bibliography, index.

3381 Jennings, David H. "President Wilson's Tour in September, 1919: A Study of Forces Operating during the League of Nations Fight." Ph.D. dissertation, Ohio State University, 1958.

In September 1919, Wilson toured the country to win popular support for the League in the mistaken belief that the Senate would yield to public opinion. Although he tailored his speeches to the concerns of the various regions he visited, the author concludes that more appeal to self-interest and less to altruism would have had more effect. DAI 19:3289.

3382 Kosberg, Roberta L. "Executive-Legislative Rhetoric regarding American Participation in an Association of Nations, 1916–1920 and 1935–1945." Ph.D. dissertation, Pennsylvania State University, 1982.

Wilson emphasized idealism rather than national self-interest in explaining why the United States needed the League of Nations, although most people at the time did not understand the changing nature of national security. He failed to use the many communications resources available to him. Franklin Roosevelt did a better job in selling the United Nations to the American people. DAI 43:3152-A.

3383 Lodge, Henry Cabot. *The Senate and the League of Nations.* New York: Scribner's, 1975.

Lodge discusses the Republican reactions to Wilson's foreign policy, especially the Treaty of Versailles and the League. Wilson was a total failure who bears all of the responsibility for the defeat of the treaty. Appendix.

3384 Logan, Rayford W. *The Senate and the Versailles Mandate System.* Washington, DC: Minorities, 1945.

During the debates over the Treaty of Versailles, the Senate paid close attention to the League Covenant's provision for mandates, with some denouncing it as a new form of colonialism, while others welcomed the opportunity to shelter persecuted and backward peoples.

3385 McGinty, Brian. " 'Remember, No Compromise': The Debate over the League of Nations." *American History Illustrated* 15 (1971): 8–17.

An overview of the struggle for ratification of the Treaty of Versailles is presented.

3386 Meaney, N. K. "The British Empire in the American Rejection of the Treaty of Versailles." *Australian Journal of Politics and History* 9 (1963): 213–34.

While the attitudes and actions of Wilson and his political enemies had much to do with the fate of the Treaty of Versailles, a contributing factor was the growing perception of the peace treaty as a British document. Notes.

3387 Rosenberger, Homer T. "The American Peace Society's Reaction to the Covenant of the League of Nations." *World Affairs* 141 (1978): 139–52.

The reaction of the American Peace Society to Wilson's many compromises at the Paris Peace Conference was decidedly mixed, although it supported the League idea.

3388 Stern, Sheldon M. "American Nationalism vs. the League of Nations: The Correspondence of Albert J. Beveridge and Louis A. Coolidge, 1918–1920." *Indiana Magazine of History* 72 (1976): 138–58.

Beveridge and Coolidge were unmoved by the "new diplomacy," remaining ardent advocates of expansionism and supernationalism.

3389 Stone, Ralph A. "The Irreconcilables' Alternatives to the League." *Mid-America* 49 (1967): 163–73.

The "irreconcilables" can be divided into three factions: supernationalists, realists who stood halfway between isolationism and the internationalism of Wilson, and idealists demanding that the League be nearly perfect. Notes.

3390 ———. *The Irreconcilables: The Fight against the League of Nations*. Lexington: University of Kentucky Press, 1970.

The hard core of opposition to Wilson's League of Nations scheme consisted of sixteen senators, fourteen of whom were Republicans. They represented the East, the Midwest, and the West, and they were united only by their bitter opposition to the treaty as an instrument of the status quo. Notes, appendix, bibliography, index.

3391 ———. "Two Illinois Senators among the Irreconcilables." *Mississippi Valley Historical Review* 50 (1963): 443–65.

Illinois Senators Medill McCormick and Lawrence Y. Sherman joined Lodge in opposing the Treaty of Versailles for different reasons.

McCormick was a supernationalist who hated Britain, while Sherman despised Wilson and his Progressive reforms. Notes.

3392 ———, ed. *Wilson and the League of Nations: Why America's Rejection?* New York: Holt, Rinehart and Winston, 1967.

Excerpts from previously published works discuss politics, ideology, and the roles of Wilson and Lodge in the ratification controversy along with lessons drawn by historians. Bibliography.

3393 Trow, Clifford W. "'Something Desperate in His Face': Woodrow Wilson in Portland at the 'Very Crisis of His Career.' " *Oregon Historical Quarterly* 82 (1981): 40–64.

Wilson's visit to Portland, Oregon, during his desperate tour to reverse the tide running against the Treaty of Versailles is described along with the position of Oregon's senators on the president and his work. Notes.

3394 Vinson, John C. *Referendum for Isolation: The Defeat of Article Ten of the League of Nations Covenant*. Athens: University of Georgia Press, 1961.

Senate rejection of the League of Nations reflected the public's growing desire for political isolation from Europe. Notes, bibliography, index.

3395 Walker, Henry P. "American Isolationism and the National Defense Act of 1920." *Military Review* 54 (1974): 14–23.

The National Defense Act was passed to keep the United States from being unprepared for future wars, but the bitter defeat of the Treaty of Versailles created a mood of isolationism which ensured that this legislation would be ignored.

3396 Wimer, Kurt. "Executive-Legislative Tensions in the Making of the League of Nations." Ph.D. dissertation, New York University, 1957.

The president and the Senate engaged in a complex struggle over power and ideology while debating the League Covenant. DAI 21:719.

3397 ———. "Woodrow Wilson Tries Conciliation: An Effort that Failed." *Historian* 25 (1963): 419–38.

During the debate over ratification of the Versailles treaty, Wilson was not as uncompromising as he has been portrayed. In July 1919 it appeared that the president would meet moderate Republicans halfway on the issues that separated them, although in the next month

Wilson decided to use public pressure to hurry the conciliation along. Notes.

3398 Wittgens, Herman J. "The German Foreign Office Campaign against the Versailles Treaty: An Examination of the Activities of the *Kriegsschuldreferat* in the United States." Ph.D. dissertation, University of Washington, 1970.

The German foreign office's propaganda campaign against the Versailles treaty concentrated on Article 231, the war guilt clause. Agents in the United States provided interested publicists and scholars with the German side of the issue. Documents were published to show that Germany was peaceful and not really responsible for starting the war. DAI 31:5342-A.

General Reference Works

13

Included in this final chapter are some of the reference aids dealing with the Wilson presidency, the Progressive era, and World War I. While these works list useful collections of primary and secondary source materials, it also should be remembered that monographs, articles, dissertations, and collections of documents listed in previous chapters often contain extensive bibliographies and citations. Because bibliographies do become dated, researchers ought to consult annual finding guides printed by specialty presses and scholarly journals as well.

While the compilation by Laura S. Turnbull, ed., *Woodrow Wilson: A Selected Bibliography* (#3405), is many years out of date, it remains valuable as a guide to early works about Wilson as well as his writings. A computer-assisted search of major databases makes Fenton S. Martin and Robert V. Goehlert, *American Presidents: A Bibliography* (#3404), an important source of materials whose titles contain Wilson's name. American Bibliographical Center's (ABC-Clio's) *The American Presidency: A Historical Bibliography* (#3399) contains annotated entries of scholarly articles on Wilson culled from the American Bibliographical Center's *America: History and Life: A Guide to Periodical Literature* (#3406), a quarterly publication subscribed to by many libraries and also accessible by DIALOG computer search. Other important general bibliographies include Arthur S. Link and William M. Leary, Jr., *The Progressive Era and the Great War, 1896–1920* (#3409), and Jack Salzman, ed., *American Studies: An Annotated Bibliography* (#3410).

For historiographic essays on writings about Wilson, see John A. Garraty, "Link's Wilson" (#3413), for a critical analysis of the leading expert, Arthur Link. See also Richard L. Watson, Jr., "Woodrow Wilson and His Interpreters, 1947–1957" (#3414), an essay that

is good enough to make researchers rue the lack of such extended bibliographic essays in other scholarly publications. William A. Williams, *Some Presidents: Wilson to Nixon* (#3415), contains a chapter on writings about Wilson.

The many controversies among historians about the Progressive era are examined in William G. Anderson, "Progressivism: An Historiographical Essay" (#3416); Louis Filler, *Progressivism and Muckraking* (#3418); Arthur Mann, "The Progressive Tradition" (#3420); George E. Mowry, *The Progressive Movement, 1900–1920: Recent Ideas and New Literature* (#3422); and Robert H. Wiebe, "The Progressive Years, 1900–1917" (#3426). For the "golden age of socialism" see Bryan Strong, "Historians and American Socialism, 1900–1920" (#3424). Useful examinations of works on Wilsonian foreign policy include Edith James, "Wilsonian Wartime Diplomacy: The Sense of the Seventies" (#3430); Gordon Martel, "America's Bid for Empire" (#3432); Eugene P. Trani, "Woodrow Wilson and the Decision to Intervene in Russia: A Reconsideration" (#3435); and Samuel F. Wells, Jr., "New Perspectives on Wilsonian Diplomacy: The Secular Evangelism of American Political Economy" (#3436). The pre-World War II revisionists who examined Wilson's motives for entering the conflict in Europe are analyzed by Warren I. Cohen, *The American Revisionists: The Lessons of Intervention in World War I* (#3439). For post-World War II interpretations, see Daniel M. Smith, "National Interest and American Intervention, 1917: An Historiographical Appraisal" (#3442).

The best annotated bibliography on the Progressive era is John D. Buenker and Nicholas C. Burckel, *Progressive Reform: A Guide to Information Sources* (#3445). On the Industrial Workers of the World, see Dione Miles, *Something in Common: An IWW Bibliography*

Woodrow Wilson at the end of his presidency, March 1921. *Library of Congress.*

(#3447). Judith Papachristou, *Bibliography in the History of Women in the Progressive Era* (#3449), covers works on women in the period from 1890 to 1930. For foreign policy, see select chapters in Richard Dean Burns, ed., *Guide to American Foreign Relations since 1700* (#3452); Wilton B. Fowler, *American Diplomatic History since 1890* (#3455); and Elmer Plischke, *U.S. Foreign Relations: A Guide to Information Sources* (#3457). The most comprehensive listing of works on America and the Great War is Ronald Schaffer, *The United States in World War I: A Selected Bibliography* (#3463).

Much can be learned about topics in domestic affairs and foreign policy by consulting appropriate biographical materials on Wilson (Chapters 1 and 2); administration and political personalities (Chapter 3); business and labor leaders (Chapter 4); and minorities, women, radicals, and the judiciary (Chapters 5, 6, 7, and 8). Brief biographies of members of the Wilson administration may be found in the *Biographical Directory of the United States Executive Branch, 1774–1971* (#3467). Leading Americans are profiled in the *Dictionary of American Biography* (#3465).

Bibliographies: Woodrow Wilson

3399 American Bibliographical Center. *The American Presidency: A Historical Bibliography.* Santa Barbara, CA: ABC-Clio, 1984.

Annotated entries of journal articles on American presidents are presented, including multiperiod works. A chapter on Theodore Roosevelt through Franklin Roosevelt covers Wilson. Index.

3400 Brown, George D. *An Essay towards a Bibliography of the Published Writings and Addresses of Woodrow Wilson, 1910–1917.* Princeton: Library of Princeton University, 1917.

This continuation of Harry Clemons's work (#3401) covers Wilson's gubernatorial career and the first term of his presidency.

3401 Clemons, Harry. *An Essay towards a Bibliography of the Published Writings and Addresses of Woodrow Wilson, 1875–1910.* Princeton: Library of Princeton University, 1913.

The earliest published bibliography on Wilson contains references to his many published speeches and writings.

3402 Davison, Kenneth E. *The American Presidency: A Guide to Information Sources.* Detroit: Gale, 1983.

Aids to research on the presidency are listed. A separate chapter on Wilson lists many biographies, monographs, and articles. Index.

3403 Leach, Howard S. *An Essay towards a Bibliography of the Published Writings and Addresses of Woodrow Wilson, March 1917 to March 1921.* Princeton: Library of Princeton University, 1922.

Books, addresses, messages, notes, and state papers from Wilson's second term are listed from such sources as government documents, *Poole's Index*, and the *Congressional Record*.

3404 Martin, Fenton S., and Goehlert, Robert V. *American Presidents: A Bibliography.* Washington, DC: Congressional Quarterly, 1987.

Over 600 books, articles, and dissertations on Wilson and his times are included.

3405 Turnbull, Laura S., ed. *Woodrow Wilson: A Selected Bibliography.* Princeton: Princeton University Press, 1948.

While this book's list of scholarly works on Wilson is useful only for works published before World War II, the bibliography of Wilson's own books and speeches is very nearly complete.

Bibliographies: General

3406 American Bibliographical Center. *America: History and Life: A Guide to Periodical Literature.* Santa Barbara: ABC-Clio, 1964–.

This quarterly publication contains annotated bibliographies of journal articles as well as lists of books, dissertations, and book reviews. Coverage is generally good, although some gaps in certain journals are apparent. Index.

3407 Cassara, Ernest. *History of the United States of America: A Guide to Information Sources.* Detroit: Gale, 1977.

Chapter 8 contains an annotated bibliography of works on the Progressive era, biographies of well-known personalities, and literature on World War I. Index.

3408 Cohen, Hennig, ed. *Articles in American Studies, 1954–1968: A Cumulation of the Annual Bibliographies from "American Quarterly."* 2 vols. Ann Arbor, MI: Pieran, 1972.

Brief annotations of articles on American studies from *American Quarterly* are presented.

3409 Link, Arthur S., and Leary, William M., Jr., eds. *The Progressive Era and the Great War, 1896–1920.* New York: Meredith, 1969.

This extensive bibliography of the Progressive movement includes the Wilson era, American foreign policy, and economic, social, and intellectual currents. Index.

3410 Salzman, Jack, ed. *American Studies: An Annotated Bibliography.* 3 vols. New York: Cambridge University Press, 1986.

The American Studies Association has compiled some 3,100 annotations on basic sources for the United States Information Agency. Volume III is an index.

3411 Schlebecker, John T. *Bibliography of Books and Pamphlets on the History of Agriculture in the United States, 1607–1967.* Santa Barbara: ABC-Clio, 1969.

Over 2,000 books and pamphlets on all aspects of the history of agriculture are included, although the alphabetical ordering by author's last name makes this work difficult to use.

Historiographical Essays

WILSON

3412 Brodie, Bernard. "A Psychoanalytic Interpretation of Woodrow Wilson." *World Politics* 9 (1957): 413–22.

In this lengthy and largely favorable review of *Woodrow Wilson and Colonel House* (#0019), the reviewer agrees that Wilson had a compulsion to refute his feelings of inadequacy. His failure to keep friends such as Edward House is explained by his inability to take criticism.

3413 Garraty, John A. "Link's Wilson." *Virginia Quarterly* 42 (1966): 149–54.

Garraty asserts that, in his recent work, Arthur Link has lost his sense of historical objectivity, since he lauds Wilsonian diplomacy excessively.

3414 Watson, Richard L., Jr. "Woodrow Wilson and His Interpreters, 1947–1957." *Mississippi Valley Historical Review* 44 (1961): 207–36.

A wealth of material on Wilson published between the end of World War II and 1957 is analyzed. The author warns of the dangers of the psychological approach to Wilson and laments that Wilson did not write more about himself. Notes.

3415 Williams, William A. *Some Presidents: Wilson to Nixon.* New York: New York Review, 1972.

Chapter 1 contains a historiographical essay by a dean of the New Left on a number of recent works about Wilson. Notes.

PROGRESSIVE ERA

3416 Anderson, William G. "Progressivism: An Historiographical Essay." *History Teacher* 6 (1973): 427–52.

Interpretations of the Progressives are discussed, beginning with the "old liberals" and moving through Richard Hofstadter, J. Joseph Huthmacher, Eric Goldman, Samuel Hays, Robert Wiebe, Gabriel Kolko, and Peter Filene.

3417 Caroli, Betty B. "Recent Writing on Italian Emigration to the United States." *Journal of American Ethnic History* 5 (1985): 65–72.

Nine Italian-language books on immigration to the United States between 1890 and 1920 are discussed. While all cover politics and economics to some degree, the experiences of women and children are passed over lightly.

3418 Filler, Louis. *Progressivism and Muckraking.* New York: Bowker, 1976.

This extended bibliographic essay discusses Progressives and muckrakers and argues that they established a tradition that led to the exposés of Watergate. Indexes.

3419 Katz, Michael B. "Child-Saving." *History of Education Quarterly* 26 (1986): 413–24.

Several recent books discuss the plight of poor children and attempts to save them during the Progressive era. Notes.

3420 Mann, Arthur. "The Progressive Tradition." In John Higham, ed. *T h e Reconstruction of American History*. New York: Harper and Row, 1962, pp. 157–79.

Several partisan historians sympathize with their Progressive subjects, while more critical historians see major flaws in Progressive thought. A third group comes down in the middle, writing monographs that are more or less objective.

3421 Margulies, Herbert F. "Recent Opinion on the Decline of the Progressive Movement." *Mid-America* 45 (1963): 250–68.

Recent historical research and opinions on the decline of the Progressive movement are discussed along with suggestions for future topics.

3422 Mowry, George E. *The Progressive Movement, 1900–1920: Recent Ideas and New Literature*. Washington, DC: American Historical Association, 1958.

Old and new interpretations of the Progressive movement are discussed along with a survey of local and state studies, economic and business histories, and general interpretations written since World War II.

3423 Richardson, James R. "Urban Political Change in the Progressive Era." *Ohio History* 87 (1978): 310–21.

Several works published in the late 1970s on the urban Progressive movement are discussed. Progressives undermined their own attempts to implement popular control of government by encouraging businessmen and other elites to participate in the process. Notes.

3424 Strong, Bryan. "Historians and American Socialism, 1900–1920." *Science and Society* 34 (1970): 387–97.

The historiography of the American socialist movement is examined with a critical eye. Most writers have not been able to transcend the politics of their own day. Notes.

3425 Vaudagna, Maurizio. "Recent Studies on 'Corporate Capitalism' " (in Italian). *Italia Contemporanea* [Italy] 32 (1980): 71–81.

Many economic histories of the Progressive period have been published in the last twenty years by the New Left and by other historians. Notes.

3426 Wiebe, Robert H. "The Progressive Years, 1900–1917." In William H. Cartwright and Richard L. Watson, Jr., eds. *T h e Reinterpretation of American History and Culture*.

Washington, DC: National Council for Social Studies, 1973, pp. 425–42.

Books published since World War II on Progressivism are discussed.

3427 Zerbe, Richard O. "Monopoly, the Emergence of Oligopoly, and the Case of Sugar Refining." *Journal of Law and Economy* 13 (1970): 501–15.

Differences between the author and Alfred Eichner over the origins and consequences of the rise of the sugar oligopoly are examined. Notes.

FOREIGN AFFAIRS

3428 Floto, Inga. "Colonel House in Paris: The Fate of a Presidential Adviser." *American Studies in Scandinavia* [Norway] 6 (1973): 21–45.

The Wilson-House break and Edward House's abilities as a diplomat have been the subject of many studies which are examined here in passing. Notes.

3429 Goodell, Stephen. "Woodrow Wilson in Latin America: Interpretations." *Historian* 28 (1965): 96–127.

Historical writings from 1920 to 1965 on Wilson's Latin American policies are examined. Notes.

3430 James, Edith. "Wilsonian Wartime Diplomacy: The Sense of the Seventies." In Gerald K. Haines and J. Samuel Walker, eds. *American Foreign Relations: A Historiographical Review*. Westport, CT: Greenwood, 1981, pp. 115–31.

The 1970s favored multicausal and multidimensional approaches to wartime diplomacy. Simple economic or political motives were de-emphasized, because the motives of American leaders included national security, moral and legal concerns, and economic and diplomatic dimensions. Notes.

3431 McDermott, John. "Varieties of International History." *Canadian Review of American Studies* [Canada] 12 (1981): 101–12.

Recent books on relations between the United States and Europe differ in their approaches but share an appreciation of the profound long-term impact of World War I on American bonds with France and Germany. Notes.

3432 Martel, Gordon. "America's Bid for Empire." *Canadian Review of American Studies* 17 (1986): 81–92.

Several books on American foreign policy published in the early 1980s discuss American imperialism during the Progressive era and World War I.

3433 Moore, James R. "Woodrow Wilson and Post-Armistice Diplomacy: Some French Views." *Reviews in American History* 2 (1974): 207–13.

French historians have taken a new look at Wilson's diplomacy after the Armistice and found evidence of an Anglo-American condominium for increased power, diplomatic confusion and military exhaustion affecting the Armistice, and Wilson's isolation contributing to his diplomacy. Notes.

3434 Timberlake, Charles E. "Russian-American Contacts, 1917–1937: A Review Article." *Pacific Northwest Quarterly* 61 (1970): 217–24.

Books on early Soviet-American relations are discussed, including some examining American reaction to the Bolshevik Revolution. Notes.

3435 Trani, Eugene P. "Woodrow Wilson and the Decision to Intervene in Russia: A Reconsideration." *Journal of Modern History* 48 (1976): 440–61.

Many interpretations have been developed to explain why Wilson intervened in the Russian civil war. He had much to think about at this crucial time, and he based his action on the importance of continued cooperation with the Allies and on advice, hunches, and lifelong beliefs about Russia.

3436 Wells, Samuel F., Jr. "New Perspectives on Wilsonian Diplomacy: The Secular Evangelism of American Political Economy." *Perspectives in American History* 6 (1972): 389–419.

Twelve recent books on Wilson are discussed, all of which cover American political and economic expansion during the Wilson years. The author suggests that greater attention be given to the religious, missionary side of Wilson's character. Notes.

3437 Wilder, Jan A. "Of the History of Soviet-American Relations" (in Polish). *Kwartalnik Historyczny* [Poland] 65 (1958): 510–16.

Reviewing George Kennan's *Russia Leaves the War*, this writer examines the diplomat-scholar's career and finds much of value in the book.

WORLD WAR I

3438 Braeman, John. "World War One and the Crisis of American Liberty." *American Quarterly* 16 (1964): 104–12.

Interest in the Red Scare of 1919–20 has been revived by recent monographs. Attorney General A. Mitchell Palmer is seen as the embodiment of the Progressive movement gone wrong.

3439 Cohen, Warren I. *The American Revisionists: The Lessons of Intervention in World War I.* Chicago: University of Chicago, 1967.

Revisionist historians who questioned American motives for entering World War I, among them Harry Barnes, Charles Beard, C. Hartley Grattan, Walter Millis, and Charles Tansill, are analyzed for the contribution they made to the isolationist mood of the 1930s. Notes, index.

3440 May, Ernest R. *American Intervention: 1917 and 1941.* Washington, DC: American Historical Association, 1960.

This bibliographic essay compares and contrasts Wilson's intervention with Franklin Roosevelt's.

3441 Miller, Sally M. "Socialist Party Decline and World War I: Bibliography and Interpretation." *Science and Society* 34 (1970): 398–411.

While historians of the 1950s and 1960s differ in their interpretations of the decline of socialism, no one yet has come to grips with efforts by the right wing of the socialist movement to rework traditional ideology. Victor Berger's work is used as an example of what can be understood by using this approach. Notes.

3442 Smith, Daniel M. "National Interest and American Intervention, 1917: An Historiographical Appraisal." *Journal of American History* 52 (1965): 5–24.

Twenty years of American writing on intervention in the European war is discussed. Most writers agree that intervention seemed to be in the national interest. Factors influencing the president's decision include his own idealism, economic concerns, fear of Germany, U-boat warfare, and American prestige.

Bibliographies: Domestic Affairs

3443 "Annual Bibliography on American Labor History." *Labor History* (1959–).

The final issue in each yearly volume of this journal contains an excellent survey of the year's publications on labor history, many of which relate to the Wilson years.

3444 Bremner, Robert H., ed. *American Social History since 1860.* New York: Meredith, 1971.

This work includes a subchapter on the Progressive era as well as more general chapters on the rise of the city, the American people, religious life, social and political thought, and social problems and reform movements. Index.

3445 Buenker, John D., and Burckel, Nicholas C. *Progressive Reform: A Guide to Information Sources.* Detroit: Gale, 1980.

Some 1,600 annotated entries on Progressivism include many books, articles, and doctoral dissertations on the Wilson period. Index.

3446 Jones, Clifton. "The Socialist Party of the United States, 1901–1920: A Bibliography of Secondary Sources, 1945–74." *Labor History* 19 (1978): 253–79.

Thirty years of writing on the golden age of socialism are listed in thirteen categories.

3447 Miles, Dione. *Something in Common: An IWW Bibliography.* Detroit: Wayne State University Press, 1986.

Over 5,000 books, journal articles, dissertations, pamphlets, and comments on the Industrial Workers of the World are arranged by topic. Index.

3448 Miller, Elizabeth W., and Fisher, Mary L., eds. *The Negro in America: A Bibliography.* 2d ed., rev. Cambridge, MA: Harvard University Press, 1970.

References to materials on blacks during Wilson's tenure are scattered through this work. Index.

3449 Papachristou, Judith, ed. *Bibliography in the History of Women in the Progressive Era.* Bronxville, NY: Sarah Lawrence College, 1985.

Works about women in the period 1890 to 1930 are arranged under such topics as women and work, gender and family, education, religion, community activism, World War I, feminism and suffrage, minorities, and biography and autobiography. Index.

3450 Seidman, Joel, ed. *Communism in the United States: A Bibliography.* Ithaca, NY: Cornell University Press, 1969.

Works by and about socialists, Communists, anarchists, syndicalists, civil liberties, and the Red Scare are included in this massive work. Index.

3451 Stroud, Gene S., and Donahue, Gilbert S., eds. *Labor History in the United States: A General Bibliography.* Urbana, IL: Institute of Labor and Industrial Relations, 1961.

Many references to labor during the Wilson administration are included, but students must already have authors in mind or be prepared to wade through the book, as references are listed alphabetically by author's name. Index.

Bibliographies: Foreign Affairs

3452 Burns, Richard Dean. *Guide to American Foreign Relations since 1700.* Santa Barbara, CA: ABC-Clio, 1983.

Over 100 American diplomatic historians contributed to this annotated bibliography. Chapter 15 covers U.S.-Latin American relations during Wilson's tenure; Chapter 18 does the same for Africa and the Middle East. Chapter 19 contains references to World War I and the peace settlement. Indexes by author, title, and subject.

3453 "Doctoral Dissertations in U.S. Foreign Affairs." *Diplomatic History* (1979–).

The second issue in each volume of this journal contains a list of dissertations written during the previous year, arranged by categories of topics.

3454 *Foreign Affairs Bibliography: A Selected and Annotated List of Books on International Affairs.* 5 vols. New York: Harper, 1933–.

Issued every ten years, these indexes contain scattered references to the Wilson years, especially in the first volume.

3455 Fowler, Wilton B. *American Diplomatic History since 1890*. Northbrook, IL: AHM, 1975.

Chapter 3 contains over 400 references to Wilson, World War I, and the Versailles settlement, 1913–1921. Index.

3456 Kunina, A. E. "American Bourgeois Historiography on U.S. Policy towards Soviet Russia in 1917–20" (in Russian). *Voprosy Istorii* [USSR] 10 (1960): 36–55.

Writing in response to various books and articles by George Kennan on Soviet-American relations, a Soviet historian examines the work of recent American historians and finds it wanting.

3457 Plischke, Elmer. *U.S. Foreign Relations: A Guide to Information Sources*. Detroit: Gale, 1980.

Books, articles, and government documents on the Wilson presidency are included under various headings. Index.

3458 Trask, David F.; Meyer, Michael C.; and Trask, Roger R., eds. *A Bibliography of United States-Latin American Relations since 1810*. Lincoln: University of Nebraska, 1968.

Over 11,000 published references are included. Students of the Wilson period will find chapters on the imperialist era and Latin America (1900–1921) and on Latin America and World War I to be very useful. Index.

3459 U.S. Department of State. *Index to Papers Relating to the Foreign Relations of the United States, 1900–1918*. Washington, DC: Government Printing Office, 1941.

This index facilitates research on foreign policy in the Progressive era using the *Foreign Relations* series.

Bibliographies: World War I and Peace Settlement

3460 Genthe, Charles V. *American War Narratives, 1917–1918: A Study and Bibliography*. New York: David Lewis, 1969.

This work discusses narratives of the war published in the United States between 1914 and 1918. Most took a romantic view of the war more appropriate to the nineteenth century than to the twentieth. Notes, bibliography, index.

3461 Lane, Jack C. *America's Military Past: A Guide to Information Sources*. Detroit: Gale, 1980.

This annotated bibliography contains over one hundred references on World War I and a few on Wilson's military interventions in Latin America and the Caribbean. Index.

3462 Rangel, Sandra K. *Records of the American Commission to Negotiate Peace*. Washington, DC: National Archives and Records Service, 1974.

The American delegation to the Paris Peace Conference left behind voluminous records, which this compiler has indexed.

3463 Schaffer, Ronald. *The United States in World War I: A Selected Bibliography*. Santa Barbara: ABC-Clio, 1978.

Over 2,900 references are listed under such categories as American intervention, military activity, unit histories, the war and American society, and peacemaking. Index.

3464 Toscano, Mario, ed. *The History of Treaties and International Politics*. Baltimore, MD: Johns Hopkins University Press, 1966.

Designed originally for Italian university students of international affairs, this book contains chapters on diplomatic documents relating to the origins of World War I and memoir sources for that war. Index.

Biographical Dictionaries and Directories

3465 Johnson, Allen, et al. *Dictionary of American Biography*. 21 vols., 3 supplements. New York: Scribner's, 1928–.

Leading scholars provide biographies of leading Americans, including many from the Wilson years. Index.

3466 Morris, Dan, and Morris, Inez. *Who Was Who in American Politics*. New York: Hawthorn, 1974.

Over 4,000 thumbnail sketches of men and women prominent in state and national politics are presented, including many from the Wilson years.

3467 Sobel, Robert, ed. *Biographical Directory of the United States Executive Branch, 1774–1971*. Westport, CT: Greenwood, 1971.

Short biographies of Wilson, Thomas R. Marshall, and the president's cabinet members are included.

3468 U.S. Congress. House. *Biographical Directory of the American Congress, 1774–1961*. 85th Cong., 2d sess., 1961. H. Doc. 442. Washington, DC: Government Printing Office, 1961.

This large volume includes paragraph-length biographies of all members of Congress between 1774 and 1961 as well as other data. A previous edition was published in 1950.

3469 U.S. Department of the Interior. *Biographical and Historical Index of American Indians and Persons Involved in Indian Affairs*. 8 vols. Boston: Hall, 1966.

Some information on congressional legislation and executive policy on Native Americans is included in this work. Bibliography.

3470 *Who Was Who in America*. 6 vols. Chicago: Marquis, 1942–.

Short biographies of prominent Americans of the Progressive era are included in Volumes I to V. Index.

Author Index

Lunt, Richard D., 0821
Luthin, Reinhard H., 0144
Lutskov, N. D., 2366
Lutter, Martin H., 2975
Lutz, Ralph, 3015
Lutzker, Michael A., 2453
Lybarger, Michael, 1090
Lyddon, W. G., 2700
Lyman, Donald R., 2343
Lynch, Edmund C., 0614
Lynn, Kenneth S., 0893
Lyon, Jessie C., 2454
Lyon, Peter, 1968
Lyons, Maurice F., 1848
Lyons, Thomas, 3218
Lyu, Kingsley K., 2001

MacDonald, Norbert, 2011
Machado, Manuel A., Jr., 2455–
56
Mackey, Thomas C., 1405
MacKinnon, Jan, 2888
MacKinnon, Steve, 2888
MacMahon, Arthur W., 0268–69
Maddox, Robert J., 0088,
0454, 3160–61
Madison, Charles A., 1578
Maga, Timothy P., 3290
Mahoney, Joseph F., 0145,
1472, 1763
Makarewicz, Joseph T., 2976
Malan, Nancy E., 2992
Malino, Sarah S., 0779
Malkasian, Mark, 3342
Mal'kov, V. L., 0817, 2096
Mamatey, Victor S., 3343
Mambretti, Catherine C., 1473
Mandel, Bernard, 0809–10
Mander, Mary S., 2889
Manijak, William, 3344
Mann, Arthur, 1579, 1641,
3420
Manners, William, 0546
Manning, Clarence A., 2285,
2701
Manning, Eugene A., 0475
Mantoux, Étienne, 3240
Mantoux, Paul, 3210
Marable, W. Manning, 1288
Maranell, Gary M., 0247–48
Marburg, Theodore, 3260–61
Marcell, David W., 0981
Marchand, C. Roland, 1922
Margulies, Herbert F., 0547,
1764, 1852, 1905, 3006,
3421
Marina, William F., 2256
Marion, David E., 0232
Markmann, Charles L., 2222
Markowitz, Gerald E., 2257
Marks, Barry A., 2826
Marks, Carole, 1330–31
Marmor, Michael F., 0105
Maroney, James C., 0846
Marsh, Margaret, 2073

Marshall, George C., 0422
Marshall, Thomas R., 0323
Marston, Frank S., 3211
Marszalek, John F., 1289
Martel, Gordon, 3432
Martelet, Penny, 2993
Martin, Albro, 0615
Martin, Fenton S., 3404
Martin, James P., 1923
Martin, Laurence W., 0191,
2286, 2702, 3304
Martin, Patricia S., 1149
Martin, Percy A., 2684
Martin, William S., Jr., 3291
Marwick, Arthur, 2703
Masingill, Eugene F., 0394
Mason, Alpheus T., 2061
Masterson, Thomas D., 0548
Mathews, Carl S., 1290–92
Mathews, F. H., 0982
Matsuda, Takeshi, 2328
Maunder, Elwood R., 1225
Maurer, John H., 3084
Maurer, Maurer, 3048
Maxwell, William J., 1406
May, Arthur J., 3345
May, Ernest R., 2616, 2666–
67, 2680, 3440
May, Henry F., 0983–84
May, Lary, 0925
May, Martha E., 0632, 1642
Mayer, Arno J., 2675, 3212
Mayer, Robert S., 0633
Mazev, V. I., 3141
Mazuzan, George T., 0648
Mazza, David L., 1906
McAdoo, Eleanor Wilson, 0086–
87
McAdoo, William G., 0320
McAlpin, William B., 1142
McArthur, Benjamin, 1091
McAvoy, Thomas T., 1143
McBride, James D., 2887
McBride, Paul W., 1523–25
McBride, Ralph L., 1569
McCaffrey, Donna T., 1092
McCallum, R. B., 3302
McCarthy, Dennis J., 3303
McCarthy, G. Michael, 1224
McCarthy, Kathleen D., 0924
McClelland, John M., Jr., 2244
McClung, John B., 1762
McClymer, John F., 1526
McCombs, William F., 1849
McConachie, Alexander S., 0682
McCorkle, James L., Jr., 2586
McCormick, John S., 0980
McCormick, Richard L., 1636
McCoy, Pressley C., 3122
McCreesh, Carolyn D., 0778
McCrum, Robert, 3341
McCulley, Richard T., 0661,
1695
McDean, Harry C., 0581
McDermott, John, 3431

McDiarmid, Alice M., 2634
McDonald, Timothy G., 2635
McDonnell, James R., 1144
McDonnell, Janet, 1351–52
McDougall, Walter A., 2509
McEnroe, Thomas H., 2095
McFarland, Charles K., 1471
McGeary, M. Nelson, 2954
McGinty, Brian, 3385
McGovern, James R., 1404,
1640
McGruder, Larry, 1287
McInery, Thomas J., 1850
McKenna, Charles D., 3032
McKenna, Edmond, 0014
McKenna, Marian C., 0453
McKeown, Elizabeth, 1145
McKinley, Silas B., 0033
McKnight, Gerald D., 1568
McKown, Paul, 0231
McLoughlin, William G., Jr.,
1146–47
McMahan, Russell S., Jr., 2755
McNamara, JoAnn K., 1389
McNaught, Kenneth, 2158
McReynolds, George E., 3194
McShane, Joseph M., 1148
McWilliams, Tennant S., 1851
Mead, David, 1093
Meagher, Timothy J., 1527
Meaney, Neville K., 2526, 3386
Medved, Michael, 0309
Megargee, Richard, 0406
Mehl, Joseph M., Jr., 2726
Mehr, Linda H., 1407
Meiburger, Anne V., 3123
Meier, August, 1251, 1293,
1332
Meier, Matt S., 1358
Mellinger, Philip J., 0793
Melvin, Patricia M., 1765
Merchant, Carolyn, 1226
Meredith, Howard L., 1969,
2159–60
Meriwether, Lee, 0549
Merritt, Richard L., 1907
Mervin, David, 0192, 0478
Metallo, Michael V., 2329–30
Meyer, Carl S., 1150
Meyer, Jonah N., 1887
Meyer, Leo J., 2357
Meyer, Melissa L., 1353
Meyer, Michael C., 2457–58,
2649, 3458
Meyer, Stephen, 0634, 0736
Meyerowitz, Joanne J., 1408
Michalski, Thomas A., 1528
Milden, James W., 0780
Miles, Dione, 3447
Miller, David Hunter, 3213,
3262
Miller, Donald H., 1151
Miller, Elizabeth W., 3448
Miller, John, 3144
Miller, John P., 1696

Subject Index

Health issues, 1005–45; behaviorism, 1006, 1025, 1029; eugenics, 1016; infant mortality, 1021; influenza, 1015, 1027, 1031–32, 1036, 1039; medical ethics, 1010; mental illness, 1037, 1088, 2018; military and, 1014; physicians, 1011, 1017, 1020, 1023, 1028; polio, 1034; psychoanalysis, 1009, 1019; psychology, 1012, 1038, 1042, 1087, 3031; public health, 1007, 1013, 1030, 1035, 1041, 1043–44, 1632, 1660; pure food, 1005, 1045; sexuality, 1008, 1059; tuberculosis, 1041; use of anesthesia, 1022, 1026; venereal disease, 1023–24, 1033, 3017, 3076

Hearst, William Randolph, 0358, 1967, 1971, 1975, 1991, 2309
Hellman, Lillian, 0859
Hemingway, Ernest, 0873, 0893
Hemphill, James Calvin, 1827
Henri, Robert, 0952
Henry, Alice, 0773
Herrick, James, 1020
Herrick, Robert, 0886
Herron, George D., 2725, 2731
Higginson, Henry Lee, 1837
Hill, Claibourne M., 1430
Hill, Joe, 2093
Hill, Leslie Pinckney, 1324
Hillquit, Morris, 1438, 2128, 2169
Hindenburg, Paul von, 2625
Hispanic Americans, 1355–62; barrios, 1355, 1360; labor, 0795, 0850, 1362; Mexican Revolution and, 1356, 1358, 1361; stereotypes, 1357
A History of the American People (Wilson), 0060, 0120
Hitchcock, Gilbert C., 0341
Hobson, Richmond P., 0500, 0557
Hofstadter, Richard, 1794, 2021
Hollingsworth, Leta, 1369
Holmes, Oliver Wendell, Jr., 1233, 1570, 2049, 2069–70, 2225
Holt, Benjamin, 0588
Holt, Hamilton, 1965, 3182
Honduras, 2371, 2396
Hoover, Herbert C., 0174, 0177, 0228, 0294–307, 2392, 2778, 2799, 2801, 3154, 3217; *see also* World War I, mobilization
Hoover, J. Edgar, 2209–10, 2215, 2223, 2226, 2234
House, Edward M.: biographies, 0308–14, 1994; diplomacy, 0381, 2059, 2512, 2534, 2587, 2599, 2607, 2611–12, 2617, 2693, 2718, 2736; influence of, 0095, 0277, 0356, 0360, 2265, 2280, 2837; Paris Peace Conference and, 3197, 3199, 3204, 3213, 3222, 3319, 3344, 3362, 3428; Wilson and, 0019, 0099, 0277
Houston, David F., 0315
Howe, Frederick C., 1517, 1577, 1620, 1664
Howells, William Dean, 0891, 0904
Huerta, Victoriano, 0393, 1957, 2407, 2415, 2418, 2442–43, 2462, 2465, 2481;

German support for, 2401, 2422, 2457, 2649; Lind mission to, 2428, 2441; U.S. recognition of, 0394, 2417, 2419, 2429, 2431, 2439
Hughes, Charles Evans, 0458–61, 1307, 1749, 1833, 1877, 1880, 1884, 1887, 2392
Hughes, W. M., 3238
Hulbert, Mary A. *see* Peck, Mary Hulbert
Hull, Cordell, 0174, 0228, 0529, 0550
Hungary, 3154, 3317
Hurley, Edward, 2805
Hutton, Laura, 1370
Hylan, John F., 2946

Igoe, William L., 0561
Immigrants and ethnic groups, 1490–1546; Americanization of, 1099, 1499, 1525–26, 1539, 1541, 1546, 2978, 3043; Anglo-Americans, 3303; Chinese, 1542–43; Danish, 2897; ethnicity and, 1490, 2852; Finnish, 1520–21, 2872; German, 1504, 1512, 1536, 1882, 1889, 2572, 2578, 2845, 2857, 2860, 2862, 2864, 2868–69, 2879, 2885, 2893, 2905, 2911–12, 2914, 2940, 2963, 2966, 3297; Hungarian, 1492, 1538; Irish, 1500, 1527, 1536, 1874–75, 1883, 2306, 2578, 2947, 2981, 2986, 3348–49, 3361; Italian, 1503, 1529, 2913, 2978, 3417; Japanese, 0345, 1320, 1519–20, *see also* Japanese Americans; Jewish, 1493, 1509, 1511, 1513–14, 1536–37, 1544, *see also* Religion, Judaism; Korean, 1516; nativism and, 1510, 1515, 1522–24, 1534, 2347; Norwegian, 1540, 2585, 2852; Polish, 1491, 3058, 3069, 3301, 3344, 3352; politics and, 2307, 3305; prostitution and, 1508; Puerto Rican, 1533; radicalism and, 1494, 2154; Romanian, 1498, 1530–31; Slavic, 1495, 1497, 1502, 1528, 1535, 1545, 2927; Ukrainian, 1532, 2701; war and, 2578, 2585, 3058; women, 1496, 1506; *see also* Hispanic Americans
Industrial Welfare Commission, 0842
Industrial Workers of the World (IWW), 0749, 0783, 0793, 0839, 0846, 2074–2105, 2836, 2867, 2883–84, 2898, 2908, 2922–23, 2925, 2930, 2932–34, 2983, 3447
Inman, Samuel Guy, 2487
"The Inquiry," 3181, 3188, 3221–22
Intellectuals, 0959–93; antimodernists, 0979; economics and, 0970; education and, 0961, 0965, 0968; historians, 0981, 1085, 2816, 2821, 2824, 3184, 3424, 3439; leftists, 0959, 0963, 0969, 0971, 0977–78, 0985; pragmatism and, 0981, 0986; war and, 0960, 0966, 0974–76, 0991–93, 2742–43, 2752
Interchurch World Movement, 0832–33
International Ideals (Wilson), 0129
International Ladies Garment Workers Union, 0770, 0781
Interstate Commerce Commission, 0705
Intervention *see* World War I
Intolerance (1916 film), 0918, 0933

Wilson, Woodrow (*cont.*)
2750, 2762, 2764, 2774, 2780–81, 2789, 2794, 2801, 3025
Winant, John Gilbert, 0507
Wise, Stephen S., 1559
Woman's Peace party, 1414
Women, 1363–1426; antisuffragism, 1372, 1466, 1481; bibliographies, 3444–45, 3449; clubs, 1381, 1389; crime and, 1363; education, 1066, 1073, 1079–80, 1083, 1367, 1400; Equal Rights Amendment and, 1385; families, 1390; feminism, 1410, 1427–37; health, 1021, 1023–24, 1033, 1387, 1397, 1399, 1409; labor and, 0759–88, 1408, 2038, 2042; lesbianism, 1431; literature and, 0868, 0881, 0888, 0890, 0894–95, 0897, 0902, 1434; prostitution, 1365–66, 1374, 1405, 1411, 1426, 1637; radicals, 1438–52, 1508; religion, 1375, 1424; settlement houses and, 1364–65, 1383, 1388, 1398, 1401, 1415–17, 1772; sexism, 1392, 1394–95, 1407, 1412, 1422; suffrage movement and, 0343, 0512, 1402, 1418–19, 1453–89, 2034–37; war and, 1404, 1413–14, 1419, 2835, 2987–97, 3056
Women's Trade Union League, 0762–65, 0771, 0773, 1429, 1592
Wood, Leonard, 0437–40, 1927
Woodbey, George Washington, 2127
Woodrow, Harriet, 0050
Woodson, Carter, 1297
World Court, 3366–67
World Peace Foundation, 1918
World War I (European war, Great War): Armistice, 0423, 2731–40; bibliographies, 3409, 3438–42, 3460–63; blacks and, 2974, 2987, 3005, 3016, 3019, 3033, 3051, 3057, 3060, 3067; civil liberties, 2844–2943, 3438, 3450; Congress and, 2951, 2959, 2985, 3011; conscription, 2851, 2854, 2858, 2973, 3018, 3034; ethnic groups and, 2578, 2585, 3058, *see also* Immigrants and ethnic groups; Everett massacre, 2075, 2083; government persecution, 2845,

2921–34; home front, 2741–68; intervention, 2654–72, 3439–40, 3442; labor and, 2771, 2788, 2798, 2836, 2948, 2967; *Lusitania* sinking, 2641–45; maritime issues, 2622–40; military dimension, 0420–25, 0428, 0430, 0432, 0441, 3014–91; mobilization, 0275–81, 0321, 0327, 0625, 0641, 2769–2815; opposition to, 2303; origins, 2562–66; preparedness, 0187, 0290, 0437–40, 1926–36, 2598; politics, 2944–62; press and, 1946, 2600, 2889, 3022–23, 3068; propaganda, 2816–43; readjustment after, 2998–3013; state and local studies, 2963–86; superpatriots and vigilantes and, 2935–43, 2966, 2973; wartime diplomacy, 2673–2730, *see also* Russia, Bolshevik Revolution; women and, 1404, 1413–14, 1419, 2835, 2987–97, 3056; Zimmermann Note, 2646–53; *see also* Neutrality; Paris Peace Conference
Wright, Frank Lloyd, 0853–55, 0857, 0871, 1597
Wright, Harold Bell, 0895

Yap, 3290
Yardley, Herbert O., 2814
Yeats, William Butler, 1298
Yerkes, Robert M., 3031
York, Alvin C., 3063
Young, Art, 0896, 1953, 2106
Young, Charles, 1319
Young, Robert J., 0666
Young Men's Christian Association (YMCA), 2847, 3037, 3140
Ypiranga (ship), 2401, 2457
Yuan Shih-k'ai, 2330
Yugoslavia, 0296, 3091, 3340, 3365

Zanuck, Darryl F., 0923
Zayas, Alberto, 2357
Zimmermann Note, 2646–53, 2671
Zionism, 0373, 1151, 1156, 1547–59, 2054–65, 2067, 2804, 3332, 3336
Znaniecki, Florian, 1061